PARENT MATTERS

SUPPORTING PARENTS OF CHILDREN AGES 0–8

Committee on Supporting the Parents of Young Children

Vivian L. Gadsden, Morgan Ford, and Heather Breiner, *Editors*

Board on Children, Youth, and Families

Division of Behavioral and Social Sciences and Education

A Report of

The National Academies of
SCIENCES · ENGINEERING · MEDICINE

THE NATIONAL ACADEMIES PRESS
Washington, DC
www.nap.edu

THE NATIONAL ACADEMIES PRESS   500 Fifth Street, NW   Washington, DC 20001

This activity was supported by contracts between the National Academies of Sciences, Engineering, and Medicine and the Bezos Family Foundation (unnumbered award); the Bill & Melinda Gates Foundation (OPP1118359); the Centers for Disease Control and Prevention (200-2011-38807); the David and Lucile Packard Foundation (2014-40233); the Foundation for Child Development (09-2014); the Health Resources and Services Administration (HHSH25034025T); the Heising-Simons Foundation (2014-64); and the Substance Abuse and Mental Health Services Administration (HHSP23320140224P). Any opinions, findings, conclusions, or recommendations expressed in this publication are those of the author(s) and do not necessarily reflect the views of the organizations or agencies that provided support for the project.

International Standard Book Number-13:   978-0-309-38854-2
International Standard Book Number-10:   0-309-38854-6
Library of Congress Control Number: 2016953420
Digital Object Identifier: 10.17226/21868

Additional copies of this report are available for sale from the National Academies Press, 500 Fifth Street, NW, Keck 360, Washington, DC 20001; (800) 624-6242 or (202) 334-3313; http://www.nap.edu.

Printed in the United States of America

Suggested citation: National Academies of Sciences, Engineering, and Medicine. (2016). *Parenting Matters: Supporting Parents of Children Ages 0-8*. Washington, DC: The National Academies Press. doi: 10.17226/21868.

The National Academies of
SCIENCES · ENGINEERING · MEDICINE

The **National Academy of Sciences** was established in 1863 by an Act of Congress, signed by President Lincoln, as a private, nongovernmental institution to advise the nation on issues related to science and technology. Members are elected by their peers for outstanding contributions to research. Dr. Marcia McNutt is president.

The **National Academy of Engineering** was established in 1964 under the charter of the National Academy of Sciences to bring the practices of engineering to advising the nation. Members are elected by their peers for extraordinary contributions to engineering. Dr. C. D. Mote, Jr., is president.

The **National Academy of Medicine** (formerly the Institute of Medicine) was established in 1970 under the charter of the National Academy of Sciences to advise the nation on medical and health issues. Members are elected by their peers for distinguished contributions to medicine and health. Dr. Victor J. Dzau is president.

The three Academies work together as the **National Academies of Sciences, Engineering, and Medicine** to provide independent, objective analysis and advice to the nation and conduct other activities to solve complex problems and inform public policy decisions. The Academies also encourage education and research, recognize outstanding contributions to knowledge, and increase public understanding in matters of science, engineering, and medicine.

Learn more about the National Academies of Sciences, Engineering, and Medicine at **www.national-academies.org**.

v

Acknowledgments

The committee and project staff would like to express their sincere gratitude to all of those who generously contributed their time and expertise to inform the development of this report.

To begin, we would like to thank the sponsors of this study for their guidance. Support for the committee's work was provided by the Administration for Children and Families, the Bezos Family Foundation, the Bill & Melinda Gates Foundation, the Centers for Disease Control and Prevention, the David and Lucile Packard Foundation, the U.S. Department of Education, the Foundation for Child Development, the Health Resources and Services Administration, the Heising-Simons Foundation, and the Substance Abuse and Mental Health Services Administration.

Many individuals volunteered significant time and effort to address and educate the committee during our public sessions (see Appendix A) and our interviews with parents. Their willingness to share their perspectives was essential to the committee's work. We express gratitude to those who provided support in identifying parents for the interviews and public session in Irvine, California, including Sunnah Kim at the American Academy of Pediatrics, Yolie Flores at The Campaign for Grade-Level Reading, Sandra Gutierrez and Debbie Ignacio at Abriendo Puertas/Opening Doors, and Michael Duncan at Native Dad Networks. We are grateful to Lucy Rivero for providing interpretation services during the public session in Irvine. We also thank the many stakeholders who offered input and shared information and documentation with the committee over the course of the study, including the Center for Law and Social Policy, the Center for the Study of Social Policy, Futures Without Violence, the National Parenting Education

Network, and ZERO TO THREE. In addition, we appreciate the generous hospitality of the organizations and providers in Omaha, Nebraska, and Washington, D.C., who opened their doors to provide us space to conduct interviews with parents. We are also immensely grateful for the planning assistance and logistical support for site visits provided to us by Lori Koker at the Buffett Early Childhood Institute, University of Nebraska. Furthermore, we extend our appreciation to the many assistants who provided scheduling, communication, and travel support for the committee members.

The committee also expresses its deep appreciation for the opportunity to work with the dedicated members of the staff of the National Academies of Sciences, Engineering, and Medicine on this important project. We are thankful to the project staff: Morgan Ford, Heather Breiner, Sarah Tracey, Kelsey Geiser, Stacey Smit, Anthony Janifer, and Katherine Gold. The committee is also thankful to Pamella Atayi, Faye Hillman, and Lisa Alston for their assistance on this project. The committee gratefully acknowledges Kimber Bogard and Bridget Kelly of the Board on Children, Youth, and Families; Robert Hauser, executive director of the Division of Behavioral and Social Sciences and Education; Mary Ellen O'Connell, deputy executive director of the Division of Behavioral and Social Sciences and Education; and Clyde Behney, executive director of the Health and Medicine Division for their leadership and the guidance they provided throughout this study. The committee would like to thank staff of the Office of Reports and Communication of the Division of Behavioral and Social Sciences and Education for their assistance with the preparation of this report, including Eugenia Grohman, Viola Horek, Patricia L. Morison, Kirsten Sampson-Snyder, Douglas Sprunger, and Yvonne Wise. We also wish to thank the staff at the Research Center for their research assistance. In addition, we thank the staff of Kentlands Travel for their assistance with the travel needs of this project.

The committee is grateful to Lauren Tobias of Maven Messaging & Communications for her work as a consultant for this study. We greatly appreciate Jessica F. Harding, Joanne Nicholson, Karen Bierman, Kyla Liggett-Creel, Lisa A. Gennetian, Pamella Morris, and Tumaini Coker for their valuable commissioned work. We thank Rona Briere and Alisa Decatur at Briere Associates, Inc., for the diligent editorial assistance they provided in preparing this report.

Reviewers

This report has been reviewed in draft form by individuals chosen for their diverse perspectives and technical expertise, in accordance with procedures approved by the National Academies of Sciences, Engineering, and Medicine. The purpose of this independent review is to provide candid and critical comments that will assist the institution in making its published report as sound as possible and to ensure that the report meets institutional standards for objectivity, evidence, and responsiveness to the study charge. The review comments and draft manuscript remain confidential to protect the integrity of the deliberative process. We wish to thank the following individuals for their review of this report: Anthony Biglan, Education and Training, Oregon Research Institute, Eugene; Deborah Daro, Hall Center for Children, University of Chicago; Julia Mendez, Department of Psychology, University of North Carolina at Greensboro; Bennett A. Shaywitz, Center for Dyslexia and Creativity, Yale University; Susan J. Spieker, Family and Child Nursing and Barnard Center for Infant Mental Health and Development, University of Washington; William H. Teale, Center for Literacy, University of Illinois; Ross A. Thompson, Department of Psychology, University of California, Davis; Richard Wasserman, Department of Pediatrics, University of Vermont College of Medicine.

Although the reviewers listed above provided many constructive comments and suggestions, they were not asked to endorse the report's conclusions or recommendations, nor did they see the final draft of the report before its release. The review of this report was overseen by Nancy E. Adler, Departments of Psychiatry and Pediatrics and Center for Health and Community, University of California, San Francisco, and Jeanne Brooks-Gunn,

Teachers College and College of Physicians and Surgeons, Columbia University. Appointed by the Academies, they were responsible for making certain that an independent examination of this report was carried out in accordance with institutional procedures and that all review comments were carefully considered. Responsibility for the final content of this report rests entirely with the authoring committee and the institution.

Contents

Boxes, Figures, and Tables

BOXES

FIGURES

TABLES

Summary

Decades of research have demonstrated that the parent-child dyad and the environment of the family—which includes all primary caregivers—are at the foundation of children's well-being and healthy development. From birth, children are learning and rely on parents and the other caregivers in their lives to protect and care for them. The impact of parents may never be greater than during the earliest years of life, when a child's brain is rapidly developing and when nearly all of her or his experiences are created and shaped by parents and the family environment. Parents help children build and refine their knowledge and skills, charting a trajectory for their health and well-being during childhood and beyond. The experience of parenting also impacts parents themselves. For instance, parenting can enrich and give focus to parents' lives; generate stress or calm; and create any number of emotions, including feelings of happiness, sadness, fulfillment, and anger.

Parenting of young children today takes place in the context of significant ongoing developments. These include a rapidly growing body of science on early childhood that has provided a more nuanced understanding of the critical periods in early childhood development and parenting. In addition, while child poverty has increased in recent years, there have been increases in funding for programs and services for families, such as early childhood education, home visiting, and income support programs, which have implications for the development of a framework for better supporting parents of young children.

In addition, the demographic characteristics of the U.S. population are changing rapidly. As of 2014, 25 percent of children ages 0-5 had at least one immigrant parent, compared with just under 14 percent in 1990. Related in part to immigration, the racial and ethnic diversity of families has increased over the past several decades, a trend that is anticipated to continue. For example, between 2000 and 2010, the percentage of Americans identifying as black, Hispanic, Asian, or "other" increased from 15 percent to 36 percent, and the percentage of children under age 10 of Hispanic ethnicity (of any race) grew from about 19 percent to 25 percent.

There also is greater diversity in family structure as a result of increases in divorce, cohabitation, new types of parental relationships (e.g., same-sex parents), and involvement of grandparents and other relatives in the raising of young children. Between 1960 and 2015, the percentage of children and youth under age 18 who lived with two married parents (biological, nonbiological, or adoptive) decreased from approximately 85 percent to 65 percent. In 2014, 7 percent of children lived in households headed by grandparents, compared with 3 percent in 1970.

Finally, parenting is increasingly being shaped by technology and increased access to information about parenting, some of which is not based in evidence. All of the above changes have implications for how best to support the parents and other caregivers of young children.

It is against this backdrop that in fall 2014 multiple federal agencies and private foundations requested that the National Academies of Sciences, Engineering, and Medicine form the Committee on Supporting Parents of Young Children to assess the research on parenting and strategies for supporting parenting in the United States. The committee's major tasks were to identify parenting knowledge, attitudes, and practices associated with positive developmental outcomes in children ages 0-8; universal/preventive and targeted strategies used in a variety of settings that have been effective with parents of young children and that support the identified knowledge, attitudes, and practices; and barriers to and facilitators for parents' use of practices that lead to healthy child outcomes as well as their participation in effective programs and services. Based on this assessment, the committee was asked to make recommendations directed at an array of stakeholders, for promoting the wide-scale adoption of effective programs and services for parents and on areas that warrant further research to inform policy and practice. The resulting report would serve as a roadmap for the future of parenting policy, research, and practice in the United States.

PARENTING KNOWLEDGE, ATTITUDES, AND PRACTICES

Research reviewed by the committee revealed that certain areas of knowledge and parenting practices are associated with children's favorable developmental outcomes, although there are some limitations to this research.

In the area of parenting knowledge, the extant research suggests that parental knowledge of child development is positively associated with quality parent-child interactions and the likelihood of parents' engagement in practices that promote their children's healthy development. Research also indicates that parents with knowledge of evidence-based parenting practices, especially those related to promoting children's physical health and safety (e.g., injury prevention, how to sooth a crying infant), are more likely than those without such knowledge to engage in those practices.

Parents' attitudes about the roles of parents and others in the raising of young children, as well as about specific practices (e.g., breastfeeding, the role of parents in children's education), contribute to some variation in practices and in the uptake of services for families among individuals and subpopulations. The committee concluded that empirical studies on parenting attitudes do not allow for the identification of core parenting attitudes consistently associated with positive child outcomes. However, the available evidence points to a need for taking parents' attitudes and beliefs into consideration in the design and implementation of programs and services to ensure that they are sensitive to parents' needs and to extend their reach.

The committee identified a number of parenting practices associated with positive child outcomes in the areas of physical health and safety, emotional and behavioral competence, social competence, and cognitive competence:

- contingent responsiveness ("serve and return")—adult behavior that occurs immediately after a child's behavior and that is related to the child's focus of attention, such as a parent smiling back at a child;
- showing warmth and sensitivity;
- routines and reduced household chaos;
- shared book reading and talking to children;
- practices that promote children's health and safety—in particular receipt of prenatal care, breastfeeding, vaccination, ensuring children's adequate nutrition and physical activity, monitoring, and household/vehicle safety; and
- use of appropriate (less harsh) discipline.

Much of the research on parenting knowledge, attitudes, and practices is correlational, making it difficult to draw firm conclusions about causation. In addition, most studies are focused on mothers, with a lack of research on fathers and other caregivers (e.g., grandparents).

Although studies suggest some variation in parenting knowledge, attitudes, and practices among racial/ethnic, cultural, and other subgroups of parents, more attention is needed as to whether and how these differences matter for child outcomes.

INTERVENTIONS TO SUPPORT PARENTS AND PARENTING

Scaling Effective Interventions

The committee identified a number of interventions that promote the parenting practices described above. These include well-identified formal sources of parenting support for many parents, such as well-child care, center-based child care (Head Start and Early Head Start), and home visiting programs that are largely preventive in their approach. Other interventions are targeted to specific populations of parents, such as parents of children with special needs (e.g., those with developmental disabilities) and parents facing adversities, such as mental illness, substance abuse, and intimate partner violence. Federal efforts also support parents through income assistance, nutrition assistance (e.g., the Special Supplemental Nutrition Program for Women, Infants, and Children [WIC]), health care, and housing programs. These programs aid large numbers of parents, primarily those with low incomes, in ensuring their own and their children's physical health and safety.

Yet many families that could benefit from these interventions neither seek out nor are referred to them. To better support parents and children, then, improved referral mechanisms are needed. Millions of parents interact with health care (e.g., well-child and mental and behavioral health care), education (e.g., early care and education and formal prekindergarten to grade 3), and other community services each year. Along with improvements in workforce preparation (see Recommendations 3 and 4 below), better leveraging the services with which many parents already have ongoing connections as points of intervention and referral would help improve the reach of effective strategies.

> **Recommendation 1: The U.S. Department of Health and Human Services, the U.S. Department of Education, state and local agencies, and community-based organizations responsible for the implementation of services that reach large numbers of families (e.g., health care, early care and education, community programs) should form a working group to identify points in the delivery of these services at which evidence-based strategies for supporting parents can be implemented and referral of parents to needed resources can be enhanced. Based on its findings, the working group should issue guidance to service delivery organizations on increasing parents' access to evidence-based interventions.**

Research on how to bring effective parenting programs to scale is limited. Although a number of programs are effective in supporting parents, their potential for helping large numbers of families often depends on factors specific to the families served and to the organizations and communities in which they will be implemented. Additional evidence is needed to inform the creation of a system for efficiently disseminating evidence-based programs and services to the field and for ensuring that communities learn about them, are able to assess their fit with community needs, develop needed adaptations, and monitor fidelity and progress toward targeted outcomes. Findings from this research could be used in an ongoing way to inform the integration of evidence-based interventions into widely used service platforms.

> **Recommendation 2:[1] The U.S. Department of Health and Human Services, the Institute of Education Sciences, the Patient-Centered Outcomes Research Institute, and private philanthropies should fund research focused on developing guidance for policy makers and program administrators and managers on how to scale effective parenting programs as widely and rapidly as possible. This research should take into account organization-, program-, and system-level factors, as well as quality improvement. Supports for scaling efforts developed through this research might include cost tools, measurement toolkits, and implementation guidelines.**

Enhancing Workforce Competence in Delivering Evidence-Based Parenting Interventions

A professional workforce with knowledge about and competencies for implementing evidence-based interventions to support parents is essential to the successful scale-up of effective approaches. Evidence-based parenting interventions often are not available as part of either routine services for parents or services not designed specifically for parents but with the potential to benefit many parents, such as treatments for mental illness and substance abuse. One reason for this is that providers of these services often lack knowledge and competencies in evidence-based parenting interventions. Graduate training for providers of children's services and behavioral health care (e.g., in schools of social work and nursing) currently includes limited or no coursework on evidence-based parenting programs or their core elements. A viable way to increase the availability of evidence-based parenting interventions is to build on the commonality of specific and non-specific elements across interventions.

---

[1] This recommendation, along with Recommendations 4, 6, and 10 were modified following the transmittal of the report to the study sponsors. In particular, the U.S. Department of Health and Human Services (HHS) was inserted to replace the names of specific agencies within HHS to allow HHS to decide the most appropriate agencies to carry out the recommendations.

Recommendation 3: The U.S. Department of Health and Human Services should continue to promote the use of evidence-based parenting interventions. In so doing, it should support research designed to further operationalize the common elements of effective parenting interventions and to compare the benefits of interventions based on the common elements of effective parenting programs with the specific evidence-based programs from which the elements originated. These efforts also should encompass (1) development of a common terminology for describing common elements and creation and testing of corresponding training materials; (2) development of an open-source curriculum, fidelity-checking strategies, and sustainability strategies for use in educating health and human service professionals in the delivery of evidence-based parenting interventions; and (3) creation of a variety of incentives and training programs to ensure knowledge of effective parenting interventions among professional groups working with young children and their families.

Enhancing Workforce Knowledge and Competence in Parent Engagement

Parents' engagement in young children's learning is associated with improvements in children's literacy, behavior, and socioemotional well-being. Parent engagement is a process that can be facilitated by provider skills in communication and joint decision making with diverse families about their children's education, but programs designed to prepare individuals to work with young children do not always include evidence-informed strategies for creating successful partnerships with families. Despite growing recognition that partnerships with families contribute to the success of early childhood programs and schools in preparing children for academic success, as well as an emphasis on family engagement in statutes and policies, programs designed to prepare teachers and providers often do not include professional development related to working with parents.

Recommendation 4: The U.S. Department of Health and Human Services and the U.S. Department of Education should convene a group of experts in teaching and research and representatives of relevant practice organizations and research associations to review and improve professional development for providers who work with families of young children across sectors (e.g., education, child welfare, health). Professional development should be evaluated as to whether its core elements include best practices in engagement of and joint decision making with parents, across diverse family structures with other parental caregivers, as well as evidence-informed programs that support parents. The expert group should identify appropriate courses to address issues of parents and develop appropriate course plans and frameworks for professional development where they are lacking. Courses and coursework on parent engagement for educators of young children should be aligned with the knowledge and competencies outlined in the 2015 Institute of Medicine and National Research Council report *Transforming the Workforce for Children Birth through Age 8.*

Developing and Disseminating Best Practices in Parent Engagement

Studies have documented the effectiveness of joint decision making (parents as partners) and other approaches to parent-teacher collaboration in education. Accordingly, the Elementary and Secondary Education Act requires that school districts develop and implement parent engagement policies designed to bolster student outcomes. Yet despite the availability of evidence-based approaches for increasing parent engagement in children's learning and thereby improving child development outcomes, limited official guidance is available on how to do so. In addition to obstacles related to workforce preparation, the implementation and sustained use of best practices in parent engagement are limited by a dearth of official guidance at the local, state, and federal levels, as well as a lack of attention to how families' culture and language may moderate the effectiveness of school districts' engagement plans.

> Recommendation 5: The U.S. Department of Health and Human Services and the U.S. Department of Education should convene experts in parent engagement to create a toolbox of evidence-informed engagement and joint decision-making models, programs, and practices for implementation in early education settings. The U.S. Department of Health and Human Services and the U.S. Department of Education should disseminate this toolbox to support state and district adherence to requirements for parent engagement such as those described in the Elementary and Secondary Education Act, as well as to support the effective use of parenting interventions by health, behavioral health, and community programs with which parents and their children often have sustained and important connections. Toolbox development and dissemination efforts should include parents from diverse language and cultural backgrounds.

Elements of Effective Interventions

The committee identified features and practices of parenting interventions that appear to influence success in engaging parents and increasing their use of effective parenting practices and in promoting parents' participation and retention in programs and services. No single approach will yield the same positive results for all parents; rather, the diversity of parent beliefs, needs, and resources requires a menu of approaches. Nonetheless, the committee found a number of elements to be successful across a wide range of programs and services for parents:

- viewing parents as equal partners in determining the types of services that would most benefit them and their children;
- tailoring interventions to meet the specific needs of families;
- integrating and collaborating in services for families with multiple service needs;
- creating opportunities for parents to receive support from peers to encourage engagement, reduce stigma, and increase the sense of connection to other parents with similar circumstances;
- addressing trauma, which affects a high percentage of individuals in some communities and can interfere with parenting and healthy child development;
- making programs culturally relevant to improve their effectiveness and participation across diverse families; and
- enhancing efforts to involve fathers, who are underrepresented in parenting research.

On the effectiveness of monetary incentives in improving parents' participation and retention in programs and services, the committee found mixed results. More recent research suggests that while monetary incentives may enhance parents' initial interest in parenting programs, they do not necessarily improve attendance over time. This outcome may reflect the fact that monetary incentives do little to address some of the most common barriers to participation cited by parents, such as irregular work schedules and a lack of transportation or child care. Preliminary experimental studies on the use of conditional cash transfers to incentivize low-income families' engagement in behaviors that can enhance their well-being show an association between receipt of cash transfers and improvements in some economic outcomes such as reduced poverty, food insecurity, and housing hardships and increased employment. However, further work is needed to confirm these findings.

Some studies show that interventions incorporating the use of motivational techniques (e.g., motivational interviewing) in combination with other supportive strategies improve attendance and retention in programs and services for some individuals. Yet, there is a lack of research focused specifically on parents and identifying for which populations of parents these techniques are most effective.

COMMUNICATING EVIDENCE-BASED
PARENTING INFORMATION

As noted above, parents with knowledge of child development compared with parents without such knowledge have higher-quality interactions with their young children and are more likely to engage in parenting practices associated with children's healthy development. Moreover, parents with knowledge of parenting practices that lead to healthy outcomes in children, particularly practices that facilitate children's physical health and safety, have been found to be more likely to implement those practices. Although simply knowing about parenting practices that promote healthy child development or the benefits of a particular parenting practice does not necessarily translate into the use of such practices, awareness is foundational for behavior that supports children.

When designed and executed carefully in accordance with rigorous scientific evidence, public health campaigns are a potentially effective low-cost way to reach large and heterogeneous groups of parents. Moreover, information and communication technologies now offer promising opportunities to tailor information to the needs of parents based on their background and social circumstances. Several important ongoing efforts by the federal government and private organizations (e.g., the Centers for Disease Control and Prevention, ZERO TO THREE) communicate information to parents on developmental milestones and parenting practices grounded in evidence. Yet inequalities exist in how such information is generated, manipulated, and distributed among social groups, as well as at the individual level in the ability to access and take advantage of the information. Parenting information that is delivered via the Internet, for example, is more difficult to access for some parents, including linguistic minorities, families in rural areas, and parents with less education.

> **Recommendation 6: The U.S. Department of Health and Human Services and the U.S. Department of Education, working with state and local departments of health and education and private partners, including businesses and employers, should lead an effort to expand and improve the communication to parents of up-to-date information on children's developmental milestones and parenting practices associated with healthy child development. This effort should place particular emphasis on communication to subpopulations that are often underserved, such as immigrant families; linguistic, racial, and ethnic minorities; families in rural areas; parents of low socioeconomic status; and fathers. Given the potential of public health campaigns to promote positive parenting practices, this effort should draw on the latest state of the science of such campaigns. The effectiveness of communication**

efforts also should be evaluated to enhance their success and to inform future efforts.

ADDRESSING GAPS IN RESEARCH

The committee identified a number of interventions that show promise in supporting parenting knowledge, attitudes, and practices for specific groups of parents and children. Further research is needed to understand whether and how these interventions should be scaled up to serve all parents who would benefit from them.

To best guide policy and practice, it is important that such research focus on major gaps in current knowledge and that it use those methodologies most likely to produce evidence that can inform policy or practice. These gaps include interventions previously subjected to rigorous evaluation but not tested in diverse populations; interventions that may have been limited by their mother-only focus; and interventions focused on parents needing services for personal issues, such as mental illness.

More research also is needed on cases in which parenting interventions have been layered onto another intervention and (1) their unique benefit (separate from that of the primary intervention) has not been adequately assessed, or (2) the parenting component was found to have no impact. Examples of parenting interventions that fall into one or both of these categories are enhanced anticipatory guidance, which can be provided as part of well-child care; parenting interventions delivered in conjunction with treatment for parents who have mental illness or substance abuse or are experiencing interpersonal violence; parenting interventions delivered using new information and communication technologies; and parenting components in Head Start, Early Head Start, and WIC. Although evaluation of these layered parenting interventions has been limited, many of them have shown promising initial findings and are supported by sizable public and private investment; thus it is important for both research and practice to optimize opportunities to learn from these investments and build on this existing work. Each of the above examples offers multiple opportunities for researchers to learn from practitioners and for practitioners to work with researchers to identify possibilities for improving both research and interventions and engaging parents.

To generate research that would produce policy-relevant findings, the federal government could sponsor a relatively small number of studies involving large and diverse samples. Most likely to produce findings that would be cumulative and translatable into policy and practice would be a research agenda based on selected parenting behaviors clearly related to child outcomes, entailing studies that would utilize the same small number of measures and instruments. This research also could focus on evaluating the cost of programs and avenues through which evidence-based programs could be funded.

The evidence-based process used by HHS to design, fund, and implement the Maternal, Infant, and Early Childhood Home Visitation (MIECHV) Program could serve as a model for future research and practice aimed at improving programs designed to support parents and parenting knowledge, attitudes, and practices associated with positive child outcomes. MIECHV began with a systematic review of the evidence, followed by a state competition for funding that required the use of a consistent small set of performance measures, rigorous local evaluation, and participation in a national evaluation. The Health Resources and Services Administration also has implemented collaborative improvement and innovation networks to facilitate ongoing learning and improve models for supporting parenting knowledge, attitudes, and practices in the areas of home visiting and infant mortality prevention that could inform the refinement and implementation of other types of parenting supports.

> **Recommendation 7: The secretary of the U.S. Department of Health and Human Services and the secretary of the U.S. Department of Education should launch a national effort to address major gaps in the research-to-practice/practice-to-research pipeline related to parenting. This effort should be based on an assessment aimed at identifying the gaps in knowledge that if filled would most advance parenting-related policy and practice. The effort should include (1) systematic review of the evidence for the selected areas; (2) further development and testing of the most promising interventions; (3) research on newly developed and existing interventions conducted through collaborative improvement and innovation networks; and (4) rigorous efficacy, effectiveness, and implementation studies of promising programs and policies. In funding decisions, priority should be given to examining interventions delivered in the context of services that reach large numbers of families, such as prenatal care, well-child care, Head Start and Early Head Start, and parent engagement in the early grades.**

Three important areas of need for additional research are described in Recommendations 8, 9, and 10 below, all of which address populations of parents on which relatively little evidence-based research has been conducted and for which few evidence-based interventions have been developed.

Strengthening the Evidence on Parents with Special Needs

Many parents in the United States cope with personal challenges, such as mental illness, substance abuse, or intimate partner violence, as well as the associated stigma, that can reduce their ability to use effective parenting practices and their access to and participation in evidence-based parenting interventions. Relatively little is known about how best to support parents and parenting practices grounded in evidence for families with such special needs. Research is needed to realize the potential of available interventions that show promise for parents with special needs, as well as to develop new interventions that reflect emerging knowledge of how to support these parents. The strengths of evidenced-based training in parenting skills offer a foundation for improving existing and developing new interventions that can serve greater numbers of families with special needs, including by providing a setting of trust in which parents can reveal their needs.

> **Recommendation 8: The U.S. Department of Health and Human Services and the U.S. Department of Education, in coordination with private philanthropies, should fund research aimed at evaluating existing interventions that have shown promise and designing and evaluating new interventions for parents with special needs. The design of new interventions should be informed by elements of successful programs, which include treating parents as equal partners, tailoring interventions to meet families' needs, making programs culturally relevant, ensuring service integration and collaboration for families with multiple needs, providing opportunities for peer support, addressing trauma, and targeting both mothers and fathers. Funders should incentivize the use of state and local data to support this research.**

Strengthening the Evidence on Fathers

Children's development is shaped by the independent and combined effects of myriad influences, especially their mothers and fathers and the interactions between them. During the early years, parents are the most proximal—and most important—influence on children's development.

Substantial evidence shows that young children have optimal developmental outcomes when they experience nurturing relationships with both fathers and mothers. Research also demonstrates that children benefit when the parents who are living in the same household are supportive of each other and are generally consistent in their expectations for the child and in their parenting behaviors. Further, there is evidence that when parents live apart, children generally benefit if they have supportive relationships with each parent, at least in those cases in which the parents do not have negative relationships with each other. In contrast, children are placed at risk when their parents experience conflict or when they have very different expectations for the child, regardless of whether the parents are living together or apart. Yet despite the importance of the father-child relationship, fathers continue to be underrepresented in research on parenting and parenting support. Moreover, very few interventions aimed at improving mother-child relationships also target father-child or mother-father-child relationships, whether the parents are living together or apart. When parents are living apart, fatherhood programs typically focus on building fathers' economic capacity to parent, such as through employment or counseling, rather than on fostering father-child relationships that can promote development.

More research is needed on how to design parenting programs so they better engage fathers and enhance the parenting of both parents. Few studies have evaluated how the dyadic and reciprocal interactions between fathers and mothers and between fathers and their children affect children's development. Research is needed to identify promising interventions for fathers and mothers both in their individual relationships with their children and in their co-parenting role.

Research also is needed to understand how nonresident fathers can establish long-lasting warm and nurturing relationships with their children. Although steps have been taken to increase evidence-based and empirically rigorous evaluations of fathering programs serving noncustodial fathers (e.g., the federally funded Fatherhood Research and Practice Network), these studies are still in their early stages and may be minimally focused on changes in child outcomes.

Recommendation 9: The U.S. Department of Health and Human Services, in coordination with the U.S. Department of Education and other relevant federal agencies, private philanthropies and foundations, researchers, and research associations focused on children and families, should increase support for studies that can inform the development and improvement of parenting interventions focused on building parents' capacity to parent both individually and together. Such studies should be designed to identify strategies that can improve fathers' knowledge and use of parenting practices associated with positive child outcomes, and should examine the unique and combined effects of individual and co-parenting practices, with special attention to building strong relationships between parents and within diverse parenting relationships. The research should focus not only on adult but also on child outcomes, and should be designed to shed light on the specific ways in which greater investments in co-parenting can lead to better outcomes for children. Existing efforts to provide parenting support for both mothers and fathers should be reinforced and expanded in such programs as the Maternal, Infant, and Early Childhood Home Visitation Program, Head Start, and Early Head Start.

Strengthening the Evidence on Diverse Populations

The U.S. population of young children and their parents is demo-graphically, culturally, linguistically, and socially diverse. As noted above, although research suggests that some parenting knowledge, attitudes, and practices vary across groups, little is known about whether and how these differences matter for children's development. Moreover, relatively little is known about how engagement with, acceptance of, retention in, and the efficacy of interventions for parents vary across culturally and linguistically diverse subgroups. Finally, despite increasing diversity in family structure, data are lacking on how parenting, engagement in interventions and services, and efficacy of services may vary for diverse family forms, kinship providers (e.g., grandparents), stepparents, and other adults assuming parental roles (e.g., foster or adoptive parents). Filling these gaps would improve the ability of evidence-based programs and policies to support the needs of the range of families and children while addressing the needs of parents from historically marginalized and underrepresented populations.

Recommendation 10: The U.S. Department of Health and Human Services and the U.S. Department of Education should launch a multi-pronged effort to support basic research on parenting and applied research on parenting interventions across diverse populations and family forms. Basic research should include the identification of (1) key constructs and measures related to successful parenting among different populations; (2) important gaps in knowledge of how parenting practices and parent-child interactions affect child outcomes in culturally, ethnically, and socially diverse groups; and (3) constraints that produce disparities in access to and utilization of resources that support parenting across groups and contribute to negative outcomes for parents and children. Applied intervention research should include the formation of a collaborative improvement and innovation network to develop new and adapt existing interventions for diverse groups, and support for rigorous efficacy, effectiveness, and implementation studies of the most promising programs and policies conducted in a manner consistent with Recommendation 7 above.

1

Introduction

Parents are among the most important people in the lives of young children.[1] From birth, children are learning and rely on mothers and fathers, as well as other caregivers acting in the parenting role, to protect and care for them and to chart a trajectory that promotes their overall well-being. While parents generally are filled with anticipation about their children's unfolding personalities, many also lack knowledge about how best to provide for them. Becoming a parent is usually a welcomed event, but in some cases, parents' lives are fraught with problems and uncertainty regarding their ability to ensure their child's physical, emotional, or economic well-being.

At the same time, this study was fundamentally informed by recognition that the task of ensuring children's healthy development does not rest solely with parents or families. It lies as well with governments and organizations at the local/community, state, and national levels that provide programs and services to support parents and families. Society benefits socially and economically from providing current and future generations of parents with the support they need to raise healthy and thriving children (Karoly et al., 2005; Lee et al., 2015). In short, when parents and other caregivers are able to support young children, children's lives are enriched, and society is advantaged by their contributions.

To ensure positive experiences for their children, parents draw on the resources of which they are aware or that are at their immediate disposal.

---

[1] In this report, "parents" refers to the primary caregivers of young children in the home. In addition to biological and adoptive parents, main caregivers may include kinship (e.g., grandparents), foster, and other types of caregivers.

15

However, these resources may vary in number, availability, and quality at best, and at worst may be offered sporadically or not at all. Resources may be close at hand (e.g., family members), or they may be remote (e.g., government programs). They may be too expensive to access, or they may be substantively inadequate. Whether located in early childhood programs, school-based classrooms, well-child clinics, or family networks, support for parents of young children is critical to enhancing healthy early childhood experiences, promoting positive outcomes for children, and helping parents build strong relationships with their children (see Box 1-1).

The parent-child relationship that the parent described in Box 1-1 sought and continues to work toward is central to children's growth and

---

BOX 1-1
A Mother's Story

A mother of a second grader shared her story with the committee during one of its open sessions. She presented a poignant picture of the isolation and fear she experienced during the first few years of her son's life. At the time of his birth and afterward, she had little knowledge of the community resources available to support her in her parenting role. In overcoming the challenges she faced over the next several years, she came to understand that parents need shared knowledge, access to resources and services, and strong community bonds. She believes these are essential components of a complex system of governmental and non-governmental services, such as child care, that support parents. She explained, "I was able to see my problems as connected to larger structural problems," as information about the complex system of services available for parents was not easily accessible.

This parent's story is one of persistence and resilience, which makes her both similar to and different from many other parents experiencing the same problems. She found information through a program from which she learned the cost of child care for her son, was introduced to the supports and services available to her as a low-income parent, and was assisted in navigating the various services and programs. Her participation in a number of services required appointments in different areas of town. Without convenient transportation, she spent much of her time commuting on the bus with her son. The stressors in her life were compounded when her son began exhibiting symptoms of asthma, which made her "dread" returning home to be with her son. Depressed, lonely, and afraid, she faced struggles "every single day, dealing with these challenges on top of just trying to make a living" while trying to build a strong relationship with her child. This parent's story illustrates how many parents who are uncertain about their ability to care for their children face multiple issues in having to use different services, all with distinctive points of entry.

SOURCE: Open session presentation (2015). See Appendix A for additional information.

development—to their social-emotional and cognitive functioning, school success, and mental and physical health. Experiences during early childhood affect children's well-being over the course of their lives. The impact of parents may never be greater than during the earliest years of life, when children's brains are developing rapidly and when nearly all of their experiences are created and shaped by their parents and by the positive or difficult circumstances in which the parents find themselves. Parents play a significant role in helping children build and refine their knowledge and skills, as well as their learning expectations, beliefs, goals, and coping strategies. Parents introduce children to the social world where they develop understandings of themselves and their place and value in society, understandings that influence their choices and experiences over the life course.

PURPOSE OF THIS STUDY

Over the past several decades, researchers have identified parenting-related knowledge, attitudes, and practices that are associated with improved developmental outcomes for children and around which parenting-related programs, policies, and messaging initiatives can be designed. However, consensus is lacking on the elements of parenting that are most important to promoting child well-being, and what is known about effective parenting has not always been adequately integrated across different service sectors to give all parents the information and support they need. Moreover, knowledge about effective parenting has not been effectively incorporated into policy, which has resulted in a lack of coordinated and targeted efforts aimed at supporting parents.

Several challenges to the implementation of effective parenting practices exist as well. One concerns the scope and complexity of hardships that influence parents' use of knowledge, about effective parenting, including their ability to translate that knowledge into effective parenting practices and their access to and participation in evidence-based parenting-related programs and services. Many families in the United States are affected by such hardships, which include poverty, parental mental illness and substance use, and violence in the home. A second challenge is inadequate attention to identifying effective strategies for engaging and utilizing the strengths of fathers, discussed later in this chapter and elsewhere in this report. Even more limited is the understanding of how mothers, fathers, and other caregivers together promote their children's development and analysis of the effects of fathers' parenting on child outcomes. A third challenge is limited knowledge of exactly how culture and the direct effects of racial discrimination influence childrearing beliefs and practices or children's development (National Research Council and Institute of Medicine, 2000). Despite acknowledgment of and attention to the importance of culture in the field of developmental science, few studies have explored differences in parenting among demographic communities that vary in race and ethnicity, culture, and immigrant experience, among other factors, and the implications for children's development.

In addition, the issue of poverty persists, with low-income working families being particularly vulnerable to policy and economic shifts. Although these families have benefited in recent years from the expansion of programs and policies aimed at supporting them (discussed further below), the number of children living in deep poverty has increased (Sherman and Trisi, 2014).[2] Moreover, the portrait of America's parents and children has changed over the past 50 years as a result of shifts in the numbers and origins of immigrants to the United States and in the nation's racial, ethnic, and cultural composition (Child Trends Databank, 2015b; Migration Policy Institute, 2016). Family structure also has grown increasingly diverse across class, race, and ethnicity, with fewer children now being raised in households with two married parents; more living with same-sex parents; and more living with kinship caregivers, such as grandparents, and in other household arrangements (Child Trends Databank, 2015b). Lastly, parenting increasingly is being shaped by technology and greater access to information about parenting, some of which is not based in evidence and much of which is only now being studied closely.

The above changes in the nation's demographic, economic, and technological landscape, discussed in greater detail below, have created new opportunities and challenges with respect to supporting parents of young children. Indeed, funding has increased for some programs designed to support children and families. At the state and federal levels, policy makers recently have funded new initiatives aimed at expanding early childhood education (Barnett et al., 2015). Over the past several years, the number of states offering some form of publicly funded prekindergarten program has risen to 39, and after slight dips during the Great Recession of 2008, within-state funding of these programs has been increasing (Barnett et al., 2015). Furthermore, the 2016 federal budget allocates about $750 million for state-based preschool development grants focused on improved access and better quality of care and an additional $1 billion for Head Start programs (U.S. Department of Education, 2015; U.S. Department of Health and Human Services, 2015). The federal budget also includes additional funding for the expansion of early childhood home visiting programs ($15 billion over the next 10 years) and increased access to child care for low-income working families ($28 billion over 10 years) (U.S. Department

---

[2] Deep poverty is defined as household income that is 50 percent or more below the federal poverty level (FPL). In 2015, the FPL for a four-person household was $24,250 (Office of the Assistant Secretary for Planning and Evaluation, 2015).

of Health and Human Services, 2015). Low-income children and families have been aided as well in recent years by increased economic support from government in the form of both cash benefits (e.g., the Earned Income Tax Credit and the Child Tax Credit) and noncash benefits (e.g., Temporary Assistance for Needy Families and the Supplemental Nutrition Assistance Program), and millions of children and their families have moved out of poverty as a result (Sherman and Trisi, 2014).

It is against this backdrop of need and opportunity that the Administration for Children and Families, the Bezos Family Foundation, the Bill & Melinda Gates Foundation, the Centers for Disease Control and Prevention, the David and Lucile Packard Foundation, the Health Resources and Services Administration, the U.S. Department of Education, the Foundation for Child Development, the Heising-Simons Foundation, and the Substance Abuse and Mental Health Services Administration (SAMHSA) requested that the National Academies of Sciences, Engineering, and Medicine empanel a committee to conduct a study to examine the state of the science with respect to parenting knowledge, attitudes, and practices tied to positive parent-child interactions and child outcomes and strategies for supporting them among parents of young children ages 0-8. The purpose of this study was to provide a roadmap for the future of parenting and family support policies, practices, and research in the United States.

The statement of task for the Committee on Supporting the Parents of Young Children is presented in Box 1-2. The committee was tasked with describing barriers to and facilitators for strengthening parenting capacity and parents' participation and retention in salient programs and services. The committee was asked to assess the evidence and then make recommendations whose implementation would promote wide-scale adoption of effective strategies for enabling the identified knowledge, attitudes, and practices. Given the multi- and interdisciplinary nature of the study task, the 18-member committee comprised individuals with an array of expertise, including child development, early childhood education, developmental and educational psychology, child psychiatry, social work, family engagement research, pediatric medicine, public and health policy, health communications, implementation science, law, and economics (see Appendix D for biosketches of the committee members).

WHAT IS PARENTING?

Conceptions of who parents are and what constitute the best conditions for raising children vary widely. From classic anthropological and human development perspectives, parenting often is defined as a primary mechanism of socialization, that is, a primary means of training and preparing children to meet the demands of their environments and take advantage

BOX 1-2
Statement of Task

An ad hoc committee will conduct a study that will inform a national framework for strengthening the capacity of parents* of young children birth to age 8. The committee will examine the research to identify a core set of parenting knowledge, attitudes, and practices (KAPs) tied to positive parent-child interactions and child outcomes, as well as evidence-based strategies that support these KAPs universally and across a variety of specific populations. These KAPs and strategies will be brought together to inform a set of concrete policy recommendations, across the private and public sectors within the health, human services, and education systems. Recommendations will be tied to promoting the wide-scale adoption of the effective strategies and the enabling of the identified KAPs. The report will also identify the most pressing research gaps and recommend three to five key priorities for future research endeavors in the field. This work will primarily inform policy makers, a wide array of child and family practitioners, private industry, and researchers. The resulting report should serve as a "roadmap" for the future of parenting and family support policies, practices, and research in this country.

Specific populations of interest include fathers, immigrant families, parents with substance abuse and/or mental health issues, low-income families, single-mother headed households, and parents of children with disabilities. Given the diversity of family characteristics in the United States, the committee will examine research across diverse populations of families and identify the unique strengths/assets of traditionally underrepresented groups in the literature, including Native Americans, African Americans, and Latinos.

Contextual areas of interest include resource poor neighborhoods, unsafe communities, rural communities, availability of quality health care and education systems and services (including early childhood education), and employment opportunities.

The committee will address the following questions:

1. What are the core parenting KAPs, as identified in the literature, that support healthy child development, birth to age 8? Do core parenting KAPs differ by specific characteristics of children (e.g., age), parents, or contexts?
2. What evidence-informed strategies to strengthen parenting capacity, including family engagement strategies, in various settings (e.g., homes,

of opportunities within those environments. As Bornstein (1991, p. 6) explains, the "particular and continuing task of parents and other caregivers is to enculturate children . . . to prepare them for socially accepted physical, economic, and psychological situations that are characteristic of the culture in which they are to survive and thrive."

Attachment security is a central aspect of development that has been schools, health care centers, early childhood centers) have been shown to be effective with parents of young children prenatal to age 8? Are there key periods of intervention that are more effective in supporting parenting capacity—beginning in high school or even earlier?

3. What types of strategies work at the universal/preventive, targeted, and intensive levels (e.g., media campaigns, information sharing, text reminders; social support groups, self-monitoring and tracking online; modeling and feedback coaching, intensive home visiting), and for which populations of parents and children? The committee will consider the appropriate balance between strategies tailored to unique parent and child needs and common strategies that can be effective and accepted with parents across groups.

4. What are the most pronounced barriers, including lack of incentives, to strengthening parenting capacity and retention in effective programs and systems designed to improve developmental, health, and education outcomes for children birth to age 8? How can programs and systems be designed to remove these barriers?

5. Are there evidence-based models of systems and programs that support parenting capacity and build upon existing assets of families, including underserved, low-income families of color?

6. What are three to five research areas that warrant further investigation, in order to inform policy and practice?

Specific recommendations to strengthen parenting capacity should target federal, state, and local governments; the private sector (e.g., faith-based communities, philanthropy, business, employers, insurance companies); public education systems; and health and human service systems. The report will recommend policies to be implemented across all levels of the public sector within the health, human services, and education systems to support parents in their parenting role. For the private sector, the report may recommend specific actions they can take to enact, implement, or fund the outlined strategies or policies. In addition, the committee will make specific recommendations about how programs and policies can be paid for (e.g., insurance waivers, family co-pay subsidies, layering on other government programs, etc.).

---

*The term "parents" in this study includes the main caregivers of children in the home. In addition, this report will include a special emphasis on fathers.

defined as a child's sense of confidence that the caregiver is there to meet his or her needs (Main and Cassidy, 1988). All children develop attachments with their parents, but how parents interact with their young children, including the extent to which they respond appropriately and consistently to their children's needs, particularly in times of distress, influences whether the attachment relationship that develops is secure or insecure. Young children who are securely attached to their parents are provided a solid foundation for healthy development, including the establishment of strong peer relationships and the ability to empathize with others (Bowlby, 1978; Chen et al., 2012; Holmes, 2006; Main and Cassidy, 1988; Murphy and Laible, 2013). Conversely, young children who do not become securely attached with a primary caregiver (e.g., as a result of maltreatment or separation) may develop insecure behaviors in childhood and potentially suffer other adverse outcomes over the life course, such as mental health disorders and disruption in other social and emotional domains (Ainsworth and Bell, 1970; Bowlby, 2008; Schore, 2005).

More recently, developmental psychologists and economists have described parents as investing resources in their children in anticipation of promoting the children's social, economic, and psychological well-being. Kalil and DeLeire (2004) characterize this promotion of children's healthy development as taking two forms: (1) material, monetary, social, and psychological resources and (2) provision of support, guidance, warmth, and love. Bradley and Corwyn (2004) characterize the goals of these investments as helping children successfully regulate biological, cognitive, and social-emotional functioning.

Parents possess different levels and quality of access to knowledge that can guide the formation of their parenting attitudes and practices. As discussed in greater detail in Chapter 2, the parenting practices in which parents engage are influenced and informed by their knowledge, including facts and other information relevant to parenting, as well as skills gained through experience or education. Parenting practices also are influenced by attitudes, which in this context refer to parents' viewpoints, perspectives, reactions, or settled ways of thinking with respect to the roles and importance of parents and parenting in children's development, as well as parents' responsibilities. Attitudes may be part of a set of beliefs shared within a cultural group and founded in common experiences, and they often direct the transformation of knowledge into practice.

Parenting knowledge, attitudes, and practices are shaped, in part, by parents' own experiences (including those from their own childhood) and circumstances; expectations and practices learned from others, such as family, friends, and other social networks; and beliefs transferred through cultural and social systems. Parenting also is shaped by the availability of supports within the larger community and provided by institutions, as well as by policies that affect the availability of supportive services.

Along with the multiple sources of parenting knowledge, attitudes, and practices and their diversity among parents, it is important to acknowledge the diverse influences on the lives of children. While parents are central to children' development, other influences, such as relatives, close family friends, teachers, community members, peers, and social institutions, also contribute to children's growth and development. Children themselves are perhaps the most essential contributors to their own development. Thus, the science of parenting is framed within the theoretical perspective that parenting unfolds in particular contexts; is embedded in a network of relationships within and outside of the family; and is fluid and continuous, changing over time as children and parents grow and develop.

In addition, it is important to recognize that parenting affects not only children but also parents themselves. For instance, parenting can enrich and give focus to parents' lives; generate stress or calm; compete for time with work or leisure; and create combinations of any number of emotions, including happiness, sadness, fulfillment, and anger.

STUDY CONTEXT

As attention to early childhood development has increased over the past 20 years, so, too, has attention to those who care for young children. A recent Institute of Medicine and National Research Council report on the early childhood workforce (Institute of Medicine and National Research Council, 2015) illustrates the heightened focus not only on whether young children have opportunities to be exposed to healthy environments and supports but also on the people who provide those supports. Indeed, an important responsibility of parents is identifying those who will care for their children in their absence. Those individuals may include family members and others in parents' immediate circle, but they increasingly include non-family members who provide care and education in formal and informal settings outside the home, such as schools and home daycare centers.

Throughout its deliberations, the committee considered several questions relevant to its charge: What knowledge and attitudes do parents of young children bring to the task of parenting? How are parents engaged with their young children, and how do the circumstances and behaviors of both parents and children influence the parent-child relationship? What types of support further enhance the natural resources and skills that parents bring to the parenting role? How do parents function and make use of their familial and community resources? What policies and resources at the local, state, and federal levels assist parents? What practices do they expect those resources to reinforce, and from what knowledge and attitudes are those practices derived? On whom or what do they rely in the absence of those resources? What serves as an incentive for participation in parenting programs? How are the issues of parenting different or the same across culture and race? What factors constrain parents' positive relationships with their children, and what research is needed to advance agendas that can help parents sustain such relationships?

The committee also considered research in the field of neuroscience, which further supports the foundational role of early experiences in healthy development, with effects across the life course (Center on the Developing Child, 2007; National Research Council and Institute of Medicine, 2009; World Health Organization, 2015). During early childhood, the brain undergoes a rapid development that lays the foundation for a child's lifelong learning capacity and emotional and behavioral health (see Figure 1-1). This research has provided a more nuanced understanding of the importance of investments in early childhood and parenting. Moreover, advances in analyses of epigenetic effects on early brain development demonstrate consequences of parenting for neural development at the level of DNA, and suggest indirect consequences of family conditions such as poverty that operate on early child development, in part, through the epigenetic consequences of parenting (Lipinia and Segretin, 2015).

This report comes at a time of flux in public policies aimed at supporting parents and their young children. The cost to parents of supporting their children's healthy development (e.g., the cost of housing, health care, child care, and education) has increased at rates that in many cases have offset the improvements and increases provided for by public policies. As noted above, for example, the number of children living in deep poverty has grown since the mid-1990s (Sherman and Trisi, 2014). While children represent approximately one-quarter of the country's population, they make up 32 percent of all the country's citizens who live in poverty (Child Trends Databank, 2015a). About one in every five children in the United States is now growing up in families with incomes below the poverty line, and 9 percent of children live in deep poverty (families with incomes below 50%

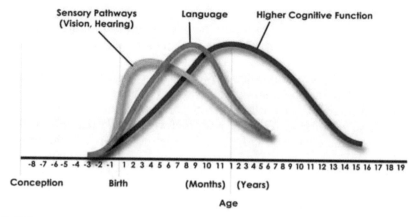

FIGURE 1-1 Human brain development: Rate of synapse formation by age.
SOURCE: Nelson (2000).

of the poverty line) (Child Trends Databank, 2015a). The risk of growing up poor continues to be particularly high for children in female-headed households; in 2013, approximately 55 percent of children under age 6 in such households lived at or below the poverty threshold, compared with 10 percent of children in married couple families (DeNavas-Walt and Proctor, 2014). Black and Hispanic children are more likely to live in deep poverty (18 and 13%, respectively) compared with Asian and white children (5% each) (Child Trends Databank, 2015a). Also noteworthy is that child care policy, including the recent increases in funding for low-income families, ties child care subsidies to employment. Unemployed parents out of school are not eligible, and job loss results in subsidy loss and, in turn, instability in child care arrangements for young children (Ha et al., 2012).

As noted earlier, this report also comes at a time of rapid change in the demographic composition of the country. This change necessitates new understandings of the norms and values within and among groups, the ways in which recent immigrants transition to life in the United States, and the approaches used by diverse cultural and ethnic communities to engage their children during early childhood and utilize institutions that offer them support in carrying out that role. The United States now has the largest absolute number of immigrants in its history (Grieco et al., 2012; Passel and Cohn, 2012; U.S. Census Bureau, 2011), and the proportion of foreign-born residents today (13.1%) is nearly as high as it was at the turn of the 20th century (National Academies of Sciences, Engineering, and Medicine, 2015). As of 2014, 25 percent of children ages 0-5 in the United States had at least one immigrant parent, compared with 13.5 percent in 1990 (Migration Policy Institute, 2016).[3] In many urban centers, such as Los Angeles, Miami, and New York City, the majority of the student body of public schools is first- or second-generation immigrant children (Suárez-Orozco et al., 2008).

Immigrants to the United States vary in their countries of origin, their reception in different communities, and the resources available to them. Researchers increasingly have called attention to the wide variation not only among but also within immigrant groups, including varying premigration histories, familiarity with U.S. institutions and culture, and childrearing

---

[3] Shifting demographics in the United States have resulted in increased pressure for service providers to meet the needs of all children and families in a culturally sensitive manner. In many cases, community-level changes have overwhelmed the capacity of local child care providers and health service workers to respond to the language barriers and cultural parenting practices of the newly arriving immigrant groups, particularly if they have endured trauma. For example, many U.S. communities have worked to address the needs of the growing Hispanic population, but it has been documented that in some cases, eligible Latinos are "less likely to access available social services than other populations" (Helms et al., 2015; Wildsmith et al., 2016).

strategies (Crosnoe, 2006; Fuller and García Coll, 2010; Galindo and Fuller, 2010; Suárez-Orozco et al., 2010; Takanishi, 2004). Immigrants often bring valuable social and human capital to the United States, including unique competencies and sociocultural strengths. Indeed, many young immigrant children display health and learning outcomes better than those of children of native-born parents in similar socioeconomic positions (Crosnoe, 2013). At the same time, however, children with immigrant parents are more likely than children in native-born families to grow up poor (Hernandez et al., 2008, 2012; National Academies of Sciences, Engineering, and Medicine, 2015; Raphael and Smolensky, 2009). Immigrant parents' efforts to raise healthy children also can be thwarted by barriers to integration that include language, documentation, and discrimination (Hernandez et al., 2012; Yoshikawa, 2011).

The increase in the nation's racial and ethnic diversity over the past several decades, related in part to immigration, is a trend that is expected to continue (Colby and Ortman, 2015; Taylor, 2014). Between 2000 and 2010, the percentage of Americans identifying as black, Hispanic, Asian, or "other" increased from 15 percent to 36 percent of the population (U.S. Census Bureau, 2011). Over this same time, the percentage of non-Hispanic white children under age 10 declined from 60 percent to 52 percent, while the percentage of Hispanic ethnicity (of any race) grew from about 19 percent to 25 percent (U.S. Census Bureau, 2011); the percentages of black/African American, American Indian/Alaska Native, and Asian children under age 10 remained relatively steady (at about 15%, 1%, and 4-5%, respectively); and the percentages of children in this age group identifying as two or more races increased from 3 percent to 5 percent (U.S. Census Bureau, 2011).

The above-noted shifts in the demographic landscape with regard to family structure, including increases in divorce rates and cohabitation, new types of parental relationships, and the involvement of grandparents and other relatives in the raising of children (Cancian and Reed, 2008; Fremstad and Boteach, 2015), have implications for how best to support families. Between 1960 and 2014, the percentage of children under age 18 who lived with two married parents (biological, nonbiological, or adoptive) decreased from approximately 85 percent to 64 percent. In 1960, 8 percent of children lived in households headed by single mothers; by 2014, that figure had tripled to about 24 percent (Child Trends Databank, 2015b; U.S. Census Bureau, 2016). Meanwhile, the proportions of children living with only their fathers or with neither parent (with either relatives or non-relatives) have remained relatively steady since the mid-1980s, at about 4 percent (see Figure 1-2). Black children are significantly more likely to live in households headed by single mothers and also are more likely to live in households where neither parent is present. In 2014, 34 percent of black

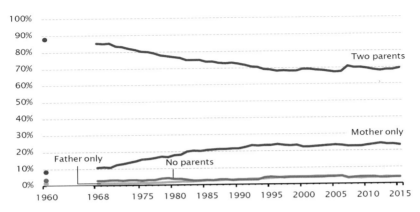

FIGURE 1-2 Living arrangements of children under age 18 in the United States, 1960-2015.
SOURCE: U.S. Census Bureau (2016).

children lived with two parents, compared with 58 percent of Hispanic children, 75 percent of white children, and 85 percent of Asian children (Child Trends Databank, 2015b).

From 1996 to 2015, the number of cohabiting couples with children rose from 1.2 million to 3.3 million (Child Trends Databank, 2015b). Moreover, data from the National Health Interview Survey show that in 2013, 30,000 children under age 18 had married same-sex parents and 170,000 had unmarried same-sex parents, and between 1.1 and 2.0 million were being raised by a parent who identified as lesbian, gay, or bisexual but was not part of a couple (Gates, 2014).

More families than in years past rely on kinship care (full-time care of children by family members other than parents or other adults with whom children have a family-like relationship). When parents are unable to care for their children because of illness, military deployment, incarceration, child abuse, or other reasons, kinship care can help cultivate familial and community bonds, as well as provide children with a sense of stability and belonging (Annie E. Casey Foundation, 2012; Winokur et al., 2014). It is estimated that the number of children in kinship care grew six times the rate of the number of children in the general population over the past decade (Annie E. Casey Foundation, 2012). In 2014, 7 percent of children lived in households headed by grandparents, as compared with 3 percent in 1970 (Child Trends Databank, 2015b), and as of 2012, about 10 percent of American children lived in a household where a grandparent was present (Ellis and Simmons, 2014). Black children are twice as likely as the overall population of children to live in kinship arrangements, with about 20 percent of black children spending time in kinship care at some point during their childhood (Annie E. Casey Foundation, 2012). Beyond kinship care, about 400,000 U.S. children under age 18 are in foster care with about one-quarter of these children living with relatives (Child Trends Databank, 2015c). Of the total number of children in foster care, 7 percent are under age 1, 33 percent are ages 1-5, and 23 percent are ages 6-10 (Child Trends Databank, 2015c). Other information about the structure of American families is more difficult to come by. For example, there is a lack of data with which to assess trends in the number of children who are raised by extended family members through informal arrangements as opposed to through the foster care system.

As noted earlier, fathers, including biological fathers and other male caregivers, have historically been underrepresented in parenting research despite their essential role in the development of young children. Young children with involved and nurturing fathers develop better linguistic and cognitive skills and capacities, including academic readiness, and are more emotionally secure and have better social connections with peers as they get older (Cabrera and Tamis-LeMonda, 2013; Harris and Marmer, 1996; Lamb, 2004; Pruett, 2000; Rosenberg and Wilcox, 2006; Yeung et al., 2000). Conversely, children with disengaged fathers have been found to be more likely to develop behavioral problems (Amato and Rivera, 1999; Ramchandani et al., 2013). With both societal shifts in gender roles and increased attention to fathers' involvement in childrearing in recent years, fathers have assumed greater roles in the daily activities associated with raising young children, such as preparing and eating meals with them, reading to and playing and talking with them, and helping them with homework (Bianchi et al., 2007; Cabrera et al., 2011; Jones and Mosher, 2013; Livingston and Parker, 2011). In two-parent families, 16 percent of fathers were stay-at-home parents in 2012, compared with 10 percent in 1989; 21 percent of these fathers stayed home specifically to care for their home or family, up from 5 percent in 1989 (Livingston, 2014). At the same time, however, fewer fathers now live with their biological children because of increases in nonmarital childbearing (U.S. Census Bureau, 2015).

In addition, as alluded to earlier, parents of young children face trans- formative changes in technology that can have a strong impact on parenting and family life (Collier, 2014). Research conducted by the Pew Internet and American Life Project shows that, relative to other household configura- tions, married parents with children under age 18 use the Internet and cell phones, own computers, and adopt broadband at higher rates (Duggan and Lenhart, 2015). Other types of households, however, such as single-parent and unmarried multiadult households, also show high usage of technology, particularly text messaging and social media (Smith, 2015). Research by the Pew Research Center (2014) shows that many parents—25 percent in one survey (Duggan et al., 2015)—view social media as a useful source of parenting information.

At the same time, however, parents also are saturated with information and faced with the difficulty of distinguishing valid information from fallacies and myths about raising children (Aubrun and Grady, 2003; Center on Media and Human Development, 2014; Dworkin et al., 2013; Future of Children, 2008). Given the number and magnitude of innovations in media and communications technologies, parents may struggle with understanding the optimal use of technology in the lives of their children.

Despite engagement with Internet resources, parents still report turning to family, friends, and physicians more often than to online sources such as Websites, blogs, and social network sites for parenting advice (Center on Media and Human Development, 2014). Although many reports allude to the potentially harmful effects of media and technology, parents generally do not report having many concerns or family conflicts regarding their children's media use. On the other hand, studies have confirmed parents' fears about an association between children's exposure to violence in media and increased anxiety (Funk, 2005), desensitization to violence (Engelhardt et al., 2011), and aggression (Willoughby et al., 2012). And although the relationship between media use and childhood obesity is challenging to disentangle, studies have found that children who spend more time with media are more likely to be overweight than children who do not (see Chapter 2) (Bickham et al., 2013; Institute of Medicine, 2011; Kaiser Family Foundation, 2004).

The benefits of the information age have included reduced barriers to knowledge for both socially advantaged and disadvantaged groups. Yet despite rapidly decreasing costs of many technologies (e.g., smartphones, tablets, and computers), parents of lower socioeconomic position and from racial and ethnic minority groups are less likely to have access to and take advantage of these resources (Center on Media and Human Development, 2014; File and Ryan, 2014; Institute of Medicine, 2006; Perrin and Duggan, 2015; Smith, 2015; Viswanath et al., 2012). A digital divide also exists between single-parent and two-parent households, as the cost of a computer and monthly Internet service can be more of a financial burden for the former families, which on average have lower household incomes (Allen and Rainie, 2002; Dworkin et al., 2013).

STUDY APPROACH

The committee's approach to its charge consisted of a review of the evidence in the scientific literature and several other information-gathering activities.

Evidence Review

The committee conducted an extensive review of the scientific literature pertaining to the questions raised in its statement of task (Box 1-2). It did not undertake a full review of all parenting-related studies because it was tasked with providing a targeted report that would direct stakeholders to best practices and succinctly capture the state of the science. The committee's literature review entailed English-language searches of databases including, but not limited to, the Cochrane Database of Systematic Reviews, Medline, the Education Resources Information Center (ERIC), PsycINFO, Scopus, and Web of Science. Additional literature and other resources were identified by committee members and project staff using traditional academic research methods and online searches. The committee focused its review on research published in peer-reviewed journals and books (including individual studies, review articles, and meta-analyses), as well as reports issued by government agencies and other organizations. The committee's review was concentrated primarily, although not entirely, on research conducted in the United States, occasionally drawing on research from other Western countries (e.g., Germany and Australia), and rarely on research from other countries.

In reviewing the literature and formulating its conclusions and recommendations, the committee considered several, sometimes competing, dimensions of empirical work: internal validity, external validity, practical significance, and issues of implementation, such as scale-up with fidelity (Duncan et al., 2007; McCartney and Rosenthal, 2000; Rosenthal and Rosnow, 2007).

With regard to *internal validity*, the committee viewed random-assignment experiments as the primary model for establishing cause-and-effect relationships between variables with manipulable causes (e.g., Rosenthal and Rosnow, 2007; Shadish et al., 2001). Given the relatively limited body of evidence from experimental studies in the parenting literature, however, the committee also considered findings from quasi-experimental studies (including those using regression discontinuity, instrumental variables, and difference-in-difference techniques based on natural experiments) (Duncan et al., 2007; Foster, 2010; McCartney et al., 2006) and from observational studies, a method that can be used to test logical propositions inherent to causal inference, rule out potential sources of bias, and assess the sensitivity of results to assumptions regarding study design and measurement. These include longitudinal studies and limited cross-sectional studies. Although quasi- and nonexperimental studies may fail to meet the "gold standard" of randomized controlled trials for causal inference, studies with a variety of internal validity strengths and weaknesses can collectively provide useful evidence on causal influences (Duncan et al., 2014).

When there are different sources of evidence, often with some differences in estimates of the strength of the evidence, the committee used its collective experience to integrate the information and draw reasoned conclusions.

With regard to *external validity*, the committee attempted to take into account the extent to which findings can be generalized across population groups and situations. This entailed considering the demographic, socio-economic, and other characteristics of study participants; whether variables were assessed in the real-world contexts in which parents and children live (e.g., in the home, school, community); whether study findings build the knowledge base with regard to both efficacy (i.e., internal validity in highly controlled settings) and effectiveness (i.e., positive net treatment effects in ecologically valid settings); and issues of cultural competence (Bracht and Glass, 1968; Bronfenbrenner, 2009; Cook and Campbell, 1979; Harrison and List, 2004; Lerner et al., 2000; Rosenthal and Rosnow, 2007; Whaley and Davis, 2007). However, the research literature is limited in the extent to which generalizations across population groups and situations are examined.

With regard to *practical significance*, the committee considered the magnitude of likely causal impacts within both an empirical context (i.e., measurement, design, and method) and an economic context (i.e., benefits relative to costs), and with attention to the salience of outcomes (e.g., how important an outcome is for promoting child well-being) (Duncan et al., 2007; McCartney and Rosenthal, 2000). As discussed elsewhere in this report, however, the committee found limited economic evidence with which to draw conclusions about investing in interventions at scale or to weigh the costs and benefits of interventions. (See the discussion of other information-gathering activities below.) Also with respect to practical significance, the committee considered the manipulability of the variables under consideration in real-world contexts, given that the practical significance of study results depend on whether the variables examined are represented or experienced commonly or uncommonly among particular families (Fabes et al., 2000).

Finally, the committee took into account issues of *implementation*, such as whether interventions can be brought to and sustained at scale (Durlak and DuPre, 2008; Halle et al., 2013). Experts in the field of implementation science emphasize not only the evidence behind programs but also the fundamental roles of scale-up, dissemination planning, and program monitoring and evaluation. Scale-up in turn requires attending to the ability to implement adaptive program practices in response to heterogeneous, real-world contexts, while also ensuring fidelity for the potent levers of change or prevention (Franks and Schroeder, 2013). Thus, the committee relied on both evidence on scale-up, dissemination, and sustainability from empirically based programs and practices that have been implemented and evaluated, and more general principles of implementation science, including considerations of capacity and readiness for scale-up and sustainability at the macro (e.g., current national politics) and micro (e.g., community resources) levels.

The review of the evidence conducted for this study, especially pertaining to strategies that work at the universal, targeted, and intensive levels to strengthen parenting capacity (questions 2 and 3 from the committee's statement of task [Box 1-2]), also entailed searches of several databases that, applying principles similar to those described above, assess the strength of the evidence for parenting-related programs and practices: the National Registry of Evidence-Based Programs and Practices (NREPP), supported by SAMHSA; the California Evidence-Based Clearinghouse for Child Welfare (CEBC), which is funded by the state of California; and Blueprints for Healthy Youth Development, which has multiple funding sources. Although each of these databases is unique with respect to its history, sponsors, and objectives (NREPP covers mental health and substance abuse interventions, CEBC is focused on evidence relevant to child welfare, and Blueprints describes programs designed to promote the health and well-being of children), all are recognized nationally and internationally and undergo a rigorous review process.

The basic principles of evaluation and classification and the processes for classification of evidence-based practices are common across NREPP, CEBC, and Blueprints. Each has two top categories—optimal and promising—for programs and practices (see Appendix B; see also Burkhardt et al., 2015; Means et al., 2015; Mihalic and Elliot, 2015; Soydan et al., 2010). Given the relatively modest investment in research on programs for parents and young children, however, the array of programs that are highly rated remains modest. For this reason, the committee considered as programs with the most robust evidence not only those included in the top two categories of Blueprints and CEBC but also those with an average rating of 3 or higher in NREPP. The committee's literature searches also captured well-supported programs that are excluded from these databases (e.g., because they are recent and/or have not been submitted for review) but have sound theoretical underpinnings and rely on well-recognized intervention and implementation mechanisms.

Other reputable information sources used in producing specific portions of this report were What Works for Health (within the County Health Rankings and Roadmaps Program, a joint effort of the Robert Wood Johnson Foundation and the University of Wisconsin); the What Works Clearinghouse of the U.S. Department of Education's Institute of Education Services; and HHS's Home Visiting Evidence of Effectiveness (HomVEE) review.

In addition, the committee chose to consider findings from research using methodological approaches that are emerging as a source of innovation and improvement. These approaches are gaining momentum in parenting research and are being developed and funded by the federal government and private philanthropy. Examples are breakthrough series collaborative approaches, such as the Home Visiting Collaborative Innovation and Improvement Network to Reduce Infant Mortality, and designs such as factorial experiments that have been used to address topics relevant to this study.

Other Information-Gathering Activities

The committee held two open public information-gathering sessions to hear from researchers, practitioners, parents, and other stakeholders on topics germane to this study and to supplement the expertise of the committee members (see Appendix A for the agendas of these open sessions). Material from these open sessions is referenced in this report where relevant.

As noted above, the committee's task included making recommendations related to promoting the wide-scale adoption of effective strategies for supporting parents and the salient knowledge, attitudes, and practices. Cost is an important consideration for the implementation of parenting programs at scale. Therefore, the committee commissioned a paper reviewing the available economic evidence for investing in parenting programs at scale to inform its deliberations on this portion of its charge. Findings and excerpts from this paper are integrated throughout Chapters 3 through 6. The committee also commissioned a second paper summarizing evidence-based strategies used by health care systems and providers to help parents acquire and sustain knowledge, attitudes, and practices that promote healthy child development. The committee drew heavily on this paper in developing sections of the report on universal/preventive and targeted interventions for parents in health care settings. Lastly, a commissioned paper on evidence-based strategies to support parents of children with mental illness formed the basis for a report section on this population.[4]

In addition, the committee conducted two sets of group and individual semistructured interviews with parents participating in family support programs at community-based organizations in Omaha, Nebraska, and Washington, D.C. Parents provided feedback on the strengths they bring to parenting, challenges they face, how services for parents can be improved, and ways they prefer to receive parenting information, among other topics. Excerpts from these interviews are presented throughout this report as "Parent Voices" to provide real-world examples of parents' experiences and to supplement the discussion of particular concepts and the committee's findings.

---

[4]The papers commissioned by the committee are in the public access file for the study and can be requested at https://www8.nationalacademies.org/cp/ManageRequest.aspx?key=49669 [October 2016].

TERMINOLOGY AND STUDY PARAMETERS

As specified in the statement of task for this study (Box 1-2), the term "parents" refers in this report to those individuals who are the primary caregivers of young children in the home. Therefore, the committee reviewed studies that involved not only biolofical and adoptive parents but also relative/kinship providers (e.g., grandparents), stepparents, foster parents, and other types of caregivers, although research is sparse on unique issues related to nontraditional caregivers. The terms "knowledge," "attitudes," and "practices" and the relationships among them were discussed earlier in this chapter, and further detail can be found in Chapter 2).

The committee recognized that to a certain degree, ideas about what is considered effective parenting vary across cultures and ecological conditions, including economies, social structures, religious beliefs, and moral values (Cushman, 1995). To address this variation, and in accordance with its charge, the committee examined research on how core parenting knowledge, attitudes, and practices differ by specific characteristics of children, parents, and contexts. However, because the research on parenting has traditionally underrepresented several populations (e.g., caregivers other than mothers), the evidence on which the committee could draw to make these comparisons was limited.

The committee interpreted "evidence-based/informed strategies" very broadly as ranging from teaching a specific parenting skill, to manualized parenting programs, to policies that may affect parenting. The term "interventions" is generally used in this report to refer to all types of strategies, while more specific terms (e.g., "program," "well-child care") are used to refer to particular types or sets of interventions. Also, recognizing that nearly every facet of society has a role to play in supporting parents and ensuring that children realize their full potential, the committee reviewed not only strategies designed expressly for parents (e.g., parenting skills training) but also, though to a lesser degree, programs and policies not designed specifically for parents that may nevertheless affect an individual's capacity to parent (e.g., food assistance and housing programs, health care policies).

As noted earlier in this chapter, this report was informed by a life-course perspective on parenting, given evidence from neuroscience and a range of related research that the early years are a critical period in shaping how individuals fare throughout their lives. The committee also aimed to take a strengths/assets-based approach (e.g., to identify strategies that build upon the existing assets of parents), although the extent to which this approach could be applied was limited by the paucity of research examining parenting from this perspective.

GUIDING PRINCIPLES

A number of principles guided this study. First, following the ideas of Dunst and Espe-Sherwindt (2016), the distinction between two types of family-centered practices—relational and participatory—informed the committee's thinking. *Relational practices* are those focused primarily on intervening with families using compassion, active and reflective listening, empathy, and other techniques. *Participatory practices* are those that actively engage families in decision making and aim to improve families' capabilities. In addition, *family-centered practices* focused on the context of successful parenting are a key third form of support for parenting. A premise of the committee is that many interventions with the most troubled families and children will require all these types of services—often delivered concurrently over a lengthy period of time.

Second, many programs are designed to serve families at particular risk for problems related to cognitive and social-emotional development, health, and well-being. Early Head Start and Head Start, for example, are means tested and designed for low-income families most of whom are known to face not just one risk factor (low income) but also others that often cluster together (e.g., living in dangerous neighborhoods, exposure to trauma, social isolation, unfamiliarity with the dominant culture or language). Special populations addressed in this report typically are at very high risk because of this exposure to multiple risk factors. Research has shown that children in such families have the poorest outcomes, in some instances reaching a level of toxic stress that seriously impairs their developmental functioning (Shonkoff and Garner, 2012). Of course, in addition to characterizing developmental risk, it is essential to understand the corresponding adaptive processes and protective factors, as it is the balance of risk and protective factors that determines outcomes. In many ways, supporting parents is one way to attempt to change that balance.

From an intervention point of view, several principles are central. First, intervention strategies need to be designed to have measurable effects over time and to be sustainable. Second, it is necessary to focus on the needs of individual families and to tailor interventions to achieve desired outcomes. The importance of personalized approaches is widely acknowledged in medicine, education, and other areas. An observation perhaps best illustrated in the section on parents of children with developmental disabilities in Chapter 5, although the committee believes this approach applies to many of the programs described in this report. A corresponding core principle of intervention is viewing parents as equal partners, experts in what both they and their children need. It is important as well that multiple kinds of services for families be integrated and coordinated. As illustrated earlier in Box 1-1, families may be receiving interventions from multiple sources delivered in different places, making coordination all the more important.

A useful framework for thinking about interventions is described in the National Research Council and Institute of Medicine (2009) report *Preventing Mental, Emotional, and Behavioral Disorders among Young People*. Prevention interventions encompass mental health promotion: universal prevention, defined as interventions that are valuable for all children; selected prevention, aimed at populations at high risk (such as children whose parents have mental illness); and indicated prevention, focused on children already manifesting symptoms. Treatment interventions include case identification, standard treatment for known disorders, accordance of long-term treatment with the goal of reduction in relapse or occurrence, and aftercare and rehabilitation (National Research Council and Institute of Medicine, 2009).

The committee recognizes that engaging and retaining children and families in parenting interventions are critical challenges. A key to promoting such engagement may be cultural relevance. Families representing America's diverse array of cultures, languages, and experiences are likely to derive the greatest benefit from interventions designed and implemented to allow for flexibility.

Finally, the question of widespread implementation and dissemination of parenting interventions is critically important. Given the cost of testing evidence-based parenting programs, the development of additional programs needs to be built on the work that has been done before. Collectively, interventions also are more likely to achieve a significant level of impact if they incorporate some of the elements of prior interventions. In any case, a focus on the principles of implementation and dissemination clearly is needed. As is discussed in this report, the committee calls for more study and experience with respect to taking programs to scale.

REPORT ORGANIZATION

This report is divided into eight chapters. Chapter 2 examines desired outcomes for children and reviews the existing research on parenting knowledge, attitudes, and practices that support positive parent-child interactions and child outcomes. Based on the available research, this chapter identifies a set of core knowledge, attitudes, and practices. Chapter 3 provides a brief overview of some of the major federally funded programs and policies that support parents in the United States. Chapters 4 and 5 describe evidence-based and evidence-informed strategies for supporting parents and enabling the identified knowledge, attitudes, and practices, including universal and widely used interventions (Chapter 4) and interventions targeted to parents of children with special needs and parents who themselves face adversities

(Chapter 5). Chapter 6 reviews elements of effective programs for strengthening parenting capacity and parents' participation and retention in effective programs and systems. Chapter 7 describes a national framework for supporting parents of young children. Finally, Chapter 8 presents the committee's conclusions and recommendations for promoting the wide-scale adoption of effective intervention strategies and parenting practices linked to healthy child outcomes, as well as areas for future research.

REFERENCES

Ainsworth, M.D.S., and Bell, S.M. (1970). Attachment, exploration, and separation: Illustrated by the behavior of one-year-olds in a strange situation. *Child Development, 41*(1), 49-67.

Allen, K., and Rainie, L. (2002). *Parents Online.* Available: http://www.pewinternet. org/2002/11/17/parents-online/ [October 2016].

Amato, P.R., and Rivera, F. (1999). Paternal involvement and children's behavior problems. *Journal of Marriage and Family, 61*(2), 375-384.

Annie E. Casey Foundation. (2012). *Stepping Up for Kids: What Government and Communities Should Do to Support Kinship Families.* Available: http://www.issuelab.org/ permalink/resource/12484 [October 2016].

Aubrun, A., and Grady, J. (2003). *Two Cognitive Obstacles to Preventing Child Abuse: The "Other Mind" Mistake and the "Family Bubble."* Washington, DC: Cultural Logic.

Barnett, W.S., Carolan, M.E., Squires, J.H., Brown, K.C., and Horowitz, M. (2015). *The State of Preschool 2014.* New Brunswick, NJ: National Institute for Early Education Research, Rutgers Graduate School of Education.

Bianchi, S.M., Robinson, J.P., and Milkie, M.A. (2007). *Changing Rhythms of American Family Life: Table 4.1.* New York: Russell Sage Foundation.

Bickham, D.S., Blood, E.A., Walls, C.E., Shrier, L.A., and Rich, M. (2013). Characteristics of screen media use associated with higher BMI in young adolescents. *Pediatrics, 131*(5), 935-941.

Bornstein, M.H. (1991). *Cultural Approaches to Parenting (The Crosscurrents in Contemporary Psychology Series).* Hillsdale, NJ: Lawrence Erlbaum Associates.

Bowlby, J. (1978). Attachment theory and its therapeutic implications. *Adolescent Psychiatry, 6,* 5-33.

Bowlby, J. (2008). *A Secure Base: Parent-Child Attachment and Healthy Human Development.* New York: Basic Books.

Bracht, G.H., and Glass, G.V. (1968). The external validity of experiments. *American Educational Research Journal, 5*(4), 437-474.

Bradley, R.H., and Corwyn, R.F. (2004). "Family process" investments that matter for child well-being. In A. Kalil and T.C. DeLeire (Eds.), *Family Investments in Children's Potential Resources and Parenting Behaviors That Promote Success* (pp. 1-32). Mahwah, NJ: Lawrence Erlbaum Associates.

Bronfenbrenner, U. (2009). *The Ecology of Human Development: Experiments by Nature and Design.* Cambridge, MA: Harvard University Press.

Burkhardt, J.T., Schroter, D.C., Magura, S., Means, S.N., and Coryn, C.L.S. (2015). An overview of evidence-based program registers (EBPRs) for behavioral health. *Evaluation and Program Planning, 48,* 92-99.

Cabrera, N., and Tamis-LeMonda, C. (2013). *Handbook of Father Involvement: Multidisciplinary Perspective* (2nd ed.). Mahwah, NJ: Routledge.

Cabrera, N. J., Hofferth, S. L, and Chae, S. (2011). Patterns and predictors of father-infant engagement across race/ethnic groups. *Early Childhood Research Quarterly, 26*(3), 365-375.

Cancian, M., and Reed, D. (2008). *Family Structure, Childbearing, and Parental Employment Implications for the Level and Trend in Poverty*. Madison: University of Wisconsin-Madison, Institute for Research on Poverty.

Center on Media and Human Development. (2014). *Parenting in the Age of Digital Technology: A National Survey*. Evanston, IL: Northwestern University.

Center on the Developing Child. (2007). *A Science-Based Framework for Early Childhood Policy: Using Evidence to Improve Outcomes in Learning, Behavior, and Health for Vulnerable Children*. Cambridge, MA: Center on the Developing Child at Harvard University.

Chen, F.M., Lin, H.S., and Li, C.H. (2012). The role of emotion in parent-child relationships: Children's emotionality, maternal meta-emotion, and children's attachment security. *Journal of Child and Family Studies, 21*(3), 403-410.

Child Trends Databank. (2015a). *Children in Poverty*. Available: http://www.childtrends.org/?indicators=children-in-poverty [May 2016].

Child Trends Databank. (2015b). *Family Structure*. Available: http://www.childtrends.org/?indicators=family-structure [October 2016].

Child Trends Databank. (2015c). *Foster Care*. Available: http://www.childtrends.org/?indicators=foster-care [May 2016].

Colby, S., and Ortman, L. (2015). *Projections of the Size and Composition of the U.S. Population: 2014 to 2060*. Available: http://www.census.gov/content/dam/Census/library/publications/2015/demo/p25-1143.pdf [May 2016].

Collier, A. (2014). Perspectives on parenting in a digital age. In A.B. Jordan and D. Romer (Eds.), *Media and the Well-Being of Children and Adolescents* (pp. 247-265). New York: Oxford University Press.

Cook, T.D., and Campbell, D.T. (1979). *Quasi-Experimentation: Design & Analysis Issues for Field Settings*. Boston, MA: Houghton Mifflin.

Crosnoe, R. (2006). *Mexican Roots, American Schools: Helping Mexican Immigrant Children Succeed*. Redwood City, CA: Stanford University Press.

Crosnoe, R. (2013). *Preparing the Children of Immigrants for Early Academic Success*. Washington, DC: Migration Policy Institute.

Cushman, P. (1995). *Constructing the Self, Constructing America: A Cultural History of Psychotherapy*. Boston, MA: Addison-Wesley.

DeNavas-Walt, C., and Proctor, B.D. (2014). *Current Population Reports: Income and Poverty in the United States: 2013*. Washington, DC: U.S. Census Bureau.

Duggan, M., and Lenhart, A. (2015). *Parents and Social Media: Mothers are Especially Likely to Give and Receive Support on Social Media*. Washington, DC: Pew Research Center.

Duggan, M., Lenhart, A., Lampe, C., and Ellison, N.B. (2015). *Parents and Social Media*. Available: http://www.pewinternet.org/2015/07/16/parents-and-social-media/#fn-13802-1 [October 2016].

Duncan, G.J., Ludwig, J., and Magnuson, K.A. (2007). Reducing poverty through preschool interventions. *The Future of Children, 17*(2), 143-160.

Duncan, G.J., Engel, M., Claessens, A., and Dowsett, C.J. (2014). Replication and robustness in developmental research. *Developmental Psychology, 50*(11), 2417-2425.

Dunst, C.J., and Espe-Sherwindt, M. (2016). Family-centered practices in early intervention. In B. Reichow, B. Boyd, E. Barton, and S. Odom (Eds.), *Handbook of Early Childhood Special Education*. New York: Springer.

Durlak, J.A., and DuPre, E.P. (2008). Implementation matters: A review of research on the influence of implementation on program outcomes and the factors affecting implementation. *American Journal of Community Psychology, 41*(3-4), 327-350.

Dworkin, J., Connell, J., and Doty, J. (2013). A literature review of parents' online behavior. *Cyberpsychology: Journal of Psychological Research on Cyberspace, 7*, 2.

Ellis, R.R., and Simmons, T. (2014). *Coresident Grandparents and Their Grandchildren: 2012.* Washington, DC: U.S. Census Bureau.

Engelhardt, C.R., Bartholow, B.D., Kerr, G.T., and Bushman, B.J. (2011). This is your brain on violent video games: Neural desensitization to violence predicts increased aggression following violent video game exposure. *Journal of Experimental Social Psychology, 47*(5), 1033-1036.

Fabes, R.A., Martin, C.L., Hanish, L.D., and Updegraff, K.A. (2000). Criteria for evaluating the significance of developmental research in the twenty-first century: Force and counterforce. *Child Development, 71*(1), 212-221.

File, T., and Ryan, C. (2014). *Computer and Internet Use in the United States: 2013.* American Community Survey Reports, ACS-28. Available: https://www.census.gov/history/pdf/2013computeruse.pdf [October 2016].

Foster, E.M. (2010). Causal inference and developmental psychology. *Developmental Psychology, 46*(6), 1454-1480.

Franks, R.P., and Schroeder, J. (2013). Implementation science: What do we know and where do we go from here? In T. Halle, A. Metz, and I. Martinez-Beck (Eds.), *Applying Implementation Science in Early Childhood Programs and Systems* (pp. 5-20). Baltimore, MD: Paul H. Brookes.

Fremstad, S., and Boteach, M. (2015). *Valuing All Our Families: Progressive Policies That Strengthen Family Commitments and Reduce Family Disparities.* Washington, DC: Center for American Progress.

Fuller, B., and García Coll, C. (2010). Learning from Latinos: Contexts, families, and child development in motion. *Developmental Psychology, 46*(3), 559-565.

Funk, J.B. (2005). Video games. *Adolescent Medicine Clinics, 16*(2), 395-411.

Future of Children. (2008). *Parenting in a Media-Saturated World.* Available: http://www.futureofchildren.org/futureofchildren/publications/highlights/18_01_highlights_05. pdf [October 2016].

Galindo, C., and Fuller, B. (2010). The social competence of Latino kindergartners and growth in mathematical understanding. *Developmental Psychology, 46*(3), 579-592.

Gates, G.J. (2014). *LGB Families and Relationships: Analyses of the 2013 National Health Interview Survey.* Available: http://williamsinstitute.law.ucla.edu/wp-content/uploads/lgb-families-nhis-sep-2014.pdf [May 2016].

Grieco, E.M., Trevelyan, E., Larsen, L., Acosta, Y.D., Gambino, C., de la Cruz, P., Gryn, T., and Walters, N. (2012). *The Size, Place of Birth, and Geographic Distribution of the Foreign-Born Population in the United States: 1960 to 2010.* Washington, DC: U.S. Census Bureau.

Ha, Y., Magnuson, K., and Ybarra, M. (2012). Patterns of child care subsidy receipt and the stability of child care. *Children and Youth Services Review, 34*(9), 1834-1844.

Halle, T., Metz, A., and Martinez-Beck, I. (Eds.). (2013). *Applying Implementation Science in Early Childhood Programs and Systems.* Baltimore, MD: Paul H. Brookes.

Harris, K.M., and Marmer, J.K. (1996). Poverty, paternal involvement, and adolescent well-being. *Journal of Family Issues, 17*(5), 614-640.

Harrison, G.W., and List, J.A. (2004). Field experiments. *Journal of Economic Literature, 42*(4), 1009-1055.

Helms, H.M., Hengstebeck, N.D., Rodriguez, Y., Mendez, J.L., and Crosby, D.A. (2015). *Mexican Immigrant Family Life in a Pre-Emerging Southern Gateway Community.* National Research Center on Hispanic Children and Families. Available: http://www. childtrends.org/wp-content/uploads/2015/09/Hispanic-Center-Unidos-Report.pdf [May 2016].

Hernandez, D.J., Denton, N.A., and Macartney, S.E. (2008). Children in immigrant families: Looking to America's future. *Society for Research in Child Development, 22*(3), 3-22.

Hernandez, D.J., Macartney, S., and Cervantes, W. (2012). Measuring social disparities via the CWI: Race-ethnicity, income, and immigrant status. In K.C. Land (Ed.), *The Well-Being of America's Children* (vol. 6, pp. 77-120). Dordrecht, The Netherlands: Springer.

Holmes, J. (2006). *John Bowlby and Attachment Theory.* New York: Routledge.

Institute of Medicine. (2006). *Examining the Health Disparities Research Plan of the National Institutes of Health: Unfinished Business.* G.E. Thomson, F. Mitchell, and M. Williams (Eds.). Board on Health Sciences Policy. Washington, DC: The National Academies Press.

Institute of Medicine. (2011). *Early Childhood Obesity Prevention Policies.* L.L. Birch, L. Parker, and A. Burns (Eds.). Committee on Obesity Prevention Policies for Young Children. Washington, DC: The National Academies Press.

Institute of Medicine and National Research Council. (2015). *Transforming the Workforce for Children Birth through Age 8: A Unifying Foundation.* L. Allen and B.B. Kelly (Eds.). Committee on the Science of Children Birth to Age 8: Deepening and Broadening the Foundation for Success; Board on Children, Youth, and Families. Washington, DC: The National Academies Press.

Jones, J., and Mosher, W.D. (2013). Fathers' involvement with their children: United States, 2006-2010. *National Health Statistics Reports, 71*, 1-22.

Kalil, A., and DeLeire, T. (Eds.). (2004). *Family Investments in Children: Resources and Parenting Behaviors That Promote Success.* Mahwah, NJ: Lawrence Erlbaum Associates.

Kaiser Family Foundation. (2004). *The Role of Media in Childhood Obesity.* Available: https:// kaiserfamilyfoundation.files.wordpress.com/2013/01/the-role-of-media-in-childhood-obesity.pdf [October 2016].

Karoly, L.A., Kilburn, M.R., and Cannon, J.S. (2005). *Early Childhood Interventions: Proven Results, Future Promise.* Available: http://www.rand.org/content/dam/rand/pubs/ monographs/2005/RAND_MG341.pdf [May 2016].

Lamb, M.E. (2004). *The Role of the Father in Child Development* (4th ed.). Hoboken, NJ: John Wiley & Sons.

Lee, S., Aos, S., and Pennucci, A. (2015). *What Works and What Does Not? Benefit-Cost Findings from the Washington State Institute for Public Policy.* Doc. No. 15-02-4101. Olympia: Washington State Institute for Public Policy.

Lerner, R.M., Fisher, C.B., and Weinberg, R.A. (2000). Toward a science for and of the people: Promoting civil society through the application of developmental science. *Child Development, 71*(1), 11-20.

Lipinia, S.J., and Segretin, M.S. (2015). Strengths and weakness of neuroscientific investigations of childhood poverty: Future directions. *Frontiers in Human Neuroscience, 9*(53), 1-5.

Livingston, G. (2014). *Growing Number of Dads Home with the Kids.* Available: http://www. pewsocialtrends.org/2014/06/05/growing-number-of-dads-home-with-the-kids/ [October 2016].

Livingston, G., and Parker, K. (2011). *A Tale of Two Fathers: More Are Active, but More Are Absent.* Washington, DC: Pew Research Center.

Main, M., and Cassidy, J. (1988). Categories of response to reunion with the parent at age 6: Predictable from infant attachment classifications and stable over a 1-month period. *Developmental Psychology, 24*(3), 415-426.

McCartney, K., and Rosenthal, R. (2000). Effect size, practical importance, and social policy for children. *Child Development, 71*(1), 173-180.

McCartney, K., Burchinal, M., and Bub, K.L. (2006). Best practices in quantitative methods for developmentalists. *Monographs of the Society for Research in Child Development, 7*(3), 1-150.

Means, S.N., Magura, S., Burkhardt, J.T., Schroter, D.C., and Coryn, C.L.S. (2015). Comparing rating paradigms for evidence-based program registers in behavioral health: Evidentiary criteria and implications for assessing programs. *Evaluation and Program Planning Evaluation and Program Planning, 48*(1), 100-116.

Migration Policy Institute. (2016). *U.S. Immigration Trends.* Available: http://www.migrationpolicy.org/programs/data-hub/us-immigration-trends#children [June 2016].

Mihalic, S.F., and Elliott, D.S. (2015). Evidence-based programs registry: Blueprints for healthy youth development. *Evaluation and Program Planning Evaluation and Program Planning, 48*(4), 124-131.

Murphy, T.P., and Laible, D.J. (2013). The influence of attachment security on preschool children's empathic concern. *International Journal of Behavioral Development, 37*(5), 436-440.

National Academies of Sciences, Engineering, and Medicine. (2015). *The Integration of Immigrants into American Society.* Panel on the Integration of Immigrants into American Society, M.C. Waters and M.G. Pineau, Eds. Committee on Population, Division of Behavioral and Social Sciences and Education. Washington, DC: The National Academies Press. doi: 10.17226/21746.

National Research Council and Institute of Medicine. (2000). *From Neurons to Neighborhoods: The Science of Early Childhood Development.* J.P. Shonkoff and D.A. Phillips (Eds.). Committee on Integrating the Science of Early Childhood Development. Board on Children, Youth, and Families; Commission on Behavioral and Social Sciences and Education. Washington, DC: National Academy Press.

National Research Council and Institute of Medicine. (2009). *Preventing Mental, Emotional, and Behavioral Disorders among Young People: Progress and Possibilities.* M.E. O'Connell, T. Boat, and K.E. Warner (Eds.). Committee on the Prevention of Mental Disorders and Substance Abuse Among Children, Youth and Young Adults: Research Advances and Promising Interventions; Board on Children, Youth and Families; Division of Behavioral and Social Sciences and Education. Washington, DC: The National Academies Press.

Nelson, C.A. (2000). The neurobiological bases of early intervention. In J.P. Shonkoff and S.J. Meisels (Eds.), *Handbook of Early Childhood Intervention* (2nd ed., pp. 204-227). Cambridge, MA: Cambridge University Press.

Office of the Assistant Secretary for Planning and Evaluation. (2015). *2015 Poverty Guidelines.* Available: http://aspe.hhs.gov/2015-poverty-guidelines [December 2, 2015].

Open session presentation. (2015). *Perspectives from Parents.* Presentation before the Committee on Supporting the Parents of Young Children, June 29, Irvine, CA.

Passel, J.S., and Cohn, D. (2012). *Unauthorized Immigrants: 11.1 Million in 2011.* Washington, DC: Pew Research Center.

Perrin, A., and Duggan, M. (2015). *Americans' Internet Access: 2000-2015.* Washington, DC: Pew Research Center.

Pew Research Center. (2014). *Internet Use Over Time.* Available: http://www.pewinternet.org/data-trend/internet-use/internet-use-over-time [November 2015].

Pruett, K. (2000). *Father-Need.* New York: Broadway Books.

Ramchandani, P.G., Domoney, J., Sethna, V., Psychogiou, L., Vlachos, H., and Murray, L. (2013). Do early father-infant interactions predict the onset of externalising behaviours in young children? Findings from a longitudinal cohort study. *Journal of Child Psychology and Psychiatry, and Allied Disciplines, 54*(1), 56-64.

Raphael, S., and Smolensky, E. (2009). Immigration and poverty in the United States. *The American Economic Review*, 41-44.

Rosenberg, J., and Wilcox, W.B. (2006). *The Importance of Fathers in the Healthy Development of Children: Fathers and Their Impact on Children's Well-Being.* Washington, DC: U.S. Children's Bureau, Office on Child Abuse and Neglect.

Rosenthal, R., and Rosnow, R. (2007). *Essentials of Behavioral Research: Methods and Data Analysis* (3rd ed.). Boston, MA: McGraw Hill.

Schore, A.N. (2005). Attachment, affect regulation, and the developing right brain: Linking developmental neuroscience to pediatrics. *Pediatrics in Review, 26*(6), 204-217.

Shadish, W.R., Cook, T.D., and Campbell, D.T. (2001). *Experimental and Quasi-Experimental Designs for Generalized Causal Inference.* Boston, MA: Houghton Mifflin.

Sherman, A., and Trisi, D. (2014). *Deep Poverty among Children Worsened in Welfare Law's First Decade.* Washington, DC: Center on Budget and Policy Priorities.

Shonkoff, J.P., and Garner, A.S. (2012). The lifelong effects of early childhood adversity and toxic stress. *Pediatrics, 129*(1), e232-e246.

Smith, A. (2015). *U.S. Smartphone Use in 2015.* Washington, DC: Pew Research Center.

Soydan, H., Mullen, E., Alexandra, L., Rehnman, J., and Li, Y.-P. (2010). Evidence-based clearinghouses in social work. *Research on Social Work Practice, 20*(6), 690-700.

Suárez-Orozco, C., Suárez-Orozco, M.M., and Todorova, I. (2008). *Learning a New Land: Immigrant Students in American Society.* Cambridge, MA: The Belknap Press of Harvard University Press.

Suárez-Orozco, C., Gaytán, F.X., and Kim, H.Y. (2010). Facing the challenges of educating Latino immigrant origin youth. In S. McHale and A. Booth (Eds.), *Growing up Hispanic: Health & Development of Children* (pp. 189-239). Washington, DC: The Urban Institute.

Taylor, P. (2014). *The Next America.* Available: http://www.pewresearch.org/next-america/#Two-Dramas-in-Slow-Motion [May 2016].

Takanishi, R. (2004). Leveling the playing field: Supporting immigrant children from birth to eight. *The Future of Children, 14*(2), 61-79.

U.S. Census Bureau. (2011). *National Intercensal Estimates (2000-2010).* Available: http://www.census.gov/popest/data/intercensal/national/nat2010.html [February 2016].

U.S. Census Bureau. (2016). *Living Arrangements of Children.* Available: http://www.census.gov/hhes/families/files/graphics/CH-1.pdf [July 2016].

U.S. Department of Education. (2015). *Fiscal Year 2016 Budget: Summary and Background Information.* Available: http://www2.ed.gov/about/overview/budget/budget16/summary/16summary.pdf [October 2016].

U.S. Department of Health and Human Services. (2015). *HHS FY2016 Budget in Brief.* Available: http://www.hhs.gov/about/budget/budget-in-brief/index.html [October 2016].

Viswanath, K., Nagler, R.H., Bigman-Galimore, C.A., McCauley, M.P., Jung, M., and Ramanadhan, S. (2012). The communications revolution and health inequalities in the 21st century: Implications for cancer control. *Cancer Epidemiology, Biomarkers & Prevention, 21*(10), 1701-1708.

Whaley, A.L., and Davis, K.E. (2007). Cultural competence and evidence-based practice in mental health services: A complementary perspective. *The American Psychologist, 62*(6), 563-574.

Wildsmith, E., Alvira-Hammond, M., and Guzman, L. (2016). *A National Portrait of Hispanic Children in Need*. National Research Center on Hispanic Children and Families. Available: http://www.childtrends.org/wp-content/uploads/2016/02/2016-15HispChildrenInNeed.pdf [May 2016].

Willoughby, T., Adachi, P.J., and Good, M. (2012). A longitudinal study of the association between violent video game play and aggression among adolescents. *Developmental Psychology, 48*(4), 1044-1057.

Winokur, M., Holtan, A., and Batchelder, K.E. (2014). Kinship care for the safety, permanency, and well-being of children removed from the home for maltreatment. *Cochrane Database of Systematic Reviews*. Available: http://www.cochrane.org/CD006546/BEHAV_kinship-care-for-the-safety-permanency-and-well-being-of-maltreated-children [May 2016].

World Health Organization. (2015). *10 Facts About Early Childhood Development as a Social Determinant of Health*. Available: http://www.who.int/maternal_child_adolescent/topics/child/development/10facts/en/ [October 2016].

Yeung, W.J., Duncan, G.J., and Hill, M.S. (2000). Putting fathers back in the picture: Parental activities and children's adult outcomes. In H.E. Peters, G.W. Peterson, S.K. Steinmetz, and R.D. Day (Eds.), *Fatherhood: Research, Interventions and Policies* (pp. 97-113). New York: Hayworth Press.

Yoshikawa, H. (2011). *Immigrants Raising Citizens: Undocumented Parents and Their Children*. New York: Russell Sage Foundation.

2

Parenting Knowledge, Attitudes, and Practices

This chapter responds to the first part of the committee's charge—to identify core parenting knowledge, attitudes, and practices that are associated with positive parent-child interactions and the healthy development of children ages birth to 8. The chapter also describes findings from research regarding how core parenting knowledge, attitudes, and practices may differ by specific characteristics of children and parents, as well as by context. The chapter begins by defining desired outcomes for children that appear frequently in the research literature and inform efforts by agencies at the federal, state, and local levels to promote child health and well-being. It then reviews the knowledge, attitudes, and practices identified in the literature as core—those most strongly associated with healthy child development—drawing primarily on correlational and experimental studies. This is followed by brief discussion of the family system as a key source of additional determinants of parenting. The chapter concludes with a summary. The core knowledge, attitudes, and practices identified in this chapter serve as a foundation, along with contextual factors that affect parenting, for the committee's review of the effectiveness of strategies for strengthening parenting capacity in subsequent chapters of this report.

DESIRED OUTCOMES FOR CHILDREN

To determine the salient features of core parenting knowledge, attitudes, and practices, the committee first identified desired outcomes for children. Identifying these outcomes grounds the discussion of core parenting knowledge, attitudes, and practices and helps researchers, practitioners, and policy makers establish priorities for investment, develop policies that provide optimal conditions for success, advocate for the adoption and implementation of appropriate evidence-based interventions, and utilize data to assess and improve the effectiveness of specific policies and programs.

Child outcomes are interconnected within and across diverse domains of development. They result from and are enhanced by early positive and supportive interactions with parents and other caregivers. These early interactions can have a long-lasting ripple effect on development across the life course, whereby the function of one domain of development influences another domain over time. In the words of Masten and Cicchetti (2010, p. 492), "effectiveness in one domain of competence in one period of life becomes the scaffold on which later competence in newly emerging domains develops . . . competence begets competence." From the literature, the committee identified the following four outcomes as fundamental to children's well-being. While the committee focused on young children (ages 0-8), these outcomes are important for children of all ages.

Physical Health and Safety

Children need to be cared for in a way that promotes their ability to thrive and ensures their survival and protection from injury and physical and sexual maltreatment. While such safety needs are important for all children, they are especially critical for young children, who typically lack the individual resources required to avoid dangers (National Research Council and Institute of Medicine, 2000). Rather, young children rely on parents and other primary caregivers, inside and outside the home, to act on their behalf to protect their safety and healthy development (Institute of Medicine and National Research Council, 2015). At the most basic level, children must receive the care, as reflected in a number of emotional and physiological protections, necessary to meet normative standards for growth and physical development, such as guidelines for healthy weight and receipt of recommended vaccinations (Institute of Medicine and National Research Council, 2015). Physical health and safety are fundamental for achieving all of the other outcomes described below.

Emotional and Behavioral Competence

Children need care that promotes positive emotional health and well-being and that supports their overall mental health, including a positive sense of self, as well as the ability to cope with stressful situations, temper emotional arousal, overcome fears, and accept disappointments and frustrations. Parents and other caregivers are essential resources for children in managing emotional arousal, coping, and managing behavior. They serve in this role by providing positive affirmations, conveying love and respect and engendering a sense of security. Provision of support by parents helps minimize the risk of internalizing behaviors, such as those associated with anxiety and depression, which can impair children's adjustment and ability to function well at home, at school, and in the community (Osofsky and Fitzgerald, 2000). Such symptoms as extreme fearfulness, helplessness, hopelessness, apathy, depression, and withdrawal are indicators of emotional difficulty that have been observed among very young children who experience inadequate parental care (Osofsky and Fitzgerald, 2000).

Social Competence

Children who possess basic social competence are able to develop and maintain positive relationships with peers and adults (Semrud-Clikeman, 2007). Social competence, which is intertwined with other areas of development (e.g., cognitive, physical, emotional, and linguistic), also may include children's ability to get along with and respect others, such as those of a different race or ethnicity, religion, sexual orientation, or economic background (Institute of Medicine and National Research Council, 2015). Basic social skills include a range of prosocial behaviors, such as empathy and concern for the feelings of others, cooperation, sharing, and perspective taking, all of which are positively associated with children's success both in school and in nonacademic settings and can be fostered by parents and other caregivers (Durlak et al., 2011; Fantuzzo et al., 2007). These skills are associated with children's future success across a wide range of contexts in adulthood (e.g., school, work, family life) (Elias, 2006; Fantuzzo et al., 2007).

Cognitive Competence

Cognitive competence encompasses the skills and capacities needed at each age and stage of development to succeed in school and in the world at large. Children's cognitive competence is defined by skills in language and communication, as well as reading, writing, mathematics, and problem solving. Children benefit from stimulating, challenging, and supportive environments in which to develop these skills, which serve as a foundation for healthy self-regulatory practices and modes of persistence required for academic success (Gottfried, 2013).

PARENTING KNOWLEDGE, ATTITUDES, AND PRACTICES

The child outcomes described above provide the context for considering the range of parenting knowledge, attitudes, and practices and identifying those that research supports as core. As noted in Chapter 1, the term "knowledge" for the purposes of this report refers to facts, information, and skills gained through experience or education and understanding of an issue or phenomenon. "Attitudes" refers to viewpoints, perspectives, reactions, or settled ways of thinking about aspects of parenting or child development, including parents' roles and responsibilities. Attitudes may be related to cultural beliefs founded in common experience. And "practices" refers to parenting behaviors or approaches to childrearing that can shape how a child develops. Generally speaking, knowledge relates to cognition, attitudes relate to motivation, and practices relate to ways of engaging or behavior, but all three may emanate from a common source.

These three components are reciprocal and intertwined theoretically, empirically, and bidirectionally, informing one another. For example, practices are related to knowledge and attitudes, and often involve the application of knowledge. According to behavior modification theory (Ajzen and Fishbein, 1980; Fishbein et al., 2001), a person's attitude often determines whether he or she will use knowledge and transform it into practice. In short, if one does not believe in or value knowledge, one is less likely to act upon it. What parents learn through the practice of parenting can also be a source of knowledge and can shape parents' attitudes. Parenting attitudes are influenced as well by parenting self-efficacy, which has been broadly defined as the level of parents' self-belief about their ability to succeed in the parenting role (Jones and Prinz, 2005).

Parenting knowledge, attitudes, and practices are shaped not only by each other but also by a number of contextual factors, including children's characteristics (e.g., gender, temperament); parents' own experiences (e.g., those from their own childhood) and circumstances; expectations learned from others, such as family, friends, and other social networks; and cultural systems. Of particular relevance to this study, the contextual factors that influence parenting knowledge, attitudes, and practices also include the supports available within the larger community and provided by institutions, as well as by policies that affect the nature and availability of supportive services.

In response to the study charge (Box 1-2 in Chapter 1), this chapter presents the evidence on core parenting knowledge, attitudes, and practices separately. However, it should be noted that in the research literature, the distinctions among these concepts, especially knowledge and attitudes, are not well-delineated and that the applications of these concepts to parenting often are equally informed by professional wisdom and historical observation.

Parenting Knowledge

Parenting is multidimensional. To respond to the varied needs of their children, parents must develop both depth and breadth of knowledge, ranging from being aware of developmental milestones and norms that help in keeping children safe and healthy to understanding the role of professionals (e.g., educators, child care workers, health care providers, social workers) and social systems (e.g., institutions, laws, policies) that interact with families and support parenting. This section describes these areas of knowledge, as well as others, identified by the available empirical evidence as supporting core parenting practices and child outcomes. It is worth noting that the research base regarding the association between parental knowledge and child outcomes is much smaller than that on parenting practices and child outcomes (Winter et al., 2012). Where data exist, they are based largely on correlational rather than experimental studies.

Knowledge of Child Development

Parent Voices

[Some parents recognized the need for education related to providing care for young children.]

"I am a new parent and even though I have a bachelor's degree from India, I do not have a particular education in child care. Just because I have a degree, it does not mean it is a degree on how to take care of a child."

—Father from Omaha, Nebraska

The importance of parents' knowledge of child development is a primary theme of many efforts to support parenting. Evidence-based recommendations issued by the American Psychological Association Task Force on Evidence-Based Practice with Children and Adolescents (2008), the Centers for Disease Control and Prevention (CDC) (2015b), and the World Health Organization (WHO) (2009) emphasize the need for policy and program initiatives to promote parenting knowledge. As they suggest, to optimize children's development, parents need a basic understanding of infant and child developmental milestones and norms and the types of parenting practices that promote children's achievement of these milestones (Belcher et al., 2007; Benasich and Brooks-Gunn, 1996, p. 1187; Bond and Burns, 2006; Bornstein and Cote, 2004; Hess et al., 2004; Huang et al., 2005; Larsen and Juhasz, 1985; Mercy and Saul, 2009).

A robust body of correlational research demonstrates tremendous variation in parents' knowledge about childrearing. Several of these studies suggest that parents with higher levels of education tend to know more about child developmental milestones and processes (Bornstein et al., 2010;

Conrad et al., 1992; Hess et al., 2004; Huang et al., 2005), as well as effective parenting strategies (Morawska et al., 2009). This greater knowledge may reflect differential access to accurate information, differences in parents' trust in the information or information source, and parents' comfort with their own abilities, among other factors. For example, research shows that parents who do not teach math in the home tend to have less knowledge about elementary math, doubt their competence, or value math less than other skills (Blevins-Knabe et al., 2000; Cannon and Ginsburg, 2008; Vukovic and Lesaux, 2013). However, parents' knowledge and willingness to increase their knowledge may change; thus, they can acquire developmental knowledge that can help them employ effective parenting practices.

Parent Voices

[Some parents recognized the need for comprehensive parenting education.]

"I always prefer education for the parents, from the beginning to the end. From pregnancy, some don't know when to go to the doctor, and after birth, when to go to the hospital or the doctor. So we need education from the beginning to the end."

—Mother from Omaha, Nebraska

The focus on parental knowledge as a point of intervention is important because parents' knowledge of child development is related to their practices and behaviors (Okagaki and Bingham, 2005). For example, mothers who have a strong body of knowledge of child development have been found to interact with their children more positively compared with mothers with less knowledge (Bornstein and Bradley, 2012; Huang et al., 2005). Parents who understand child development also are less likely to have age-inappropriate expectations for their child, which affects the use of appropriate discipline and the nature and quality of parent-child interactions (Goodnow, 1988; Huang et al., 2005).

Support for the importance of parenting knowledge to parenting practices is found in multiple sources and is applicable to a range of cognitive and social-emotional behaviors and practices. Several correlational studies show that mothers with high knowledge of child development are more likely to provide books and learning materials tailored to children's interests and age and engage in more reading, talking, and storytelling relative to mothers with less knowledge (Curenton and Justice, 2004; Gardner-Neblett et al., 2012; Grusec, 2011). Fathers' understanding of their young children's development in language and literacy is associated with being better prepared to support their children (Cabrera et al., 2014). And parents who do not know that learning begins at birth are less likely to engage in practices that promote learning during infancy (e.g., reading to infants) or appreciate the importance of exposing infants and young children to hearing words and using language. For example, mothers who assume that very young children are not attentive have been found to be less likely to respond to their children's attempts to engage and interact with them (Putnam et al., 2002).

Stronger evidence of the role of knowledge of child development in supporting parenting outcomes comes from intervention research. Randomized controlled trial interventions have found that parents of young children showed increases in knowledge about children's development and practices pertaining to early childhood care and feeding (Alkon et al., 2014; Yousafzai et al., 2015).

Some studies have found a direct association between parental knowledge and child outcomes, including reduced behavioral challenges and improvements on measures of cognitive and motor performance (Benasich and Brooks-Gunn, 1996; Dichtelmiller et al., 1992; Hunt and Paraskevopoulos, 1980; Rowe et al., 2015). In an analysis of data from a prospective cohort study that controlled for potential confounders, children of mothers with greater knowledge of child development at 12 months were less likely to have behavior problems and scored higher on child IQ tests at 36 months relative to children of mothers with less developmental knowledge (Benasich and Brooks-Gunn, 1996). This and other observational studies also show that parental knowledge is associated with improved parenting and quality of the home environment, which, in turn, is associated with children's outcomes (Benasich and Brooks-Gunn, 1996; Parks and Smeriglio, 1986; Winter et al., 2012), in addition to being contingent on parental attitudes and competence (Conrad et al., 1992; Hess et al., 2004; Murphy et al., 2015).

Experimental studies of parent education interventions support these associational findings. In an experimental study of parent education for first-time fathers, fathers, along with home visitors, reviewed examples of parental sensitivity and responsiveness from videos of themselves playing with their children (Magill-Evans et al., 2007). These fathers showed a significant increase in parenting competence and skills in fostering their children's cognitive growth as well as sensitivity to infant cues 2 months after the program, compared with fathers in the control group, who discussed age-appropriate toys with the home visitor (Magill-Evans et al., 2007). Another experimental study examined a 13-week population-level behavioral parenting program and found intervention effects on parenting knowledge for mothers and, among the highest-risk families, increased involvement in children's early learning and improved behavior management practices. Lower rates of conduct problems for boys at high risk of problem behavior also were found (Dawson-McClure et al., 2015).

Knowledge of Parenting Practices

Parents' knowledge of how to meet their children's basic physical (e.g., hunger) and emotional (e.g., wanting to be held or soothed) needs, as well as of how to read infants' cues and signals, can improve the synchronicity between parent and child, ensuring proper child growth and development. Specifically, parenting knowledge about proper nutrition, safe sleep environments, how to sooth a crying baby, and how to show love and affection is critical for young children's optimal development (Bowlby, 2008; Chung-Park, 2012; Regalado and Halfon, 2001; Zarnowiecki et al., 2011).

For many parents, for example, infant crying is a great challenge during the first months of life. Parents who cannot calm their crying babies suffer from sleep deprivation, have self-doubt, may stop breastfeeding earlier, and may experience more conflict and discord with their partners and children (Boukydis and Lester, 1985; Karp, 2008). Correlational research indicates that improvement in parental knowledge about normal infant crying is associated with reductions in unnecessary medical emergency room visits for infants (Barr et al., 2015). That knowledge leads to changes in behavior is further supported in systematic reviews by Bryanton and colleagues (2013) of randomized controlled trials and Middlemiss and colleagues (2015) of studies with various design types, with both groups reporting that increases in mother's knowledge about infant behavior is associated with positive changes in the home environment, as well as improvements in infant sleep time.

Specific knowledge about health and safety—including knowledge about how to access health care, protect children from physical harm (e.g., the importance of wearing a seat belt or a helmet), and promote good hygiene and nutrition—is a key parenting competency. Experimental studies show, for example, a positive link between parents' knowledge of nutrition and both children's intake of nutritious foods and reduced calorie and sodium intake (Campbell et al., 2013; Katz et al., 2011). In a randomized controlled trial, Campbell and colleagues (2013) found that children whose parents received knowledge, skills, and social support related to infant feeding, diet, physical activity, and television viewing consumed fewer sweet snacks and spent fewer minutes daily viewing television relative to children whose parents were in the control group (Campbell et al., 2013). Also associated with children's intake of nutritious foods is parents' modeling of good eating habits and nutritional practices (Mazarello Paes et al., 2015).

In addition, although limited in scope, correlational evidence shows that parents with knowledge about immunization are more likely to understand its purpose and comply with the timetable for vaccinations (Smailbegovic et al., 2003); that parents with more knowledge about effective injury prevention practices are more likely to create safer home environments for their children and reduce unintentional injuries (Corrarino, 2013; Dowswell et al., 1996; Middlemiss et al., 2015; Morrongiello and Kiriakou, 2004); and that parents with knowledge about asthma are more likely to use an asthma management plan (Bryant-Stephens and Li, 2004; DeWalt et al., 2007; Harrington et al., 2015). Other studies have found that parents with more information about the purpose of vaccinations had greater knowledge of immunization than parents in the control group (Hofstetter et al., 2015; Jackson et al., 2011), and parents with more knowledge about sun safety provided sunscreen and protective clothing for their children, who presented with fewer sunburns (Crane et al., 2012).

Still, knowledge alone may not be sufficient in some cases. For example, knowing about the importance of using car seats does not always translate into good car seat practices (Yanchar et al., 2012, 2015), and knowledge about the advantages of vaccines may not result in parents choosing to vaccinate their children. Some findings suggest that using multiple modes of delivery is important to advancing parents' knowledge. In an experimental study, for example, Dunn and colleagues (1998) found that parents who received educational information about child vaccinations via videotape as well as in written form showed greater gains in understanding about vaccinations than parents who received the information in written form alone.

The evidence linking parental knowledge about the specific ways in which parents can help children develop cognitive and academic skills, including skills in math, is limited. However, the available correlational data show that parents who know about how children develop language are more likely to have children with emergent literacy skills (e.g., letter sound awareness) relative to parents who do not (Ladd et al., 2011). Several studies over the past 20 years have described parents' increasing knowledge and use of approaches for supporting children's literacy (Clark, 2007; National Research Council, 1998; Sénéchal and LeFevre, 2002). Much of this work has focused on book reading and parent-child engagement around reading (Hindman et al., 2008; Mol et al., 2008; Morrow et al., 1990). As early as the 1960s, Durkin (1966) and others referred to the important role of the home literacy environment and parents' beliefs about reading in children's early literacy development.

Knowledge of Supports, Services, and Systems

Little is known about parents' knowledge of various supports—such as educators, social workers, health care providers, and extended family—and the relationship between their conceptions of the roles of these supports and their use of them.

To take an example, parents' knowledge about child care and their school decision-making processes are informed in a variety of ways through these different supports. In their literature review of child care decision making, Forry and colleagues (2013) found that many low-income parents learn about their child care options through their social networks rather than through professionals or referral agencies. While many parents say they highly value quality, their choices also may reflect a range of other factors that are valued. Parents tend to make child care decisions based on structural (teacher education and training) and process (activities, parent-provider communication) features, although their choices also vary by family income, education, and work schedules. Sosinsky and Kim (2013), for example, found that higher maternal education and income and being white were associated with the likelihood of parents choosing higher-quality child care programs that were associated with better child outcomes. Based on a survey of parents of children in a large public school system, Goldring and Phillips (2008) found that parents' involvement, not satisfaction with their child's school, was associated with school decision making. It should be noted that while parents may know what constitutes high-quality child care and education, structural (availability of quality programs and schools), individual (work, income, belief), and child (temperament, age) factors also influence these decision-making processes (Meyers and Jordan, 2006; Shlay, 2010).

Taking another example, limited studies have looked at parental awareness of services for children with special needs. A study that utilized a survey and qualitative interviews with parents of children with autism indicated that parents' autism spectrum disorder service knowledge partially mediates the relationship between socioeconomic status and use of services for their children (Pickard and Ingersoll, 2015).

Parenting Attitudes

Although considerable discussion has focused on attitudes and beliefs broadly, less research attention has been paid to the effects of parenting attitudes on parents' interactions with young children or on parenting practices. Few causal analyses are available to test whether parenting attitudes actually affect parenting practices, positive parent-child interaction, and child development. Even less research exists on fathers' attitudes about parenting. Given this limited evidence base, the committee drew primarily on correlational and qualitative studies in examining parenting attitudes.

Parents' attitudes toward parenting are a product of their knowledge of parenting and the values and goals (or expectations) they have for their children's development, which in turn are informed by cultural, social, and societal images, as well as parents' experiences and their overall values and goals (Cabrera et al., 2000; Cheah and Chirkov, 2008; Iruka et al., 2015; Okagaki and Bingham, 2005; Rogoff, 2003; Rosenthal and Roer-Strier, 2006; Whiting and Whiting, 1975). People in the United States hold several universal, or near universal, beliefs about the types of parental behaviors that promote or impair child development. For example, there is general agreement that striking a child in a manner that can cause severe injury, engaging in sexual activity with a child, and failing to provide adequate food for and supervision of young children (such as leaving toddlers unattended) pose threats to children's health and safety and are unacceptable. At the same time, some studies identify differences in parents' goals for child development, which may influence attitudes regarding the roles of parents and have implications for efforts to promote particular parenting practices.

While there is variability within demographic groups in parenting attitudes and practices, some research shows differences in attitudes and practices among subpopulations. For example, qualitative research provides some evidence of variation by culture in parents' goals for their children's socialization. In one interview study, mothers who were first-generation immigrants to the United States from Central America emphasized long-term socialization goals related to proper demeanor for their children, while European American mothers emphasized self-maximization (Leyendecker et al., 2002). In another interview study, Anglo American mothers stressed the importance of their young children developing a balance between autonomy and relatedness, whereas Puerto Rican mothers focused on appropriate levels of relatedness, including courtesy and respectful attentiveness (Harwood et al., 1997). Other ethnographic and qualitative research shows that parents from different cultural groups select cultural values and norms from their country of origin as well as from their host country, and that their goal is for their children to adapt and succeed in the United States (Rogoff, 2003).

Similarly, whereas the larger U.S. society has historically viewed individual freedom as an important value, some communities place more emphasis on interdependence (Elmore and Gaylord-Harden, 2013; Sarche and Spicer, 2008). The importance of intergenerational connections (e.g., extended family members serving as primary caregivers for young children) also varies among and within cultural communities (Bertera and Crewe, 2013; Mutchler et al., 2007). The values and traditions of cultural communities may be expressed as differences in parents' views regarding gender roles, in parents' goals for children, and in their attitudes related to childrearing.

Parent Voices

[One parent described differences between men and women in parenting roles.]

"Mothers play the main role as parents in [certain cultures]. Culturally men aren't that involved. The dad is the outer worker; the mother is the inner worker. If you are talking about the mom, they are the ones who care about the kids. They aren't typically working outside the home. But now, in the United States, the mothers are working outside the home."

—Father from Omaha, Nebraska

Although slowly changing, attitudes about the roles of men and women in the raising of young children often differ between men and women and among various communities in the United States. Longitudinal research on mothers' attitudes toward fathers' involvement in childrearing has made reference to the "gatekeeping" role of mothers of children with nonresidential fathers (Fagan and Barnett, 2003; Schoppe-Sullivan et al., 2008). Research has shown that fathers of young children participate in child caregiving activities in increasing numbers (Cabrera et al., 2011), but has not examined the specific attitudes that fathers bring to particular parenting behaviors across the life span. Parents' values and goals related to childrearing, both overall and for specific demographic groups, also may shift from one generation to the next in the United States based on changing norms and viewpoints within social networks and cultural communities, as well as parents' knowledge of and access to new research and information provided by educators, health care providers, and others who work with families.

Relatively little research has been conducted on parents' attitudes toward specific parenting-related practices. Much of the extant research focuses on practices related to promoting children's physical health and safety. Studies of varying designs indicate that parental attitudes and beliefs about the need for and safety of vaccination influence vaccination practices (Mergler et al., 2013; Salathé and Bonhoeffer, 2008; Vannice et al., 2011; Yaqub et al., 2014). Maternal attitudes and beliefs about breastfeeding (e.g., views about breastfeeding in public, the belief that it will be uncomfortable) are associated with initiation and continuation of breastfeeding and appear to factor into differences in breastfeeding rates and practices observed across cultural and other demographic groups in cross-sectional survey and qualitative research (Vaaler et al., 2010; Wojcicki et al., 2010). Other studies have found differences among parents (e.g., those living in rural versus urban areas) in attitudes about the importance of monitoring children's activities and whereabouts (Armistead et al., 2002; Jones et al., 2003) and parents' beliefs about young children's literacy development (Lynch et al., 2006).

Parental involvement in children's education has been linked to academic readiness (Fan and Chen, 2001). However, parents differ in their attitudes about the role of parents in children's learning and education (Hammer et al., 2007). Some see parents as having a central role, while others view the school as the primary facilitator of children's education and see parents as having less of a role (Hammer et al., 2007). These attitudinal differences may be related to cultural expectations or parents' own education or comfort with teaching their children certain skills. Some parents, for example, may have lower involvement in their children's education because of insecurity about their own skills and past negative experiences in school (Lareau, 1989; Lawrence-Lightfoot, 2003). And as discussed above, some parents view math skills as less important for their children relative to other types of skills and therefore are less likely to teach them in the home.

Parents within and across different communities vary in their opinions and practices with respect to the role and significance of discipline. Some of the parenting literature notes that some parents use *control* to discipline children, while others aim to *correct* but not to control children (Nieman and Shea, 2004). In a small cross-cultural ethnographic study, Mosier and Rogoff (2003) found that some parents regard rules and punishment as inappropriate for infants and toddlers. The approach valued by these parents to help children understand what is expected of them is to cooperate with them, perhaps distracting them but not forcing their compliance. In contrast, many middle-class U.S. parents display a preference for applying the same rules to infants and toddlers that older children are expected to follow, although with some lenience (Mosier and Rogoff, 2003). And ethnographic research provides some evidence of differences in African American and European American mothers' beliefs about spoiling and infant intentionality (whether infants can intentionally misbehave) related to the use of physical punishment with young children (Burchinal et al., 2010).

Parents' attitudes not only toward parenting but also toward providers in societal agencies—such as educators, social service personnel, health care providers, and police—which can be shaped by a variety of factors, including discrimination, are important determinants of parents' access to and ability to obtain support. Studies show a relationship between parents' distrust of agencies and their likelihood of rejecting participation in an intervention. For example, in systematic reviews of studies of various types, parents who distrust the medical community and government health agencies are less likely to have their children vaccinated (Brown et al., 2010; Mills et al., 2005). Racial and ethnic minority parents whose attitudes about appropriate remedies for young children vary from those of the Western medical establishment often distrust and avoid treatment by Western medical practitioners (Hannan, 2015). While not specific to parents, studies using various methodologies show that individuals who have experienced racial and other forms of discrimination, both within and outside of health care settings, are less likely to utilize various health services or to engage in other health-promoting behaviors (Gonzales et al., 2013; Institute of Medicine, 2003; Pascoe and Smart Richman, 2009; Shavers et al., 2012). In a survey study, African American parents' racism awareness was negatively associated with involvement in activities at their children's school (McKay et al., 2003). Longitudinal studies, mostly involving families with older children, indicate that, like other sources of stress, parents' experience of discrimination can have a detrimental effect on parenting and the quality of the parent-child relationship (Murray et al., 2001; Sanders-Phillips et al., 2009). Adverse outcomes for youth associated with their own experience of discrimination may be weakened by more nurturing/involved parenting (Brody et al., 2006; Gibbons et al., 2010; Simons et al., 2006).

As noted earlier, attitudes are shaped in part by parenting self-efficacy—a parent's perceived ability to influence the development of his or her child. Parenting self-efficacy has been found to influence parenting competence (including engagement in some parenting practices) as well as child functioning (Jones and Prinz, 2005). Studies show associations between maternal self-efficacy and children's self-regulation, social, and cognitive skills (Murry and Brody, 1999; Swick and Hassell, 1990). Self-efficacy also may apply to parents' confidence in their capacity to carry out specific parenting practices. For example, parents who reported a sense of efficacy in influencing their elementary school-age children's school outcomes were more likely to help their children with school activities at home (Anderson and Minke, 2007). A multimethod study of African American families found that maternal self-efficacy was related to children's regulatory skills through its association with competence-promoting parenting practices, which included family routines, quality of mother-child interactions based on observer ratings, and teachers' reports of mothers' involvement with their children's schools (Brody et al., 1999). Henshaw and colleagues (2015) found in a longitudinal study that higher breastfeeding self-efficacy predicted exclusive breastfeeding at 6 months postpartum, as well as better emotional adjustment of mothers in the weeks after giving birth.

Parenting Practices

Parenting practices have been studied extensively, with some research showing strong associations between certain practices and positive child outcomes. This section describes parenting practices that research indicates are central to helping children achieve basic outcomes in the areas discussed at the beginning of the chapter: physical health and safety, emotional and behavioral competence, social competence, and cognitive competence. While these outcomes are used as a partial organizing framework for this section, several specific practices—contingent responsiveness of parents, organization of the home environment and the importance of routines, and behavioral discipline practices—that have been found to influence child well-being in more than one of these four outcome areas are discussed separately.

Practices to Promote Physical Health and Safety

Parents influence the health and safety of their children in many ways. However, the difficulty of using random assignment designs to examine parenting practices that promote children's health and safety has resulted in a largely observational literature. This section reviews the available evidence on a range of practices in which parents engage to ensure the health and safety of their children. It begins with breastfeeding—a subject about which there has historically been considerable discussion in light of generational shifts and commercial practices that have affected children in poor families.

Breastfeeding Breastfeeding has myriad well-established short- and long-term benefits for both babies and mothers. Breast milk bolsters babies' immunity to infectious disease, regulates healthy bacteria in the intestines, and overall is the best source of nutrients to help babies grow and develop. Breastfeeding also supports bonding between mothers and their babies. According to a meta-analysis by the WHO (Horta and Victora, 2013), breastfeeding is associated with a small increase in performance on intelligence tests in children and adolescents, reduced risk for the development of type 2 diabetes and overweight/obesity later in life, and a potential decreased risk for the development of cardiovascular disease. Breastfeeding may benefit mothers' health as well by lowering risk for postpartum depression, certain cancers, and chronic diseases such as diabetes (U.S. Department of Health and Human Services, 2011). Current guidelines from the American Academy of Pediatrics (2012) and the WHO (2011) recommend mothers breastfeed exclusively until infants are 6 months old. Thereafter and until the child is either age 1 year (American Academy of Pediatrics, 2012) or 2 years (World Health Organization, 2011), it is recommended that children continue to be breastfed while slowly being introduced to other foods.

According to 2011 data from the CDC (2015a), about 80 percent of babies born in the United States are breastfed (including fed breast milk) for some duration, and about 50 percent and 27 percent are breastfed (to any extent with or without the addition of complementary liquids or solids) at

6 and 12 months, respectively. Forty percent and 19 percent are exclusively breastfed through 3 and 6 months, respectively.

Mothers in the United States often cite a number of reasons for not initiating or continuing breastfeeding, including lack of knowledge about how to breastfeed, difficulty or pain during breastfeeding, embarrassment, perceived inconvenience, and return to work (Hurley et al., 2008; Ogbuanu et al., 2009; U.S. Department of Health and Human Services, 2011). Low-income women with less education are less likely than women of higher socioeconomic status to breastfeed (Heck et al., 2006). Some research with immigrant mothers shows that rates of breastfeeding decrease with each generation in the United States, possibly because of differences in acceptance of bottle feeding here as compared with other countries (e.g., Sussner et al., 2008).

Nutrition and physical activity Parents play an important role in shaping their young children's nutrition and physical activity levels (Institute of Medicine, 2011; Sussner et al., 2006). Among toddlers and preschool-age children, parents' feeding practices are associated with their children's ability to regulate food intake, which can affect weight status (Faith et al., 2004; Farrow et al., 2015). Parents' modeling of healthful eating habits for their children and offering of healthful foods, particularly during toddlerhood, when children are often reluctant to try new foods, may result in children being more apt to like and eat such foods (Hill, 2002; Natale et al., 2014; Sussner et al., 2006). The extant observational research generally shows that children's dietary intake (particularly fruit and vegetable consumption) is associated with food options available in the home and at school, and that parents are important role models for their children's dietary behaviors (Cullen et al., 2003; Pearson et al., 2009; Wolnicka et al., 2015). Conversely, the presence of less nutritious food and beverage items in the home may increase children's risk of becoming overweight. For example, Dennison and colleagues (1997) and Welsh and colleagues (2005) found positive associations between overweight in children and their consumption of sugar-sweetened beverages. On the other hand, there are some indications that overly strict diets may increase children's preferences for high-fat, energy-dense foods, perhaps causing an imbalance in children's self-regulation of hunger and satiety and increasing the risk that they will become overweight (Birch and Fisher, 1998; Farrow et al., 2015).

A few cross-sectional and longitudinal studies, coupled with conventional wisdom, suggest that eating dinner together as a family is associated with increased consumption of fruits, vegetables, and whole grains and reduced consumption of fats and soda (Gillman et al., 2000), as well as with reduced risk for overweight and obesity (Gable et al., 2007; Taveras et al., 2005). However, these studies involved primarily older children and adolescents.

Physical activity is a complement to good nutrition. Even in young children, physical activity is essential for proper energy balance and prevention of childhood obesity (Institute of Medicine, 2011; Kohl and Hobbs, 1998). It also supports normal physical growth. Parents may encourage activity in young children through play (e.g., free play with toys or playing on a playground) or age-appropriate sports. Children who spend more time outdoors may be more active (e.g., Institute of Medicine, 2011; Sallis et al., 1993) and also have more opportunity to explore their community and interact with other children. For many parents living in high-crime neighborhoods, however, most of whom are racial and ethnic minorities, the importance of safety overrides the significance of physical activity. In some neighborhoods, safety issues and lack of access to parks and other places for safe recreation make it difficult for families to spend time outdoors, leading parents to keep their children at home (Dias and Whitaker, 2013; Gable et al., 2007; Powell et al., 2003).

Although more of the research on screen time and sedentary behavior has focused on adolescents than on young children, several cross-sectional and longitudinal studies on younger children show an association between television viewing and overweight and inactivity (Ariza et al., 2004; Carson et al., 2016; Dennison et al., 2002; DuRant et al., 1994; Gable et al., 2007; Tremblay et al., 2011). An analysis of data on 8,000 children participating in a longitudinal cohort study showed that those who watched more television during kindergarten and first grade were significantly more likely to be clinically overweight by the spring semester of third grade (Gable et al., 2007). Although television, computers, and other screen media often are used for educational purposes with young children, these findings suggest that balancing screen time with other activities may be one way parents can promote their children's overall health. As with diet, children's sedentary behavior can be influenced by parents' own behaviors. For example, De Lepeleere and colleagues (2015) found an association between parents' screen time and that of their children ages 6-12 in a cross-sectional study.

Vaccination Parents protect their own and other children from potentially serious diseases by making sure they receive recommended vaccines. Among children born in a given year in the United States, childhood vaccination is estimated to prevent about 42,000 deaths and 20 million cases of disease (Zhou et al., 2014). In 2013, 82 percent of children ages 19-35 months received combined-series vaccines (for diphtheria, tetanus, and pertussis [DTP]; polio; measles, mumps, and rubella [MMR]; and Haemophilus influenzae type b [Hib]), up from 69 percent in 1994 (Child Trends Databank, 2015b). Vaccination rates are lower among low-income children;

71 percent of children ages 19-35 months living below the poverty level received the combined-series vaccines listed above in 2014 (Child Trends Databank, 2015b). Although much of the media coverage on this subject has focused on middle-income parents averse to having their children vaccinated, it is in fact poverty that is thought to account for much of the disparity in vaccination rates by race and ethnicity (Hill et al., 2015). As discussed earlier in this chapter, parental practices around vaccination may be influenced by parents' knowledge and interpretation of information on and their attitudes about vaccination.

Preconception and prenatal care The steps women take with their health care providers before becoming pregnant can promote healthy pregnancy and birth outcomes for both mothers and babies. These include initiating certain supplements (e.g., folic acid, which reduces the risk of birth defects), quitting smoking, attaining healthy weight for women who are obese, and treating preexisting physical and mental health conditions (Aune et al., 2014; Gold and Marcus, 2008; Institute of Medicine and National Research Council, 2009).

During pregnancy, receipt of recommended prenatal care can help parents reduce the risk of pregnancy complications and poor birth outcomes by promoting healthy behaviors (e.g., smoking cessation, adequate rest and nutrition), as well as identifying and managing any complications that do arise. Prior to the birth of a child, health care providers also can educate parents on the importance of breastfeeding, infant injury and illness prevention, and other practices.

Infants born to mothers who do not receive prenatal care or who do not receive it until late in their pregnancy are more likely than those born to mothers who receive such care early in pregnancy to be born premature and at a low birth weight and are more likely to die. Since the 1970s, there has been a decline in the number of women in the United States receiving late or no prenatal care, with the majority of pregnant women now receiving recommended prenatal care (Child Trends Databank, 2015a). Yet disparities among subgroups persist. In 2014, American Indian and Alaska Native (11% of births), black (10% of births), and Hispanic (8% of births) women were more than twice as likely as white mothers (4% of births) to receive late or no prenatal care (Child Trends Databank, 2015a). The proportion of women receiving timely prenatal care increases with age: in 2014, 25 percent of births to females under age 15 and 10 percent of births to females ages 15-19 were to mothers receiving late or no prenatal care, compared with 7.8 percent for females ages 20-24 and 5.6 percent for those ages 25-29 (Child Trends Databank, 2015a). Women whose pregnancies are unintended also are less likely to receive timely prenatal care. Despite the importance of timely and quality prenatal care, moreover, many parents experience barriers to receiving such care, including poor access and rural residence, limited knowledge of its importance, and mental illness (Heaman et al., 2014).

Injury prevention Unintentional injuries are the leading cause of death among children ages 1-9 (Centers for Disease Control and Prevention, 2015c) and a leading cause of disability for both younger and older children in the United States. In addition to motor vehicle-related injuries, children sustain unintentional injuries (due, for example, to suffocation, falls, poisoning, and drowning) in the home environment. About 1,700 children under age 9 in the United States die each year from injuries in the home (Mack et al., 2013).

Parents can protect their children from injury through various measures, such as ensuring proper use of automobile passenger restraints, insisting that children wear helmets while bike riding and playing sports, and creating a safe home environment (e.g., keeping medicines and cleaning products out of children's reach, installing safety gates to keep children from falling down stairs). Yet the limited available research on parents' use of safety measures suggests there is room for improvement in some areas. For instance, appropriate use of child restraint systems is known to reduce the risk of child motor vehicle-related injuries and deaths (Arbogast et al., 2009; Durbin, 2011); nonetheless, data show that many children ride in automobiles without appropriate restraints (Greenspan et al., 2010; Lee et al., 2015; Macy et al., 2014). Likewise, using data from a national survey conducted during 2001-2003, Dellinger and Kresnow (2010) show that less than one-half of children ages 5-14 always wore bicycle helmets while riding, and 29 percent never did so. More recent data on parents' home safety practices and on helmet usage among young children are lacking.

Evidence that families' home safety practices affect child safety comes from intervention research. A large meta-analysis of randomized and nonrandomized controlled trials of home safety education interventions for families (Kendrick et al., 2013) showed that the education was generally effective in increasing the proportion of families that stored medicines and cleaning products out of reach and that had fitted stair gates, covers on unused electrical sockets, safe hot tap water temperatures, functional smoke alarms, and a fire escape system. There was also some evidence for reduced injury rates among children. As discussed in Chapter 4, helping parents reduce hazards in the home is a component of some home visiting programs.

Parents also protect their children's safety by monitoring their whereabouts and activities to prevent them from both physical and psychological harm. The type of supervision may vary based on a child's needs and age as well as parents' values and economic circumstances. For all young children, monitoring for the purposes of preventing exposure to hazards is an important practice. As children grow older, knowing their friends and where the children are when they are not at home or in school also becomes important. As noted previously, research suggests the importance of monitoring screen time to children's well-being. And monitoring of children's Internet usage may prevent them from being exposed to online predators (Finkelhor et al., 2000).

Practices to Promote Emotional and Behavioral Competence and Social Competence

Fundamental to children's positive development is the opportunity to grow up in an environment that responds to their emotional needs (Bretherton, 1985) and that enables them to develop skills needed to cope with basic anxieties, fears, and environmental challenges. Parents' ability to foster a sense of belonging and self-worth in their children is vital to the children's early development. In much the same way, parents contribute to children's emerging social competence by teaching them skills—such as self-control, cooperation, and taking the perspective of others—that prepare them to develop and maintain positive relationships with peers and adults. Parents can promote the learning and acquisition of social skills by establishing strong relationships with their children. The importance of early parent-child interactions for children's social competence is embedded in many theoretical frameworks, such as attachment (Ainsworth and Bowlby, 1991), family system theories (Cox and Paley, 1997), and ecocultural theories (Weisner, 2002). Parents socialize their children to adopt culturally appropriate values and behaviors that enable them to be socially competent and act as members of a social group.

Research suggests that children who are socially competent are independent rather than suggestible, responsible rather than irresponsible, cooperative instead of resistive, purposeful rather than aimless, friendly rather than hostile, and self-controlled rather than impulsive (Landy and Osofsky, 2009). In short, the socially competent child exhibits social skills (e.g., has positive interactions with others, expresses emotions effectively), is able to establish peer relationships (e.g., being accepted by other children), and has certain individual attributes (e.g., shows capacity to empathize, has coping skills). Parents help children develop these social skills through parenting practices that include fostering and modeling positive relationships and providing enriching and stimulating experiences and opportunities for children to exercise these skills (Landy and Osofsky, 2009). Parents also help their children acquire these skills by having them participate in routine activities (e.g., chores, taking care of siblings) and family rituals (e.g., going to church) (Weisner, 2002). These activities are shared with and initiated by parents, siblings, and other kin; unfold within the home; and are structured by cultural and linguistic practices, expectations, and behaviors (Rogoff, 2003; Weisner, 2002). In this context, young children interact with their mothers, fathers, siblings, and grandparents who teach them implicitly or explicitly to acquire appropriate social behaviors, adapt to expected norms, and learn linguistic conventions and cognitive skills (Sameroff and Fiese, 2000).

Another important aspect of parent-supported social development pertains to parents aiding their children in acquiring executive function skills needed to adapt to changing needs of the environment and regulate their impulses and responses to distressing situations (Blair and Raver, 2012; Malin et al., 2014; Thompson, 1994). Evidence, primarily from correlational research, suggests that parents who help their children regulate the difficulty of tasks and who model mature performance during joint participation in activities are likely to have socially competent children (Eisenberg et al., 1998). Parents also facilitate their children's development of friendships by engaging in positive social interaction with them and by creating opportunities for them to be social with peers (McCollum and Ostrosky, 2008). In one correlational study, children whose parents initiated peer contacts had more playmates and more consistent play companions in their preschool peer networks (Ladd et al., 2002). Research also shows that children who have increased opportunities for playing or interacting with children from diverse backgrounds are likely to develop less prejudice and more empathy toward others (Bernstein et al., 2000; Perkins and Mebert, 2005; Pettigrew and Tropp, 2000).

Findings from experimental studies on parent training provide evidence of the types of parental practices that are associated with child emotional and behavioral health (i.e., fewer internalizing and externalizing problems) and social competence (i.e., relationship building skills, moral dispositions, and prosocial behaviors such as altruism). In one study for example, parent training designed to decrease the use of harsh discipline and increase supportive parenting reduced mother-reported child behavior problems in children ages 3-9 (Bjørknes and Manger, 2013). In another randomized study, mothers who received parent training to improve their empathy toward their children became less permissive with their 2- to 3-year-olds, who became less aggressive (Christopher et al., 2013).

These relationships have been found to hold in experimental studies involving diverse samples. Brotman and colleagues (2005) found that a program designed to reduce parents' use of negative parenting and increase their provision of stimulation for child learning increased social competence with peers in young African American and Latino children who had a sibling who had been involved in the juvenile justice system. In a European study, Berkovits and colleagues (2010) studied ethnically diverse parents participating in an abbreviated parent skills training delivered in pediatric primary care aimed at encouraging children's prosocial behavior. The findings show significant increases in effective parenting strategies and in parents' beliefs about personal controls, as well as declines in child behavior problems. Improvements in child behavior as a consequence of parent training have been found not only for programs emphasizing better and more consistent discipline and contingency management, but also for those providing training that led to parents' greater emotional support for their children (McCarty et al., 2005). In addition, Stormshak and colleagues (2000) found that punitive interactions between parents and children were associated with higher rates of child disruptive behavior problems, and that low levels of warm involvement were characteristic of parents of children who showed oppositional behaviors.

Internalizing disorders in young children include depression (withdrawal, persistent sadness) and anxiety (Tandon et al., 2009). They may occur simultaneously with and/or independently of externalizing disorders (e.g., noncompliance, aggression, coercive behaviors directed at the environment and others) (Dishion and Snyder, 2016). Studies focusing exclusively on the causes of internalizing disorders in young children are relatively limited. However, the results of the available studies lead to similar conclusions about the relationships among training, changes in parenting practices, and child internalizing problems. First, there is evidence that parental behaviors matter for child emotional functioning. Specifically, parents' sense of personal control and behaviors such as autonomy granting are inversely related to child anxiety in cross-sectional research (McLeod et al., 2007). Similarly, in another nonexperimental study, Duncombe and colleagues (2012) show that inconsistent discipline, parents' negative emotion, and mental health are related to child problems with emotion regulation. Second, there is evidence that parent training interventions can modify the parenting practices that matter. Third, some parent training interventions have positive effects on children's emotional functioning. In a review of randomized controlled studies of the effects of group-based parenting programs on behavioral and emotional adjustment, Barlow and colleagues (2010) found significant effects of the programs on parent-reported outcomes of children under age 4. Herbert and colleagues (2013) conducted a randomized clinical trial of parent training and emotion socialization for hyperactive preschool children in which the target outcome was emotion regulation. Not only did the intervention group mothers report lower hyperactivity, inattention, and emotional lability in their children, but also changes in children's functioning were correlated with more positive and less negative parenting and with less verbosity, greater support, and use of emotion socialization practices on the part of mothers.

With respect to social competence, a number of studies point to a relationship with parenting practices and suggest that parent training may have an impact on both parenting practices related to and children's development of social competence. An experimental evaluation of the Incredible Years Program (discussed further in Chapter 5), for instance, found that parent training contributed to improved parenting practices, defined as lower negative parenting and increased parental stimulation for learning (Brotman et al., 2005), which, in turn, are related to children's social competence. Gagnon and colleagues (2014) found that preschool children with a combination of reactive temperament and authoritarian parents demonstrated low social competence (high levels of disruptive play and low levels of interactive play). In a community trial by Havighurst and colleagues (2010), training focused on helping parents tune in to their own and their children's emotions resulted in significant improvement in the parents' emotion awareness and regulation, as well as the practice of emotion coping. The intervention decreased emotionally dismissive beliefs and behaviors among parents, who also used emotion labels and discussed the causes and consequences of emotions with their children more often than was the case prior to the training. The program improved parental beliefs and relationships with their children, and these improvements were related to reductions in child behavior problems (Havighurst et al., 2010).

Practices to Stimulate Cognitive Development

As explained in the National Research Council (2000) report *How People Learn: Brain, Mind, Experience, and School*, individuals learn by actively encountering events, objects, actions, and concepts in their environments. For an individual to become an expert in any particular knowledge or skill area, he or she must have substantial experience in that area which is usually guided (Dweck and Leggett, 2000; National Research Council, 2000). As children's first teachers, parents play an important role in their cognitive development, including their acquisition of such competencies as language, literacy, and numerical/math skills that are related to future success in school and society more generally. Enriching and stimulating sets of experiences for children can help develop these skills.

Evidence of the potential importance of parenting for language development is found across studies of parent talk. This research offers compelling correlational evidence that providing children with labels (e.g., for objects, numbers, and letters) to promote and reinforce knowledge, responding contingently to their speech, eliciting and sustaining conversation with them, and simply talking to them more often are related to vocabulary development (Hart and Risley, 1995; Hirsh-Pasek et al., 2015; Hoff, 2003). In addition to the frequency of talking with children, research is beginning to show that the quality of language used by parents when interacting with their children may matter for children's vocabulary development. Studies using various types of designs have shown that children whose fathers are more educated and use complex and diverse language when interacting with them develop stronger vocabulary skills relative to other children (Malin et al., 2012; Pancsofar and Vernon-Feagans, 2006; Rowe et al., 2004).

Language development studies have found that providing an instructional platform in a child's early language experience, such as offering a social context for communication and asking more "what," "where," and "why" questions, is associated with language acquisition (Baumwell et al., 1997; Bruner, 1983; Leech et al., 2013). Similar findings are provided by experimental research on dialogic reading, in which adults engage children in discussion about the reading material rather than simply reading to them (Mol et al., 2008; Whitehurst et al., 1988). A meta-analytic review of 16 interventions by Mol and colleagues (2008) showed that, relative to reading as usual, dialogic reading interventions, especially use of expressive language, were more effective at increasing children's vocabulary. The effect was stronger for children ages 2-3 and more modest for those ages 4-5 and those at risk for language and literacy impairment (Mol et al., 2008).

Frequency of shared book reading by mothers and fathers is linked to young children's acquisition of skills and knowledge that affect their later success in reading, writing, and other areas (Baker, 2014; Duursma et al., 2008; Malin et al., 2014). Studies demonstrate that through shared book reading, young children learn, among other skills, to recognize letters and words and develop understanding that print is a visual representation of spoken language, develop phonological awareness (the ability to manipulate the sounds of spoken language), begin to understand syntax and grammar, and learn concepts and story structures (Duursma et al., 2008; Malin et al., 2014). Shared literacy activities such as book reading also expose children to new words and words they may not encounter in spoken language, stimulating vocabulary development beyond what might be obtained through toy-play or other parent-child interactions (Isbell et al., 2004; Ninio, 1983; Whitehurst et al., 1988). Regular book reading also may play a role in establishing routines for children and shaping wake and sleep patterns, as well as provide them with knowledge about relationships and coping that can be applied in the real world (Duursma et al., 2008).

Children of low socioeconomic status and minority children frequently have smaller vocabularies relative to children of higher socioeconomic status and white children, and these differences increase over time (Markman and Brooks-Gunn, 2005). Some experts have theorized that this differential arises from variations in "speech cultures" of families, which are linked to socioeconomic status and race/ethnicity. The middle- and upper-class (primarily white) speech culture is associated with more and more varied language and more conversation, which contributes to bigger vocabularies and improved school readiness among children in these homes (Hart and

Risley, 1999). Little research has focused on whether reducing these variations would help close the racial/ethnic gap in school readiness, however (Markman and Brooks-Gunn, 2005). Relative to their middle- and upper-class, mainly white, counterparts, low-income and immigrant parents are less likely to report that they read to their children on a regular basis and to have books and other learning materials in the home (Markman and Brooks-Gunn, 2005). Besides culture, this difference may be due to such factors as access to books (including those in parents' first language), parents' own reading and literacy skills, and erratic work schedules (which could interfere with regular shared book reading before children go to bed, for example).

As discussed in Chapter 4, limited experimental research suggests that interventions designed to promote parents' provision of stimulating learning experiences support children's cognitive development, primarily on measures of language and literacy (Chang et al., 2015; Garcia et al., 2015; Mendelsohn et al., 2005; Roberts and Kaiser, 2011). In one study, for example, interactions between high-risk parents and their children over developmentally stimulating, age-appropriate learning material (e.g., a book or a toy), followed by review and discussion between parents and child development specialists, were found to improve children's cognitive and language skills at 21 months compared with a control group, and also reduced parental stress (Mendelsohn et al., 2005).

Early numeracy and math skills also are building blocks for young children's academic achievement (Claessens and Engel, 2013). To instill early math skills in young children, parents sometimes employ such strategies as playing with blocks, puzzles, and legos; assisting with measuring ingredients for recipes; solving riddles and number games; and playing with fake money (Benigno and Ellis, 2008; Hensen, 2005). Such experiences may facilitate children's math-related competencies, but compared with the research on strategies to foster children's language development, the evidence base on how parenting practices promote math skills in young children is small.

A growing literature identifies general aspects of home-based parental involvement in children's early learning—such as parents' expectations and goals for their children, parent-child communication, and support for learning—that appear to be associated with greater academic achievement, including in math (Fan and Chen, 2001; Galindo and Sonnenschein, 2015; Ginsburg et al., 2010; Jeynes, 2003, 2005). More work is needed, however, to distill specific actions parents can take to promote math-related skills in their young children. At the same time, as noted earlier, some parents appear to be reluctant to engage their children in math learning—some because they lack knowledge about early math and may engage in few math-related activities in the home relative to activities related to language, and some because they view math skills as less important than other skills for their children (Blevins-Knabe et al., 2000; Cannon and Ginsburg, 2008; Vukovic and Lesaux, 2013). Given the demonstrated importance of early math skills for future academic achievement and the persistent gap in math knowledge related to socioeconomic status (Galindo and Sonnenschein, 2015), additional research is needed to elucidate how parents can and do promote young children's math skills and how they can better be supported in providing their children with these skills.

Finally, there is some evidence for differences across demographic groups in the United States with respect to parents' use of practices to promote children's cognitive development. Barbarin and Jean-Baptiste (2013), for example, found that poor and African American parents employed dialogic practices less often than nonpoor and European American parents in a study that utilized in-home interviews and structured observations of parent-child interactions.

Contingent Responsiveness of Parents

Broadly defined, contingent responsiveness denotes an adult's behavior that occurs immediately after and in response to a child's behavior and is related to the child's focus of attention (Roth, 1987). Dunst and colleagues (1990) argue that every time two or more people are together, there is a communicative exchange in which the behavior (nonverbal or verbal) affects the other person, is interpreted, and is responded to with a "discernible outcome" (p. 1). Such communication exchanges between parents and their children are considered foundational for building healthy relationships between parents and children, as well as between parents (Cabrera et al., 2014).

Within the multiple relationships and systems that surround parents and children, the quality of the relationship they share is vital for the well-being of both (Bronfenbrenner and Morris, 1998). The science is clear on the importance of positive parent-child relationships for children. Emotionally responsive parenting, whereby parents respond in a timely and appropriate way to children's needs, is a major element of healthy relationships, and is correlated with positive developmental outcomes for children that include emotional security, social facility, symbolic competence, verbal ability, and intellectual achievement (Ainsworth et al., 1974). The majority of children who are loved and cared for from birth and develop healthy and reciprocally nurturing relationships with their caregivers grow up to be happy and well adjusted (Armstrong and Morris, 2000; Bakermans-Kranenburg et al., 2003). Conversely, children who grow up in neglectful or abusive relationships with parents who are overly intrusive and controlling are at high risk for a variety of adverse health and behavioral outcomes (Barber, 2002; Egeland et al., 1993).

The development of health-promoting relationships between parents and their children is rooted in evolutionary pressures that lead children to be born wired to interact with their social environment in ways that will ensure their survival and promote their eventual development (Bowlby, 2008). Through reaching out, babbling, facial expressions, and gestures, very young children signal to caregivers when they are ready to engage with them. Caregivers may respond by producing similar vocalizations and gestures to signal back to infants that they have heard and understood (Masataka, 1993). Cabrera and colleagues (2007) found that children of fathers who react to their behavior in a sensitive way by following their cues, responding, and engaging them are more linguistically and socially competent relative to children of fathers who do not react in these ways (Cabrera et al., 2007).

This "serve and return" interaction between caregivers and children, which continues throughout childhood, is fundamental for growth-promoting relationships (Institute of Medicine and National Research Council, 2015; National Research Council and Institute of Medicine, 2000). A consistent give and take with responsive caregivers provides the child with tailored experiences that are enriching and stimulating; forms an emotional connection between caregiver and child; builds on the child's interests and capacities; helps the child develop a sense of self; and stimulates the child's intellectual, social, physical, and emotional and behavioral growth (Institute of Medicine and National Research Council, 2015; National Research Council and Institute of Medicine, 2000). This give and take is particularly important for language development. It is believed that through this process, the child learns that she or he is loved and will love others in return, and that she or he is accepted and cared for and will also eventually accept and care for others.

For infants, social expectations and a sense of self-efficacy in initiating social interactions are influenced by their early interactions with their caregivers. McQuaid and colleagues (2009) found that mothers' contingent smiles (i.e., those in response to infant smiles) in an initial interactive study phase predicted infant social bids when mothers were still-faced in a subsequent study phase, a finding consistent with results of earlier research (Bigelow, 1998). The adult's response to the child's overtures for interaction needs to be contingent on the child's behaviors. Infants' spontaneous vocalizations are characterized by pauses that enable caregivers to respond vocally. Children who have experience with turn taking are able to vocalize back to the caregiver in a synchronized manner (Masataka, 1993). Young children's social and emotional development is influenced by the degree to which primary caregivers engage them in this kind of growth-promoting interaction (Cassidy, 2002).

As described in Chapter 1, securely attached infants develop basic trust in their caregivers and seek the caregiver's comfort and love when alarmed because they expect to receive protection and emotional support. Infants who trust their caregivers to respond to their needs in a sensitive and timely manner are able to explore and learn freely because they can return to their "safe base" if they encounter unfamiliar things and events (Bowlby, 2008; Cassidy, 2002). In the face of the demands of daily life, with parents being unable to offer individualized responsiveness and synchronized, attuned interactions all of the time, sensitive caregiving makes it possible to manage and repair disruptions that inevitably occur in day-to-day parenting.

High-quality "serve and return" parenting skills do not always develop spontaneously, especially during infancy and toddlerhood, before children have learned to speak. Some research indicates that lower-income families are at higher risk for not engaging in these types of interactions with their children (Paterson, 2011), but there is variability within and across economic and cultural groups (Cabrera et al., 2006). Differences among racial/ethnic groups in mothers' interactive behaviors with their young children have also been noted (e.g., Brooks et al., 2013; Cho et al., 2007). In a study of mothers of premature infants, for example, American Indian mothers relative to African American mothers looked and gestured more with their infants based on observer ratings (Brooks et al., 2013). Such differences may be related to variation in sociocultural norms or to other factors. Parents who experience such stressors as low income, conflict with partners or other adults, depression, and household chaos face more challenges to engaging in emotionally responsive parenting because of the emotional toll these stressors can exact (Conger and Donnellan, 2007; Markman and Brooks-Gunn, 2005; McLoyd, 1998). Building the capacities of all caregivers to form responsive and nurturing relationships with their children is crucial to promoting child well-being.

As detailed in Chapters 4 and 5, experimental studies largely confirm evidence from correlational studies showing that sensitive parenting and attachment security are related to children's social-emotional development (Van Der Voort et al., 2014). One international study found that an intervention focused on responsive stimulation could promote positive caregiving behaviors among impoverished families (Yousafzai et al., 2015). Another study found that home visiting for parents of preterm infants that entailed promotion of more sensitive and responsive parenting skills modestly improved parent-infant interactions (Goyal et al., 2013).

These and other interventions that successfully promote positive parent-child interactions, secure attachment, and healthy child development have been developed for parents of both infants (Armstrong and Morris, 2000) and preschoolers (Bagner and Eyberg, 2007). Some research shows that such an intervention provided first in infancy, followed by a second dose during the toddler/preschool years, is most effective at improving maternal behaviors and child outcomes (Landry et al., 2008). However, the success of preventive interventions in improving the quality of parent-infant attachment, a parent's relationship with her or his child, and the resulting child mental and physical outcomes depends upon the quality of the intervention (Chaffin et al., 2004), the number of sessions (a moderate number may be better than either more or less) (Moss et al., 2011), and the degree to which other parts of the parent-child system (e.g., separation due to parental incarceration or other reasons) are considered (Barr et al., 2011). Although much of the literature has focused on non-Hispanic white and black families, and mainly on mothers, preventive interventions with successful maternal and child outcomes have also been developed for Hispanic and Asian families (Ho et al., 2012; McCabe and Yeh, 2009) and can be designed to include fathers (Barr et al., 2011).

Organization of the Home Environment and the Importance of Routines

Observational research suggests that children's development is enhanced by parents' use of predictable and orderly routines. Family routines, such as those related to feeding, sleeping, and learning, help structure children's environment and create order and stability that, in turn, help children develop self-regulatory skills by teaching them that events are predictable and there are rewards for waiting (Evans et al., 2005; Hughes and Ensor, 2009; Martin et al., 2012). Conversely, an unpredictable environment may undermine children's confidence in their ability to influence their environment and predict consequences, which may in turn result in children's having difficulty with regulating their behavior according to situational needs (Deater-Deckard et al., 2009; Evans and English, 2002).

Although family routines vary widely across time and populations, studies have associated such routines with children's developmental outcomes (Fiese et al., 2002; Spagnola and Fiese, 2007). It is particularly difficult, however, to infer causal effects of routines on child outcomes in correlational studies because of the many contextual factors (e.g., parental depression or substance abuse, erratic work schedules) or factors related to economic strain (e.g., homelessness, poverty) that may make keeping routines difficult and at the same time adversely affect child development in other ways.

Several literatures have developed around routines thought to promote particular developmental targets. For example, Mindell and colleagues (2009) describe results from a randomized controlled trial in which mothers instructed in a specific bedtime routine reported reductions in sleep problems for their infants and toddlers (see also Staples et al., 2015, for a recent nonexperimental analysis of bedtime routines and sleep outcomes). De Castilho and colleagues (2013) found in a systematic review of randomized controlled trials consistent associations between children's oral health and elements of their family environment such as parents' toothbrushing habits. And in a nationally representative cross-sectional study, Anderson and Whitaker (2010) report strong associations between exposure to various household routines, such as eating meals as a family, obtaining adequate sleep, and limiting screen time, and risk for obesity in preschool-age children. As discussed above, a growing body of literature also reports associations between more general aspects of children's healthy development, such as social competence, and the organization and predictability of a broader set of day-to-day experiences in the home (see Evans and Wachs, 2010).

In some cases, however, routines are difficult to establish because of demands on parents, such as the nonstandard work schedules some parents are forced to keep. Reviewing the cross-sectional and longitudinal literature on nonstandard work schedules, for example, Li and colleagues (2014) found that 21 of the 23 studies reviewed reported associations between nonstandard work schedules and adverse child developmental outcomes. They found that while parents working nonstandard schedules, particularly those who work night or evening shifts, may be afforded more parent-child time during the day, such schedules can lead to fatigue and stress, with detrimental effects on the parent's physical and psychological capacity to provide quality parenting.

Other research has looked at the impacts on children of living in home environments that are marked by high levels of "chaos," or instability and disorganization (Evans and Wachs, 2010; Vernon-Feagans et al., 2012). A few studies have found a relationship between measures of household instability and disorganization and risk of adverse cognitive, social, and behavioral outcomes in young children. In a longitudinal study, for example, Vernon-Feagans and colleagues (2012) found that a higher level of household disorganization in early childhood (e.g., household density, messiness, neighborhood and household noise) was predictive of poorer performance on measures of receptive and expressive vocabulary at age 3. This finding held after taking into account a wide range of variables known to influence children's language development. Household instability (e.g., number of people moving in and out of the household, changes in residence and care providers) was not predictive of adverse language outcomes (Vernon-Feagans et al., 2012). In another longitudinal study, a questionnaire was used to assess household chaos based on whether parents had a regular morning routine, whether a television was usually on in the home, how calm the home atmosphere was, and the like when children were in kindergarten. Parent-reported chaos accounted for variations in child IQ and conduct problems in first grade beyond other home environment predictors of these outcomes such as lower parental education and poorer home literacy environment (Deater-Deckard et al.,

2009). In other studies, children rating their homes as more chaotic have been found to earn lower grades (Hanscombe et al., 2011) and to show more pronounced conduct and hyperactivity problems (Fiese and Winter, 2010; Hildyard and Wolfe, 2002; Jaffee et al., 2012; Repetti et al., 2002; Sroufe et al., 2005).

Household chaos has strong negative associations with children's abilities to regulate attention and arousal (Evans and Wachs, 2010). Children raised in chaotic environments may adapt to these contexts by shifting their attention away from overstimulating and unpredictable stimuli, essentially "tuning out" from their environment (Evans, 2006). In the short term, this may be an adaptive solution to reduce overarousal. In the long term, however, it may also lessen children's exposure to important aspects of socialization and, in turn, negatively affect their cognitive and social-emotional development.

Emerging evidence suggests that the relationship between household chaos and poorer child outcomes may involve other aspects of the home environment, such as maternal sensitivity. In chaotic environments, for example, longitudinal research shows that parents' abilities to read, interpret, and respond to their children's needs accurately are compromised (Vernon-Feagans et al., 2012). Furthermore, supportive and high-quality exchanges between caregivers and young children, thought to support young children's abilities to maintain and volitionally control their attention, are fewer and of lower quality in such environments (Conway and Stifter, 2012; Vernon-Feagans et al., 2012). This association is likely to be of particular importance in infancy, when children lack the self-regulatory capacities to screen out irrelevant stimuli without adult support (Conway and Stifter, 2012; Posner and Rothbart, 2007).

Even ambient noise from the consistent din of a television playing in the background is associated with toddlers' having difficulty maintaining sustained attention during typical play—a building block for the volitional aspects of executive attentional control (Blair et al., 2011; Posner and Rothbart, 2007). Studies with older children and adults show that chronic exposure to noise is related to poorer attention during visual and auditory search tasks (see Evans, 2006; Evans and Lepore, 1993).

In addition, household chaos likely serves as a physiological stressor that undermines higher-order executive processes. Theoretical and empirical work indicates that direct physiological networks link the inner ear with the myelinated vagus of the 10th cranial nerve—a key regulator of parasympathetic stress response (Porges, 1995). Very high or very low frequencies of auditory stimuli such as those present in ambient and unpredictable noise directly trigger vagal responses indicative of parasympathetic stress modulation (Porges et al., 2013). In the same way, novel unpredictable and uncontrollable experiences can activate the hypothalamic-pituitary-adrenal

(HPA)[1] axis (Dickerson and Kemeny, 2004). General levels of chaos play a role in children's autonomic nervous system and HPA axis functioning (Blair et al., 2011; Evans and English, 2002) in ways that may negatively affect executive functioning (Berry et al., 2012; Oei et al., 2006).

Highly chaotic environments also may affect children's language and early literacy development through similar mechanisms. Overstimulation, which may overtax children's attentional and executive systems, may challenge young children's ability to encode, process, and interpret linguistic information (Evans et al., 1999). The lack of order in such an environment also may impair children's emerging executive functioning abilities (see Schoemaker et al., 2013). Better executive functioning has been found in longitudinal research to be strongly associated with larger receptive vocabularies in early childhood (Blair and Razza, 2007; Hughes and Ensor, 2007), as well as with lower levels of externalizing behaviors (Hughes and Ensor, 2011). Other longitudinal studies have found positive relationships between family routines and children's executive functioning skills during the preschool years (e.g., Hughes and Ensor, 2009; Martin et al., 2012; Raver et al., 2013).

Behavioral Discipline Practices

Parental guidance or discipline is an essential component of parenting. When parents discipline their children, they are not simply punishing the children's bad behavior but aiming to support and nurture them for self-control, self-direction, and their ability to care for others (Howard, 1996). Effective discipline is thought to require a strong parent-child bond; an approach for teaching and strengthening desired behaviors; and a strategy for decreasing or eliminating undesired or ineffective behaviors (American Academy of Pediatrics, 1998).

Effective discipline entails some of the parenting practices discussed earlier. In children's earliest years, for example, discipline includes parents' use of routines that not only teach children about the behaviors in which people typically engage but also help them feel secure in their relationship with their parent because they can anticipate those daily activities. As infants become more mobile and begin to explore, parents need to create safe environments for them. Beginning in early childhood and continuing as children get older, positive child behavior may be facilitated through parents' clear communication of expectations, modeling of desired behaviors, and positive reinforcement for positive behaviors (American Academy of

---

[1] The HPA axis "regulates the release of cortisol, an important hormone associated with psychological, physiological, and physical health functioning" (Dickerson and Kemeny, 2004, p. 355).

Pediatrics, 2006). Over time, children internalize the attitudes and expectations of their caregivers and learn to self-regulate their behavior.

Parents' use of corporal punishment as a disciplinary measure is a controversial topic in the United States. Broadly defined as parents' intentional use of physical force (e.g., spanking) to cause a child some level of discomfort, corporal punishment is assumed to have as its goal correcting children's negative behavior. Many researchers and professionals who work with children and families have argued against the use of physical punishment by parents as well as in schools (American Psychological Association, 2016; Hendrix, 2013). Although illegal in several countries, in no U.S. state is parents' use of corporal punishment entirely prohibited, with some variation in where states draw the line between corporal punishment and physical abuse (Coleman et al., 2010; duRivage et al., 2015).

The state laws are consistent with the views of many Americans who approve of the use of spanking, used by many parents as a disciplinary measure with their own children (Child Trends Databank, 2015a; MacKenzie et al., 2013). In a 2014 nationally representative survey of attitudes about spanking, 65 percent of women and 78 percent of men ages 18-65 agreed that children sometimes need to be spanked (Child Trends Databank, 2015a). Among parents participating in the Fragile Families and Child Well-Being Study, 57 percent of mothers and 40 percent of fathers reported spanking their children at age 3, and 52 percent of mothers and 33 percent of fathers reported doing so when their children were age 5 (MacKenzie et al., 2013).

Although physical punishment often results in immediate cessation of behavior that parents view as undesirable in young children, the longer-term consequences for child outcomes are mixed, with research showing a relationship with later behavioral problems. In a systematic review of studies using randomized controlled, longitudinal, cross-sectional, and other design types, Larzelere and Kuhn (2005) found that, compared with other disciplinary strategies, physical punishment was either the primary means of discipline or was severe was associated with less favorable child outcomes. In particular, children who were spanked regularly were more likely than children who were not to be aggressive as children as well as during adulthood.

More recent analyses of data from large longitudinal studies conducted in the United States show positive associations between corporal punishment and adverse cognitive and behavioral outcomes in children (Berlin et al., 2009; Bodovski and Youn, 2010; MacKenzie et al., 2013; Straus and Paschall, 2009). Using data from two cohorts of young children (ages 2-4 and 5-9) in the National Longitudinal Survey of Youth, Straus and Paschall (2009) found that children whose mothers reported at the beginning of the study that they used corporal punishment performed worse on measures of cognitive ability 4 years later relative to children whose mothers stated that they did not use corporal punishment. In the Early Head Start National Research and Evaluation Project, Berlin and colleagues (2009) found that spanking at age 1 predicted aggressive behavior problems at age 2 and lower developmental scores at age 3, but did not predict childhood aggression at age 3 or development at age 2. The overall effects of spanking were not large. In the Fragile Families and Child Well-Being Study, MacKenzie and colleagues (2013) found that children whose mothers spanked them at age 5 relative to those whose mothers did not had higher levels of externalizing behavior at age 9. High-frequency spanking by fathers when the children were age 5 was also associated with lower child-receptive vocabulary at age 9. These studies controlled for a number of factors besides parents' use of physical punishment (e.g., parents' education, child birth weight) that in other studies have been found to be associated with negative child outcomes.

Some have proposed that the circumstances in which physical discipline takes place (e.g., whether it is accompanied by parental warmth) may influence the meaning of the discipline for the child as well as its effects on child outcomes (Landsford et al., 2004). Using data from a large longitudinal survey, McLoyd and Smith (2002) found that spanking was associated with an increase in problem behaviors in African American, white, and Hispanic children when mothers exhibited low levels of emotional support but not when emotional support from mothers was high.

Time-out is a discipline strategy recommended by the American Academy of Pediatrics for children who are toddlers or older (American Academy of Pediatrics, 2006), and along with redirection appears to be used increasingly by parents instead of more direct verbal or physical punishment (Barkin et al., 2007; LeCuyer et al., 2011). Yet for some parents, use of time-out may not be optimal, and parents who consult the Internet for how best to use this disciplinary technique may find the information to be incomplete and/or erroneous (Drayton et al., 2014). Research on best practices for the use of time-out continues to emerge, generally pointing to relatively short time-outs that are shortened further if the child responds rapidly to the request to go into time-out and engages in appropriate behavior during time-out (Donaldson et al., 2013), or may be lengthened if the child engages in inappropriate behavior during time-out (Donaldson and Vollmer, 2011). However, these studies are limited by very small sample sizes. States, seeking to shape briefer and more effective uses of the technique and to avoid prolonged seclusion, are just beginning to prescribe how time-out should be administered in schools (Freeman and Sugai, 2013).

PARENTING WITHIN FAMILY SYSTEMS

As discussed in Chapter 1, while focusing on the parenting knowledge, attitudes, and practices that can help children develop successfully, the committee recognized that "human development is too complicated, nuanced, and dynamic to assert that children's parents alone determine the course and outcome of their ontogeny" (Bornstein and Leventhal, 2015, p. 107). Parenting knowledge, attitudes, and practices are embedded in various ecologies that include family composition, social class, ethnicity, and culture, all of which are related to how parents treat their children and what they believe about their children as they grow, and all of which affect child outcomes.

Family systems theory offers a useful perspective from which to view parenting behavior, to understand what shapes it, and to explain its complex relation to child outcomes. As a system, the family operates according to an evolving set of implicit rules that establish routines, regulate behavior, legitimate emotional support and expression, provide for communication, establish an organized power structure or hierarchy, and provide for negotiating and problem solving so that family tasks can be carried out effectively (Goldenberg and Goldenberg, 2013). Families as systems also create a climate or internal environment with features that shape parenting behavior and influence child outcomes. Family climates can be characterized along various dimensions, such as cohesive-conflictual, supportive-dismissive, tightly or loosely controlled, orderly-chaotic, oriented toward academic achievement or not, expressive of positive or negative emotions, hierarchical-democratic, fostering autonomy versus dependence, promoting stereotypical gender roles or not, and fostering strong ethnic and cultural identity or not.

Roles are defined within the family system in ways that may influence parenting. Family members may operate with a division of labor based on their own personal resources, mental health, skills, and education, in which one member specializes in and is responsible for one set of functions, such as garnering economic resources needed by the family, and another takes responsibility for educating the children. When these differences work well, family members complement and compensate for one another in ways that may soften the rough edges of one and make up for the inadequacies of another.

As discussed in this chapter and throughout the report, children do best when they develop sustaining and supportive relationships with parents. Yet while attachment theory has been useful in understanding mainly how mothers form relationships with children, it has been less useful at guiding research with fathers (Grossmann et al., 2002), and relatively little research has examined other relations of the family system and microsystems where family members spend time (e.g., school, church, work). As systems, however, families are interdependent with the broader world and thus are susceptible to influences and inputs from their environments. Actions occurring in one system can result in reactions in another. For example, children who have not developed healthy relationships with their parents may have difficulty developing positive relationships with teachers.

In short, family systems are influenced by the evolving cultural, political, economic, and geographic conditions in which they are embedded. Members of a cultural group share a common identity, heritage, and values, which also reflect the broad economic and political circumstances in which they live. An understanding of salient macrolevel societal shifts (e.g., rates of cohabitation or divorce), along with microsystem influences (e.g., attachments with multiple caregivers and shifts in attachment patterns across childhood into adulthood) that are the subject of more recent research, can be helpful for rethinking parenting processes, what influences them, and how they matter for children. This rethinking in turn highlights the need to understand how complex living systems function and how they reorganize to accommodate changes in their environments (Wachs, 2000).

SUMMARY

The following key points emerged from the committee's examination of core parenting knowledge, attitudes, and practices:

- Parental knowledge of child development is positively associated with quality parent-child interactions and the likelihood of parents' engagement in practices that promote their children's healthy development. Research also indicates that parents with knowledge of evidence-based parenting practices, especially those related to promoting children's physical health and safety, are more likely than those without such knowledge to engage in those practices. Although there is currently limited empirical evidence on how parents' knowledge of available services affects uptake of those services, parenting, and child outcomes, parents with this knowledge are likely better equipped to access services for their families.
- As mediators of the relationship between knowledge and practice, parental attitudes about the roles of parents and others in the raising of young children, as well as about specific practices (e.g., breastfeeding, immunization), can contribute to some variation in practices and in the uptake of services among individuals and subpopulations. The committee found that empirical studies on parenting attitudes do not allow for the identification of core parenting attitudes consistently associated with positive child out-

comes. However, the available evidence points to a need for taking parents' attitudes and beliefs into consideration in the design and implementation of programs and services in order to improve their reach.

- The committee identified several parenting practices that are associated with improvements in the four domains introduced at the beginning of this chapter (physical health and safety, emotional and behavioral competence, social competence, and cognitive competence):

  — contingent responsiveness (serve and return);
  — showing warmth and sensitivity;
  — routines and reduced household chaos;
  — shared book reading and talking to children;
  — practices related to promoting children's health and safety—in particular, receipt of prenatal care, breastfeeding, vaccination, ensuring children's adequate nutrition and physical activity, monitoring, and household/vehicle safety; and
  — use of appropriate (less harsh) discipline.

- Much of the existing research is focused on mothers. A lack of research exists on how parenting knowledge, attitudes, and practices may differ for fathers and other caregivers (e.g., grandparents). Studies suggest some variation in parenting knowledge, attitudes, and practices among racial/ethnic, cultural, and other demographic groups, but more attention is needed to whether and how these differences matter for child outcomes.

- With regard to practices that promote children's cognitive skills, research to date has examined primarily the effect of parenting on children's language and literacy skills. Research on how parenting affects other cognitive domains, such as math and problem-solving skills, would deepen understanding of the relationship between parenting and children's cognitive development.

REFERENCES

Ainsworth, M.D.S., Bell, S.M., and Stayton, D.J. (1974). Infant-mother attachment and social development: "Socialisation" as a product of reciprocal responsiveness to signals. In M.P. Richards (Ed.), *The Integration of a Child into a Social World* (pp. 9-135). London, UK: Cambridge University Press.

Ainsworth, M.S., and Bowlby, J. (1991). An ethological approach to personality development. *American Psychologist, 46*(4), 333.

Ajzen, I., and Fishbein, M. (1980). *Understanding Attitudes and Predicting Social Behavior.* Englewood Cliffs, NJ: Prentice-Hall.

Alkon, A., Crowley, A.A., Neelon, S.E.B., Hill, S., Pan, Y., Nguyen, V., Rose, R., Savage, E., Forestieri, N., Shipman, L., and Kotch, J.B. (2014). Nutrition and physical activity: Randomized control trial in child care centers improves knowledge, policies, and children's body mass index. *BMC Public Health, 14*(1), 1-13.

American Academy of Pediatrics. (1998). Guidance for effective discipline. *Pediatrics, 101*(4 Pt. 1), 723-728.

American Academy of Pediatrics. (2006). *Practice Guide: Effective Discipline, Child Development.* Elk Grove Village, IL: American Academy of Pediatrics.

American Academy of Pediatrics. (2012). Policy statement: Breastfeeding and the use of human milk. *Pediatrics, 129*(3), e827-e841.

American Psychological Association. (2016). *Corporal Punishment.* Available: http://www.apa.org/about/policy/corporal-punishment.aspx [May 2016].

American Psychological Association Task Force on Evidence-Based Practice with Children and Adolescents. (2008). *Disseminating Evidence-Based Practice for Children and Adolescents.* Washington, DC: American Psychological Association.

Anderson, K.J., and Minke, K.M. (2007). Parent involvement in education: Toward an understanding of parents' decision making. *The Journal of Educational Research, 100*(5), 311-323.

Anderson, S.E., and Whitaker, R.C. (2010). Household routines and obesity in U.S. preschool-aged children. *Pediatrics, 125*(3).

Arbogast, K.B., Jermakian, J.S., Kallan, M.J., and Durbin, D.R. (2009). Effectiveness of belt positioning booster seats: An updated assessment. *Pediatrics, 124*(5), 1281-1286.

Ariza, A.J., Chen, E.H., Binns, H.J., and Christoffel, K.K. (2004). Risk factors for overweight in five-to six-year-old Hispanic-American children: A pilot study. *Journal of Urban Health, 81*(1), 150-161.

Armistead, L., Forehand, R., Brody, G., and Maguen, S. (2002). Parenting and child psychosocial adjustment in single-parent African American families: Is community context important? *Behavior Therapy, 33*(3), 361-375.

Armstrong, K., and Morris, J. (2000). Promoting secure attachment, maternal mood and child health in a vulnerable population: A randomized controlled trial. *Journal of Paediatrics and Child Health, 36*(6), 555-562.

Aune, D., Saugstad, O.D., Henriksen, T., and Tonstad, S. (2014). Maternal body mass index and the risk of fetal death, stillbirth, and infant death: A systematic review and meta-analysis. *Journal of the American Medical Association, 311*(15), 1536-1546.

Bagner, D.M., and Eyberg, S.M. (2007). Parent-child interaction therapy for disruptive behavior in children with mental retardation: A randomized controlled trial. *Journal of Clinical Child and Adolescent Psychology, 36*(3), 418-429.

Baker, C.E. (2014). African American fathers' contributions to children's early academic achievement: Evidence from two-parent families from the Early Childhood Longitudinal Study—Birth Cohort. *Early Education & Development, 25*(1), 19-35.

Bakermans-Kranenburg, M.J., Van Ijzendoorn, M.H., and Juffer, F. (2003). Less is more: Meta-analyses of sensitivity and attachment interventions in early childhood. *Psychological Bulletin, 129*(2), 195-215.

Barbarin, O., and Jean-Baptiste, E. (2013). The relation of dialogic, control, and racial socialization practices to early academic and social competence: Effects of gender, ethnicity, and family socioeconomic status. *American Journal of Orthopsychiatry, 83*(2 Pt. 3), 207-217.

Barber, B.K. (2002). Reintroducing parental psychological control. In B.K. Barber (Ed.), *Intrusive Parenting: How Psychological Control Affects Children and Adolescents* (pp. 3-13). Washington, DC: American Psychological Association.

Barkin, S., Scheindlin, B., Ip, E.H., Richardson, I., and Finch, S. (2007). Determinants of parental discipline practices: A national sample from primary care practices. *Clinical Pediatrics, 46*(1), 64-69.

Barlow, J., Smailagic, N., Ferriter, M., Bennett, C., and Jones, H. (2010). Group-based parent-training programmes for improving emotional and behavioural adjustment in children from birth to three years old. *Cochrane Database of Systematic Reviews, 3,* CD003680.

Barr, R.G., Brito, N., Zocca, J., Reina, S., Rodriguez, J., and Shauffer, C. (2011). The Baby Elmo Program: Improving teen father-child interactions within juvenile justice facilities. *Children and Youth Services Review, 33*(9), 1555-1562.

Barr, R.G., Rajabali, F., Aragon, M., Colbourne, M., and Brant, R. (2015). Education about crying in normal infants is associated with a reduction in pediatric emergency room visits for crying complaints. *Journal of Developmental & Behavioral Pediatrics, 36*(4), 252-257.

Baumwell, L., Tamis-LeMonda, C.S., and Bornstein, M.H. (1997). Maternal verbal sensitivity and child language comprehension. *Infant Behavior and Development, 20*(2), 247-258.

Belcher, H.M., Watkins, K., Johnson, E., and Ialongo, N. (2007). Early Head Start: Factors associated with caregiver knowledge of child development, parenting behavior, and parenting stress. *NHSA Dialog: A Research-to-Practice Journal for the Early Intervention Field, 10*(1), 6-19.

Benasich, A.A., and Brooks-Gunn, J. (1996). Maternal attitudes and knowledge of child-rearing: Associations with family and child outcomes. *Child Development, 67*(3), 1186-1205.

Benigno, J., and Ellis, S. (2008). Do parents count? The socialization of children's numeracy. In O.N. Saracho and B. Spodek (Eds.), *Contemporary Perspectives on Mathematics in Early Childhood Education* (pp. 291-308). Charlotte, NC: Information Age.

Berkovits, M.D., O'Brien, K.A., Carter, C.G., and Eyberg, S.M. (2010). Early identification and intervention for behavior problems in primary care: A comparison of two abbreviated versions of parent-child interaction therapy. *Behavior Therapy, 41*(3), 375-387.

Berlin, L.J., Ispa, J.M., Fine, M.A., Malone, P.S., Brooks-Gunn, J., Brady-Smith, C., Ayoub, C., and Bai, Y. (2009). Correlates and consequences of spanking and verbal punishment for low-income white, African American, and Mexican American toddlers. *Child Development, 80*(5), 1403-1420.

Bernstein, J., Zimmerman, T.S., Werner-Wilson, R.J., and Vosburg, J. (2000). Preschool children's classification skills and a multicultural education intervention to promote acceptance of ethnic diversity. *Journal of Research in Childhood Education, 14*(2), 181-192.

Berry, J.G., Poduri, A., Bonkowsky, J.L., Zhou, J., Graham, D.A., Welch, C., Putney, H., and Srivastava, R. (2012). Trends in resource utilization by children with neurological impairment in the United States inpatient health care system: A repeat cross-sectional study. *PLoS Medicine, 9*(1), e1001158.

Bertera, E.M., and Crewe, S.E. (2013). Parenthood in the twenty-first century: African American grandparents as surrogate parents. *Journal of Human Behavior in the Social Environment, 23*(2), 178-192.

Bigelow, A.E. (1998). Infants' sensitivity to familiar imperfect contingencies in social interaction. *Infant Behavior and Development, 21*(1), 149-162.

Birch, L.L., and Fisher, J.O. (1998). Development of eating behaviors among children and adolescents. *Pediatrics, 101*(Suppl. 2), 539-549.

Bjørknes, R., and Manger, T. (2013). Can parent training alter parent practice and reduce conduct problems in ethnic minority children? A randomized controlled trial. *Prevention Science, 14*(1), 52-63.

Blair, C., and Raver, C.C. (2012). Child development in the context of adversity: Experiential canalization of brain and behavior. *American Psychologist, 67*(4), 309-318.

Blair, C., and Razza, R.P. (2007). Relating effortful control, executive function, and false belief understanding to emerging math and literacy ability in kindergarten. *Child Development, 78*(2), 647-663.

Blair, C., Granger, D.A., Willoughby, M., Mills-Koonce, R., Cox, M., Greenberg, M.T., Kivlighan, K.T., and Fortunato, C.K. (2011). Salivary cortisol mediates effects of poverty and parenting on executive functions in early childhood. *Child Development, 82*(6), 1970-1984.

Blevins-Knabe, B., Austin, A.B., Musun, L., Eddy, A., and Jones, R.M. (2000). Family home care providers' and parents' beliefs and practices concerning mathematics with young children. *Early Child Development and Care, 165*(1), 41-58.

Bodovski, K., and Youn, M.-J. (2010). Love, discipline and elementary school achievement: The role of family emotional climate. *Social Science Research, 39*(4), 585-595.

Bond, L.A., and Burns, C.E. (2006). Mothers' beliefs about knowledge, child development, and parenting strategies: Expanding the goals of parenting programs. *Journal of Primary Prevention, 27*(6), 555-571.

Bornstein, M.H., and Bradley, R.H. (2012). *Socioeconomic Status, Parenting, and Child Development.* New York: Routledge.

Bornstein, M.H., and Cote, L.R. (2004). "Who is sitting across from me?" Immigrant mothers' knowledge of parenting and children's development. *Pediatrics, 114*(5), e557-e564.

Bornstein, M., and Leventhal, T. (2015). *Handbook of Child Psychology and Developmental Science* (vol. 4, 7th ed.). Hoboken, NJ: Wiley.

Bornstein, M.H., Cote, L.R., Haynes, O.M., Hahn, C.S., and Park, Y. (2010). Parenting knowledge: Experiential and sociodemographic factors in European American mothers of young children. *Developmental Psychology, 46*(6), 1677-1693.

Boukydis, C.Z., and Lester, B.M. (1985). *Infant Crying: Theoretical and Research Perspectives.* New York: Plenum Press.

Bowlby, J. (2008). *A Secure Base: Parent-Child Attachment and Healthy Human Development.* New York: Basic Books.

Bretherton, I. (1985). Attachment theory: Retrospect and prospect. *Monographs of the Society for Research in Child Development, 50*(1/2), 3-35.

Brody, G.H., Flor, D.L., and Gibson, N.M. (1999). Linking maternal efficacy beliefs, developmental goals, parenting practices, and child competence in rural single-parent African American families. *Child Development, 70*(5), 1197-1208.

Brody, G.H., Murry, V.M., Ge, X., Simons, R.L., Gibbons, F.X., Gerrard, M., and Cutrona, C.E. (2006). Perceived discrimination and the adjustment of African American youths: A five-year longitudinal analysis with contextual moderation effects. *Child Development, 77*(5), 1170-1189.

Bronfenbrenner, U., and Morris, P.A. (1998). The ecology of developmental processes. In W. Damon and R.M. Lerner (Eds.), *Handbook of Child Psychology* (vol. 1, 5th ed., pp. 993-1028). Hoboken, NJ: John Wiley & Sons.

Brooks, J.L., Holditch-Davis, D., and Landerman, L.R. (2013). Interactive behaviors of ethnic minority mothers and their premature infants. *Journal of Obstetric, Gynecologic, & Neonatal Nursing, 42*(3), 357-368.

Brotman, L.M., Gouley, K.K., Chesir-Teran, D., Dennis, T., Klein, R.G., and Shrout, P. (2005). Prevention for preschoolers at high risk for conduct problems: Immediate outcomes on parenting practices and child social competence. *Journal of Clinical Child and Adolescent Psychology, 34*(4), 724-734.

Brown, K.F., Kroll, J.S., Hudson, M.J., Ramsay, M., Green, J., Long, S.J., Vincent, C.A., Fraser, G., and Sevdalis, N. (2010). Factors underlying parental decisions about combination childhood vaccinations including MMR: A systematic review. *Vaccine, 28*(26), 4235-4248.

Bruner, J. (1983). The acquisition of pragmatic commitments. In R.M. Golinkoff (Ed.), *The Transition from Prelinguistic to Linguistic Communication* (pp. 27-42). Hillsdale, NJ: Lawrence Erlbaum Associates.

Bryant-Stephens, T., and Li, Y. (2004). Community asthma education program for parents of urban asthmatic children. *Journal of the National Medical Association, 96*(7), 954.

Bryanton, J., Beck, C.T., and Montelpare, W. (2013). Postnatal parental education for optimizing infant general health and parent-infant relationships. *Cochrane Database of Systematic Reviews, 1*, CD004068.

Burchinal, M., Skinner, D., and Reznick, J.S. (2010). European American and African American mothers' beliefs about parenting and disciplining infants: A mixed-method analysis. *Parenting: Science and Practice, 10*(2), 79-96.

Cabrera, N., Tamis-LeMonda, C.S., Bradley, R.H., Hofferth, S., and Lamb, M.E. (2000). Fatherhood in the twenty-first century. *Child Development, 71*(1), 127-136.

Cabrera, N.J., Shannon, J.D., West, J., and Brooks-Gunn, J. (2006). Parental interactions with Latino infants: Variation by country of origin and English proficiency. *Child Development, 77*(5), 1190-1207.

Cabrera, N.J., Shannon, J.D., and Tamis-LeMonda, C. (2007). Fathers' influence on their children's cognitive and emotional development: From toddlers to pre-K. *Applied Development Science, 11*(4), 208-213.

Cabrera, N.J., Hofferth, S.L., and Chae, S. (2011). Patterns and predictors of father-infant engagement across race/ethnic groups. *Early Childhood Research Quarterly, 26*(3), 365-375.

Cabrera, N.J., Fitzgerald, H.E., Bradley, R.H., and Roggman, L. (2014). The ecology of father-child relationships: An expanded model. *Journal of Family Theory and Review, 6*(4), 336-354.

Campbell, K.J., Lioret, S., McNaughton, S.A., Crawford, D.A., Salmon, J., Ball, K., McCallum, Z., Gerner, B.E., Spence, A.C., and Cameron, A.J. (2013). A parent-focused intervention to reduce infant obesity risk behaviors: A randomized trial. *Pediatrics, 131*(4), 652-660.

Cannon, J., and Ginsburg, H.P. (2008). "Doing the math": Maternal beliefs about early mathematics versus language learning. *Early Education and Development, 19*(2), 238-260.

Carson, V., Hunter, S., Kuzik, N., Gray, C.E., Poitras, V.E., Chaput, J.P., Saunders, T.J., Katzmarzyk, P.T., Okely, A.D., Gorber, C., Kho, M.E., Sampson, M., Lee, H., and Tremblay, M.S. (2016). Systematic review of sedentary behavior and health indicators in school-aged children and youth: An update. *Applied Physiology, Nutrition, and Metabolism, 41*(6 Suppl. 3), S240-S265.

Cassidy, J. (2002). *Handbook of Attachment: Theory, Research, and Clinical Applications*. London, UK: Rough Guides.

Centers for Disease Control and Prevention. (2015a). *Breastfeeding Report Card*. Available: http://www.cdc.gov/breastfeeding/pdf/2014breastfeedingreportcard.pdf [February 2016].

Centers for Disease Control and Prevention. (2015b). *Parent Information*. Available: http://www.cdc.gov/parents/index.html [February 2016].

Centers for Disease Control and Prevention. (2015c). *Ten Leading Causes of Death and Injury*. Available: http://www.cdc.gov/injury/wisqars/leadingcauses.html [February 2016].

Chaffin, M., Silovsky, J.F., Funderburk, B., Valle, L.A., Brestan, E.V., Balachova, T., Jackson, S., Lensgraf, J., and Bonner, B.L. (2004). Parent-child interaction therapy with physically abusive parents: Efficacy for reducing future abuse reports. *Journal of Consulting and Clinical Psychology, 72*(3), 500-510.

Chang, S.M., Grantham-McGregor, S.M., Powell, C.A., Vera-Hernández, M., Lopez-Boo, F., Baker-Henningham, H., and Walker, S.P. (2015). Integrating a parenting intervention with routine primary health care: A cluster randomized trial. *Pediatrics, 136*(2), 272-280.

Cheah, C.S., and Chirkov, V. (2008). Parents' personal and cultural beliefs regarding young children: A cross-cultural study of aboriginal and Euro-Canadian mothers. *Journal of Cross-Cultural Psychology, 39*(4), 402-423.

Child Trends Databank. (2015a). *Attitudes Toward Spanking: Indicators on Children and Youth.* Bethesda, MD: Child Trends.

Child Trends Databank. (2015b). *Immunization.* Bethesda, MD: Child Trends.

Cho, J., Holditch-Davis, D., and Belyea, M. (2007). Gender and racial differences in the looking and talking behaviors of mothers and their 3-year-old prematurely born children. *Journal of Pediatric Nursing, 22*(5), 356-367.

Christopher, C., Saunders, R., Jacobvitz, D., Burton, R., and Hazen, N. (2013). Maternal empathy and changes in mothers' permissiveness as predictors of toddlers' early social competence with peers: A parenting intervention study. *Journal of Child and Family Studies, 22*(6), 769-778.

Chung-Park, M.S. (2012). Knowledge, opinions, and practices of infant sleep position among parents. *Military Medicine, 177*(2), 235-239.

Claessens, A., and Engel, M. (2013). How important is where you start? Early mathematics knowledge and later school success. *Teachers College Record, 115*(6), 1-29.

Clark, C. (2007). *Why It Is Important to Involve Parents in Their Children's Literacy Development: A Brief Research Summary.* London, UK: National Literacy Trust.

Coleman, D.L., Dodge, K.A., and Campbell, S.K. (2010). Where and how to draw the line between reasonable corporal punishment and abuse. *Law and Contemporary Problems, 73*(2), 107-166.

Conger, R.D., and Donnellan, M.B. (2007). An interactionist perspective on the socioeconomic context of human development. *Annual Review of Psychology, 58*, 175-199.

Conrad, B., Gross, D., Fogg, L., and Ruchala, P. (1992). Maternal confidence, knowledge, and quality of mother-toddler interactions: A preliminary study. *Infant Mental Health Journal, 13*(4), 353-362.

Conway, A., and Stifter, C.A. (2012). Longitudinal antecedents of executive function in preschoolers. *Child Development, 83*(3), 1022-1036.

Corrarino, J.E. (2013). Health literacy and women's health: Challenges and opportunities. *Journal of Midwifery & Women's Health, 58*(3), 257-264.

Cox, M.J., and Paley, B. (1997). Families as systems. *Annual Review of Psychology, 48*(1), 243-267.

Crane, L.A., Asdigian, N.L., Barón, A.E., Aalborg, J., Marcus, A.C., Mokrohisky, S.T., Byers, T.E., Dellavalle, R.P., and Morelli, J.G. (2012). Mailed intervention to promote sun protection of children: A randomized controlled trial. *American Journal of Preventive Medicine, 43*(4), 399-410.

Cullen, K.W., Baranowski, T., Owens, E., Marsh, T., Rittenberry, L., and de Moor, C. (2003). Availability, accessibility, and preferences for fruit, 100% fruit juice, and vegetables influence children's dietary behavior. *Health Education & Behavior, 30*(5), 615-626.

Curenton, S.M., and Justice, L.M. (2004). African American and Caucasian preschoolers' use of decontextualized language: Literate language features in oral narratives. *Language, Speech, and Hearing Services in Schools, 35*(3), 240-253.

Dawson-McClure, S., Calzada, E., Huang, K.-Y., Kamboukos, D., Rhule, D., Kolawole, B., Petkova, E., and Brotman, L.M. (2015). A population-level approach to promoting healthy child development and school success in low-income, urban neighborhoods: Impact on parenting and child conduct problems. *Prevention Science, 16*(2), 279-290.

De Lepeleere, S., De Bourdeaudhuij, I., Cardon, G., and Verloigne, M. (2015). Do specific parenting practices and related parental self-efficacy associate with physical activity and screen time among primary schoolchildren? A cross-sectional study in Belgium. *BMJ Open*, 5(9), e007209.

Deater-Deckard, K., Mullineaux, P.Y., Beekman, C., Petrill, S.A., Schatschneider, C., and Thompson, L.A. (2009). Conduct problems, IQ, and household chaos: A longitudinal multi-informant study. *Journal of Child Psychology and Psychiatry, 50*(10), 1301-1308.

De Castilho, A.R., Mialhe, F.L., Barbosa, Tde S., and Puppin-Rontani, R.M. (2013). Influence of family environment on children's oral health: A systematic review. *Jornal de Pediatria, 89*(2), 116-123.

Dellinger, A.M., and Kresnow, M.-J. (2010). Bicycle helmet use among children in the United States: The effects of legislation, personal and household factors. *Journal of Safety Research, 41*(4), 375-380.

Dennison, B.A., Rockwell, H.L., and Baker, S.L. (1997). Excess fruit juice consumption by preschool-aged children is associated with short stature and obesity. *Pediatrics, 99*(1), 15-22.

Dennison, B.A., Erb, T.A., and Jenkins, P.L. (2002). Television viewing and television in bedroom associated with overweight risk among low-income preschool children. *Pediatrics, 109*(6), 1028-1035.

DeWalt, D.A., Dilling, M.H., Rosenthal, M.S., and Pignone, M.P. (2007). Low parental literacy is associated with worse asthma care measures in children. *Ambulatory Pediatrics, 7*(1), 25-31.

Dias, J.J., and Whitaker, R.C. (2013). Black mothers' perceptions about urban neighborhood safety and outdoor play for their preadolescent daughters. *Journal of Health Care for the Poor and Underserved, 24*(1), 206-219.

Dickerson, S.S., and Kemeny, M.E. (2004). Acute stressors and cortisol responses: A theoretical integration and synthesis of laboratory research. *Psychological Bulletin, 130*(3), 355.

Dichtelmiller, M., Meisels, S.J., Plunkett, J.W., Bozytnski, M.E.A., Claflin, C., and Mangelsdorf, S.C. (1992). The relationship of parental knowledge to the development of extremely low birth weight infants. *Journal of Early Intervention, 16*(3), 210-220.

Dishion, T.J., and Snyder, J.J. (Eds.). (2016). *The Oxford Handbook of Coercive Relationship Dynamics*. New York: Oxford University Press.

Donaldson, J.M., and Vollmer, T.R. (2011). An evaluation and comparison of time-out procedures with and without release contingencies. *Journal of Applied Behavior Analysis, 44*(4), 693-705.

Donaldson, J.M., Vollmer, T.R., Yakich, T.M., and Van Camp, C. (2013). Effects of a reduced time-out interval on compliance with the time-out instruction. *Journal of Applied Behavior Analysis, 46*(2), 369-378.

Dowswell, T., Towner, E., Simpson, G., and Jarvis, S. (1996). Preventing childhood unintentional injuries—what works? A literature review. *Injury Prevention, 2*(2), 140-149.

Drayton, A.K., Andersen, M.N., Knight, R.M., Felt, B.T., Fredericks, E.M., and Dore-Stites, D.J. (2014). Internet guidance on time out: Inaccuracies, omissions, and what to tell parents instead. *Journal of Developmental and Behavioral Pediatrics, 35*(4), 239-246.

Duncombe, M.E., Havighurst, S.S., Holland, K.A., and Frankling, E.J. (2012). The contribution of parenting practices and parent emotion factors in children at risk for disruptive behavior disorders. *Child Psychiatry & Human Development, 43*(5), 715-733.

Dunn, R.A., Shenouda, P.E., Martin, D.R., and Schultz, A.J. (1998). Videotape increases parent knowledge about poliovirus vaccines and choices of polio vaccination schedules. *Pediatrics, 102*(2), e26.

Dunst, C.J., Lowe, L.W., and Bartholomew, P.C. (1990). Contingent social responsiveness, family ecology, and infant communicative competence. *National Student Speech Language Hearing Association Journal, 17*(39-49), 1989-1990.

DuRant, R.H., Baranowski, T., Johnson, M., and Thompson, W.O. (1994). The relationship among television watching, physical activity, and body composition of young children. *Pediatrics, 94*(4), 449-455.

Durbin, D.R. (2011). Child passenger safety. *Pediatrics, 127*(4), e1050-e1066.

duRivage, N., Keyes, K., Leray, E. Pez, O., Bitfoi, A., Koc, C., Dietmar, G. Kuijpers, R., Lesinskiene, S., Mihova, Z., Otten, R., Fermanian, C., and Kovess-Masfety, V. (2015). Parental use of corporal punishment in Europe: Intersection between public health and policy. *PLoSOne, 10*(2), e0118059. doi:10.1371/journal.pone.0118059.

Durkin, D. (1966). *Children Who Read Early.* New York: Columbia University, Teachers College Press.

Durlak, J.A., Weissberg, R.P., Dymnicki, A.B., Taylor, R.D., and Schellinger, K.B. (2011). The impact of enhancing students' social and emotional learning: A meta-analysis of school-based universal interventions. *Child Development, 82*(1), 405-432.

Duursma, E., Augustyn, M., and Zuckerman, B. (2008). Reading aloud to children: The evidence. *Archives of Disease in Childhood, 93*(7), 554-557.

Dweck, C.S., and Leggett, E.L. (2000). A social-cognitive approach to motivation and personality. In E.T. Higgins and A.W. Kruglanski (Eds.), *Motivational Science: Social and Personality Perspectives. Key Reading in Social Psychology* (pp. 394-415). New York: Psychology Press.

Egeland, B., Pianta, R., and O'Brien, M.A. (1993). Maternal intrusiveness in infancy and child maladaptation in early school years. *Development and Psychopathology, 5*(3), 359-370.

Eisenberg, N., Cumberland, A., and Spinrad, T.L. (1998). Parental socialization of emotion. *Psychological Inquiry, 9*(4), 241-273.

Elias, M.J. (2006). The connection between academic and social-emotional learning. In M.J. Elias and H.A. Arnold (Eds.), *The Educator's Guide to Emotional Intelligence and Academic Achievement* (pp. 4-14). Thousands Oak, CA: Corwin Press.

Elmore, C.A., and Gaylord-Harden, N.K. (2013). The influence of supportive parenting and racial socialization messages on African American youth behavioral outcomes. *Journal of Child and Family Studies, 22*(1), 63-75.

Evans, G.W. (2006). Child development and the physical environment. *Annual Review of Psychology, 57*, 423-451.

Evans, G.W., and English, K. (2002). The environment of poverty: Multiple stressor exposure, psychophysiological stress, and socioemotional adjustment. *Child Development, 73*(4), 1238-1248.

Evans, G.W., and Lepore, S.J. (1993). Nonauditory effects of noise on children: A critical review. *Children's Environments*, 31-51.

Evans, G.W., and Wachs, T.D. (2010). *Chaos and Its Influence on Children's Development.* Washington, DC: American Psychological Association.

Evans, G.W., Maxwell, L.E., and Hart, B. (1999). Parental language and verbal responsiveness to children in crowded homes. *Developmental Psychology, 35*(4), 1020-1023.

Evans, G.W., Gonnella, C., Marcynyszyn, L.A., Gentile, L., and Salpekar, N. (2005). The role of chaos in poverty and children's socioemotional adjustment. *Psychological Science, 16*(7), 560-565.

Fagan, J., and Barnett, M. (2003). The relationship between maternal gatekeeping, paternal competence, mothers' attitudes about the father role, and father involvement. *Journal of Family Issues, 24*(8), 1020-1043.

Faith, M.S., Scanlon, K.S., Birch, L.L., Francis, L.A., and Sherry, B. (2004). Parent-child feeding strategies and their relationships to child eating and weight status. *Obesity Research, 12*(11), 1711-1722.

Fan, X., and Chen, M. (2001). Parental involvement and students' academic achievement: A meta-analysis. *Educational Psychology Review, 13*(1), 1-22.

Fantuzzo, J., Bulotsky-Shearer, R., McDermott, P.A., and McWayne, C. (2007). Investigation of dimensions of social-emotional classroom behavior and school readiness for low-income urban preschool children. *School Psychology Review, 36*(1), 44-62.

Farrow, C.V., Haycraft, E., and Blissett, J.M. (2015). Teaching our children when to eat: How parental feeding practices inform the development of emotional eating—a longitudinal experimental design. *The American Journal of Clinical Nutrition, 101*(5), 908-913.

Fiese, B.H., and Winter, M.A. (2010). The dynamics of family chaos and its relation to children's socioemotional well-being. In G.W. Evans and T.D. Wachs (Eds.), *Chaos and Its Influence on Children's Development: An Ecological Perspective* (pp. 49-66). Washington, DC: American Psychological Association.

Fiese, B.H., Tomcho, T.J., Douglas, M., Josephs, K., Poltrock, S., and Baker, T. (2002). A review of 50 years of research on naturally occurring family routines and rituals: Cause for celebration? *Journal of Family Psychology, 16*(4), 381-390.

Finkelhor, D., Mitchell, K.J., and Wolak, J. (2000). *Online Victimization: A Report on the Nation's Youth.* Alexandria, VA: National Center for Missing & Exploited Children.

Fishbein, M., Triandis, H.C., Kanfer, F.H., Becker, M., and Middlestadt, S.E. (2001). Factors influencing behavior and behavior change. *Evaluation & the Health Professions, 24*(4), 363-384.

Forry, N.D., Tout, K., Rothenberg, L., Sandstrom, H., and Vesely, C. (2013). *Child Care Decision-Making Literature Review.* OPRE Brief 2013-45. Washington, DC: Office of Planning, Research and Evaluation, Administration for Children and Families, U.S. Department of Health and Human Services.

Freeman, J., and Sugai, G. (2013). Recent changes in state policies and legislation regarding restraint or seclusion. *Exceptional Children, 79*(4), 427-438.

Gable, S., Chang, Y., and Krull, J.L. (2007). Television watching and frequency of family meals are predictive of overweight onset and persistence in a national sample of school-aged children. *Journal of the American Dietetic Association, 107*(1), 53-61.

Gagnon, S.G., Huelsman, T.J., Reichard, A.E., Kidder-Ashley, P., Griggs, M.S., Struby, J., and Bollinger, J. (2014). Help me play! Parental behaviors, child temperament, and preschool peer play. *Journal of Child and Family Studies, 23*(5), 872-884.

Galindo, C., and Sonnenschein, S. (2015). Decreasing the SES math achievement gap: Initial math proficiency and home learning environments. *Contemporary Educational Psychology, 43*, 25-38.

Garcia, D., Bagner, D.M., Pruden, S.M., and Nichols-Lopez, K. (2015). Language production in children with and at risk for delay: Mediating role of parenting skills. *Journal of Clinical Child & Adolescent Psychology, 44*(5), 814-825.

Gardner-Neblett, N., Pungello, E.P., and Iruka, I.U. (2012). Oral narrative skills: Implications for the reading development of African American children. *Child Development Perspectives, 6*(3), 218-224.

Gibbons, F.X., Etcheverry, P.E., Stock, M.L., Gerrard, M., Weng, C., Kiviniemi, M., and O'Hara, R.E. (2010). Exploring the link between racial discrimination and substance use: What mediates? What buffers? *Journal of Personality and Social Psychology, 99*(5), 785-801.

Gillman, M.W., Rifas-Shiman, S.L., Frazier, A.L., Rockett, H.R., Camargo, Jr., C.A., Field, A.E., Berkey, C.S., and Colditz, G.A. (2000). Family dinner and diet quality among older children and adolescents. *Archives of Family Medicine, 9*(3), 235-240.

Ginsburg, M., Block, P.H., and McWayne, C. (2010). Partnering to foster achievement in reading and mathematics. In S.L. Christenson and A.L. Reschly (Eds.), *Handbook of School-Family Partnerships* (pp. 175-203). New York: Routledge.

Gold, K.J., and Marcus, S.M. (2008). Effect of maternal mental illness on pregnancy outcomes. *Expert Review of Obstetrics & Gynecology, 3*(3), 391-401.

Goldenberg, H., and Goldenberg, I. (2013). *Family Therapy: An Overview*. Boston, MA: Cengage Learning.

Goldring, E.B., and Phillips, K.J. (2008). Parent preferences and parent choices: The public-private decision about school choice. *Journal of Education Policy, 23*(3), 209-230.

Gonzales, K.L., Harding, A.K., Lambert, W.E., Fu, R., and Henderson, W.G. (2013). Perceived experiences of discrimination in health care: A barrier for cancer screening among American Indian women with type 2 diabetes. *Women's Health Issues, 23*(1), e61-e67.

Goodnow, J.J. (1988). Parents' ideas, actions, and feelings: Models and methods from developmental and social psychology. *Child Development, 59*(2), 286-320.

Gottfried, A.W. (2013). *Home Environment and Early Cognitive Development: Longitudinal Research*. London, UK: Academic Press.

Goyal, N.K., Teeters, A., and Ammerman, R.T. (2013). Home visiting and outcomes of preterm infants: A systematic review. *Pediatrics, 132*(3), 502-516.

Greenspan, A.I., Dellinger, A.M., and Chen, J. (2010). Restraint use and seating position among children less than 13 years of age: Is it still a problem? *Journal of Safety Research, 41*(2), 183-185.

Grossmann, K., Grossmann, K.E., Fremmer-Bombik, E., Kindler, H., and Scheuerer-Englisch, H. (2002). The uniqueness of the child-father attachment relationship: Fathers' sensitive and challenging play as a pivotal variable in a 16-year longitudinal study. *Social Development, 11*(3), 301-337.

Grusec, J.E. (2011). Socialization processes in the family: Social and emotional development. *Annual Review of Psychology, 62*, 243-269.

Hammer, C.S., Rodriguez, B.L., Lawrence, F.R., and Miccio, A.W. (2007). Puerto Rican mothers' beliefs and home literacy practices. *Language, Speech, and Hearing Services in Schools, 38*(3), 216-224.

Hannan, J. (2015). Minority mothers' healthcare beliefs, commonly used alternative healthcare practices, and potential complications for infants and children. *Journal of the American Association of Nurse Practitioners, 27*(6), 338-348.

Hanscombe, K.B., Haworth, C., Davis, O.S., Jaffee, S.R., and Plomin, R. (2011). Chaotic homes and school achievement: A twin study. *Journal of Child Psychology and Psychiatry, 52*(11), 1212-1220.

Harrington, K.F., Zhang, B., Magruder, T., Bailey, W.C., and Gerald, L.B. (2015). The impact of parent's health literacy on pediatric asthma outcomes. *Pediatric Allergy, Immunology, and Pulmonology, 28*(1), 20-26.

Hart, B., and Risley, T.R. (1995). *Meaningful Differences in the Everyday Experience of Young American Children*. Baltimore, MD: Paul H. Brookes.

Hart, B., and Risley, T.R. (1999). *The Social World of Children: Learning to Talk*. Baltimore, MD: Paul H. Brookes.

Harwood, R.L., Miller, J.G., and Irizarry, N.L. (1997). *Culture and Attachment: Perceptions of the Child in Context*. New York: Guilford Press.

Havighurst, S.S., Wilson, K.R., Harley, A.E., Prior, M.R., and Kehoe, C. (2010). Tuning in to kids: Improving emotion socialization practices in parents of preschool children—findings from a community trial. *Journal of Child Psychology and Psychiatry, 51*(12), 1342-1350.

Heaman, M.I., Moffatt, M., Elliott, L., Sword, W., Helewa, M.E., Morris, H., Gregory, P., Tjaden, L., and Cook, C. (2014). Barriers, motivators and facilitators related to prenatal care utilization among inner-city women in Winnipeg, Canada: A case-control study. *BMC Pregnancy and Childbirth, 14*(1), 1.

Heck, K.E., Braveman, P., Cubbin, C., Chávez, G.F., Kiely, J.L., and Chárez, G.F. (2006). Socioeconomic status and breastfeeding initiation among California mothers. *Public Health Reports, 121*(1), 51-59.

Hendrix, S. (2013). The end of spanking. *The Washington Post Magazine*, January 3. Available: https://www.washingtonpost.com/lifestyle/magazine/the-end-of-spanking/2013/01/02/d328cf1e-3273-11e2-bb9b-288a310849ee_story.html [May 2016].

Hensen, L.E. (2005). ABCs of early mathematics experiences. *Teaching Children Mathematics, 12*(4), 208.

Henshaw, E.J., Fried, R., Siskind, E., Newhouse, L., and Cooper, M. (2015). Breastfeeding self-efficacy, mood, and breastfeeding outcomes among primiparous women. *Journal of Human Lactation, 31*(3), 511-518.

Herbert, S.D., Harvey, E.A., Roberts, J.L., Wichowski, K., and Lugo-Candelas, C.I. (2013). A randomized controlled trial of a parent training and emotion socialization program for families of hyperactive preschool-aged children. *Behavior Therapy, 44*(2), 302-316.

Hess, C.R., Teti, D.M., and Hussey-Gardner, B. (2004). Self-efficacy and parenting of high-risk infants: The moderating role of parent knowledge of infant development. *Journal of Applied Developmental Psychology, 25*(4), 423-437.

Hildyard, K.L., and Wolfe, D.A. (2002). Child neglect: Developmental issues and outcomes. *Child Abuse & Neglect, 26*(6), 679-695.

Hill, A.J. (2002). Developmental issues in attitudes to food and diet. *Proceedings of the Nutrition Society, 61*(2), 259-266.

Hill, H.A., Elam-Evans, L.D., Yankey, D., Singleton, J.A., and Kolasa, M. (2015). National, state, and selected local area vaccination coverage among children aged 19-35 months—United States, 2014. *Morbidity and Mortality Weekly Report, 64*(33), 889-896.

Hindman, A.H., Connor, C.M., Jewkes, A.M., and Morrison, F.J. (2008). Untangling the effects of shared book reading: Multiple factors and their associations with preschool literacy outcomes. *Early Childhood Research Quarterly, 23*(3), 330-350.

Hirsh-Pasek, K., Adamson, L.B., Bakeman, R., Owen, M.T., Golinkoff, R.M., Pace, A., Yust, P.K., and Suma, K. (2015). The contribution of early communication quality to low-income children's language success. *Psychological Science, 26*(7), 1071-1083.

Ho, J., Yeh, M., McCabe, K., and Lau, A. (2012). Perceptions of the acceptability of parent training among Chinese immigrant parents: Contributions of cultural factors and clinical need. *Behavior Therapy, 43*(2), 436-449.

Hoff, E. (2003). The specificity of environmental influence: Socioeconomic status affects early vocabulary development via maternal speech. *Child Development, 74*(5), 1368-1378.

Hofstetter, A.M., Vargas, C.Y., Camargo, S., Holleran, S., Vawdrey, D.K., Kharbanda, E.O., and Stockwell, M.S. (2015). Impacting delayed pediatric influenza vaccination: A randomized controlled trial of text message reminders. *American Journal of Preventive Medicine, 48*(4), 392-401.

Horta, B.L., and Victora, C.G. (2013). *Long-Term Effects of Breastfeeding: A Systematic Review*. Geneva, Switzerland: World Health Organization.

Howard, B.J. (1996). Advising parents on discipline: What works. *Pediatrics, 98*(4), 809-815.

Huang, K.-Y., Caughy, M.O.B., Genevro, J.L., and Miller, T.L. (2005). Maternal knowledge of child development and quality of parenting among white, African-American and Hispanic mothers. *Journal of Applied Developmental Psychology, 26*(2), 149-170.

Hughes, C.H., and Ensor, R.A. (2007). Executive function and theory of mind: Predictive relations from ages 2 to 4. *Developmental Psychology, 43*(6), 1447-1559.

Hughes, C.H., and Ensor, R.A. (2009). How do families help or hinder the emergence of early executive function? *New Directions for Child and Adolescent Development, 2009*(123), 35-50.

Hughes, C.H., and Ensor, R.A. (2011). Individual differences in growth in executive function across the transition to school predict externalizing and internalizing behaviors and self-perceived academic success at 6 years of age. *Journal of Experimental Child Psychology, 108*(3), 663-676.

Hunt, J.M., and Paraskevopoulos, J. (1980). Children's psychological development as a function of the inaccuracy of their mothers' knowledge of their abilities. *The Journal of Genetic Psychology, 136*(2), 285-298.

Hurley, K.M., Black, M.M., Papas, M.A., and Quigg, A.M. (2008). Variation in breastfeeding behaviours, perceptions, and experiences by race/ethnicity among a low-income statewide sample of Special Supplemental Nutrition Program for Women, Infants, and Children (WIC) participants in the United States. *Maternal & Child Nutrition, 4*(2), 95-105.

Institute of Medicine. (2003). *Unequal Treatment: Confronting Racial and Ethnic Disparities in Health Care.* B.D. Smedley, A.Y. Stith, and A.R. Nelson (Eds.). Committee on Understanding and Eliminating Racial and Ethnic Disparities in Health Care, Board on Health Sciences Policy. Washington, DC: The National Academies Press.

Institute of Medicine. (2011). *Early Childhood Obesity Prevention Policies.* L.L. Birch, L. Parker, and A. Burns (Eds.). Committee on Obesity Prevention Policies for Young Children. Washington, DC: The National Academies Press.

Institute of Medicine and National Research Council. (2009). *Weight Gain during Pregnancy: Reexamining the Guidelines.* K.M. Rasmussen and A.L. Yaktine (Eds.). Committee to Reexamine IOM Pregnancy Weight Guidelines; Food and Nutrition Board; Board on Children, Youth and Families; Division of Behavioral and Social Sciences and Education. Washington, DC: The National Academies Press.

Institute of Medicine and National Research Council. (2015). *Transforming the Workforce for Children Birth through age 8: A Unifying Foundation.* L. Allen and B.B. Kelly (Eds.). Committee on the Science of Children Birth to Age 8: Deepening and Broadening the Foundation for Success; Board on Children, Youth, and Families. Washington, DC: The National Academies Press.

Iruka, I.U., Durden, T., and Kennel, P. (2015). Changing faces: Parenting, culture, and child learning and development. *ZERO TO THREE Journal, 35*(4), 10.

Isbell, R., Sobol, J., Lindauer, L., and Lowrance, A. (2004). The effects of storytelling and story reading on the oral language complexity and story comprehension of young children. *Early Childhood Education Journal, 32*(3), 157-163.

Jackson, C., Cheater, F.M., Harrison, W., Peacock, R., Bekker, H., West, R., and Leese, B. (2011). Randomised cluster trial to support informed parental decision-making for the MMR vaccine. *BMC Public Health, 11*(1), 475.

Jaffee, S.R., Hanscombe, K.B., Haworth, C.M., Davis, O.S., and Plomin, R. (2012). Chaotic homes and children's disruptive behavior a longitudinal cross-lagged twin study. *Psychological Science, 23*(6), 643-650.

Jeynes, W.H. (2003). A meta-analysis the effects of parental involvement on minority children's academic achievement. *Education and Urban Society, 35*(2), 202-218.

Jeynes, W.H. (2005). A meta-analysis of the relation of parental involvement to urban elementary school student academic achievement. *Urban Education, 40*(3), 237-269.

Jones, D.J., Forehand, R., Brody, G., and Armistead, L. (2003). Parental monitoring in African American, single mother-headed families: An ecological approach to the identification of predictors. *Behavior Modification, 27*(4), 435-457.

Jones, T.L., and Prinz, R.J. (2005). Potential roles of parental self-efficacy in parent and child adjustment: A review. *Clinical Psychology Review, 25*(3), 341-363.

Karp, H.N. (2008). Safe swaddling and healthy hips: Don't toss the baby out with the bathwater. *Pediatrics, 121*(5), 1075-1076.

Katz, D.L., Katz, C.S., Treu, J.A., Reynolds, J., Njike, V., Walker, J., Smith, E., and Michael, J. (2011). Teaching healthful food choices to elementary school students and their parents: The Nutrition Detectives™ Program. *Journal of School Health, 81*(1), 21-28.

Kendrick, D., Young, B., Mason-Jones, A.J., Ilyas, N., Achana, F.A., Cooper, N.J., Hubbard, S.J., Sutton, A.J., Smith, S., and Wynn, P. (2013). Home safety education and provision of safety equipment for injury prevention (review). *Evidence-Based Child Health: A Cochrane Review Journal, 8*(3), 761-939.

Kohl, III, H., and Hobbs, K. (1998). Development of physical activity behaviors among children and adolescents. *Pediatrics, 101*(3 Pt. 2), 549-554.

Ladd, G.W., Pettit, G.S., and Bornstein, M. (2002). Parenting and the development of children's peer relationships. In M.H. Bornstein (Ed.), *Handbook of Parenting. Volume 5: Practical Issues in Parenting* (pp. 268). Mahwah, NJ: Lawrence Erlbaum Associates.

Ladd, M., Martin-Chang, S., and Levesque, K. (2011). Parents' reading-related knowledge and children's reading acquisition. *Annals of Dyslexia, 61*(2), 201-222.

Landy, S., and Osofsky, J.D. (2009). *Pathways to Competence: Encouraging Healthy Social and Emotional Development in Young Children, Second Edition.* Baltimore, MD: Paul H. Brookes.

Landry, S.H., Smith, K.E., Swank, P.R., and Guttentag, C. (2008). A responsive parenting intervention: The optimal timing across early childhood for impacting maternal behaviors and child outcomes. *Developmental Psychology, 44*(5), 1335-1353.

Lansford, J.E., Deater-Deckard, K., Dodge, K.A., Bates, J.E., and Pettit, G.S. (2004). Ethnic differences in the link between physical discipline and later adolescent externalizing behaviors. *Journal of Child Psychology and Psychiatry, 45*(4), 801-812.

Lareau, A. (1989). *Home Advantage: Social Class and Parental Intervention in Elementary Education.* New York: Falmer Press.

Larsen, J.J., and Juhasz, A.M. (1985). The effects of knowledge of child development and social-emotional maturity on adolescent attitudes toward parenting. *Adolescence, 20*(80), 823-839.

Larzelere, R.E., and Kuhn, B.R. (2005). Comparing child outcomes of physical punishment and alternative disciplinary tactics: A meta-analysis. *Clinical Child and Family Psychology Review, 8*(1), 1-37.

Lawrence-Lightfoot, S. (2003). *The Essential Conversation: What Parents and Teachers Can Learn from Each Other.* New York: Random House.

LeCuyer, E.A., Christensen, J.J., Kearney, M.H., and Kitzman, H.J. (2011). African American mothers' self-described discipline strategies with young children. *Issues in Comprehensive Pediatric Nursing, 34*(3), 144-162.

Lee, L.K., Farrell, C.A., and Mannix, R. (2015). Restraint use in motor vehicle crash fatalities in children 0 year to 9 years old. *Journal of Trauma and Acute Care Surgery, 79*(3 Suppl. 1), S55-S60.

Leech, K.A., Salo, V.C., Rowe, M.L., and Cabrera, N.J. (2013). Father input and child vocabulary development: The importance of wh-questions and clarification requests. *Seminars in Speech and Language, 34*(4), 249-259.

Leyendecker, B., Lamb, M.E., Harwood, R.L., and Schölmerich, A. (2002). Mothers' socialisation goals and evaluations of desirable and undesirable everyday situations in two diverse cultural groups. *International Journal of Behavioral Development, 26*(3), 248-258.

Li, J., Johnson, S.E., Han, W.-J., Andrews, S., Kendall, G., Strazdins, L., and Dockery, A. (2014). Parents' nonstandard work schedules and child well-being: A critical review of the literature. *The Journal of Primary Prevention, 35*(1), 53-73.

Lynch, J., Anderson, J., Anderson, A., and Shapiro, J. (2006). Parents' beliefs about young children's literacy development and parents' literacy behaviors. *Reading Psychology, 27*(1), 1-20.

Mack, K.A., Rudd, R.A., Mickalide, A.D., and Ballesteros, M.F. (2013). Fatal unintentional injuries in the home in the U.S., 2000-2008. *American Journal of Preventive Medicine, 44*(3), 239-246.

MacKenzie, M.J., Nicklas, E., Waldfogel, J., and Brooks-Gunn, J. (2013). Spanking and child development across the first decade of life. *Pediatrics, 132*(5), e1118-e1125.

Macy, M.L., Cunningham, R.M., Resnicow, K., and Freed, G.L. (2014). Disparities in age-appropriate child passenger restraint use among children aged 1 to 12 years. *Pediatrics, 133*(2), 262-271.

Magill-Evans, J., Harrison, M.J., Benzies, K., Gierl, M., and Kimak, C. (2007). Effects of parenting education on first-time fathers' skills in interactions with their infants. *Fathering, 5*(1), 42.

Malin, J.L., Karberg, E., Cabrera, N.J., Rowe, M., Cristaforo, T., and Tamis-LeMonda, C.S. (2012). Father-toddler communication in low-income families: The role of paternal education and depressive symptoms. *Family Science, 3*(3-4), 155-163.

Malin, J.L., Cabrera, N.J., Karberg, E., Aldoney, D., and Rowe, M.L. (2014). Low-income, minority fathers' control strategies and their children's regulatory skills. *Infant Mental Health Journal, 35*(5), 462-472.

Markman, L., and Brooks-Gunn, J. (2005). The contribution of parenting to ethnic and racial gaps in school readiness. *The Future of Children, 15*(1), 139-168.

Martin, A., Razza, R.A., and Brooks-Gunn, J. (2012). Specifying the links between household chaos and preschool children's development. *Early Child Development and Care, 182*(10), 1247-1263.

Masataka, N. (1993). Effects of contingent and noncontingent maternal stimulation on the vocal behaviour of three-to four-month-old Japanese infants. *Journal of Child Language, 20*(2), 303-312.

Masten, A.S., and Cicchetti, D. (2010). Developmental cascades. *Development and Psychopathology, 22*(3), 491-495.

Mazarello Paes, V., Hesketh, K., O'Malley, C., Moore, H., Summerbell, C., Griffin, S., Sluijs, E., Ong, K.K., and Lakshman, R. (2015). Determinants of sugar-sweetened beverage consumption in young children: A systematic review. *Obesity Reviews, 16*(11), 903-913.

McCabe, K., and Yeh, M. (2009). Parent-child interaction therapy for Mexican Americans: A randomized clinical trial. *Journal of Clinical Child & Adolescent Psychology, 38*(5), 753-759.

McCarty, C.A., Zimmerman, F.J., Digiuseppe, D.L., and Christakis, D.A. (2005). Parental emotional support and subsequent internalizing and externalizing problems among children. *Journal of Developmental & Behavioral Pediatrics, 26*(4), 267-275.

McCollum, J.A., and Ostrosky, M.M. (2008). Family roles in young children's emerging peer-related social competence. In W.H. Brown, S.L. Odom and S.R. McConnell (Eds.), *Social Competence of Young Children: Risk, Disability, and Intervention* (pp. 31-60). Baltimore, MD: Paul H. Brookes.

McKay, M.M., Atkins, M.S., Hawkins, T., Brown, C., and Lynn, C.J. (2003). Inner-city African American parental involvement in children's schooling: Racial socialization and social support from the parent community. *American Journal of Community Psychology, 32*(1), 107-114.

McLeod, B.D., Wood, J.J., and Weisz, J.R. (2007). Examining the association between parenting and childhood anxiety: A meta-analysis. *Clinical Psychology Review, 27*(2), 155-172.

McLoyd, V.C. (1998). Socioeconomic disadvantage and child development. *American Psychologist, 53*(2), 185-204.

McLoyd, V.C., and Smith, J. (2002). Physical discipline and behavior problems in African American, European American, and Hispanic children: Emotional support as a moderator. *Journal of Marriage and Family, 64*(1), 40-53.

McQuaid, N.E., Bibok, M.B., and Carpendale, J.I. (2009). Relation between maternal contingent responsiveness and infant social expectations. *Infancy, 14*(3), 390-401.

Mendelsohn, A.L., Dreyer, B.P., Flynn, V., Tomopoulos, S., Rovira, I., Tineo, W., Pebenito, C., Torres, C., Torres, H., and Nixon, A.F. (2005). Use of videotaped interactions during pediatric well-child care to promote child development: A randomized, controlled trial. *Journal of Developmental and Behavioral Pediatrics, 26*(1), 34-41.

Mercy, J.A., and Saul, J. (2009). Creating a healthier future through early interventions for children. *Journal of the American Medical Association, 301*(21), 2262-2264.

Mergler, M.J., Omer, S.B., Pan, W.K., Navar-Boggan, A.M., Orenstein, W., Marcuse, E.K., Taylor, J., Patricia deHart, M., Carter, T.C., and Damico, A. (2013). Association of vaccine-related attitudes and beliefs between parents and health care providers. *Vaccine, 31*(41), 4591-4595.

Meyers, M.K., and Jordan, L.P. (2006). Choice and accommodation in parental child care decisions. *Community Development, 37*(2), 53-70.

Middlemiss, W., Yaure, R., and Huey, E.L. (2015). Translating research-based knowledge about infant sleep into practice. *Journal of the American Association of Nurse Practitioners, 27*(6), 328-337.

Mills, E., Jadad, A.R., Ross, C., and Wilson, K. (2005). Systematic review of qualitative studies exploring parental beliefs and attitudes toward childhood vaccination identifies common barriers to vaccination. *Journal of Clinical Epidemiology, 58*(11), 1081-1088.

Mindell, J.A., Meltzer, L.J., Carskadon, M.A., and Chervin, R.D. (2009). Developmental aspects of sleep hygiene: Findings from the 2004 National Sleep Foundation Sleep in America Poll. *Sleep Medicine, 10*(7), 771-779.

Mol, S.E., Bus, A.G., de Jong, M.T., and Smeets, D.J. (2008). Added value of dialogic parent-child book readings: A meta-analysis. *Early Education and Development, 19*(1), 7-26.

Morawska, A., Winter, L., and Sanders, M. (2009). Parenting knowledge and its role in the prediction of dysfunctional parenting and disruptive child behaviour. *Child: Care, Health and Development, 35*(2), 217-226.

Morrongiello, B.A., and Kiriakou, S. (2004). Mothers' home-safety practices for preventing six types of childhood injuries: What do they do, and why? *Journal of Pediatric Psychology, 29*(4), 285-297.

Morrow, L.M., O'Connor, E.M., and Smith, J.K. (1990). Effects of a story reading program on the literacy development of at-risk kindergarten children. *Journal of Literacy Research, 22*(3), 255-275.

Mosier, C.E., and Rogoff, B. (2003). Privileged treatment of toddlers: Cultural aspects of individual choice and responsibility. *Developmental Psychology, 39*(6), 1047.

Moss, E., Dubois-Comtois, K., Cyr, C., Tarabulsy, G.M., St-Laurent, D., and Bernier, A. (2011). Efficacy of a home-visiting intervention aimed at improving maternal sensitivity, child attachment, and behavioral outcomes for maltreated children: A randomized controlled trial. *Development and Psychopathology, 23*(1), 195-210.

Murphy, D.A., Armistead, L., Marelich, W.D., and Herbeck, D.M. (2015). Parenting deficits of mothers living with HIV/AIDS who have young children. *Vulnerable Children and Youth Studies, 10*(1), 41-54.

Murry, V.M., and Brody, G.H. (1999). Self-regulation and self-worth of black children reared in economically stressed, rural, single mother-headed families: The contribution of risk and protective factors. *Journal of Family Issues, 20*(4), 458-484.

Murry, V.B., Brown, P.A., Brody, G.H., Cutrona, C.E., and Simons, R.L. (2001). Racial discrimination as a moderator of the links among stress, maternal psychological functioning, and family relationships. *Journal of Marriage and Family, 63*(4), 915-926.

Mutchler, J.E., Baker, L.A., and Lee, S. (2007). Grandparents responsible for grandchildren in Native-American families. *Social Science Quarterly, 88*(4), 990-1009.

Natale, R.A., Messiah, S.E., Asfour, L., Uhlhorn, S.B., Delamater, A., and Arheart, K.L. (2014). Role modeling as an early childhood obesity prevention strategy: Effect of parents and teachers on preschool children's healthy lifestyle habits. *Journal of Developmental & Behavioral Pediatrics, 35*(6), 378-387.

National Research Council. (1998). *Preventing Reading Difficulties in Young Children.* C.E. Snow, M.S. Burns, and P. Griffin (Eds.). Committee on the Prevention of Reading Difficulties in Young Children, Commission on Behavioral and Social Sciences and Education. Washington, DC: National Academy Press.

National Research Council. (2000). *How People Learn: Brain, Mind, Experience, and School.* J.D. Bransford (Ed.). Committee on Developments in the Science of Learning and Committee on Learning Research and Educational Practice, Commission on Behavioral and Social Sciences and Education. Washington, DC: National Academy Press.

National Research Council and Institute of Medicine. (2000). *From Neurons to Neighborhoods: The Science of Early Childhood Development.* J.P. Shonkoff and D.A. Phillips (Eds.). Committee on Integrating the Science of Early Childhood Development; Board on Children, Youth, and Families; Commission on Behavioral and Social Sciences and Education. Washington, DC: National Academy Press.

Nieman, P., and Shea, S. (2004). Effective discipline for children. *Pediatrics & Child Health, 9*(1), 37-41.

Ninio, A. (1983). Joint book reading as a multiple vocabulary acquisition device. *Developmental Psychology, 19*(3), 445-451.

Oei, N., Everaerd, W., Elzinga, B., Van Well, S., and Bermond, B. (2006). Psychosocial stress impairs working memory at high loads: An association with cortisol levels and memory retrieval. *Stress, 9*(3), 133-141.

Ogbuanu, C.A., Probst, J., Laditka, S.B., Liu, J., Baek, J., and Glover, S. (2009). Reasons why women do not initiate breastfeeding: A southeastern state study. *Women's Health Issues, 19*(4), 268-278.

Okagaki, L., and Bingham, G.E. (2005). Parents' social cognitions and their parenting behaviors. In T. Luster and L. Okagaki (Eds.), *Parenting: An Ecological Perspective* (2nd ed., pp. 3-33). Mahwah, NJ: Lawrence Erlbaum Associates.

Osofsky, J.D., and Fitzgerald, H.E. (2000). *WAIMH Handbook of Infant Mental Health* (Vol. 1: Perspectives on Infant Mental Health). Chichester, UK: Wiley.

Pancsofar, N., and Vernon-Feagans, L. (2006). Mother and father language input to young children: Contributions to later language development. *Journal of Applied Developmental Psychology, 27*(6), 571-587.

Parks, P.L., and Smeriglio, V.L. (1986). Relationships among parenting knowledge, quality of stimulation in the home and infant development. *Family Relations, 35*(3), 411-416.

Pascoe, E.A., and Smart Richman, L. (2009). Perceived discrimination and health: A meta-analytic review. *Psychological Bulletin, 135*(4), 531-540.

Paterson, C. (2011). *Parenting Matters.* London, UK: Centre Forum.

Pearson, N., Timperio, A., Salmon, J., Crawford, D., and Biddle, S.J. (2009). Family influences on children's physical activity and fruit and vegetable consumption. *International Journal of Behavioral Nutrition and Physical Activity, 6*(1), 34.

Perkins, D.M., and Mebert, C.J. (2005). Efficacy of multicultural education for preschool children a domain-specific approach. *Journal of Cross-Cultural Psychology, 36*(4), 497-512.

Pettigrew, T.F., and Tropp, L.R. (2000). Does intergroup contact reduce prejudice: Recent meta-analytic findings. In S. Oskamp (Ed.), *Reducing Prejudice and Discrimination* (pp. 93-114). Mahwah, NJ: Lawrence Erlbaum Associates.

Pickard, K.E., and Ingersoll, B.R. (2015). Quality versus quantity: The role of socioeconomic status on parent-reported service knowledge, service use, unmet service needs, and barriers to service use. *Autism*. DOI: 10.1177/1362361315569745.

Porges, S.W. (1995). Cardiac vagal tone: A physiological index of stress. *Neuroscience & Biobehavioral Reviews, 19*(2), 225-233.

Porges, S.W., Macellaio, M., Stanfill, S.D., McCue, K., Lewis, G.F., Harden, E.R., Handelman, M., Denver, J., Bazhenova, O.V., and Heilman, K.J. (2013). Respiratory sinus arrhythmia and auditory processing in autism: Modifiable deficits of an integrated social engagement system? *International Journal of Psychophysiology, 88*(3), 261-270.

Posner, M.I., and Rothbart, M.K. (2007). Research on attention networks as a model for the integration of psychological science. *Annual Review of Psychology, 58*, 1-23.

Powell, K.E., Martin, L.M., and Chowdhury, P.P. (2003). Places to walk: Convenience and regular physical activity. *American Journal of Public Health, 93*(9), 1519-1521.

Putnam, S.P., Sanson, A.V., and Rothbart, M.K. (2002). Child temperament and parenting. In M.H. Bornstein (Ed.), *Handbook of Parenting* (vol. 1, pp. 255-277). Mahwah, NJ: Lawrence Erlbaum Associates.

Raver, C.C., Blair, C., and Willoughby, M. (2013). Poverty as a predictor of 4-year-olds' executive function: New perspectives on models of differential susceptibility. *Developmental Psychology, 49*(2), 292-304.

Regalado, M., and Halfon, N. (2001). Primary care services promoting optimal child development from birth to age 3 years: Review of the literature. *Archives of Pediatrics & Adolescent Medicine, 155*(12), 1311-1322.

Repetti, R.L., Taylor, S.E., and Seeman, T.E. (2002). Risky families: Family social environments and the mental and physical health of offspring. *Psychological Bulletin, 128*(2), 330-366.

Roberts, M.Y., and Kaiser, A.P. (2011). The effectiveness of parent-implemented language interventions: A meta-analysis. *American Journal of Speech-Language Pathology, 20*(3), 180-199.

Rogoff, B. (2003). *The Cultural Nature of Human Development*. New York: Oxford University Press.

Rosenthal, M.K., and Roer-Strier, D. (2006). "What sort of an adult would you like your child to be?": Mothers' developmental goals in different cultural communities in Israel. *International Journal of Behavioral Development, 30*(6), 517-528.

Roth, P.L. (1987). Temporal characteristics of maternal verbal styles. In K.E. Nelson and A. van Kleek (Eds.), *Children's Language* (vol. 6, pp. 137-158). Hillsdale, NJ: Lawrence Erlbaum Associates.

Rowe, M.L., Coker, D., and Pan, B.A. (2004). A comparison of fathers' and mothers' talk to toddlers in low-income families. *Social Development, 13*(2), 278-291.

Rowe, M.L., Denmark, N., Harden, B.J., and Stapleton, L.M. (2015). The role of parent education and parenting knowledge in children's language and literacy skills among white, black, and Latino families. *Infant and Child Development* [E-pub ahead of print].

Sallis, J.F., Nader, P.R., Broyles, S.L., Berry, C.C., Elder, J.P., McKenzie, T.L., and Nelson, J.A. (1993). Correlates of physical activity at home in Mexican-American and Anglo-American preschool children. *Health Psychology, 12*(5), 390-398.

Sameroff, A.J., and Fiese, B.H. (2000). Transactional regulation: The developmental ecology of early intervention. In S.J. Meisels and J.P. Shonkoff (Eds.), *Handbook of Early Childhood Intervention* (2nd ed., pp. 135-159). New York: Cambridge University Press.

Sanders-Phillips, K., Settles-Reaves, B., Walker, D., and Brownlow, J. (2009). Social inequality and racial discrimination: Risk factors for health disparities in children of color. *Pediatrics, 124*(3), S176-S186.

Sarche, M., and Spicer, P. (2008). Poverty and health disparities for American Indian and Alaska Native children. *Annals of the New York Academy of Sciences, 1136*(1), 126-136.

Schoemaker, K., Mulder, H., Dekovi , M., and Matthys, W. (2013). Executive functions in preschool children with externalizing behavior problems: A meta-analysis. *Journal of Abnormal Child Psychology, 41*(3), 457-471.

Schoppe-Sullivan, S.J., Brown, G.L., Cannon, E.A., Mangelsdorf, S.C., and Sokolowski, M.S. (2008). Maternal gatekeeping, coparenting quality, and fathering behavior in families with infants. *Journal of Family Psychology, 22*(3), 389-398.

Semrud-Clikeman, M. (2007). *Social Competence in Children.* New York: Springer.

Sénéchal, M., and LeFevre, J.-A. (2002). Parental involvement in the development of children's reading skill: A five-year longitudinal study. *Child Development, 73*(2), 445-460.

Shavers, V.L., Fagan, P., Jones, D., Klein, W.M.P., Boyington, J., Moten, C., and Rorie, E. (2012). The state of research on racial/ethnic discrimination in the receipt of health care. *American Journal of Public Health, 102*(5), 953-966.

Shlay, A.B. (2010). African American, white and Hispanic child care preferences: A factorial survey analysis of welfare leavers by race and ethnicity. *Social Science Research, 39*(1), 125-141.

Simons, R.L., Simons, L.G., Burt, C.H., Drummund, H., Stewart, E., Brody, G.H., Gibbons, F.X., and Cutrona, C. (2006). Supportive parenting moderates the effect of discrimination upon anger, hostile view of relationships, and violence among African American boys. *Journal of Health and Social Behavior, 47*(4), 373-389.

Smailbegovic, M.S., Laing, G.J., and Bedford, H. (2003). Why do parents decide against immunization? The effect of health beliefs and health professionals. *Child: Care, Health and Development, 29*(4), 303-311.

Sosinsky, L.S., and Kim, S.-K. (2013). A profile approach to child care quality, quantity, and type of setting: Parent selection of infant child care arrangements. *Applied Developmental Science, 17*(1), 39-56.

Spagnola, M., and Fiese, B.H. (2007). Family routines and rituals: A context for development in the lives of young children. *Infants & Young Children, 20*(4), 284-299.

Sroufe, L.A., Egeland, B., Carlson, E.A., and Collins, W.A. (2005). *The Development of the Person: The Minnesota Study of Risk and Adaptation from Birth to Adulthood.* New York: Guilford Press.

Staples, A.D., Bates, J.E., and Petersen, I.T. (2015). IX. Bedtime routines in early childhood: Prevalence, consistency, and associations with nighttime sleep. *Monographs of the Society for Research in Child Development, 80*(1), 141-159.

Stormshak, E.A., Bierman, K.L., McMahon, R.J., and Lengua, L.J. (2000). Parenting practices and child disruptive behavior problems in early elementary school. *Journal of Clinical Child Psychology, 29*(1), 17-29.

Straus, M.A., and Paschall, M.J. (2009). Corporal punishment by mothers and development of children's cognitive ability: A longitudinal study of two nationally representative age cohorts. *Journal of Aggression, Maltreatment & Trauma, 18*(5), 459-483.

Sussner, K.M., Lindsay, A.C., Gortmaker, S.L., and Kim, J. (2006). The role of parents in preventing childhood obesity. *The Future of Children, 16*(1), 169-186.

Sussner, K.M., Lindsay, A.C., and Peterson, K.E. (2008). The influence of acculturation on breast-feeding initiation and duration in low-income women in the U.S. *Journal of Biosocial Science, 40*(5), 673-696.

Swick, K.J., and Hassell, T. (1990). Parental efficacy and the development of social competence in young children. *Journal of Instructional Psychology, 17*(1), 24.

Tandon, M., Cardeli, E., and Luby, J. (2009). Internalizing disorders in early childhood: A review of depressive and anxiety disorders. *Child and Adolescent Psychiatric Clinics of North America*, 18(3), 593–610.

Thompson, R.A. (1994). Emotion regulation: A theme in search of definition. *Monographs of the Society for Research in Child Development*, 59(2-3), 25-52.

Tremblay, M.S., LeBlanc, A.G., Kho, M.E., Saunders, T.J., Larouche, R., Colley, R.C., Goldfield, G., and Gorber, S.C. (2011). Systematic review of sedentary behaviour and health indicators in school-aged children and youth. *International Journal of Behavioral Nutrition and Physical Activity*, 8(1), 98.

U.S. Department of Health and Human Services. (2011). *The Surgeon General's Call to Action to Support Breastfeeding*. Washington, DC: U.S. Department of Health and Human Services.

Vaaler, M.L., Stagg, J., Parks, S.E., Erickson, T., and Castrucci, B.C. (2010). Breast-feeding attitudes and behavior among WIC mothers in Texas. *Journal of Nutrition Education and Behavior*, 42(3), S30-S38.

Van Der Voort, A., Linting, M., Juffer, F., Bakermans-Kranenburg, M.J., Schoenmaker, C., and van IJzendoorn, M.H. (2014). The development of adolescents' internalizing behavior: Longitudinal effects of maternal sensitivity and child inhibition. *Journal of Youth and Adolescence*, 43(4), 528-540.

Vannice, K.S., Salmon, D.A., Shui, I., Omer, S.B., Kissner, J., Edwards, K.M., Sparks, R., Dekker, C.L., Klein, N.P., and Gust, D.A. (2011). Attitudes and beliefs of parents concerned about vaccines: Impact of timing of immunization information. *Pediatrics*, 127(Suppl. 1), S120-S126.

Vernon-Feagans, L., Garrett-Peters, P., Willoughby, M., Mills-Koonce, R., and Family Life Project Key Investigators. (2012). Chaos, poverty, and parenting: Predictors of early language development. *Early Childhood Research Quarterly*, 27(3), 339-351.

Vukovic, R.K., and Lesaux, N.K. (2013). The language of mathematics: Investigating the ways language counts for children's mathematical development. *Journal of Experimental Child Psychology*, 115(2), 227-244.

Wachs, T.D. (2000). *Necessary but Not Sufficient: The Respective Roles of Single and Multiple Influences on Individual Development*. Washington, DC: American Psychological Association.

Weisner, T.S. (2002). Ecocultural understanding of children's developmental pathways. *Human Development*, 45(4), 275-281.

Welsh, J.A., Cogswell, M.E., Rogers, S., Rockett, H., Mei, Z., and Grummer-Strawn, L.M. (2005). Overweight among low-income preschool children associated with the consumption of sweet drinks: Missouri, 1999-2002. *Pediatrics*, 115(2), e223-e229.

Whitehurst, G.J., Falco, F.L., Lonigan, C.J., Fischel, J.E., DeBaryshe, B.D., Valdez-Menchaca, M.C., and Caulfield, M. (1988). Accelerating language development through picture book reading. *Developmental Psychology*, 24(4), 552-559.

Whiting, B.B., and Whiting, J.W. (1975). *Children of Six Cultures: A Psycho-Cultural Analysis*. Cambridge, MA: Harvard University Press.

Winter, L., Morawska, A., and Sanders, M. (2012). The Knowledge of Effective Parenting Scale (KEPS): A tool for public health approaches to universal parenting programs. *The Journal of Primary Prevention*, 33(2-3), 85-97.

Wojcicki, J.M., Gugig, R., Tran, C., Kathiravan, S., Holbrook, K., and Heyman, M.B. (2010). Early exclusive breastfeeding and maternal attitudes towards infant feeding in a population of new mothers in San Francisco, California. *Breastfeeding Medicine*, 5(1), 9-15.

Wolnicka, K., Taraszewska, A.M., Jaczewska-Schuetz, J., and Jarosz, M. (2015). Factors within the family environment such as parents' dietary habits and fruit and vegetable availability have the greatest influence on fruit and vegetable consumption by Polish children. *Public Health Nutrition, 18*(15), 2705-2711.

World Health Organization. (2009). *Preventing Violence through the Development of Safe, Stable, and Nurturing Relationships between Children and Their Parents and Caregivers.* Geneva, Switzerland: World Health Organization.

World Health Organization. (2011). *Exclusive Breastfeeding for Six Months Best for Babies Everywhere.* Available: http://www.who.int/mediacentre/news/statements/2011/breastfeeding_20110115/en [March 2016].

Yanchar, N.L., Kirkland, S.A., LeBlanc, J.C., and Langille, D.B. (2012). Discrepancies between knowledge and practice of childhood motor vehicle occupant safety in Nova Scotia—A population-based study. *Accident Analysis and Prevention, 45*, 326-333.

Yanchar, N.L., Young, J.B., and Langille, D.B. (2015). Knowledge and practice of childhood motor vehicle restraint use in Nova Scotia: Phase II. *Accident Analysis and Prevention, 74*, 150-156.

Yaqub, O., Castle-Clarke, S., Sevdalis, N., and Chataway, J. (2014). Attitudes to vaccination: A critical review. *Social Science & Medicine, 112*, 1-11.

Yousafzai, A.K., Rasheed, M.A., Rizvi, A., Armstrong, R., and Bhutta, Z.A. (2015). Parenting skills and emotional availability: An RCT. *Pediatrics, 135*(5), e1247-e1257.

Zarnowiecki, D., Sinn, N., Petkov, J., and Dollman, J. (2011). Parental nutrition knowledge and attitudes as predictors of 5-6-year-old children's healthy food knowledge. *Public Health Nutrition, 15*(7), 1284-1290.

Zhou, F., Shefer, A., Wenger, J., Messonnier, M., Wang, L.Y., Lopez, A., Moore, M., Murphy, T.V., Cortese, M., and Rodewald, L. (2014). Economic evaluation of the routine childhood immunization program in the United States, 2009. *Pediatrics, 133*(4), 577-585.

3

Federal Policies and Investments Supporting Parents and Children in the United States

Many of the parenting competencies described in Chapter 2 are reflected in federal policies and investments designed to improve the well-being of children and support parents in their efforts to create safe, supportive, and nurturing environments for their children. The U.S. government has a more than 100-year history of investing in programs and services for families that are designed to promote positive outcomes and reduce negative circumstances for children (see Box 3-1 for an overview). The parent- and child-focused policies and programs funded with public dollars and administered or augmented at the state and local levels by government agencies, businesses, community-based organizations, and foundations are aimed at promoting a host of positive outcomes, including keeping children safe from harm; making sure they do not go to bed hungry; and reducing disparities in outcomes associated with parental characteristics, especially those related to income, race/ethnicity, and place of birth. Each year billions of dollars are spent on these policies and programs at the federal level.

This chapter is intended to serve as a bridge between the description of core parenting knowledge, attitudes, and practices in Chapter 2 and the review of available evidence on what works to support and enhance these knowledge, attitudes, and practices in Chapters 4 and 5. The policies and investments described suggest an implicit governmental goal of promoting parenting knowledge, attitudes, and practices; facilitating the job of parenting; and ensuring that children are well cared for. However, no explicit link is evident between these policies and investments and a well-organized and articulated effort to promote the knowledge, attitudes, and practices they are designed to support. Likewise, the connection between the policies and

BOX 3-1
The Founding and Evolution of the Children's Bureau:
The First Agency Focused Solely on Children and Families

To understand what some have termed the current U.S. "nonsystem" of supports for children and families and the many agency budgets, policies, and programs that exist in this area, it is useful to look back at the creation of the first agency focused solely on meeting the needs of children and how its focus on supporting parents began and changed over time. The restructuring that transferred responsibility for the work originally conducted by the Children's Bureau to other agencies is also of interest and may be relevant when this report considers barriers to and facilitators for the effectiveness of salient policies and programs. Below are some highlights from the 113-year history of the Children's Bureau.

- 1909—The White House Conference on the Care of Dependent Children focused on the needs of vulnerable children experiencing abandonment, neglect, destitution, and routine institutionalization. Recommendations included a call for a federal children's bureau.
- 1912—President Taft signed legislation establishing the Children's Bureau as part of the Department of Commerce and Labor, which then moved to the new Department of Labor. Julia Lathrop was the Bureau's first leader.
- The Bureau was charged with understanding and reporting on all matters relevant to the welfare of children and child life. Early research topics included infant mortality, child labor, juvenile delinquency, mothers' pensions, and illegitimacy.
- 1923—The Bureau published *Juvenile-Court Standards* and *Foster-Home Care for Dependent Children*. Support focused on keeping children with families and preventing institutionalization. The Bureau also partnered with Yale School of Medicine to study rickets and risks of ancillary health problems.
- 1926—The Bureau published *Public Aid to Mothers of Dependent Children*, an overview of legislation and work that supported mothers.
- 1930—The Third White House Conference on Children resulted in the Children's Charter, which included 19 points focused on the health, welfare, protection, and educational needs of children.
- 1935—Passage of the Social Security Act authorized the Bureau to administer maternal and child health services, medical care for children with disabilities, and child welfare services.
- 1930s—The Fair Labor Standards Act, containing child labor requirements that the Bureau worked with the states to enforce, was passed.
- 1940s—The Fourth White House Conference on Children focused on the principles, conditions, and services that contribute to all children's well-being, not just those in need or those with a disability. Of special interest was the development of standards for daycare.
- 1946—The Children's Bureau moved to the Social Security Administration within the Federal Security Agency; responsibility for child labor regulatory enforcement remained with the Department of Labor.

- 1950—The White House Conference on Children and Youth focused on the emotional well-being of children and resulted in creation of a handbook for parents on supporting healthy personality development.
- 1953—The Federal Security Agency became the Department of Health, Education, and Welfare (DHEW). *A Research Program for the Children's Bureau*, based on a review of previous research and input from experts, was published.
- Early 1960s—The Bureau's work emphasized the needs of children in foster care and continued to focus on child health. Supports for foster care for refugee children from Cuba were also a focus.
- 1965—Head Start was created within the Children's Bureau.
- 1968—A federal Panel on Early Childhood was created to coordinate programs and plan funding.
- 1969—DHEW housed the Office of Child Development (OCD), which in turn housed the Children's Bureau, Head Start Bureau, and Bureau of Program Development and Resources.
- 1970—The White House Child Conference was organized around 16 areas of well-being, including comprehensive family-oriented child development programs.
- 1974—Passage of the Child Abuse Prevention and Treatment Act led to increased reporting of child abuse and neglect, services for abused children, and research.
- 1980—Passage of the Adoption Assistance and Child Welfare Act expanded the role of the Children's Bureau related to accountability of the federal and state child welfare systems by means of annual reporting requirements to Congress and state audits.
- 1980s—The Bureau's work focused on improving adoption rates for special-needs children, use of family-based services, and prevention. Improvement in data quality was a priority, leading to the Adoption and Foster Care Analysis and Reporting System and the National Child Abuse and Neglect Data System.
- 1990s—The Bureau focused on high-quality child abuse and neglect prevention, foster care, and adoption.
- 1997—The Adoption and Safe Families Act, which codified the three responsibilities of child welfare—safety, permanency, and well-being—was passed.
- 2000-2010—National rates of children in foster care declined by 25 percent. Investment continued in discretionary programs and research in areas including crack and substance use among parents, support for evidence-based home visiting, and abandoned infants.
- 2012—The Bureau published *Promoting Social and Emotional Well-Being of Children and Youth Receiving Child Welfare Services*, a research-based framework and roadmap for child welfare agencies' use of the latest in research and practice in their work with children and families.

SOURCE: Administration for Children and Families (2016b).

investments and the evidence, taken as a whole, is tenuous and at times incongruous. It is important to note that the policies and investments were instituted and amended over many years, reflecting various political and philosophical approaches, and often predate the evidence on what works that is described in the next two chapters. The connections across and among the knowledge, attitudes, and practices; federal policies and investments; and the evidence are relatively haphazard. As a result, the collection of policies and investments designed to strengthen and support parenting represents a piecemeal approach rather than a coherent system that has interconnected and cohesive goals and is informed by current knowledge about what works.

This chapter begins by describing examples of recent public health successes in changing parenting knowledge, attitudes, and practices to achieve better outcomes for children. Next, the chapter provides a brief overview of the federal budget supporting parents and children to help the reader understand the overall scale of the federal investment in promoting positive outcomes for children and families. The chapter then turns to a description of federal policies and investments supporting parents and children, which include policies and investments that are universal or near-universal and those that are more targeted. The latter category encompasses economic support for low-income families and children, investments in child and parent education, support for parents of children with special needs and parents facing adversity, and policies and programs focused on family and parental leave. Note that the discussion here is intended as an overview and does not include all federal policies and investments that support parents and children. The impacts on outcomes for families, including parenting, for several but not all of the programs reviewed in this chapter are discussed in Chapter 4. The chapter concludes with a summary.

PUBLIC HEALTH SUCCESSES

A central premise of this study is that, based on historical data, it is possible to shift the knowledge, attitudes, and practices of parents, and the nation, so as to create a safer and healthier environment for children. Three major successes in the field of public health illustrate this point: child passenger safety, the Safe to Sleep campaign, and reductions in smoking and drinking during pregnancy. These initiatives have been successful, in part, because their behavior change messages are relatively straightforward and consistently reinforced and are presented to parents through multiple, influential media and trusted sources. In most cases, these positive messages are coupled with society's changing norms and expectations regarding the behavior of parents. These three examples demonstrate what can be accomplished when policy and practice are aligned across service systems and provide some idea of what is possible in improving parenting behavior. They are focused to a large extent, though not exclusively, on the parents of young children, and all three have advantaged young children and their families in notable ways. Taken together, these examples demonstrate how parenting knowledge about what to do and why it matters for keeping children safe and well can lead to changes in parenting practices within a relatively short period of time based on the advice, recommendations, and encouragement of trusted information sources, as well as the potential benefit of a penalty for not complying (child passenger safety in particular). While not exhaustive, they also illustrate how marrying evidence, policies, and financing and supporting parents and families can lead to better outcomes for children.

Child Passenger Safety

Progress has been seen in child passenger safety, although motor vehicle collisions remain a leading cause of death for young children (Centers for Disease Control and Prevention, 2015a). Less than 40 years ago, children were allowed to play unrestrained while riding in a car; today, multiple efforts are focused on ensuring that all children have the right size of car seat and are properly buckled up. Advocacy for child passenger safety by families and community members, physicians, traffic safety experts, and researchers has influenced state and federal policy makers, car manufacturers, and an entire industry with respect to making car seats for babies, toddlers, and children. Among children ages 0-8, use of restraints increased from 51 percent in 1999 to 80 percent in 2007 (Children's Hospital of Philadelphia, 2008). Parents face potential social pressure from family members and friends to buckle up themselves and their children, and fines are levied if they are stopped for a moving violation and found not to be using proper restraints.

The Safe to Sleep Campaign

A second example of a major shift in parenting behavior accomplished in less than a generation is what was originally launched as the Back to Sleep public education campaign in 1995 and is now called Safe to Sleep. This initiative, led by the *Eunice Kennedy Shriver* National Institute of Child Health and Human Development, is designed to reduce the incidence of sudden infant death syndrome (SIDS) by having all caregivers place children to sleep on their backs rather than their bellies, remove all soft bedding in sleeping areas, and ensure that sleeping spaces outside of the home (e.g., at child care, when traveling) are just as safe as those in the home. From 1990 to 2014, the rate of SIDS decreased from 130.3 to 38.7 deaths per 100,000 live births (Centers for Disease Control and Prevention, 2015b).

Reduced Smoking and Drinking during Pregnancy

Finally, prenatal care visits and an emphasis on the known toxic effects of exposure to tobacco and alcohol on the developing fetus have led to dramatic decreases in the numbers of women who smoke and drink while pregnant in the past 25 years. Women are exposed to reminders not to smoke and drink during prenatal visits with health care providers and through signage in many restaurants and bars. Approximately 20 percent of women reported smoking during pregnancy in 1989, compared with 8.5 percent in 2013, although rates remain much higher among Native Americans (Child Trends, 2015). In surveys conducted before 2001, 20 percent of women reported consuming alcohol during pregnancy (Bhuvaneswar et al., 2007); in a Centers for Disease Control and Prevention analysis of Behavioral Risk Factor Surveillance System data for 2006 to 2010, this percentage had declined to 8 percent (Centers for Disease Control and Prevention, 2012).

FEDERAL BUDGET SUPPORTING PARENTS AND CHILDREN

As noted earlier, significant federal fiscal support is dedicated to children and to helping their parents provide for their basic needs. This funding and the selected policies and investments described in the sections below, among others, are interrelated and form a platform upon which a national framework for more robustly meeting the needs of parents and improving outcomes for children could be organized, as described in Chapter 2.

It is important to note that this federal spending is augmented publicly and privately in various ways by states and localities, private businesses, organizations, and foundations.[1] Therefore, none of the estimates provided herein represents a full picture of national spending on children and families. Estimates of the total amount of federal money spent on children and families also vary based on the methodology used. The committee drew on data from Kids' Share (Isaacs et al., 2015), which describes the share of the federal budget dedicated to children and to families with children through age 18. To the committee's knowledge, a review of the budget specifically with respect to parenting does not exist, and the amount spent on improving parenting knowledge, attitudes, and practices cannot be isolated in the federal budget.

In 2014, 10 percent of total federal expenditures—amounting to $463 billion—was on children (see Figure 3-1) (Isaacs et al., 2015). Most spending on children in 2014 was for child-related tax provisions (e.g., the

---

[1] Three-fifths of the total public funding for children is provided by state and local governments, the bulk of which is spent on public schools. In 2011, for example, 62 percent of the total funds spent on children ($12,770 per child) was from state and local sources (Isaacs et al., 2015).

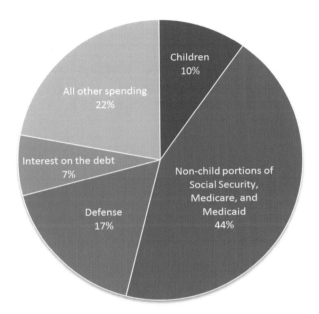

FIGURE 3-1 Share of federal budget outlays spent on children (ages 0-18), 2014.
SOURCE: Adapted from Isaacs et al. (2015).

Earned Income Tax Credit [EITC], the Child Tax Credit, the dependent exemption), followed by health, nutrition, income security (e.g., Temporary Assistance for Needy Families [TANF]), education, early education and care, and social services and housing (see Figure 3-2 and Table 3-1).

FEDERAL POLICIES AND INVESTMENTS
SUPPORTING PARENTS AND CHILDREN

Some of the federal expenditures that provide families with direct economic support or services to enable them to better meet the needs of their children are universal, while others are tied to family income. Federal funding is also directed at a number of programs available to parents seeking information and support in caring for their children. This section highlights some of the programs that are discussed further in Chapter 4; while this review is not exhaustive, it should serve to illustrate the scale of these investments.

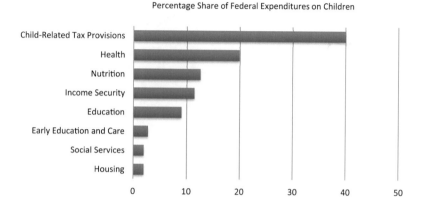

FIGURE 3-2 Percentage share of federal expenditures on children (ages 0-18) by program type, 2014.
NOTES: Categories representing less than 1 percent of federal expenditures are not depicted. The Child-Related Tax Provision estimate was calculated by adding estimates (from Table 3-1 below) for refundable portions of tax credits, tax expenditures, and the dependent exemption and dividing by total expenditures on children ($463 billion). Table 3-1 lists programs included in these and each of the other categories shown on the figure.
SOURCE: Adapted from Isaacs et al. (2015).

Universal and Near-Universal Policies and Investments

Child-Related Tax Provisions

By far the largest portion of the budget that goes to helping families with children is in the form of tax provisions that include (1) refundable components of tax credits, such as the EITC, the Child Tax Credit, and a set of other smaller credits (almost $76 billion in 2014) and (2) tax expenditures, such as exclusions for employer-sponsored health insurance, the nonrefundable portions of the EITC and the Child Tax Credit, and other small expenditures ($71 billion in 2014) (Isaacs et al., 2015).

Established by Congress in 1975, the EITC is currently the largest poverty alleviation program for the nonelderly in the United States. In 2013, it is estimated to have lifted 6.2 million people, including 3.2 million children, out of poverty (Center on Budget and Policy Priorities, 2015e). EITC benefits are paid by the federal government, as well as 26 states and the District of Columbia, which set their own EITCs as a percentage of the federal credit (Center on Budget and Policy Priorities, 2015e). Benefits are

TABLE 3-1 Federal Expenditures on Children by Program, 2014 (in billions of dollars)

	2014
Health	**92.6**
Medicaid	77.6
Children's Health Insurance Program (CHIP)	9.0
Vaccines for children	3.6
Other health	2.4
Nutrition	**58.3**
Supplemental Nutrition Assistance Program (SNAP) (formerly the Food Stamp Program)	33.4
Child nutrition	19.4
Special Supplemental Nutrition Program for Women, Infants, and Children (WIC)	5.5
Commodity Supplemental Food Program (CSFP)	*
Income Security	**52.6**
Social Security	21.0
Temporary Assistance for Needy Families	12.2
Supplemental Security Income	11.3
Veterans disability compensation	3.9
Child support enforcement	3.4
Other income security	0.8
Education	**41.8**
Education for the Disadvantaged (Title I, part A)	15.8
Special education/Individuals with Disabilities Education Act	12.6
School improvement	4.4
Impact Aid	1.1
Dependents' schools abroad	1.2
Innovation and improvement	1.2
State Fiscal Stabilization Fund	1.1
Other education	4.3
Early Education and Care	**12.8**
Head Start (including Early Head Start)	7.7
Child Care and Development Fund	5.1

continued

TABLE 3-1 Continued

	2014
Social Services	9.3
Foster care	4.3
Adoption assistance	2.3
Other social services	2.7
Housing	9.3
Section 8 low-income housing assistance	7.3
Low-rent public housing	1.1
Other housing	1.0
Training	1.2
Refundable Portions of Tax Credits	75.9
Earned Income Tax Credit	53.6
Child Tax Credit	21.5
Other refundable tax credits	0.8
Tax Expenditures	71.3
Exclusion for employer-sponsored health insurance	33.8
Child Tax Credit (nonrefundable portion)	25.6
Dependent care credit	4.3
Earned Income Tax Credit (nonrefundable portion)	3.3
Other tax expenditures	4.4
Dependent Exemption	37.9
TOTAL EXPENDITURES ON CHILDREN	463.1
Outlays Subtotal	353.8
Tax Expenditures Subtotal (including tax expenditures and dependent exemption)	109.2

NOTES: * = Less than $50 million. Does not sum to 100 because of rounding.
SOURCE: Isaacs et al. (2015).

paid as a function of earned income and thus are intended to incentivize employment (i.e., encourage individuals to leave welfare for work and increase work hours). Despite the benefits of this credit, there is significant underparticipation (about 21% nationally) (Internal Revenue Service, 2015b). While there are no data to explain this underparticipation, it may be due, in part, to lack of awareness and clarity about the credit, eligibility criteria, and how to apply. In 2014, federal expenditures for the refundable portion of the EITC were 53.6 billion (Isaacs et al., 2015).

The EITC reduces the amount owed in federal taxes. If the credit exceeds a worker's income tax liability, the remainder is provided as a refund (Center on Budget and Policy Priorities, 2015e). Eligibility and the amount of the credit received depend on filing status, income, and number of qualifying children (Internal Revenue Service, 2015a).[2] In the 2015 tax year, the credit ranged from a maximum of $503 for filers with no qualifying children, to $3,359 for those with one qualifying child, to $6,242 for those with three or more qualifying children (Internal Revenue Service, 2015a). Eligibility for the federal EITC has been expanded several times (Marr et al., 2015).

The Child Tax Credit, enacted in 1997, helps offset the costs of raising children for working families with qualifying children up to age 16. Like the EITC, the Child Tax Credit is designed to incentivize employment, increasing with earnings up to a certain level. Families receive a tax refund that amounts to 15 percent of their earnings above $3,000, with a maximum $1,000 refund per child (Center on Budget and Policy Priorities, 2015a). Whereas the EITC is aimed at low-income families, both low- and middle-income families are eligible for the Child Tax Credit; for married individuals filing jointly, phaseout begins at $110,000 (Internal Revenue Service, 2015c). Also like the EITC, the Child Tax Credit has lifted many families out of poverty. In 2013, it moved 3.1 million people and 1.7 million children out of poverty and reduced poverty for another 13.7 million people, including 6.8 million children (Center on Budget and Policy Priorities, 2016). The Child Tax Credit is paid by the federal government and a few states that have their own programs. In the early and late 2000s, the federal program underwent expansions that vastly increased the number of eligible families (Mattingly, 2009). Expenditures for the refundable portion of the Child Tax Credit were $21.5 billion in 2014 (Isaacs et al., 2015).

Finally, the Child and Dependent Care Tax Credit refunds individuals for 20 to 35 percent of the amount paid to someone to care for a qualifying child under age 13 (or for a spouse or dependent who is unable to care for him- or herself) so that filers can work or look for work (Internal Revenue Service, 2015d). Allowable expenses are up to $3,000 for one child or other dependent and $6,000 for two or more dependents. Families with lower incomes qualify for higher refunds. It is estimated that 6.3 million returns claimed the credit in 2013 (Tax Policy Center, 2015). How many of these were for children is unclear.

[2]For individuals who were single or widowed in 2015, both earned income and adjusted gross income limits to qualify for the credit were $39,131 for those with one child, $44,454 for those with two children, and $47,747 for those with three or more children. For married couples filing jointly in 2015, income limits were $44,651 for one child, $49,974 for two children, and $53,267 for three or more children (Internal Revenue Service, 2015a).

Support for Health Care

The second largest category of federal investments in children and families focuses on helping parents access health care for their children and themselves. Health care policies and programs can benefit the health of children directly, as well as benefit the health and financial well-being of parents, with potential spillover effects on their children.

The passage of the Patient Protection and Affordable Care Act (ACA) of 2010 resulted in a number of policy changes that increase access to health care and supportive services for parents. Among other enhancements, the ACA expanded Medicaid and improved child coverage; increased access to essential health benefits such as maternity and newborn care, pediatric services, and mental health and substance abuse services; and allowed parents to select a pediatrician for their child.

Medicaid ($77.6 billion in federal expenditures for children in 2014) and the Children's Health Insurance Program (CHIP) ($9 billion) play an important role in child coverage, and as of fiscal year (FY) 2014 provided insurance coverage for more than one in three (more than 43 million) U.S. children (Burwell, 2016; Isaacs et al., 2015). CHIP gives states federal aid to provide programs for children in families whose incomes exceed Medicaid thresholds but are not high enough for them to afford private health insurance. Among disadvantaged populations, Medicaid and CHIP are principally responsible for increasing children's health insurance coverage. The programs have had positive effects not only on coverage but also on access to care and health status among participants (American Academy of Pediatrics, 2014; Paradise, 2014). Previous state public health insurance expansions for parents show that such expansions may lead to higher rates of child participation in Medicaid (Dubay and Kenney, 2003).

The Maternal, Infant, and Early Childhood Home Visiting Program (established in 2010 as part of the ACA and currently funded through FY 2017) helps expectant and new at-risk parents prepare for and support children from birth to kindergarten. The implementation of evidence-based home visiting is a defining feature of this program. Health, social service, and child development specialists make regularly scheduled visits to provide hands-on guidance and referrals based on family needs. The program is designed to help parents develop and refine the skills they need to promote the well-being of children so they are physically and emotionally healthy and ready to learn. In FY 2014, more than 115,000 parents and their children received home visits through this program (Health Resources Services Administration, 2015). Both congressionally mandated performance measures and a rigorous impact evaluation are used to determine the program's effectiveness in enhancing parent-child outcomes and improving child outcomes in the health and psychoeducational domains. Total funding from

2011 through 2015 was more than $1.5 billion (Health Resources Services Administration, 2015). Home visiting also is provided nationally through many other funding streams.

Economic Support for Lower-Income Families and Children

Nutrition Assistance Policies and Programs

Proper nutrition can help people reach and maintain a healthy weight, reduce chronic disease risk, lower pregnancy-related risks, support fetal development, and promote overall health. Conversely, food insecurity[3] is associated with health issues, such as diabetes, heart disease, depression, and obesity, and can cause difficulty during pregnancy (Institute of Medicine, 2011; Lee et al., 2012). In 2014, federal investment in nutrition-related programs for children was $58.3 billion (Isaacs et al., 2015). Such programs include the Supplemental Nutrition Assistance Program (SNAP), the Special Supplemental Nutrition Program for Women, Infants, and Children (WIC), and the National School Breakfast and National School Lunch Programs.

SNAP, formerly known as the Food Stamp Program, is the largest nutrition program in the United States. Almost 60 percent of federal expenditures on children for nutrition in 2014 ($33.4 billion) was for SNAP (Isaacs et al., 2015). Administered by the U.S. Department of Agriculture, SNAP provides nutrition assistance to low-income individuals and families, with eligibility requirements that are less restrictive than those of other programs. In FY 2015, an average of 45 million people participated in SNAP each month, with an average monthly per household benefit of approximately $258 (U.S. Department of Agriculture, 2016c). Most households receiving SNAP (76% in 2014) include a child or an elderly or disabled individual (Gray and Kochhar, 2015), and many are very poor (with incomes less than 59% of the federal poverty level) (Food Research Action Center, 2015).

WIC, another long-standing program, is a federal grant program that provides vouchers for the purchase of nutritious food, as well as nutrition education, breastfeeding support, and referrals to social services and community supports for low-income women who are pregnant, postpartum, and breastfeeding as well as their children up to age 5. In FY 2015, the program served more than 8 million women, infants, and children, providing an average of $43.37 in monthly benefits per person (U.S. Department

---

[3] Food insecurity is defined as limited or uncertain availability of nutritionally adequate and safe foods or limited or uncertain ability to acquire such foods in a socially acceptable way (National Research Council, 2006; U.S. Department of Agriculture, 2015).

of Agriculture, 2016d). The 2014 expenditures totaled $5.5 billion (Isaacs et al., 2015).

Federal programs promoting child nutrition also include the National School Breakfast Program and the National School Lunch Program, both of which are offered in schools as well as in residential child care institutions. While meals are available to all children through both programs, children from families meeting income requirements are eligible to receive meals at low or no cost. In FY 2015, an average of 12 million and 20 million children per month received reduced-price or free meals through the National School Breakfast and National School Lunch Programs, respectively (U.S. Department of Agriculture, 2016a, 2016b). After-school snacks also are provided to children meeting income eligibility criteria (U.S. Department of Agriculture, 2013). Additional school-based nutrition programs include the Special Milk Program, the Fresh Fruit and Vegetable Program, and the Summer Food Service Program. In addition to ensuring children's nutrition, these programs can be viewed as income supports to parents and also as stress reducers because they reduce time demands on parents.

Income Security Policies and Programs

Another large area of federal spending on children takes the form of income security, totaling about $53 billion in 2014 (Isaacs et al., 2015). The largest income support to help parents and caregivers raise children after the death of a parent is Old Age and Survivors Insurance, part of Social Security, which covers insured workers. While not traditionally regarded as a program targeting children and their parents, it represents the largest income support for families with children. Child-related expenditures in 2014 were $21 billion for Social Security benefits to survivors and dependents (Isaacs et al., 2015).

TANF helps families achieve self-sufficiency through an assortment of services, such as direct cash payments, child care, education, job training, and transportation assistance. Block grants are provided to states, territories, and tribes, which have some discretion in determining eligibility criteria and services, so the program varies by location (Center on Budget and Policy Priorities, 2015b). Created through the Personal Responsibility and Work Opportunity Reconciliation Act of 1996, which was designed to increase labor market participation among individuals receiving public assistance, TANF requires jurisdictions to impose work requirements for participation, and assistance is reduced or eliminated for work-eligible individuals not meeting those requirements. In FY 2015, the average number of families served by TANF monthly was 1.35 million; these families included 3.12 million total recipients, 2.37 million of whom were children (Office of Family Assistance, 2015). Expenditures on children for TANF in 2014 totaled $12.2 billion (Isaacs et al., 2015).

The federal Child Support Enforcement Program aims to encourage parental responsibility "so that children receive financial, emotional, and medical support from both parents, even when they live in separate households" (Office of Child Support Enforcement, 2015a). The program's services, which may include assistance in locating parents, establishing legal paternity, enforcing support orders, increasing health care coverage for children, and removing barriers to child support payment (e.g., providing referrals for employment services, supporting healthy co-parenting), are available through local child support offices to any family with children in which one parent is not living in the same home as the children (First Focus, 2015; Office of Child Support Enforcement, 2016). Either parent may apply for services, as may grandparents or other custodians. Services are automatically provided to all families participating in TANF that could benefit. In FY 2014, the Child Support Enforcement Program served 16 million children and collected nearly $32 billion in child support, 95 percent of which went to families (Office of Child Support Enforcement, 2015b). Federal expenditures for child support enforcement in 2014 totaled $3.4 billion (Isaacs et al., 2015).

Housing Policies and Programs

Housing programs support parents in meeting various objectives for their children—including their health; safety; and emotional, social, and cognitive well-being—by offsetting a number of stressors. Across various income groups, housing-related expenses (e.g., shelter, utilities, furniture) accounted for the largest share of families' expenditures on children in 2013, totaling 30-33 percent of all expenses in mother and father families with two children (Lino, 2014).

Federal support helps millions of low-income households with children afford housing in the United States (Center on Budget and Policy Priorities, 2015c). The funding flows mainly through programs in the U.S. Department of Housing and Urban Development, including Tenant-Based Rental Assistance, Project-Based Rental Assistance, and the Public Housing Operating Fund. Together, these funding streams contributed more than $9 billion to federal spending on children in 2015, representing nearly 80 percent of all housing investments that impact children (Isaacs et al., 2015).

The Housing Choice Voucher Program (HCVP) (often referred to as Section 8) helps more than 5 million people in low-income families access affordable rental housing in the private market that meets health and safety standards (Center on Budget and Policy Priorities, 2015d; U.S. Department of Housing and Urban Development, 2016b), supporting families in creating safe households for their children. Seventy-five percent of the vouchers distributed to new participants each year are provided to extremely low-income households.[4] Currently, children reside in 46 percent of households that are HCVP recipients (Center on Budget and Policy Priorities, 2015d). Family unification vouchers are provided to families participating in HCVP that are at risk of having their children placed in out-of-home care because of a lack of adequate housing and to those for whom reunification is de-layed because of lack of adequate housing (U.S. Department of Housing and Urban Development, 2016a).

Investments in Child and Parent Education

In terms of state and local funding as well as federal investments, edu-cation is by far the largest form of societal investment in children in the United States. In addition to direct expenditures on education, from early childhood through college, the federal government provides or supports ac-cess to child care for children through both tax credits and direct support.

While most child care and education expenditures are focused exclu-sively on the care and education of children, the U.S. Department of Health and Human Services (HHS) and the U.S. Department of Education fund and administer a number of early childhood care and education programs for children ages 0-8, many of which are focused on helping parents engage in parenting practices associated with healthy child development. HHS manages two large programs—Head Start (including Early Head Start) and the Child Care and Development Fund (CCDF). The U.S. Department of Education manages more than 80 federally funded education programs, including special education programs, benefiting children of all ages, from infants to high school students preparing for college; from all states and territories; and across all income groups. State and local funding for public education for children ages 5-8 dwarfs federal funding for children in this age range.

The Head Start Program was established in 1965 to support the school readiness of low-income children ages 3-5 through the provision of pre-school education and supportive services to families. Early Head Start, which became a part of Head Start programming following the reautho-rization of the Head Start Act in 1994, provides services for low-income pregnant women and families of children ages 0-3 for the purpose of supporting children's healthy development and strengthening family and community partnerships (U.S. Department of Health and Human Services, 2015). Delivered in about 1,700 community agencies located throughout

---

[4]Defined as household income not above 30 percent of the local median or the federal poverty line, whichever is higher (Center on Budget and Policy Priorities, 2015d).

the United States (U.S. Department of Health and Human Services, 2015), Head Start and Early Head Start represent scaled-up, means-tested, and rigorously evaluated approaches to two-generation programs, which target parents and children from the same family. In addition to education services directed at children, they typically provide parenting education; self-sufficiency services; and resources and referrals to community providers to meet families' needs in a range of areas, such as transportation, housing, and health care. The government spent $7.7 billion on Head Start and Early Head Start in 2014 (Isaacs et al., 2015). In the 2014-2015 program year, almost 1.1 million children ages 0-5 and pregnant women were served by the two programs (Office of Head Start, 2015).

CCDF makes funding available to states, tribes, and territories to help qualifying low-income families obtain child care so that parents can work or attend classes or training. The program works to improve the quality of child care so that children will have positive and enriching experiences. Nearly 1.5 million children receive a child care subsidy from the program every month (Administration for Children and Families, 2015). State Quality Rating and Improvement Systems (QRIS), developed to help states evaluate the quality of care and education programs for children, are funded largely through CCDF and include incentives for child care providers to improve the quality of their programs (Administration for Children and Families, 2016a). Implementation of QRIS was encouraged by their inclusion in the U.S. Department of Education's Race-to-the-Top Early Learning Challenge grants, which also required QRIS validation studies. Many of these efforts were joint HHS-Department of Education early care and education initiatives with funding targeted to different parts of the service delivery system that supports parents of young children. Programs such as CCDF may positively impact parenting by providing parents access to services that promote self-sufficiency and parenting practices associated with healthy child development.

Preschool Development Grants support states in building or enhancing infrastructure for preschool programs to enable the delivery of high-quality preschool services to children, as well as in expanding high-quality preschool programs in targeted communities that can serve as models for extending preschool to all 4-year-olds from low- and moderate-income families. In 2015, 18 states were awarded $237 million for year 2 of this grant program (U.S. Department of Education, 2015).

Support for Parents of Children with Special Needs and Parents Facing Adversity

In addition to the policies and programs discussed above that are directed at ensuring the well-being of children of all ages and that reach a large number of families, particularly low-income families, investments are made to support parents who face situational or personal challenges. Although families may face singular challenges, such as intimate partner violence, challenges often cluster together. Substance abuse, mental illness, involvement with the child welfare system, financial hardship, and other challenges can overlap in families, with profound consequences for the development and well-being of young children. A variety of federal investments are designed to support parents who face such challenges. Many families experiencing these challenges have access to and utilize the universal and widely used supports discussed above, but these, even along with community and family supports, often are insufficient.

Some investments for such families are part of broader spending on health and education, such as that for programs for children with mental, behavioral, and developmental disabilities. The Individuals with Disabilities Education Act (IDEA) Part C, Grants for Children and Families, for example, assists states in providing early intervention services for young children with disabilities and their families. IDEA Part C allocations in 2015 totaled $438.6 million (First Focus, 2015), and those funds are included in the federal budget for education described above.

In the area of child welfare, there are investments in programs that are aimed at preventing and addressing child maltreatment and that provide assistance to kinship and foster parents. In 2015, for instance, nearly $445 million in mandatory funding was allocated for the Promoting Safe and Stable Families Program, which, through state grants, aims to prevent unnecessary separation of children from their families and promote child permanency. In 2015, $99 million was allocated for assistance payments to grandparents and other kinship caregivers with legal guardianship of children (First Focus, 2015).

Family and Parental Leave Policies and Programs

Newborns and infants require substantial, focused, and responsive care. Parents of newborns need time to bond with their child and adjust to the demands of caring for an infant while also overseeing their child's healthy development. In addition, parents need time to rest and recover from pregnancy and childbirth. As described in Chapter 2, breastfeeding is a critical nutritional issue for infants. Mothers who are breastfeeding need to be available to their infants and toddlers or need time to pump breast milk during the day when they are not with their baby. Also, children have considerable preventive (e.g., routine well-child visits), acute, and chronic health care needs to which parents need to attend. Nonetheless, current state and federal policies regarding parental and family medical leave cover some but not all parents and employers, and among those covered, the policies address some but not all of their needs. For some parents, taking time off from work to care for a newborn or a sick child means losing income or even risking their job.

Most parents of young children are in the labor force (Bureau of Labor Statistics, 2016). To meet their children's needs, employees in the United States tend to rely on a mix of support that combines employer benefits (if offered) with federal, state, and local leave laws and programs (Schuster et al., 2011). The Pregnancy Discrimination Act of 1978 requires that employers provide women who have medical conditions associated with pregnancy and childbirth the same leave as is provided to employees who are temporarily unable to work because of other medical conditions (e.g., a broken leg or a heart attack) (U.S. Equal Employment Opportunity Commission, 2016). The act does not require employers to provide paid leave, but if they provide paid leave or disability benefits for some medical conditions, they must do so for conditions related to pregnancy and childbirth as well.

The Family and Medical Leave Act of 1993 (FMLA) provides up to 12 weeks a year of unpaid leave with job protection to eligible employees for their own serious health conditions; for the birth of a child or to care for the employee's newly born, adopted, or foster child; or to care for a family member (spouse, child, or parent) with a serious health condition. Eligibility is restricted to those who work for employers with 50 or more employees and have worked at least 1,250 hours for the same employer in the past 12 months (U.S. Department of Labor, 2016). Although 60 percent of employees meet all eligibility criteria for FMLA (U.S. Department of Labor, 2015), many employees cannot afford to take unpaid leave (Han and Waldfogel, 2003).

Finally, although not federal policy, some states currently have or are considering paid parental leave policies. The implications of these policies for parents and children, as well as for employers, the economy, and society, are yet to be determined.

SUMMARY

Federal funding that supports parents and children in the United States is distributed across the federal budget, and responsibility for administering the funded programs resides with a range of agencies, including those at the state and local levels. There is no easy way to map the evidence-based parenting knowledge, attitudes, and practices identified in Chapter 2 to the federal budget; however, a review of the budget and a general understanding of the policy and funding structure provides an overview of the existing framework for the programs reviewed in Chapters 4 and 5. Although many children interface with specific programs, the committee notes that there is no simple way to compute how many children receive services through multiple programs at the same time or what percentage of those serve young children ages 0-8—an important question for understanding the return on investment in programs. What the existing funding streams and service delivery platforms do provide are settings and systems with the potential to be linked more systematically to offer support for parenting knowledge, attitudes, and practices that is grounded in evidence-based programming and practice (see Chapter 7). As noted in subsequent chapters, new approaches to developing interventions are being tested. Understanding how federal funding flows into programs directly and indirectly to support parents and children informs the development and financing of a new framework for providing this support.

The following key points emerged from the committee's review of federal policies and investments supporting parents and children:

- The United States has a long history of funding policies and programs with the goal of improving children's outcomes and the well-being of families and society. These policies and programs are not limited to young children; however, young children and their parents are within the larger populations served.
- Large-scale policies and programs designed to change parenting behavior in some areas have been effective in improving targeted outcomes at the population level. However, support for parents is not isolated in these policies and programs, and there is little information about parents' awareness of how various policies and programs can support them in their parenting role.
- The specific policy and program approaches reflected in the federal budget are a mix of child-related tax provisions, policies and programs designed to promote well-being and positive outcomes for all children and families, and policies and programs targeted at providing a safety net for children and families facing adversity and various risk factors.

REFERENCES

Administration for Children and Families. (2015). *Administration for Children and Families: Child Care Development Fund*. Available: https://www.acf.hhs.gov/sites/default/files/olab/sec2c_ccdf_2015cj_complete.pdf [January 2016].

Administration for Children and Families. (2016a). About QRIS. Available: https://qrisguide.acf.hhs.gov/index.cfm?do=qrisabout [May 2016].

Administration for Children and Families. (2016b). History. Available: http://www.acf.hhs.gov/programs/cb/about/history [May 2016].

American Academy of Pediatrics. (2014). Children's Health Insurance Program (CHIP): Accomplishments, challenges, and policy recommendations. *Pediatrics, 133*(3), e784-e793.

Bhuvaneswar, C.G., Chang, G., Epstein, L.A., and Stern, T.A. (2007). Alcohol use during pregnancy: Prevalence and impact. *Primary Care Companion to The Journal of Clinical Psychiatry, 9*(6), 455-460.

Bureau of Labor Statistics. (2016). *Employment Characteristics of Families Summary*. Available: http://www.bls.gov/news.release/famee.nr0.htm [May 2016].

Burwell, S.M. (2016). *The Department of Health and Human Services 2015 Annual Report on the Quality of Care for Children in Medicaid and CHIP*. Washington, DC: U.S. Department of Health and Human Services.

Center on Budget and Policy Priorities. (2015a). *Chart Book: The Earned Income Tax Credit and Child Tax Credit*. Available: http://www.cbpp.org/research/federal-tax/chart-book-the-earned-income-tax-credit-and-child-tax-credit#PartOne [February 2016].

Center on Budget and Policy Priorities. (2015b). *Policy Basics: An Introduction to TANF*. Available: http://www.cbpp.org/research/policy-basics-an-introduction-to-tanf [October 2016].

Center on Budget and Policy Priorities. (2015c). *Policy Basics: Federal Rental Assistance*. Available: http://www.cbpp.org/research/housing/policy-basics-federal-rental-assistance [October 2016].

Center on Budget and Policy Priorities. (2015d). *Policy Basics: The Housing Choice Voucher Program*. Available: http://www.cbpp.org/research/housing/policy-basics-the-housing-choice-voucher-program [October 2016].

Center on Budget and Policy Priorities. (2015e). *Policy Basics: The Earned Income Tax Credit*. Available: http://www.cbpp.org/research/policy-basics-the-earned-income-tax-credit [August 2015].

Center on Budget and Policy Priorities. (2016). *Policy Basics: The Child Tax Credit*. Available: http://www.cbpp.org/research/policy-basics-the-child-tax-credit [October 2016].

Centers for Disease Control and Prevention. (2012). Alcohol use and binge drinking among women of childbearing age—United States, 2006-2010. *Morbidity and Mortality Weekly Report, 61*(28), 534-538.

Centers for Disease Control and Prevention. (2015a). *Leading Causes of Death Reports: National and Regional, 1999-2014*. Available: http://webappa.cdc.gov/sasweb/ncipc/leadcaus10_us.html [May 2016].

Centers for Disease Control and Prevention. (2015b). *Sudden Unexpected Infant Death and Sudden Infant Death Syndrome: Data and Statistics*. Available: http://www.cdc.gov/sids/data.htm [January 2016].

Child Trends. (2015). *Mothers Who Smoke While Pregnant: Indicators on Children and Youth*. Bethesda, MD: Child Trends.

Children's Hospital of Philadelphia. (2008). *2008 Partners for Child Passenger Safety (PCPS): Fact and Trend Report*. Available: https://injury.research.chop.edu/sites/default/files/documents/2008_ft.pdf [January 2016].

Dubay, L., and Kenney, G. (2003). Expanding public health insurance to parents: Effects on children's coverage under Medicaid. *Health Services Research, 38*(5), 1283-1302.

First Focus. (2015). *Children's Budget 2015*. Washington, DC: First Focus.

Food Research Action Center. (2015). SNAP: The latest research on participant characteristics and program. *Food Insecurity and Hunger in the U.S.: New Research, 6*.

Gray, K.F., and Kochhar, S. (2015). *Characteristics of Supplemental Nutrition Assistance Program Households: Fiscal Year 2014*. Report No. SNAP-15-CHAR. Alexandria, VA: U.S. Department of Agriculture, Food and Nutrition Service, Office of Policy Support.

Han, W.J., and Waldfogel, J. (2003). Parental leave: The impact of recent legislation on parents' leave taking. *Demography, 40*(1), 191-200.

Health Resources Services Administration. (2015). *Maternal, Infant, and Early Childhood Home Visiting*. Available: http://mchb.hrsa.gov/programs/homevisiting [January 2016].

Institute of Medicine. (2011). *Hunger and Obesity: Understanding a Food Insecurity Paradigm—Workshop Summary.* L.M. Troy, E.A. Miller, and S. Olson (Rapporteurs). Food and Nutrition Board. Washington, DC: The National Academies Press.

Internal Revenue Service. (2015a). *2015 EITC Income Limits, Maximum Credit Amounts and Tax Law Updates.* Available: https://www.irs.gov/credits-deductions/individuals/earned-income-tax-credit/eitc-income-limits-maximum-credit-amounts [October 2016].

Internal Revenue Service. (2015b). *EITC Participation Rate by States.* Available: https://www.eitc.irs.gov/EITC-Central/Participation-Rate [February 2016].

Internal Revenue Service. (2015c). *Ten Facts about the Child Tax Credit.* Available: https://www.irs.gov/uac/Ten-Facts-about-the-Child-Tax-Credit [February 2016].

Internal Revenue Service. (2015d). *Reduce your Taxes with the Child and Dependent Care Tax Credit.* Available: https://www.irs.gov/uac/Reduce-Your-Taxes-with-the-Child-and-Dependent-Care-Tax-Credit [February 2016].

Isaacs, J., Edelstein, S., Hahn, H., Steele, E., and Stuerle, C.E. (2015). *Kids' Share 2015: Report on Federal Expenditures on Children in 2014 and Future Projections.* Washington, DC: Urban Institute.

Lee, J.S., Gundersen, C., Cook, J., Laraia, B., and Johnson, M.A. (2012). Food insecurity and health across the lifespan. *Advances in Nutrition: An International Review Journal,* 3(5), 744-745.

Lino, M. (2014). *Expenditures on Children by Families, 2013.* Publication No. 1528-2013. Washington, DC: U.S. Department of Agriculture, Center for Nutrition Policy and Promotion.

Marr, C., Huang, C., Sherman, A., and DeBot, B. (2015). *EITC and Child Tax Credit Promote Work, Reduce Poverty, and Support Children's Development, Research Finds.* Washington, DC: Center on Budget and Policy Priorities.

Mattingly, M.J. (2009). *Child Tax Credit Expansion Increases Number of Families Eligible for a Refund.* Issue Brief No. 4. Durham: University of New Hampshire, Carsey Institute.

National Research Council. (2006). *Food Insecurity and Hunger in the United States: An Assessment of the Measure.* G.S. Wunderlich and J.L. Norwood (Eds.). Panel to Review the U.S. Department of Agriculture's Measurement of Food Insecurity and Hunger; Committee on National Statistics, Division of Behavioral and Social Sciences and Education. Washington, DC: The National Academies Press.

Office of Child Support Enforcement. (2015a). *About the Office of Child Support Enforcement (OCSE).* Available: http://www.acf.hhs.gov/css/about [October 2016].

Office of Child Support Enforcement. (2015b). *Child Support 2014: More Money for Families.* Available: https://www.acf.hhs.gov/sites/default/files/programs/css/2014_preliminary_report_infographic.pdf [May 2016].

Office of Child Support Enforcement. (2016). *OCSE Fact Sheet.* Available: http://www.acf.hhs.gov/programs/css/resource/ocse-fact-sheet [May 2016].

Office of Family Assistance. (2015). *TANF Caseload Data 2015.* Available: http://www.acf.hhs.gov/programs/ofa/resource/tanf-caseload-data-2015 [October 2016].

Office of Head Start. (2015). *Office of Head Start—Services Snapshot: National All Programs (2014-2015).* Available: http://eclkc.ohs.acf.hhs.gov/hslc/data/psr/2015/services-snapshot-all-programs-2014-2015.pdf [January 2016].

Paradise, J. (2014). *The Impact of the Children's Health Insurance Program (CHIP): What Does the Research Tell Us?* Available: https://kaiserfamilyfoundation.files.wordpress.com/2014/07/8615-the-impact-of-the-children_s-health-insurance-program-chip-what-does-the-research-tell-us.pdf [May 2016].

Schuster, M.A., Chung, P.J., and Vestal, K.D. (2011). Children with health issues. *Future Child,* 21(2), 91-116.

Tax Policy Center. (2015). *Historical Dependent Care Credits*. Available: http://www. taxpolicycenter.org/taxfacts/displayafact.cfm?Docid=180 [February 2016].

U.S. Department of Agriculture. (2013). *The School-Based After School Snack Program*. Available: http://www.fns.usda.gov/sites/default/files/AfterschoolFactSheet.pdf [May 2016].

U.S. Department of Agriculture. (2015). *Supplemental Nutrition Assistance Program Participation and Costs*. Available: http://www.fns.usda.gov/sites/default/files/pd/SNAP summary.pdf [October 2016].

U.S. Department of Agriculture. (2016a). *National School Lunch Program: Participation and Lunches Served*. Available: http://www.fns.usda.gov/sites/default/files/pd/slsummar.pdf [May 2016].

U.S. Department of Agriculture. (2016b). *School Breakfast Program Participation and Meals Served*. Available: http://www.fns.usda.gov/sites/default/files/pd/sbsummar.pdf [May 2016].

U.S. Department of Agriculture. (2016c). *Supplemental Nutrition Assistance Program: FY13 through FY16 National View Summary*. Available: http://www.fns.usda.gov/sites/default/ files/pd/34SNAPmonthly.pdf [June 2016].

U.S. Department of Agriculture. (2016d). *WIC Program Participation and Costs*. Available: http://www.fns.usda.gov/sites/default/files/pd/wisummary.pdf [May 2016].

U.S. Department of Education. (2015). *U.S. Departments of Education and Health and Human Services Award $237M in Early Education Grants to 18 States*. Available: http://www.ed.gov/news/press-releases/us-departments-education-and-health-and-human-services-award-237m-early-education-grants-18-states [January 2016].

U.S. Department of Health and Human Services. (2015). *Head Start Services*. Available: http:// www.acf.hhs.gov/programs/ohs/about/head-start [February 2016].

U.S. Department of Housing and Urban Development. (2016a). *Family Unification Program*. Available: http://portal.hud.gov/hudportal/HUD?src=/program_offices/public_indian_ housing/programs/hcv/family [May 2016].

U.S. Department of Housing and Urban Development. (2016b). *Housing Choice Vouchers Fact Sheet*. Available: http://portal.hud.gov/hudportal/HUD?src=/program_offices/public_ indian_housing/programs/hcv/about/fact_sheet [May 2016].

U.S. Department of Labor. (2015). *FMLA Is Working*. Available: http://www.dol.gov/whd/ fmla/survey/FMLA_Survey_factsheet.pdf [May 2016].

U.S. Department of Labor. (2016). *Family and Medical Leave Act. Overview*. Available: https://www.dol.gov/whd/fmla/index.htm [May 2016].

U.S. Equal Employment Opportunity Commission. (2016). *Pregnancy Discrimination*. Available: https://www.eeoc.gov/eeoc/publications/fs-preg.cfm [May 2016].

4

Universal/Preventive and
Widely Used Interventions

This chapter reviews the evidence on interventions for strengthening parenting capacity and supporting parents of young children, from the prenatal period through age 8. The focus is on universal and widely used interventions that touch large numbers of families and that are primarily preventive, such as those delivered in health care settings; those delivered in connection with child care, early education, and K-3 schooling; and public education approaches.[1] These interventions and approaches generally emphasize providing parents with knowledge and guidance about children's development and successful parenting practices; many also connect parents to a variety of needed support services. Following this review, the chapter turns to a discussion of the use of information and communication technologies to support parenting. The chapter then examines the research evaluating the impact on parenting of income, nutrition, health care, and housing support programs and parental and family leave policies described in Chapter 3. The chapter concludes with a summary.

UNIVERSAL/PREVENTIVE INTERVENTIONS

Parents seek knowledge about how to raise their children from many sources, including both formal programs and information they obtain on

---

[1] A useful framework for thinking about interventions is described in the National Research Council and Institute of Medicine (2009) report *Preventing Mental, Emotional, and Behavioral Disorders among Young People*. In the prevention area, this framework specifies mental health promotion; universal interventions defined as those that are valuable for all children; and selective interventions, which are targeted at populations at high risk.

their own. Numerous books, magazine articles, and Websites provide information about parenting. Whereas earlier generations may have relied on books such as Benjamin Spock's *Baby and Child Care* (e.g., Spock, 1957, 1968, 1976) and later generations on guidance from T. Berry Brazelton and Harvey Karp (Brazelton, 1992; Karp, 2002; Karp and Spencer, 2004), parents today are seeking information from a more diverse array of print, online, and human resources. Some of the information that is available is not grounded in evidence.

Parents seek information and guidance in particular about actions they can take that apply to the developmental stage of their child (e.g., infancy, toddlerhood, early childhood, early school age). They naturally look to their extended family (e.g., their own parents, siblings), the community (including others who are raising their own children), faith-based institutions, and community organizations for guidance and support. All of these sources contribute to parents' knowledge, attitudes, and practices with respect to raising their children. In the best cases, parents have access to and knowledge of multiple resources and are able to draw on them as needed.

There are also a variety of formal sources of parenting information, guidance, and support. These sources include primary care practitioners who provide guidance on early learning, well-child care and guidance, and other health care for children. In some communities, this role also is filled by visiting nurses and others in both lay and professional disciplines with experience in parenting. Other formal programs discussed in this chapter include center-based child care and comprehensive early care and education (ECE) programs (e.g., Head Start and Early Head Start). These programs, sometimes referred to as universal interventions, reflect the shared needs of children and families for health care, educational preparation, and general support.

Well-Child Care[2]

Well-child care refers to preventive care visits for children that include not only basic health care, vaccination, and developmental assessment but also anticipatory guidance (counseling and education on a broad variety of topics aimed at supporting parents) and identification of family concerns that can serve as a barrier to good parenting. Conducted by pediatricians, family physicians, and other primary care providers, well-child care is a

---

[2]Portions of this section are based on a paper commissioned for this study, authored by Tumaini R. Coker, assistant professor of pediatrics at the David Geffen School of Medicine and Mattel Children's Hospital, and associate director of health services research at the Children's Discovery and Innovation Institute, University of California, Los Angeles. The paper can be requested from the study public access file at https://www8.nationalacademies.org/cp/ManageRequest.aspx?key=49669 [October 2016].

mainstay of families' interaction with the health care system. In 2013, 92 percent of children under the age of 6 and covered by health insurance had had a well-child visit in the past year (Child Trends Databank, 2014). In the 0-8-year age range, the American Academy of Pediatrics (AAP) recommends a regular schedule of multiple well-child visits during the first 2 years and annual visits thereafter and specifies that each visit should include a physical exam, anticipatory guidance, and developmental/behavioral assessment (American Academy of Pediatrics and Bright Futures, 2016). Several other organizations, including the U.S. Preventive Services Task Force and the American Academy of Family Physicians have developed similar well-child care recommendations (American Academy of Family Physicians, 2005; U.S. Preventive Services Task Force, 2015). Visits may be conducted either individually or in a group format.

Anticipatory guidance is intended to help parents prepare for and deal with issues and concerns—such as anticipated developmental steps and situational crises—they may encounter as their child grows. Guidelines for anticipatory guidance encompass a broad variety of topics pertinent to supporting evidence-based parenting knowledge and practices, ranging from promoting children's health and safety (e.g., guidance on helmet use, gun safety, treatment and counseling on overweight and obesity, guidance for parents on tobacco cessation), to appropriate discipline techniques, to managing difficult child behavior (e.g., sibling rivalry, tantrums) (American Academy of Pediatrics, 2000, 2002; Green and Palfrey, 2002). Multiple randomized controlled studies have examined tools for enhancing anticipatory guidance, such as telephone advice lines, supplemental parent education via DVD, Websites, and waiting-room kiosks (Bergman et al., 2009; Christakis et al., 2006; Kempe et al., 1999; Paradis et al., 2011; Sanghavi, 2005). Most of these supplemental interventions have failed to show substantial benefits, but efforts to improve safe sleep by means of video education modules and nurse education for parents have shown promising results in uncontrolled trials (Canter et al., 2015; Goodstein et al., 2015). (See also the section on information and communication technologies later in this chapter.)

Unfortunately, many families do not receive all of the parenting support and guidance that is recommended in well-child care guidelines. A shortage of provider time to cover the full range of topics may be one of the most important factors in the observed variation in the quality of well-child care. Longer well-child visits have been associated with more anticipatory guidance, more psychosocial risk assessment, and better ratings of family-centeredness of care in survey research with parents (Halfon et al., 2011). Yet the AAP has estimated that it would take a clinician 90 minutes to complete just one visit if all of its guidelines were followed (American Academy of Pediatrics, 2004). Given the time limitations for well-child visits (often constrained to 15-30 minutes), there have been efforts to expand the scope of visits by partnering families with nonphysician providers who can offer education, guidance, and counseling services to augment the care provided during formal visits, either within or outside of those visits (Farber, 2009; Zuckerman et al., 2004). However, the qualified personnel needed to provide those services are lacking.

In general, although well-child visits, including anticipatory guidance, likely support parenting and the achievement of evidence-based parenting knowledge, attitudes, and practices (e.g., vaccination), and several interventions have been designed to enhance the effectiveness of well-child care, evaluation of these interventions is limited. In addition, there is a lack of objective measures with which to evaluate effects of these interventions on parenting behavior or to identify the optimal mode of delivery of well-child care (O'Connell et al., 2015).

Some models of care and enhanced anticipatory guidance have proven successful, particularly by extending the resources provided during the initial visit through regular contact and support. Healthy Steps for Young Children is a model of care and enhanced anticipatory guidance in which a pediatric health care provider and a child specialist with training in child development (e.g., nurse, social worker) partner to provide well-child care. The specialist spends extra time with the family after the physician visit, offering home visits and connecting the family with telephone help lines, parent support groups, and community resources (Zuckerman et al., 2004). Most of the evaluations of Healthy Steps have focused on parenting outcomes rather than child outcomes (Piotrowski et al., 2009). A systematic review of experimental and quasi-experimental studies (Piotrowski et al., 2009) found that this model provided parents with effective developmental screening and anticipatory guidance (Caughy et al., 2003, 2004; Huebner et al., 2004; Johnston et al., 2006; Kinzer et al., 2004; McLearn et al., 2004; Minkovitz et al., 2003; Niederman et al., 2007). For example, parents reported improved parenting practices with respect to discipline, safety, and promotion of early reading (Minkovitz et al., 2003a). Other positive outcomes from Healthy Steps include parents reporting greater knowledge of infant development, better recognition of appropriate discipline, improved compliance with immunization and well-child visit schedules, and increased satisfaction with pediatric care (Johnston et al., 2006; Minkovitz et al., 2003).

Another program, the Parent-focused Redesign for Encounters, Newborns to Toddlers (PARENT) intervention (Coker et al., 2016), employs a team-based approach to care in which a parent coach provides the bulk of services at well-child visits and addresses specific needs faced by families in low-income communities. An initial randomized evaluation of this model among 251 parents found positive effects on parents' receipt of anticipatory guidance and health information, psychosocial assessment, and other services. Parents participating in the intervention had significantly reduced emergency department use (22% of control parents versus 10% of intervention parents reported two or more emergency department visits in the past 12 months) (Coker et al., 2016).

Finally, a well-known program designed to support early literacy, Reach Out and Read, provides caregivers of young children with free, age-appropriate books and anticipatory guidance on the importance of child literacy at each well-child care visit to promote caregiver-child reading. As noted in a recent review, the existing evidence on this program is limited by nonrandom designs, data collected by self-report, and high participant dropout rates (Yeager Pelatti et al., 2014). That said, a recent cross-sectional survey of eight Reach Out and Read sites found that caregivers provided with at least four books read to their children more often than those who received fewer books (Rikin et al., 2015). Other observational studies of the program also have found that it is associated with improvement in the home literacy environment for children, particularly for parents who might otherwise face obstacles in this regard, with parents participating in the program being more likely to report having books in the home and reading aloud to and looking at books with their children (Needlman et al., 2005; Zuckerman, 2009). However, there have been no studies of the reading scores of children whose caregivers participate in Reach Out and Read.

Patient-Centered Medical Homes and Shared Decision Making

The patient-centered medical home is a relatively new model of care in which primary care providers serve as the medical home for patients, offering team-based and coordinated care to increase the receipt of preventive services and reduce the need for specialty or emergency room care. Early findings from a review of randomized controlled trials and longitudinal studies suggest that interventions based on this model have a small positive impact on patient experiences with health care and a small to moderate effect on the delivery of primary care services (Jackson et al., 2013). Family-centered care recognizes a partnership among patients, families, and health care professionals and encourages shared decision making (Scholle et al., 2010), which can improve patients' knowledge about treatment options and risk perceptions and help them take a more active role in decisions about their care (Stacey et al., 2014). In meta-analyses of studies using various designs, shared decision-making interventions designed to engage pediatric patients, parents, or both in medical decisions significantly reduced decisional conflict and improved parents' knowledge of their children's health conditions and how to manage them (Wyatt et al., 2015).

Universal Health Interventions for Parents
for Specific Parenting Behaviors

Many interventions for parents that occur within health care settings support parents in engaging in empirically grounded parenting practices outlined in Chapter 2 that promote the physical health of their children. Examples of these practices include receiving preconception and prenatal care, breastfeeding, complying with recommended immunization schedules, limiting children's screen time, helping children avoid overweight and obesity, reducing children's exposure to environmental tobacco smoke, and educating caregivers on normal infant crying to reduce shaken baby syndrome/abusive head trauma.

Preconception and Prenatal Interventions

Self-identification as a parent often begins long before the birth of a baby. Pregnancy and the postpartum period serve as the transition period for becoming a parent as both mothers and fathers anticipate changes in their roles, prepare for the upcoming birth, and recall important aspects of their own childhoods (Leon, 2009). Parental attachment starts to develop during pregnancy, facilitated by fetal movement as well as biological and hormonal changes in the mother. Feeling the baby move or seeing the fetus on ultrasound has been shown to significantly increase feelings of attachment, and there are even surveys for measuring maternal-fetal attachment during pregnancy (Pisoni et al., 2014).

As a universal parenting intervention, family planning helps optimize the timing of pregnancy and defer conception for individuals who do not desire children or do not feel ready to have a child under their current circumstances. More than one-half of pregnancies in the United States are unintended. These pregnancies can have serious negative consequences for parents as well as for children, including complications with pregnancy and delivery; exposure to illicit substances in utero; low birth weight; and higher risk of infant death, abuse, and developmental delays (Finer and Zolna, 2014; Institute of Medicine, 1995; Sawhill and Venator, 2015). Family planning can include efforts both to delay the onset of sexual activity among young people and to increase access to and use of birth control among those who are sexually active but do not currently desire pregnancy (Finer and Zolna, 2014). Family planning can be particularly valuable for populations at high risk for unintended pregnancy, including adolescents, individuals who abuse substances, and parents with severe mental illness (Institute of Medicine, 1995; Seeman, 2010; Strunk, 2008). A randomized intervention in North Carolina enrolled adolescent mothers with their first child in the Adolescent Parenting Program, which offers case management and peer group meetings aimed at keeping adolescents in school and preventing a rapid second pregnancy (Sangalang et al., 2006). Compared with usual care, the program did not reduce time to second birth among participants as a whole, but the time to next birth was significantly longer for 12- to 16-year-olds participating in the program. (The Adolescent Parenting Program is discussed further in Chapter 5.) In a longitudinal study, adolescent mothers offered subdermal contraceptive implants immediately postpartum had significant reductions in rapid repeat pregnancy compared with controls, as most had retained the implant 1 year after delivery (Tocce et al., 2012).

Preconception and prenatal health visits are universal strategies for optimizing maternal health and well-being prior to and during pregnancy and promoting healthy child development. As discussed in Chapter 1, exposures in the in utero environment can affect the developing fetus in ways that shape health across the life span (Institute of Medicine and National Research Council, 2009; Tsankova et al., 2007; van Ijzendoorn et al., 2011). Prior to conception, people can initiate many health behaviors with strong evidence for improving child birth and developmental outcomes. These behaviors include folic acid supplementation to reduce neural tube defects (De-Regil et al., 2010); weight loss for obese mothers to prevent stillbirth and infant death (Aune et al., 2014); and cessation of tobacco use (discussed further below) to reduce the risk for pregnancy complications, low birth weight, and preterm delivery. Preconception and prenatal services also are important for identifying and providing intervention for women with such conditions as psychosocial stress (e.g., depression, anxiety, job strain), which during pregnancy is associated with preterm birth and low birth weight (Gold and Marcus, 2008; Loomans et al., 2013), and mental illness, which can increase the risk of fetal death and behavioral and mental health problems in children (Lancaster et al., 2010; O'Donnell et al., 2014).

After conception, universal parenting programs promote healthy pregnancy and delivery, often through education and counseling to increase parents' knowledge of child development and use of effective parenting practices. For example, California tested a Kit for New Parents available through prenatal care providers, delivery hospitals, home visits, and other means that provides new and expecting parents with free pregnancy and early childhood information. The kit led to a significant increase in parent knowledge at 2-month follow-up (based on an assessment of sleep safety, infant feeding and nutrition, early learning, accessing child care, low-cost medical care for babies, and smoking cessation) compared with controls in a quasi-experimental study (Neuhauser et al., 2007). Also, nearly half of mothers who received the kit reported improved parenting practices, with significant differences seen between participants and controls at 14-month follow-up in frequency of reading to their children, steps taken to child-proof their homes, taking children for routine medical visits, and use of safer bottle-feeding practices. These gains were particularly strong for Spanish-speaking mothers, suggesting that videos and written materials may be useful for such interventions as they can be easily translated into other languages (Neuhauser et al., 2007).

Childbirth classes for expecting parents are widely available. Some medical and community centers also offer classes in newborn care, first aid, breastfeeding, and infant sleep. However, such classes have not been studied for their effects on promoting evidence-based knowledge, attitudes, and practices.

The use of group visits for prenatal care has attracted strong interest because of the potential for peer support. While group care appears to result in high participant satisfaction, however, a recent Cochrane review found only four eligible studies of group prenatal care and noted no differences in either maternal or infant birth or health outcomes (Catling et al., 2015). Centering Pregnancy is a proprietary model for group prenatal care (Mittal, 2011) that has been given a "strong" evidence rating by the Agency for Healthcare Research and Quality (2015). Groups of 8 to 10 women meet with a health care provider to discuss nutrition, stress management, breastfeeding, and other issues. One large randomized controlled trial examined the impact of this model on key outcomes, including adequacy of prenatal care and rates of preterm birth. Analysis of data from individuals who enrolled and participated (N = 993) showed that those in the intervention received better prenatal care, had fewer preterm births, were more likely to initiate breastfeeding, and had better prenatal knowledge relative to those receiving usual care (Ickovics et al., 2007). Sites using the model have reported an enhanced capacity to serve nonpregnant patients, as the group sessions free up resources previously used to provide individual visits (Agency for Healthcare Research and Quality, 2015).

All of these programs address knowledge, attitudes, and practices focused on improving children's physical and mental health at birth and beyond. However, some researchers have asserted that the sources of disparities in birth outcomes (e.g., the increased risk for preterm birth and infant mortality among African American women relative to other women) are isolated not only to the 9 months of pregnancy but also arise from parents' own developmental trajectories (Lu and Halfon, 2003). This view implies that support for parents may need to start with support for positive environments, health behaviors, and opportunities focused on reducing risks for women long before they actually conceive. As discussed further in Chapter 5, some evidence indicates that school-based clinics that provide prenatal care for teenagers in the school setting increase the uptake of health care and also encourage adolescents to stay in school. These programs have been shown to reduce absenteeism and dropout rates, help in identifying potential developmental delays among children born to teenagers, improve birth weights, and encourage the use of contraception in correlational and qualitative research (Griswold et al., 2013; Strunk, 2008).

Breastfeeding

A systematic review of 10 randomized controlled studies of primary care-based educational interventions designed to improve breastfeeding practices among low-income women found that such interventions are effective in encouraging mothers to initiate breastfeeding as well as to continue breastfeeding 3 months postpartum. Successful programs often involved ongoing brief follow-up sessions with health care providers (Ibanez et al., 2012). In another review of randomized controlled studies conducted primarily in the United States and other Western nations, breastfeeding interventions using lactation consultants and counselors who provide antenatal education and postnatal support were found to be associated with increased initiation of breastfeeding and increased exclusive breastfeeding rates (Patel and Patel, 2015).

A lack of research exists on how to support breastfeeding effectively among adolescent mothers in the United States, whose breastfeeding rates are disproportionately low (Sipsma et al., 2013; Wambach et al., 2011). In one randomized study (N = 289), predelivery and postnatal education and counseling from lactation consultants who were registered nurses and peer counselors significantly increased breastfeeding duration, but not initiation or exclusive breastfeeding, in adolescent mothers (Wambach et al., 2011).

Complying with Recommended Immunization Schedules

Health care providers and educational interventions delivered in health care settings play an important role in parents' immunization practices (Dunn et al., 1998; Hofstetter et al., 2015; Mergler et al., 2013; Vannice et al., 2011; Wallace et al., 2014; Yaqub et al., 2014). Such simple tools as patient reminders and health care providers talking to parents about vaccination are associated with higher rates of child immunization (Hofstetter et al., 2015; Szilagyi et al., 2000). Experimental studies indicate that moderately intensive interventions also are effective. In a cluster randomized trial, parents recruited from primary health care centers who received an information leaflet on the measles, mumps, rubella vaccine and/or participated in a parent meeting addressing immunization experienced a decrease in decisional conflict regarding child immunization after receiving the intervention. Those who participated in the parent meeting were significantly more likely to have a fully vaccinated child than those who only received the information leaflet (Jackson et al., 2011). In another randomized trial, Dunn and colleagues (1998) found that videotape was more effective than written material in increasing parents' knowledge about immunization, but actual uptake of the practice was not measured. Little evidence exists on how to reduce parental refusal of vaccination (Sadaf et al., 2013).

Limiting Screen Time

Newer health interventions have focused on helping parents limit young children's screen time, such as the time they spend watching television and using computers and hand-held devices, including playing video games. As discussed in Chapter 2, limiting young children's screen time can reduce sedentary behavior associated with increased risk for future overweight (see also the discussion of overweight and obesity below) (Gable et al., 2007; Lumeng et al., 2006). In randomized controlled trials, family-based interventions designed to reduce screen time that include a parental component of medium to high intensity have been the most effective, and these programs appear to be most beneficial for preschool-age children (Marsh et al., 2014). Brief primary care interventions also may be effective. In an experimental study involving English- and Spanish-speaking parents, parents who watched a short video or received a handout on reducing children's exposure to television violence, compared with parents who received standard primary care, were more likely to report reductions in their children's media viewing habits and exposure to media violence 2 weeks postintervention. Parents who watched the brief video were slightly less likely to report a change in media viewing habits and slightly more likely to report a reduction in exposure to media violence relative to parents who received the handout (Aragon et al., 2013).

Helping Children Avoid Overweight and Obesity

The rapid increase in the percentage of children who are considered overweight or obese in the United States (currently about 30%) has led to efforts to address the issue through multiple settings, including primary care (Taveras et al., 2011). Obesity in childhood often persists into adulthood and is related to a myriad of adverse health outcomes, including diabetes, hyperlipidemia, and hypertension, among others. Most health care settings with interventions related to child obesity focus on children who are already overweight or obese rather than on primary prevention. One systematic review found that only 8 of 31 randomized controlled trials in primary care demonstrated significant benefits with respect to child weight (Seburg et al., 2015). The review also noted that all of the interventions with positive outcomes—particularly those focused on young children—included a parent-targeted component. Newer research examining the role of motivational interviewing for parents of overweight children in primary care shows promising outcomes although this work is still in early develop-ment (Resnicow et al., 2015).

Reducing Environmental Tobacco Exposure

One of the most extensively evaluated interventions is cessation of tobacco for parents who smoke. In the United States, about 9 percent of women overall self-report smoking during pregnancy, and rates are much higher in some communities (Child Trends Databank, 2015). Tobacco use during pregnancy is associated with prematurity, growth restriction, and infant death. While the U.S. Preventive Services Task Force does not specifi-cally target parents, it has issued Grade A recommendations that clinicians ask all adults and all pregnant women about tobacco use and provide counseling for smokers (U.S. Preventive Services Task Force, 2009). Many tobacco cessation programs for parents also involve identifying smokers at well-child exams, in the hospital during delivery, and during postpartum care, although some of the longitudinal interventions take place in the home setting or via telephone. While several programs targeted to parents of young children focus on outpatient settings (Winickoff et al., 2003), there has been growing interest in hospital interventions targeting caregivers who smoke for cases in which children are hospitalized for tobacco-sensitive ill-nesses, such as asthma, other respiratory diseases, or infection (Chan et al., 2005; Ralston and Roohi, 2008).

A systematic review identified 13 experimental and quasi-experimental studies on interventions designed to assist families of young children with smoking reduction and cessation (Brown et al., 2015). Ten of these studies were focused on reducing child exposure to environmental tobacco smoke, and most of them found positive outcomes, such as use of household re-strictions on smoking or less smoking. Approaches that focused on smok-ing cessation and relapse prevention among parents were less successful. However, the heterogeneity among the interventions reviewed prevented the authors from drawing firm conclusions about essential components associated with success (Brown et al., 2015). In a separate meta-analysis of randomized controlled trials and controlled clinical trials of interventions aimed at preventing children's exposure to tobacco smoke delivered primar-ily in the context of health care (including such components as provision of educational materials, counseling, and telephone check-ins), a small but sta-tistically significant benefit was noted based on parent self-report. Studies in which child biomarkers were collected showed lower exposure to tobacco smoke for those whose parents participated in the interventions, but these findings were not significant (Rosen et al., 2014). Finally, a novel approach to promoting cessation of tobacco use among parents through primary care is a pilot program that includes electronic health record prompts for exposure to tobacco smoke at well-child visits, as well as decision support, education, and a referral to the state quit hotline (Sharifi et al., 2014).

Educating Caregivers on Normal Infant Crying

Typically delivered by health care professionals, the Period of PURPLE Crying Program aims to educate caregivers about normal infant crying given where the infant is in his or her development and thereby prevent shaken baby syndrome/abusive head trauma. Caregivers learn that there is a unique developmental phase beginning at age 2 weeks through age 3-4 months during which infants may cry for hours despite efforts to soothe them, that shaking a baby can be fatal, and that alternatives (such as walking away) can be used instead (Barr, 2012; Reese et al., 2014). Even though this program is currently classified as promising by the California Evidence-Based Clearinghouse for Child Welfare, the concern about crying as a precursor to abuse (especially abusive head trauma) is supported by evidence showing that teaching parents about typical crying and how to respond effectively is beneficial. In one study, the program's approach was associated with a significant reduction in cases of infants ages 0-5 months who were brought to the emergency department primarily because of crying (with no other underlying medical condition) by 29.5 percent relative to before the program was implemented (Barr et al., 2015). The Period of PURPLE Crying Program has been or is in the process of being implemented in a number of health care facilities throughout the United States (National Center on Shaken Baby Syndrome, 2013).

Public Education Approaches

As noted in Chapter 3, public education has increased general awareness of some positive parenting knowledge, attitudes, and practices among parents and families. Some public education initiatives use media to disseminate information relevant to promoting parenting knowledge, attitudes, and practices to a broad audience. An example is the universal component of the Triple P-Positive Parenting Program, referred to as Triple P level 1. (The full Triple P system is described in Chapter 5.) Triple P level 1 uses a coordinated media and communication strategy targeting all parents and other members of the community to destigmatize parents' seeking and participating in parenting support programs, counter parent-blaming messages in the media, and connect parents with supportive resources and programs. Messages are delivered using newsletters, brochures, posters, radio and televisions spots, and other media (Shapiro et al., 2015; Triple P-Positive Parenting Program, 2016a). A number of controlled evaluations have found that parents who participate in Triple P show improved quality of parenting compared with controls (Hoath and Sanders, 2002; Sanders et al., 2000; Turner and Sanders, 2006; Zubrick et al., 2005). To the committee's knowledge, however, no studies have evaluated the specific effects of Triple P level 1 in changing parenting-related knowledge, attitudes, or practices at the individual or community level.

Other media efforts focused on parenting are organization driven. ZERO TO THREE, for example, is a nonprofit organization founded by experts in child development, health, and mental health that disseminates evidence-based parenting information nationwide. Based on the premise that children's earliest years are a period of substantial growth during which experiences can have lasting impacts, ZERO TO THREE has created a variety of resources to educate parents about how to nurture children during this important developmental stage. Tools include tip sheets, brochures, podcasts, and videos on a range of parenting-related topics, such as what parents should expect from their children given their age and steps parents can take at each developmental stage to help their children acquire various skills (e.g., language, communication, thinking, self-control); how to promote young children's social-emotional development and school readiness; and how to address challenging behaviors (ZERO TO THREE, 2015).

The Centers for Disease Control and Prevention also has developed a number of parenting resources, including information on developmental milestones and parenting tips in such areas as creating structure and rules for children, using consequences, giving directions, and using time-out. Videos and other tools are designed to help parents practice these skills (Centers for Disease Control and Prevention, 2016).

Several public health education campaigns in clinics and hospitals have proven successful. An example, reviewed in Chapter 3, is the Safe to Sleep campaign (previously known as Back to Sleep), which was thought to have played a significant role in reducing the incidence of sudden infant death syndrome (SIDS) over the past two decades (U.S. Department of Health and Human Services, 2015b). Much of the Safe to Sleep information is provided in hospital settings prior to postpartum discharge and in outpatient clinics. Similarly, use of media for wide dissemination of information about helmet safety, coupled with distribution of free and reduced-price helmets, in the National Safe Kids campaign is believed to have increased knowledge among parents about the importance of children wearing helmets during bicycling and other wheeled sports and increased children's helmet use (Morris et al., 1994; Rouzier and Alto, 1995). Other examples with documented success range from tobacco control, to seat belt use, to reduced use of illicit drugs (Hornik, 2002).

The literature on successful public health campaigns identifies characteristics conducive to success (Randolph and Viswanath, 2004). These include maximizing exposure to targeted messages among the audience; using social marketing tools to create the appropriate messages for distribution, drawing on "message effect" theories (Storey et al., 2008); and creating associated structural conditions, such as a supportive environment or opportunities to support the audience in making the recommended changes. The reach of the communication effort, as well as the campaign's intensity (e.g., how often individuals are exposed to the message), duration, and messaging approach and whether it is used in combination with other elements, also may influence the extent of its impact (Boles et al., 2014; Friend and Levy, 2002).

Likewise, certain factors can reduce the success of public health campaigns. This is the case, for example, when individuals become confused or they develop distrust as a result of competing messages advocating behaviors inconsistent with or contradictory to those being promoted by a campaign (Carpenter et al., 2015; Nagler, 2014). Another characteristic of the contemporary information environment that presents a significant challenge to public health campaigns is the generation of a large body of information and data on a range of topics and the dissemination of such information on increasingly proliferating information delivery platforms (Viswanath et al., 2012). Also posing a challenge are differences among social groups in the generation, manipulation, and distribution of information at the group level and differences in access to and ability to take advantage of information at the individual level, a phenomenon characterized as communication inequalities (Viswanath, 2006).

Despite these challenges, public health campaigns can be an effective tool for reaching a large and heterogeneous population at a much lower cost than many other forms of interventions. And information and communication technologies make it possible to customize and tailor information to the needs of the parents based on their background and social circumstances. The use of information and communication technologies is discussed further later in this chapter.

Instruction in Parenting for Adolescents in the General Population

Part of the committee's task was to describe "key periods of intervention that are more effective in supporting parenting capacity—beginning in high school or even earlier" (see Box 1-2 in Chapter 1). The committee interpreted this part of its task as including individuals of high school age and younger in the general population who are not pregnant or parents. (See Chapter 5 for a discussion of interventions for adolescent parents.) However, scarce scientific evidence supports the premise that informing individuals about the challenges of parenting during high school or earlier will help lower pregnancy rates or improve future parenting among those who do become parents. Evaluations of infant simulation programs, including the well-known "Baby Think it Over" (BTIO: now marketed by

Realityworks as "RealCare Baby"), have not yet demonstrated a direct relationship between participating in such programs and reduced pregnancy rates or improved parenting.

Some evidence from longitudinal research does point to a prospective association between perceived benefits of childbearing and subsequent pregnancy among young women wishing to avoid pregnancy (Rocca et al., 2013). Additional longitudinal data show that positive attitudes toward an adolescent birth may be predictive of a subsequent birth (Rosengard et al., 2004). The converse also may be true—that adverse attitudes toward adolescent parenting may be predictive of delayed childbearing, although this has not been shown.

Some, but not unequivocal, evidence indicates that participating in BTIO resulted in changes in adolescents' perceptions with regard to the costs and rewards of adolescent parenting. For example, Somers (2013) used an experimental design and a 1-year follow-up with middle schoolers from low-income families in an urban district to test BTIO. The program instilled a more realistic perception of their lack of readiness among the BTIO groups; however, none of the other expected outcomes—changes in sexual behavior, contraceptive use, personal intentions to avoid teenage pregnancy, sexual attitudes, and actual pregnancy rates—was seen. Some of these effects could be due to the relatively low rate of sexual activity even after 1 year.

Roberts and McCowan (2004) implemented a randomized controlled trial of an intervention combining the New York State parenting curriculum (which focused on reflection-based parenting skills with specific child care competencies) and exposure to BTIO, with the control group experiencing only the BTIO curriculum. Their findings, based on a sample of high school students in a rural community, show that the infant simulator is an effective tool for teaching child care skills in that the students more often expressed their belief that parenting is a skill that takes time and patience to learn, that teenagers cannot afford to raise a baby, that raising a child and continuing one's education is difficult, and that teenagers should abstain from sexual behaviors.

Herrman and colleagues (2011) concluded that 79 teens in a single-group study using a pre- and post-test design showed no changes in perceptions following six weekly BTIO classes and a weekend infant simulator experience. The committee agrees with their conclusion that "until such a time as a multiple site, large sample, randomized study with control groups using a valid instrument to measure outcomes is conducted, the use of infant stimulators will remain controversial" (Herrman et al., 2011, p. 327). It is possible that the use of infant simulators as part of a more comprehensive pregnancy prevention program providing accurate information about both abstinence and contraception could change attitudes about becoming pregnant and encourage a reduction in unprotected sexual intercourse. Many effective pregnancy prevention programs do include exercises aimed at getting adolescents to consider the untoward impact on their lives if they become parents. Programs such as BTIO could reinforce this message, although this is not a known effect of the program. However, the committee found no direct evidence as to whether teaching youth in the general population about parenting has an impact on their future behavior as parents.

Couple Relationship Education

Over the past two decades, concerns about the state of family life in the United States have led to the creation of many general programs designed to strengthen couple relationships, prevent the emergence of conflict and violence, and increase fathers' positive involvement with their children. Generally characterized as couple relationship education (Cowan et al., 2010; Panter-Brick et al., 2014), these programs have focused primarily on improving couples' communication, although a very few, using clinically trained staff, also focus on parenting. Couple relationship education programs initially were targeted to middle-class couples early in their marriage and not already in marital or relationship distress. More recently, there have been efforts to provide services for couples that are at risk by virtue of low income but not otherwise identified as experiencing serious relationship difficulties.

Two relatively large-scale couple relationship education initiatives have been funded and evaluated by the federal government. Building Strong Families (Wood et al., 2014), which included three different couple relationship intervention approaches, was conducted across eight U.S. sites, with 5,102 low-income, unmarried couples being randomly assigned to intervention and control conditions. The couples were not identified as having specific relationship difficulties. The Supporting Healthy Marriage Program (Hsueh et al., 2012) was a randomized controlled trial involving 6,298 low-income married couples, expecting or with a child, at eight sites assigned randomly either to one of four couples-group programs plus a family support worker or to a no-treatment control condition. The results for Building Strong Families appear to be limited, although there is some evidence for a possible impact on conflict in low-income families. Self-report and observational measures suggest that the Supporting Healthy Marriage Program changed the way participants viewed their marriage, as well as the extent to which they were able to implement the skills taught by the program curricula (Cowan and Cowan, 2014).

A number of smaller programs have shown evidence of success (Cowan and Cowan, 2014; Faircloth et al., 2011; Feinberg et al., 2010; Pinquart and Teubert, 2010). One of these programs (Supporting Father Involvement) works with parents about to have a child. A consistent body of research finds that marital satisfaction often decreases following the birth of a child, and marital conflict emerges or worsens. This program provides a 16-week group course to either the couple or just the father. Randomized controlled research involving several hundred families found reductions in parenting stress; stability in couples' relationship satisfaction; and stability or reductions in children's hyperactivity, social withdrawal, and psychological symptoms compared with families in a control group (Cowan and Cowan, 2000). Reduction in parents' violent problem solving was linked to reductions in children's aggression. In another randomized controlled trial involving parents of children entering kindergarten, positive effects were found on both mothers' and fathers' marital satisfaction and the children's adaptation (hyperactivity and aggression), according to their teachers (Cowan et al., 2011).

WIDELY USED INTERVENTIONS

Beyond the health care system, the most widely used approaches to strengthening and supporting parenting are home visiting programs; programs focused on helping parents provide cognitive stimulation in the home through educational activities involving reading, language, and math; efforts at providing parenting education in the context of classroom-based ECE programs; and efforts to increase parent engagement in school settings and school-related activities (prekindergarten through grade 3). These are usually voluntary programs aimed at enhancing parenting knowledge, skills, and practices; improving the parent-child relationship and the quality of parent-child interactions; improving children's school readiness and well-being; and preventing poor outcomes for children. The programs vary in their core features (e.g., requirements for staff training, number of sessions, cost to implement), target populations, and the amount of evidence of effectiveness available to guide policy and program decision making. Because these programs may cost several thousand dollars per participant per year, they often are targeted to those families considered to be in greatest need of additional support. Some programs, such as Head Start, require that families meet income requirements (e.g., a certain poverty level), and others, such as the home visiting program Durham Connects, are limited to individuals living within a specific geographic area. In addition, as described in Chapter 3, the actual numbers of families enrolled in these programs represent only a fraction of those who are eligible for them.

Home Visiting Programs

Prenatal, infant, and early childhood home visiting is a relationship-based mode of service delivery in which a professional or paraprofessional home visitor provides services in the family home using a prescribed home visiting model or curriculum. Home visiting programs have specific goals and range from truly universal programs for new parents in the community in which it is offered to targeted programs that select families based on important descriptive characteristics (e.g., first-time pregnant woman early in her pregnancy) or key risk factors. Across models, the home visitor's aims generally include supporting parents in their parenting role, facilitating positive parent-child interactions and relationships, reducing risks of harm, and promoting good parenting practices. Because the intervention is provided where families' daily lives take place, a potential benefit of home visiting is the ability to tailor services to meet families' specific needs (Johnson, 2009). Visits usually last 60 to 90 minutes and occur regularly over the course of 6 months to 2 years, with some long-term models serving families prenatally through age 5. These relatively intensive services usually are targeted to families with children at the highest risk for poor outcomes and those who are unlikely to enter kindergarten with the preacademic skills needed to make the most of formal schooling. Home visiting services generally are voluntary, although in some cases they may be court mandated (for example, in cases of child abuse and neglect). Although many home visiting programs target pregnant women and mothers, some include fathers in visits, and others provide separate visits for mothers and fathers (Sandstrom et al., 2015).

The roots of home visiting in the United States trace back to nurse and teacher home visiting in 19th-century England (Wasik and Bryant, 2001). The more than 250 home visiting programs implemented and studied at the state and local levels in the United States during the late 20th and early 21st centuries reflected those public health and education roots as well as an emphasis on prevention of child maltreatment (Boller et al., 2010; Paulsell et al., 2010). Programs focused on pregnant women and newborns often were run by public health departments and child welfare agencies, and those focused on ECE or on special education services often were run by a human service or education agency (Boller et al., 2010; Daro, 2006).

In fiscal year 2015, the federal home visiting program served about 145,500 parents and children in all 50 states, the District of Columbia, and 5 territories (Health Resources and Services Administration, 2016). There are also a number of state-based home visiting programs. In 2009, the most recent year for which the committee could find data, 40 states reported that they had state-based home visiting programs. Most states supported one or two models (Johnson, 2009), with 5 states reporting that they supported three or more, for a total of 70 state-based home visiting programs across the 40 states (Johnson, 2009). Over the past 20 years, the development of national home visiting programs with national offices and a support infrastructure for implementation has grown (Daro, 2011; Daro and Benedetti, 2014). States, counties, and municipalities around the country have implemented different models, some that are branded and have some evidence of effectiveness and some that are home grown and have not been evaluated (Johnson, 2009).

Home Visiting Logic Model: Changing Parenting Knowledge, Attitudes, and Practices to Improve Child Outcomes

As depicted by the prenatal and early childhood home visiting logic model in Figure 4-1, some of the problems home visiting is designed to address include poor birth outcomes (low birth weight), child maltreatment, and lack of school readiness. Historically, funding agencies and communities that developed home visiting programs or selected from existing programs chose models that best suited the needs of the families they served and the particular outcomes they were trying to improve. Regardless of the specific mode, the underlying assumption of these programs is that the home is a comfortable, convenient setting for expectant parents and parents of young children to receive supports and services. As described below, a growing body of research points to the importance of high-quality implementation (such as collaboration among local public and private partners, program developers, and funders and oversight of service provision [training, quality assurance]) in achieving impacts on targeted knowledge, attitudes, and practices and child outcomes. Assuming an implementation system that brings families into services and provides high-quality visits as intended, targeted short-term outcomes include decreased parenting stress, depression, and isolation and improved parenting knowledge, attitudes, and practices.

As depicted in Figure 4-1, home visiting programs aim to support several evidence-based parenting knowledge, attitudes, and practices identified in Chapter 2. Visits are designed to improve parents' knowledge of children's development and how adults can support children's exploration and learning. Some programs attempt to enhance parents' attitudes about their own efficacy in the parenting role, given that parents who do not believe they can be effective in supporting their child's development and learning may be unable to overcome that mind-set and engage fully in the home visits. Home visiting's primary pathway to the targeted long-term child outcomes is through improvements in the parent-child emotional relationship and the quality of parent-child interactions (e.g., how sensitive and responsive parents are when interacting with their young children). Other specific aims of programs may include increasing parents' use of positive guidance and decreasing their use of harsh punishment. Some programs target household and vehicular safety.

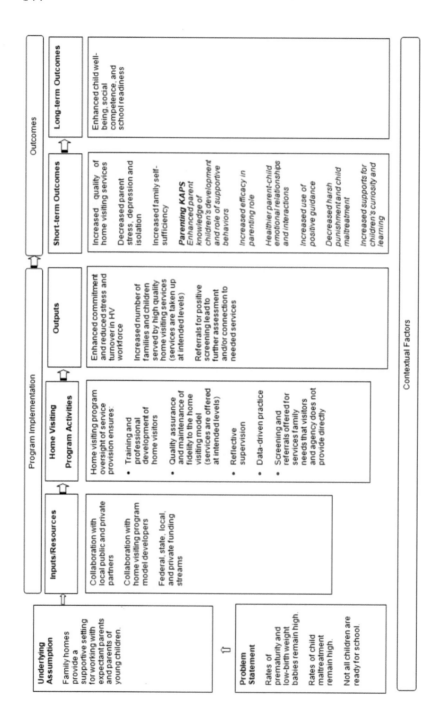

FIGURE 4-1 Illustrative prenatal and early childhood home visiting logic model.
NOTE: HIV = home visiting; KAPs = knowledge, attitudes, and practices.

Throughout this section, three home visiting models are profiled to illustrate how model activities are linked to outcomes and to highlight examples of the evidence for their impacts on parenting knowledge, attitudes, and practices and child outcomes. Box 4-1 describes the Nurse-Family Partnership (NFP)®, a model rooted in a public health approach for which multiple longitudinal impact studies have been conducted. Box 4-2 describes Parents as Teachers (PAT)®, a model with roots in ECE for which a number of studies exist. Finally, Durham Connects, described in Box 4-3, is one of the newer models, focused on universal strategies for ensuring that families receive the services they need, for which two studies were included in the U.S. Department of Health and Human Services' (HHS) 2014 Home Visiting Evidence of Effectiveness (HomVee) review.[3]

Home Visiting and Evidence-Based Policy Making

The Maternal, Infant, and Early Childhood Home Visiting (MIECHV) Program, funded under the Patient Protection and Affordable Care Act (ACA) of 2010, changed the national home visiting landscape considerably by providing $1.5 billion in funding to states, territories, and tribal entities to serve very high-risk families. A distinctive feature of the legislation is its emphasis on research evidence as the basis for the home visiting models states could select (75% of funds had to be allocated to models with evidence of effectiveness [see below], and the other 25% could be used to fund models that were promising if they met certain criteria and states agreed to conduct a rigorous study). In addition, the legislation identified the specific outcome areas that had to be impacted by the selected programs and the performance measures on which the states would have to report each year, which included positive parenting practices and three child outcome areas—child health, child development and school readiness, and reductions in child maltreatment.[4] A national evaluation is also under way to assess MIECHV implementation and impacts (Michalopoulos et al., 2013).

Based on a systematic review of the evidence and the application of strict criteria for what counted as evidence (adapted in part from the U.S. Department of Education's What Works Clearinghouse), the HomVEE project team identified seven national models that met the HHS evidence

---

[3] See http://homvee.acf.hhs.gov/ [August 2016].

[4] It is important to note that requirements for territories and tribal entities were different from those for the states given the available research evidence—no existing home visiting models were originally found that had evidence of effectiveness for tribal populations. Thus, HHS allowed grantees to choose from existing models but required them to conduct an evaluation.

BOX 4-1
Nurse-Family Partnership (NFP)

NFP is designed to improve prenatal health and outcomes, child health and development, and families' economic self-sufficiency and/or maternal life-course development for first-time, low-income mothers. The program consists of one-on-one visits between trained registered nurses and mothers, beginning at pregnancy and concluding when the child turns 2. Along with their professional nursing experience, nurses use input from parents and principles of motivational interviewing (discussed in Chapter 6) to meet program objectives.

NFP has strong evaluation results from randomized controlled trials conducted in New York (Olds et al., 1997), Tennessee (Kitzman et al., 1997), and Colorado (Olds et al., 2002). In all, 135 studies for NFP were released from 1979 to 2012, 31 of which were found to be eligible for review by HomVEE. Of these, 18 were rated high for outcomes in child health and development, maternal health, and family economic self-sufficiency. Specific program effects have included improved prenatal health, fewer childhood injuries, increased intervals between births, improved school readiness, and higher rates of maternal employment.

SOURCE: Administration for Children and Families (2015b).

BOX 4-2
Parents as Teachers (PAT)

PAT serves families from pregnancy through kindergarten entry. Services include one-on-one visits by parent educators, group hands-on learning activities, health and developmental screenings for children, and a resource network. Programs offer families a minimum of 12 home visits annually and are required to provide services for at least 2 years. The goals of PAT include increased parental knowledge of child development, early detection of developmental and health-related issues, prevention of child abuse and neglect, and improved school readiness. Target populations and program duration are identified by program sites.

Between 1979 and 2011, 60 studies of PAT were conducted, 23 of which were eligible for review through HomVEE (2 rated PAT high, and the rest rated PAT moderate or low or overlapped with another study and were not rated). Evidence showed small and inconsistent overall positive effects on parents' knowledge, attitudes, and behavior; no overall improvement in child development or health; and significant improvement in cognitive, communication, social, and self-help development for children in Spanish-speaking households. PAT services have been found to provide the greatest benefit to those also receiving case management services.

SOURCE: Administration for Children and Families (2015c).

BOX 4-3
Durham Connects

Durham Connects is a universal nurse home visiting program available to all families in a defined service area that have newborns between 2 and 12 weeks old. The goals of Durham Connects are to help families promote their children's health and well-being and reduce child abuse and neglect. Visits are conducted by trained nurses who utilize a structured interview protocol to examine families' strengths and potential needs in domains associated with mother and infant well-being and connect families to needed supportive services. Child weight and health checks are also provided. Home visits may start 2-3 weeks after the child's birth. Two additional follow-up home visits are available from the nurse home visitor or through local social services employees.

Evaluations of Durham Connects have found favorable primary and secondary impacts on child health (e.g., reductions in child receipt of emergency care), positive parenting practices, and use of community resources.

SOURCE: Administration for Children and Families (2015a).

---

criteria[5] and to which 75 percent or more of funds had to be allocated (Paulsell et al., 2010): Early Head Start-Home Visiting (EHS-HV), Family Check-Up® for Children, Healthy Families America (HFA)®, Healthy Steps, Home Instruction for Parents of Preschool Youngsters (HIPPY)®, NFP®, and PAT®. In a second HomVEE review, published in 2012, six more models that met the evidence criteria were identified: Child FIRST, Early Intervention Program for Adolescent Mothers (EIP), Early Start (New Zealand), Oklahoma's Community-Based Family Resource and Support (CBFRS) Program, Play and Learning Strategies-Infant (PALS Infant), and SafeCare® Augmented (Avellar et al., 2012). In 2014, 40 models were re-

---

[5] In order to meet HHS' criteria for an evidence-based home visiting program, models must have at least one high- or moderate-quality impact study with favorable, statistically significant impacts for two or more outcomes, or at least two high- or moderate-quality impact studies of the model using nonoverlapping participant samples with one or more favorable, statistically significant impacts in the same domain. In either case, impacts must be found for either the full sample or, if found for subgroups only, be replicated in the same domain in at least two studies using nonoverlapping participant samples. For models meeting these criteria based on randomized trials only, significant impacts must be sustained for at least 1 year after participants were enrolled and must be reported in a peer-reviewed journal. Single-case studies may be considered if at least five studies on the intervention meet the What Works Clearing-houses' pilot design standards, are conducted by three research teams without overlapping authorship, and the combined number of cases is at least 20 (U.S. Department of Health and Human Services, 2016).

viewed, and 4 more met the HHS criteria (Avellar et al., 2014): Durham
Connects/Family Connects, Family Spirit®, Maternal Early Childhood Sus-
tained Home-Visiting (MECSH) Program, and Minding the Baby®. Two
additional models were included in a September 2015 update: the Health
Access Nurturing Development Services (HANDS) Program and Healthy
Beginnings (Avellar et al., 2015).

Table 4-1 shows the number of favorable primary positive parent and
child outcomes compared with the total number of outcomes reviewed for
all of the models reviewed in 2010, 2012, 2014, and 2015.[6] The table also
notes where unfavorable or ambiguous outcomes were found.

A Note on Program and Evaluation Logic

It is important to note that the logic of home visiting programs and
their evaluations may not always align. As depicted in the generic home
visiting logic model in Figure 4-1, for example, parenting knowledge, attitudes, and practices are among the hypothesized short-term outcomes en
route to the longer-term outcome of child well-being. As seen in Table 4-1,
positive parenting practices were not measured in the evaluations of some
programs; however, this does not necessarily mean that parenting was not
part of the program logic model. For example, the program description for
Child FIRST states that parenting enhancements are expected as a result of
the program, but parenting practices were not measured in the study that
provided evidence of the program's effectiveness based on impacts on child
outcomes (Lowell et al., 2011).

Home Visiting Program Impacts

In addition to findings from the HomVEE review, this section draws
on findings from a paper commissioned by the committee on evidence for
investing in parenting programs at scale, which includes six programs that
were not included in the HomVEE review. These programs have rigorous
designs that differ from MIECHV in either program delivery approach or
outcomes.[7]

---

[6]Primary outcomes refer to those that were measured through direct observation or assessment, administrative data, or self-report using a standardized instrument. Table 4-1 does
not include impacts on "secondary outcomes"—those self-reported by means other than a
standardized instrument.

[7]The papers commissioned by the committee are in the study public access file and can be
requested at https://www8.nationalacademies.org/cp/ManageRequest.aspx?key=49669 [Oc-
tober 2016].

TABLE 4-1 Number of Favorable Impacts of Home Visiting for Primary Outcomes Compared with Total Number of Outcomes Reviewed for Models with Evidence of Effectiveness, by Outcome Domain

	Outcome				
	Positive Parenting Practices	Family Economic Self-Sufficiency	Child Health	Child Development and School Readiness	Reductions in Child Maltreatment
Child FIRST	Not measured	Not measured	Not measured	5/16	1/3
Durham Connects/Family Connects	Not measured	Not measured	6/9	Not measured	Not measured
Early Head Start-Home Visiting	3/28	Not measured	Not measured	2/36	Not measured
Early Intervention Program for Adolescent Mothers	0/9	Not measured	8/18	Not measured	Not measured
Early Start (New Zealand)	3/3	Not measured	2/4	2/6	1/2
Family Check-Up for Children	2/2	Not measured	Not measured	3/14	Not measured
Family Spirit	0/5	Not measured	Not measured	10/40	Not measured
Health Access Nurturing Development Services	Not measured	2/3[e]	6/9	Not measured	1/1
Healthy Beginnings	Not measured	Not measured	1/3	Not measured	Not measured
Healthy Families America	2/50	Not measured	0/9	9/43	1/34
Healthy Steps[f]	0/1	Not measured	2/2	0/2	Not measured
Home Instruction for Parents of Preschool Youngsters	1/10	Not measured	Not measured	3/20	Not measured
Maternal Early Childhood Sustained Home-Visiting Program	1/6	Not measured	0/3	Not measured	Not measured

continued

TABLE 4-1 Continued

	Outcome				
	Positive Parenting Practices	Family Economic Self-Sufficiency	Child Health	Child Development and School Readiness	Reductions in Child Maltreatment
Minding the Baby	0/2	Not measured	1/2	Not measured	0/1
Nurse-Family Partnership	4/22	4/21[a]	4/30	5/59	7/25
Oklahoma's Community-Based Family Resource and Support Program	2/7	Not measured	Not measured	Not measured	Not measured
Parents as Teachers	3/50[b]	1/1	0/1	7/66[c]	1/3
Play and Learning Strategies-Infant	11/24[d]	Not measured	Not measured	1/16	Not measured
SafeCare Augmented	Not measured	Not measured	Not measured	Not measured	1/6

NOTE: The table shows the number of favorable outcomes relative to the total number of outcomes. Footnotes indicate when the total number of outcomes includes an unfavorable or ambiguous outcome(s). In accordance with www.homvee.acf.hhs.gov/models.aspx, descriptions of the outcomes are as follows: (1) Favorable: a statistically significant impact on an outcome measure in a direction that is beneficial for children and parents. An impact could be statistically positive or negative, and is determined "favorable" based on the end result. (2) No effect: findings for a program model that are not statistically significant. (3) Unfavorable or ambiguous: a statistically significant impact on an outcome measure in a direction that may indicate potential harm to children and/or parents. An impact could statistically be positive or negative, and is determined "unfavorable or ambiguous" based on the end result. While some outcomes are clearly unfavorable, for other outcomes it is not as clear which direction is desirable. (4) Not measured: current research (meeting HomVEE standards for a high or moderate rating) includes no measures in this domain.

[a]One of the three outcomes were unfavorable or ambiguous.

[b]This report focuses on Healthy Steps as implemented in the 1996 evaluation. HHS has determined that home visiting is not the primary service delivery strategy and the model does not meet current requirements for MIECHV program implementation

[c]One of the 21 outcomes were unfavorable or ambiguous.

[d]Four of the 50 outcomes were unfavorable or ambiguous.

[e]One of the 66 outcomes were unfavorable or ambiguous.

[f]One of the 24 outcomes were unfavorable or ambiguous.

SOURCES: Adapted from www.homvee.acf.hhs.gov/models.aspx; Avellar et al. (2012, 2014, 2015); Paulsell et al. (2010).

Positive parenting practices PALS Infant and NFP had the highest number of favorable impacts on parenting practices (Table 4-1). Across two studies, the HomVEE evidence review found 11 favorable impacts of PALS Infant on parenting behaviors such as contingent responsiveness and maintaining child foci, although it also found a negative impact on redirecting child foci (Landry et al., 2006, 2008). The HomVEE review identified favorable impacts of NFP on a number of parenting beliefs and practices, including cognitive stimulation in the home, reductions in dangerous exposures in the home, beliefs, worry, mother-infant interaction, and sensitive interaction across a number of studies (Kitzman et al., 1997; Olds et al., 1986, 1994). Among other models with impacts on parenting practices, the specific parenting outcomes affected within and across models vary, even for those programs that share a similar theoretical grounding or logic model.

In addition, as can be seen in Table 4-1 for several programs, the number of outcomes for which no impacts were found is high, exceeding the number of outcomes for which significant impacts were found; moreover, impacts may have been found at one point of measurement but not another. For example, EHS-HV participants were no more likely than controls to report reading to their children every day at the end of the program. Two years after the program ended, however, participants were significantly more likely than controls to say that they read to their children daily (Jones Harden et al., 2012). Getting Ready, an add-on to EHS-HV that provides parents with additional training in effective engagement in routine activities that support child behavior and learning, showed changes in parent warmth, encouragement of autonomy, and supports for children's skills and appropriate guidance, but no changes in the quality of behavior supporting children's learning (Knoche et al., 2012). The effect of Getting Ready on child outcomes was not assessed.

Overall, while many individual evaluations of home visiting programs have shown impacts on parenting practices tied to positive developmental outcomes, the average impacts of home visiting on parenting practices are not large. Nor is there a strong pattern of effects on parenting practices across evaluation studies and home visiting models.

Family economic self-sufficiency Relatively few home visiting programs target or measure effects of home visits on family economic self-sufficiency. The HomVEE review identified several studies in which participation in NFP was associated with reduced rates of subsequent childbearing (Kitzman et al., 1997; Olds et al., 2002, 2004) and lowered use of some forms of public assistance (Olds et al., 2010). In two impact studies, participation in HANDS was associated with significant increases in maternal receipt of WIC (Williams et al., 2014a, 2014b). Other models had positive effects on aspects of parents' self-sufficiency, such as reductions in rates of subsequent childbearing in Minding the Baby (Sadler et al., 2013). Taking into account secondary outcomes (i.e., those self-reported by means other than a standardized instrument), Early Head Start and EIP showed improvements in parents' receipt of education and training (Jones Harden et al., 2012; Koniak-Griffin et al., 2000; U.S. Department of Health and Human Services et al., 2001, 2002).

Child health Several programs, including EIP, Durham Connects (Box 4-3), HANDS, and NFP have had favorable impacts on child health, with some consistent findings across studies. Effects for measures of infant health, such as fewer hospitalizations and emergency room visits, were found for both EIP and Durham Connects (Dodge et al., 2013; Koniak-Griffin et al., 2002, 2003). Participation in HANDS was associated with reductions in preterm births and low birth weight across studies (Williams et al., 2014a, 2014b, 2014c). Two programs included not in the HomVEE review but in the commissioned paper—Rest Routine and the MOM Program—showed impacts on child health. Rest Routine, which focuses on reducing infant irritability or colic, a hypothesized precursor to child maltreatment, was found to reduce the number of hours of child crying and some aspects of parenting stress (Keefe et al., 2006a, 2006b). The MOM Program provides up to 11 home visits to encourage care for the health and development of the baby and use of well-child care and early intervention services if needed (Schwarz et al., 2012). The program had an impact on use of early intervention services, but no differences were seen in rates of developmental delays or cognitive outcomes. Parenting knowledge, attitudes, and practices were not assessed.

Child development and school readiness Family Spirit, HFA, PAT, Child FIRST, and NFP showed the greatest number of favorable impacts on child development and school readiness in the HomVEE review, although there were many null effects for each of these programs. Three programs showed clear evidence of effectiveness: Child FIRST (effects on externalizing problems and language problems [Lowell et al., 2011]); HFA (effects on some behavioral and academic outcomes in at least in two of the three trials in which child outcomes were measured [Caldera et al., 2007; Kirkland and Mitchell-Herzfeld, 2012]); and NFP (but only based on longer-term follow-up [Eckenrode et al., 2010; Kitzman et al., 2010; Olds et al., 2004]). In the commissioned paper, the University of California at Los Angeles Family Development Project is identified as improving child behavior but not cognitive skills (Heinicke et al., 2001). Minding the Baby (Sadler et al., 2013) also demonstrated evidence of efficacy but only for the child's security of attachment, which may or may not translate to long-term benefits (other behavioral and academic skills were not measured in the study of that program).

Effects were less clear for the EHS-HV model (U.S. Department of Health and Human Services et al., 2002), with effects being found only on parent-reported child behavioral measures and only at a later follow-up point (and no effects on cognitive skills being found at any time point). Both trials of Family Spirit showed mixed findings across parent-reported behavioral outcomes, including significant reductions in externalizing problems but not in many other similar behaviors (Barlow et al., 2013; Walkup et al., 2009); academic skills were not measured here. Effects of Healthy Steps on children were not evaluated during the intervention, and no effects were found 2 years after the intervention (Minkovitz et al., 2001, 2007).

Reductions in child maltreatment Of the programs reviewed by HomVEE, NFP showed the greatest number of favorable impacts on child maltreatment. The program had effects on hospitalizations for accidents and injuries and involvement in child protective services (CPS) in some sites and follow-ups, but not consistently across sites and studies (Administration for Children and Families, 2015b). There is also evidence of effects of Child FIRST on reductions in CPS involvement and general child maltreatment (Lowell et al., 2011). The review found improvements in measures of child maltreatment for other programs as well (e.g., HANDS and PAT).

Home Visiting Collaborative for Improvement and Innovation Network

Mary Catherine Arbour, Harvard Medical School and Brigham and Women's Hospital, was invited to present before the committee at one of its open sessions on lessons learned in continuous quality improvement from the Home Visiting Collaborative for Improvement and Innovation Network (HV CoIIN). The HV CoIIN is operated by the Education Development Center, Inc., with funding from the Health Resources and Services Administration (HRSA). Dr. Arbour is the Improvement Advisor for this national initiative that supports the work of a set of MIECHV state grantees. HV CoIIN aims to achieve improvement in outcomes in four areas targeted by home visiting programs: breastfeeding, maternal depression, family engagement, and child development.

HV CoIIN uses the Institute for Healthcare Improvement's Breakthrough Series Collaborative Model (Institute for Healthcare Improvement, 2003), which combines the Model for Improvement and a structured, time-limited collaborative learning model. This model is designed to close the gap between what is known from science about what works and what is happening on the ground to achieve results and facilitate the implementation of improved programs (Arbour, 2015). The collaborative's first step is to select a topic that has a good evidence base but is not always applied in practice. Faculty are recruited to develop a framework and set of changes expected to improve service quality and outcomes, and teams are then formed to participate in the collaborative (including leadership, front-line workers, and end-users). These teams test changes and adapt them to specific contexts, collect data on a number of indicators over time to demonstrate improvement, and share experiences to facilitate learning (Arbour, 2015). HV CoIIN is using this approach to build a culture of inquiry and improvement and enhance the implementation of improvements across a number of the home visiting models included in the MIECHV Program and across the participating states.

HV CoIIN is the first national initiative to apply continuous quality improvement (CQI) methods to evidence-based home visiting programs to improve critical outcomes for vulnerable families with young children ages 0-5. Participating home visiting teams receive training and coaching in the basic quality improvement skills of rapid-cycle hypothesis testing and data use based on the Model for Improvement. The model uses three questions to guide teams to set short-term specific aims: (1) "What are we trying to accomplish?" asks them to define aims specific to their context; (2) "What ideas do we have that can result in improvement?" asks them to use their own ideas to make home visiting work in their specific setting; and (3) "How will we know that a change is an improvement?" asks them to collect and use data to determine how well those ideas work to advance their aims. Drawing on the manufacturing and business sector, teams then subject their ideas to small, rapid-cycle testing using Plan, Do, Study, Act (PDSA).

In addition to applying the Model for Improvement in their local work, the CQI teams apply the Breakthrough Series Collaborative Model by participating in three "Learning Sessions" that bring together local teams, expert faculty, and stakeholders (including model developers and state leaders). Between Learning Sessions, CQI teams test changes in their local settings and gather data to measure the effect of those changes during 4- to 6-month-long "Action Periods." At the first Learning Session, expert faculty presented a vision for home visiting quality and specific changes proposed by HV CoIIN, and CQI teams learned about the Model for Improvement and PDSA cycles. At the second and third Learning Sessions, teams learned from one another as they reported on successes, barriers, and lessons learned in formal presentations, workshops, and informal dialogue and exchange.

Participants in HV CoIIN commit to pursuing shared aims and to reporting a set of shared measures. Every month, data are displayed on run charts and shared transparently across the collaborative and with state and local representatives to facilitate shared learning and rapid diffusion of good ideas.

The mission of HV CoIIN is to achieve breakthrough improvements in selected process and outcome measures, including benchmark areas legislatively mandated for the federal MIECHV Program, while reducing or maintaining program costs. Its mission also includes developing the means to diffuse the learning and improvements resulting from its efforts more widely within participating organizations and to other MIECHV grantees and home visiting agencies. During its first phase (May 2014-August 2015), the collaborative enrolled 12 states and tribes and 33 home visiting agencies using five evidence-based home visiting models serving 3,500 families. HV CoIIN integrates CQI methodologies into existing evidence-based home visiting programs with the goal of disseminating practices known to work, innovating, achieving results more rapidly, building leaders in quality improvement and sustainability in home visiting, and demonstrating the effectiveness of home visiting in large-scale implementation.

Initial data indicate that the learning and improvements resulting from the HV CoIIN efforts have enabled agencies and staff to change their practices so as to affect behaviors in ways that are associated with quality improvements that support outcomes targeted by the collaborative (Arbour, 2015). The collaborative's approach shows promise as a way to work with staff in programs that target parenting knowledge, attitudes, and practices, and has been used in a variety of other health and related fields, including efforts focused on reducing infant mortality (McPherson et al., 2015; Selk et al., 2015).

Programs Promoting Parent Educational Activities in the Early Home Learning Environment

As discussed in Chapter 2, in recent years there has been increased attention to parent behaviors that are associated with children's cognitive development as well as social-emotional skills. Designing interventions that generate large impacts on parent practices in promoting children's cognitive skills has proved difficult. Two large meta-analyses of randomized controlled trials have included evaluations of parent skills training in relation to children's cognitive outcomes. One found that parent training in promoting children's cognitive, academic, and social skills was associated with smaller effects relative to parent training programs that did not include those components (Kaminski et al., 2008). The other found that interventions for new and expecting at-risk parents that focus on the promotion of children's cognitive development (e.g., teaching parents how to use stimulating materials) generate small to very small effects on various noncognitive childhood outcomes, including parent-child relations (Pinquart and Teubert, 2010).

There is, however, some experimental research suggesting that interventions designed to promote parents' provision of stimulating learning experiences do support children's cognitive development, primarily on measures of language and literacy. Intensive parent training in the home or a community setting provided by coaches who visit parents frequently (as often as weekly) have been shown to increase responsive and developmentally stimulating parenting and, in turn, children's early achievement and positive social behavior. Evidence-based models of this approach include Play and Learning Strategies (PALS) (Landry et al., 2006, 2008, 2012); My Baby and Me (which used the PALS curriculum for responsive parenting plus additional training on such topics as developmental milestones, health and safety, and literacy) (Guttentag et al., 2014); Let's Play in Tandem (Ford et al., 2009); the Head Start Research-based Developmentally Informed Parent (REDI-P) Program (Bierman et al., 2015); and the Getting Ready for School Program (Noble et al., 2012).

In PALS and My Baby and Me, parents of infants are coached during 90-minute in-home sessions on contingent responsiveness, joint engagement, interactive communication, and emotional support for their children. Multiple randomized trials of these programs have indicated increased contingent responsiveness, verbal stimulation, and warmth from socially disadvantaged mothers and, in turn, later improvements in children's receptive and/or expressive language skills and complexity of play, as well as more prosocial play with their mothers and fewer behavior problems (Guttentag et al., 2014; Landry et al., 2006, 2008, 2012). It is worth noting, however, that while My Baby and Me produced gains for mothers and children when administered from 4 to 30 months of age, PALS administered during the toddler years produced more positive outcomes for children than it did during infancy alone or across both infancy and toddlerhood. Let's Play in Tandem (Ford et al., 2009) and REDI-P have (Bierman et al., 2015) demonstrated effectiveness in randomized controlled trials with respect to parent engagement during the preschool years, at ages 3 and 4-5, respectively. For Let's Play in Tandem, weekly home visits for 1 year were used to train parents in how to engage children in activities designed to promote vocabulary, emergent literacy, and numeracy skills, as well as self-regulation. Although changes in parenting behaviors were not examined following treatment, significant child-level effects included improved vocabulary, literacy, numeracy, and general academic skills, as well as inhibitory control and social-behavioral skills. For REDI-P, parent training during home visits was focused primarily on developing parenting skills directed at children's social-emotional, self-regulatory, and literacy outcomes, including how to better engage in literacy-based play and learning activities that support children's learning skills and motivation. The intervention improved the richness of parent-child conversations and interactive reading activities.

When the children entered kindergarten, significant differences between treatment and control groups included better self-directed learning, literacy skills, and academic performance for those whose parents had received the trainings (Bierman et al., 2015).

Although generally less intensive than the other in-home and workshop trainings discussed above, several dialogic reading interventions (Arnold et al., 1994; Lonigan and Whitehurst, 1998; Whitehurst et al., 1988, 1994) have been designed to increase parents' engagement with their children during storybook reading by training them to ask open-ended questions, respond to and encourage children's comments and interests, and teach children vocabulary. Experimental evaluations of these interventions have shown them to be effective for improving literacy or language outcomes (e.g., expressive language skills), although these effects appear to be limited to immediately after the end of the intervention and may be most pronounced when complemented by similar interventions within child care/preschool. Similarly, programs designed to tutor parents in reading effectively with their children have demonstrated short-term but not long-term improvements in children's literacy (Mehran and White, 1988). Notably, in these dialogic reading interventions, there is some evidence that video-based instruction and modeling that is complemented by discussion with parents is effective for training parents to better engage in their children's early learning (Arnold et al., 1994; Whitehurst et al., 1988).

There are several other programs with some evidence of impact. In one randomized controlled study, interactions between high-risk parents and their children over developmentally stimulating, age-appropriate learning material (e.g., a book or a toy) followed by review and discussion between parents and child development specialists, were found to improve children's cognitive and language skills at 21 months compared with a control group, and also reduced parental stress (Mendelsohn et al., 2005). In another experimental study, children of mothers who watched a series of short films on talking to children, using praise, using bath time to learn, and looking at books and puzzles, among other topics, followed by discussion with community health workers to encourage mothers to practice the activities with their children, showed significant benefits on measures of cognitive development predictive of academic achievement compared with controls (Chang et al., 2015).

Language interventions for parents of children with developmental disabilities and delays also have shown an impact. An 18-study meta-analysis found that language interventions implemented by parents had a significant and positive effect on the development of receptive and expressive language skills in children ages 18-60 months with and without intellectual disabilities (Roberts and Kaiser, 2011). In another randomized controlled study, Parent-Child Interaction Therapy, which targets child behavior problems through mother's use of child-directed play, improved language production among children ages 20 to 70 months with and at risk of developmental delays compared with a control group (Garcia et al., 2015).

In the Getting Ready for School intervention (Noble et al., 2012), 2-hour weekly workshops with parents over a 15-week period were used to complement existing Head Start teacher-parent workshops for families of children in randomly selected intervention classrooms. The complementary workshops, led by a trained facilitator, focused on teaching parents how to engage with their children at home in activities focused on literacy (e.g., helping their children learn the letters in their names), language (e.g., learning how to ask questions of their children), and math (e.g., helping their children recognize and extend patterns). Although parenting behaviors were not measured, compared with children in comparison classrooms, children of parents in the intervention evidenced improved language and literacy as well as applied problem and math concept scores.

There is also some evidence that aligning home learning contexts for literacy with early elementary school literacy learning is valuable, at least for increasing the frequency of literacy activities in the home of socially disadvantaged children. The Family Literacy Program (Morrow and Young, 1997), for example, encouraged parents to create home centers for parent-child literacy activities that paralleled 1st- to 3rd-grade classroom centers, while also encouraging reading daily, sharing stories, and writing journals together. Parents were guided through monthly group meetings and one-on-one mentorship. In an experimental study, according to parents and children, in-home literacy activities increased in the intervention group relative to controls, and teacher-rated literacy ability and interest improved, although no improvements were evident on a standardized reading assessment.

There is also evidence that transmedia interventions—focused on media content delivered across multiple platforms (e.g., videos, online games, and apps)—can be used to promote parent engagement in the home. From 2010 to 2015, the U.S. Department of Education supported the Ready to Learn initiative, a series of descriptive and experimental studies on parent-caregiver outcomes in supporting children's cognitive (literacy and math) engagement and social-emotional skills. A randomized controlled evaluation study, Supporting Parent-Child Experiences with PEG+CAT Early Math Concepts, conducted by SRI International, addressed the question of how time spent viewing and playing with PBS KIDS educational, non-commercial media at home, in family settings, can foster positive outcomes for children and parents/caregivers (Moorthy et al., 2014). Using videos, online games, and tablet-based apps that allowed caregivers and children to engage with PEG+CAT characters, parents and caregivers in the treatment group reported a higher frequency of joint parent-child use of technology, more joint gameplay, and more conversation connecting digital media and daily life than did nontreatment parents and caregivers. In addition, the study report indicates that children participating in the intervention exhibited statistically significant improvements in the mathematics skill areas of ordinal numbers, spatial relationships, and 3-D shapes compared with children in the nontreatment group. Important study limitations, however, included reliance on parent self-reports, selection bias, and inadequate assessments targeted by the study experience.

Finally, it is worth noting recent findings indicating that information about the importance of engaging in children's learning may not be enough to achieve meaningful behavioral changes among parents. In a randomized field experiment of the Parent and Children Together Program (Mayer et al., 2015)—a 6-week intervention with English- and Spanish-speaking parents of children enrolled in Head Start programs—three behavioral tools were employed (text reminders, goal setting, and social rewards), and parents were provided with information about the importance of reading to children. Findings indicated large increases in usage of a reading app after the 6-week intervention with increases due to the behavioral tools rather than the increased information.

Parenting Education Delivered in the Context of Classroom-Based Early Care and Education Programs

ECE programs provide full- or part-time classroom-based services (center or family child care) for children from birth to age 5. They often include parenting education and other services for families (sometimes starting prenatally) designed to improve the overall circumstances of families and promote parenting knowledge, attitudes, and practices that support children's cognitive and social-emotional development and success in school (Brooks-Gunn et al., 2000; Chase-Lansdale and Brooks-Gunn, 2014; Fantuzzo et al., 2013; Seitz, 1990). ECE programming that involves parents can be structured in several different ways, including (1) comprehensive two-generation programs with components that include multipronged, intensive classroom-based services for children, parenting education, and parent self-sufficiency support (as in Head Start, Early Head Start, and Educare); (2) primarily classroom-based services for children with some parenting education services; and (3) primarily classroom-based services for children with some parent self-sufficiency services.

The logic behind ECE programming that involves parents is the potential for additive effects for the child and family. Children's positive experiences in care can have a direct effect on their outcomes, and if parenting education or parent self-sufficiency outcomes also are achieved, additional benefits may accrue. However, coupling ECE programs with parenting components does entail costs, and with a fixed budget it is difficult to maintain high-quality efforts on both components. Indeed, a meta-analysis showed significant effects of preschool education on children's cognitive and social development but found that provision of additional services tended to be associated with smaller gains (Camilli et al., 2010). Thus, it is important to identify two-generation models likely to generate benefits that justify their added expense and administrative complications.

This section summarizes findings from studies evaluating how ECE programs support parenting and healthy child development. The committee was unable to identify clearinghouses or reviews of classroom-based ECE programs that included parenting supports and thus drew on rigorous studies published in the peer-reviewed literature. Note that the discussion in this section excludes approaches used in the early intervention/special education system.

Head Start and Early Head Start

Head Start and Early Head Start are rigorously evaluated two-generation programs. (A brief description of both programs and numbers of families served can be found in Chapter 3.) In addition to education services directed at children, Head Start and Early Head Start programs are required to provide parents with activities that may include (1) parenting education, including at least two home visits per year whereby teachers give parents information about their children's current classroom activities; (2) group parenting support classes on topics of interest to parents; and (3) opportunities to volunteer in the child's classroom (Administration for Children and Families, 2016). Parent policy councils and center committees also provide opportunities for parents to participate in program leadership. Services are intended to be responsive to the needs and cultural and linguistic heritage of families in the communities served (Administration for Children and Families, 2016).

Parental engagement and service take-up, which have become a focus of attention because of the cost of nonparticipation and the potential impact of nonengagement on school readiness outcomes, are far from 100 percent (Administration for Children and Families, 2015d).[8] Recent data show that just 41 percent of parents whose children were enrolled in Head Start attended parenting classes, although this percentage was 14 percent higher than that for control group parents. Attendance at goal-setting classes also was significantly higher for Head Start than for non-Head Start parents,

---

[8] In June 2015, a Notice of Proposed Rulemaking on Head Start Program Performance Standards was issued, focused on the development of new targets for program participation (Administration for Children and Families, 2015d).

but take-up rates for nutrition, income, housing, utilities, education and job training assistance programs did not differ significantly between parents who won and lost lotteries for their children to enter the Head Start Program to which they had applied. Parents' participation in the programs offered by Early Head Start was higher than was the case for Head Start parents, and almost always significantly higher for Early Head Start parents than for their control group counterparts (based on full-sample estimates) (Auger, 2015).

Head Start impacts on knowledge, attitudes, and practices and child outcomes Puma and colleagues (2012) provide a random-assignment evaluation of parenting impacts in the National Head Start Impact Study. Parenting-related measures included disciplinary practices, educational supports, parenting styles, parent participation in and communication with the school, and parent and child time together. Two cohorts of children (those entering Head Start for the first time at ages 3 and 4) were analyzed separately.

Looking first at impacts at the end of the Head Start year, in no case did any of the parenting measures differ significantly for the two cohorts of children. Practices for which significant impacts were found for only one cohort included an unexpected negative impact on the amount of time parents reported reading to their children (for the 3-year-old cohort) and beneficial impacts on spanking, reading, and cultural enrichment for the 4-year-old cohort. None of the beneficial impacts found at the end of the Head Start year persisted across the kindergarten, 1st-, and 3rd-grade follow-ups, and in no case did safety practices differ significantly between the Head Start and control groups. For the 4-year-old cohort, only 1 of 28 parenting impacts emerged as statistically significant (time spent with child in 3rd grade). For the 3-year-old cohort, there was some indication that parenting styles were more authoritative (characterized by high warmth and control) and less authoritarian for the Head Start group, although these patterns were seen in less than one-half of the tests conducted. Overall, despite the program's stated goals of improving parenting, the Head Start evaluation found virtually no consistent evidence that this goal was achieved.

With respect to child outcomes, both cohorts showed statistically significant impacts on children's language and literacy development while they were in Head Start, although these effects dissipated when children reached elementary school. By the end of 3rd grade, the only favorable impact was on reading, and this was only for the 4-year-old cohort. Results in the social-emotional domain differed by both cohort and source of information. In the 3-year-old cohort, early favorable impacts on social-emotional measures (problem behaviors, social skills) were sustained through 3rd grade based on parent-reported measures, but data reported by teachers suggested

no impacts on social-emotional outcomes in either the kindergarten or
1st-grade year. No social-emotional impacts were observed in the 4-year-
old cohort through kindergarten, while favorable impacts were reported
by parents and unfavorable impacts by teachers at the end of the 1st and
3rd grades. There was strong evidence of improved receipt of dental care at
the end of the Head Start year in both cohorts (Puma et al., 2012).

One of the challenges of programs that include both direct and indirect
pathways to child outcomes is the inability to assess the extent to which
observed impacts are the result of any one component of the intervention.
It is impossible to know in this case whether the parenting impacts noted
(scattered as they were) had any role in the observed impacts on child outcomes. Nonexperimental analyses could provide exploratory answers to
these types of questions.

*Early Head Start center-based impacts on knowledge, attitudes, and prac-
tices and child outcomes* Evidence of the impact of Early Head Start
on parenting comes from the Early Head Start Research and Evaluation
Project, a large-scale randomized evaluation following 3,001 children and
families in 17 community sites. Sites delivered services primarily through
home visits (discussed in the previous section), center-based services, or a
mixed program approach whereby families received home visiting and/or
center-based services (Love et al., 2005; U.S. Department of Health and
Human Services et al., 2002).

A random-assignment evaluation of Early Head Start in four center-
based programs found one positive impact of the program on the quality
of parent-child play when the children were age 3 and one negative impact
on parent knowledge of how to use a car seat correctly (U.S. Department
of Health and Human Services et al., 2002). Mothers in the Early Head
Start group reported lower levels of severe depression and were more likely
than controls to be employed or in an education or training program.
Overall, none of the other many parenting, parent well-being, home, and
self-sufficiency outcomes studied was affected by Early Head Start among
the families in the center-based sites. With regard to child outcomes at age
3, children in the Early Head Start group were less likely to show negativity
toward their parent during a parent-child play task. There were no other
impacts on child outcomes for the Early Head Start center-based group.

In sites using the mixed approach (center-based and/or home visiting
services), families would in some cases receive home visiting services when
they started in the program and then transition to center-based services
when their children were older and the mother went to work. At age 3
and beyond, analysis indicated that among the three service delivery approaches, sites employing the mixed approach tended to have the greatest
concentration of impacts with respect to both parenting and child outcomes

(U.S. Department of Health and Human Services et al., 2002). These findings may have implications for the need for increased flexibility in programming that allows families to shift from one mode of service delivery to another as their needs change.

Smaller-Scale Classroom-based ECE Interventions

Other classroom-based ECE programs that include parenting supports also have some evidence of effectiveness and provide insights into ways to reach parents. Effective interventions target improving parents' engagement in preschool/elementary school, as well as parents' roles as collaborators with teachers in decision making about children's academic experiences. In some cases, these targets are complemented by attempts to improve alignment between home and classroom learning contexts.

The Companion Curriculum, for example, uses Head Start teachers to encourage parents' participation in the classroom and provide workshops and activity spaces in the classroom that are focused on training parents to engage in parent-child learning activities. Although the program did not demonstrate benefits for parents' involvement in the classroom or general engagement in home learning activities, it led to increased frequency of parent-child reading and improved children's vocabulary in a quasi-experimental study (Mendez, 2010).

The Kids in Transition to School (KITS) Program is a short-term, targeted, evidence-based intervention aimed at increasing early literacy, social skills, and self-regulatory skills among children who are at high risk for school difficulties. This program provides a 24-session readiness group for children that promotes social-emotional skills and early literacy as well as a 12-session parent workshop focused on promoting parent involvement in early literacy and the use of positive parenting practices. In a pilot efficacy trial with 39 families, Pears and colleagues found that children in families who received the KITS intervention demonstrated early literacy and social skill improvements as compared with their peers who did not receive the intervention (Pears et al., 2014). In randomized controlled studies, foster children who received the intervention exhibited improvements in social competence, self-regulation skills, and early literacy skills (Pears et al., 2007, 2012, 2013).

Two-Generation Approaches

One class of early intervention programs uses a two-generation approach with an explicit focus on human capital skill building. As described by Chase-Lansdale and Brooks-Gunn (2014, p. 14), these programs "intentionally link education, job training, and career-building services for low-income parents simultaneously with early education for their young children."

Early versions of these kinds of two-generation programs focused on adolescent mothers, providing them with a host of education- and job-related services. Developed during a time when the nation was focusing on welfare reform and had not begun to appreciate the potential of high-quality early childhood education programs with respect to skill building for children, these programs typically viewed child care services as a means of supporting the self-sufficiency efforts of mothers rather than promoting the school readiness of their children.

Four prominent programs conducted during the 1980s and 1990s (Project Redirection, the New Chance Demonstration, Ohio's Learning and Earning Program, and the Teen Parent Demonstration) offered adolescent mothers a wide range of services, including, in some cases, parenting classes, job training, and mandatory schooling (Granger and Cytron, 1999; Polit, 1989). Project Redirection was the earliest. It offered education and training programs for low-income adolescent mothers combined with intensive support services that included individual counseling, training in parenting and employability skills, and referrals to community services. Its evaluation, which was not based on random assignment, showed virtually no differences in parents' education or training but some promising improvements in the quality of their children's home environments and early literacy and behavior (Polit, 1989).

Evaluations of the other three programs were based on random assignment and showed a less positive set of impacts (Granger and Cyrton, 1999). In terms of parenting knowledge, attitudes, and practices, the New Chance Demonstration provided parenting education designed to promote positive parenting practices and better mother-child relationships and to reduce the stresses associated with parenthood. The Teen Parent Demonstration also included parenting workshops. The effects of these programs on mothers were not very promising, with virtually no impacts being seen on educational advances (New Chance increased GED holding, possibly at the expense of high school diplomas) or on mothers' earning, employment, or welfare participation. Maternal mental health was assessed in evaluations of New Chance and the Teen Parent Demonstration, but in neither case did the program improve scores on the mental health measures employed. Moreover, mothers in the New Chance Demonstration experimental group reported significantly more parenting stress relative to their control counterparts.

Consistent with the view of child care as merely a support for the mother's employment and education activities, none of these three programs affected any of the assessed dimensions of children's school readiness. In fact, New Chance mothers reported higher rates of child behavioral problems relative to their control group counterparts.

Another example of a rigorously evaluated comprehensive two-generation program was the Comprehensive Child Development Program (CCDP). Developed in the 1990s, this program was an ambitious attempt to provide low-income families with a range of social services designed to support infants' and children's cognitive, social-emotional, and physical development, as well as to enhance parents' ability to support their children's development and achieve economic and social self-sufficiency (St. Pierre et al., 1997). Services were intended to extend from birth through kindergarten or 1st grade but, in contrast to Head Start and some Early Head Start programs, were not built on a high-quality classroom-based program for children. The comprehensive nature of CCDP services is reflected in the program's cost, which amounted to $15,768 per family per year, or about $47,000 per family over the entire course of the program (St. Pierre et al., 1997). (In 2014 dollars, this amounts to approximately $23,250 per family per year, or nearly $70,000 per family over the entire course of the program.)[9]

CCDP service delivery relied heavily on case managers and appeared to be implemented effectively (St. Pierre et al., 1997). For children, the program supported and in fact increased parents' use of center-based child care, although evaluators did not systematically assess the quality of this care. Most sites offered biweekly home visits by a case manager or early childhood specialist between birth and age 3 in which training was provided to parents on infant and child development and, in some cases, modeling of ways to interact with children. Results of CCDP's random-assignment evaluation 5 years after the program began showed no statistically significant impacts on parenting skills or self-sufficiency among participating mothers or on the cognitive or social-emotional development of participating children (St. Pierre et al., 1997). Nor did consistent impacts emerge for any demographic subgroups or among the families that participated in the program for most of the service period. Evaluators speculated that the lack of impacts may have been the result of some combination of the dilution of service quality caused by the overly ambitious scope of program services and, for children, the program's reliance on indirect effects through parents rather than direct effects that might have come from high-quality classroom-based early education services.

In contrast to CCDP, the Child-Parent Center (CPC) Program in Chicago is a center-based early intervention program that offers comprehensive educational and family support services designed to increase academic success among low-income children ages 3-9 residing in disadvantaged Chicago neighborhoods (University of Minnesota, 2013). CPC employs a number of components directed at children and parents to meet the program objec-

---

[9]Calculated based on the Consumer Price Index (Crawford et al., 2016).

tives, such as structured and diverse language-based instructional activities; low child-to-teacher ratios; a multifaceted program for parents that takes place under the supervision of a parent-resource teacher (e.g., volunteering in the classroom, attending school events, enrolling in educational courses); outreach activities (resource mobilization, home visitation); ongoing staff development; health and nutrition services; and supports to help children from 1st to 3rd grade transition to elementary school (Reynolds, 2000). Longitudinal analyses of CPC show participation to be associated with children's improved future performance in school, such as reading and math achievement, especially for those who remain in the program for several years (Reynolds, 1997; Reynolds and Temple, 1998; Reynolds et al., 2004). Parents' involvement in school was found to be a mediator of the program's effects, suggesting that the program components targeting parents played a role in its success (Reynolds et al., 2004).

New in two-generation programming are so-called "Two Generation 2.0" human capital programs (Chase-Lansdale and Brooks-Gunn, 2014), which assign a key role to high-quality ECE. Examples of such programs for which evaluations are planned or under way include the CareerAdvance® Community Action Project of Tulsa, Oklahoma; the Annie E. Casey Foundation Atlanta Partnership; and the Housing Opportunity and Services Together project (see Chase-Lansdale and Brooks-Gunn, 2014, for others). In effect, these programs view ECE as an important and independent source of human capital training for children rather than merely a means of providing child care in order to promote the careers of mothers. ECE is coupled with postsecondary workforce skill development for parents, with training taking place in community colleges, job training programs, or workplaces. The theory of change behind these models is focused on the education benefits to children of high-quality ECE programs and higher parental levels of education and labor force motivation. Parenting knowledge, attitudes, and practices may be improved, but the improvement comes indirectly through higher parental job skills and education and reduced household stress rather than explicit programming directed at parenting skills.

Within programs designed to enhance school readiness, a subset of programs target children's cognitive skills (language, literacy, and math) and focus as well on children's social-emotional development, given the reciprocal nature of these skills. For example, Educare, based in 12 Educare schools and on Head Start's parent involvement objectives, focuses on receptive language, vocabulary, and early reading, and children's social-emotional skills. To date, implementation studies have shown promise for the program in addressing the quality gap of service delivery and parent engagement. A randomized controlled trial currently under way is comparing children at age 3 who are cared for at home or in other settings with children who are served in Educare on cognitive, language, executive function and social-emotional measures, and examining whether performance on these measures differs for dual language learners. No strong evidence on program impacts is available, however, so it is impossible to determine whether this new generation of programs will change parenting knowledge, attitudes, and practices or improve child well-being.

A brief summary of two ECE programs developed in the latter half of the 20th century, in which children assigned to comparison groups faced different and often worse conditions than they do today, is provided in Box 4-4.

Parent Engagement in School Settings and School-Related Activities, Prekindergarten through Grade 3

Beyond stimulation of and support for learning activities in the home, parents engage in their children's early learning and education through an array of practices aimed collectively at promoting educational success and well-being. These practices may include participation in school functions (e.g., classroom volunteering), communication with school personnel (e.g., parent-teacher conferences), supervision and assistance with school-related home activities (e.g., help with homework), and education-related communication and connections with other families and community members (e.g., parent social networks).

Although the terminology used to describe parenting behaviors relative to children's learning and education varies in the empirical literature (e.g., *parent engagement, parent involvement, family-school partnerships*), most researchers emphasize the ways in which such engagement requires connections between parent and child and relationships across home, school, and community contexts. The parent engagement literature generally treats schools and communities as parents' partners and collaborators because parents' power to act on behalf of their children's educational interests is determined, in large part, by the extent to which schools and communities make parents aware of opportunities, give them access to resources, and enable them to take advantage of these opportunities and resources (Dearing et al., 2015; Henderson and Mapp, 2002). In the parent-engagement intervention literature, programs generally take one of two approaches: (1) focusing primarily on improving parents' level and quality of engagement in the home environment with regard to learning stimulation and behavior regulation, or (2) focusing on connecting parents with their children's schools to promote academic achievement and/or positive behaviors.

Theory on parent engagement is built largely on ecological systems frameworks, particularly those focused on how aligning child, family, school, and community assets can help promote positive development in

BOX 4-4
Parenting in Older-Model Early Care and Education Programs

It is difficult to draw lessons from older-model early care and education (ECE) programs because children assigned to comparison groups faced much different and typically worse conditions relative to those faced today. Family sizes were much larger, parents' education levels were much lower, and very few poor children attended center-based preschool (Duncan and Magnuson, 2013). These conditions combined to set a very low standard of care for low-income children for programs developed in the 1960s, 1970s, and 1980s to improve upon. That said, it is still useful to mention the knowledge, attitudes, and practices components of the most prominent of these early programs—the High/Scope Perry Preschool Study (Perry) and the Abecedarian Project.

Perry provided 1-2 years of part-day educational services plus weekly home visits by teachers to 58 low-income, low-IQ African American children ages 3 and 4 in Ypsilanti, Michigan, during the 1960s. Meetings with groups of parents were also organized (Weikart and Lambie, 1970). The home visits focused mainly on instructional activities between the teacher and children, although the teachers were encouraged to engage in informal conversation with the mothers about the teaching materials brought to the home, childrearing practices, and the academic needs of the children when they started school. Perry's evaluation included teachers' ratings of the degree of cooperation shown by mothers; predictions of mothers' future school relationship, which were collected in kindergarten through 3rd grade; and, when the children reached age 15, both their and their parents' reports of the quality of parenting. No treatment/control group differences were found for any of these items (personal communication with Larry Schweinhart, August 8, 2015).

The Abecedarian program served 57 low-income African American families from Chapel Hill, North Carolina (Campbell and Ramey, 1994). Enrolling participants in the first year of life, the program was considerably more intensive than Perry Preschool, providing center-based education and other services to children 8 hours a day, 5 days a week, 50 weeks a year, and generating costs totaling about $80,000 per child (in 2014 dollars). Supportive social services were available to families facing problems with housing, food, transportation, and the like, although these services also were made available to families in the control group, making it impossible to assess program impacts on these social services. Unique to the Abecedarian group were opportunities for parents to serve on the advisory boards of the daycare center and participate in a series of voluntary programs covering such topics as nutrition and behavior management (Burchinal et al., 1997). Although Abecedarian boosted children's IQs and academic skills and had lasting effects on their educational attainment and health (Barnett and Masse, 2007), it had no impact on the parenting measures gathered in the study (personal communication with Peg Burchinal, August 8, 2015).

In summary, these two best-known early ECE programs both included parenting components, and both generated child impacts well into adulthood. But for neither program was there evidence of impact on parenting knowledge, attitudes, and practices.

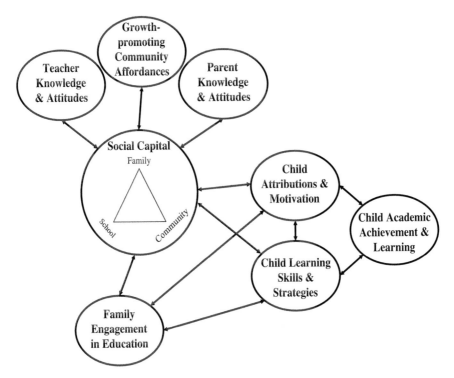

FIGURE 4-2 Hypothesized benefits of parents' engagement in children's early education for children's achievement and school success.
SOURCE: Dearing et al. (2015).

contexts characterized by multipronged social and economic disadvantage (García Coll et al., 1996; Huston and Bentley, 2009). More specifically, theory on parents' engagement in children's early education has hypothesized benefits for achievement and school success through three primary mechanisms (see Figure 4-2).

First, collaboration among families, schools, and communities can help build the capacity to stimulate and support children's learning. This linkage holds if (and only if) the information channels and norm reinforcement provided by the social network members emphasize knowledge, attitudes, and practices that are beneficial for children's achievement (e.g., teachers sharing with parents knowledge about best practice for promoting learning, and parents sharing with teachers nuanced information about their children as learners).

Second, it is expected that when parents are involved in their children's schooling with developmentally appropriate levels of autonomy and emotional support, they communicate positive beliefs about the children's learning potential. In turn, the children are likely to have positive feelings toward learning and themselves as learners, identify positively with their parents' achievement values, and meet learning challenges with effort and feelings of self-efficacy (Pomerantz et al., 2007).

Third, parents play a direct role in building children's learning strategies and skills, including approaches to problem solving, study skills, domain-specific and domain-general knowledge, and meta-cognitive skills. For a review, see Dearing and Tang (2010).

As noted in a recent review of parent engagement programs, policies, and practices (Sheridan et al., 2016), practice recommendations for interventions targeting parent engagement in early childhood education tend to emphasize the value of cultivating positive parenting through connections between home and school. Also emphasized is the importance of ensuring that these partnerships can be "*culturally sensitive* (responsive to values, priorities, and interaction styles of families), *developmentally responsive* (appropriate to children's needs across the developmental spectrum), *intentional* (focused on specific objectives), *strengths-based* (building on family and child competencies and interests), and *collaborative* (structured around mutual—parent and teacher—goals)." In turn, interventions proving successful in randomized experimental evaluations share such characteristics as a strong emphasis on (1) frequent communication and sharing of information between parents and early childhood teachers, (2) collaborative goal setting in which parents and teachers work in partnership to develop an educational plan for their children, and (3) improvements in parenting skills and parenting efficacy (Sheridan et al., 2016).

Evidence-Based Programs for Promoting
Parent Engagement in Young Children's Schooling

Much of the research on parents and children's schooling has focused on the association between parent involvement and children's academic outcomes. Studies have found that specific parent involvement behaviors, such as participation in school activities and direct communication with teachers, are linked to higher academic achievement in both reading and mathematics (El Nokali et al., 2010; Fan and Chen, 2001; Fantuzzo et al., 2004, 2013). Furthermore, parent involvement in the home, such as monitoring assigned homework and participating in learning activities, as well as having conversations with their children about school, is linked to higher reading and writing scores and report card grades. With some exceptions, the research on the effects of fathers' similar involvement has been sparse.

Many attempts have been made to improve parent engagement through interventions in the home and through home-school connections. The focus here is on interventions with socially disadvantaged children and families targeting home-school connections between prekindergarten and 3rd grade for which evidence of efficacy has been derived from randomized experimental evaluations.

A family mathematics curriculum intervention (Starkey and Klein, 2000) used an approach similar to that of the Family Literacy Program for improving parent engagement in children's math learning. Specifically, Head Start teachers trained parents in the use of math learning activities and games designed to promote developmentally sequenced learning of number concepts, arithmetic operations, logical reasoning, geometric concepts, and patterns. One notable feature of this program was that Head Start teachers were matched ethnically with parents. Families also were given learning activities to use at home. Although parenting behaviors were not observed in the home, this 4-month (eight classes) intervention resulted in improved math performance among children in the treatment group compared with the control condition.

In the Parent Corps Program, parent groups—cofacilitated by preschool teachers and mental health professionals with expertise in behavior management—are used to help parents establish structure and routines for children, to teach positive parenting practices (e.g., use of positive reinforcement and consistent consequences), and to provide opportunities for facilitator-observed parent-child interactions. Parent Corps evaluators note that a critical component of the intervention model is the "numerous opportunities to directly increase parent–teacher communication. Parents heard from teachers about their use of effective behavior management practices at school and in turn shared ideas based on how their child responded to the practices at home. Teachers heard parents' perspectives about daily struggles and the challenges of implementing these practices at home" (Brotman et al., 2011, p. 263). More effective parenting practices in the treatment compared with the control groups were evident, including parent reports of using more effective disciplinary practices, higher scores on tests of knowledge of effective behavior management strategies, and higher-quality parenting in researcher-observed parent-child interactions (Brotman et al., 2011). The intervention also resulted in reduced behavior problems among children.

Getting Ready is an evidence-supported intervention targeting parents' decision-making role at school (Sheridan et al., 2010). This program uses structured interactions between early childhood teachers and parents during home visits, parent-teacher conferences, and monthly family socialization activities that are designed to engage parents actively in learning and behavior goal setting and decision making. Together, teachers and parents identify learning opportunities at home and school and plan how educators and parents can complement each other's efforts to promote learning and track children's growth. Priorities include affirming parents' competence, increasing their access to information on child development, and reinforcing positive parenting practices. Treatment effects have, in fact, been evident for parental warmth and sensitivity, learning support, and autonomy support (Knoche et al., 2012). In one study involving children of mothers with depression, children in the Getting Ready intervention experienced a significantly greater decline in some problem behaviors (e.g., difficulty standing still, tendency to run around) relative to children in the control group. However, no differences were observed for other learning-related behaviors (Sheridan et al., 2014). In addition, the Getting Ready intervention has been found to improve children's language and literacy (Sheridan et al., 2011), with some evidence that its effects on achievement are largest for children at greatest risk for underachievement (e.g., those whose parents have less than a high school education and those who did not speak English prior to treatment [Sheridan et al., 2011]).

Applying a similar collaborative model focused exclusively on child behavior, the Parent-Child Action Teams intervention uses a parent liaison to create and guide partnerships among parents, teachers, and other school professionals focused on assessing and monitoring children's learning progress. In addition to parent-reported improvements in empowerment, intervention children were found to have significant reductions in externalizing and internalizing behavior problems compared with control children.

USE OF INFORMATION AND COMMUNICATION TECHNOLOGIES TO SUPPORT PARENTING

Information and communication technologies can contribute to parenting in two ways: (1) socialization with respect to what parenting is and means through the media, especially entertainment media, and (2) development and maintenance of parenting skills through interventions that use these technologies. New information and communication technologies provide numerous opportunities to deliver interventions with the potential to improve parenting. Digital delivery of parenting interventions has been explored as a way to overcome barriers to participation and to increase the reach, sustainability, and impact of interventions. In theory, at least, parents who can access a training program from a computer or mobile device when and where it is convenient for them to do so may face fewer logistical and financial barriers (e.g., child care, transportation) to participation. The new technologies also make it possible to tailor services to special parent populations.

Established and emerging communication technologies are now common in American households and are reframing the context of modern parenting. The majority of U.S. households have a computer and Internet access, making digital modes of intervention a promising strategy for improving program reach. In 2013, approximately 84 percent of households reported having a computer (with 78.5% having a desktop or laptop computer and 63.6% having a handheld computer), and approximately 74 percent of households reported Internet use (File and Ryan, 2014). According to data from the Pew Internet and American Life Project's Networked Families Survey, married parents with minor children living at home relative to other household configurations have the highest rates of Internet and cell phone usage, computer ownership, and broadband adoption (Kennedy et al., 2008). Nontraditional family arrangements, such as single-parent and unmarried multiadult households, also tend to be heavy users of these technologies, particularly with respect to text messaging and use of social media (Kennedy et al., 2008). Contrary to concerns that these technologies could divide families and impede their meaningful interaction, results of nationally representative surveys from the Pew Research Center reveal that technology—particularly mobile phones and the Internet—is enabling new forms of family connectedness (Kennedy et al., 2008). In fact, the majority of parents believe technology allows their families to be as close, or closer, than their families were when they grew up (Kennedy et al., 2008). Parents use the Internet to help research, organize, and improve various aspects of their lives. As far back as 2002, one study found that 73 percent of online parents used the Internet to learn new things, and 52 percent said their use of the Internet improved the way they connected with their family members (Allen and Rainie, 2002).

While the penetration of new information and communication technologies is widespread, significant inequalities in access to the technologies persist (Viswanath et al., 2012). For example, young adults, members of minority groups, and individuals with low educational attainment and low household income are more likely to say that their phone is their main source of Internet access. In contrast to Internet access, African Americans and whites are equally likely to own a cell phone of some kind and also have similar rates of smartphone ownership (File and Ryan, 2014; Zickuhr and Smith, 2012). Nonetheless, data suggest that low-income and minority groups are more likely to experience disruptions in service due to lack of payment of bills, relocation, or a change in phone number (Smith, 2015). Furthermore, although the Internet may be widely used (Smith, 2014), disparities in access by income, education, race/ethnicity, and other factors need to be considered in the implementation of programs for the diverse population of primary caregivers of young children (see Table 4-2). In 2013, for example, just 62 percent of households earning less than $25,000 had a computer, and only 48 percent had some form of Internet access, whereas among households earning $150,000 or more, 98 percent had a computer, and 95 percent had Internet access. Blacks and Hispanics (of any race),

TABLE 4-2 Computer and Internet Use among U.S. Households, 2013

Household Characteristic	Total Households (in thousands)	Percentage of Households with a Computer	Percentage of Households with an Internet Subscription
Race and Hispanic Origin of Householder			
White alone, non-Hispanic	80,699	85.4	77.4
Black alone, non-Hispanic	13,816	75.8	61.3
Asian alone, non-Hispanic	4,941	92.5	86.6
Hispanic (of any race)	14,209	79.7	66.7
Limited English-Speaking Household			
Yes	111,084	84.7	75.5
No	5,207	63.9	51.4
Metropolitan Status			
Metropolitan area	98,607	85.1	76.1
Nonmetropolitan area	17,684	76.5	64.8
Household Income			
Less than $25,000	27,605	62.4	48.4
$25,000-$49,999	27,805	81.1	69.0
$50,000-$99,999	34,644	92.6	84.9
$100,000-$149,999	14,750	97.1	92.7
$150,000+	11,487	98.1	94.9
Educational Attainment of Householder			
Less than high school	12,855	56.0	43.8
High school graduate	28,277	73.9	62.9
Some college/associate's degree	34,218	89.0	79.2
Bachelor's degree or higher	36,349	95.5	90.1

SOURCE: Adapted from File and Ryan (2014).

those with a high school education or less, those living in nonmetropolitan areas, and those living in households in which limited English is spoken also were much less likely to have computer and Internet access in 2013 (File and Ryan, 2014).

Another challenge is that, compared with previous generations, parents today are exposed to a much greater amount of information via a variety of channels, including entertainment media such as television and digital platforms such as the World Wide Web and DVDs. Much of the available information is untested and sometimes contradictory, and the sheer amount of information and the fact that it may be contradictory may confuse parents and families.

Parent Voices

[One parent acknowledged that the Internet can be a platform for communication of information to parents.]

"Parents need education on how to find the right information on the Internet. Only a few parents use Internet access to get information on parenting, but most of them, they always rely on others."

—Father from Omaha, Nebraska

As discussed in Chapter 6, despite the effectiveness of a number of various face-to-face parenting interventions, there are a number of barriers to parents' participation and retention in these programs. According to Breitenstein and colleagues (2014), studies of involvement in face-to-face interventions for parents of children in preschool through grade school show that only 10 to 34 percent of parents enroll (Baker et al., 2011; Garvey et al., 2006; Heinrichs et al., 2005; Thornton and Calam, 2011). Among those who do participate, average attendance rates range from 35 to 50 percent of sessions (Breitenstein et al., 2012; Coatsworth et al., 2006; Scott et al., 2010). Creating online-based content may be one strategy for increasing participation in interventions by providing a more convenient way to receive the information. In addition, digital delivery of parenting interventions may reduce challenges associated with uneven implementation that often occur with face-to-face interventions, including those provided across multiple sites, where adherence to protocols may vary (Breitenstein et al., 2014, 2015). Digital modes of delivery also may decrease demands on providers' time and reduce costs and other resources associated with providing the intervention in person. This can be an important advantage for some communities, as the costs of hiring, training, and maintaining professionals for evidence-based programs can be prohibitive for isolated and poorly resourced agencies

(Baggett et al., 2010), while rural communities may have limited numbers of professionals available to provide evidence-based programs.

The body of research on the use of technology and media to improve parenting knowledge and skills and provide social support for parents is relatively small but growing. This research has included evaluations of parenting programs, several of which are discussed in Chapter 5, that have been adapted from a face-to-face to an online format (e.g., Triple P Online, the Incredible Years), as well as programs developed at the outset for delivery in a digital format.

A recent systematic review included 11 experimental and quasi-experimental studies of seven parent training interventions utilizing digital delivery methods (electronic text, audio, video, or interactive components delivered via the Internet, DVD, or CD-ROM) for administering a portion of or the entire program (Breitenstein et al., 2014). Eight of these interventions supplemented text and other instructional content with videos of parent-child interactions (an effective teaching strategy in face-to-face interventions that is easily translated to digital formats). In the four programs for which parent and child behavioral outcomes were reported—InfantNet, Internet-Parent Management Training, Parenting Wisely, and Triple P Online—medium to large effect sizes were observed in the areas of infant and parent positive behaviors, child behavioral problems (e.g., conduct, hyperactivity), parental disciplinary practices, parental self-efficacy and satisfaction, and postpartum depression. When reported, participants' satisfaction with the interventions was high, ranging from 87 to 95 percent (Breitenstein et al., 2014). Although these findings suggest that the programs had a positive effect, it is difficult to draw firm conclusions given the small number of studies. Furthermore, in 6 of the 11 studies, 75 percent or more of the sample was white; only one intervention had a sample with a more diverse distribution among racial groups (Scholer et al., 2010, 2012), possibly limiting the generalizability of the findings. Future studies including parents from diverse racial/ethnic and socioeconomic backgrounds are needed. The studies reviewed also relied primarily on parents' self-reports rather than electronic tracking methods to assess completion of the intervention, and parents may misreport their completion rates. In the 2 studies that did use electronic tracking, the intervention doses were 92 percent (Baggett et al., 2010) and 67 percent (Sanders et al., 2012)—as high as or higher than those reported by parents in the other studies. Finally, as none of the interventions reviewed had been formatted for mobile devices, the review showed a need for further experimental research on parenting interventions formatted for such devices.

Other studies have examined the feasibility of adapting evidence-based training in parenting skills to information and communication technologies. A recent evaluation of the adaptation of the face-to-face Chicago Parent

Program (CPP), designed for low-income, diverse families, to an Android tablet application showed that it is feasible to accomplish such adaptation and maintain the core components of the original program when key stakeholders (parents, program developers, and designers) are engaged (Breitenstein and Gross, 2013; Breitenstein et al., 2015). The adapted program, eCPP, includes interactive activities, video examples and explanations of parenting strategies, reflection questions, evaluation of parent knowledge with feedback, and practice assignments.

Taylor and colleagues (2008) evaluated the feasibility of adapting the Incredible Years Program to a technology-based format. The study collaborators combined a computer and Web-based intervention that presented a large portion of the original Incredible Years content through technology (including video vignettes, sound files, and pictures) with support from a coach delivered through phone calls, electronic messages, and home visits. Ninety Head Start families with high levels of child behavior issues joined the study, which was implemented as part of a randomized controlled trial. Participation rates were comparable to those in the group-based Incredible Years Program, and among a subset of participants (45 families) 30 reported achieving at least one of their self-determined goals. Although further study is needed to demonstrate the effectiveness of the approach, this study showed the feasibility of using technology for adaptation and dissemination of evidence-based parenting interventions (Taylor et al., 2008).

Triple P Online is a Web version of the Triple P-Positive Parenting Program for parents of children ages 2 to 12 with behavioral problems that can be completed by parents at their own pace over a 16-week period. Triple P Online consists of eight interactive modules, each of which takes 30 to 60 minutes, on such topics as encouraging child behaviors that parents like, managing misbehavior and disobedience, and raising confident and capable children. Each of the eight modules includes video demonstrations of positive parenting skills and activities to help parents utilize these skills. After completing an initial module, parents gain access to such resources as worksheets, podcasts, and text message summaries (Triple P-Positive Parenting Program, 2016b). A focus group and survey study involving African American and Hispanic parents residing in economically depressed areas in Los Angeles County showed the feasibility of using social media in Triple P Online to reach high-risk, high-poverty families (Love et al., 2013). In a subsequent relatively small randomized study comparing two self-help versions of Triple P—Triple P Online and a self-help workbook—no differences in short-term intervention effects were observed for dysfunctional parenting and disruptive child behavior; both versions were associated with significant declines in levels of disruptive child behavior, dysfunctional parenting styles, risk of child maltreatment, and interparental conflict on both mother and father report measures. Results were largely sustained at 6-month follow-up (Sanders et al., 2014).

SafeCare®, designed specifically to prevent and reduce the recurrence of child maltreatment among families of children ages 0-5, has used technology-based hybrid approaches for the delivery of skills training during home visits. Cellular phone technology is incorporated into the Parent-Child Interaction (PCI) module of SafeCare, from which parents learn skills to increase positive interactions with their children. In a randomized controlled trial involving 371 mother-child dyads, mothers who received cellular phone-enhanced training from home visitors (i.e., tailored cell phone text messages about skill usage delivered twice a day and weekly phone calls to discuss the text message content and other issues raised by mothers) used significantly more positive parenting skills relative to waitlist controls. Perhaps as a result of increased contact with the home visitors due to use of the technology, these mothers showed more positive parenting strategies, reduced depression, and increased child-adaptive behaviors 6 months postintervention relative to parents who received traditional training, as well as waitlist controls. They also showed greater retention in services (Bigelow, 2014; Carta et al., 2013). In a small feasibility study involving three families, use of iPhone™ video in the SafeCare home safety module showed promise as a way to identify and reduce child safety hazards. Parents used the phone between home visits to capture video of rooms in their home. They then sent these videos to the home visitor, who evaluated them for hazards and provided feedback to parents. The safety module of SafeCare is typically completed in six in-home sessions lasting between 90 and 120 minutes. As a result of the use of this technology, face-to-face time for the home visits was progressively reduced and replaced by the video data collection (Jabaley et al., 2011).

Behavioral parent training (BPT) is designed to promote changes in attitudes and practices related to harsh discipline among parents of young children with attention deficit hyperactivity disorder who display conduct problems and antisocial behaviors (Chacko et al., 2009; Cowart-Osborne et al., 2014; Kaminski et al., 2008; van den Hoofdakker et al., 2007; Webster-Stratton et al., 2011). This training has been found to be effective for preventing child maltreatment and reducing child maltreatment recidivism (Barth, 2009; Cowart-Osborne et al., 2014; Kaminski et al., 2008; Whitaker et al., 2005). In-person, group-based BPT typically takes place over several weeks and involves instruction, modeling, and practice of positive parenting behaviors; supportive group discussions; and home practice assignments. Studies provide preliminary evidence that incorporating media, such as an Internet program, videotapes supplemented by telephone or in-person coaching, and multimedia CD-ROMs into BPT is effective for improving parenting skills (Cefai et al., 2010; Irvine et al., 2014; Webster-

Stratton and Reid, 2010). For example, in a recent randomized trial of an Internet BPT program (Parenting Toolkit) using a scenario-based video hybrid instructional design conducted at urban community centers, test scores of parents of youth ages 11-14 who viewed the toolkit and completed a 1-month follow-up (N = 90) indicated that they would be less likely than controls (N = 140) to overreact and respond harshly during disciplinary interactions with their children and more likely to follow through with promised consequences. These parents also reported a reduction in their children's problem behaviors and greater gains in their own self-efficacy and intention to engage in positive parenting practices (Irvine et al., 2014).

Another emerging area of research is parents' use of technology and media as a source of social support. In a recent survey of parents by the Pew Research Institute, nearly three-quarters of respondents reported receiving social support from others on social media (Duggan et al., 2015). Forty-two percent of parents using social media (more mothers than fathers) reported that they had received social or emotional support specifically for a parenting issue on social media in the past month. Eight percent and 16 percent of parents, respectively, said they received social or emotional support for a parenting issue "frequently" or "sometimes" over the past month (Duggan et al., 2015).

The use of social media (e.g., Facebook, Twitter) among mothers with young children to share information about their children is an emerging trend. One correlational study of new mothers (N = 157) evaluated whether blogging and social networking is associated with improvement in maternal well-being by providing social support (McDaniel et al., 2012). Maternal well-being was assessed by means of psychological and emotional measures, such as marital functioning, parenting stress, and depression. The study demonstrated an association between the frequency of blogging and feelings of connection to extended family and friends, perceived social support, and maternal well-being, showing that blogging may be a powerful tool for developing a new mother's sense of increased connection to the outside world and eventually improving her well-being (McDaniel et al., 2012).

In a quasi-experimental study involving 1,300 mothers of infants, intervention participants were provided with online interactive resources that offered information and social support. These resources included an information database, an online peer discussion forum, and an online answering service staffed by nurses and midwives, covering such topics as how to respond to infants' cues and needs. The study found that the intervention had no effect on mothers' perceptions of parenting satisfaction and depressive symptoms. Yet relative to mothers in the control group, mothers in the intervention experienced higher infant centrality at 6 weeks (Salonen et al., 2014).

Differences in preferred channels of information may depend on the type of parenting information sought. In primary care settings, especially in pediatrician offices, parents' preferred channel of delivery for patient educational materials may vary based on the type of message and the complexity of the information. A review of 114 studies of patient education in primary care settings using primarily randomized controlled designs looks at parents' preference for delivery formats for information on such topics as positive parenting practices, children's behavioral self-management, and skills for improving the well-being of both children and families (Glascoe et al., 1998). The authors report that media, including advertising campaigns and office posters, helped extend parents' interests to new areas, while parents preferred verbal communication for brief and concrete messages. Modeling and role playing were particularly beneficial for addressing problematic parenting or child behavior. However, there may be challenges to delivering long, complex verbal messages to parents in primary care settings; limitations of memory and understanding of content may make the information difficult to absorb, particularly in stressful situations such as discussing problematic child behaviors or other family concerns. The authors suggest that written form may be more beneficial for communicating complex medical information.

Web-based strategies have also been tested among foster, adoptive, and kinship parents, who may need to deal with particularly difficult behavioral issues (Pacifici et al., 2006). In a pre- and post-test study, Pacifici and colleagues (2006) investigated the effectiveness of two interactive Web-based courses on lying and sexualized behavior in children developed for foster, adoptive, and kinship parents. Findings demonstrated significant improvement in parental knowledge for both courses and a significant increase in competency-based parenting perceptions for the course on lying. This Web-based program also led to new connections and interactions among users, and overall user satisfaction was high (Pacifici et al., 2006).

In summary, while early research on the use of information and communication technologies to support parenting has had promising results, much more remains to be done. Future research needs to include study populations that are more culturally and socioeconomically diverse and incorporate electronic tracking to monitor usage. In addition, more work is needed to develop formatting for mobile devices to extend the availability of interventions to those without access to a computer (Breitenstein et al., 2014). While some research supports the use of the Internet and other technologies for the delivery of parent training, interventions that utilize in-person support group formats (e.g., Triple P, the Incredible Years) have shown significant effects on parenting practices, some of which can be measured years later. It is not yet clear whether self-administered, technology-based interventions can replicate the effects of these interventions (Irvine et al., 2014). One attractive feature of technology-based interventions is providing parents with the ability to learn at their own pace, although there is a risk that parents will move too quickly without taking the time to practice new skills or too slowly so they lose momentum and interest (Breitenstein et al., 2014). If programs are to remain relevant and engage a broad population, however, they would need to adapt to Americans' growing reliance on technology for information relevant to parenting. This may be especially true for younger, including adolescent, parents, who are accustomed to communication through technologies that have been available to them their entire lives (Cowart-Osborne et al., 2014). As is the case for all parenting interventions, if technology-based parenting support interventions are to have a positive effect on parenting practices, their developers need to apply theories of behavior change (e.g., the theory of reasoned action and the theory of planned behavior) that can inform influential mechanisms through which such interventions can impact parenting knowledge, attitudes, and practices. In addition, ecological approaches that intervene at multiple levels are called for as multilevel interventions may have more lasting effects on behavior change.

Finally, a gap in the research on information and communication technologies is work on how entertainment media socialize young parents on norms of parenting. While formal avenues of classes and structured curricula are important for developing and reinforcing certain norms about parenting, entertainment media are also likely to have a significant influence. This is an area ripe for additional work.

SUPPORTING PARENTING: INCOME, NUTRITION ASSISTANCE, HEALTH CARE, AND HOUSING PROGRAMS

As described in Chapter 3, a number of programs and policies at the federal level are designed to provide resources for families. Some provide direct cash assistance, others help ensure the health of children, and some provide services and parenting education in conjunction with the material assistance. This section focuses on research evaluating the impact of these programs, both directly on children and parents and with respect to facilitating better parenting.

The Earned Income Tax Credit and Child Tax Credit

As discussed in Chapter 3, the Earned Income Tax Credit (EITC), which offsets the amount owed in taxes for low-income working families, is one of the largest poverty alleviation programs for the nonelderly in the United States (Center on Budget and Policy Priorities, 2016). The credit is paid by the federal government, as well as by 26 states and the District of Columbia, which set their own EITCs as a percentage of the federal credit

(Center on Budget and Policy Priorities, 2016). Federal benefits were as high as $6,269 for families with three or more qualifying children in 2016 (Internal Revenue Service, 2016). Single mothers are the group most likely to be eligible for the EITC. Noncustodial parents who qualify as childless workers may claim the EITC, although payments under this category are much smaller than those to custodial parents (Marr and Huang, 2015; Marr et al., 2015). The Child Tax Credit, up to $1,000 per child, offsets the costs of raising children for low- to moderate-income working families (Center on Budget and Policy Priorities, 2016). The credit is paid by the federal government and a few states that have their own programs.

A growing literature, none of it relying on random assignment, has demonstrated associations between the generosity of EITC payments and maternal work, stress, and health-related outcomes and behaviors; parenting practices discussed in Chapter 2, such as receipt of prenatal care and breastfeeding; and child well-being.

Consistent evidence suggests that tax credits improve employment-related outcomes for most recipients. Analyses of the EITC expansions that took place in the 1990s show that they contributed to significant increases in work and wage growth among single mothers and female heads of households compared with women who were otherwise similar but did not receive the EITC (Blank, 1997; Herbst, 2010; Hotz and Scholz, 2003). According to Meyer and Rosenbaum (2001), more than one-half of the large increase in employment among single mothers that occurred during the late 20th century can be attributed to the EITC expansions that took place between 1984 and 1996.

Benefits such as the EITC that are designed to encourage parents to work are not unambiguously beneficial for children and their parents, however, especially when they are provided to single low-income, parents who are particularly likely to hold jobs that are stressful and require them to work long hours or unusual shifts (Heinrich, 2014). While the income that working parents earn may benefit themselves and their children in some ways, the stress they bring home from work may undermine their parenting practices and the atmosphere in the home (Duncan et al., 2001; Heinrich, 2014). Working parents who lack access to or cannot afford quality child care may place their young children in lower-quality care or leave them unsupervised or with older child siblings. If policies such as the EITC aimed at increasing employment rates among parents are to be beneficial, these kinds of problems need to be prevented (Heinrich, 2014).

A considerable body of research has explored how the EITC may influence adult recipients' health and health-related behaviors although a 2013 review of many of these studies found that they carry a high risk of bias from confounding and insufficient control of underlying time trends (Pega et al., 2013). One of the stronger studies links expansions of the EITC to data from the Behavioral Risk Factor Surveillance System and the National Health and Nutrition Examination Survey (Evans and Garthwaite, 2010). In particular, between 1993 and 1996, the generosity of the EITC increased sharply, especially for mothers with two or more children. If income matters for maternal stress and health, the authors argue, greater improvement should be seen for children and mothers in two-child low-income families than in single-child low-income families. Indeed, the study found that, compared with mothers with one child, low-income mothers with two or more children experienced larger reductions in risky biomarkers and self-reported better mental health.

Additional studies have shown that the generosity of EITC payments is associated with improvement in several health-related outcomes/behaviors, including food security, smoking cessation, and efforts to lose weight. The EITC also may improve working mothers' access to health insurance (Averett and Yang, 2012; Cebi and Woodbury, 2009). At the same time, however, the generosity of EITC payments has been found to be associated with detrimental effects on metabolic factors among women (Rehkopf et al., 2014) and morbidity indictors such as weight gain (Schmeiser, 2009).

As for child outcomes, studies have found that EITC expansions in the early 1990s contributed to improved academic achievement in the form of higher test scores (especially in math) and higher high school/GED completion rates (Chetty et al., 2011; Dahl and Lochner, 2012; Maxfield, 2013). The Maxfield (2013) study also found effects of higher EITC payments on college enrollment by age 19 or 20. An analysis of reading and math test scores among 2.5 million children in grades 3 to 8 in an urban school district and corresponding tax record data for their families, spanning the school years 1988-1989 through 2008-2009, found that additional income from the EITC resulted in significant increases in students' test scores; a $1,000 increase in the tax credit raised students' test scores by 6 percent of a standard deviation (Chetty et al., 2011). Students with higher test scores were more likely to attend college, have higher-paying jobs, and live in better neighborhoods as adults and less likely to have a child during adolescence. These findings led the authors to conclude that a substantial portion of the cost of tax credits may be offset by earnings gained in the longer term.

In addition, available evidence suggests an association between parents' receipt of the EITC and improved birth and perinatal outcomes. An analysis by Arno and colleagues (2009) found that each 10 percent increase in EITC penetration (within or across states) was associated with a 23.2 per 100,000 reduction in infant mortality (P = .013). However, it is unclear how differences among states in poverty and unemployment rates, as well as in welfare programs other than the EITC, may have influenced these findings (Arno et al., 2009). Some research has found the size of EITC payments to be associated with improvements in such indicators of perinatal health as mothers' utilization of prenatal and postnatal care, mothers' use of tobacco and alcohol during pregnancy, term birth, and birth weight (Baker, 2008; Rehkopf et al., 2014).

Because the Child Tax Credit is newer than the EITC, it has not been studied as extensively. The two credits share several features, however, so the benefits for families may be similar as well. Like the EITC, the Child Tax Credit alleviates poverty for working families by supplementing wages and incentivizing work (Marr et al., 2015). In terms of child outcomes, income support from the Child Tax Credit is associated with better academic achievement for elementary and middle-school students (Chetty et al., 2011; Dahl and Lochner, 2012; Duncan et al., 2011).

Temporary Assistance for Needy Families (TANF)

TANF is an income support program created to help families achieve self-sufficiency. The program provides block grants to states to be used for an assortment of services, such as income support, child care, education, job training, and transportation assistance, with services and eligibility varying by state (Center on Budget and Policy Priorities, 2015b). Additionally, states are required to include work requirements for participants, and assistance is reduced or stopped if an individual does not work. In general, TANF recipients are less educated and poorer with more mental and physical health problems relative to low-income nonrecipients, and those with larger families are impacted more than those with small families (Hildebrandt and Stevens, 2009; Muenning et al., 2015)

When TANF was created, the economy was strong, and during the first year of the program, 73 percent of funds went to cash assistance (Hahn et al., 2012). Over time, cash assistance has decreased, and states have used the block grants for other purposes. Today, they spend approximately 25 percent of TANF funds on basic assistance; 25 percent on child care and connecting families to work; and about one-third on other types of services, such as child welfare, emergency assistance, early education, teen pregnancy prevention, and two-parent family formation and marriage support (Schott et al., 2015).

Since TANF was initiated, few evaluations of the program have been conducted, and only a few studies have used national or recent data (Acs and Loprest, 2007; Bloom et al., 2011; Hildebrandt and Stevens, 2009). States are not required to report whom they serve with TANF funds or what outcomes are achieved. This lack of accountability and transparency means that little is known about TANF's effectiveness. It has been found in analyses of studies that included randomized controlled trials that TANF has saved money for both individuals and government (Muennig et al.,

2015) and overall has increased employment and earnings among participants (Ziliak, 2015). However, there is currently no evidence that giving
states broad flexibility in use of the funds has improved outcomes for poor
families (Schott et al., 2015).

Health

It has been found that women with relatively smaller families who are
able to work have better health and longevity outcomes under TANF, while
those with disabilities or family obligations that prevent them from working
are better off under Aid to Families with Dependent Children (AFDC), and
in fact many of these women have enrolled in the Supplemental Security
Income Program instead of TANF (Muenning et al., 2015). Over the average TANF recipient's working life, AFDC would cost about $28,000 more
than TANF, but it would increase life by an additional .44 year (Muenning
et al., 2015).

Work Participation

TANF's work incentives allow participants to work and receive assistance. The work participation rate is the primary measure of state performance for TANF. Hence, states can have an incentive not to help those
who may be difficult to employ since they often need extra assistance to
find work and stay employed (Hahn et al., 2012). Little evidence indicates
that TANF helps participants obtain better jobs than they could have found
on their own, and the jobs they find through TANF often do not help them
move on to better jobs thereafter (Lower-Basch, 2013). There has been
some evaluation of models aimed at helping those who are difficult to
employ. It has been found that state approaches to providing such service
vary. Random assignment studies have found some positive effects from
employment- and treatment-focused strategies. PRIDE in Philadelphia, for
example, increased employment, with impacts that lasted several years. At
the end of the program, however, most participants did not have jobs, and
80 percent still were receiving cash assistance; 2 years later, only 23 percent of participants had a job (Bloom et al., 2011). Overall, employment-
focused interventions have had weak longer-term employment effects, while
treatment-focused interventions have increased service use but do not have
strong evidence for increasing employment (Bloom et al., 2011).

Education and Future Earnings

Encouraging TANF recipients' participation in and completion of additional education can help improve their families' economic position. Many

states provide some basic education classes, vocational training, and post-secondary education, which may be supplemented by other supports, such as child care and tuition assistance. However, states also encourage TANF recipients to work at the same time.

Studies evaluating TANF's education initiatives have found mixed results (Hamilton and Scrivener, 2012). Using random assignment research designs, one evaluation found an increase in enrollment in education and training, especially among single parents (Hamilton and Scrivener, 2012). Even when enrollment has increased, however, the challenge has been increasing the percentage of participants who complete the education or training. Studies suggest that the following are beneficial: financial incentives to encourage attendance, academic progress, acquisition of marketable skills, community college exposure, job search aids, and student support assistance (Hamilton and Scrivener, 2012). TANF recipients also often face challenges to pursuing postsecondary education, particularly since many recipients do not have a GED or high school diploma (Hamilton and Scrivener, 2012).

Some argue that expanding TANF's educational support may make the program less effective at helping recipients become employed (Greenberg et al., 2009). In an analysis of results from 28 cost-benefit studies that used random assignment evaluation, programs for GED completion and basic education that recipients are required to take did not appear to increase income (Greenberg et al., 2009). Unpaid work experience programs that are mandatory after a period of unsuccessful job searching have shown limited benefits (Greenberg et al., 2009).

Nutrition Assistance Programs

Many households today are food insecure. In 2014, an estimated 14 percent of households were food insecure at some point during the past year (Coleman-Jensen et al., 2015); the proportion was 19.2 percent among households with children under age 18. Nutrition assistance programs reach millions of low-income families in the United States each year. Major programs are the Special Supplemental Nutrition Program for Women, Infants, and Children (WIC), the Supplemental Nutrition Assistance Program (SNAP), and the National School Breakfast and National School Lunch Programs.

Special Supplemental Nutrition Program for Women, Infants, and Children (WIC)

WIC helps parents obtain knowledge and adopt practices that promote their own and their young children's health by providing nutrition education and vouchers for the purchase of healthy foods, breastfeeding support, and health and social service referrals. The program reaches millions of low-income pregnant, postpartum, and breastfeeding women and their children under age 5 each year (U.S. Department of Agriculture, 2016d).

WIC nutrition education is provided in a manner that is easy for participants to understand and that acknowledges the real-world interactions among nutritional needs, living circumstances, and cultural preferences. Mothers meet with WIC staff either individually or in groups to learn about the role of nutrition and physical activity in health, as well as to discuss nutrition-related practices (e.g., how to read nutrition labels and prepare healthy meals) (Carlson and Neuberger, 2015). Traditionally, nutrition education has taken place in person at WIC offices, but online education is available in many jurisdictions. Parents may use WIC vouchers to purchase infant formula and baby food as well as fruits and vegetables, whole grains, and other healthy foods. For breastfeeding mothers, counseling and educational materials, as well as peer support, are provided. To promote breastfeeding, breastfeeding mothers are eligible for WIC benefits for a longer period relative to nonbreastfeeding mothers, and those who breastfeed exclusively have a broader selection of foods from which to choose for voucher purchases. Referral services may include child immunizations and health and dental care, as well as counseling for women who smoke and abuse alcohol (Carlson and Neuberger, 2015).

Since WIC was initiated about 40 years ago, abundant research has shown evidence of its effectiveness. WIC participation during pregnancy is consistently associated with longer gestations and higher birth weights, with effects tending to be greatest among children born to disadvantaged mothers. Other outcomes include improved child nutrition (e.g., increased vitamin and mineral intake, reduced consumption of fat and added sugars), better infant feeding practices, and greater receipt of preventive and curative care (Carlson and Neuberger, 2015; Fox et al., 2004). Evidence also indicates that updates to WIC-approved foods in 2007 to bring them more in line with the latest nutrition science, made in response to recommendations in the Institute of Medicine (2006) report *WIC Food Packages: Time for a Change* enhanced the impact of WIC on the purchase and consumption of healthy foods among families participating in the program (Carlson and Neuberger, 2015). These changes included, among others, adding whole grain and soy products; reducing milk, cheese, and juice allowances; and giving states and other jurisdictions more flexibility to accommodate food preferences of cultural groups.

Despite efforts to promote breastfeeding, mothers participating in WIC have been found to be less likely to breastfeed than those not participating. It is unclear whether this differential is related to the availability of formula through WIC or other factors. Also in response to the 2006 Institute of

Medicine report, the U.S. Department of Agriculture took steps to encourage breastfeeding among mothers participating in WIC, such as no longer routinely providing them with formula for the first month after birth and providing a limited amount of formula in subsequent months to mothers of partially breastfeeding infants. Whether these changes have had an impact on breastfeeding rates among WIC participants is thus far unknown (Carlson and Neuberger, 2015).

Research on the nonhealth benefits of WIC is limited. One recent study that analyzed data from two nationally representative longitudinal surveys showed that children whose mothers participated in WIC while pregnant performed better than those of mothers not participating on measures of cognitive skills at age 2. This finding persisted into children's early school years based on reading assessment (Jackson, 2015).

An evaluation of the Early Developmental Screening and Intervention (EDSI) initiative among WIC participants in California illustrates how WIC can support parents' interactions with health care professionals. The initiative used a health education class to teach parents about child development and how to talk to their child's health care professional(s) about the child's development. Before the class, 42 percent of parents reported by survey that they had concerns about their child's development, learning, or behavior, and only 26 percent of them had been asked about these concerns at their child's last health care visit (Early Developmental Screening and Intervention Initiative, 2011). The evaluation found that the parent education class was associated with increases in parents' preparation before health care meetings, with about one-third of these parents reporting that they used material they had learned in class. However, there was no change in parents' actions during their child's health care visits or their attitudes while talking to their child's health care professional based on the survey findings (Early Developmental Screening and Intervention Initiative, 2011). Another evaluation found that 30 to 40 percent of parents participating in a Parent Activation/Developmental Surveillance pilot reported discussing their concerns about their child's development with a developmental specialist (Early Developmental Screening and Intervention Initiative, 2011).

SNAP and National School Breakfast and National School Lunch Programs

SNAP is the largest nutrition assistance program in the United States, reaching an average of 22.5 million households each month in 2015 (U.S. Department of Agriculture, 2016c). Many households receiving SNAP (76% in 2014) include a child or an elderly or disabled individual (Gray and Kochhar, 2015). By providing assistance for the purchase of food, SNAP reduces poverty among disadvantaged populations, especially for two-parent families (Center on Budget and Policy Priorities, 2015a; Tiehen et al., 2013). A number of studies have found that SNAP reduces food insecurity, while findings on improvements in diet quality have been mixed (Andreyeva et al., 2015; Gregory et al., 2013; Hartline-Grafton, 2013). In analyses of longitudinal data, SNAP participation has been found to decrease the probability of being food insecure by approximately 30 percent and the likelihood of being very food insecure by 20 percent (Ratcliffe et al., 2011) in both urban and rural areas (Mabli, 2014). Other longitudinal analyses found that SNAP participation increased preschool children's intake of iron, zinc, niacin, thiamin, and vitamin A (Rose et al., 1998), while another showed that young children participating in SNAP and/or WIC had lower rates of nutritional deficit relative to nonparticipants (Lee and Mackey-Bilever, 2007). However, other evidence shows that while SNAP alleviates food insecurity, participants appear to be no more likely than income-eligible nonparticipants to be meeting dietary guidelines. In a systematic review of peer-reviewed studies, diet quality among children and adults was similar for SNAP and low-income nonparticipants and of lower quality than for higher-income individuals (Andreyeva et al., 2015).

The National School Breakfast and National School Lunch Programs provide nutritionally balanced, low-cost or free breakfasts and lunches to millions of children in public and nonprofit private schools and residential child care institutions each day (U.S. Department of Agriculture, 2016a, 2016b). The evidence on the effects of these and other school-based nutrition programs on child nutrition outcomes is limited (Gundersen et al., 2012). Using National Health and Nutrition Examination Survey data for 2001-2004, Gundersen and colleagues (2012) estimate that the National School Lunch Program reduced the rate of poor health among children by at least 29 percent, the rate of obesity by at least 17 percent, and food insecurity by at least 3.8 percent.

Health Care

As reviewed in Chapter 2 and above, various elements of the health care system have the potential to affect parents positively in promoting the health of their children. Health care providers have multiple contacts with parents through the care of both children and the parents themselves.

Since the passage of the ACA in 2010, the number of adults without health insurance is estimated to have fallen by 16.4 million (U.S. Department of Health and Human Services, 2015a). This increase in insurance coverage has expanded access to a number of services for families, such as maternity care and pediatric services, preventive services, and screening and treatment for mental health disorders.

Relative to insured children, uninsured children are more likely to have problems with access to health care and unmet health care needs. They are less likely to receive preventive care (well-child care, immunizations, basic dental care) and almost 27 percent less likely to have had a routine checkup in the past year (Alker and Kenney, 2014; White House, 2015). Medicaid and the Children's Health Insurance Program (CHIP) play an important role in child coverage, currently providing coverage to more than one in three children (Burwell, 2016). Evidence indicates that health insurance has improved access to care for children, and utilization of primary and preventive care appears to increase after CHIP enrollment (American Academy of Pediatrics, 2014; McMorrow et al., 2014). Evaluations within and across states generally have found that enrollees report improvements in having a usual source of care, in visiting physicians or dentists, and in having fewer unmet health needs after enrollment (American Academy of Pediatrics, 2014; Damiano et al., 2003; Fox et al., 2003; Selden and Hudson, 2006; Szilagyi et al., 2004). Moreover, pre-post survey research with parents suggests that racial/ethnic disparities in health care access and utilization detected before enrollment are eliminated or greatly reduced after enrollment (American Academy of Pediatrics, 2014; Shone et al., 2005). In a cross-sectional analysis of data from the Health Reform Monitoring Survey, compared with parents with employer-sponsored insurance, parents whose children were covered under Medicaid or CHIP reported less difficulty paying children's medical bills (9.7% versus 19%) and paying less out of pocket on health care (McMorrow et al., 2014).

McMorrow and colleagues (2014) found that 40 percent of children with Medicaid or CHIP had a parent who obtained information on all recommended anticipatory guidance topics during well-child visits (how to keep a child from getting injured, how much or what kind of food a child should eat and how much exercise a child should get, how smoking indoors is bad for a child's health, how a child should behave and get along with parents and others), versus 26 percent of those with insurance through their parent's employer (McMorrow et al. 2014). However, some research has found that children with public coverage have more difficulty accessing specialist care, family-centered care, and after-hours care (Bethell et al., 2011; Kenney and Coyer, 2012; McMorrow et al., 2014).

Parent Voices

[Issues around health are a concern for many parents.]

"A father from Omaha, Nebraska, who had always provided for his family experienced a medical condition that keeps him from working, and he found it difficult to accept that he is no longer able to provide for his family."

—Father from Omaha, Nebraska

"Some parents in this country, based on income, rely on government benefits, but when you have higher income, you are not eligible. So when you are not eligible for Medicaid, some parents won't take their kids to see the doctor. At work, they can get insurance, but they have to pay more. From my own experience, when a kid doesn't have Medicaid, they stop seeing the doctor."

—Mother from Omaha, Nebraska

Housing Programs

Housing-related expenses (shelter, utilities, furniture) account for families' largest share of expenditures on children across income groups, representing 30-33 percent of total expenditures on a child in two-child, husband-wife families in 2013 (Lino, 2014). Balancing housing-related expenses with expenses for other necessities, such as nutritious foods and quality child care, can be especially difficult for low-income families.

The Housing Choice Voucher Program (HCVP) (often referred to as Section 8) helps more than 5 million people in low-income families access affordable rental housing that meets health and safety standards (Center on Budget and Policy Priorities, 2015c). Studies show potential benefits of participation in HCVP, including improved nutrition due to greater food security, increased household stability after the first year, and reductions in measures of concentrated poverty and the incidence of homelessness (Carlson et al., 2012; Lindberg et al., 2010; Wood et al., 2008). A study of 8,731 families in six locations where housing vouchers were randomly assigned to eligible participants found that over a period of about 5 years the vouchers reduced the incidence of homelessness and living with relatives: 45 percent of nonrecipients versus 9 percent of recipients spent time without a place of their own in the 4th year of the study) (Wood et al., 2008). In a review of published research on neighborhood-level housing interventions, Lindberg and colleagues (2010) found that voucher holders were less likely than nonvoucher holders to experience malnutrition due to food insecurity, poverty, and overcrowding.

Another scientifically supported housing initiative—housing rehabilitation loan and grant programs—provides financial assistance to enable low-income homeowners to repair, improve, modernize, or remove health and safety hazards from their dwellings (U.S. Department of Housing and

Urban Development, 2015). Low-interest loans and grants are offered to homeowners at the federal and state levels through local lenders based on income level and rural versus urban residence. Evidence from systematic reviews and randomized controlled research suggests that housing improvements, especially those aimed at increasing household warmth, may positively impact physical and mental health and respiratory outcomes, as well as absences from school for children and from work for adults (Gibson et al., 2011; Howden-Chapman et al., 2007; Thomson et al., 2013).

PARENTAL AND FAMILY LEAVE POLICIES

The United States is the only advanced industrialized nation that does not mandate paid maternity leave and one of only a few industrialized countries that do not require paid leave for children's health needs by national law. Of the 189 countries included in Heymann and McNeill's (2013) examination of the World Policy Analysis Centre Adult Labour Database, nearly all offer paid leave for new mothers, although less than one-half provide paid leave to new fathers. Moreover, 48 countries have policies that provide paid leave to parents when their child is ill. Just over half of high-income countries and one-quarter of middle-income countries have policies supporting paid leave for parents for children's health needs (Heymann and Earle, 2010; World Adult Labour, 2015). Current state and federal leave policies regarding parental and family medical leave in the United States do not cover all parents and employers; among those who are covered, the relevant policies do not cover all their needs (Schuster et al., 2011). This section characterizes the needs of new parents and the health care needs of children; existing employer, federal, and state support for families with children; and the impact of such programs and legislation on children and families.

Needs of New Parents and Young Children's Health Care Needs

Newborns and infants require substantial, focused, and responsive care. Parents of newborns need time to bond with their child and adjust to the demands of caring for an infant while also overseeing their child's healthy development. In addition, mothers need time to rest and recover from pregnancy and childbirth. Mothers who are breastfeeding also need to be available for the needs of their newborns.

All children, even those who are healthy, have preventive and acute health care needs (Schuster et al., 2011). In addition, about 20 percent of children ages 0-17 in the United States are considered children with special health care needs, defined as children "who have or are at increased risk for a chronic physical, developmental, behavioral, or emotional condition and who also require health and related services of a type or amount beyond that required by children generally" (Child and Adolescent Health Measurment Initiative, 2012; McPherson et al., 1998, p. 138). This category may include children with such conditions as ADHD, asthma, autism, cancer, cerebral palsy, cystic fibrosis, depression, and diabetes (Newacheck and Taylor, 1998).

Children's health care needs can be roughly divided into three categories: preventive care, intermittent acute care, and ongoing chronic care. All children are expected to receive a substantial amount of routine preventive care, including immunizations, most of which require multiple doses at multiple visits; developmental surveillance, which detects delays in speech and language development, gross and fine motor skills, and behavioral, social, and emotional growth; screening for early or hidden illness; anticipatory guidance; and dental care. At present, the American Academy of Pediatrics and Bright Futures jointly recommend a minimum of seven visits in a child's first year and seven more in the following 3 years, followed by annual visits through age 21 (American Academy of Pediatrics, 2008).

Nearly all children will experience one or more episodes of illness serious enough to require a visit to the emergency room, hospitalization, or care at home. Three in four children under age 18 have at least one office visit in a given year, with most averaging about four visits per year, exceeding the recommended preventive visit schedule (Schuster et al., 2011). According to a 2008 study on pediatric injuries across 14 states, one-third of emergency department visits were for pediatric injuries (Owens et al., 2008). In 2014, 23 percent of children under age 6 had visited an emergency department one or more times in the past year (National Center for Health Statistics, 2015). In addition to these acute health care issues, children experience minor illnesses that may prevent them from attending day care or school, which requires the presence of an adult in the home. Nearly two-thirds of elementary school-age children miss some school each year because of illness or injury, and nearly 11 percent of these children miss more than 1 week (Bloom et al., 2013).

Children with special health care needs generally require ongoing care that may involve frequent monitoring, interventions for preventing and managing illness complications, and acute care for severe episodes of illness (see also Chapter 5). At home, parents of children with serious or complex illnesses may be required to provide treatment and care (e.g., respiratory treatments, feeding tube care, intravenous nutrition, physical and occupational therapy, developmental interventions) in addition to cleaning and maintaining devices, ordering supplies, obtaining technical support for machines, and training other caregivers (Schuster et al., 2011). Children with serious and complex illnesses account for a vastly disproportionate number of hospital days, health care encounters, and school absences.

Because children are unable to care for themselves, their parents are expected to provide an array of health care services that are integral to the current health care system for children, including, but not limited to, providing care at home, scheduling and attending outpatient visits, and supervision during emergency ward visits and hospitalizations (Schuster et al., 2011). Parents are expected to be present whether the care is preventive, acute, or chronic. Health care providers and public health officials recommend that children experiencing acute illnesses stay home from school in addition to visiting a clinician as needed. Otherwise, their illnesses can worsen or spread to others, health care costs can increase, and small problems can become serious threats (Schuster and Chung, 2014).

Types of Support for Employed Parents

Many employed parents who must take time away from work to care for a newborn or a sick child lose wages for hours not worked. Many even risk losing their job. Employees in the United States rely on various types of support to meet the health needs of their children, including a combination of employer benefits (if offered) and federal, state, and local leave laws and programs.

Employers—Parental Leave

Policies on offering parents of newborns time off to care for their child vary by employer; some employers provide the option of taking time off from work, while others do not. Moreover, the absence of a federal-level paid parental leave policy in the United States leaves many workers in a situation of combining a number of employee-provided benefits that may include sick leave, holiday and vacation leave, disability insurance, and paid or unpaid family leave in order to take time away from work to care for a newborn.

Employers—Family Medical Leave

The patchwork of formal and informal support provided by employers to parents includes sick days; flexible paid time off that combines vacation, sick time, and family leave; telecommuting; and programs that allow employees to donate or share unused paid leave. Parents who rely on sick days to care for their children without explicit employer approval may place themselves at risk for termination. Some supervisors may informally allow parents to leave work for hours or days to care for their child (Schuster et al., 2011). Some employers offer employee assistance or work-life programs that can help families use employee benefits and access public and private resources more effectively. According to data from the 2010 National Paid Sick Days study, more than 60 percent of all workers reported that their employer provided them with paid sick leave, which could include a combination of sick leave, vacation, and other reasons. Less than one-half reported that they received paid sick leave that they could use for sick family members (Schuster et al., 2011; Smith and Kim, 2010).

Federal and State Programs and Legislation

The Pregnancy Discrimination Act of 1978 requires that employers provide leave to women with medical conditions that are linked to pregnancy and childbirth, just as they would to any other employee with a medical condition or temporary disability, such as a heart attack or broken leg. Although the act does not require employers to provide paid leave, they must provide the same leave (paid or unpaid) or disability benefits for conditions related to pregnancy that they provide for other disabilities (U.S. Equal Employment Opportunity Commission, 2016).

Five states offer Temporary Disability Insurance (TDI) programs, which typically provide up to one-half of an employee's wage for up to 52 weeks of temporary disability; this includes disability or conditions related to pregnancy (Lovell and Rahmanou, 2000). These programs are funded through employee contributions or a combination of employer and employee contributions. Women with newborn children often take 6-10 weeks of temporary disability leave for pregnancy, and those requiring longer leave may take up to the maximum allowable by their state's law. As this program is intended to provide wages for leave related to disabilities or medical conditions associated with pregnancy and childbirth, fathers and adopted parents are not eligible for TDI (Hartmann et al., 2013).

With respect to family medical leave, while the federal government does not mandate paid leave, it does guarantee unpaid leave to some workers. Under the Family and Medical Leave Act of 1993 (FMLA), employees may be eligible for up to 12 weeks a year of unpaid leave with job protection for the following circumstances: serious health condition; birth of a child or to care for the employee's newly born, adopted, or foster child; or to care for an immediate family member (spouse, child, or parent) with a serious health condition. Eligibility is limited to employees who work for employers with 50 or more employees and have worked for at least 1,250 hours for the same employer in the past 12 months. Approximately one-half of employees meet these eligibility requirements, and many are unable to take unpaid leave (Han and Waldfogel, 2003; Schuster et al., 2011). Cantor and colleagues estimated that more than three-quarters of the 3.5 million employees in need of leave in 2000 did not take it in order to avoid loss of wages. The majority of these employees would have taken leave had they received partial or additional pay (Cantor et al., 2001; Han and Waldfogel, 2003; Schuster et al., 2011).

The proposed Healthy Families Act (H.R. 932, S. 497) would require certain employers to allow employees to earn paid sick leave that could be used to meet their own medical needs or care for a child or other family member. The proposed Family and Medical Leave Insurance Act (FAMILY Act, H.R. 3712, S. 1810) would guarantee up to 12 weeks of paid family leave, which parents could use to provide care for serious health conditions faced by themselves or family members or to meet care needs associated with the birth or adoption of a child.

At the state level, California, New Jersey, and Rhode Island have established Paid Family Leave Insurance programs that provide wage replacement to employees who take leave to care for a new child or an ill family member; employees fund the leave through payroll deductions to state-wide pools. California's program covers most part- and full-time employees at about 55 percent of their salary, limited to $1,129 weekly in 2016 (California Employment Development Department, 2016), although prior research indicates that many parents were not aware of the benefits (Schuster et al., 2008). Some states and municipalities have laws that entitle employees with access to sick leave to use their leave to care for a new-born or an ill family member. Further, Connecticut, New York City, San Francisco, and Washington, D.C., among others, require employers to offer paid sick leave to their employees. At present, more than 24 other states and municipalities are working on legislation related to paid sick leave (National Partnership for Women and Families, 2015).

Despite these developments, approximately one-half of employees in the United States are not eligible to receive paid sick leave that they are allowed to use to care for family members (Smith and Kim, 2010). Parents without sick leave risk being penalized or losing their job when they must stay home from work to care for a newborn or a sick child.

Disparities in Access

Rates of access to paid leave among employed parents tends to vary with income, and are lower among lower-income relative to higher-income families (Clemans-Cope et al., 2008; Heymann et al., 2006; Phillips, 2004). Among women employed during pregnancy, rates of access to paid leave were found to be higher for women who are married, ages 25 and over, and college graduates (Laughlin, 2011).

Impact of Family Leave on Children and Families

Parental Leave

Research suggests that access to parental leave is associated with increases in breastfeeding rates and duration, reduced risk of infant mortality, and increased likelihood of infants receiving well-baby care and vaccinations. For instance, cohort and case-control studies have shown that women who take maternity leave are more likely to breastfeed, and longer leaves are associated with an increase in both the likelihood and duration of breastfeeding; by contrast, early return to work is associated with an increased probability of early cessation of breastfeeding (Chuang et al., 2010; Guendelman et al., 2009; Hawkins et al., 2007; Staehelin et al., 2007; Visness and Kennedy, 1997). Mothers who took paid leave through California's Paid Family Leave Program were found to breastfeed twice as long as those who did not take leave based on a cross-sectional survey and interviews (Appelbaum and Milkman, 2011). Moreover, children whose mothers take leave from work after childbirth are more likely to receive well-baby checkups and receive all of their recommended vaccinations (Berger et al., 2005; Daku et al., 2012). Analyses of international data have found that paid leave is associated with lower mortality rates for infants and young children, whereas this association is not seen for leave that is neither paid nor job protected (Heymann, 2011; Ruhm, 1998; Tanaka, 2005).

Access to parental leave can benefit maternal health as well. Longitudinal survey data show that women who take longer maternity leaves (more than 12 weeks) tend to experience fewer depressive symptoms and a reduction in severe depression. Additionally, paid leave is associated with improvement in overall mental health (Chatterji and Markowitz, 2012).

Paid leave also is associated with improved labor force attachment among women. Research suggests that women who have access to parental leave tend to utilize that leave period and stay home longer than those without access to such leave, but they are also more likely to return to work after that period of leave (Baum and Ruhm, 2013; Berger and Waldfogel, 2004; Houser and Vartanian, 2012; Rossin-Slater et al., 2013). While women with access to leave were less likely to return to work within the first 12 weeks of giving birth, analysis of data from a longitudinal survey has found that they were 69 percent more likely to return after 12 weeks than new mothers without leave (Berger and Waldfogel, 2004). Offering paid leave is associated with increases in the amount of leave that women take, with higher uptake among women who have less education, are unmarried, or are black or Hispanic, which was found to largely reduce the pre-existing disparities in the amount of leave taken (Berger and

Waldfogel, 2004). Multiple studies have also found that availability of paid leave is associated with increases in the number of hours that a woman works after returning to work, which corresponds to a small increase in wage income (Baum and Ruhm, 2013; Berger and Waldfogel, 2004; Rossin-Slater et al., 2013).

Access to paid paternity leave appears to increase the use of leave among fathers in the early weeks after childbirth and is associated with greater paternal engagement in caregiving in cross-sectional research (Milkman and Appelbaum, 2013). In a correlational analysis of data from Australia, Denmark, the United Kingdom, and the United States to examine the effects of leave policies, fathers who took paternity leave of at least 2 weeks were more likely to engage in activities with the infant during the first several months of the child's life relative to fathers who did not take leave (Huerta et al., 2013).

Family Medical Leave

There are many benefits for children and parents when parents have the ability to take leave that allows them to access recommended preventive care for their children and to properly care for their children when they are ill. Preventive care is crucial to child health and development. For instance, immunizations protect recipients and the public against serious and potentially debilitating diseases. Short- and long-term health benefits, as well as improved educational and economic outcomes, have been linked to the early detection and treatment of diseases (Levy, 2010; Whitlock et al., 2005; Wilcken and Wiley, 2008).

Parents who have access to paid leave can keep an ill child home from daycare or school, which minimizes the chances that their illness will spread to others and maximizes the chances that they will receive timely medical care, if needed, so their illness does not worsen. A 2010 survey found that employees who are eligible for paid sick leave are less likely than employees without this benefit to report sending an ill child to school (Smith and Kim, 2010).

When children are hospitalized, whether for acute or chronic conditions, extended parental presence is crucial in many respects. For instance parents may be required to wait with their child for long periods for an opportunity to speak with the child's health care provider(s) about the child's current clinical status, the anticipated course of illness, and treatment plans going forward. Parents are also valuable sources of information for clinicians, particularly when multiple clinicians are engaged in the child's diagnosis and treatment. In this setting, parents are expected to act as an additional, and sometimes essential, line of supervision and safety for their children. Additionally, parents are able to provide care and comfort to their hospitalized child, who may be frightened and dependent on their presence to minimize anxiety. Indeed, family presence during health care procedures has been shown to decrease anxiety for the child as well as for the parents. The immediate presence of parents before and after surgery has been linked in randomized controlled and quality improvement monitoring research to faster recovery and earlier discharge (Fina et al., 1997; Kain et al., 2007; Shelton and Stepanek, 1994).

For a child to be discharged from the hospital, parents must be present to receive training and to demonstrate their understanding of care for their child upon discharge from the hospital. Moreover, without adequate time and resources for meeting the responsibilities for home care, there may be an increase in emergency room visits, hospital readmissions, and health care costs. Giving parents additional responsibilities without providing them with more time and resources for meeting those responsibilities may lead to increases in return visits to the emergency department, hospital readmissions, morbidity, mortality, and health care costs (Schuster and Chung, 2014).

Research has shown that parents, particularly parents of chronically ill children, experience an unmet need for family medical leave (Chung et al., 2007). Many parents of children with special health care needs who have been able to take leave to care for their child believe it had positive effects on the child's physical and emotional health. However, being away from work may cause financial strain as well as job instability (Schuster et al., 2009).

SUMMARY

An overarching finding of this chapter is that several of the interventions discussed have shown a mix of positive and null findings in evaluation studies. In addition, the variability in the body of literature available for various approaches (e.g., some having been tested in one or two randomized controlled trials, and others having been tested in multiple evaluations that utilized different designs) makes it challenging to draw conclusions about the relative effectiveness of the various approaches. The following points emerged from the committee's review of evidence-based and evidence-informed strategies for strengthening parenting capacity in the areas of universal/preventive and widely used interventions; information and communication technologies; income, nutrition assistance, health care, and housing programs; and parental and family leave policies.

Universal/Preventive Interventions

- Well-child visits reach the majority of children in the United States and support parents in meeting goals for their children's health (e.g., receipt of vaccinations), but few evaluations of well-child care as a parenting intervention have been conducted. Some evidence suggests that enhanced anticipatory guidance, such as that provided in Healthy Steps, is associated with improved parental knowledge of child development and improved parenting practices with respect to vaccination, as well as discipline, safety practices, and reading.
- Preconception and prenatal care optimize maternal health and well-being prior to and during pregnancy. Most women in the United States receive prenatal care, making it an important opportunity for intervention. Although further research is needed, there is some evidence that providing pregnant women with information on pregnancy and early childhood as part of prenatal care increases parental knowledge of parenting practices that promote positive child development and knowledge of how to access such services as child care and medical care. Evidence also suggests that group prenatal care is associated with improved birth outcomes, initiation of breastfeeding, and parental knowledge.
- Primary care-based educational interventions have been found to be associated with improvements in parents' breastfeeding and vaccination practices and with reductions in children's screen time, their exposure to environmental tobacco smoke, and infants being brought to the emergency room because of crying. Health care interventions with a parenting component versus those without a parenting component have been found to be more effective in reducing children's screen time and child overweight and obesity.
- Few studies have explored the effect of public education efforts on parenting knowledge or practices. However, mass public education campaigns targeting safe sleep and child helmet use have been followed by improvements in parental safety practices in these areas. Likewise, evidence in other areas of public health (smoking cessation, obesity prevention) indicates that broad public education efforts can increase awareness of the benefits of health-related behaviors.
- No existing studies show that teaching parenting-related skills to youth of high school age or younger in the general population (who are not pregnant or parents), as in infant simulator programs, supports later parenting capacity or use of evidence-based parenting practices. Since many adolescent parents face obstacles to continuing their education, however, potentially impacting their future em-

ployment and income, adolescent pregnancy prevention programs may strengthen future parental self-sufficiency and parenting.

Widely Used Interventions

- Many individual evaluations of home visiting programs show positive effects on parenting, such as gaining knowledge of child development, practicing contingent responsiveness, creating a safe home environment, and reading to children, among others. However, no strong pattern of effects has emerged across studies (even within the same model). For several models, moreover, the list of outcomes showing no effect is longer than the list showing impacts. Benefits for child development and school readiness and for child maltreatment have been observed for some models. Little assessment has been done in the area of family economic self-sufficiency, although some models show improvements in measures of education and training, use of public assistance, and reductions in rapid repeat pregnancies.

- In the area of two-generation ECE interventions, national longitudinal data on the impact of Head Start provide little evidence that the program's parent components have a positive impact on the use of evidence-based parenting practices. Data on child outcomes are mixed, depending on the time of measurement and whether the data are reported by parents or teachers. It is unclear whether the observed changes in child outcomes are related to changes in parenting or to other Head Start program components. Data on Early Head Start indicate that sites using both center-based and home visiting services tended to have more positive impacts on parenting and child outcomes, perhaps indicating a need for flexibility in programming.

- Evidence from smaller-scale classroom-based and home visiting studies indicates that programs aimed at improving parents' engagement in their children's schooling and parents' decision making about their children's academic experiences, as well as aligning home and classroom learning, are associated with improvements in child reading and language skills and other outcomes.

- Multiple studies have found that intensive (as often as weekly) parent training in the home aimed at promoting parent engagement in the early home learning environment improves parenting practices, such as contingent responsiveness, verbal stimulation, and warmth, among socially disadvantaged mothers of infants and preschool-age children. Such interventions also have been found to improve child language skills and behavior problems. Less intensive interventions that coach parents in dialogic reading have been found to improve child literacy and language outcomes at least in the short term.

Information and Communication Technologies

- Information and communication technologies represent an opportunity to improve the reach of evidence-based parenting information and interventions. Preliminary research shows that integration of the Internet and other technologies into parenting interventions can be effective, but it remains to be seen whether the effects of such approaches are equal to those observed for face-to-face interventions. Further studies are needed that include study populations that are more culturally and socioeconomically diverse than those included to date in studies of the use of these technologies to support parenting, that incorporate electronic tracking to monitor usage, that use formatting for mobile devices, and that examine how entertainment media socialize parents into norms of parenting.

Income, Nutrition Assistance, Health Care, and Housing Programs

- A number of federal income, nutrition assistance, health care, and housing programs support families by providing financial assistance and reducing other stressors that can interfere with parenting, as well as by supporting parents in meeting the nutritional, safety, and health care needs of their children.
- In the area of income support, nonrandomized studies show that the generosity of EITC payments is associated with increases in maternal work, improvements in maternal health-related outcomes and behaviors (including food security and receipt of prenatal and postnatal care), and better child academic and birth outcomes, as well as reductions in maternal stress. Children whose parents receive the Child Tax Credit also have been found to have better academic outcomes. Evidence currently is mixed concerning the effectiveness of TANF in improving health, employment, and education outcomes among adults.
- With regard to nutrition assistance programs, WIC participation is associated with improved birth outcomes, especially among the most disadvantaged mothers, as well as improved child and parent nutrition, infant feeding practices, and receipt of medical care. Mothers participating in WIC have been found to be less likely than nonparticipants to breastfeed. Preliminary evidence shows that children whose mothers participated in WIC while they were

pregnant have improved cognitive outcomes, but further research is needed to confirm this association. Similarly, adults and children who participate in SNAP have improved food security and dietary intake and reduced poverty. Findings on the effects of SNAP on dietary quality have been mixed, with some research showing no difference in this regard between SNAP participants and eligible nonparticipants. Sparse data are available on how the National School Breakfast and National School Lunch Programs impact children's nutritional status.

- The passage of the ACA has expanded access to health care coverage to millions more Americans, including children. This expanded coverage has increased families' access to maternity care and pediatric services, preventive services, and screening and treatment for mental health disorders. Children with health care coverage (e.g., Medicaid, CHIP) are more likely than those without coverage to receive recommended services such as well-child care and immunizations.

- Housing assistance programs help millions of parents find affordable and safe housing for themselves and their young children, resulting in improved food security and reduced poverty and homelessness.

Parental and Family Leave Policies

- Parental leave is associated with positive maternal and child health outcomes. Women who take maternity leave are more likely to breastfeed than those who do not take such leave, and longer leaves are associated with greater likelihood and duration of breastfeeding. In addition, children whose mothers take leave are more likely to receive well-child visits and vaccinations. Other benefits of parental leave based on correlational research include fewer depressive symptoms for women, improved labor force attachment, and increases in fathers' use of leave in the early weeks after childbirth, as well as greater paternal engagement and caregiving. Family medical leave allows parents to better care for their children when they are sick and ensure that they receive appropriate preventive care.

REFERENCES

Acs, G., and Loprest, P. (2007). *TANF Caseload Composition and Leavers Synthesis Report: Final Report.* Washington, DC: Urban Institute.

Administration for Children and Families. (2015a). *Home Visiting Evidence of Effectiveness: Durham Connects/Family Connects.* Available: http://homvee.acf.hhs.gov/Model/1/Durham-Connects-Family-Connects/59/1 [February 2016].

Administration for Children and Families. (2015b). *Home Visiting Evidence of Effectiveness: Nurse Family Partnership*. Available: http://homvee.acf.hhs.gov/Model/1/Nurse-Family-Partnership--NFP--In-Brief/14 [June 2016].

Administration for Children and Families. (2015c). *Home Visiting Evidence of Effectiveness: Parents as Teachers*. Available: http://homvee.acf.hhs.gov/Model/1/Parents-as-Teachers--PAT--sup---sup-/16/1 [June 2016].

Administration for Children and Families. (2015d). *Notice of Proposed Rule Making on Head Start Program Performance Standards*. Washington, DC: Head Start.

Administration of Children and Families. (2016). *Office of Head Start*. Available: http://www.acf.hhs.gov/programs/ohs [February 2016].

Agency for Healthcare Research and Quality. (2015). *Group Visits Focused on Prenatal Care and Parenting Improve Birth Outcomes and Provider Efficiency*. Available: https://innovations.ahrq.gov/profiles/group-visits-focused-prenatal-care-and-parenting-improve-birth-outcomes-and-provider [October 2016].

Alker, J., and Kenney, G. (2014). *A First Look at How the Affordable Care Act Is Affecting Coverage Among Parents and Children*. Available: http://healthaffairs.org/blog/2014/09/09/a-first-look-at-how-the-affordable-care-act-is-affecting-coverage-among-parents-and-children [March 2016].

Allen, K., and Rainie, L. (2002). *Parents Online*. Available: http://www.pewinternet.org/2002/11/17/parents-online [February 2016].

American Academy of Family Physicians. (2005). *Policy Recommendations for Periodic Health Examinations*. Available: http://www.aafp.org/exam.xml [February 2016].

American Academy of Pediatrics. (2000). Recommendations for preventive pediatric health care. *Pediatrics, 105*, 645-646.

American Academy of Pediatrics. (2002). *Guidelines for Health Supervision III*. Elk Grove Village, IL: American Academy of Pediatrics.

American Academy of Pediatrics. (2004). *Using Time as the Key Factor for Evaluation and Management Visits*. Elk Grove Village, IL: American Academy of Pediatrics.

American Academy of Pediatrics. (2008). *Recommendations for Preventive Pediatric Health Care*. Elk Grove Village, IL: American Academy of Pediatrics.

American Academy of Pediatrics. (2014). Children's Health Insurance Program (CHIP): Accomplishments, challenges, and policy recommendations. *Pediatrics, 133*(3), e784-e793.

American Academy of Pediatrics and Bright Futures. (2016). *Recommendations for Preventive Pediatric Health Care*. Elk Grove Village, IL: American Academy of Pediatrics.

Andreyeva, T., Tripp, A.S., and Schwartz, M.B. (2015). Dietary quality of Americans by Supplemental Nutrition Assistance Program participation status. *American Journal of Preventive Medicine, 49*(4), 594-604.

Appelbaum, E., and Milkman, R. (2011). *Leaves That Pay: Employer and Worker Experiences with Paid Family Leave in California*. Available: https://cepr.net/documents/publications/paid-family-leave-1-2011.pdf [February 2016].

Aragon, N.J., Hudnut-Beumler, J., White Webb, M., Chavis, A., Dietrich, M.S., Bickman, L., and Scholer, S.J. (2013). The effect of primary care interventions on children's media viewing habits and exposure to violence. *Academic Pediatrics, 13*(6), 531-539.

Arbour, M. (2015). *Lessons on Home Visiting Program Implementation from the Collaborative for Improvement and Innovation Network (HV CoIIN): Promoting Wide-Scale Adoption of Evidence-Based Strategies with Continuous Quality Improvement Methodologies*. Paper presented at the Committee on Supporting the Parents of Young Children Open Session, June 29, Irvine, CA.

Arno, P.S., Sohler, N., Viola, D., and Schechter, C. (2009). Bringing health and social policy together: The case of the earned income tax credit. *Journal of Public Health Policy, 30*(2), 198-207.

Arnold, D.H., Lonigan, C.J., Whitehurst, G.J., and Epstein, J.N. (1994). Accelerating language development through picture book reading: Replication and extension to a videotape training format. *Journal of Educational Psychology, 86*(2), 235-243.

Auger, A. (2015). *Child Care and Community Services: Characteristics of Service Use and Effects on Parenting and the Home Environment.* Ph.D. dissertation, University of California Irvine School of Education.

Aune, D., Saugstad, O.D., Henriksen, T., and Tonstad, S. (2014). Maternal body mass index and the risk of fetal death, stillbirth, and infant death: A systematic review and meta-analysis. *Journal of the American Medical Association, 311*(15), 1536-1546.

Avellar, S., Paulsell, D., Sama-Miller, E., and Del Grosso, P. (2012). *Home Visiting Evidence of Effectiveness Review: Executive Summary.* Washington, DC: Office of Planning, Research and Evaluation; Administration for Children and Families; U.S. Department of Health and Human Services.

Avellar, S., Paulsell, D., Sama-Miller, E., Del Grosso, P., Akers, L., and Kleinman, R. (2014). *Home Visiting Evidence of Effectiveness Review: Executive Summary.* Washington, DC: Office of Planning, Research and Evaluation; Administration for Children and Families; U.S. Department of Health and Human Services.

Avellar, S., Paulsell, D., Sama-Miller, E., Del Grosso, P., Akers, L., and Kleinman, R. (2015). *Home Visiting Evidence of Effectiveness Review: Executive Summary.* Washington, DC: Office of Planning, Research and Evaluation; Administration for Children and Families; U.S. Department of Health and Human Services.

Averett, S.L., and Yang, W. (2012). *The Effects of EITC Payment Expansion on Maternal Smoking.* Available: http://ftp.iza.org/dp6680.pdf [April 2016].

Baggett, K.M., Davis, B., Feil, E.G., Sheeber, L.L., Landry, S.H., Carta, J.J., and Leve, C. (2010). Technologies for expanding the reach of evidence-based interventions: Preliminary results for promoting social-emotional development in early childhood. *Topics in Early Childhood Special Education, 29*(4), 226-238.

Baker, K. (2008). *Do Cash Transfer Programs Improve Infant Health?: Evidence from the 1993 Expansion of the Earned Income Tax Credit.* Working Paper. Notre Dame, IN: University of Notre Dame.

Baker, C.N., Arnold, D.H., and Meagher, S. (2011). Enrollment and attendance in a parent training prevention program for conduct problems. *Prevention Science, 12*(2), 126-138.

Barlow, A., Mullany, B., Neault, N., Compton, S., Carter, A., Hastings, R., Billy, T., Coho-Mescal, V., Lorenzo, S., and Walkup, J.T. (2013). Effect of a paraprofessional home-visiting intervention on American Indian teen mothers' and infants' behavioral risks: A randomized controlled trial. *American Journal of Psychiatry, 170*(1), 83-93.

Barnett, W.S., and Masse, L.N. (2007). Comparative benefit-cost analysis of the Abecedarian program and its policy implications. *Economics of Education Review, 26*(1), 113-125.

Barr, R.G. (2012). Preventing abusive head trauma resulting from a failure of normal inter-action between infants and their caregivers. *Proceedings of the National Academy of Sciences, 109*(Suppl. 2), 17294-17301.

Barr, R.G., Rajabali, F., Aragon, M., Colbourne, M., and Brant, R. (2015). Education about crying in normal infants is associated with a reduction in pediatric emergency room visits for crying complaints. *Journal of Developmental & Behavioral Pediatrics, 36*(4), 252-257.

Barth, R.P. (2009). Preventing child abuse and neglect with parent training: Evidence and opportunities. *The Future of Children, 19*(2), 95-118.

Baum, C.L., and Ruhm, C.J. (2013). *The Effects of Paid Family Leave in California on Labor Market Outcomes.* Working Paper No. 19741. Cambridge, MA: National Bureau of Economic Research.

Berger, L.M., and Waldfogel, J. (2004). Maternity leave and the employment of new mothers in the United States. *Journal of Population Economics, 17*(2), 331-349.

Berger, L.M., Hill, J., and Waldfogel, J. (2005). Maternity leave, early maternal employment and child health and development in the U.S. *The Economic Journal, 115*(501), F29-F47.

Bergman, D.A., Beck, A., and Rahm, A.K. (2009). The use of Internet-based technology to tailor well-child care encounters. *Pediatrics, 124*(1), 37-43.

Bethell, C.D., Kogan, M.D., Strickland, B.B., Schor, E.L., Robertson, J., and Newacheck, P.W. (2011). A national and state profile of leading health problems and health care quality for U.S. children: Key insurance disparities and across-state variations. *Academic Pediatrics, 11*(Suppl. 3), S22-S33.

Bierman, K.L., Welsh, J.A., Heinrichs, B.S., Nix, R.L., and Mathis, E.T. (2015). Helping Head Start parents promote their children's kindergarten adjustment: The research-based developmentally informed parent program. *Child Development, 86*(6), 1877-1891.

Bigelow, K. (2014). *Cellular-Phone Enhanced Home Visitation Parenting Intervention: A Randomized Trial.* Paper presented at the Society for Prevention Research 22nd Annual Meeting, May 27-30, 2013, Washington, DC.

Blank, R.M. (1997). *It Takes a Nation: A New Agenda for Fighting Poverty.* New York: Russell Sage Foundation and Princeton, NJ: Princeton University Press.

Bloom, B., Cohen, R.A., and Freeman, G. (2013). Summary health statistics for U.S. children: National Health Interview Survey, 2012. *Vital Health Statistics, 10*(258).

Bloom, D., Loprest, P.J., and Zedlewski, S.R. (2011). *TANF Recipients with Barriers to Employment.* Washington, DC: Urban Institute.

Boles, M., Adams, A., Gredler, A., and Manhas, S. (2014). Ability of a mass media campaign to influence knowledge, attitudes, and behaviors about sugary drinks and obesity. *Preventive Medicine, 67*(Suppl. 1), S40-S45.

Boller, K., Strong, D.A., and Daro, D. (2010). Home visiting: Looking back and moving forward. *ZERO TO THREE Journal, 30*(6), 4-9.

Brazelton, T.B. (1992). *Touchpoints: Your Child's Emotional and Behavioral Development.* Reading, MA: Addison-Wesley.

Breitenstein, S.M., and Gross, D. (2013). Web-based delivery of a preventive parent training intervention: A feasibility study. *Journal of Child and Adolescent Psychiatric Nursing, 26*(2), 149-157.

Breitenstein, S.M., Gross, D., Fogg, L., Ridge, A., Garvey, C., Julion, W., and Tucker, S. (2012). The Chicago parent program: Comparing 1-year outcomes for African American and Latino parents of young children. *Research in Nursing & Health, 35*(5), 475-489.

Breitenstein, S.M., Gross, D., and Christophersen, R. (2014). Digital delivery methods of parenting training interventions: A systematic review. *Worldviews on Evidence-Based Nursing, 11*(3), 168-176.

Breitenstein, S.M., Shane, J., Julion, W., and Gross, D. (2015). Developing the eCPP: Adapting an evidence-based parent training program for digital delivery in primary care settings. *Worldviews on Evidence-Based Nursing, 12*(1), 31-40.

Brooks-Gunn, J., Berlin, L.J., and Fuligni, A.S. (2000). Early childhood intervention programs: What about the family? In J.P. Shonkoff and S.J. Meisels (Eds.), *Handbook of Early Childhood Intervention* (2nd ed., pp. 549-588). New York: Cambridge University Press.

Brotman, L.M., Calzada, E., Huang, K.Y., Kingston, S., Dawson-McClure, S., Kamboukos, D., Rosenfelt, A., Schwab, A., and Petkova, E. (2011). Promoting effective parenting practices and preventing child behavior problems in school among ethnically diverse families from underserved, urban communities. *Child Development, 82*(1), 258-276.

Brown, N., Luckett, T., Davidson, P., and Di Giacomo, M. (2015). Interventions to reduce harm from smoking with families in infancy and early childhood: A systematic review. *International Journal of Environmental Research and Public Health, 12*(3), 3091-3119.

Burchinal, M.R., Campbell, F.A., Bryant, D.M., Wasik, B.H., and Ramey, C.T. (1997). Early intervention and mediating processes in cognitive performance of children of low-income African American families. *Child Development, 68*(5), 935-954.

Burwell, S.M. (2016). *The Department of Health and Human Services 2015 Annual Report on the Quality of Care for Children in Medicaid and CHIP.* Available: https://www.medicaid.gov/medicaid-chip-program-information/by-topics/quality-of-care/downloads/2015-child-sec-rept.pdf [April 2016].

Caldera, D., Burrell, L., Rodriguez, K., Shea Crowne, S., Rohde, C., and Duggan, A. (2007). Impact of a statewide home visiting program on parenting and on child health and development. *Child Abuse and Neglect, 31*(8), 829-852.

California Employment Development Department. (2016). *Disability Insurance (DI) and Paid Family Leave (PFL) Benefit Amounts.* Available: http://www.edd.ca.gov/disability/State_Disability_Insurance_(SDI)_Benefit_Amounts.htm [April 2016].

Camilli, G., Vargas, S., Ryan, S., and Barnett, W.S. (2010). Meta-analysis of the effects of early education interventions on cognitive and social development. *Teachers College Record, 112*(3), 579-620.

Campbell, F.A., and Ramey, C.T. (1994). Effects of early intervention on intellectual and academic achievement: A follow-up study of children from low-income families. *Child Development, 65*(2), 684-698.

Canter, J., Rao, V., Patrick, P.A., Alpan, G., and Altman, R.L. (2015). The impact of a hospital-based educational video on maternal perceptions and planned practices of infant safe sleep. *Journal for Specialists in Pediatric Nursing, 20*(3), 187-192.

Cantor, D., Waldfogel, J., Kerwin, J., Wright, M.M., Levin, K., Rauch, J., Hagerty, T., and Kudela, M.S. (2001). *Balancing the Needs of Families and Employers. The Family and Medical Leave Surveys, 2000 Update: A Report.* Washington, DC: U.S. Department of Labor.

Carlson, S., and Neuberger, Z. (2015). *WIC Works: Addressing the Nutrition and Health Needs of Low-Income Families for 40 Years.* Available: http://www.cbpp.org/research/food-assistance/wic-works-addressing-the-nutrition-and-health-needs-of-low-income-families [October 2016].

Carlson, D., Haveman, R., Kaplan, T., and Wolfe, B. (2012). Long-term effects of public low-income housing vouchers on neighborhood quality and household composition. *Journal of Housing Economics, 21*(2), 101-120.

Carpenter, D. M., Geryk, L.L., Chen, A.T., Nagler, R.H., Dieckmann, N.F., and Han, P.K. (2015). Conflicting health information: A critical research need. *Health Expectations* [E-pub ahead of print].

Carta, J.J., Lefever, J.B., Bigelow, K., Borkowski, J., and Warren, S.F. (2013). Randomized trial of a cellular phone-enhanced home visitation parenting intervention. *Pediatrics, 132*(Suppl. 2), S167-S173.

Catling, C.J., Medley, N., Foureur, M., Ryan, C., Leap, N., Teate, A., and Homer, C.S. (2015). Group versus conventional antenatal care for women. *Cochrane Database of Systematic Reviews, 2.*

Caughy, M.O., Miller, T.L., Genevro, J.L., Huang, K.-Y., and Nautiyal, C. (2003). The effects of healthy steps on discipline strategies of parents of young children. *Journal of Applied Developmental Psychology, 24*(5), 517-534.

Caughy, M.O., Huang, K.-Y., Miller, T., and Genevro, J.L. (2004). The effects of the healthy steps for young children program: Results from observations of parenting and child development. *Early Childhood Research Quarterly, 19*(4), 611-630.

Cebi, M., and Woodbury, S.A. (2009). *Health Insurance Tax Credits and Health Insurance Coverage of Low-Earning Single Mothers.* Available: http://www.upjohninstitute.org/publications/wp/09-158.pdf [April 2016].

Cefai, J., Smith, D., and Pushak, R.E. (2010). Parenting wisely: Parent training via CD-ROM with an Australian sample. *Child and Family Behavior Therapy, 32*(1), 17-33.

Center on Budget and Policy Priorities. (2015a). *Chart Book: SNAP Helps Struggling Families Put Food on the Table.* Washington, DC: Center on Budget and Policy Priorities.

Center on Budget and Policy Priorities. (2015b). *Policy Basics: An Introduction to TANF.* Washington, DC: Center on Budget and Policy Priorities.

Center on Budget and Policy Priorities. (2015c). *Policy Basics: The Housing Choice Voucher Program.* Washington, DC: Center on Budget and Policy Priorities.

Center on Budget and Policy Priorities. (2016). *Chart Book: The Earned Income Tax Credit and Child Tax Credit.* Washington, DC: Center on Budget and Policy Priorities.

Centers for Disease Control and Prevention. (2016). *Essentials for Parenting Toddlers and Preschoolers.* Available: http://www.cdc.gov/ncbddd/childdevelopment/index.html [October 2016].

Chacko, A., Wymbs, B.T., Wymbs, F.A., Pelham, W.E., Swanger-Gagne, M.S., Girio, E., Pirvics, L., Herbst, L., Guzzo, J., Phillips, C., and O'Connor, B. (2009). Enhancing traditional behavioral parent training for single mothers of children with ADHD. *Journal of Clinical Child & Adolescent Psychology, 38*(2), 206-218.

Chan, S.S.C., Lam, T.H., Salili, F., Leung, G.M., Wong, D.C.N., Botelho, R.J., Lo, S.L., and Lau, Y.L. (2005). A randomized controlled trial of an individualized motivational intervention on smoking cessation for parents of sick children: A pilot study. *Applied Nursing Research, 18*(3), 178-181.

Chang, S.M., Grantham-McGregor, S.M., Powell, C.A., Vera-Hernández, M., Lopez-Boo, F., Baker-Henningham, H., and Walker, S.P. (2015). Integrating a parenting intervention with routine primary health care: A cluster randomized trial. *Pediatrics, 136*(2), 272-280.

Chase-Lansdale, P.L., and Brooks-Gunn, J. (2014). Two-generation programs in the twenty-first century. *The Future of Children, 24*(1), 13-39.

Chatterji, P., and Markowitz, S. (2012). Family leave after childbirth and the mental health of new mothers. *The Journal of Mental Health Policy and Economics, 15*(2), 61-76.

Chetty, R., Friedman, J.N., and Rockoff, J. (2011). New evidence on the long-term impacts of tax credits. *Proceedings. Annual Conference on Taxation and Minutes of the Annual Meeting of the National Tax Association, 104,*116-124.

Child and Adolescent Health Measurement Initiative. (2012). *Who Are Children with Special Health Care Needs (CSHCN).* Data Resource Center, supported by Cooperative Agreement 1-U59-MC06980-01 from the U.S. Department of Health and Human Services, Health Resources and Services Administration (HRSA), Maternal and Child Health Bureau (MCHB). Available: http://www.childhealthdata.org [August 2016].

Child Trends Databank. (2014). *Child Trends Databank: Well-Child Visits.* Bethesda, MD: Child Trends.

Child Trends Databank. (2015). *Mothers Who Smoke while Pregnant: Indicators on Children and Youth.* Bethesda, MD: Child Trends.

Christakis, D.A., Zimmerman, F.J., Rivara, F.P., and Ebel, B. (2006). Improving pediatric prevention via the Internet: A randomized, controlled trial. *Pediatrics, 118*(3), 1157-1166.

Chuang, C.-H., Chang, P.-J., Chen, Y.-C., Hsieh, W.-S., Hurng, B.-S., Lin, S.-J., and Chen, P.-C. (2010). Maternal return to work and breastfeeding: A population-based cohort study. *International Journal of Nursing Studies, 47*(4), 461-474.

Chung, P.J., Garfield, C.F., Elliott, M.N., Carey, C., Eriksson, C., and Schuster, M.A. (2007). Need for and use of family leave among parents of children with special health care needs. *Pediatrics, 119*(5), 1047-1055.

Clemans-Cope, L., Perry, C.D., Kenney, G.M., Pelletier, J.E., and Pantell, M.S. (2008). Access to and use of paid sick leave among low-income families with children. *Pediatrics, 122*(2), 480-486.

Coatsworth, J.D., Duncan, L.G., Pantin, H., and Szapocznik, J. (2006). Retaining ethnic minority parents in a preventive intervention: The quality of group process. *Journal of Primary Prevention, 27*(4), 367-389.

Coker, T.R., Chacon, S., Elliott, M.N., Bruno, Y., Chavis, T., Biely, C., Bethell, C.D., Contreras, S., Mimila, N.A., Mercado, J., and Chung, P.J. (2016). A parent coach model for well-child care among low-income children: A randomized controlled trial. *Pediatrics, 137*(3), 1-10.

Coleman-Jensen, A., Gregory, C., and Rabbitt, M. (2015). *Food Security Status of U.S. Households in 2014*. Available: http://www.ers.usda.gov/topics/food-nutrition-assistance/food-security-in-the-us/key-statistics-graphics.aspx#children [June 2016].

Cowan, C.P., Cowan, P.A., and Barry, J. (2011). Couples' groups for parents of preschoolers: Ten-year outcomes of a randomized trial. *Journal of the Division of Family Psychology of the American Psychological Association (Division 43), 25*(2), 240-250.

Cowan, C.P., and Cowan, P.A. (2000). *When Partners Become Parents: The Big Life Change for Couples*. Mahwah, NJ: Lawrence Erlbaum Associates.

Cowan, P.A., and Cowan, C.P. (2014). Controversies in couple relationship education (CRE): Overlooked evidence and implications for research and policy. *Psychology, Public Policy, and Law, 20*(4), 361-383.

Cowan, P.A., Cowan, C.P., and Knox, V. (2010). Marriage and fatherhood programs. *The Future of Children, 20*(2), 205-230.

Cowart-Osborne, M., Jackson, M., Chege, E., Baker, E., Whitaker, D., and Self-Brown, S. (2014). Technology-based innovations in child maltreatment prevention programs: Examples from SafeCare®. *Social Sciences, 3*(3), 427-440.

Crawford, M., Church, J., and Akin, B. (2016). *CPI Detailed Report: Data for March 2016*. Available: http://www.bls.gov/cpi/cpid1603.pdf [May 2016].

Dahl, G.B., and Lochner, L. (2012). The impact of family income on child achievement: Evidence from the Earned Income Tax Credit. *The American Economic Review, 102*(5), 1927-1956.

Daku, M., Raub, A., and Heymann, J. (2012). Maternal leave policies and vaccination coverage: A global analysis. *Social Science and Medicine, 74*(2), 120-124.

Damiano, P.C., Willard, J.C., Momany, E.T., and Chowdhury, J. (2003). The impact of the Iowa S-SCHIP Program on access, health status, and the family environment. *Ambulatory Pediatrics, 3*(5), 263-269.

Daro, D. (2006). *Home Visitation: Assessing Progress, Managing Expectations*. Chicago, IL: Chapin Hall Center for Children.

Daro, D. (2011). Home visitation. In E. Zigler, W. Gilliam, and S. Barnett (Eds.), *The Pre-K Debates: Current Controversies and Issues* (pp. 169-173). Baltimore, MD: Paul H. Brookes.

Daro, D., and Benedetti, G. (2014). *Sustaining Progress in Preventing Child Maltreatment: A Transformative Challenge*. Chicago, IL: Chapin Hall, University of Chicago.

Dearing, E., and Tang, S. (2010). The home learning environment and achievement during childhood. In S.L. Christenson and A.L. Reschly (Eds.), *Handbook of School-Family Partnerships* (pp. 131-157). New York: Routledge.

Dearing, E., Sibly, E., and Nguyen, H.N. (2015). Achievement mediators of family engagement in children's education: A family-school-community systems model. In S.M. Sheridan and E. Moorman Kim (Eds.), *Processes and Pathways of Family-School Partnerships across Development* (vol. 2, pp. 17-39). Basel, Switzerland: Springer International.

De-Regil, L.M., Fernández-Gaxiola, A.C., Dowswell, T., and Peña-Rosas, J.P. (2010). Effects and safety of periconceptional folate supplementation for preventing birth defects. *Cochrane Database of Systematic Reviews, 10*.

Dodge, K.A., Goodman, W.B., Murphy, R.A., O'Donnell, K., and Sato, J. (2013). Randomized controlled trial of universal postnatal nurse home visiting: Impact on emergency care. *Pediatrics, 132*(Suppl. 2), S140-S146.

Duggan, M., Lenhart, A., Lampe, C., and Ellison, N.B. (2015). *Seeking Parenting Advice on Social Media.* Available: http://www.pewinternet.org/2015/07/16/seeking-parenting-advice-on-social-media [October 2016].

Duncan, G.J., and Magnuson, K. (2013). The long reach of early childhood poverty. In W.-J. Yeung and M.T. Yap (Eds.), *Economic Stress, Human Capital, and Families in Asia* (pp. 57-70). Dordrecht, Netherlands: Springer.

Duncan, G.J., Dunifon, R.E., Doran, M.B.W., and Yeung, W.J. (2001). How different are welfare and working families? And do these differences matter for children's achievement? In G.J. Duncan and P.L. Chase-Lansdale (Eds.), *For Better and for Worse: Welfare Reform and the Well-Being of Children and Families* (pp. 103-131). New York: Russell Sage Foundation.

Duncan, G.J., Morris, P.A., and Rodrigues, C. (2011). Does money really matter? Estimating impacts of family income on young children's achievement with data from random-assignment experiments. *Developmental Psychology, 47*(5), 1263-1279.

Dunn, R.A., Shenouda, P.E., Martin, D.R., and Schultz, A.J. (1998). Videotape increases parent knowledge about poliovirus vaccines and choices of polio vaccination schedules. *Pediatrics, 102*(2), e26.

Early Developmental Screening and Intervention Initiative. (2011). *Roles for Women, Infants and Children (WIC) Program in Promoting Quality Developmental Care for Young Children: A Report on Lessons Learned and Options.* Available: http://www.first5la.org/files/RolesforWICPrograminPromotingQuality.pdf [February 2016].

Eckenrode, J., Campa, M., Luckey, D.W., Henderson, C.R., Jr., Cole, R., Kitzman, H., Anson, E., Sidora-Arcoleo, K., Powers, J., and Olds, D. (2010). Long-term effects of prenatal and infancy nurse home visitation on the life course of youths: 19-year follow-up of a randomized trial. *Archives of Pediatrics & Adolescent Medicine, 164*(1), 9-15.

El Nokali, N.E., Bachman, H.J., and Votruba-Drzal, E. (2010). Parent involvement and children's academic and social development in elementary school. *Child Development, 81*(3), 988-1005.

Evans, W.N., and Garthwaite, C.L. (2010). *Giving Mom a Break: The Impact of Higher EITC Payments on Maternal Health.* NBER Working Paper No. 16296. Cambridge, MA: National Bureau of Economic Research.

Faircloth, W.B., Schermerhorn, A.C., Mitchell, P.M., Cummings, J.S., and Cummings, E.M. (2011). Testing the long-term efficacy of a prevention program for improving marital conflict in community families. *Journal of Applied Developmental Psychology, 32*(4), 189-197.

Fan, X., and Chen, M. (2001). Parental involvement and students' academic achievement: A meta-analysis. *Educational Psychology Review, 13*(1), 1-22.

Fantuzzo, J., McWayne, C., Perry, M.A., and Childs, S. (2004). Multiple dimensions of family involvement and their relations to behavioral and learning competencies for urban, low-income children. *School Psychology Review, 33*(4), 467-480.

Fantuzzo, J., Gadsden, V., Li, F., Sproul, F., McDermott, P., Hightower, D., and Minney, A. (2013). Multiple dimensions of family engagement in early childhood education: Evidence for a short form of the family involvement questionnaire. *Early Childhood Research Quarterly, 28*(4), 734-742.

Farber, M.L. (2009). Parent mentoring and child anticipatory guidance with Latino and African American families. *Health & Social Work, 34*(3), 179-189.

Feinberg, M.E., Jones, D.E., Kan, M.L., and Goslin, M.C. (2010). Effects of family foundations on parents and children: 3.5 years after baseline. *Journal of the Division of Family Psychology of the American Psychological Association (Division 43)*, 24(5), 532-542.

File, T., and Ryan, C. (2014). *Computer and Internet Use in the United States: 2013*. Available: http://www.census.gov/history/pdf/2013computeruse.pdf [October 2016].

Fina, D.K., Lopas, L.J., Stagnone, J.H., and Santucci, P.R. (1997). Parent participation in the postanesthesia care unit: Fourteen years of progress at one hospital. *Journal of PeriAnesthesia Nursing*, 12(3), 152-162.

Finer, L.B., and Zolna, M.R. (2014). Shifts in intended and unintended pregnancies in the United States, 2001-2008. *American Journal of Public Health*, 104(Suppl. 1), S43-S48.

Ford, R.M., McDougall, S.J., and Evans, D. (2009). Parent-delivered compensatory education for children at risk of educational failure: Improving the academic and self-regulatory skills of a sure start preschool sample. *British Journal of Psychology*, 100(4), 773-797.

Fox, M.H., Moore, J., Davis, R., and Heintzelman, R. (2003). Changes in reported health status and unmet need for children enrolling in the Kansas Children's Health Insurance Program. *American Journal of Public Health*, 93(4), 579-582.

Fox, M.K., Hamilton, W., and Lin, B.-H. (2004). *Effects of Food Assistance and Nutrition Programs on Nutrition and Health*. Food Assistance and Nutrition Research Report Number 19-3. Washington, DC: Economic Research Service, U.S. Department of Agriculture.

Friend, K., and Levy, D.T. (2002). Reductions in smoking prevalence and cigarette consumption associated with mass-media campaigns. *Health Education Research*, 17(1), 85-98.

Gable, S., Chang, Y., and Krull, J.L. (2007). Television watching and frequency of family meals are predictive of overweight onset and persistence in a national sample of school-aged children. *Journal of the American Dietetic Association*, 107(1), 53-61.

Garcia, D., Bagner, D.M., Pruden, S.M., and Nichols-Lopez, K. (2015). Language production in children with and at risk for delay: Mediating role of parenting skills. *Journal of Clinical Child & Adolescent Psychology*, 44(5), 814-825.

García Coll, C., Lamberty, G., Jenkins, R., McAdoo, H.P., Crnic, K., Wasik, B.H., and Garcia, H.V. (1996). An integrative model for the study of developmental competencies in minority children. *Child Development*, 67(5), 1891-1914.

Garvey, C., Julion, W., Fogg, L., Kratovil, A., and Gross, D. (2006). Measuring participation in a prevention trial with parents of young children. *Research in Nursing & Health*, 29(3), 212-222.

Gibson, M., Petticrew, M., Bambra, C., Sowden, A.J., Wright, K.E., and Whitehead, M. (2011). Housing and health inequalities: A synthesis of systematic reviews of interventions aimed at different pathways linking housing and health. *Health & Place*, 17(1), 175-184.

Glascoe, F.P., Oberklaid, F., Dworkin, P.H., and Trimm, F. (1998). Brief approaches to educating patients and parents in primary care. *Pediatrics*, 101(6), E10.

Gold, K.J., and Marcus, S.M. (2008). Effect of maternal mental illness on pregnancy outcomes. *Expert Review of Obstetrics & Gynecology*, 3(3), 391-401.

Goodstein, M.H., Bell, T., and Krugman, S.D. (2015). Improving infant sleep safety through a comprehensive hospital-based program. *Clinical Pediatrics*, 54(3), 212-221.

Granger, R.C., and Cytron, R. (1999). Teenage parent programs a synthesis of the long-term effects of the new chance demonstration, Ohio's learning, earning, and parenting program, and the teenage parent demonstration. *Evaluation Review*, 23(2), 107-145.

Gray, K.F., and Kochhar, S. (2015). *Characteristics of Supplemental Nutrition Assistance Program Households: Fiscal Year 2014*. Report No. SNAP-15-CHAR. Alexandria, VA: U.S. Department of Agriculture.

Green, M., and Palfrey, J. (2002). *Bright Futures: Guidelines for Health Supervision of Infants, Children, and Adolescents.* Arlington, VA: National Center for Education in Maternal and Child Health, Georgetown University.

Greenberg, D., Deitch, V., and Hamilton, G., and Manpower Demonstration Research. (2009). *Welfare-to-Work Program Benefits and Costs: A Synthesis of Research.* New York: Manpower Demonstration Research Corporation.

Gregory, C., Ver Ploeg, M., Andrews, M., and Coleman-Jensen, A. (2013). *Supplemental Nutrition Assistance Program (SNAP) Participation Leads to Modest Changes in Diet Quality.* Economic Research Report No. 147. Washington, DC: Economic Research Service, U.S. Department of Agriculture.

Griswold, C.H., Nasso, J.T., Swider, S., Ellison, B.R., Griswold, D.L., and Brooks, M. (2013). The prenatal care at school program. *The Journal of School Nursing: The Official Publication of the National Association of School Nurses, 29*(3), 196-203.

Guendelman, S., Kosa, J.L., Pearl, M., Graham, S., Goodman, J., and Kharrazi, M. (2009). Juggling work and breastfeeding: Effects of maternity leave and occupational characteristics. *Pediatrics, 123*(1), 38-46.

Gundersen, C., Kreider, B., and Pepper, J. (2012). The impact of the National School Lunch Program on child health: A nonparametric bounds analysis. *Journal of Econometrics, 166*(1), 79-91.

Guttentag, C.L., Landry, S.H., Williams, J.M., Baggett, K.M., Noria, C.W., Borkowski, J.G., Swank, P.R., Farris, J.R., Crawford, A., and Lanzi, R.G. (2014). "My Baby & Me": Effects of an early, comprehensive parenting intervention on at-risk mothers and their children. *Developmental Psychology, 50*(5), 1482-1496.

Hahn, H., Kassabian, D., and Zedlewski, S. (2012). *TANF Work Requirements and State Strategies to Fulfill Them.* Washington, DC: Urban Institute.

Halfon, N., Stevens, G.D., Larson, K., and Olson, L.M. (2011). Duration of a well-child visit: Association with content, family-centeredness, and satisfaction. *Pediatrics, 128*(4), 657-664.

Hamilton, G., and Scrivener, S. (2012). *Increasing Employment Stability and Earnings for Low-Wage Workers: Lessons from the Employment Retention and Advancement (ERA) Project.* Report 2012-19. Washington, DC: Office of Planning, Research and Evaluation; Administration for Children and Families; U.S. Department of Health and Human Services.

Han, W.-J., and Waldfogel, J. (2003). Parental leave: The impact of recent legislation on parents leave taking. *Demography, 40*(1), 191-200.

Hartline-Grafton, H. (2013). *SNAP and Public Health: The Role of the Supplemental Nutrition Assistance Program in Improving the Health and Well-Being of Americans.* Washington, DC: Food Research & Action Center.

Hartmann, H., Reichlin, L., Milli, J., Gault, B., and Hegewisch, A. (2013). *Paid Parental Leave in the United States.* Washington, DC: U.S. Department of Labor.

Hawkins, S.S., Griffiths, L.J., Dezateux, C., Law, C., and Millennium Cohort Study Child Health Group. (2007). The impact of maternal employment on breast-feeding duration in the UK millennium cohort study. *Public Health Nutrition, 10*(9), 891-896.

Health Resources and Services Administration. (2016). *The Maternal, Infant, and Early Childhood Home Visiting Program: Partnering with Parents to Help Children Succeed.* Washington, DC: U.S. Department of Health and Human Services,.

Heinicke, C.M., Fineman, N.R., Ponce, V.A., and Guthrie, D. (2001). Relation-based intervention with at-risk mothers: Outcome in the second year of life. *Infant Mental Health Journal, 22*(4), 431-462.

Heinrich, C.J. (2014). Parents' employment and children's well-being. *The Future of Children, 24*(1), 121-146.

Heinrichs, N., Bertram, H., Kuschel, A., and Hahlweg, K. (2005). Parent recruitment and retention in a universal prevention program for child behavior and emotional problems: Barriers to research and program participation. *Prevention Science, 6*(4), 275-286.

Henderson, A.T., and Mapp, K.L. (2002). *A New Wave of Evidence: The Impact of School, Family, and Community Connections on Student Achievement. Annual Synthesis 2002.* Austin, TX: National Center for Family and Community Connections with Schools.

Herbst, C.M. (2010). The labor supply effects of child care costs and wages in the presence of subsidies and the Earned Income Tax Credit. *Review of Economics of the Household, 8*(2), 199-230.

Herrman, J.W., Waterhouse, J.K., and Chiquoine, J. (2011). Evaluation of an infant simulator intervention for teen pregnancy prevention. *Journal of Obstetric, Gynecologic, & Neonatal Nursing, 40*(3), 322-328.

Heymann, J. (2011). Creating and using new data sources to analyze the relationship between social policy and global health: The case of maternal leave. *Public Health Reports, 126*(Suppl. 3), 127-134.

Heymann, J., and Earle, A. (2010). *Raising the Global Floor Dismantling the Myth That We Can't Afford Good Working Conditions for Everyone.* Stanford, CA: Stanford Politics and Policy.

Heymann, J., and McNeill, K. (2013). *Children's Chances: How Countries Can Move from Surviving to Thriving.* Cambridge, MA: Harvard University Press.

Heymann, J., Penrose, K., and Earle, A. (2006). Meeting children's needs: How does the United States measure up? *Merrill-Palmer Quarterly, 52*(2), 189-215.

Hildebrandt, E., and Stevens, P. (2009). Impoverished women with children and no welfare benefits: The urgency of researching failures of the Temporary Assistance for Needy Families Program. *American Journal of Public Health, 99*(5), 793-801.

Hoath, F.E., and Sanders, M.R. (2002). A feasibility study of Enhanced Group Triple P-Positive Parenting Program for parents of children with attention-deficit/hyperactivity disorder. *Behaviour Change, 19*(4), 191-206.

Hofstetter, A.M., Barrett, A., and Stockwell, M.S. (2015). Factors impacting influenza vaccination of urban low-income Latino children under nine years requiring two doses in the 2010-2011 season. *Journal of Community Health: The Publication for Health Promotion and Disease Prevention, 40*(2), 227-234.

Hornik, R.C. (Ed). (2002). *Public Health Communication: Evidence for Behavior Change.* New York: Lawrence Erlbaum Associates.

Hotz, V.J., and Scholtz, J.K. (2003). The Earned Income Tax Credit. In R.A. Moffitt (Ed.), *Means-tested Transfer Programs in the United States* (pp. 141-197). Chicago, IL: University of Chicago Press.

Houser, L., and Vartanian, T.P. (2012). *Pay Matters: The Positive Economic Impacts of Paid Family Leave for Families, Businesses, and the Public.* Available: http://go.nationalpartnership.org/site/DocServer/Pay_Matters_-_Positive_Economic_Impacts_of_Paid_Family_L.pdf?docID=9681 [March 2016].

Howden-Chapman, P., Matheson, A., Crane, J., Viggers, H., Cunningham, M., Blakely, T., Cunningham, C., Woodward, A., Saville-Smith, K., O'Dea, D., Kennedy, M., Baker, M., Waipara, N., Chapman, R., and Davie, G. (2007). Effect of insulating existing houses on health inequality: Cluster randomised study in the community. *British Medical Journal, 334*(7591), 460.

Hsueh, J., Principe Alderson, D., Lundquist, E., Michalopoulos, C., Gubits, D., Fein, D., and Knox, V. (2012). *The Supporting Healthy Marriage Evaluation: Early Impacts on Low-Income Families.* Report 11. Washington, DC: Office of Planning, Research and Evaluation; Administration for Children and Families; U.S. Department of Health and Human Services.

Huebner, C.E., Barlow, W.E., Tyll, L.T., Johnston, B.D., and Thompson, R.S. (2004). Expanding developmental and behavioral services for newborns in primary care: Program design, delivery, and evaluation framework. *American Journal of Preventive Medicine,* 26(4), 344-355.

Huerta, M.D.C., Adema, W., Baxter, J., Han, W.-J., and Lausten, M. (2013). *Fathers' Leave, Fathers' Involvement and Child Development: Are They Related? Evidence from Four OECD Countries.* OECD Social, Employment and Migration Working Paper No. 140. Paris, France: OECD.

Huston, A.C., and Bentley, A.C. (2009). Human development in societal context. *Annual Review of Psychology,* 61, 411-437.

Ibanez, G., de Reynal de Saint Michel, C., Denantes, M., Saurel-Cubizolles, M.-J., Ringa, V., and Magnier, A.-M. (2012). Systematic review and meta-analysis of randomized controlled trials evaluating primary care-based interventions to promote breastfeeding in low-income women. *Family Practice,* 29(3), 245-254.

Ickovics, J.R., Kershaw, T.S., Westdahl, C., Magriples, U., Massey, Z., Reynolds, H., and Rising, S.S. (2007). Group prenatal care and perinatal outcomes: A randomized controlled trial. *Obstetrical & Gynecological Survey,* 62(12), 766.

Institute of Medicine. (1995). *The Best Intentions: Unintended Pregnancy and the Well-Being of Children and Families.* S.S. Brown and L. Eisenberg (Eds.). Committee on Unintended Pregnancy. Washington, DC: National Academy Press.

Institute of Medicine. (2006). *WIC Food Packages: Time for a Change.* Committee to Review the WIC Food Packages, Food and Nutrition Board. Washington, DC: The National Academies Press.

Institute of Medicine and National Research Council. (2009). *Weight Gain During Pregnancy: Reexamining the Guidelines.* K.M. Rasmussen and A.L. Yaktine (Eds.). Committee to Reexamine IOM Pregnancy Weight Guidelines; Food and Nutrition Board; Board on Children, Youth, and Families. Washington, DC: The National Academies Press.

Institute for Healthcare Improvement. (2003). *The Breakthrough Series: IHI's Collaborative Model for Achieving Breakthrough Improvement.* IHI Innovation Series white paper. Boston, MA: Institute for Healthcare Improvement.

Internal Revenue Service. (2016). *2016 EITC Income Limits, Maximum Credit Amounts and Tax Law Updates.* Available: https://www.irs.gov/credits-deductions/individuals/earned-income-tax-credit/eitc-income-limits-maximum-credit-amounts-next-year [June 2016].

Irvine, A.B., Gelatt, V.A., Hammond, M., Seeley, J.R., and Irvine, A.B. (2014). A randomized study of Internet parent training accessed from community technology centers. *Prevention Science,* 16(4), 597-608.

Jabaley, J., Lutzker, J., Whitaker, D., and Self-Brown, S. (2011). Using iPhones™ to enhance and reduce face-to-face home safety sessions within SafeCare®: An evidence-based child maltreatment prevention program. *Journal of Family Violence,* 26(5), 377-385.

Jackson, C., Cheater, F.M., Harrison, W., Peacock, R., Bekker, H., West, R., and Leese, B. (2011). Randomised cluster trial to support informed parental decision-making for the MMR vaccine. *BMC Public Health,* 11(1), 1-11.

Jackson, G.L., Powers, B.J., Chatterjee, R., Bettger, J.P., Kemper, A.R., Hasselblad, V., Dolor, R.J., Irvine, R.J., Heidenfelder, B.L., Kendrick, A.S., Gray, R., and Williams, J.W. (2013). Improving patient care. The patient-centered medical home. A systematic review. *Annals of Internal Medicine,* 158(3), 169-178.

Jackson, M.I. (2015). Early childhood WIC participation, cognitive development and academic achievement. *Social Science & Medicine,* 126, 145-153.

Johnson, K. (2009). *State-Based Home Visiting: Strengthening Programs through State Leadership.* New York: National Center for Children in Poverty.

Johnston, B.D., Huebner, C.E., Anderson, M.L., Tyll, L.T., and Thompson, R.S. (2006). Healthy steps in an integrated delivery system: Child and parent outcomes at 30 months. *Archives of Pediatrics & Adolescent Medicine, 160*(8), 793-800.

Jones Harden, B., Chazan-Cohen, R., Raikes, H., and Vogel, C. (2012). Early Head Start home visitation: The role of implementation in bolstering program benefits. *Journal of Community Psychology, 40*(4), 438-455.

Kain, Z.N., Caldwell-Andrews, A.A., Mayes, L.C., Weinberg, M.E., Wang, S.M., MacLaren, J.E., and Blount, R.L. (2007). Family-centered preparation for surgery improves perioperative outcomes in children: A randomized controlled trial. *Anesthesiology, 106*(1), 65-74.

Kaminski, J.W., Valle, L.A., Filene, J.H., and Boyle, C.L. (2008). A meta-analytic review of components associated with parent training program effectiveness. *Journal of Abnormal Child Psychology, 36*(4), 567-589.

Karp, H. (2002). *The Happiest Baby on the Block: The New Way to Calm Crying and Help Your Baby Sleep Longer.* New York: Bantam Books.

Karp, H., and Spencer, P. (2004). *The Happiest Toddler on the Block: The New Way to Stop the Daily Battle of Wills and Raise a Secure and Well-Behaved One- to Four-Year-Old.* New York: Bantam Books.

Keefe, M.R., Lobo, M.L., Froese-Fretz, A., Kotzer, A.M., Barbosa, G.A., and Dudley, W.N. (2006a). Effectiveness of an intervention for colic. *Clinical Pediatrics, 45*(2), 123-133.

Keefe, M.R., Kajrlsen, K.A., Lobo, M.L., Kotzer, A.M., and Dudley, W.N. (2006b). Reducing parenting stress in families with irritable infants. *Nursing Research, 55*(3), 198-205.

Kempe, A., Dempsey, C., and Poole, S.R. (1999). Introduction of a recorded health information line into a pediatric practice. *Archives of Pediatrics & Adolescent Medicine, 153*(6), 604-610.

Kennedy, T.L.M., Smith, A., Wells, A.T., and Wellman, B. (2008). *Networked Families.* Available: http://www.pewinternet.org/2008/10/19/networked-families [February 2016].

Kenney, G.M., and Coyer, C. (2012). *National Findings on Access to Health Care and Service Use for Children Enrolled in Medicaid or CHIP.* Washington, DC: Urban Institute.

Kinzer, S.L., Dungy, C.I., and Link, E.A. (2004). Healthy Steps: Resident's perceptions. *Clinical Pediatrics, 43*(8), 743-748.

Kirkland, K., and Mitchell-Herzfeld, S. (2012). *Evaluating the Effectiveness of Home Visiting Services in Promoting Children's Adjustment in School: Final Report to the Pew Center on the States.* Rensselaer, NY: New York State Office of Children and Family Services, Bureau of Evaluation and Research.

Kitzman, H., Olds, D.L., Henderson, C.R., Jr., Hanks, C., Cole, R., Tatelbaum, R., McConnochie, K.M., Sidora, K., Luckey, D.W., Shaver, D., Engelhardt, K., James, D., and Barnard, K. (1997). Effect of prenatal and infancy home visitation by nurses on pregnancy outcomes, childhood injuries, and repeated childbearing. A randomized controlled trial. *Journal of the American Medical Association, 278*(8), 644-652.

Kitzman, H.J., Cole, R.E., Anson, E.A., Olds, D.L., Knudtson, M.D., Holmberg, J.R., Hanks, C.A., Arcoleo, K.J., Luckey, D.W., and Henderson, Jr., C.R. (2010). Enduring effects of prenatal and infancy home visiting by nurses on children: Follow-up of a randomized trial among children at age 12 years. *Archives of Pediatrics & Adolescent Medicine, 164*(5), 412-418.

Knoche, L.L., Edwards, C.P., Sheridan, S.M., Kupzyk, K.A., Marvin, C.A., Cline, K.D., and Clarke, B.L. (2012). Getting ready: Results of a randomized trial of a relationship-focused intervention on the parent-infant relationship in rural Early Head Start. *Infant Mental Health Journal, 33*(5), 439-458.

Koniak-Griffin, D., Anderson, N.L.R., Verzemnieks, I., and Brecht, M.-L. (2000). A public health nursing early intervention program for adolescent mothers: Outcomes from pregnancy through 6 weeks postpartum. *Nursing Research Nursing Research, 49*(3), 130-138.

216

PARENTING MATTERS

Koniak-Griffin, D., Anderson, N.L., Brecht, M.-L., Verzemnieks, I., Lesser, J., and Kim, S. (2002). Public health nursing care for adolescent mothers: Impact on infant health and selected maternal outcomes at 1 year postbirth. *Journal of Adolescent Health, 30*(1), 44-54.

Koniak-Griffin, D., Verzemnieks, I.L., Anderson, N.L., Brecht, M.-L., Lesser, J., Kim, S., and Turner-Pluta, C. (2003). Nurse visitation for adolescent mothers: Two-year infant health and maternal outcomes. *Nursing Research, 52*(2), 127-136.

Lancaster, C.A., Gold, K.J., Flynn, H.A., Yoo, H., Marcus, S.M., and Davis, M.M. (2010). Risk factors for depressive symptoms during pregnancy: A systematic review. *American Journal of Obstetrics and Gynecology, 202*(1), 5-14.

Landry, S.H., Smith, K.E., and Swank, P.R. (2006). Responsive parenting: Establishing early foundations for social, communication, and independent problem-solving skills. *Developmental Psychology, 42*(4), 627-642.

Landry, S.H., Smith, K.E., Swank, P.R., and Guttentag, C. (2008). A responsive parenting intervention: The optimal timing across early childhood for impacting maternal behaviors and child outcomes. *Developmental Psychology, 44*(5), 1335-1353.

Landry, S.H., Smith, K.E., Swank, P.R., Zucker, T., Crawford, A.D., and Solari, E.F. (2012). The effects of a responsive parenting intervention on parent-child interactions during shared book reading. *Developmental Psychology, 48*(4), 969-986.

Laughlin, L.L. (2011). *Maternity Leave and Employment Patterns of First-Time Mothers: 1961-2008.* Washington, DC: U.S. Department of Commerce, Economics and Statistics Administration, U.S. Census Bureau.

Lee, B.J., and Mackey-Bilaver, L.M. (2007). Effects of WIC and Food Stamp participation on child outcomes. *Children and Youth Services Review, 19*(4), 501-517.

Leon, I.G. (2009). *Psychology of Reproduction: Pregnancy, Parenthood, and Parental Ties.* Available: http://www.glowm.com/section_view/heading/Psychology%20of%20 Reproduction:%20Pregnancy,%20Parenthood,%20and%20Parental%20Ties/item/418 [April 2016].

Levy, P.A. (2010). An overview of newborn screening. *Journal of Developmental and Behavioral Pediatrics, 31*(7), 622-631.

Lindberg, R.A., Shenassa, E.D., Acevedo-Garcia, D., Popkin, S.J., Villaveces, A., and Morley, R.L. (2010). Housing interventions at the neighborhood level and health: A review of the evidence. *Journal of Public Health Management and Practice, 16*(5), S44-S52.

Lino, M. (2014). *Expenditures on Children by Families, 2013.* Washington, DC: U.S. Department of Agriculture, Center for Nutrition Policy and Promotion.

Lonigan, C.J., and Whitehurst, G.J. (1998). Relative efficacy of parent and teacher involvement in a shared-reading intervention for preschool children from low-income backgrounds. *Early Childhood Research Quarterly, 13*(2), 263-290.

Loomans, E.M., van Dijk, A.E., Vrijkotte, T.G., van Eijsden, M., Stronks, K., Gemke, R.J., and van den Bergh, B.R. (2013). Psychosocial stress during pregnancy is related to adverse birth outcomes: Results from a large multi-ethnic community-based birth cohort. *European Journal of Public Health, 23*(3), 485-491.

Love, J.M., Kisker, E.E., Ross, C., Raikes, H., Constantine, J., Boller, K., Brooks-Gunn, J., Chazan-Cohen, R., Tarullo, L.B., Brady-Smith, C., Fuligni, A.S. Schocet, P.Z., Paulsell, D., and Vogel, C. (2005). The effectiveness of Early Head Start for 3-year-old children and their parents: Lessons for policy and programs. *Developmental Psychology, 41*(6) 885-901.

Love, S.M., Sanders, M.R., Metzler, C.W., Prinz, R.J., and Kast, E.Z. (2013). Enhancing accessibility and engagement in evidence-based parenting programs to reduce maltreatment: Conversations with vulnerable parents. *Journal of Public Child Welfare, 7*(1), 20-38.

Lovell, V., and Rahmanou, H. (2000). *Paid Family and Medical Leave: Essential Support for Working Women and Men: Fact Sheet #A124*. Washington, DC: Institute for Women's Policy Research.

Lowell, D.I., Carter, A.S., Godoy, L., Paulicin, B., and Briggs-Gowan, M.J. (2011). A randomized controlled trial of child first: A comprehensive home-based intervention translating research into early childhood practice. *Child Development, 82*(1), 193-208.

Lower-Basch, E. (2013). *TANF Policy Brief: Goals for TANF Reauthorization*. Washington, DC: Center for Law and Social Policy.

Lu, M.C., and Halfon, N. (2003). Racial and ethnic disparities in birth outcomes: A life-course perspective. *Maternal and Child Health Journal, 7*(1), 13-30.

Lumeng, J.C., Rahnama, S., Appugliese, D., Kaciroti, N., and Bradley, R.H. (2006). Television exposure and overweight risk in preschoolers. *Archives of Pediatrics & Adolescent Medicine, 160*(4), 417-422.

Mabli, J. (2014). *SNAP Participation and Urban and Rural Food Security*. Washington, DC: Mathematica Policy Research.

Marr, C., and Huang, C. (2015). *Strengthening the EITC for Childless Workers Would Promote Work and Reduce Poverty*. Washington, DC: Center on Budget and Policy Priorities.

Marr, C., Huang, C., Sherman, A., and DeBot, B. (2015). *EITC and Child Tax Credit Promote Work, Reduce Poverty, and Support Children's Development, Research Finds*. Washington, DC: Center on Budget and Policy Priorities.

Marsh, S., Foley, L.S., Wilks, D.C., and Maddison, R. (2014). Family-based interventions for reducing sedentary time in youth: A systematic review of randomized controlled trials. *Obesity Reviews, 15*(2), 117-133.

Maxfield, M. (2013). *Panel Paper: The Effects of the Earned Income Tax Credit on Child Achievement and Long-Term Educational Attainment*. Paper presented at the Annual Fall Research Conference, November 7-9, Washington, D.C.

Mayer, S.E., Kalil, A., Oreopoulos, P., and Gallegos, S. (2015). *Using Behavioral Insights to Increase Parental Engagement: The Parents and Children Together (PACT) Intervention*. Working Paper No. 21602. Cambridge, MA: National Bureau of Economic Research.

McDaniel, B.T., Coyne, S.M., and Holmes, E.K. (2012). New mothers and media use: Associations between blogging, social networking, and maternal well-being. *Maternal and Child Health Journal, 16*(7), 1509-1517.

McLearn, K.T., Strobino, D.M., Hughart, N., Minkovitz, C.S., Scharfstein, D., Marks, E., and Guyer, B. (2004). Developmental services in primary care for low-income children: Clinicians perceptions of the Healthy Steps for Young Children Program. *Journal of Urban Health: Bulletin of the New York Academy of Medicine, 81*(2), 206-221.

McMorrow, S., Kenney, G.M., Anderson, N., Clemans-Cope, L., Dubay, L., Long, S.K., and Wissoker, D. (2014). Trade-offs between public and private coverage for low-income children have implications for future policy debates. *Health Affairs, 33*(8), 1367-1374.

McPherson, M., Arango, P., Fox, H., Lauver, C., McManus, M., Newacheck, P.W., Perrin, J.M., Shonkoff, J.P., and Strickland, B. (1998). A new definition of children with special health care needs. *Pediatrics, 102*(1), 137-140.

McPherson, M.E., Gloor, P.A., and Smith, L.A. (2015). Using collaborative improvement and innovation networks to tackle complex population health problems. *JAMA Pediatrics, 169*(8), 709-710.

Mehran, M., and White, K.R. (1988). Parent tutoring as a supplement to compensatory education for first-grade children. *Remedial and Special Education, 9*(3), 35-41.

Mendelsohn, A.L., Dreyer, B.P., Flynn, V., Tomopoulos, S., Rovira, I., Tineo, W., Pebenito, C., Torres, C., Torres, H., and Nixon, A.F. (2005). Use of videotaped interactions during pediatric well-child care to promote child development: A randomized, controlled trial. *Journal of Developmental and Behavioral Pediatrics, 26*(1), 34-41.

Mendez, J.L. (2010). How can parents get involved in preschool? Barriers and engagement in education by ethnic minority parents of children attending Head Start. *Cultural Diversity and Ethnic Minority Psychology, 16*(1), 26-36.

Mergler, M.J., Omer, S.B., Pan, W.K., Navar-Boggan, A.M., Orenstein, W., Marcuse, E.K., Taylor, J., DeHart, M.P., Carter, T.C., Damico, A., Halsey, N., and Salmon, D.A. (2013). Association of vaccine-related attitudes and beliefs between parents and health care providers. *Vaccine, 31*(41), 4591-4595.

Meyer, B.D., and Rosenbaum, D.T. (2001). Welfare, the earned income tax credit, and the labor supply of single mothers. *The Quarterly Journal of Economics, 116*(3), 1063-1114.

Michalopoulos, C., Duggan, A., Knox, V., Filene, J.H., Lee, H., Snell, E.E., Crowne, S., Lundquist, E., Corso, P.S., and Ingels, J.B. (2013). *Revised Design for the Mother and Infant Home Visiting Program Evaluation.* OPRE Report No. 2013-18. Washington, DC: Office of Planning Research and Evaluation.

Milkman, R., and Appelbaum, E. (2013). *Unfinished Business: Paid Family Leave in California and the Future of U.S. Work-Family Policy.* Ithaca, NY: Cornell University Press.

Minkovitz, C.S., Strobino, D., Hughart, N., Scharfstein, D., Guyer, B., and Healthy Steps Evaluation Team. (2001). Early effects of the Healthy Steps for Young Children Program. *Archives of Pediatrics & Adolescent Medicine, 155*(4), 470-479.

Minkovitz, C.S., Hughart, N., Strobino, D., Scharfstein, D., Grason, H., Hou, W., Miller, T., Bishai, D., Augustyn, M., McLearn, K.T., and Guyer, B. (2003). A practice-based intervention to enhance quality of care in the first 3 years of life: The Healthy Steps for Young Children Program. *Journal of the American Medical Association, 290*(23), 3081-3091.

Minkovitz, C.S., Strobino, D., Mistry, K.B., Scharfstein, D.O., Grason, H., Hou, W., Ialongo, N., and Guyer, B. (2007). Healthy Steps for Young Children: Sustained results at 5.5 years. *Pediatrics, 120*(3), e658-e668.

Mittal, P. (2011). Centering parenting: Pilot implementation of a group model for teaching family medicine residents well-child care. *The Permanente Journal, 15*(4), 40-41.

Moorthy, S., Llorente, C., Hupert, N., and Pasnik, S. (2014). *PEG + CAT Content Study. A Report to the CPB-PBS Ready to Learn Initiative.* New York, NY and Menlo Park, CA: Education Development Center and SRI International.

Morris, B.A.P., Trimble, N.E., and Fendley, S.J. (1994). Increasing bicycle helmet use in the community: Measuring response to a wide-scale, 2-year effort. *Canadian Family Physician, 40*(6), 1126.

Morrow, L.M., and Young, J. (1997). A family literacy program connecting school and home: Effects on attitude, motivation, and literacy achievement. *Journal of Educational Psychology, 89*(4), 736-742.

Muennig, P., Caleyachetty, R., Rosen, Z., and Korotzer, A. (2015). More money, fewer lives: The cost effectiveness of welfare reform in the United States. *American Journal of Public Health, 105*(2), 324-328.

Nagler, R.H. (2014). Adverse outcomes associated with media exposure to contradictory nutrition messages. *Journal of Health Communication, 19*(1), 24-40

National Center for Health Statistics. (2015). *Health, United States, 2015: With Special Feature on Racial and Ethnic Health Disparities.* Hyattsville, MD: National Center for Health Statistics.

National Center on Shaken Baby Syndrome. (2013). *Guidebook for Program Implementation and Management 2013.* Available: http://www.dontshake.org/lms/files/lmspdf/PURPLE-ProgramGuidebook.pdf [March 2016].

The National Partnership for Women and Families. (2015). *State and Local Action on Paid Sick Days.* Available: http://www.nationalpartnership.org/research-library/campaigns/psd/state-and-local-action-paid-sick-days.pdf [February 2016].

National Research Council and Institute of Medicine. (2009). *Preventing Mental, Emotional, and Behavioral Disorders among Young People.* M.E. O'Connell, T. Boat, and K.E. Warner (Eds.). Committee on the Prevention of Mental Disorders and Substance Abuse Among Children, Youth and Young Adults: Research Advances and Promising Interventions; Board on Children, Youth and Families. Division of Behavioral and Social Sciences and Education. Washington, DC: The National Academies Press.

Needlman, R., Toker, K.H., Dreyer, B.P., Klass, P., and Mendelsohn, A.L. (2005). Effectiveness of a primary care intervention to support reading aloud: A multicenter evaluation. *Ambulatory Pediatrics, 5*(4), 209-215.

Neuhauser, L., Constantine, W.L., Constantine, N.A., Sokal-Gutierrez, K., Obarski, S.K., Clayton, L., Desai, M., Sumner, G., and Syme, S.L. (2007). Promoting prenatal and early childhood health: Evaluation of a statewide materials-based intervention for parents. *American Journal of Public Health, 97*(10), 1813-1819.

Newacheck, P.W., and Taylor, W.R. (1998). Childhood chronic illness: Prevalence, severity, and impact. *American Journal of Public Health, 82*(3), 364-371.

Niederman, L.G., Schwartz, A., Connell, K.J., and Silverman, K. (2007). Healthy Steps for Young Children Program in pediatric residency training: Impact on primary care outcomes. *Pediatrics, 120*(3), 596-603.

Noble, K.G., Duch, H., Darvique, M.E., Grundleger, A., Rodriguez, C., and Landers, C. (2012). "Getting Ready for School": A preliminary evaluation of a parent-focused school-readiness program. *Child Development Research, 2012,* Art. ID 259598. doi:10.1155/2012/259598. Available: http://www.columbia.edu/cu/needlab/Publications/Noble%20et%20al.,%202012%20Hindawi.pdf [August 2016].

O'Connell, L.K., Davis, M.M., and Bauer, N.S. (2015). Assessing parenting behaviors to improve child outcomes. *Pediatrics, 135*(2), e286-e288.

O'Donnell, K.J., Glover, V., Barker, E.D., and O'Connor, T.G. (2014). The persisting effect of maternal mood in pregnancy on childhood psychopathology. *Development and Psychopathology, 26*(2), 393-403.

Olds, D.L., Henderson, C.R., Jr., Chamberlin, R., and Tatelbaum, R. (1986). Preventing child abuse and neglect: A randomized trial of nurse home visitation. *Pediatrics, 78*(1), 65-78.

Olds, D.L., Henderson, C.R., Jr., and Kitzman, H. (1994). Does prenatal and infancy nurse home visitation have enduring effects on qualities of parental caregiving and child health at 25 to 50 months of life? *Pediatrics, 93*(1), 89-98.

Olds, D.L., Eckenrode, J., Henderson, C.R., Jr., Kitzman, H., Powers, J., Cole, R., Sidora, K., Morris, P., Pettitt, L.M., and Luckey, D. (1997). Long-term effects of home visitation on maternal life course and child abuse and neglect. Fifteen-year follow-up of a randomized trial. *Journal of the American Medical Association, 278*(8), 637-643.

Olds, D.L., Robinson, J., O'Brien, R., Luckey, D.W., Pettitt, L.M., Henderson, C.R., Jr., Ng, R.K., Sheff, K.L., Korfmacher, J., Hiatt, S., and Talmi, A. (2002). Home visiting by paraprofessionals and by nurses: A randomized, controlled trial. *Pediatrics, 110*(3), 486-496.

Olds, D.L., Kitzman, H., Cole, R., Robinson, J., Sidora, K., Luckey, D.W., Henderson, C.R., Jr., Hanks, C., Bondy, J., and Holmberg, J. (2004). Effects of nurse home-visiting on maternal life course and child development: Age 6 follow-up results of a randomized trial. *Pediatrics, 114*(6), 1550-1559.

Olds, D.L., Kitzman, H.J., Cole, R.E., Hanks, C.A., Arcoleo, K.J., Anson, E.A., Luckey, D.W., Knudtson, M.D., Henderson, C.R., Jr., Bondy, J., and Stevenson, A.J. (2010). Enduring effects of prenatal and infancy home visiting by nurses on maternal life course and government spending: Follow-up of a randomized trial among children at age 12 years. *Archives of Pediatrics & Adolescent Medicine, 164*(5), 419-424.

Owens, P.L., Zodet, M.W., Berdahl, T., Dougherty, D., McCormick, M.C., and Simpson, L.A. (2008). Annual report on health care for children and youth in the United States: Focus on injury-related emergency department utilization and expenditures. *Ambulatory Pediatrics: The Official Journal of the Ambulatory Pediatric Association, 8*(4), 219-240.

Pacifici, C., Delaney, R., White, L., Nelson, C., and Cummings, K. (2006). Web-based training for foster, adoptive, and kinship parents. *Children and Youth Services Review, 28*(11), 1329-1343.

Panter-Brick, C., Burgess, A., Eggerman, M., McAllister, F., Pruett, K., and Leckman, J.F. (2014). Practitioner review: Engaging fathers—Recommendations for a game change in parenting interventions based on a systematic review of the global evidence. *Journal of Child Psychology and Psychiatry, 55*(11), 1187-1212.

Paradis, H.A., Conn, K.M., Gewirtz, J.R., and Halterman, J.S. (2011). Innovative delivery of newborn anticipatory guidance: A randomized, controlled trial incorporating media-based learning into primary care. *Academic Pediatrics, 11*(1), 27-33.

Patel, S., and Patel, S. (2015). The effectiveness of lactation consultants and lactation counselors on breastfeeding outcomes. *Journal of Human Lactation.* Available: http://jhl.sagepub.com/content/early/2015/12/03/0890334415618668.full.pdf+html [August 2016].

Paulsell, D., Avellar, S., Sama Martin, E., and Del Grosso, P. (2010). *Home Visiting Evidence of Effectiveness Review: Executive Summary.* Washington, DC: Office of Planning, Research and Evaluation; Administration for Children and Families; U.S. Department of Health and Human Services.

Pears, K.C., Fisher, P.A., and Bronz, K.D. (2007). An intervention to promote social emotional school readiness in foster children: Preliminary outcomes from a pilot study. *School Psychology Review, 36*(4), 665.

Pears, K.C., Kim, H.K., and Fisher, P.A. (2012). Effects of a school readiness intervention for children in foster care on oppositional and aggressive behaviors in kindergarten. *Children and Youth Services Review, 34*(12), 2361-2366.

Pears, K.C., Fisher, P.A., Kim, H.K., Bruce, J., Healey, C.V., and Yoerger, K. (2013). Immediate effects of a school readiness intervention for children in foster care. *Early Education & Development, 24*(6), 771-791.

Pears, K.C., Healey, C.V., Fisher, P.A., Braun, D., Gill, C., Conte, H.M., Newman, J., and Ticer, S. (2014). Immediate effects of a program to promote school readiness in low-income children: Results of a pilot study. *Education & Treatment of Children, 37*(3), 431-460.

Pega, F., Carter, K., Blakely, T., and Lucas, P.J. (2013). In-work tax credits for families and their impact on health status in adults. *Cochrane Database of Systematic Reviews, 8.*

Phillips, K.R. (2004). *Getting Time Off: Access to Leave among Working Parents.* Washington, DC: Urban Institute.

Pinquart, M., and Teubert, D. (2010). Effects of parenting education with expectant and new parents: A meta-analysis. *Journal of Family Psychology, 24*(3), 316-327.

Piotrowski, C.C., Talavera, G.A., and Mayer, J.A. (2009). Healthy Steps: A systematic review of a preventive practice-based model of pediatric care. *Journal of Developmental and Behavioral Pediatrics, 30*(1), 91-103.

Pisoni, C., Garofoli, F., Tzialla, C., Orcesi, S., Spinillo, A., Politi, P., Balottin, U., Manzoni, P., and Stronati, M. (2014). Risk and protective factors in maternal-fetal attachment development. *Early Human Development, 90*(Suppl. 2), S45-S46.

Polit, D.F. (1989). Effects of a comprehensive program for teenage parents: Five years after project redirection. *Family Planning Perspectives, 21*(4), 164-187.

Pomerantz, E.M., Moorman, E.A., and Litwack, S.D. (2007). The how, whom, and why of parents' involvement in children's academic lives: More is not always better. *Review of Educational Research, 77*(3), 373-410.

Puma, M., Bell, S., Cook, R., Heid, C., Broene, P., Jenkins, F., Mashburn, A., and Downer, J. (2012). *Third Grade Follow-up to the Head Start Impact Study: Final Report.* Report 2012-45. Washington, DC: Office of Planning, Research and Evaluation; Administration for Children and Families; U.S. Department of Health and Human Services.

Ralston, S., and Roohi, M. (2008). A randomized, controlled trial of smoking cessation counseling provided during child hospitalization for respiratory illness. *Pediatric Pulmonology, 43*(6), 561-566.

Randolph, W., and Viswanath, K. (2004). Lessons from mass media public health campaigns: Marketing health in a crowded media world. *Annual Review of Public Health, 25*, 419-437.

Ratcliffe, C., McKernan, S.M., and Zhang, S. (2011). How much does the Supplemental Nutrition Assistance Program reduce food insecurity? *American Journal of Agricultural Economics, 93*(4), 1082-1098.

Reese, L.S., Heiden, E.O., Kim, K.Q., and Yang, J. (2014). Evaluation of Period of PURPLE Crying, an abusive head trauma prevention program. *Journal of Obstetric, Gynecologic & Neonatal Nursing, 43*(6), 752-761.

Rehkopf, D.H., Strully, K.W., and Dow, W.H. (2014). The short-term impacts of Earned Income Tax Credit disbursement on health. *International Journal of Epidemiology, 43*(6), 1884-1894.

Resnicow, K., McMaster, F., Bocian, A., Harris, D., Zhou, Y., Snetselaar, L., Schwartz, R., Myers, E., Gotlieb, J., Foster, J., Hollinger, D., Smith, K., Woolford, S., Mueller, D., and Wasserman, R.C. (2015). Motivational interviewing and dietary counseling for obesity in primary care: An RCT. *Pediatrics, 135*(4), 649-657.

Reynolds, A.J. (1997). *The Chicago Child-Parent Centers: A Longitudinal Study of Extended Early Childhood Intervention.* Madison: Institute for Research on Poverty, University of Wisconsin–Madison.

Reynolds, A.J. (2000). *Success in Early Intervention: The Chicago Child Parent Centers.* Lincoln: University of Nebraska Press.

Reynolds, A.J., and Temple, J.A. (1998). Extended early childhood intervention and school achievement: Age thirteen findings from the Chicago Longitudinal Study. *Child Development, 69*(1), 231-246.

Reynolds, A.J., Ou, S.-R., and Topitzes, J.W. (2004). Paths of effects of early childhood intervention on educational attainment and delinquency: A confirmatory analysis of the Chicago child-parent centers. *Child Development, 75*(5), 1299-1328.

Rikin, S., Glatt, K., Simpson, P., Cao, Y., Anene-Maidoh, O., and Willis, E. (2015). Factors associated with increased reading frequency in children exposed to Reach Out and Read. *Academic Pediatrics, 15*(6), 651-657.

Roberts, S.W., and McCowan, R.J. (2004). The effectiveness of infant simulators. *Adolescence, 39*(155), 475.

Roberts, M.Y., and Kaiser, A.P. (2011). The effectiveness of parent-implemented language interventions: A meta-analysis. *American Journal of Speech-Language Pathology, 20*(3), 180-199.

Rocca, C.H., Harper, C.C., and Raine-Bennett, T.R. (2013). Young women's perceptions of the benefits of childbearing: Associations with contraceptive use and pregnancy. *Perspectives on Sexual and Reproductive Health, 45*(1), 23-32.

Rose, D., Habicht, J.P., and Devaney, B. (1998). Household participation in the food stamp and WIC programs increases the nutrient intakes of preschool children. *Journal of Nutrition, 128*(3), 548-555.

Rosen, L.J., Myers, V., Hovell, M., Zucker, D., and Ben Noach, M. (2014). Meta-analysis of parental protection of children from tobacco smoke exposure. *Pediatrics, 133*(4), 698-714.

Rosengard, C., Phipps, M.G., Adler, N.E., and Ellen, J.M. (2004). Adolescent pregnancy intentions and pregnancy outcomes: A longitudinal examination. *Journal of Adolescent Health, 35*(6), 453-461.

Rossin-Slater, M., Ruhm, C.J., and Waldfogel, J. (2013). The effects of California's Paid Family Leave Program on mothers' leave-taking and subsequent labor market outcomes. *Journal of Policy Analysis and Management, 32*(2), 224-245.

Rouzier, P., and Alto, W.A. (1995). Evolution of a successful community bicycle helmet campaign. *Journal of the American Board of Family Practice, 8*(4), 283-287.

Ruhm, C.J. (1998). *Parental Leave and Child Health*. Cambridge, MA: National Bureau of Economic Research.

Sadaf, A., Richards, J.L., Glanz, J., Salmon, D.A., and Omer, S.B. (2013). A systematic review of interventions for reducing parental vaccine refusal and vaccine hesitancy. *Vaccine, 31*(40), 4293-4304.

Sadler, L.S., Slade, A., Close, N., Webb, D.L., Simpson, T., Fennie, K., and Mayes, L.C. (2013). Minding the Baby: Enhancing reflectiveness to improve early health and relationship outcomes in an interdisciplinary home-visiting program. *Infant Mental Health Journal, 34*(5), 391-405.

Salonen, A.H., Pridham, K.F., Brown, R.L., and Kaunonen, M. (2014). Impact of an Internet-based intervention on Finnish mothers' perceptions of parenting satisfaction, infant centrality and depressive symptoms during the postpartum year. *Midwifery, 30*(1), 112-122.

Sanders, M.R., Montgomery, D.T., and Brechman-Toussaint, M.L. (2000). The mass media and the prevention of child behavior problems: The evaluation of a television series to promote positive outcomes for parents and their children. *Journal of Child Psychology and Psychiatry, 41*(7), 939-948.

Sanders, M.R., Baker, S., and Turner, K.M.T. (2012). A randomized controlled trial evaluating the efficacy of Triple P Online with parents of children with early-onset conduct problems. *Behaviour Research and Therapy, 50*(11), 675-684.

Sanders, M.R., Dittman, C.K., Farruggia, S.P., and Keown, L.J. (2014). A comparison of online versus workbook delivery of a self-help positive parenting program. *The Journal of Primary Prevention, 35*(3), 125-133.

Sandstrom, H., Gearing, M., Peters, E., Heller, C., Healy, O., and Pratt, E. (2015). *Approaches to Father Engagement and Fathers' Experiences in Home Visiting Programs*. Washington, DC: Office of Planning, Research and Evaluation; Administration for Children and Families; U.S. Department of Health and Human Services.

Sangalang, B.B., Barth, R.P., and Painter, J.S. (2006). First-birth outcomes and timing of second births: A statewide case management program for adolescent mothers. *Health & Social Work, 31*(1), 54-63.

Sanghavi, D.M. (2005). Taking well-child care into the 21st century: A novel, effective method for improving parent knowledge using computerized tutorials. *Archives of Pediatrics & Adolescent Medicine, 159*(5), 482-485.

Sawhill, I., and Venator, J. (2015). *Improving Children's Life Chances through Better Family Planning*. Washington, DC: Center on Children and Families at Brookings.

Schmeiser, M.D. (2009). Expanding wallets and waistlines: The impact of family income on the BMI of women and men eligible for the Earned Income Tax Credit. *Health Economics, 18*(11), 1277-1294.

Scholer, S.J., Hudnut-Beumler, J., and Dietrich, M.S. (2010). A brief primary care intervention helps parents develop plans to discipline. *Pediatrics, 125*(2), e242-e249.

Scholer, S.J., Hudnut-Beumler, J., and Dietrich, M.S. (2012). Why parents value a brief required primary care intervention that teaches discipline strategies. *Clinical Pediatrics, 51*(6), 538-545.

Scholle, S.H., Torda, P., Peikes, D., Han, E., and Genevro, J. (2010). *Engaging Patients and Families in the Medical Home*. Rockville, MD: Agency for Healthcare Research and Quality, U.S. Department of Health and Human Services.

Schott, L., Pavetti, L., and Floyd, I. (2015). *How States Use Federal and State Funds under the TANF Block Grant*. Washington, DC: Center on Budget and Policy Priorities.

Schuster, M.A., and Chung, P.J. (2014). Time off to care for a sick child: Why family-leave policies matter. *New England Journal of Medicine, 371*(6), 493-495.

Schuster, M.A., Chung, P.J., Elliott, M.N., Garfield, C.F., Vestal, K.D., and Klein, D.J. (2008). Awareness and use of California's paid family leave insurance among parents of chronically ill children. *Journal of the American Medical Association, 300*(9), 1047-1055.

Schuster, M.A., Chung, P., Elliot, M., Garfield, C., Vestal, K., and Klein, D. (2009). Perceived effects of leave from work and the role of paid leave among parents of children with special health care needs. *American Public Health Association, 99*(4), 698-705.

Schuster, M.A., Chung, P.J., and Vestal, K.D. (2011). Children with health issues. *The Future of Children, 21*(2), 91-116.

Schwarz, D.F., O'Sullivan, A.L., Guinn, J., Mautone, J.A., Carlson, E.C., Zhao, H., Zhang, X., Esposito, T.L., Askew, M., and Radcliffe, J. (2012). Promoting early intervention referral through a randomized controlled home-visiting program. *Journal of Early Intervention, 34*(1), 20-39.

Scott, S., O'Connor, T.G., Futh, A., Matias, C., Price, J., and Doolan, M. (2010). Impact of a parenting program in a high-risk, multi-ethnic community: The PALS trial. *Journal of Child Psychology and Psychiatry, and Allied Disciplines, 51*(12), 1331-1341.

Seburg, E.M., Olson-Bullis, B.A., Bredeson, D.M., Hayes, M.G., and Sherwood, N.E. (2015). A review of primary care-based childhood obesity prevention and treatment interventions. *Current Obesity Reports, 4*(2), 157-173.

Seeman, M.V. (2010). Parenting issues in mothers with schizophrenia. *Current Women's Health Reviews, 6*(1), 51-57.

Seitz, V. (1990). Intervention programs for impoverished children: A comparison of educational and family support models. *Annals of Child Development, 7*, 73-103.

Selden, T.M., and Hudson, J.L. (2006). Access to care and utilization among children: Estimating the effects of public and private coverage. *Medical Care, 44*(5), 119-126.

Selk, S., Finnerty, P., Fitzgerald, E., Levesque, Z., and Taylor, J. (2015). Collaborative improvement and innovation network: Increasing capacity of data systems to help save babies' lives. *BMJ Quality & Safety, 24*(11), 738-739.

Shapiro, C.J., Prinz, R.J., and Sanders, M.R. (2015). Sustaining use of an evidence-based parenting intervention: Practitioner perspectives. *Journal of Child and Family Studies, 24*(6), 1615-1624.

Sharifi, M., Adams, W.G., Winickoff, J.P., Guo, J., Reid, M., and Boynton-Jarrett, R. (2014). Enhancing the electronic health record to increase counseling and quit-line referral for parents who smoke. *Academic Pediatrics, 14*(5), 478-484.

Shelton, T.L., and Stepanek, J.S. (1994). *Family-Centered Care for Children Needing Specialized Health and Developmental Services*. Bethesda, MD: Association for the Care of Children's Health.

Sheridan, S.M., Knoche, L.L., Edwards, C.P., Bovaird, J.A., and Kupzyk, K.A. (2010). Parent engagement and school readiness: Effects of the getting ready intervention on preschool children's social-emotional competencies. *Early Education and Development, 21*(1), 125-156.

Sheridan, S.M., Knoche, L.L., Kupzyk, K.A., Edwards, C.P., and Marvin, C.A. (2011). A randomized trial examining the effects of parent engagement on early language and literacy: The Getting Ready Intervention. *Journal of School Psychology, 49*(3), 361-383.

Sheridan, S.M., Knoche, L.L., Edwards, C.P., Kupzyk, K.A., Clarke, B.L., and Kim, E.M. (2014). Efficacy of the Getting Ready Intervention and the role of parental depression. *Early Education and Development, 25*(5), 746-769.

Sheridan, S.M., Holmes, S.R., Smith, T.E., and Moen, A.L. (2016). Complexities in field-based partnership research: Exemplars, challenges, and an agenda for the field. In M.S. Sheridan and E. Moorman Kim (Eds.), *Family-School Partnerships in Context* (pp. 1-23). Cham, Switzerland: Springer International.

Shone, L.P., Dick, A.W., Klein, J.D., Zwanziger, J., and Szilagyi, P.G. (2005). Reduction in racial and ethnic disparities after enrollment in the state Children's Health Insurance Program. *Pediatrics, 115*(6), e697-e705.

Sipsma, H.L., Magriples, U., Divney, A., Gordon, D., Gabzdyl, E., and Kershaw, T. (2013). Breastfeeding behavior among adolescents: Initiation, duration, and exclusivity. *The Journal of Adolescent Health: Official Publication of the Society for Adolescent Medicine, 53*(3), 394-400.

Smith, A. (2014). *African Americans and Technology Use—A Demographic Portrait.* Washington, DC: Pew Research Center.

Smith, A. (2015). *U.S. Smartphone Use in 2015.* Available: http://www.pewinternet.org/2015/04/01/us-smartphone-use-in-2015 [February 2016].

Smith, T.W., and Kim, J. (2010). *Paid Sick Days: Attitudes and Experiences.* Chicago, IL: NORC, University of Chicago.

Somers, C.L. (2013). Effects of infant simulators on urban, minority, middle school students. *Health Promotion Practice, 15*(1), 35-43.

Spock, B. (1957). *Dr. Benjamin Spock's Baby and Child Care* (1st ed.).New York: Pocket Books.

Spock, B. (1968). *Baby and Child Care* (2nd ed.). New York: Meredith Press.

Spock, B. (1976). *Baby and Child Care* (3rd ed.). New York: Pocket Books.

St. Pierre, R.G., Layzer, J.I., Goodson, B.D., and Bernstein, L.S. (1997). *National Impact Evaluation of the Comprehensive Child Development Program: Final Report.* Cambridge, MA: Abt Associates.

Stacey, D., Légaré, F., Col, N.F., Bennett, C.L., Barry, M.J., Eden, K.B., Holmes-Rovner, M., Llewellyn-Thomas, H., Lyddiatt, A., Thomson, R., Trevena, L., and Wu, J.H. (2014). Decision aids for people facing health treatment or screening decisions. *Cochrane Database of Systematic Reviews, 1.*

Staehelin, K., Bertea, P.C., and Stutz, E.Z. (2007). Length of maternity leave and health of mother and child—A review. *International Journal of Public Health, 52*(4), 202-209.

Starkey, P., and Klein, A. (2000). Fostering parental support for children's mathematical development: An intervention with Head Start families. *Early Education and Development, 11,* 659-680.

Storey, J.D., Saffitz, G.B., and Rimon, J.G. (2008). Social marketing. In K. Glanz, B. Rimer, and K. Viswanath (Eds.), *Health Behavior and Health Education: Theory, Research, and Practice* (4th ed., pp. 435-464). San Francisco, CA: Jossey-Bass.

Strunk, J.A. (2008). The effect of school-based health clinics on teenage pregnancy and parenting outcomes: An integrated literature review. *The Journal of School Nursing: The Official Publication of the National Association of School Nurses, 24*(1), 13-20.

Szilagyi, P.G., Bordley, C., Vann, J.C., Chelminski, A., Kraus, R.M., Margolis, P.A., and Rodewald, L.E. (2000). Effect of patient reminder/recall interventions on immunization rates: A review. *Journal of the American Medical Association, 284*(14), 1820-1827.

Szilagyi, P.G., Dick, A.W., Klein, J.D., Shone, L.P., Zwanziger, J., and McInerny, T. (2004). Improved access and quality of care after enrollment in the New York State Children's Health Insurance Program (SCHIP). *Pediatrics, 113*(5), e395-e404.

Tanaka, S. (2005). Parental leave and child health across OECD countries. *The Economic Journal, 115*(501), F7-F28.

Taveras, E.M., Gortmaker, S.L., Hohman, K.H., Horan, C.M., Kleinman, K.P., Mitchell, K., Price, S., Prosser, L.A., Rifas-Shiman, S.L., and Gillman, M.W. (2011). Randomized controlled trial to improve primary care to prevent and manage childhood obesity: The High Five for Kids Study. *Archives of Pediatrics & Adolescent Medicine, 165*(8), 714-722.

Taylor, T.K., Webster-Stratton, C., Feil, E.G., Broadbent, B., Widdop, C.S., and Severson, H.H. (2008). Computer-based intervention with coaching: An example using the Incredible Years Program. *Cognitive Behaviour Therapy, 37*(4), 233-246.

Thomson, H., Thomas, S., Sellstrom, E., and Petticrew, M. (2013). Housing improvements for health and associated socio-economic outcomes. *Cochrane Database of Systematic Reviews, 2013, 2*(CD008657). doi: 10.1002/14651858.CD008657.pub2.

Thornton, S., and Calam, R. (2011). Predicting intention to attend and actual attendance at a universal parent-training programme: A comparison of social cognition models. *Clinical Child Psychology and Psychiatry, 16*(3), 365-383.

Tiehen, L., Jolliffe, D., and Smeeding, T. (2013). *The Effect of SNAP on Poverty*. Discussion Paper No. 1415-13. Madison, WI: Institute for Research on Poverty.

Tocce, K.M., Sheeder, J.L., and Teal, S.B. (2012). Rapid repeat pregnancy in adolescents: Do immediate postpartum contraceptive implants make a difference? *American Journal of Obstetrics and Gynecology, 206*(6), 1-7.

Triple P-Positive Parenting Program. (2016a). *Communications*. Available: http://www.triplep.net/glo-en/the-triple-p-system-at-work/training-and-delivery/communications [April 2016].

Triple P-Positive Parenting Program. (2016b). *Triple P-Positive Parenting Program*. Available: http://www.triplep.net/glo-en/home [February 2016].

Tsankova, N., Renthal, W., Kumar, A., and Nestler, E.J. (2007). Epigenetic regulation in psychiatric disorders. *Nature Reviews. Neuroscience, 8*(5), 355-367.

Turner, K.M.T., and Sanders, M.R. (2006). Help when it's needed first: A controlled evaluation of brief, preventive behavioral family intervention in a primary care setting. *Behavior Therapy, 37*(2), 131-142.

U.S. Department of Agriculture. (2016a). *National School Lunch Program*. Available: http://www.fns.usda.gov/nslp/national-school-lunch-program-nslp [April 2016].

U.S. Department of Agriculture. (2016b). *School Breakfast Program*. Available: http://www.fns.usda.gov/sbp/school-breakfast-program-sbp [April 2016].

U.S. Department of Agriculture. (2016c). *Supplemental Nutrition Assistance Program: FY13 through FY16 National View Summary*. Available: http://www.fns.usda.gov/sites/default/files/pd/34SNAPmonthly.pdf [June 2016].

U.S. Department of Agriculture. (2016d). *WIC Program Participation and Costs*. Available: http://www.fns.usda.gov/sites/default/files/pd/wisummary.pdf [May 2016].

U.S. Department of Health and Human Services. (2015a). *Health Insurance Coverage and the Affordable Care Act*. Available: https://aspe.hhs.gov/sites/default/files/pdf/139211/ib_uninsured_change.pdf [February 2016].

U.S. Department of Health and Human Services. (2015b). *Sudden Unexpected Infant Death and Sudden Infant Death Syndrome: Data and Statistics*. Available: http://www.cdc.gov/sids/data.htm [February 2016].

U.S. Department of Health and Human Services, Administration for Children and Families, Administration on Children, Youth and Families, Commissioner's Office of Planning, Research and Evaluation, and Head Start Bureau. (2001). *Building Their Futures: How Early Head Start Programs Are Enhancing the Lives of Infants and Toddlers in Low-Income Families*. Available: http://www.acf.hhs.gov/sites/default/files/opre/bldg_vol1.pdf [March 2016].

U.S. Department of Health and Human Services, Administration for Children and Families, Office of Planning, Research and Evaluation, and Administration on Children, Youth and Families. (2002). *Making a Difference in the Lives of Infants and Toddlers and Their Families the Impacts of Early Head Start.* Available: http://www.acf.hhs.gov/sites/default/files/opre/impacts_vol1.pdf [March 2016].

U.S. Department of Housing and Urban Development. (2015). *Home Improvements. 2015,* Available: http://portal.hud.gov/hudportal/HUD?src=/topics/home_improvements [March 2016].

U.S. Equal Employment Opportunity Commission. (2016). *Pregnancy Discrimination.* Available: https://www.eeoc.gov/eeoc/publications/fs-preg.cfm [May 2016].

U.S. Preventive Services Task Force. (2009). Counseling and interventions to prevent tobacco use and tobacco-caused disease in adults and pregnant women: U.S. Preventive Services Task Force reaffirmation recommendation statement. *Annals of Internal Medicine, 150*(8), 551-555.

U.S. Preventive Services Task Force. (2015). *Published Recommendations.* Available: http://www.uspreventiveservicestaskforce.org/BrowseRec/Index [February 2016].

University of Minnesota. (2013). *Chicago Longitudinal Study.* Available: http://www.cehd.umn.edu/icd/research/cls/Component.html [February 2016].

van den Hoofdakker, B.J., van der Veen-Mulders, L., Sytema, S., Emmelkamp, P.M., Minderaa, R.B., and Nauta, M.H. (2007). Effectiveness of behavioral parent training for children with ADHD in routine clinical practice: A randomized controlled study. *Journal of the American Academy of Child & Adolescent Psychiatry, 46*(10), 1263-1271.

van Ijzendoorn, M.H., Bakermans-Kranenburg, M.J., and Ebstein, R.P. (2011). Methylation matters in child development: Toward developmental behavioral epigenetics. *Child Development Perspectives, 5*(4), 305-310.

Vannice, K.S., Salmon, D.A., Shui, I., Omer, S.B., Kissner, J., Edwards, K.M., Sparks, R., Dekker, C.L., Klein, N.P., and Gust, D.A. (2011). Attitudes and beliefs of parents concerned about vaccines: Impact of timing of immunization information. *Pediatrics, 127*(Suppl. 1), S120-S126.

Visness, C.M., and Kennedy, K.I. (1997). Maternal employment and breast-feeding: Findings from the 1988 National Maternal and Infant Health Survey. *American Journal of Public Health, 87*(6), 945-950.

Viswanath, K. (2006). Public communications and its role in reducing and eliminating health disparities. In Institute of Medicine, *Examining the Health Disparities Research Plan of the National Institutes of Health: Unfinished Business* (pp. 215-253). Committee on the Review and Assessment of NIH's Strategic Research Plan and Budget to Reduce and Ultimately Eliminate Health Disparities. G.E. Thomson, F. Mitchell, and M.B. Williams (Eds.). Board of Health Sciences Policy. Washington, DC: The National Academies Press.

Viswanath, K., Nagler, R.H., Bigman-Galimore, C.A., McCauley, M.P., Jung, M., and Ramanadhan, S. (2012). The communications revolution and health inequalities in the 21st century: Implications for cancer control. *Cancer Epidemiology, Biomarkers & Prevention: A Publication of the American Association for Cancer Research, Cosponsored by the American Society of Preventive Oncology, 21*(10), 1701-1708.

Walkup, J.T., Barlow, A., Mullany, B.C., Pan, W., Goklish, N., Hasting, R., Cowboy, B., Fields, P., Baker, E.V., Speakman, K., Ginsburg, G., and Reid, R. (2009). Randomized controlled trial of a paraprofessional-delivered in-home intervention for young reservation-based American Indian mothers. *Journal of the American Academy of Child and Adolescent Psychiatry, 48*(6), 591-601.

Wallace, A.S., Mantel, C., Mayers, G., Mansoor, O., Gindler, J.S., and Hyde, T.B. (2014). Experiences with provider and parental attitudes and practices regarding the administration of multiple injections during infant vaccination visits: Lessons for vaccine introduction. *Vaccine, 32*(41), 5301-5310.

Wambach, K.A., Aaronson, L., Breedlove, G., Domian, E.W., Rojjanasrirat, W., and Yeh, H.W. (2011). A randomized controlled trial of breastfeeding support and education for adolescent mothers. *Western Journal of Nursing Research, 33*(4), 486-505.

Wasik, B.H., and Bryant, D.M. (2001). *Home Visiting: Procedures for Helping Families* (2nd ed.). Thousands Oak, CA: Sage.

Webster-Stratton, C., and Reid, M.J. (2010). The Incredible Years parents, teachers, and children training series: A multifaceted treatment approach for young children with conduct disorders. In J.R. Weisz and A.E. Kazdin (Eds.), *Evidence-Based Psychotherapies for Children and Adolescents* (2nd ed., pp. 194-210). New York: Guilford Press.

Webster-Stratton, C.H., Reid, M.J., and Beauchaine, T. (2011). Combining parent and child training for young children with ADHD. *Journal of Clinical Child and Adolescent Psychology, 40*(2), 191-203.

Weikart, D.P., and Lambie, D. (1970). Early enrichment in infants. In V.H. Denenberg (Ed.), *Education of the Infant and the Young Child* (pp. 83-107). New York: Academic Press.

Whitaker, D.J., Lutzker, J.R., and Shelley, G.A. (2005). Child maltreatment prevention priorities at the Centers for Disease Control and Prevention. *Child Maltreatment, 10*(3), 245-259.

White House. (2015). *The Affordable Care Act Gives Parents Greater Control Over Their Children's Health Care.* Available: https://www.whitehouse.gov/files/documents/health_reform_for_children.pdf [March 2016].

Whitehurst, G.J., Falco, F.L., Lonigan, C.J., Fischel, J.E., DeBaryshe, B.D., Valdez-Menchaca, M.C., and Caulfield, M. (1988). Accelerating language development through picture book reading. *Developmental Psychology, 24*(4), 552-559.

Whitehurst, G.J., Arnold, D.S., Epstein, J.N., Angell, A.L., Smith, M., and Fischel, J.E. (1994). A picture book reading intervention in day care and home for children from low-income families. *Developmental Psychology, 30*(5), 679-689.

Whitlock, E.P., Williams, S.B., Gold, R., Smith, P.R., and Shipman, S.A. (2005). Screening and interventions for childhood overweight: A summary of evidence for the U.S. Preventive Services Task Force. *Pediatrics, 116*(1), e125-e144.

Wilcken, B., and Wiley, V. (2008). Newborn screening. *Pathology, 40*(2), 104-115.

Williams, C.M., Asaolu, I., English, B., Jewell, T., Smith, K., and Robl, J. (2014a). *Child Health Improvement by Hands Home Visiting Program.* Lexington: University of Kentucky Department of Obstetrics and Gynecology.

Williams, C.M., Asaolu, I., English, B., Jewell, T., Smith, K., and Robl, J. (2014b). *Maternal and Child Health Improvement by Hands Home Visiting Program in the Bluegrass Area Development District.* Lexington: University of Kentucky Department of Obstetrics and Gynecology.

Williams, C.M., Asaolu, I., English, B., Jewell, T., Smith, K., and Robl, J. (2014c). *Maternal and Child Health Improvement by Hands Home Visiting Program in the KIPDA Area Development District, Kentucky.* Lexington: University of Kentucky Department of Obstetrics and Gynecology.

Winickoff, J.P., Buckley, V.J., Palfrey, J.S., Perrin, J.M., and Rigotti, N.A. (2003). Intervention with parental smokers in an outpatient pediatric clinic using counseling and nicotine replacement. *Pediatrics, 112*(5), 1127-1133.

Wood, M., Turnham, J., and Mills, G. (2008). Housing affordability and family well-being: Results from the housing voucher evaluation. *Housing Policy Debate, 19*(2), 367-412.

Wood, R.G., Moore, Q., Clarkwest, A., and Killewald, A. (2014). The long-term effects of building strong families: A program for unmarried parents. *Journal of Marriage and Family, 76*(2), 446-463.

World Adult Labour, (2015). *Raising the Global Floor: Adult Labour Leave for Children's Health Needs.* Montreal: McGill Institute for Health and Social Policy.

Wyatt, K.D., List, B., Brinkman, W.B., Prutsky Lopez, G., Asi, N., Erwin, P., Wang, Z., Domecq Garces, J.P., Montori, V.M., and LeBlanc, A. (2015). Shared decision making in pediatrics: A systematic review and meta-analysis. *Academic Pediatrics, 15*(6), 573-583.

Yaqub, O., Castle-Clarke, S., Sevdalis, N., and Chataway, J. (2014). Attitudes to vaccination: A critical review. *Social Science & Medicine, 112*, 1-11.

Yeager Pelatti, C., Pentimonti, J.M., and Justice, L.M. (2014). Methodological review of the quality of Reach Out and Read: Does it "work"? *Clinical Pediatrics, 53*(4), 343-350.

ZERO TO THREE. (2015). *Behavior and Development.* Available: http://www.zerotothree. org/child-development [February 2016].

Zickuhr, K., and Smith, A. (2012). *Digital Differences.* Available: http://www.pewinternet. org/2012/04/13/digital-differences [February 2016].

Ziliak, J.P. (2015). *Temporary Assistance for Needy Families.* Working Paper No. 21038. Cambridge, MA: National Bureau of Economic Research.

Zubrick, S., Ward, K., Silburn, S., Lawrence, D., Williams, A., Blair, E., Robertson, D., and Sanders, M. (2005). Prevention of child behavior problems through universal implementation of a group behavioral family intervention. *Prevention Science, 6*(4), 287-304.

Zuckerman, B. (2009). Promoting early literacy in pediatric practice: Twenty years of Reach Out and Read. *Pediatrics, 124*(6), 1660-1665.

Zuckerman, B., Parker, S., Kaplan-Sanoff, M., Augustyn, M., and Barth, M.C. (2004). Healthy Steps: A case study of innovation in pediatric practice. *Pediatrics, 114*(3), 820-826.

5

Targeted Interventions Supporting Parents of Children with Special Needs, Parents Facing Special Adversities, and Parents Involved with Child Welfare Services

The previous chapter describes universal and widely available interventions designed to strengthen parenting and support parents of young children. This chapter turns to evidence-based and evidence-informed interventions used in a variety of settings (e.g., health care, education, the home) with some evidence of effectiveness in supporting parents and parenting knowledge, attitudes, and practices among (1) parents of children with special needs; (2) parents facing special personal and situational adversities; and (3) parents who have in some way been involved with the child welfare system, including those who have a history of or are believed to be at risk for maltreatment and foster parents. These interventions target specific populations of interest named in the committee's statement of task (Box 1-2 in Chapter 1), such as parents of children with disabilities, parents with mental health conditions, and parents with a history of substance abuse, as well as other populations of parents the committee believes also warrant specific attention based on its review of the evidence. The chapter concludes with a summary.

In a well-known book published some years ago titled *Disadvantaged Children: What Have They Compelled Us to Learn?*, Julius Richmond advances the idea that much can be learned about the needs of all children by studying populations at risk (Richmond, 1970). In much the same way, the committee believes that examining the needs of specific populations of parents and children, such as those with disabilities and families dealing with mental illness or other challenges, can highlight important principles that extend beyond the needs of those particular populations.

PARENTS OF CHILDREN WITH SPECIAL NEEDS

Among the challenges facing many parents is support and care of their young children who are either born with special needs or develop such needs early in life. This section describes research-based interventions for parents of children with developmental disabilities, behavioral and mental health disorders,[1] and serious or chronic medical illnesses, as well as very-low-birthweight, premature infants. Parents often seek out these programs to help them develop skills, learn problem-solving approaches, or receive support because of the challenges they face in carrying out the type of parenting they wish to provide. They recognize that their child's characteristics may demand special skills in addition to the general knowledge, attitudes, and practices needed by parents.

Parent Voices

[One parent noted that parents of special needs children need to take on many roles and responsibilities.]

"With a special needs child, a parent has to learn to be patient, to be a nurse, to be a lawyer because I have to be a good mediator for all the things that happen to my child."

—Mother from Omaha, Nebraska

Parents of Children with Developmental Disabilities

Parents, and indeed family members, of children with developmental disabilities experience challenges that differ from those experienced by parents of typically developing children (Woodman, 2014). When a child with one or more disabilities is born into a family or when parents receive the diagnosis of their child's disability, they often experience a range of emotions (e.g., shock, grief, anger) that are somewhat similar to those experienced upon learning about the death of a loved one (Kandel and Merrick, 2003). Parents experiencing such emotional reactions require a period of time to adjust, and during that time, parenting and caregiving may be affected.

Some children with disabilities pose particular challenges because of developmental needs and behaviors that require specific parenting skills

---

[1] It is important to note that behavioral and mental disorders in children may represent an adaptive response to adverse circumstances. In such cases, interventions need to focus on improving the child's circumstances in addition to addressing the behavioral or mental health disorder.

or actions not required for children who are developing typically (Durand et al., 2013). In addition, parents of children with disabilities tend to experience challenges at certain points of transition during the early childhood years (e.g., hospital to home, entry to early intervention programs, movement from early intervention to preschool programs, movement from preschool to kindergarten) (Malone and Gallagher, 2008, 2009). Young children with disabilities affect families in different ways, but a common finding in the literature is that parents of children with disabilities experience more stress than parents of typically developing children (Woodman, 2014). Given the difficulties faced by parents of children with disabilities, a range of programs focus on parenting skills and engagement for these parents.

Several entities at the federal level define disability. The *Eunice Kennedy Shriver* National Institute on Child Health and Human Development (2012), drawing on definitions issued by the American Association on Intellectual and Developmental Disabilities (2013) and the Centers for Disease Control and Prevention (n.d.), states

> Intellectual and developmental disabilities are disorders that are usually present at birth and that negatively affect the trajectory of the individual's physical, intellectual, and/or emotional development. Many of these conditions affect multiple body parts or systems. Intellectual disability starts any time before a child turns 18 and is characterized by problems with both: intellectual functioning or intelligence, which include the ability to learn, reason, problem solve, and other skills; and adaptive behavior, which includes everyday social and life skills. The term "developmental disabilities" is a broader category of often lifelong disability that can be intellectual, physical, or both.

The U.S. Department of Education also has established numerous definitions for disabilities that qualify children and families for early intervention and special education services through the Individuals with Disabilities Education Act (IDEA) (U.S. Department of Education, 2015b). The definition of "developmental delay" is particularly relevant in the present context in that it is used most commonly in early intervention and early childhood programs, with carryover through the later grades. IDEA notes that states are required to define developmental delay, but the term usually refers to a rate of development that is slower than normative rates in one or more of the following areas: physical development, cognitive development, communication, social or emotional development, or adaptive (behavioral) development. In addition, a growing population of infants and young children are being diagnosed with autism spectrum disorder (ASD). Although IDEA defines autism as one of its eligibility categories, the ASD definition that researchers and practitioners typically use is from the *Diagnostic and Statistical Manual of Mental Disorders* (DSM), fifth edition (DSM-5) (American

Psychiatric Association, 2013). According to DSM-5, defining features of ASD are "persistent deficits in social communication and social interaction across multiple contexts (and) . . . restricted, repetitive patterns of behavior, interests, or activities."

For parents of children with developmental disabilities, the committee expands on the scope of parenting to encompass family-centered care as foundational for parenting practice (Dunst and Trivette, 2010). Family-centered care is a critical concept in programs for young children with disabilities and is written into the provisions of IDEA, which outlines how services to children with disabilities should be provided (see below). The committee draws on a conceptual framework developed by Dunst and Espe-Sherwindt (2016) that explains the linkage among family-centered practices, early childhood intervention practices, and child outcomes (see Figure 5-1) to organize the literature in this section. Dunst and Espe-Sherwindt propose two primary types of family-centered practice— relational practices and participatory practices—that underlie early childhood intervention. The early childhood intervention practices then lead to child outcomes.

IDEA requires for each child and family receiving services establishment of an Individualized Family Service Plan that includes "family-directed assessment of the resources, priorities, and concerns of the family and the identification of the supports and services necessary to enhance the family's capacity to meet the developmental needs of the infant or toddler" (U.S. Department of Education, 2015a). This provision applies to children with disabilities from birth to age 3. After age 3, children with disabilities may

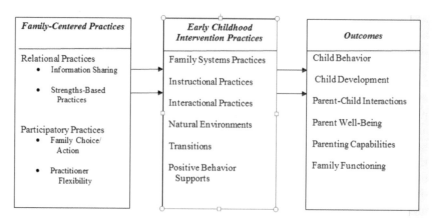

FIGURE 5-1 Linkage among family-centered practices, early childhood intervention practices, and child outcomes.
SOURCE: Dunst and Espe-Sherwindt (2016).

begin special education services that public school programs are required to provide. Families are involved in the development of their child's Individualized Education Plan.

The three clearinghouses reviewed by the committee for this study (the National Registry of Evidence-based Programs and Practices [NREPP], Blueprints, and the California Evidence-Based Clearinghouse for Child Welfare [CEBC]) do not cover the literature on programs for parents of children with developmental disabilities, although some of the programs developed for other populations that are included in these clearinghouses have been used with families of children with disabilities (e.g., the Triple P-Positive Parenting Program and Incredible Years, which are described in greater detail in the following section). When available, the committee drew on information from evaluations of those programs that is relevant to children with disabilities, but the discussion in this section also includes findings from studies accessed directly from the research literature. In all cases, the findings reviewed here are from studies that employed randomized controlled trials, high-quality quasi-experimental designs, and/or high-quality meta-analyses published in peer-reviewed journals.

Intervention Strategies

Interventions designed to support parents of children with developmental disabilities fall into four overlapping areas: family systems programs, instructional programs, interactional programs, and positive behavior support. Each is discussed in turn below.

Family systems programs Family systems programs follow a systems approach in that they most commonly focus on parents' internal variables, such as stress, depression, or coping, based on the assumption that changes in those variables will affect the quality of parenting. Singer and colleagues (2007) conducted a meta-analysis examining the primary and secondary effects of parenting and stress management interventions for parents of children with developmental disabilities. Among the 17 studies with experimental or quasi-experimental designs that qualified for the analysis based on the quality of their research methodology, the authors identified three classes of interventions: behavioral parent training (i.e., teaching parents behavior management skills); coping skills interventions, based on principles of cognitive-behavioral therapy; and a combination of the two. They found that interventions in all three groups had significant effects on reducing psychological distress among mothers and fathers of children with developmental disabilities. In a randomized controlled trial involving 70 families of children with ASD, for example, Tonge and colleagues (2006) provided parent education and behavior management training in group and individual sessions. They found significantly positive outcomes for parents on the General Health Questionnaire postintervention and in follow-up. Feldman and Werner (2002) provided behavior management training with follow-up over a 3- to 6-month period for parents of children with developmental delays and found significantly lower levels of depression for parents randomized into the treatment group. In their summary, Singer and colleagues (2007) note that interventions occurring over a longer period of time and having multiple components (e.g., those that address parents' well-being as well as parenting skills) produced greater reductions in parental stress relative to those of shorter duration and a simpler design.

In a recent randomized controlled trial of 59 parents of children with autism, parents received six individual sessions in a problem-solving education program, adapted from the well-known problem-solving treatment (PST) (Feinberg et al., 2014). Each session focused on working through a problem identified by the mother using the steps of PST (goal setting, brainstorming, evaluating solutions, choosing a solution, and action planning). Study findings showed that the intervention reduced parents' depressive symptoms, but not their stress levels.

A more recent trend has been the application of mindfulness training for parents of children with developmental disabilities, with the goal of reducing stress and potentially increasing self-efficacy. Benn and colleagues (2012) conducted randomized controlled trials to examine the effects of mindfulness-based stress reduction techniques, and found significantly positive effects on stress reduction and associated variables (e.g., personal growth). Collateral effects of these techniques are seen in caregiver competence as reported by parents (Benn et al., 2012) and in fewer behavior problems reported by teachers (Neece, 2014).

Instructional programs A large literature documents the effectiveness of programs designed to instruct parents in implementing approaches that promote the skills (e.g., developmental, language, social, play) of their children with disabilities (Girolametto et al., 1998; Green et al., 2010). Roberts and Kaiser (2011), for example, found strong positive effects on the receptive and expressive language skills of young children with intellectual disabilities in a meta-analysis of 18 studies of parent-implemented language training programs that utilized a control group. Effect sizes ranged from .35 to .81 in studies in which parent-implemented treatment was compared with nontreatment or business-as-usual comparison groups. Smaller effects were found for studies comparing parent-delivered and professional-delivered treatment. This finding suggests that children receiving the treatment from parents and speech pathologists made comparable progress, which indicates in turn that, when appropriately trained, parents can be effective facilitators of the language development of children with disabilities.

Programs that have instructed parents in promoting the reading skills of their young children with disabilities have likewise documented positive effects. Two randomized controlled studies (Crain-Thoreson and Dale, 1999; Dale et al., 1996) document the efficacy of parent-implemented dialogic (shared) reading approaches in improving the reading skills of young children with language delays. Using a version of the dialogic reading approach, parents read a book to their child, monitor the child's understanding through questions, give the child opportunities to respond, repeat and elaborate on what the child says, refer to illustrations to enhance meaning, praise and encourage the child, and focus on making reading a fun activity. The What Works Clearinghouse (2014) has examined this literature and found that these studies meet their standards of acceptability.

Particularly for children with ASD, interventions involving parents have generated positive outcomes. Many comprehensive treatment programs have been designed for children with ASD, and almost all have a parenting component (Odom et al., 2014). These comprehensive programs comprise a set of practices that are based on an organizing conceptual framework, address a variety of developmental needs of the child, and generally occur over an extended period of time (e.g., 1-2 years or more). These elements are detailed in program manuals. Some programs begin in a clinical setting, with the clinician taking the lead, and also are implemented at home by the parent. The Early Start Denver Model (ESDM) is the best and most well-validated example of this approach. Dawson and colleagues (2010) conducted an experimental evaluation of the ESDM, finding significant effects on cognitive developmental and adaptive behavior. They also found differences in brain activation for children in the treatment and control groups (Dawson et al., 2012), and the effects of the ESDM were partially replicated with families in community settings (Rogers et al., 2012). In a quasi-experimental design study of Project ImPACT (Improving Parents as Communication Teachers) (Ingersoll and Wainer, 2013), an evidence-based program that teaches parents of children with autism how to promote their children's social-communication skills during daily routines and activities, Stadnick and colleagues (2015) found that parents could implement the intervention with fidelity, and the program produced positive child outcomes. In a review of eight intervention programs for toddlers with ASD, Siller and colleagues (2013) document the variety of approaches used by these programs, nearly all involving families and most employing experimental designs to document efficacy (although this summative review does not include effect sizes).

Other studies have documented the positive effects of early intensive behavior therapy delivered by parents. For example, in a meta-analysis of 13 studies conducted in 2009-2011 using experimental and other design types, Strauss and colleagues (2013) found that early intensive behavioral interventions delivered by parents were more effective than those delivered only by a therapist. In summary, it appears that involving parents is an essential element of early interventions for children with ASD and in some cases may produce stronger positive outcomes than such interventions in which parents are not directly involved.

Interactional programs Interactional programs are designed to promote positive social interactions between caregivers and young children with disabilities. They are based on research showing that some young children with disabilities have difficulty engaging in positive interactions with their parents and others (Adamson et al., 2012), and parents at times may interact with their children in ways that discourage social interaction (e.g., they may be overly directive) (Cress et al., 2008; Lussier et al., 1994). In these interventions, parents are taught how to set up play situations that encourage interaction and to respond in particularly encouraging ways. In a number of randomized studies, Mahoney and colleagues (2006) employed a responsive parenting approach that resulted in increased social interactions among children with disabilities (Karaaslan and Mahoney, 2013; Karaaslan et al., 2013). For many young children with ASD, joint attention—a specific form of parent-child interaction that is a building block for later communication development—is limited or fails to develop. Several investigators have developed interventions designed to promote joint attention among young children with ASD and their parents that have demonstrated positive effects in randomized studies (Kasari et al., 2010; Schertz et al., 2013).

Positive behavior support For parents of young children with disabilities, their child's behavior often poses challenges, results in negative parent-child interaction, and creates great stress for the parents (Hastings, 2002). A variety of approaches have been developed to promote parenting practices related to behavior management. One such approach—positive behavior intervention and support (PBIS)—is a multicomponent program involving problem-behavior prevention strategies and increasing levels of behavioral intervention (Dunlap and Fox, 2009). In a randomized controlled study, Durand and colleagues (2013) examined the effects of PBIS on parents and their children with a developmental disability and serious challenging behavior. They found significant improvement in challenging behavior, as well as reduction in parent pessimism. Effects of the PBIS model were stronger when it was paired with a complementary program of optimism training aimed at helping parents identify and restructure their parenting-related thought patterns.

The Triple P-Positive Parenting Program (Triple P) (Sanders et al., 2008) was initially designed for school-age children with conduct disorders, and has been used with parents of young children with behavioral and mental health challenges (described in the next section). An adaptation of this program—Stepping Stones—has been used with parents of young children with disabilities. Individual randomized controlled studies (Sofronoff et al., 2011) and a meta-analysis (Tellegen and Sanders, 2013) of Stepping Stones revealed strong effects on reducing challenging behavior and improving broader parenting variables (e.g., style, adjustment, parental relationship). Similarly, the Incredible Years Program was initially designed for parents of school-age children with conduct disorders (Webster-Stratton, 1984), but has been adapted for and applied with parents of young children with disabilities. In a randomized trial, McIntyre (2008) found that the Incredible Years Program reduced negative parent-child interactions and child behavioral problems.

In another study focused on parents of children with autism, investigators evaluated a pilot study of 16 families with children ages 3-6 with a diagnosis of autism and parent-reported disruptive behaviors (Bearss et al., 2013). This study evaluated the RUPP (Research Units on Pediatric Psychopharmacology) Autism Network Parent Training Program, an 11-session structured program designed to teach parents of children with autism and serious behavioral problems skills needed to reduce their children's disruptive behavior. In a single group pre-post evaluation, parents reported a reduction in their children's disruptive behaviors and improvements in their adaptive functioning (Bearss et al., 2013).

Research Gaps

There are significant research gaps in the area of interventions for parents of children with developmental disabilities, such as implementation of interventions in natural environments and support for child and family transitions. Although a primary feature of early intervention programs funded through IDEA—a feature required by the federal government—is that they must occur in natural settings, and although IDEA encourages the creation of a transition plan for children moving from early intervention to preschool, the committee found that little or no such experimental research has been conducted, nor do these gaps appear to inform directions for future program development and research.

Parents of Children with Behavioral Challenges and Mental Health Disorders

Behavioral and mental health challenges encompass a range of behaviors and conditions. The psychiatric, psychological, and educational professional communities use somewhat different terminologies, but they agree in identifying these behaviors and conditions as occurring in children who present with externalizing (e.g., aggression, tantrums) or internalizing (e.g., childhood depression, social withdrawal) behavior. In addition, attention deficit hyperactivity disorder (ADHD), while overlapping to some extent with these behaviors, manifests more distinctly in high levels of physical activity, difficulty with attention, and difficulty in completing tasks (American Psychiatric Association, 2013).

Aggression and antisocial behavior in young children appear to reach a peak between the ages of 2 and 4 and then decline, only to reemerge in the adolescent years (Wahl and Metzner, 2012). Lavigne and colleagues (1996) report that during the early years (ages 2-5), the prevalence of such behavior problems in a sample of 3,860 children averages 8.3 percent, with gender differences (boys having a higher prevalence than girls). In a small proportion of children, however, studies have found that aggressive/antisocial behavior is severe and persists through early childhood (Wahl and Metzner, 2012). It is these children that are diagnosed as having oppositional defiant disorder (ODD) (American Psychiatric Association, 2013). Children with ODD may lose their temper; argue with adults; actively defy rules; and harm people, animals, and/or property.

Intervention Strategies: Parents of Children with Externalizing Behavior

A number of interventions have focused on improving the knowledge, attitudes, and practices of parents of children with externalizing behavior. For the most part, effective interventions have been designed to provide parents with skills needed to better manage their children's behavior. These interventions have included applications of general parent management training to parents of children with challenging behavior, as well as parent training developed specifically for this population.

Triple P One of the most frequently used and internationally replicated interventions for helping parents prevent and address behavioral challenges in their children is Triple P (Sanders et al., 2008), a multilevel system of support that provides increasingly intensive interventions based on parents' and children's needs. The interventions range from basic information on parenting at the least intensive level to behavior management through different modalities (e.g., group, one-on-one, or self-directed learning) (see Box 5-1).

In experimental and quasi-experimental studies of the Primary Care, Standard and Group, and Enhanced Triple P levels conducted in the United States and in other countries, parents have reported less frequent use of dysfunctional parenting practices in such areas as discipline, laxness, and over-reactivity and greater parenting competence. Improvements in observed and parent-reported negative behavior in children relative to controls also have been found (Hoath and Sanders, 2002; Sanders et al., 2000; Turner and Sanders, 2006; Zubrick et al., 2005). A systematic review and meta-analysis of the multilevel Triple P system that includes 101 studies shows significant short-term improvements in parenting practices; parenting satisfaction and self-efficacy; parental adjustment; parental relationship; and children's social, emotional, and behavioral well-being (Sanders et al., 2014).[2] Triple P has an average NREPP rating of 3 out of 4, where programs rated 4 have the strongest evidence of effectiveness (National Registry of Evidence-based Programs and Practices, 2016e). Triple P level 4 has a CEBC rating of 1 (out of 5), and the entire Triple P system has a CEBC rating of 2, where programs rated 1 have the strongest evidence of effectiveness (California Evidence-Based Clearinghouse, 2016n). The positive results from these assessments provide empirical support for Triple P and a blending of universal and targeted parenting interventions to promote child, parent, and family well-being (Sanders et al., 2014).

The Incredible Years The Incredible Years Program is a developmentally based training intervention for children ages 0-12 and their parents and teachers. Children of families in the program often have behavioral problems. Drawing on developmental theory, the program consists of parent, teacher, and child components that are designed to work jointly to promote emotional and social competence and prevent, reduce, and treat behavioral and emotional problems in young children (National Registry of Evidence-based Programs and Practices, 2016a). Incredible Years received an average NREPP rating of 3.5 out of 4 in a July 2012 review and 3.7 out of 4 in an August 2007 review. It has a CEBC rating of 1 (California Evidence-Based Clearinghouse, 2016g).

The Incredible Years Program addresses parental attitudes by helping parents increase their empathy for their children and educates parents about

---

[2] Some concerns regarding Triple P studies that report child-based outcomes are raised in a 2012 review of 33 such studies (Wilson et al., 2012). Among the concerns are the use of wait list or no-treatment comparison groups in most of the studies reviewed and potential reporting bias attributed to author affiliation with Triple P and the fact that few of the abstracts for the studies reviewed reported negative findings. A follow-up commentary (Sanders et al., 2012) challenges the findings of this review, noting that it includes a limited subsample of Triple P studies and pools findings from interventions of various intensities and types. Further, the commentary notes that most of the studies reviewed included maintenance probes many of which showed that post-treatment improvements were maintained over various lengths of follow-up. With regard to author affiliation, the commentary states that while developers are often authors of evaluations of Triple P and other parenting programs, the claim that most Triple P evidence is authored by affiliates of the program is untrue (Sanders et al., 2012). The controversy about the proper treatment of the Wilson and Sanders reviews continues in a series of published papers, blog postings, and policy decisions in Australia, the United States, and Europe.

BOX 5-1
The Triple P-Positive Parenting Program

Triple P is designed to prevent and treat social, emotional, and behavioral problems in children by improving parents' knowledge, skills, and confidence in their parenting role. Drawing on social learning, cognitive, developmental, and public health theories, Triple P incorporates five levels of intervention on a tiered continuum of increasing strength and narrowing population reach for parents of children from birth to age 16 (see Figure 5-1-1 below) (National Registry of Evidence-based Programs and Practices, 2016e; Sanders et al., 2014).

Universal Triple P (level 1) takes a public health approach by using media to increase awareness of parenting resources, programs, and solutions to common child behavioral and developmental concerns at the community level. *Selected Triple P* (level 2) gives parents who are generally coping well advice on practices for accommodating common developmental issues, such as toilet training and minor child behavior problems, via one to three telephone, face-to-face, or group sessions. *Primary Care Triple P* (level 3) targets parents with children who have mild to moderate behavioral challenges. Parents receive active skills training that combines advice, skill rehearsal, and self-evaluation in three to four one-on-one sessions in person or by telephone, or in a series of 2-hour group discussion sessions. *Standard and Group Triple P* (level 4), designed for parents of children with more severe behavioral challenges, provides parents with more intensive training in how to manage a range of children's problem behaviors. It is delivered in eight to ten sessions in individual, group, or self-directed (online or workbook) formats. Finally, *Enhanced Triple P* (level 5) is designed for families whose parenting challenges are heightened by other sources of family distress, such as parental depression or relationship conflict. This level includes practice sessions to enhance parenting, mood management, stress coping, and partner support skills using adjunct individual or group sessions (National Registry of Evidence-based Programs and Practices, 2016e; Sanders et al., 2014). Variants of Triple P have been developed for parents of children with developmental disabilities (Stepping Stones Triple P), parents at high risk for maltreatment (Pathways Triple P), parents of children with obesity (Lifestyles Triple P), and divorcing parents (Transitions Triple P), as well as for delivery over the Internet (Online Triple P) (Sanders and Prinz, 2005).

---

healthy child development, positive parent-child interaction techniques, and positive child behaviors (Marcynyszyn et al., 2011). Sessions focus on building skills to strengthen the parent-child relationship; reduce the use of harsh discipline; and support children's social, emotional, and language development, as well as their school readiness. The parent program varies in length from 12 to 20 weekly group sessions, each of which lasts 2 to 3 hours. In the teacher program, presented in a workshop format, early childhood and elementary school teachers learn strategies for building positive

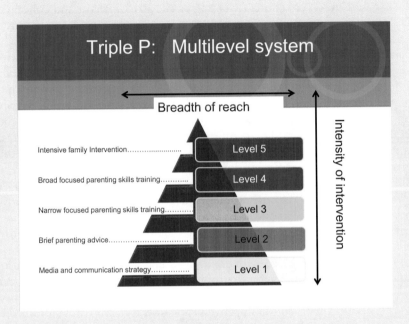

Triple P: Multilevel system

Breadth of reach

Intensity of intervention

Intensive family Intervention.......................... Level 5

Broad focused parenting skills training........... Level 4

Narrow focused parenting skills training........... Level 3

Brief parenting advice................................ Level 2

Media and communication strategy................ Level 1

FIGURE 5-1-1 Schematic of the Triple P system of tiered levels of intervention.
SOURCE: Prinz (2014).

All levels of Triple P are designed to encourage in parents developmentally appropriate expectations, beliefs, and assumptions about children's behavior and the importance of the family environment in children's development; impart knowledge and teach practices related to providing a safe, supervised, and protective environment and alternatives to coercive discipline practices; and teach parents to take good care of themselves in order to be more effective parents (Sanders and Prinz, 2005).

relationships with students and families, discipline techniques, and how to stimulate and support children's academic achievement. The child arm of the program aims to improve children's social and emotional competence through more than 60 classroom lesson plans lasting about 45 minutes each, delivered by teachers at least twice weekly over consecutive years. Incredible Years has been implemented in almost every U.S. state and is delivered in a variety of education, health, and social service settings.

A systematic review and meta-analysis of 39 randomized controlled studies of Incredible Years found intervention effects in reducing disruptive behavior and increasing prosocial behavior in children based on parent, teacher, and observer reports (Menting et al., 2013). Perrin and colleagues (2014) conducted a randomized trial of a 10-week Incredible Years parent training program involving families in pediatric practices with toddlers with disruptive behaviors. They found greater improvements in the intervention group compared with the control group for parent-reported and observed child disruptive behavior, negative parenting, and negative child-parent interactions. In another primary care-based experimental study involving 117 parents of children with ODD, however, Lavigne and colleagues (2008) compared Incredible Years led by a nurse, led by a psychologist, or using materials only with no in-person sessions. Findings suggested that all groups showed short- and long-term improvement, but there was no intervention effect. In a randomized controlled trial (independent from the developer, Webster-Stratton), Brotman and colleagues (2003) identified low-income families with a child ages 2-5 at risk for disruptive behaviors as a result of having a sibling or other relative with ODD or conduct disorder or a criminal history. Using a fairly intensive version of Incredible Years, they found that, compared with children receiving usual care, intervention children had fewer behavioral problems, and intervention parents performed better on observed parenting practices of responsiveness and affection. These postintervention improvements, however, were not sustained at 6-month follow-up (Brotman et al., 2003).

Parent Management Training One of the earliest training programs for parents, Parent Management Training (PMT), involving parents of children with externalizing behavior, originated with Gerald Patterson and colleagues. Parents participate in therapy sessions to learn behavior management techniques they would use with their children. In an initial experimental study (Patterson et al., 1982), observations revealed significant reductions in children's externalizing behavior relative to the control group. In a subsequent randomized study, Hughes and Wilson (1988) followed the PMT model to teach parents of children with conduct disorders to use contingency management. They also found significantly greater changes in child behavior and parent attitudes for the intervention relative to the control group.

Parent-Child Interaction Therapy Elaborating on the model used by Patterson and colleagues (1982), Eyberg and Boggs (1998) designed the parent-child interaction therapy (PCIT) approach, which not only includes a therapy-based child management component but also incorporates elements of play therapy that involve the child directly in clinic sessions. PCIT is an evidence-based intervention developed as a treatment for children ages 2-7 with emotional and behavioral disorders and their parents. Evaluations of PCIT have involved children ages 0-12. Parents learn skills to encourage prosocial behavior and discourage negative behavior in their children, with the ultimate goal of developing nurturing and secure parent-child relationships.

The intervention has two phases. In the first phase—child-directed interaction—parents learn nondirective play skills and engage their child in a play situation with the objective of strengthening the parent-child relationship. In the second phase—parent-directed interaction—parents learn to use age-appropriate instructions and consistent messages about consequences to direct their child's behavior, with the goal of improving the child's compliance with parental instruction. At the beginning of the child- and parent-directed phases, parents attend a didactic session with a PCIT professional to learn interaction skills. The entire intervention is typically delivered in weekly 1-hour sessions over a 15-week period in an outpatient clinic or school setting. PCIT has been applied with families with a history of child abuse, as well as families of children who have developmental disabilities or were exposed to substances prior to their birth (National Registry of Evidence-based Programs and Practices, 2016c; Parent-Child Interaction Therapy International, 2015).

In a randomized controlled efficacy study of PCIT involving parents of children with externalizing behavior and noncompliance, Schuhmann and colleagues (1998) found that parents in the PCIT group interacted more positively with their child, were more successful in gaining their child's compliance, experienced less stress, and reported more internal locus of control relative to parents in the control group. Other randomized studies comparing outcomes for parents participating in PCIT and those participating in standardized community-based parenting classes or wait-list controls have shown improvements resulting from the intervention in parenting skills (reflective listening, physical proximity, prosocial verbalization), parent-child interactions and child compliance with parental instruction, and child behavior. In addition, compared with controls, parents who participate in PCIT are more likely to report reductions in parenting stress and improvement in parenting locus of control (Bagner and Eyberg, 2007; Boggs et al., 2005; Chaffin et al., 2004; Nixon et al., 2003; Parent-Child Interaction Therapy International, 2015). Participants in evaluations of PCIT have been relatively diverse in terms of race and ethnicity (National Registry of Evidence-based Programs and Practices, 2016c). PCIT received an average NREPP rating of 3.4 out of 4 and a CEBC rating of 1 (California Evidence-Based Clearinghouse, 2016k; National Registry of Evidence-based Programs and Practices, 2016c).

Several randomized controlled evaluation studies have documented the efficacy of a PCIT intervention delivered in a pediatric setting to mothers of infants and toddlers. Bagner and colleagues (2010) found significant effects on positive parenting and reductions in ineffective parenting practices (as reported by parents). Berkovits and colleagues (2010) compared a PCIT intervention that included anticipatory guidance (i.e., receiving materials ahead of time) with a standard PCIT intervention among mothers of young children expressing subclinical levels of behavior problems. They found that both groups of mothers reported positive effects on their parenting, with no difference between versions at postintervention or 6-month follow-up groups.

Other interventions for externalizing behavior Although Triple P, The Incredible Years, and PCIT have the strongest evidence of efficacy, documented through randomized controlled studies and international replications, a variety of other interventions have been designed to promote parenting (primarily behavior management) skills among parents of children with externalizing behavior. Play Nicely is a video-based training program provided to parents during well-baby visits that is focused on discipline. Randomized controlled studies have found effects on parents' attitudes toward spanking, as measured immediately after the training (Chavis et al., 2013; Scholer et al., 2010). Early Pathways is an in-home therapy intervention for low-income children with severe externalizing behavioral and emotional problems (e.g., aggression and oppositional behavior) and their parents. In experimental evaluations of standard and culturally adapted versions of Early Pathways, Fung and Fox (2014) and Harris and colleagues (2015) found improvements in parenting (caregiver limit setting and nurturing), parent-child relationships, and child behavior and a decrease in clinical diagnoses following treatment. Results were sustained several weeks postintervention. Intervention components delivered in families' homes over 8-10 sessions were child-led play to improve the parent-child relationship and parent skills training related to maintaining developmentally appropriate expectations of children and improving parents' disciplinary practices (time-outs, redirection, ignoring). Early Pathways has been rated by NREPP as having strong evidence of a favorable effect.

Interventions for children with ADHD As noted, children with ADHD have characteristics and presenting issues that differ from those of children with externalizing or internalizing behaviors; thus interventions targeting ADHD address different issues from those addressed by the interventions reviewed above. Lehner-Dua (2001) compared a 10-week program of parent skills training based on the Defiant Children Program (Barkley, 1997) with a parent support group for parents of children newly diagnosed with ADHD ages 6-10. Parents in both groups reported significant improvement in parenting-related competence, while parents randomized to skills training were more likely to report reductions in children's problem behavior.

Mikami and colleagues (2010) in a randomized controlled study provided the Parental Friendship Coaching intervention to parents to teach them strategies they could use to promote the social skills and peer relationships of their children with ADHD ages 6-10. The intervention resulted in parents' greater provision of corrective feedback and reduced criticism, and improvement in children's social skills based on parent but not teacher reports.

Working with fathers of children with ADHD (average age around 8), Fabiano and colleagues (2009) developed a program called COACHES (Coaching Our Acting-Out Children: Heightening Essential Skills), which included parent behavioral training and sports skill training. Although investigators found no significant intervention effects on child ADHD-related behavioral outcomes, fathers participating in the program scored higher on satisfaction measures and were significantly more likely to attend sessions (76% of intervention fathers versus 57% of controls attended ≥ 75% of sessions) and complete parent training "homework" compared with the control group of fathers who only received parent behavioral training.

Intervention Strategies: Parents of Children with Internalizing Behavior and Mental Illness

Internalizing behavior and mental illness are manifest in young children primarily as anxiety and depression. Most of the literature on interventions that involve parents has focused on externalizing behavior, given that internalizing behavior is less prevalent (McKee et al., 2008). Yet the trajectory of internalizing behavior across childhood is often persistent, serious, and linked to adult outcomes (Dekker et al., 2007). DSM-5 (American Psychiatric Association, 2013) includes diagnostic classification and criteria for both anxiety disorder and depression that extend to young children. Some internalizing conditions have been inversely associated with certain parenting practices, such as those that are overinvolved and those that display low warmth (Bayer et al., 2006). Empirically validated intervention approaches have been developed to address both anxiety disorder and depression in children.

Anxiety disorder Anxiety in some situations is normal for young children, such as when very young children are anxious around strangers or in new places. However, severe and debilitating forms of anxiety may manifest in phobias, sleep terrors, posttraumatic stress disorder (PTSD), and separation anxiety. Recent systematic, critical reviews by Anticich and colleagues (2012) and Luby (2013) have identified empirically supported interventions for anxiety disorder in young children. Cognitive-behavioral therapy, once used primarily with older children and youth and in clinical settings, has been adapted for young children in several approaches that involve parents directly (Cohen and Mannarino, 1996; Deblinger et al., 2001; Hirshfeld-Becker et al., 2010; Kennedy et al., 2009). PCIT, described earlier as treatment for externalizing conditions, also has been adapted for anxiety in young children (Comer et al., 2012; Pincus et al., 2008). In addition, other supported treatments have employed psychoeducational approaches addressing anxiety disorders (Rapee et al., 2005) and play therapy (Santacruz et al., 2006). All of these studies used experimental designs with active control, passive control, or wait list control groups.

Childhood depression The intervention studies discussed above for anxiety have at times included children with depression. Luby and colleagues (2012) adapted the PCIT intervention specifically for parents and their young children with depression. They found significant improvements in children's executive functioning and decreases in parents' stress relative to randomly assigned active control group participants.

Parents of Children with Serious or Chronic Medical Illness

For parents of children with serious or chronic medical illness, the concern for their child's welfare and the challenges related to health care provision and coverage may affect their ability to provide positive parenting. One of the most promising approaches for supporting these parents is problem-solving therapy. Bright IDEAS is a problem-solving skills training program provided by a mental health professional over eight 1-hour individual sessions (Sahler et al., 2002, 2005, 2013). It has been tested in a randomized controlled trial involving mothers of children newly diagnosed with cancer at hospitals/cancer centers in the United States and Israel (Sahler et al., 2002); in a second, larger trial involving mothers at U.S. hospitals/cancer centers, with the intervention being expanded to include Spanish-speaking participants (Sahler et al., 2005); and in a third trial using an active therapy control (Sahler et al., 2013) (the first two trials used standard psychosocial services in the hospital as the control). Significant differences between intervention and control mothers were documented for the mother's report of her mood, depressive symptoms, and stress across multiple studies (Sahler et al., 2005, 2013).

Melnyk and colleagues developed an educational-behavioral intervention called Creating Opportunities for Parent Empowerment (COPE) for mothers of critically ill children in pediatric intensive care units. In this intervention, mothers are provided information about their child's course of treatment and recovery, and then trained in structured interaction activities in which to engage when the child is discharged. In two randomized controlled studies (Melnyk et al., 1997, 2007), researchers found that, compared with mothers in the control group, mothers in the COPE group provided more emotional support for their child during invasive procedures and experienced less stress, and their children showed less internalizing or externalizing behavior after discharge. Researchers also found that treatment effects were mediated by parent beliefs and (inversely) negative maternal mood state.

A number of other programs have tested cognitive-behavioral approaches as well as training in communication and social support for parents of children with illnesses ranging from cancer to diabetes to other chronic diseases. Unfortunately, most of these studies have either been underpowered or shown no significant benefits.

Parents of Very Low-Birth Weight, Premature Infants

Very low birthweight is defined as less than 1,500 grams at birth and extremely low birthweight as less than 1,000 grams. The terms are most commonly used to designate an infant as being born prematurely. Very-low-birth weight infants are admitted to neonatal intensive care units (NICUs), may reside in those units for weeks to months, and at times sustain chronic health or developmental conditions. Because these infants do not come home immediately after birth, a concern is that the normal formation of attachment and transition to parenthood (especially for first-time parents) may be disrupted (Odom and Chandler, 1990). In addition, the children may have ongoing and significant medical needs (e.g., use of respirators or heart monitors) after transitioning home to which the parents must attend.

A range of studies have focused on supporting parents of infants admitted to the NICU (Heidari et al., 2013; Obeidat et al., 2009). Some have evaluated parenting training designed to support effective early parenting skills, while others have looked at psychosocial support for parents to prevent or address posttraumatic stress or depressive symptoms. An approach that has been used for decades is called Kangaroo Mother Care (KMC). This program involves mothers and infants having consistent skin-to-skin contact during the hospitalization period and care providers supporting mothers' appropriate interactions with their child. In a Cochrane-like quantitative review, Athanasopoulou and Fox (2014) evaluated 13 experimental and quasi-experimental studies of KMC. They found that, although the outcomes of these studies were mixed, mothers in the KMC groups experienced significantly less negative mood and more positive interactions with their infant relative to mothers in the control groups.

Schroeder and Pridham (2006) examined a guided participation approach to supporting mothers' competencies in relating to their preterm (less than 28 weeks' gestation) infants admitted to the NICU. Compared with mothers receiving standard care teaching, mothers in the guided participation group developed expectations and intentions that were more attuned and adaptive to their infants' needs and showed consistently higher relationship competencies in a randomized clinical trial. In a study of the impact of providing information about prematurity to mothers of preterm infants, Browne and Talmi (2005) provided educational materials about the infants' behavior and development delivered either through videos and slides and written information or one-on-one teaching sessions. Mothers receiving both interventions scored higher on knowledge of preterm infants' behavior and reported lower parenting stress at 1-month postdischarge from the NICU relative to control mothers who participated in an informal discussion about care for preterm infants (Browne and Talmi, 2005). To examine the effects of the COPE model, described previously, applied with mothers with very low-birth weight infants in the NICU, Melnyk and colleagues (2008) conducted a secondary analysis of a larger randomized controlled study. They found that mothers experiencing COPE had less anxiety and depression and higher parent-child interaction scores compared with the control group. Segre and colleagues (2013) used the Listening Visits intervention, consisting of six 45- to 60-minute individual sessions provided by a trained neonatal nurse practitioner. The sessions entailed empathic listening on the part of the nurse practitioner to understand the mother's situation and collaborative problem solving. Improvements were detected in primary outcomes of maternal depressive and anxiety symptoms, as well as quality-of-life measures in a single group pre-post test trial (Segre et al., 2013).

Much of the research in this area has focused on low-birth weight infants in the NICU, and there is a set of well-articulated programs that can be beneficial to these parents. Given the stress created by a premature birth, the psychological trauma associated with prolonged stays in the NICU, and the possible chronic health and developmental conditions that may emerge in these infants, these programs may produce ongoing benefits. It is also important to note the long-standing finding that low-birth weight children born to families living in poverty often have poorer outcomes relative to those born to families not living in poverty (Sameroff and Chandler, 1975), even when interventions are implemented to support their early development (Brooks-Gunn et al., 1995). Parents with limited financial resources or social supports who have premature and low-birth weight children may well need more assistance than their better-off counterparts.

PARENTS FACING SPECIAL ADVERSITIES

This section reviews programs addressing the needs of parents facing special adversities related to mental illness, substance abuse disorders, intimate partner violence, and parental developmental disabilities, as well as adolescent parents, who often face a number of challenges. It is important to emphasize that approaches for intimate partner violence differ from those applied, for example, with parents with mental illness in that concerns about the safety of the child—even removing the child from the home—must be the priority rather than providing treatment for parents and supporting them in their parental role. Certainly, concerns about the safety of the child are part of the evaluation in the latter cases, but they are not the central focus. It should also be noted that, because of the lack of definitive research on support for parents facing other adversities, such as homelessness or incarceration, the discussion does not address these adversities, even though they affect the lives of millions of children.

The fact that parents are experiencing one or more of these adversities does not necessarily mean that they need help with parenting. Many parents facing such problems are able to provide adequate parenting. However, these adversities can impair parents' ability to provide their children with the safe, nurturing environment they wish to provide. Coping with these adversities can reduce parents' overall coping ability and their ability to engage in the types of positive parenting behaviors identified in Chapter 2. As discussed below, it is well established that children living with parents facing these adversities are less likely to attain the desired outcomes identified in Chapter 2 relative to children whose parents are of similar socioeconomic status but do not face these adversities. Providing effective interventions for these parents to support and strengthen their parenting is therefore critical for both them and their children.

At present, the majority of parents experiencing one or more of these adversities are receiving no services for their condition. For higher-risk families most in need of effective treatment programs, engagement rates may be even lower (Ingoldsby, 2010). Although not specific to parents, one study estimates the percentage of persons who needed but did not receive substance abuse treatment to be about 90 percent (Batts et al., 2014). With respect to mental health, a national study of low-income women found that just one-quarter of those with any mental health disorder had sought treatment in the past month (Rosen et al., 2006). Again, even when individuals do receive services, the services generally focus on the presenting problem but do not address parenting issues; in fact, individuals receiving treatment for mental health or substance abuse disorders frequently are not asked whether they are parents.

Three interrelated factors are particularly common barriers to seeking and receiving support among the parent populations discussed in this section: stigma (e.g., that associated with having a mental illness or substance use disorder),[3] parents' fear that they will be reported to child protection agencies, and distrust of service providers. Parents facing adversities may have an internalized sense of stigma about their condition that affects their sense of self-worth and competence (Borba et al., 2012; Krumm et al., 2013; Nicholson et al., 1998; Wittkowski et al., 2014). The widespread stigma associated with mental illness often increases parental and family stress and poses a barrier to seeking any parenting support, even basic health care (Blegen et al., 2010; Borba et al., 2012, Byatt et al., 2013, Dolman et al., 2013; Gray et al., 2008; Henderson et al., 2013; Krumm et al., 2013; Lacey et al., 2015; Rose and Cohen, 2010; Wittkowski et al., 2014). This appears to be particularly true for parents with severe mental illnesses. Similarly, societal stigma may increase the self-blame, remorse, and shame already felt by mothers with substance abuse disorders, pushing them further away from seeking help and contributing to the denial that is a hallmark of the disease of addiction. Substance abusing mothers cite enormous guilt and shame for "failing" as mothers as a major barrier to accessing treatment (Nicholson et al., 2006).

In addition, many adults living with mental illness, substance abuse, developmental disabilities, or intimate partner violence are cognizant that their condition negatively influences other people's beliefs about their parenting abilities. Mothers report feeling significant vulnerability based on fear of not being perceived as a good mother. They recognize that as a result of their condition, they can be at risk for involvement of child protective services and loss of child custody, a perception that is based in fact (Berger et al., 2010; Cook and Mueser, 2014; Fletcher et al., 2013; Niccols and Sword, 2005; Park et al., 2006; Seeman, 2012). For example, using Medicaid and child welfare system data, a large study of Medicaid-eligible mothers with severe mental illness found almost three times higher odds of being involved with child welfare services and a four-fold higher risk of losing custody at some point compared with mothers without psychiatric diagnoses (Park et al., 2006). In the case of mothers with substance abuse, caseworkers may be more likely to perceive that children have experienced severe risk and harm (Berger et al., 2010). And the law in many states requires that reports of domestic violence be investigated by child welfare agencies (Blegen et al., 2010; Cook and Mueser, 2014; Dolman et al., 2013; Wittkowski et al., 2014), which makes some victims reticent to invite service providers into their homes (Brown, 2007).

---

[3] The Substance Abuse and Mental Health Services Administration and other stakeholders are moving away from the use of the term "stigma," as noted in the recent report *Ending Discrimination Against People with Mental and Substance Use Disorders: The Evidence for Stigma Change* (2016). Because the word "stigma" continues to be widely accepted in the research community, the committee chose to use this term in this report.

These factors also contribute to parents' distrust of service providers. Ambivalent feelings about parenting support programs may come from past experiences, as well as familial or social histories or perceptions (McCurdy and Daro, 2001). Some parents report stigmatizing remarks or comments from health care or social service providers. Parents with substance use problems, for example, frequently report that they experience anger and blame from medical and other treatment professionals instead of being viewed as suffering from an illness and treated as such (Camp and Finkelstein, 1997; Nicholson et al., 2006). In the case of parents with mental illness, the distrust may be part of the general attitudes associated with paranoia or delusions (Healy et al., 2015; Stepp et al., 2012).

Although generating participation can be challenging, a wide range of programs are available that are designed to meet the needs of these populations, both by addressing the underlying problems and with respect to supporting and strengthening parenting. High-quality trials of such interventions are limited, however. Although there have been randomized controlled trials, many smaller studies, observational research, and case-control studies provide some guidance on best practices. This section reviews the available evidence on interventions designed specifically to support parents facing adversities related to mental illness, substance abuse disorders, intimate partner violence, and parental developmental disabilities, since each has unique needs that should be considered in offering services to strengthen and support parenting. As noted, many parents face two or more of these challenges, and some face nearly all of them. There has been almost no rigorous evaluation of interventions for these very complex cases, and many of these families are referred to child welfare agencies. Later in this chapter, the committee assesses parenting interventions offered through the child welfare system.

Parents with Mental Illness

Many parents struggle with mental illness at the same time they are trying to provide a safe, nurturing environment for their family. It is estimated that 43.6 million adults in the United States experience mental illness annually, and 9.8 million of them are living with serious mental illness (Center for Behavioral Health Statistics and Quality, 2015). Research indicates that one-half of all lifetime cases of diagnosable mental illness occur by age 14 and three-fourths by age 24 (Institute of Medicine and National Research Council, 2009; Kessler et al., 2005), suggesting that the onset of mental illness precedes or overlaps with the parenting years in most cases.

Determining the prevalence of mental illness specifically among parents is more challenging. Depression is the most common mental illness. A report issued by the National Research Council (NRC) and Institute of Medicine (IOM) estimates that in a given year, as many as 15 million children may live in a household with a parent experiencing an episode of major depression (Institute of Medicine and National Research Council, 2009). Depression occurring around the time of childbearing is common, with 13 to 19 percent of women experiencing postpartum depression and many others experiencing depressive symptoms during pregnancy (O'Hara and McCabe, 2013). But many parents who experience mental illness have not been formally diagnosed, and patients with a diagnosis of mental illness often are not identified as being parents. It is particularly challenging to estimate the number of parents with severe mental illness (often defined as schizophrenia, psychosis, and bipolar disorder). The relevant research typically has assessed individuals in community settings (community service agencies, mental health clinics, child welfare agencies, prisons, or hospitals), who likely do not represent the broader population (Nicholson et al., 2006). Analysis of data from the National Co-Morbidity Survey suggests that approximately one-half of mothers (46.8%) and one-third of fathers (29.5%) have had a psychiatric disorder at some point during their lifetime (Nicholson et al., 2002). In another study, among adults identified with severe persistent mental illness, approximately two-thirds of women and three-quarters of men were also parents (Gearing et al., 2012; Nicholson et al., 2002).

Mental health disorders encompass a wide spectrum of illnesses and levels of severity, and symptoms may wax and wane over time; thus their impact on parenting and the supports these parents need can be quite variable. As with prevalence, far more is known about the impact of depression on parenting (Institute of Medicine and National Research Council, 2009) than about the impact of severe mental illness (Bee et al., 2014; Schrank et al., 2015). The 2009 IOM and NRC report describes research showing that parental depression is associated with more negative and withdrawn parenting and with worse physical health and well-being of children. But the same report describes a number of promising two-generational programs focused on prevention and emphasizes the potential for helping parents with treatment and parenting programs.

For individuals with mental illness, being a parent is not only a challenge but also often one of the most rewarding parts of their lives (Dolman et al., 2013; Lacey et al., 2015; Wittkowski et al., 2014). Many of these parents are motivated to cope with their own symptoms by focusing on meeting their children's needs, and they value these relationships (Barrow et al., 2014; Oyserman et al., 2000; Wittkowski et al., 2014). However, mental illness also can interfere with the quality of parenting. A cross-sectional study using video observation of 251 depressed mothers with their toddlers demonstrated that those with more severe depressive symptoms engaged in fewer positive interactions and more negative interactions with their children and also provided less developmental stimulation (Beeber et al., 2014). Children of parents with mental illness also have a higher risk of developing their own mental health issues, developmental delays, and behavioral problems (Beardslee et al., 2011; Craig, 2004; Dean et al., 2012; Friesen et al., 2009; Gearing et al., 2012; McCoy et al., 2014). Children's development of these problems can add to the challenges parents face in childrearing and also can increase the fear and guilt they may feel about the impact of their own illness on their child.

There have been few high-quality large-scale evaluations of interventions designed for parents with mental illness and even fewer of those for parents with severe mental illness. The 2009 IOM and NRC report notes that few studies of parental depression focus on parental outcomes or issues specific to parents (Institute of Medicine and National Research Council, 2009). However, many universal interventions have the potential to prevent or mitigate mental illness before it has serious impacts on parenting, and a number of smaller studies have shown positive or promising results of such interventions. For example, the MOMS Partnership, operated by Yale University, interviewed more than 1,300 low-income urban mothers of young children to create a set of developmental and community-based mental health and workforce supports (Smith, 2014). These supports included cognitive-behavioral therapy delivered by community "mental health ambassadors," along with phone applications to help strengthen mothers' executive functioning skills and capacity for stress management and reduce depression. Early results based on a participant questionnaire reveal an increase in positive parenting and reduction in depression (Smith, 2014).

Interventions for Parents with Depressive Disorders

A number of programs are designed to prevent adverse child outcomes among families with known parental mental illness. For postpartum depression, limited controlled research indicates that simply treating the illness leads to gains in the quality of parenting (O'Hara and McCabe, 2013). An analysis of the Sequence Treatment Alternatives to Relieve Depression (STAR*D) trial found that treatment leading to remission of mothers' depression was associated with improved mental health among their children in a nonexperimental study, although the mechanism of change was not assessed (Institute of Medicine and National Research Council, 2009; Weissman et al., 2006). The evidence for treating maternal depression for mothers of infants, however, is mixed. Several reviews found that while sustained interventions may improve the cognitive development of the child, additional research is needed to determine the success of these treatments over time, particularly with regard to the benefits for the child as well as the mother (Nylen et al., 2006; Pooblan et al., 2007). Forman and colleagues

(2007) found in an experimental study that relieving maternal depression alone affected only parenting stress and did not necessarily improve the mother-infant relationship or child outcomes (Forman et al., 2007).

Nonetheless, most studies have demonstrated that interventions combining mental health treatment and parenting support, or at least including a component focused on parenting, often lead to better outcomes relative to programs that focus solely on the illness. A systematic review of the impact of maternal-infant dyadic interventions on postpartum depression included 19 single group pre-post and randomized controlled studies. The author concluded that strategies focused on the dyad and maternal coaching were most effective at reducing psychiatric symptoms and demonstrated modest improvements in the mother-child relationship and maternal responsiveness (Tsivos et al., 2015). Not all such approaches are successful, however. A 2015 Cochrane review assessing the impact specifically of parent-infant psychotherapy versus control or an alternative intervention found no significant effects of the psychotherapy on maternal depression or the mother-child dyad (Barlow et al., 2015).

With the advent of primary care medical homes and the resultant integration of physical, mental, and behavioral health care, there has been growing interest in incorporating parenting interventions and support into primary care settings. This may be a particularly effective way of diagnosing and addressing parental mental health issues. Parents may be more willing to seek health care for their children than for themselves, but during pediatric visits, health care providers may identify a parent who would benefit from mental health treatment (Nicholson and Clayfield, 2004). Screening adults for depression in primary care settings with the capacity to provide accurate diagnosis, effective treatment, and follow-up is endorsed by the U.S. Preventive Services Task Force (2009). Models of stepped collaborative care entail screening for and identifying depression in primary care settings and providing straightforward care in those locations while referring patients with more severe or resistant illness to mental health specialists (Dennis, 2014).

Additional primary prevention programs for parental depression have focused on the period from conception through age 5, although most address parents with infants rather than those with toddlers (Bee et al., 2014; Craig, 2004). Selective primary prevention of depression among parents has been tested most frequently in the perinatal period, with most programs targeting high-risk groups, such as mothers with preterm infants or those at increased risk for postpartum depression (Ammerman et al., 2013; Beardslee et al., 2010; Dennis, 2014; Silverstein et al., 2011). The perinatal period appears to be an effective time to reach a broad population of parents.

Home visiting programs (discussed in detail in Chapter 4) serve parents with high rates of depression, interpersonal trauma, and PTSD, yet less than one-half of state-based home visiting programs currently have improving parental mental health as an objective (Johnson, 2009). Early studies examining the mental health benefits of home visiting interventions for parents had mixed results, but the results of more recent studies have been positive. In recent studies, for example, home visiting that includes psychotherapy for mothers has been found to improve depression, and as depression improves, so do many measures of parenting (Ammerman et al., 2011, 2013, 2015; Paradis et al., 2013; Tandon et al., 2014). A randomized controlled trial enrolled women in home visiting programs who were identified as being at risk for perinatal depression (Tandon et al., 2014). The intervention consisted of six 2-hour group sessions focused on cognitive-behavioral therapy, with skills being reinforced during regular home visits. At 6-month follow-up, 15 percent of mothers in the intervention group versus 32 percent of the control mothers had experienced an episode of major depression (Tandon et al., 2014). In a randomized trial of the Building Healthy Children Collaborative, there was no difference in rate of referral to child protective services for mothers who received mental health services as part of home visits and women in a comparison group who did not receive such services; in both groups, almost all mothers avoided referral to child protective services (Paradis et al., 2013).

There also have been efforts to help parents with children in center-based care. In a randomized controlled trial of depressed mothers who had infants and toddlers in Early Head Start, investigators tested interpersonal therapy combined with parenting enhancement training versus just treatment for the depression (Beeber et al., 2013). Both groups had a significant improvement in depression scores, but only the group with parent training showed enhanced parent-child interaction skills. Beardslee and colleagues (2010) describe a nonrandomized, multiyear, multicomponent pilot intervention with parents, staff, and administration in an Early Head Start program serving up to 200 children a year. The intervention, Family Connections, was intended to help staff with strategies for addressing mental health problems in the families they served. The program, which was provided to all the families, not just those identified as suffering from depression, utilized widespread education of staff and parents and a parent support group. It resulted in improved parent self-reported parenting knowledge and social support and increased parent engagement with the center.

Other approaches have been tried in public health settings. A randomized study tested two different parenting interventions (Family Talk Intervention and Let's Talk about Children) in families with a parent diagnosed with a mood disorder (Solantaus et al., 2010). Both interventions improved child mental health symptoms and behaviors. Family Talk utilizes manual-based psychoeducation prevention strategies. One study of 93 families with at least one depressed parent and one child ages 8-15 found significant and sustained improvement in parental attitudes toward parenting and reduction in internalizing symptoms (predictive of future depression) in the children whose families were assigned to a lecture or clinician-facilitated intervention, although outcomes in terms of levels of parental depression are not described (Beardslee et al., 2003, 2011).

Interventions for Parents with Severe Mental Illness

While parents with brief or time-limited mental health problems can benefit from brief interventions, those with severe mental illness or more complex mental health disorders are likely to need ongoing support and crisis intervention services. Unfortunately, interventions to support and strengthen parenting for parents with severe mental illness have typically not been rigorously evaluated using the types of well-designed randomized controlled trials used to test other parenting interventions described in this report, and this is an identified area of need (Schrank et al., 2015). Shrank and colleagues (2015) conducted a systematic review of parenting studies involving parents who had severe mental illness (psychosis or bipolar disorder) and at least one child between the ages of 1-18. The review included a heterogeneous range of interventions, and child outcomes were evaluated. Four of six randomized controlled trials included in the review showed significant benefits from the interventions, which included intensive home visits, parenting lectures, clinician counseling, and Online Triple P; the lower-quality studies showed mixed results.

A 3-year observational study of mothers with severe mental illness with children ages 4-16 demonstrated that over time, as serious symptoms remitted, parents became more nurturing, raising the hope that treatment could lead to improved child outcomes (Kahng et al., 2008). A meta-analysis of a variety of parenting interventions found a medium to large effect size in improving short-term parent mental health but noted that these benefits may wane over time, again emphasizing the need for longer and more enduring programs (Bee et al., 2014).

One approach for parents with severe mental illness that appears to be promising is to provide parenting interventions during intensive outpatient treatment or inpatient treatment for mental health crises (Krumm et al., 2013). A few hospitals in the United States (many more in Europe and Australia) have mother-baby mental health units where the baby can stay with the mother while she is hospitalized. A systematic review of inpatient parenting programs for women with schizophrenia evaluated 29 studies of interventions in mother-baby units and found improved maternal outcomes, but the review included no randomized controlled studies, and most such studies have been descriptive, observational, and/or quasi-experimental designs (Gearing et al., 2012; Hinden et al., 2006). A newer observational study in the United Kingdom using a video feedback intervention found that between the time of admission and discharge, mothers with schizophrenia, severe depression, and mania became more sensitive and less unresponsive, and their infants became more cooperative and less passive (Kenny et al., 2013). Notably, mothers at discharge had better outcomes on all parenting measures than both a comparison group of nonhospitalized mothers with mental illness of comparable severity and a group of mothers without mental illness in the community.

Interventions and treatment for parents with mental illness have been found to significantly reduce the risk of children developing the same mental health problems as well as behavior challenges. A meta-analysis included 1,490 children in 13 randomized controlled trials of interventions with cognitive, behavioral, or psychoeducational elements for parents with a variety of mental illnesses and substance use problems (Siegenthaler et al., 2012). The studies included in the review focused on maternal stress reduction, family interventions, home visits, or parenting skills, and reported a 40 percent reduction in the risk of new diagnoses of mental health disorders in the children as well as a significant decrease in the children's internalizing and externalizing symptoms.

Given the enormous complexity of comorbidities and varieties of presentation in mental illness, sorting out which risks to children derive from parental mental illness and which should be attributed to other stressors is challenging. Doing so is critical, however, for identifying the best strategies for helping families and in considering interventions at both the micro and macro levels. For example, many parents living with severe mental illness will need support in learning parenting knowledge, attitudes, and practices, specifically in understanding normal child development and milestones and how to provide emotional support for their children. They, like all parents, may also benefit from training in such skills as getting children to have a consistent bedtime routine, feeding them, administering nonphysical discipline, and providing emotional support (Nicholson and Henry, 2003; Stepp et al., 2012). Mothers living with severe mental illness themselves have identified generic parenting issues for which they may need help—both in accessing essential resources and in developing critical parenting skills (Nicholson and Henry, 2003).

Tailoring of Services to Individual Needs

Mental illnesses include a wide range of conditions. One mother may have severe depression and struggle with lifelong, recurrent episodes, while another may have a single episode of mild postpartum depression. One disorder may cause symptoms that make it difficult to recognize the emotions or affect of others, while another may cause a parent to display odd behaviors or make unusual comments, and still another may lead to social withdrawal (Healy et al., 2015; Stepp et al., 2012). Even a single diagnosis can manifest with different symptoms and severity at different stages of the illness, and the illness itself can lead to complications. Parents with severe or recurrent illness also may face separation from their children due to hospitalization or temporary or permanent loss of custody, which can impact parental self-efficacy as well as attachment (Gearing et al., 2012; Nicholson et al., 2006). Thus it is important for programs to tailor services to the individual needs of parents. Programs that offer service coordination are likely to be effective for parents with mental illness who face other adversities as well, such as poverty, family violence, housing instability, and substance abuse. Providers and policy makers also need to be mindful of the multiple layers of risk these co-occurring conditions pose to families, since childhood outcomes will be affected by far more than the parenting behaviors or knowledge targeted by many programs.

Parents with or Recovering from Substance Abuse Disorders

Like mental health conditions, substance use and abuse can affect parenting attitudes and practices, as well as engagement and retention in parenting programs. It has been estimated that nearly 22 million Americans have a substance use disorder (Center for Behavioral Health Statistics and Quality, 2015). Yet in 2014, only 4.1 million out of 21.6 million people ages 12 and older with illicit drug or alcohol dependence or abuse received treatment (Substance Abuse and Mental Health Services Administration, 2014b). Moreover, both research and clinical practice have seen little integration of child development and parenting with addiction prevention and treatment. Most studies on substance abuse to date have measured mainly retention in treatment and reduction in maternal substance use as the primary outcomes, with less attention to parenting and work with children (Finkelstein, 1994, 1996; Nicholson et al., 2006).

Abuse of alcohol and drugs can impact parenting in multiple ways. Prenatal exposure to substances can significantly affect infants, resulting in behaviors that are extremely challenging to parents (O'Connor and Paley, 2006; Preece and Riley, 2011; Schuetze et al., 2007). Potential neonatal effects include prematurity and low birth weight; greater reactivity to stress; increased arousal; higher irritability and restlessness; disordered sleep and feeding; tremulousness, high-pitched cry, and startled response; difficulties with sensory integration, such as abnormal responses to light, visual stimuli, and sounds; and hyperactivity (Iqbal et al., 2002; U.S. Department of Health and Human Services, 2014a). An infant who cannot regulate sleep, wakefulness, or stress is therefore often partnered with a mother who has reduced capacity to deal with stress and to respond to infant cues (Beeghly and Tronick, 1994; Pajulo et al., 2012).

Research has recently combined the neurobiology of addiction with the neurobiology of parenting, and has examined how the disregulation of the stress-reward neural circuits in addiction may impact the capacity to parent (Rutherford et al., 2013). It is well documented that increases in stress result in increases in cravings and substance use (Sinha, 2001). More specifically, the rewarding value of drugs for a substance-dependent individual comes from ameliorating withdrawal and other stressful situations, and this value may diminish biochemically the rewarding and pleasurable aspects of parenting (Rutherford et al., 2013).

One suggested mechanism by which substance abuse impairs parenting is its impact on the neurocircuitry of the mother's brain, particularly the oxytocin and dopamine systems (Strathearn and Mayes, 2010). Oxytocin motivates social behavior by stimulating a reward response to proximity and social interaction and has been shown to increase significantly in both mother and infant during periods of close contact and breastfeeding (Strathearn et al., 2008). Substance abuse interferes with this process. For example, cocaine specifically coopts this neuropathway by decreasing the production of oxytocin and thereby making maternal care less rewarding for a cocaine user (Elliott et al., 2001). Dopamine operates similarly: it rewards social behavior and regulates the production of stress-response chemicals. Most addictive substances affect dopamine production by providing drug-induced surges of dopamine, decreasing the body's natural production of the chemical, and nullifying the rewarding effects of normal human behavior. The dysregulation of dopamine also impairs a mother's ability to regulate stress, making her more susceptible to the exhaustion and frustration inherent in early parenting (Strathearn and Mayes, 2010). From a neurobiological perspective, therefore, the motivation to engage with and respond to infants may be compromised in the presence of addiction, and this diminished motivation may result in part from infant signals holding less reward value (Rutherford et al., 2013). In addition, the increased stress inherent in the parenting role may increase cravings, drug-seeking behaviors, and relapse to substance use (Rutherford et al., 2013).

The few studies that have been conducted on parenting and substance use/abuse have focused primarily on adults entering treatment, who account for a relatively small share of the broader population of parents with substance abuse disorders (Mayes and Truman, 2002). From this limited sample, studies have described a range of parenting deficits and consequences, sometimes associated with specific drugs (including alcohol), as well as the amount, frequency and duration of use.

Chronic substance abuse affects parents' ability to regulate their own emotions, to provide safe and consistent care for their child, and to be mentally alert for bonding and intellectual development (Suchman et al., 2013). Parents may become preoccupied by drug cravings and drug-seeking behaviors, which in turn may lead to physical absences and multiple disruptions in parenting. Studies have found a strong association between substance abuse and emotional/physical neglect and physical abuse (Suchman et al., 2004, 2008).

Further complicating this picture is that all too frequently, the substance-dependent mother has herself been a victim of violence and abuse. High levels of trauma history and moderate to high levels of PTSD diagnosis co-occur among both men and women with substance abuse disorders (Back et al., 2003; Miller et al., 2000; Najavits et al., 1997; Read et al., 2004). Women whose childhood history includes sexual abuse are significantly more likely than women without such a history to report substance use and abuse, as well as depression, anxiety, and other mental health problems (Camp and Finkelstein, 1997).

Although prenatal substance exposure and early mother-child interactions characterized by intoxication and withdrawal have independent affects, it is the cumulative risk of chemical, psychological, and environmental disturbances related to substance abuse disorders that interferes with parenting and child development (Huxley and Foulger, 2008; Mayes and Truman, 2002). These secondary risk factors are amenable to early intervention, identification, and comprehensive treatment modalities, offering an avenue for improved outcomes for both mother and child (Barnard and McKeganey, 2004). Indeed, childrearing conditions appear to greatly outweigh substance abuse in predicting adolescent outcomes for drug-exposed children (Fisher et al., 2011b).

Parenting status is nonetheless frequently neglected in the development of treatment interventions for parents with substance abuse, and rarely are critical needs for child care or children's services taken into account in developing services and parenting programs for these parents (Finkelstein, 1994, 1996). In addition, most adult and infant/child mental health professionals view families affected by addiction as highly challenging to treat, frequently eliciting feelings of frustration, helplessness, and lack of empathy. The result too often is that individuals suffering from addiction are excluded from community programs, as well as research and evaluation studies (Camp and Finkelstein, 1997; U.S. Department of Health and Human Services, 1999). This exclusion includes home visiting programs, which may screen out parents who use alcohol and drugs. According to the Department of Health and Human Services' recent report on the Maternal, Infant, and Early Childhood Home Visiting (MIECHV) Program (discussed in Chapter 4), only 12 percent of enrolled families had substance use issues, and only 21 percent of grantees selected alcohol, tobacco, or other drug use as issues to monitor in their families (U.S. Department of Health and Human Services, 2014b).

Substance abuse can be successfully treated. However, while there is good reason to believe that decreased substance use should lead to improved parenting, there have been no experimental evaluations of whether successful treatment of substance abuse disorders, in and of itself, leads to better parenting. Described below are interventions for substance abuse that include a specific focus on parenting.

Residential Treatment Programs for Mothers with Their Children

The standard of care for women's residential treatment for substance abuse disorders has shifted over the past 15-20 years from mothers being treated in single-adult programs apart from their children to women and children residing together and mothers receiving integrated addiction treatment and parenting education and services (Bromberg et al., 2010). Research suggests that mothers who reside with their children are more likely to enter, remain in, and complete treatment, as well as remain drug free for longer periods of time, relative to mothers who are separated from their children (Clark, 2001; d'Arlach et al., 2006; Grella et al., 2000; Lundgren et al., 2003; Metsch et al., 2001; Pajulo et al., 2006, 2012).

The literature describes a number of specific residential treatment programs for mothers with their children. The majority of studies report positive parent and child outcomes using pre-post evaluation designs (Allen and Larson, 1998; Conners et al., 2001; Grella et al., 2000; Jackson, 2004; Metsch et al., 2001; Moore and Finkelstein, 2001; Porowski et al., 2004; Szuster et al., 1996; Wobie et al., 1997). The Substance Abuse and Mental Health Services Administration (SAMHSA) conducted a national cross-site study of 24 of its funded residential treatment programs for pregnant and parenting women and their children. Data on 1,847 women showed positive results, including an infant mortality rate 57 percent lower than that in the general population. Seventy-five percent of 97 mothers at one site reported improved relationships with their children and learned better stress coping skills (Clark, 2001).

Family Drug Courts

In response to high rates of nonviolent drug-related arrests in the early 1990s, the United States began utilizing drug courts as an alternative to traditional sentencing procedures. These courts often mandate treatment for substance abuse disorders, frequent drug testing, and periodic court appearances for status hearings (Mitchell et al., 2012). If drug court sentences are completed successfully, the individual will have the charges against him/her dropped or, if postconviction, will receive a sentence of time served.

As of 2014, nearly 3,400 drug courts were operating in the United States (National Institute of Justice, 2016).

An expansion of the adult drug court model, family treatment drug courts (FTDCs) were created as an alternative pathway to reunification in child protective cases. Parental substance abuse is one of five recognized risk factors for involvement in the child welfare system; once child protective services are involved, children of parents with substance abuse disorders tend to stay in the system longer and spend more time out of their home of origin (Child Welfare Information Gateway, 2014). The aim of FTDCs is to combat these trends by giving parents with these disorders access to treatment, accountability, support, and a system of structured rewards and sanctions aimed at their ultimately regaining full custody of their children.

One large-scale outcome study compared 301 families served through three FTDCs with a matched control group of more than 1,200 families with substance abuse issues who received traditional child welfare services. This study found that the FTDC mothers were more likely to enter treatment, entered treatment more quickly, and were twice as likely to complete at least one treatment relative to the control group. Also, children of mothers who participated in FTDCs were more likely than children in the control group to be reunited with their mothers (Worcel et al., 2008). Another, smaller, quasi-experimental study showed that parents participating in FTDCs were significantly more likely than those not participating to enter treatment, entered treatment more quickly, received more treatment, and were more likely to complete treatment successfully. The FTDC-group children spent less time placed out of home, their involvement with child welfare services ended sooner, and they were more likely to return to parental care upon discharge (Bruns et al., 2012). Other nonexperimental research has found FTDCs to be one of the most effective ways to increase initiation and completion of treatment for substance abuse disorders among those involved in the child welfare system (Marlowe and Carey, 2012). Reviews of FTDCs have found some evidence of positive findings related to reunification, completion of treatment episodes, fewer parental criminal arrests, and significant cost savings for the child welfare system (Brook et al., 2015; Marlowe and Carey, 2012). However, the lack of rigorous, randomized, intent-to-treat studies leaves unaddressed the possibility that those women who elect to participate in FTDCs are different from those who do not.

Parenting Skills Training for Parents with or Recovering from Substance Abuse Disorders

While research has demonstrated that family and parenting skills can be improved when specific parenting programs are integrated into treatment for substance abuse (Camp and Finkelstein, 1997; Kerwin, 2005; Suchman et al., 2008, 2010), few targeted parenting interventions have been developed for parents who have or are recovering from such disorders. A study published in 2013 sampled 125 addiction programs in the United States with respect to the extent and nature of parenting skills interventions offered. Only 43 percent of addiction programs surveyed reported offering formal classes on parenting. Of programs that did offer such classes, only 19 percent stated that they had a standardized curriculum. In general, programs did not rate parenting as a high priority relative to other issues addressed in treatment (Arria et al., 2013). Few programs have reached the threshold of a high evidence rating by NREPP and CEBC.

Strengthening Families and the Nurturing Parenting Programs (NPP) are two of the few highly rated group-based parenting programs. Strengthening Families and the NPP for Families in Substance Abuse Treatment and Recovery specifically target substance abuse and parenting. Both of these curriculums are widely used in substance abuse treatment programs nationally, often within residential, day treatment, or FTDC settings. Both emphasize reducing parents' alcohol and drug use while helping them learn new patterns of nurturing their children to replace existing, possibly abusive patterns. Strengthening Families also has a youth prevention focus, with the goal of reducing risk factors and building resilience against children's future alcohol and drug use. Strengthening Families and NPP have average NREPP ratings of 3.1 and 3.0, respectively, and the NPP received a CEBC rating of 3 for the version of the program for parents of 5- to 12-year-olds (however, the specific adaptation for substance abuse was not rated independently) (California Evidence-Based Clearinghouse, 2016j; National Registry of Evidence-based Programs and Practices, 2016b, 2016d).

Strengthening Families is one of the first structured group parenting programs developed within an addiction framework (reviewed by NREPP in 2007) (National Registry of Evidence-based Programs and Practices, 2016d). Developed by a university-based research team, the program has been able to gather higher-quality data relative to most other parenting programs that address parental substance abuse. A family-skills training program targeting parents of children ages 3-16, Strengthening Families consists of three courses—parenting skills for parents; life skills for children; and family life skills for the entire family, consisting of structured family activities. All three courses have a strong emphasis on communication skills, effective discipline, reinforcing positive behaviors, and planning family activities together. The goal is to reduce risk factors for behavioral and emotional problems such as substance use. Findings from evaluations of this intervention include improvements in children's behavior, mental health, and social skills and in parental involvement, parenting supervision, and parenting efficacy. Improvements also have been found in family cohesion and communication, including a decrease in family conflict, as well as reduced alcohol and drug use (Kumpfer et al., 2007).

The NPP was developed specifically for families involved with child welfare services. The emphasis is on participants learning how to nurture themselves while developing nurturing families and parenting skills. The five core domains of the intervention are age-appropriate expectations; empathy, bonding, and attachment; nonviolent nurturing discipline; self-awareness and self-worth; and empowerment, autonomy, and healthy independence. Multiple adaptations, focused on the same core domains, include the NPP for Families in Substance Abuse Treatment and Recovery, which integrates recovery from substance abuse disorders with improved parenting and nurturing relationships with children. Correlational evidence relevant to parenting practices indicates improvements in such parenting outcomes as parental empathy, reduced child abuse and neglect recidivism, decreased family conflict, and decreased support for corporal punishment (Bavolek et al., 1983, 1988; Camp and Finkelstein, 1997; Hodnett et al., 2009).

Other well-supported programs—adult-focused family behavioral therapy and behavioral couples therapy for alcoholism and drug abuse—utilize individual therapy for addressing co-occurring problems so as to improve family relationships and parenting skills. Both of these interventions are conducted primarily in outpatient mental health settings. Adult-focused family behavioral therapy, with a CEBC rating of 2 ("supported by research evidence"), focuses on adults with drug abuse, as well as other co-occurring problems such as depression, trauma, and child maltreatment (California Evidence-Based Clearinghouse, 2016b). This intervention, based in outpatient behavioral health systems, requires delivery by licensed mental health professionals. It includes a focus on improving family relationships; communication skills; and child management skills, including effective discipline. Outcomes in randomized and longitudinal studies that utilized control groups include improvements in family relationships and parental employment as well as reductions in parental substance use and depression (Azrin et al., 1994, 1996; Donohue et al., 2014). Behavioral couples therapy for alcoholism and drug abuse, rated highly by NREPP, is an intervention for couples focused on reducing alcohol and drug use and intimate partner violence and increasing treatment compliance. Although not used solely with parents, its outcomes, in addition to reduction in intimate partner violence, have been found to include improvement in children's psychosocial functioning and decline in children's clinical impairment in randomized controlled research (Kelley and Fals-Stewart, 2002).

Schaeffer and colleagues (2013) describe a pilot study of Multisystemic Therapy-Building Stronger Families (MST-BSF), an integrated treatment model designed to address parental substance abuse and child maltreatment among families in the child welfare system. A quasi-experimental study of 43 mother-youth dyads (25 MST-BSF participants and 18 comparison dyads) found fewer substantiated maltreatment reports and reduced time out of the home in the MST-BSF group (Schaeffer et al., 2013). This home-based intervention is currently being studied in a large, randomized clinical trial funded by the National Institute on Drug Abuse.

A recent review of 21 outcome studies on parenting programs used in substance abuse disorder treatment included 17 different parenting interventions. Studies consisted of 9 randomized controlled trials, 3 quasi-experimental studies, and 9 studies with no comparison group. Results indicate that combining substance abuse treatment with a parenting intervention may be more effective than substance abuse treatment alone for reducing parental substance use and improving parenting. Parents appeared to benefit the most when, prior to learning specific parenting techniques, they learned general psychological coping strategies, such as developing emotional regulation. In addition, many of the parenting programs showed common obstacles to attendance, including lack of transportation, hunger, unsupervised children, and stigma (Neger and Prinz, 2015).

Helping Parents Nurture Child Security

Given the complexity of addiction and the way it impacts parenting and the parent-child relationship, a number of newer, promising interventions grounded in attachment theory and focused on the parent-child relationship have been developed and described in the literature (Pajulo and Kalland, 2013; Pajulo et al., 2006; Suchman et al., 2008). These newer interventions focus mainly on assisting parents in being more emotionally attuned to their children and in developing their own capacity for emotional regulation. They include individual and dyadic interventions, such as child-parent psychotherapy, parental reflective functioning (Fonagy et al., 2012), and mentalization-based therapy—that is, keeping the child in mind (Suchman et al., 2013). They also include parenting program adaptations for adults with substance abuse disorders that have been the subject of several small pilot studies.

Berlin and colleagues (2014) in a randomized study piloted Attachment and Behavioral Catch Up, a residential treatment program for new mothers focused on coaching parents in nurturing that follows the child's lead and reducing frightening caregiving behaviors. Mothers who received 10 sessions of this attachment-based parenting program revealed more supportive parenting behaviors relative to controls. However, the pilot was very small, with only 11 mothers in the intervention group and 10 in the control group (Berlin et al., 2014). In a randomized pilot study testing the efficacy of the Mothers and Toddlers Program (MTP), a 12-week attachment-based parenting intervention for mothers enrolled in methadone treatment, mothers participating in MTP demonstrated better caregiving behaviors compared with mothers enrolled in a traditional parenting education program (Suchman et al., 2010). This individual psychotherapy intervention emphasized reflective functioning and mentalization and targeted mothers of children ages 0-3. MTP, now known as Mothering from the Inside Out, is currently undergoing a 5-year randomized clinical trial targeting children 12-60 months of age (Suchman et al., 2013).

Preventing Substance Use during Pregnancy

Another promising intervention, known as the Parent-Child Assistance Program (PCAP), follows pregnant and parenting mothers with alcohol and/or drug abuse to prevent substance-exposed births. The program provides office- and home-based substance abuse treatment and case management services over several years that include attention to parenting, family planning, education and employment, and reunification with children. Evaluations of PCAP in experimental and single group pre-post studies show increased substance use disorder treatment completion rates and reductions in substance-exposed births and disrupted parenting (Grant and Ernst, 2014; Grant et al., 2005; Ryan et al., 2008). In one experimental study, 12 percent of mothers participating in PCAP had a subsequent alcohol- or drug-exposed infant within 3 years, compared with 21 percent of similar mothers in typical substance abuse disorder treatment that did not include case management (Ryan et al., 2008). Data from Washington State for the period 2007-2014 show that after 3 years in PCAP, 90 percent (of 924) of mothers had completed substance abuse treatment, and 83 percent of children whose mothers were in the program were living with their own families (Grant and Ernst, 2014).

Recently, several federal agencies have evaluated programs and systems of care that coordinate substance abuse disorder treatment with children's physical and mental health services (including trauma-specific services), as well as child welfare. In the Children Affected by Methamphetamine (CAM) Grant Program, SAMHSA funded 12 grantees to develop integrated and coordinated approaches to care for parents with substance abuse disorders and child welfare involvement, as well as to expand and enhance services for children ages 0-17 in families participating in an FTDC. Specialized client outreach and engagement strategies, as well as strengthened care coordination, were part of the program design. Data from 1,850 families served through the end of program year 3 show that parents stayed in substance abuse treatment an average of 6 months, and 42 percent completed treatment. The percentage of adults with reduced substance use at treatment discharge ranged from approximately 33 to 63 percent, depending on the substance. Families showed statistically significant improvements in overall child well-being and family functioning, including safety and parental capabilities (Substance Abuse and Mental Health Services Administration, 2014a). This was not a randomized controlled demonstration.

A second program designed to enhance collaborative projects between child welfare and substance abuse treatment services—the Regional Partnership Grant Program—has been funded by the U.S. Children's Bureau. Fifty-three grantees representing state, county, and tribal partnerships were funded initially, during 2007-2012, and a 2-year extension was awarded to eight of these grantees. A second 5-year cohort of 17 grantees is funded for 2012-2017, with a more specific focus on both trauma and child well-being, as well as participation in a national cross-state evaluation. All grantees were required to provide activities addressing child maltreatment; safety; parenting capacity; family well-being; and substance abuse treatment, including reduced substance use, care coordination, and cross-system collaboration. Grantees were not required to implement a specific intervention or program model. Interim findings from a subset of 10 grantees based on the North Carolina Family Assessment Scale showed that the percentage of overall parental capability with a rating of mild to clear strength increased from 16.6 to 49.7 percent. Parents in the grant program showed significant improvements in four of seven parental capability areas, including development/enrichment opportunities and supervision of children (U.S. Department of Health and Human Services, 2014a).

Parents Affected by Intimate Partner Violence

A major issue to be addressed in designing any approach for strengthening and supporting parenting is the impact of high levels of intimate partner violence on the quality of parenting and on outcomes for children. Intimate partner violence often affects parenting capacity and can have a direct effect on children who witness its occurrence. While most attention has focused on the impact of physical intimate partner violence, children exposed to a parent's threatening or otherwise verbally abusing a partner also are at elevated risk for a variety of mental health and other developmental problems, especially when such behavior is frequent, intense, and poorly resolved (Geffner et al., 2014; Repetti et al., 2002). For example, a child who regularly watches or hears one parent[4] threaten or scream at the other may feel fear, anxiety, and anger similar to what is experienced by a child who regularly sees one parent slap or shove the other. Infants, toddlers, and preschoolers in particular cannot distinguish between the severity of aggressive verbal threats and that of mild physical violence.

---

[4]The term "parent" here refers to biological parents as well as to any other intimate partners who are regularly a part of the household.

While a number of national studies have found that as many as one-third of women and one-fourth of men are exposed to intimate partner violence at some point, the evidence regarding the number of exposed children is limited, and there are no data on the number of children exposed to all forms of high family conflict (Black et al., 2011; Finkelhor et al., 2009). According to the 2008 National Survey on Children's Exposure to Violence, 6.1 percent of all children in the United States had witnessed an interparental assault in the past year, and 17.3 percent had witnessed an interparental physical assault at some point in their lifetime (Finkelhor et al., 2015).[5]

Like parents with mental illness or substance abuse, parents experiencing intimate partner violence often feel ashamed and guilty about what has happened to their children. These feelings, plus fear of being reported to child welfare, discourage many victims from reporting the violence and may affect parents' willingness and capacity to engage in parenting programs, as well as other support services (Lieberman et al., 2005).

Impact

Various studies have found that, across a number of measures, 4-20 percent of individual differences in children's functioning can be attributed to exposure to intimate partner violence (Davies and Cummings, 2006). Numerous studies have found that children living in households with intimate partner violence evidence a variety of emotional and developmental problems (Edleson, 1999; Holt et al., 2008; Wolfe et al., 2003). Witnessing intimate partner violence is a traumatic event for children and can directly impact their mental health and behaviors by undermining their sense of safety, security, and support (Lieberman et al., 2011). School-age children and adolescents exposed to intimate partner violence perform more poorly than their peers in school (Kitzmann et al., 2003; Koenen et al., 2003) and are more likely to display externalizing behaviors, conduct and oppositional defiant disorder, and aggressive interactions with peers (Cummings and Davies, 2011; Voisin and Hong, 2012). Exposure to intimate partner violence also is associated with depression and anxiety, poorer physical health, and increased risk of involvement in teen pregnancy (Anda et al., 2001), as well as juvenile delinquency (Herrera and McCloskey, 2001). Additionally, longitudinal studies have found an association between childhood exposure to intimate partner violence and adult alcohol abuse, particularly in

---

[5]This study was based on interviews with parents and children, with assault broadly defined. It included pushing and shoving, as well as more serious forms of violence. The lifetime exposure percentage was almost three times as high as the past year exposure percentage, suggesting that many of the children who had witnessed domestic violence in the past had not recently been exposed to this particular form of violence (Finkelhor et al., 2015).

women (Repetti et al., 2002). Moreover, one analysis of school and court record data of 3rd through 5th graders and their families found that being in a class with children exposed to domestic violence was associated with significantly decreased reading and math scores and significantly increased misbehavior among other children in the classroom (Carrell and Hoekstra, 2010).

Mechanisms

Many researchers have sought to identify the mechanisms through which exposure to intimate partner violence affects children's development. Summarizing this research, Davies and Cummings (2006, p. 88) conclude that "interspousal conflict increases child vulnerability to maladaptive trajectories through multiple mechanisms and pathways."

Physical or verbal violence in the home can impair parental functioning, the parent-child relationship, and the co-parenting relationship and can impact children directly. For example, parents in a violent home often suffer from trauma and physical and mental problems. As a result, they may be unable to provide consistent nurturing and support or appropriate discipline for their children, which may in turn have an effect on children's externalizing or internalizing behaviors, thereby making parenting more difficult. Parents experiencing intimate partner violence often engage in overly harsh or overly permissive parenting or have difficulty responding to children in a consistent and positive manner (Conger et al., 2011; Cowan et al., 2014; Cummings and Davies, 2011). In some situations involving intimate partner violence, children are subjected to physical punishment that constitutes legal child abuse.

Not all exposed children will experience adverse outcomes. There is evidence that parenting practices can either buffer or exacerbate the effects of intimate partner violence on children's behavior. For example, longitudinal research has found that high maternal control and appropriate authority mitigate the effects of a partner's violence on children's externalizing behaviors (Tajima et al., 2011). But while a body of research has tested various theories, "the nature of the interplay between marital conflict and parenting practices is not well understood" (Davies and Cummings, 2006, p. 103).

The majority of families reporting intimate partner violence face a host of other challenges in their daily lives. Common co-occurring risk factors include drug and alcohol abuse, low parental educational attainment, and maternal depression (Riggs et al., 2000; Stover et al., 2009). The highly violent neighborhoods in which many families live may increase the likelihood of intimate partner violence (Benson et al., 2003). The complexity of understanding the mechanisms by which intimate partner violence affects both adults and children and the associated variations in family and child dynamics poses challenges for designing interventions that can improve parenting in these families.

Interventions Designed to Address Intimate Partner Violence and Parenting

While the harmful impact of intimate partner violence on children and adults is widely recognized, no system is in place for identifying these families and providing assistance to all family members, including children. The nature of the response and services provided generally depends on how the violence comes to light, the attitudes of the parent suffering the violence, and the nature of the available local services. Most interventions focus primarily on mothers. Programs often focus solely on the intimate partner violence, without addressing parenting strategies in general or parenting behaviors that might buffer children from the risks stemming from the violence.

Intimate partner violence raises a special issue with respect to interventions designed to strengthen and support parenting in these families, in that such interventions must consider the repetitive nature of the violence in many families, which may pose an ongoing threat to the safety of one of the adults. Many researchers and clinicians believe the use of violence often is part of perpetrators' need to exercise complete control over their partner (and often the children in the home), which is harmful to both the nonviolent partner and the children (Bancroft et al., 2011). As discussed below, this raises both policy and programmatic issues related to determining whether interventions should target just one or both partners.

Programs in connection with a parental report of violence Intimate partner violence comes to official attention most commonly when a victim, usually female, calls the police (although most female victims do not report their victimization to the police [Catalano et al., 2009]), requests protection from a court, seeks shelter, or is treated for injuries in an emergency room, or the issue of violence is raised in the context of divorce and child custody proceedings. While historically, few of these families received parenting services, recent years have seen the provision of such services, most commonly to the mother and children, and in a small number of cases to the perpetrating father. (Although more women are now being arrested for intimate partner violence, there is little information on what happens in these situations.)

Parenting services may become available when the custodial mother enters a domestic violence shelter (which occurs for only a small portion of families), and such services are offered during the stay or when the parent leaves the shelter. Some shelters now offer structured parenting programs, although there is very little evidence on the nature or effectiveness of these programs (Sullivan, 2012). Moreover, many women bring their young children with them to shelters, and over time, shelter-based programs have been developed to meet some of the children's basic needs (e.g., periodic visits from a public health nurse). Many shelters also offer counseling for children.

Increasing numbers of community programs outside of the shelter system work with mothers, couples, and children experiencing intimate partner violence. Mothers may enter these programs following a stay in shelter care; through a referral from police, a court, or a domestic violence support agency; or on their own initiative (few programs serve fathers who have been subject to intimate partner violence). Prosecutors in a number of cities have established specialized domestic violence units, and there are now more than 100 specialized domestic violence courts (Labriola et al., 2010).

These programs use a variety of approaches. Four programs focused on parenting are considered evidence-based as the result of randomized controlled trials: child-parent psychotherapy, parent-child interaction therapy (PCIT, discussed earlier), Kids' Club and Moms' Empowerment, and Project Support (Chamberlain, 2014). These programs have been found effective in reducing children's behavioral problems, reducing mental health issues for mothers and children, and reducing mothers' stress and improving their parenting (Chamberlain, 2014; Lieberman et al., 2005; Van Horn and Reyes, 2014).

Three interventions focused on helping children exposed to intimate partner violence also have proven effective. Trauma-focused cognitive-behavioral therapy works directly with children to reduce posttraumatic stress. Cognitive-Behavioral Intervention for Trauma in Schools, developed for children who have experienced trauma, including witnessing domestic violence, is delivered by school-based mental health clinicians—primarily to children, but there are sessions for parents. Finally, Child and Family Traumatic Stress Intervention provides brief psychoeducation and early intervention to address posttraumatic stress reactions and prevent the onset of PTSD among children and adolescents ages 7-18 who experience trauma, including intimate partner violence. Each of these programs has been shown to reduce symptoms resulting from trauma in children (Chamberlain, 2014), but not through changes in parenting.

Men also may receive counseling services for intimate partner violence, often through the criminal justice system. These programs focus largely or exclusively on trying to prevent further violence rather than on improving the couple or parent-child relationship. A few programs, such as Caring Dads, are available to batterers who have not been arrested or convicted of intimate partner violence, and these programs may also focus on family issues. A small number of studies have evaluated programs for men who commit intimate partner violence, with recidivism being the measured outcome. Meta-analyses of experimental and quasi-experimental studies of these programs have found small to no effects on recidivism, and dropout rates are very high (Babcock et al., 2004; Feder and Wilson, 2005; Stith et al., 2012). Some evidence suggests that men are more likely to change their violent behavior when they understand the impact of the violence on their children.

Debates are ongoing in the field about the best approach to strengthening and supporting parenting following reports of intimate partner violence. Reports to the police or a court may lead to the arrest of the perpetrator and his or her removal from the home; many jurisdictions have mandatory or preferred arrest policies if a victim calls the police (Goodmark, 2012).

In recent years, many in the field have questioned the heavy reliance on arrest and prosecution in these cases (Goodmark, 2012), arguing that these actions often fail to promote the well-being of the parent experiencing violence or that of the children, although some people with extensive experience strongly advocate for separating all perpetrators of violence from the family and against working jointly with the parents (Bancroft et al., 2011). Clearly, it often is inappropriate to treat couples together, at least initially, since doing so may pose a threat to a parent or child (Babcock et al., 2004). There is some evidence from experimental and quasi-experimental research, however, that working with couples can be beneficial to the parents and children (Babcock et al., 2004). It may be that interventions at the couple level best follow after some initial individual work and assessment of the potential danger to the victim of working with the couple.

In some states, a report of intimate partner violence can lead to involvement by child welfare services. There is high overlap between intimate partner violence and physical abuse of children, which often justifies that involvement. In many jurisdictions, the fact that a child has witnessed intimate partner violence is a basis for investigation by child welfare services. The appropriateness and impact of these interventions are discussed in the section below on child welfare services.

Court-affiliated parenting education for divorcing parents As noted, family conflict, including intimate partner violence, may come to light through divorce and child custody proceedings. In most jurisdictions, public policy or case law favors continued involvement of both divorcing parents in custody of the child through various living or visitation arrangements. Yet substantial clinical evidence shows that high conflict following divorce has extremely negative impacts on children (Amato and Keith, 1991).

A small number of states have mandated that all divorcing parents participate in court-affiliated parenting education programs, with the goals of preventing future parental conflict and minimizing negative effects of the divorce on children (Sandler et al., 2015). A number of small studies have evaluated such programs using a no-treatment control group design. Over-all, these studies have found a moderate positive effect in reducing conflict and improving parenting after divorce (Pruett and Barker, 2010; Sandler et al., 2015). However, most of these programs "were conducted under controlled, experimental conditions. Several studies suggest that parenting programs are less effective when implemented as community-based services delivered at scale. . . ." (Sandler et al., 2015, p. 169).

These studies, moreover, have not examined mandatory counseling in situations involving intimate partner violence. Some experts oppose re-quired counseling, especially joint counseling, in these cases. Joint counsel-ing, and especially any form of joint custody, can entail continued efforts at coercive control by the violent parent, with traumatic effects on the other parent and the children. Some evidence shows that courts may ignore these potential harms and may even penalize the parent who has suffered the violence if she or he resists contact with the other parent (Meier, 2015). No studies on the impact of court decisions or procedures in custody disputes involving intimate partner violence have been conducted.

Parents seeking help in dealing with children's problem behaviors associ-ated with intimate partner violence As discussed earlier in this chapter, many programs, such as PCIT, Incredible Years, and Triple P, are available for parents seeking help when their child is exhibiting problem behaviors. Children's problem behaviors often are associated with living in a family experiencing intimate partner violence (Bancroft et al., 2011; Chamberlain, 2014; Tajima et al., 2011). Child-parent psychotherapy has been used with preschoolers exposed to domestic violence and showing symptoms of PTSD and behavioral problems. In randomized controlled studies, child-parent psychotherapy has led to significant declines in these problems compared with a control group, as well as improvements in maternal behaviors (Ippen et al., 2011; Lieberman et al., 2005, 2006). PCIT, which works with families in which intimate partner violence no longer exists, has been found in a non-randomized controlled study to be effective in helping children and reducing parental conflict as long as the violence has ceased (Timmer et al., 2010).

Couples seeking relationship counseling Many couples experiencing high levels of conflict seek family therapy. This conflict may include intimate partner violence that has not been reported to the police or led to separa-tion (Jose and O'Leary, 2009). Many family therapists now regularly screen for intimate partner violence and try to assess whether joint therapy is safe, although practices in this regard are highly uneven (Stith et al., 2012).

Several specific approaches for addressing violence in couples therapy have been evaluated with respect to whether the treatment reduces inti-mate partner violence. None of these studies has examined the impact of the treatment on parenting behaviors or on the well-being of children in the family. Behavioral couples treatment is a dyadic intervention used to treat adults with substance abuse disorders. Studies of this intervention, including several large, federally funded randomized controlled clinical trials, have found significant reductions in both alcohol use and violent behaviors among both males and females (Fals-Stewart et al., 2005, 2009). Domestic violence-focused couples treatment is aimed at eliminating all forms of violence (psychological, physical, sexual, and stalking); promoting self-responsibility; and, if the couple chooses to remain together, enhancing their relationship (Stith and McCollum, 2009; Stith et al., 2012). Finally, the Couples Abuse Prevention Program is a cognitive-behavioral treatment intended to address the risk factors for intimate partner violence in couples with a history of minor to moderate physical and/or psychological aggression when there is no threat of imminent harm (LaTaillade et al., 2006). The small number of studies that have assessed these approaches have found that they decreased future violence and risk factors for violence (LaTaillade et al., 2006; Moore, 2012). None of these studies looked at the process for such change, for whom the interventions are successful, or how they work with different cultural groups. Based on the preliminary results from these small-scale studies, the federal government funded two randomized trials of systemic interventions to prevent intimate partner violence: Couples Together Against Violence (CTAV) and Couple Care for Parents (CCP). One study showed improvements in relationship satisfaction for both men and women in CCP relative to participants in a mother-focused program, but found little effect on parenting outcomes (Petch et al., 2012).

Although therapy for couples experiencing intimate partner violence is relatively new, there is a long history of therapy for couples experiencing high levels of conflict without intimate partner violence (Gottman et al., 2010). While little of this therapy has undergone evaluation, experimental studies have found that therapies based on cognitive-behavioral principles can reduce verbal aggression and coercion and help couples develop more positive ways of interacting with each other (Shadish and Baldwin, 2005).

Parent Voices

[Some parents recognize that co-parenting is difficult in practice.]

"I want to talk to a therapist and I want [us] to sit down so we can both open up . . . we're not together but I think we still need to co-parent a little bit to see what is really going on."

—Mother from Washington, DC

Home visiting Few home visiting programs have focused on reducing intimate partner violence as an outcome, although studies have found that up to 48 percent of the women receiving such services have reported incidents of domestic violence since the birth of the study child (Eckenrode et al., 2000). One randomized follow-up study found that the positive effects of home visitation were reduced when a mother was experiencing intimate partner violence, and for those experiencing high rates of intimate partner violence, the beneficial effects of home visiting in terms of preventing child abuse disappeared completely (Eckenrode et al., 2000).

A number of clinicians and advocates have proposed that all home visiting programs be redesigned to address intimate partner violence and that home visitors be trained accordingly (Futures Without Violence, 2010). Home visitors well trained in the dynamics of intimate partner violence might be able to identify situations involving intimate partner violence, link mothers to appropriate community resources, and help the mother improve her safety and the safety and stability of her children. In recent years, a small number of home visiting programs have been developing, implementing, and testing interventions designed specifically to address intimate partner violence as part of the home visitor's activities (Chamberlain, 2014; Futures Without Violence, 2010; Sharps et al., 2013). Few of these interventions have as yet been evaluated. Results from an evaluation of the Enhanced Yakima County Nurse-Family Partnership at Children's Village in Yakima, Washington, indicate decreased family conflict/family management problems, improved parent-child interaction, and reduced child maltreatment (Yakima Valley Farm Workers Clinic, 2013).

Many home visitors, however, are not well trained in recognizing intimate partner violence. They may have a suspicion that it is occurring based on the child's or caregiver's behavior. But confirming this suspicion presents significant challenges. The visitor may encounter hostility from one or both caregivers if the issue is raised. Furthermore, many professionals who work with young children have not been trained to communicate effectively with women victimized by domestic violence and thus may be uncomfortable having such conversations. There is concern that without training, a home visitor may make an inappropriate report of child abuse or neglect that results in the needless separation of a nonoffending mother and her child.

Parents with Developmental Disabilities

Although exact numbers are not available, many of the estimated 15 percent of children and adolescents with developmental disabilities (Boyle et al., 2011) go on to become parents. Whether and the extent to which such disabilities may impair parenting has been a subject of debate over many years (Reinders, 2008).

Several studies have examined the predictors of success or difficulty in parenting for individuals with intellectual disabilities. To differentiate "high-risk" and "low-risk" parents with such disabilities, McGaw and colleagues (2010) conducted a secondary analysis of data on a sample of mothers and children from the United Kingdom. They found that risk was not predicted by intellectual ability; rather, the major predictors were mothers' reports of their own trauma in childhood, the presence and characteristics of their partner, other special needs the parent might have, and special needs of the children.

For many parents, individualized programs based on assessment of needs, level of stress in everyday life, and parenting skills appear beneficial (Aunos et al., 2008). Systematic reviews of experimental and quasi-experimental efficacy studies (Feldman, 1994; Wade et al., 2008) indicate that home-based, didactic programs can result in improved childrearing skills for parents with developmental disabilities, although the effects on family functioning and other family measures remain unexamined. A Cochrane review by Coren and colleagues (2011) found three randomized controlled studies of such programs that met their criteria for inclusion. First, in a Canadian sample of mothers with intellectual disabilities and their children, Feldman and colleagues (1992) implemented a home-based individualized intervention to teach the mothers infant and child care skills, and found significantly more competent parenting in child care routines during the day at postintervention and follow-up. Working with mothers with such disabilities in the United States, Keltner and colleagues (1995) developed and implemented the Support to Access to Rural Services intervention, which focused on building sensitivity to children's cues; increases in maternal-child interaction, including providing children with verbal feedback, were seen at 12 months postintervention. A third program for parents with intellectual disabilities, conducted in Australia, delivered a home-based intervention focusing on child health and home safety, finding significantly more positive health outcomes for children in the experimental group (Llewellyn et al., 2003). Finally, although falling below the scientific threshold for inclusion in a Cochrane review because it employed only a single-group, pretest-posttest design, an adaptation of Triple P was provided to a group of Belgian parents with intellectual disabilities. All parents completed the program and reported significant reductions in psychological stress, maladaptive parenting, and child conduct problems (Glazemakers and Deboutte, 2013).

Adolescent Parents

While adolescent childbearing (births to a mother between the ages of 15-19) in the United States has fallen to an historic low in recent years,[6] 6 percent of live births were to females under age 20 in 2014 (Hamilton et al., 2015). Most adolescents who give birth are 18 or older; in 2014, about 73 percent of adolescent females who gave birth were ages 18-19, while 23 percent were 16-17 and 4 percent were 15 or under (Hamilton et al., 2015). It is estimated that 77 percent of births to 15- to 19-year-olds during 2006-2010 were unintended (Mosher et al., 2012).

Pregnant adolescents and adolescent parents may need special attention and support with respect to parenting for a number of reasons. Relative to older females, pregnant adolescents are less likely to receive adequate prenatal care and are more likely to smoke and have inadequate nutrition during pregnancy, posing risks to the development of the fetus. Adolescent parenthood also is associated with worse mental health outcomes among mothers, which may affect the parent-child relationship (Anderson and McGuinness, 2008; Boden et al., 2008; Hodgkinson et al., 2010, 2014; Siegel and Brandon, 2014). In particular, having a child during adolescence is associated with poorer mental health in mothers, including depression, suicidal ideation, anxiety disorders, and PTSD, both prenatally and postpartum (Anderson and McGuinness, 2008; Boden et al., 2008; Hodgkinson et al., 2010, 2014; Siegel and Brandon, 2014). While adolescent parenthood does not necessarily end the mother's education or pursuit of career or other goals (Assini-Meytin and Green, 2015; Gruber, 2012), adolescent mothers compared with their nonparent peers are much more likely to drop out of high school, although many go on to complete their general education diploma (GED) (Jutte et al., 2010; Perper et al., 2010). Adolescent mothers and fathers also are more likely than those who have children at a later age to face poverty and unemployment and to depend on welfare (Asheer et al., 2014).

Many adolescent mothers (12-49%, according to one study [Meade and Ickovics, 2005]) become pregnant for a second time within 1 year of a first delivery. In 2014, 17 percent of births to 15- to 19-year-olds were to females who already had one or more children (Hamilton et al., 2015). These rapid repeat pregnancies have been linked to even poorer health, education, and economic outcomes for adolescent mothers and their children (Chen et al., 2007; Hoffman and Maynard, 2008; Manlove et al., 2000; Stevens-Simon et al., 2001). Accordingly, avoiding repeat births among adolescents is a goal of federal initiatives such as the Office of Adolescent

---

[6]The birth rate for teenagers fell 9 percent between 2013 and 2014 among females ages 15-19. The rate has declined 42 percent since 2007 (the most recent peak) and 61 percent since 1991 (Martin et al., 2015).

Health's Pregnancy Assistance Fund grants to states and tribes (Office of Adolescent Health, 2015).

The children of adolescent parents relative to those of older parents are more likely to be born preterm and at a low birth weight and have a greater risk of developmental challenges (Chen et al., 2007; Pinzon et al., 2012). In longitudinal research, children born to adolescent mothers on average fare worse in cognitive, academic, and behavioral domains during childhood and adolescence relative to those born to older parents. They also have worse employment outcomes and are at higher risk for mental illness and substance abuse in adulthood (Dahinten et al., 2007; Morinis et al., 2013; Pogarsky et al., 2006). The children of adolescent parents themselves are more likely than their peers with older parents to become parents during adolescence (Meade et al., 2008; Pogarsky et al., 2006; Wu et al., 2012).

For many underserved adolescents, pregnancy and parenthood represent an opportunity to enter a comprehensive system of supportive care that can address multiple needs for themselves and their children. Some researchers argue that the experience of parenthood orients many adolescent parents toward self-improvement and enhances their sense of responsibility, making this an important time for intervention (Gruber, 2012; Hotz et al., 2005; Shanok and Miller, 2007).

The core parenting knowledge, attitudes, and practices for adolescent parents are not different from those for other parents. As described above, however, adolescent parents are at increased risk for adversities that affect their parenting capacity. Strategies discussed below that are used in evidence-based and evidence-informed interventions have targeted some of these risks, focusing on preventing rapid repeat births, promoting economic self-sufficiency, and improving birth and developmental outcomes for children of adolescents. Multigenerational approaches also are discussed, as many adolescent parents reside with their own parents or other individuals who may play a role in the parenting and development of young children.

The Nurse-Family Partnership

The Nurse-Family Partnership (NFP), discussed in the previous chapter, is an evidence-based program involving prenatal and postpartum home visitation by nurses for low-income first-time mothers, many of whom are adolescent. Home visits begin as early as the mother's first trimester and continue until the child's second birthday. Among NFP's many objectives are to promote the economic self-sufficiency of young mothers by supporting educational attainment and employment and delaying subsequent pregnancy. NFP also aims to improve child health and development (Middlemiss and McGuigan, 2005).

A number of experimental studies have found participation in NFP to be associated with a decrease in rapid-succession second pregnancies (Bouris et al., 2012; Conroy et al., 2013; Kitzman et al., 2000; Olds et al., 2004, 2007). In one relatively large randomized trial involving primarily adolescent mothers, those who received NFP home visits had fewer births and longer intervals between births of first and second children at 7-year follow-up compared with mothers who did not receive visits (Olds et al., 2007). In general, NFP has been found to have little to no effect on indicators of continued education, such as graduation from high school and highest level of education completed for parents. However, some studies have found positive short- and long-term effects on indicators of family economic self-sufficiency, such as reduced use of Temporary Assistance for Needy Families (TANF) and the Supplemental Nutrition Assistance Program (SNAP, formerly the Food Stamp program) (Administration for Children and Families, 2015). Studies of NFP that have evaluated birth outcomes generally have found no effects on gestational age or birth weight, but have found longer-term positive effects for children in the areas of school readiness, substance use, and adolescent parenthood years postintervention (Administration for Children and Families, 2005). In addition, several experimental evaluations of NFP have found positive effects on parenting related to the knowledge, attitudes, and practices identified in Chapter 2, including using appropriate discipline and creating a safe home environment.

The Adolescent Parenting Program

The Adolescent Parenting Program (APP), rated by CEBC as having a "promising" level (3) of research evidence, provides support to first-time pregnant and parenting adolescents who are enrolled in school or a GED-completion program and their children ages 0-5 (California Evidence-Based Clearinghouse, 2016a). Through intensive monthly home visiting (using either the Partners for a Healthy Baby or Parents as Teachers home visiting curriculum), goal-setting and case management services, and peer group education, APP aims to delay subsequent pregnancies and increase graduation and GED completion rates, as well as enrollment in postsecondary education or vocational training, employment, and safe and stable housing. APP also focuses on improving the developmental outcomes of the young children of adolescent parents through prenatal and postnatal support (California Evidence-Based Clearinghouse, 2014).

In a 2006 quasi-experimental study of 2,520 adolescent pregnant and parenting females, participation in APP was associated with significantly longer intervals between first and second births and increased likelihood of normal birth weight and full-term birth. The groups had similar rates of use of prenatal care (Sangalang et al., 2006). The authors point to case management and provision of direct services as central to helping adolescent mothers postpone subsequent births and achieve favorable birth outcomes (Sangalang et al., 2006). In a more recent study, APP graduates were found to have greater enrollment in higher education, job stability, and focus on career goals relative to other adolescent parents, but the study was not experimental and involved a very small number of participants (Gruber, 2012). In another nonexperimental study, a pre- and post-intervention comparison showed improvement in use of contraception and parenting knowledge postintervention among 91 adolescents participating in APP (Sangalang and Rounds, 2005). Although research on APP to date has yielded promising initial findings, further experimental research with larger study populations is needed to confirm those findings.

Other evidence-based home visiting programs that likely reach a large number of adolescent parents (e.g., Family Check-Up, Home Instruction for Parents of Preschool Youngsters [HIPPY], Durham Connects) also have shown positive child health and developmental outcomes, but fewer positive effects have been observed for parents' economic self-sufficiency (see Table 4-1 in Chapter 4).

Computer-Assisted Motivational Interviewing

Computer-assisted motivational interviewing (CAMI) is another intervention used with adolescent mothers to reduce rapid repeat births by promoting consistent use of condoms and other forms of contraception. It has been rated by CEBC as having a promising level of evidence (California Evidence-Based Clearinghouse, 2016d). CAMI entails at least two 60-minute sessions conducted in two parts by trained counselors, who meet one on one with pregnant and parenting adolescent mothers in the home or in a community agency or outpatient clinic. In one study, adolescents randomized to CAMI plus intensive home visiting or CAMI only who participated in sessions at quarterly intervals until 2 years postpartum had nonsignificantly lower birth rates compared with participants receiving usual care. Significant effects were seen for those adolescent mothers in the CAMI-only group who received two or more sessions of CAMI (Barnet et al., 2009). In a follow-up study with the same participants, adolescent mothers in the CAMI plus home visiting and CAMI-only groups had significantly reduced repeat births compared with those in the usual-care group (Barnet et al., 2010).

In an older, nonequivalent control group study of a multicomponent community-based intervention (the Family Growth Center [FGC]) designed to provide adolescent mothers in high-risk neighborhoods with a range of educational and support services for the prevention of rapid repeat pregnancy and school dropout, mothers participating in FGC followed over 3 years had a significantly lower rate of repeat pregnancy and significantly higher rate of school completion compared with nonparticipating adolescent mothers. However, the study sample was very small (Solomon and Liefeld, 1998). FGC has received a rating of promising from CEBC (California Evidence-Based Clearinghouse, 2016f).

School-Based Interventions

Provision of parenting-related interventions and child care in the school setting may serve as a means of providing multidisciplinary services to adolescents while keeping them engaged in school, but additional research on the benefits of this approach is needed (Crean et al., 2001; Pinzon et al., 2012; Sadler et al., 2003, 2007). In one study, adolescent mothers and their children receiving on-site child care while participating in a school-based program that included parenting classes and referral services were found to have better school attendance than nonparticipants, with 70 percent and 28 percent, respectively, graduating from high school (Crean et al., 2001). Some states have implemented their own programs for pregnant and parenting adolescents in schools as well as home settings, with positive impacts on education (e.g., completion of high school) and economic self-sufficiency (National Association of County and City Health Officials, 2009). However, findings from evaluations of these programs often are not published in the peer-reviewed literature.

Multigenerational Households

As noted above, many adolescent parents live with their own parents or rely on family members for support in raising young children. Multigenerational households are becoming more common in the United States, especially among racial and ethnic minorities, but a dearth of research has examined the nature and quality of parenting in these homes. Preliminary research on multigenerational households indicates that parenting and child development are influenced by interactions between parents and grandparents in the household (Barnett et al., 2012). A few well-supported parenting programs, such as NFP, take family-level functioning into account, but the committee was unable to identify any comparisons of the use and nonuse of multigenerational approaches. The FGC model described above did include an explicit focus on involving the mothers of adolescent parents in the intervention (Solomon and Liefeld, 1998).

Summary

In summary, with the exception of NFP, many of the studies reviewed are limited by small sample sizes and lack of follow-up. Taken together, the studies reviewed provide good evidence that intensive home visiting with adolescent mothers, as provided in NFP, APP, and CAMI plus home visiting, is effective for reducing rapid repeat pregnancy and improving birth and developmental outcomes in children of adolescent parents. While other strategies (e.g., motivational interviewing provided in one version of CAMI and services designed to address families' multiple needs as provided in the FGC model) also show promise with respect to these outcomes, those preliminary findings need to be replicated. With respect to parent self-sufficiency, intensive home visiting in NFP is associated in several studies with improvements in indicators of economic well-being but not continued education, although CAMI and school-based interventions and child care have shown positive effects on continuation of schooling among adolescent mothers. As with research on parenting in general, fathers are underrepresented in evaluations of interventions to support adolescent parents. Finally, because many adolescent parents live with their own parents and rely on other family members to assist with childrearing, the lack of research on the effectiveness of multigenerational approaches is a gap in research on interventions for adolescent parents.

FAMILIES INVOLVED WITH CHILD WELFARE SERVICES

Child welfare services play a unique role in parenting policy and programming. They represent the only universal set of services addressing parenting in every state. These services are, however, a residual system. Child welfare services become involved with families when the quality of parenting falls below what society considers a minimally adequate threshold. The purpose of the services is to investigate allegations of child maltreatment and intervene when it is established that the quality of parenting is deficient and that as a result, the safety and/or basic physical or mental health of a child has been put at substantial risk. In a large percentage of substantiated cases of maltreatment, the threat to the child's safety requires monitoring of the parent's care; in almost a quarter of substantiated cases, the child is removed altogether from parental care, and parents must participate in parenting interventions if they want to regain custody.

The focus of child welfare services is protecting children's safety, although once involvement with a family is initiated, the focus extends to enhancing children's well-being. Parents involved with child welfare services are most often formally designated by "child neglect: failure to supervise" or "child neglect: failure to provide," which indicates they have not addressed basic safety concerns, largely as the result of omission of effective parenting. Together, these designations represent more than one-half of child maltreatment reports (Administration for Children and Families, 2005; Casanueva et al., 2012). In about a quarter of all cases, the parent has engaged in behaviors that constitute physical abuse; a smaller and declining percentage involve sexual involvement with the child by the parent or a family member.

Even though child welfare services are recognized as a last-resort or residual response for children whose parents are not meeting their responsibility to provide a safe home environment, some contact with these services is now broadly experienced. In 2014, an investigation or other intervention by child welfare services was conducted for more than 3 million children (a rate of 42.9 per 1,000 children) (Administration for Children and Families, 2016). Approximately 702,000 of these children (a rate of 9.4 per 1,000 children) were determined to have a substantiated or indicated finding of abuse and/or neglect (Administration for Children and Families, 2016). A study in California found that 5.2 percent of all children younger than age 1 are reported for child maltreatment each year (Putnam-Hornstein et al., 2015), and 2.1 percent of children experience confirmed maltreatment by age 1 (Wildeman et al., 2014). Although national data are lacking on the reasons for these reports, they appear to be strongly associated with maternal substance abuse (Wulczyn et al., 2002).

These findings reflect yearly contacts. Taking a longitudinal perspective, one study concluded that one in eight children experience a substantiated instance of maltreatment by age 18, and nearly 6 percent do so by age 5 (Wildeman et al., 2014). For African American children, the latter figure is 1 in 5, and for Native American children, it is 1 in 7 (Wildeman et al., 2014). Within some subpopulations—for example, the children of young adult parents who were clients of child welfare services as children—interaction with child welfare services is experienced by more than one-half of children (Putnam-Hornstein et al., 2015).

The Impact of Inadequate Parenting on Children

In addition to threats to their safety, the children involved with child welfare services have high rates of behavioral and developmental problems—about twice the rates found among children in the general population (Burns et al., 2004; Casanueva et al., 2012). The largest study of children receiving child welfare services—the National Survey of Child and Adolescent Well-Being (NSCAW)—found that at the time of entry into child welfare, about one-third (37%) of children had a mental or medical condition with a high probability of resulting in developmental delays and/ or of being 2 or more standard deviations below the mean in at least one developmental area or 1.5 standard deviations below the mean in two areas (Casanueva et al., 2014). Among children ages 0-2, 3-5, and 7-10, only 83 percent, 84 percent, and 78 percent, respectively, were in very good or excellent health. Among children ages 3-5, fully 15.7 percent were reported by their parents as having behavioral problems in the clinical range on the Child Behavior Checklist (CBCL) (Achenbach, 1991a; Achenbach and Rescorla, 2001). Among children ages 6-17, a significantly higher proportion (about 26%) had a score in the clinical range for behavioral health problems (as measured by the CBCL), about three times what would be expected in the general population (Achenbach, 1991b).

The Impact of Child Welfare Services

A full evaluation of the functioning of child welfare services is beyond the scope of this report, but a number of issues related to these services have been identified in prior IOM and NRC reports (Institute of Medicine and National Research Council, 2014; National Research Council, 1993). As noted in those and many other reports, agencies providing child welfare services throughout the country face many challenges both in protecting the long-term development of children and in providing adequate services to parents.

Given the scope and impact on children of parental behaviors constituting "maltreatment," it is essential that these parents receive high-quality parenting interventions. An effective response by child welfare services is especially needed for parents of young children. It appears clear, however, that too many families are not receiving effective services. A large proportion of children—perhaps exceeding 80 percent—remain in the home following the initial report to child welfare services (Institute of Medicine and National Research Council, 2014). A recent California using a longitudinal dataset of birth and child protective service records found that nearly 70 percent of infants who received ongoing in-home family child welfare services were re-reported during the first 5 years (Putnam-Hornstein et al., 2015). Infants whose reports were screened out were as likely to be re-reported as those who received services. This finding is consistent with decades of research showing that the future risks for "unsubstantiated cases" remain high (e.g., The Center for Community Partnerships in Child Welfare, 2006; Drake and Jonson-Reid, 1999a, 1999b).

Caregiver instability is a significant factor in the lives of children who have been maltreated and reported to child welfare services. Even though most infants who come to the attention of child welfare services do not go immediately into foster care, Casanueva and colleagues (2012) in an analysis of longitudinal data from the NSCAW found that nearly all such infants (about 86%) had one or more changes in caregivers by the end of 2 years, and approximately 40 percent had four or more placement changes between infancy and entering school.

Children of any age with child welfare services involvement have a high risk of continuing to experience developmental, cognitive, and behavioral health problems regardless of whether they are placed in foster care or provided with ongoing services (Dolan et al., 2012). In another NSCAW analysis that followed 5,872 children under the supervision of child welfare for a 5-year period, by 3-year follow-up, the proportion of children in any type of placement setting who had developmental problems remained largely unchanged from the high levels described above (Casanueva et al., 2014).

The impact of living in poverty is a critical factor. After controlling for maltreatment type and severity, demographic traits, and a few caregiver characteristics, the NSCAW revealed that infants who had remained in foster care for the first 5 years of life were developing more slowly than children who had been returned home or adopted (Lloyd and Barth, 2011). Living in poverty in the final setting in which they were studied predicted decreased cognitive development as well as academic problems and tended to explain behavioral health. The well-being of children was powerfully influenced by ongoing exposure to poverty, regardless of the poverty level in which they lived at the time of original placement or the placement type at the end of placement.

Intervention Strategies

According to the NSCAW, in about two-thirds of cases that enter child welfare services, a recommendation for parent training is made, and nearly three-fourths of cases also involve a referral for mental health counseling or substance abuse treatment for the caregiver (Dolan et al., 2011). The form of parent training is rarely specified, and no assessment is made of whether parenting improved as a result of the training; at most, the courts learn only whether parents have attended parenting classes (Barth et al., 2005).

While parent training has always been common for families receiving child welfare services, those services have lagged behind other mental and physical health services both in the assessment of interventions and in the adoption of evidence-based practices. In the past, lack of access to research-based information about the effectiveness of parent training programs and limited comfort with selecting and implementing evidence-based interventions resulted in sluggish adoption of these practices among child welfare services (Horwitz et al., 2009). It was not until 2004 and thereafter, when resources such as the *Journal of Evidence-Based Social Work* and CEBC became available that information on effective practices became more widely available. As recently as 2006, a Cochrane review of parenting programs for the treatment of physical child abuse and neglect (Barlow et al., 2006) found insufficient evidence to support the use of the reviewed programs, although limited evidence showed that some programs could be effective in addressing outcomes associated with physically abusive parenting practices.

Recent years have seen much greater focus on the use of evidence-based practices among child welfare agencies, perhaps reflecting increased federal policy direction and support for the use of these practices. In some cases, agencies are adopting evidence-based programs used in helping parents not involved with the child welfare system, such as Incredible Years, sometimes adapting the program to better meet the characteristics of families that are involved with the system. Interventions also have been developed specifically for parents involved with child welfare services. Given that the implementation of evidence-based practices is relatively new in child welfare services, the literature on evidence-based strategies to support these families is emergent.

Skills Training and Family-Centered Treatment for Families with a History of Child Maltreatment or with Child Maltreatment Risk Factors

Three parent skills training programs reviewed earlier (PCIT, Incredible Years, and Triple P), often delivered in a group setting, have been found in randomized controlled studies to be suitable for implementation in the child welfare context (Linares et al., 2006, 2012, 2015) and effective for reducing child abuse recidivism and coercive and punitive discipline practices (Chaffin et al., 2004, 2011), as well as reducing parental stress associated with childrearing and increasing parental confidence. A high cost for the Incredible Years materials and a small number of approved trainers have slowed the adoption of Incredible Years by child welfare services—a problem that applies as well to other evidence-based practices (Powers et al., 2010).

A number of programs have been designed specifically for families involved with child welfare services. ABC (Attachment and Bio-Behavioral Catch-up) is an evidence-based home visiting intervention (CEBC evidence rating of 1) that utilizes videotape feedback to teach parenting skills over a 10-week period (California Evidence-Based Clearinghouse, 2016c). The program helps caregivers reinterpret children's behavioral signals to offer more nurturance, provide a responsive and predictable environment to help children with self-regulation, follow their child's lead, and decrease the use of behaviors that overwhelm and frighten the child. Randomized controlled research has shown that children in families who participate in the intervention are less disorganized in their attachment with their parents and display less sadness and anger compared with controls (Bernard et al., 2012). The attitudes and behaviors that change as a result of receiving ABC are, arguably, fundamental to helping parents and children reduce stress-inducing interactions and enhance parent-child closeness. There is, however, no direct evidence that child maltreatment is lowered by such approaches.

Another program, discussed in Chapter 4, SafeCare® (Lutzker and Chaffin, 2012) (CEBC rating of 2), was designed for parents whose children had been reported for neglect and who needed explicit, easily implemented strategies for improving home safety and increasing the use of needed medical or behavioral interventions (California Evidence-Based Clearinghouse, 2016l). During weekly or biweekly sessions, home visitors conduct baseline and follow-up assessments, observations, and trainings with parents and provide parents with feedback. The trainings focus on practices related to reducing the incidence of child maltreatment, enhancing home safety and supervision, and improving the parent-child relationship. SafeCare home visitors are required only to have a bachelor's degree, and the program uses competency-based training approaches that make its replication highly dependable and scalable. SafeCare has been the focus of considerable implementation research—including studies focused on variation in supervision, American Indian populations, and culturally enhanced training methods for working with Latino professionals and parents (Beasley et al., 2014). In randomized and single group pre-post design studies, caregivers who participate in SafeCare have been found to be less likely to abuse their children. Participation also is associated with improvements in home safety (Chaffin et al., 2012; Gershater-Molko et al., 2002, 2003). In a small pilot study of SafeCare that incorporated use of flash cards to improve parents' knowledge of developmental milestones—one of the core knowledge areas identified in Chapter 2—the intervention was found to be effective in improving parental knowledge in this area; however, the findings of this study are preliminary, and additional research is needed (Guastaferro, 2011).

Multisystemic Therapy for Child Abuse and Neglect (MST-CAN) (CEBC rating of 2) and Trauma Adapted Family Connections (TA-FC) are programs used with caregivers and/or children who have experienced trauma. Both programs work with the entire family to address concerns in the home so as to keep children safe (California Evidence-Based Clearinghouse, 2016i).

MST-CAN is an adaptation of MST for child welfare-involved families that is supported by research evidence for children ages 6-17 (Swenson and Schaeffer, 2011; Swenson et al., 2010) and founded on basic principles of care coordination. Treatment entails safety planning, cognitive-behavioral therapy for managing anger and addressing the impact of trauma, counseling for adult substance misuse, family therapy, and getting parents to take responsibility for events that brought the family to child protection. Research indicates that MST-CAN is significantly more effective than enhanced outpatient treatment in reducing parents' psychiatric distress and behaviors associated with maltreatment, increasing parents' social support, improving children's mental health symptoms, and reducing children's out-of-home placements and changes in children's placement. Yet no statistically significant difference was found for incidents of reabuse among participants and families receiving outpatient treatment in a randomized effectiveness trial (Swenson et al., 2010). One evaluation showed that MST was effective in addressing the dual needs of families involved with child welfare services and substance abuse (Swenson et al., 2009).

TA-FC builds on the service components of the Family Connections model, a promising program (CEBC rating of 3) designed to reduce risk factors for child maltreatment through family assessment and individual and family counseling, emergency assistance, and service planning and referral (California Evidence-Based Clearinghouse, 2016e). TA-FC integrates a focus on trauma into family assessment and counseling, such as by assisting families with identification of trauma symptoms and teaching trauma-informed parenting practices (Collins et al., 2011, 2015). TA-FC has not identified specific parenting knowledge, attitudes, and practices that may be the active ingredient in reducing the likelihood of maltreatment, but pilot noncontrolled evaluation of the program demonstrates reductions in child problem behaviors (Collins et al., 2011, 2015). Even though this is not the explicit program target, these findings suggest that reducing parental stress, recognizing and addressing a range of parental risk factors, and matching services (e.g., special education) to parents can benefit family functioning (DePanfilis et al., 2008).

Supporting Foster and Kinship Families to Improve Placement Stability

Many children involved with child welfare services are placed with relatives or nonrelative foster parents. Foster and kinship providers often need training in parenting skills that addresses the unique challenges associated with parenting children who have experienced maltreatment. Treatment Foster Care Oregon for Preschoolers (TFCO-P) (Chamberlain and Fisher, 2003; Fisher et al., 1999) is a well-supported treatment model (CEBC rating of 2) designed for children ages 3-6 (California Evidence-Based Clearinghouse, 2016m). The intervention is delivered through a treatment team approach that incorporates training and ongoing consultation with foster parents, skills training and therapeutic playgroups for children, and family therapy for birth parents, with the goal of promoting secure attachment with foster parents and successful permanent placement with birth parents or through adoption. Randomized controlled evaluations comparing TFCO-P with conventional foster care have shown that children who experience the consistent, contingent, responsive parenting that is taught in TFCO-P, along with other services, have reduced rates of problem behaviors (as reported daily by the foster parents), and the foster parents demonstrate less stress. As a result, children in TFCO-P have more stable placements relative to those in conventional foster care (Fisher et al., 2005, 2006, 2009, 2011a).

Keeping Foster and Kin Parents Supported and Trained (KEEP) (CEBC rating of 3) is a derivative of Multidimensional Treatment Foster Care created for use with children of elementary school age who are in out-of-home care supervised by child welfare services (California Evidence-Based Clearinghouse, 2016h). The program model includes weekly group work among foster families to learn effective parenting methods and daily or weekly calls to check on problems with parenting, which are addressed using a flexible curriculum (Price et al., 2009). KEEP is being implemented with diverse populations in both urban and rural areas in a number of states. Randomized controlled research has found foster family satisfaction and improvements in child behavior and placement outcomes (e.g., chances of a child being reunited with his or her biological parents) (Chamberlain et al., 2008; Price et al., 2009), although a replication study does not show effects of the same size (Greeno et al., 2016). A program modeled after KEEP showed increased positive behavior for foster youth in Chicago (Leathers et al., 2011), and KEEP for preschoolers is under development as a plausible alternative to TFCO-P.

Knowledge, Attitudes, and Practices and Child Welfare Services

The knowledge, attitudes, and practices needed by parents who become involved with child welfare services are not different from those needed by other parents. Knowledge of child development generally is considered a necessary precursor to reducing maltreatment. Evidence indicates that maltreating parents often have unrealistic expectations for what a child is able to do and may misinterpret a young child's actions and/or lack of capacity as intentional. Further, parents who are depressed or angry about other matters may be more likely than those who are not to view their children's behavior as controllable and negatively intended (Leung and Slep, 2006). Yet changes in parental attitudes are not well articulated as a mediator of the effectiveness of parenting training in achieving better outcomes with respect to child maltreatment. Even when modest changes in knowledge are achieved, an impact on reducing future child maltreatment is not highly likely given the array of adverse influences on parents' responses to their children's perceived misbehavior. As demonstrated by studies referenced above, parenting programs based heavily on providing information are typically outperformed by those with more of a behavioral focus (e.g., ABC, SafeCare, PCIT).

Improving the executive functioning, actions, and circumstances of parents is necessary for avoiding neglect and abuse, as is developing alternatives to neglectful and abusive practices (Knerr et al., 2013; Leung and

Slep, 2006). None of the programs reviewed here focus on specific measurement of attitude change as an indicator of whether progress is being made; instead, the programs require demonstration of desired behaviors during the course of treatment. A potential limitation of current approaches for families with a history of or at high risk for child maltreatment is that, with the exception of ABC, they generally do not address how parents' current parenting styles developed or what trauma they themselves experienced as children or parents, although ABC does systematically explore the way experience as a child affects parents' views about parenting.

Emerging knowledge about the core components that make evidence-based practices successful can support the broader distribution of what works, earlier rather than later, to the parents who need it the most. Barth and Liggett-Creel (2014) explored the common elements of programs for parents of children ages 0-8 involved with the child welfare system by building on prior work in this area (Chorpita et al., 2005; Geeraert et al., 2004; Kaminski et al., 2008). In a review of well-supported interventions in CEBC, common elements were identifiable in training programs for parents of children ages 4-8, but far less so in programs for parents of children ages 0-3 (Barth and Liggett-Creel, 2014). CEBC includes four programs (Incredible Years, PCIT, PMT-Oregon [PMT-O], and 1-2-3 Magic) with a very similar history and operational components for the older age group. Common treatment elements include being offered in a clinic setting (two of the four are also offered in the home to allow for practicing newly acquired skills) and the use of a group format. All four models have social learning theory as their foundation. PCIT also uses attachment theory to guide its work. The use of social learning theory across the four models and the core set of parenting skills taught (i.e., attending, positive reinforcement, and use of time-out) means that certain common practice elements are likely to contribute to the success of interventions for child abuse and neglect.

SUMMARY

The following key points emerged from the committee's review of evidence-based and evidence-informed interventions for parents of children with special needs, parents facing special adversities, and parents involved with child welfare services.

Parents of Children with Special Needs

- The efficacy research on programs designed to promote different dimensions of parenting for young children with special needs suggests that efficacious programs and resources are available to support parenting knowledge, attitudes, and practices for these parents. The strongest evidence is for programs that (1) teach parents how to support the learning and development of their children with disabilities, (2) promote positive parent-child interactions, and (3) focus on reducing the children's problem behaviors. Some of these programs do appear to have secondary outcomes that affect the larger family system, such as increased parental optimism, decreased parental stress, and generalized changes in parenting style.

Parents of Children with Developmental Disabilities

- Research indicates the effectiveness of family interventions designed to reduce stress among parents of children with developmental disabilities, especially when such interventions occur over a relatively long period and have multiple components (e.g., a combination of group and individual elements).
- Instructional interventions that teach parents how to facilitate the language, social, and play skills of children with developmental disabilities are effective in achieving these outcomes, indicating that with appropriate supports, parents can help their children develop these skills. For parents of children with ASD, instructional interventions focused on promoting children's social-communication skills show positive effects on children's cognitive development when they are based on a conceptual framework, address a variety of developmental needs, and occur over an extended period (1-2 years). Furthermore, interventions that involve parents appear to be more effective than other approaches for these children.
- Interventions that teach parents dialogic reading skills show positive impacts on the reading skills of young children with language delays.
- Interactional practice interventions that promote positive social interactions between parents and young children with disabilities by teaching parents how to arrange play in a way that encourages parent-child interaction and facilitates parental responsiveness have been found to improve responsive parenting and increase social interactions among these children.
- Parent training in support of positive behavior, such as that provided by the widely used Triple P and Incredible Years, including in a group format, is associated with improved parent-child interactions and reduced challenging behavior in children with developmental disabilities.
- Gaps in research and practice relevant to interventions for parents of children with developmental disabilities include the development and evaluation of interventions that take place in natural environ-

ments and that support parents and children during important life transitions, such as that from early intervention to preschool.

Parents of Children with Behavioral Challenges and Mental Health Disorders

- Active skills training with rehearsal for parents of children with externalizing behavior problems delivered in a series of one-on-one and/or group sessions in community-based settings (as in Triple P and Incredible Years) can lead to improved parent-child relationships, less frequent dysfunctional parenting (e.g., harsh discipline), improved parenting competence, and reduced child behavior problems. Multiple evaluations have found that therapy-based child management combined with play therapy (PCIT), delivered in weekly sessions in outpatient and clinic settings to teach parents the skills to encourage prosocial behavior in their children, improves parent-child interactions, imparts parenting skills related to gaining children's compliance, and reduces parental stress, among other benefits. PCIT and cognitive-behavioral therapy have been found to be effective among parents of children with internalizing behavior problems such as anxiety and depression.
- Other interventions have focused directly on a particular type of externalizing or internalizing condition. More examples of these interventions exist for externalizing conditions, although efficacy studies for children with anxiety disorders also have been documented. Few interventions have been developed to help parents address childhood depression, perhaps because depression is a fairly low-prevalence disorder in children. However, the role of parents in moderating the effects of childhood depression and potential impacts on life outcomes certainly deserves more attention and activity in intervention research.

Parents of Children with Serious or Chronic Medical Illness

- Efficacious programs (e.g., COPE) are available to support families of children with critical illnesses that require hospitalization and intensive medical services. In general, much research has been conducted on support for parents within other portions of the health care sector, but such studies often are not well powered and lack adequate evaluation. Data on long-term outcomes and on fathers are lacking, and both of these areas deserve increased attention.

Parents of Very Low-Birth Weight, Premature Infants

- Research on mothers of very-low-birth weight infants shows that interventions designed to encourage and support interactions and physical contact between mothers and infants result in improved mother-infant relationships, better maternal mood, and reduced anxiety.

Parents Facing Special Adversities

- Common barriers to receipt of support for parents facing special adversities are stigma, such as that which can be associated with having a mental illness, substance abuse disorder, or other condition; concerns that because of one's mental health, substance use, or other condition, or because of a history of maltreatment, one will be reported to child protective services; and distrust of service providers.

Parents with Mental Illness

- Recognition of individuals with mental illness as also being parents is frequently lacking among service providers.
- There have been few high-quality large-scale evaluations of interventions designed for parents with mental illness, especially those with serious mental illness.
- For parents with depressive disorders, interventions that combine mental health treatment and parenting support lead to better outcomes in terms of reducing psychiatric symptoms and increasing maternal responsiveness relative to programs focused solely on mental illness.
- Integrating parenting interventions and support into primary care may be an effective way of diagnosing and treating parents' mental health issues. The perinatal period appears to be an opportune time to reach a broad population of parents.
- Research provides preliminary evidence that home visiting programs that include therapy for parental depression improve parental mental health and parenting. Yet many home visiting programs do not include mental health as an objective, and further research is needed to confirm these preliminary findings. Efforts within Early Head Start and public health settings also show promising effects on depression, parenting practices, and child behavior, but further research on these efforts is needed as well.

- Research on strategies for supporting parents with severe mental illness who may need ongoing and intensive support is lacking. Some evidence indicates significant benefits for the parenting skills of parents with severe mental illness and the behavior of their children from interventions involving home visits, parenting lectures, and clinician counseling. Triple P in particular has shown promise, and intensive outpatient or inpatient treatment (e.g., in mother-baby mental health units) may be effective as well. Available data on interventions and treatment for parents with severe mental illness indicate an association with significantly reduced risk that children will develop the same mental health problems.

Parents with or Recovering from Substance Use Disorders

- Mothers who are permitted to reside with their children during substance abuse treatment are more likely to enter, remain in, and complete treatment and remain drug free for longer. Evaluations of specific residential treatment programs show improved parent-child relationships as well as child outcomes.
- FTDCs that provide parents with access to substance abuse treatment along with accountability, support, and rewards and sanctions aimed at regaining child custody result in improved entry into and completion of treatment. Children of parents participating in these programs are more likely to be reunited with their parents relative to children of nonparticipants. However, these findings may be biased by the fact that women who enter FTDCs may be more motivated to change their behavior than women who do not enter these programs.
- Few targeted parenting interventions have been developed for parents who have or are recovering from a substance abuse disorder. However, available evidence indicates that combining substance abuse treatment with parenting intervention improves parenting beyond the improvement achieved with substance abuse treatment alone. Parents may benefit most when instruction in specific parenting techniques is preceded by instruction in psychological coping strategies.
- Data from evidence-based parenting programs (Strengthening Families and the Nurturing Parent Program) indicate that family skills training in residential, day treatment, and FTDC settings that emphasizes reducing parents' alcohol and drug use while helping them learn new patterns of parenting results in reduced substance use and also is associated with improved parenting (involvement, supervision) and less family conflict and child maltreatment. In

addition, therapy in outpatient mental health settings designed to improve family relationships and communication and child management is associated with improvements in family relationships and other outcomes.

- Substance use can interfere with parent-child attachment. Preliminary data from pilot studies show that parent coaching sessions aimed at improving parents' nurturing of young children provided in combination with substance abuse treatment improve attachment-related parenting behaviors.

- Findings from office- and home-based substance abuse treatment and case management programs for pregnant and parenting women focused on parenting, family planning, education, and other areas indicate that these programs are associated with reduced likelihood that a woman will give birth to a drug-exposed infant.

Parents Affected by Intimate Partner Violence

- Community programs for mothers, couples, and children experiencing intimate partner violence that target parenting and/or child outcomes have been found to be effective in reducing children's behavior problems, mental health problems among both mothers and children, and maternal stress and improving parenting. Programs focused on reducing the effects of trauma in children have been found to be effective, but not through changes in parenting. There is little evidence that counseling services for men prevent further violence, and although more women are now being arrested for intimate partner violence, data on intimate partner violence perpetrated by women are scarce. With regard to couples involved in intimate partner violence who seek services, some research shows that PCIT with families reduces conflict between parents if the violence has ceased. Dyadic interventions designed to treat adults with substance abuse disorders (behavioral couples treatment) show reductions in alcohol use and violent behaviors among both men and women.

- Few home visiting programs have focused on intimate partner violence, but many women who receive home visiting services report incidents of domestic violence. Some home visiting programs are developing, implementing, and testing strategies for reducing intimate partner violence, but findings from evaluations of these strategies are not yet available.

- A small number of studies on programs for couples designed to prevent intimate partner violence have found that these programs can reduce future violence and violence risk factors, but these studies have not assessed the process for change or how the intervention works with different cultural groups.

Parents with Developmental Disabilities

- Many parents with intellectual disabilities provide adequate care-giving and parenting for their young children, but for a substantial minority, programs providing support for child caregiving, health care, and home safety may be important. A moderate level of evidence suggests that these programs have positive effects. The Triple P program, which has been effective with other populations of parents, is being adapted for parents with intellectual disabilities.

Adolescent Parents

- Adolescents' participation in intensive home visiting is associated with a reduction in rapid repeat pregnancies and improved birth and developmental outcomes in children of adolescent parents. Several studies have found that the intensive home visiting offered in NFP is associated with improvements in indicators of economic well-being. While other strategies (e.g., motivational interviewing and provision of services to address families' multiple needs) also show promise in improving these outcomes, preliminary findings need to be replicated.
- Many adolescent parents face barriers to continuing their school-ing, although many go on to complete their GED. There is some evidence that home visiting programs and school-based interven-tions that provide child care have positive effects on continuation of schooling among adolescent mothers, but further research in this area is needed.
- As with research on parenting in general, fathers are under-represented in evaluations of interventions designed to support adolescent parents. Another gap in research on adolescent parents is the effectiveness of multigenerational approaches, given that many adolescent parents live with their own parents and rely on them and other family members to help with parenting.

Families Involved with Child Welfare Services

- Effective parenting programs in child welfare are rooted largely in social learning theory. They focus on encouraging the use of antici-patory guidance and timely attention to increase parents' positive behavior and, in turn, teach them to use these tools more effectively with their children. The underlying theory is that positive changes in children's behavior will reinforce parents' positive attitudes and beliefs about their children and about the possibility of successful parenting.

- In families with a history of child maltreatment or at high risk for maltreatment, both skills training in home and community settings that involves observation and corrective feedback and multi-pronged family-system approaches that address trauma and other co-occurring challenges (e.g., substance use) can be effective for improving child behavior and the parent-child relationship, parents' psychiatric distress, and behaviors associated with child maltreatment. In addition, successful interventions for prevention of child abuse and neglect appear to include detailed, active methods for increasing the frequency of effective parenting practices, often without much attention to how parents originally began to rely on ineffective methods.

- Training and ongoing consultation with foster and kinship families are associated with reduced rates of problematic behaviors among children in these family arrangements, indicators of attachment between caregivers and children, and greater placement stability.

REFERENCES

Achenbach, T.M. (1991a). *Manual for Child Behavior Checklist/2-3 and 1991 Profile.* Burlington: University of Vermont Department of Psychiatry.

Achenbach, T.M. (1991b). *Manual for Child Behavior Checklist/4-18 and 1991 Profile.* Burlington: University of Vermont Department of Psychiatry.

Achenbach, T.M., and Rescorla, L.A. (2001). *Manual for the ASEBA School-Age Forms & Profiles: An Integrated System of Multi-Informant Assessment.* Burlington: University of Vermont, Research Center for Children, Youth, & Families.

Adamson, L.B., Bakeman, R., Deckner, D.F., and Nelson, P.B. (2012). Rating parent-child interactions: Joint engagement, communication dynamics, and shared topics in autism, Down syndrome, and typical development. *Journal of Autism and Developmental Disorders, 42*(12), 2622-2635.

Administration for Children and Families. (2005). *National Survey of Child and Adolescent Well-Being (NSCAW): CPS Sample Component Wave 1 Data Analysis Report.* Available: http://www.acf.hhs.gov/sites/default/files/opre/cps_report_revised_090105.pdf [January 2016].

Administration for Children and Families. (2016). *Child Maltreatment 2014.* Washington, DC: U.S. Department of Health and Human Services; Administration for Children and Families; Administration on Children, Youth and Families; Children's Bureau.

Allen, M., and Larson, J. (1998). *Healing the Whole Family: A Look at Family Care Programs.* Washington, DC: Children's Defense Fund.

Amato, P.R., and Keith, B. (1991). Parental divorce and the well-being of children: A meta-analysis. *Psychological Bulletin, 110*(1), 26-46.

American Association on Intellectual and Developmental Disabilities. (2013). *Definition of Intellectual Disability*. Available: http://aaidd.org/intellectual-disability/definition#. Vk35DHarTGg [October 2016].

American Psychiatric Association. (2013). *Diagnostic and Statistical Manual of Mental Disorders (DSM5®)* (5th ed.). Arlington, VA: American Psychiatric Association.

Ammerman, R.T., Putnam, F.W., Stevens, J., Bosse, N.R., Short, J.A., Bodley, A.L., and van Ginkel, J.B. (2011). An open trial of in-home CBT for depressed mothers in home visitation. *Maternal and Child Health Journal, 15*(8), 1333-1341.

Ammerman, R.T., Putnam, F.W., Altaye, M., Stevens, J., Teeters, A.R., and van Ginkel, J.B. (2013). A clinical trial of in-home CBT for depressed mothers in home visitation. *Behavior Therapy, 44*(3), 359-372.

Ammerman, R.T., Altaye, M., Putnam, F.W., Teeters, A.R., Zou, Y., and van Ginkel, J.B. (2015). Depression improvement and parenting in low-income mothers in home visiting. *Archives of Women's Mental Health, 18*(3), 555-563.

Anda, R.F., Felitti, V.J., Chapman, D.P., Croft, J.B., Williamson, D.F., Santelli, J., Dietz, P.M., and Marks, J.S. (2001). Abused boys, battered mothers, and male involvement in teen pregnancy. *Pediatrics, 107*(2), E19.

Anderson, C., and McGuinness, T.M. (2008). Do teenage mothers experience childbirth as traumatic? *Journal of Psychosocial Nursing and Mental Health Services, 46*(4), 21-24.

Anticich, S.A.J., Barrett, P.M., Gillies, R., and Silverman, W. (2012). Recent advances in intervention for early childhood anxiety. *Journal of Psychologists and Counsellors in Schools, 22*(Special Issue 2), 157-172.

Arria, A.M., Mericle, A.A., Rallo, D., Moe, J., White, W.L., Winters, K.C., and O'Connor, G. (2013). Integration of parenting skills education and interventions in addiction treatment. *Journal of Addiction Medicine, 7*(1), 1-7.

Asheer, S., Berger, A., Meckstroth, A., Kisker, E., and Keating, B. (2014). Engaging pregnant and parenting teens: Early challenges and lessons learned from the evaluation of adolescent pregnancy prevention approaches. *Journal of Adolescent Health, 54*(Suppl. 3), S84-S91.

Assini-Meytin, L.C., and Green, K.M. (2015). Long-term consequences of adolescent parenthood among African-American urban youth: A propensity score matching approach. *Journal of Adolescent Health, 56*(5), 529-535.

Athanasopoulou, E., and Fox, J.R. (2014). Effects of kangaroo mother care on maternal mood and interaction patterns between parents and their preterm, low birth weight infants: A systematic review. *Infant Mental Health Journal, 35*(3), 245-262.

Aunos, M., Feldman, M., and Goupil, G. (2008). Mothering with intellectual disabilities: Relationship between social support, health and well-being, parenting and child behaviour outcomes. *Journal of Applied Research in Intellectual Disabilities, 21*(4), 320-330.

Azrin, N.H., McMahon, P.T., Donohue, B., Besalel, V.A., Lapinski, K.J., Kogan, E.S., Acierno, R.E., and Galloway, E. (1994). Behavior therapy for drug abuse: A controlled treatment outcome study. *Behaviour Research & Therapy, 32*(8), 857-866.

Azrin, N.H., Acierno, R., Kogan, E.S., Donohue, B., Besalel, V.A., and McMahon, P.T. (1996). Follow-up results of supportive versus behavioral therapy for illicit drug use. *Behaviour Research & Therapy, 34*(1), 41-46.

Babcock, J.C., Green, C.E., and Robie, C. (2004). Does batterers' treatment work? A meta-analytic review of domestic violence treatment. *Clinical Psychology Review, 23*(8), 1023-1053.

Back, S.E., Sonne, S.C., Killeen, T., Dansky, B.S., and Brady, K.T. (2003). Comparative profiles of women with PTSD and comorbid cocaine or alcohol dependence. *American Journal of Drug and Alcohol Abuse, 29*(1), 169-189.

Bagner, D.M., and Eyberg, S.M. (2007). Parent-child interaction therapy for disruptive behavior in children with mental retardation: A randomized controlled trial. *Journal of Clinical Child and Adolescent Psychology, 36*(3), 418-429.

Bagner, D.M., Sheinkopf, S.J., Vohr, B.R., and Lester, B.M. (2010). Parenting intervention for externalizing behavior problems in children born premature: An initial examination. *Journal of Developmental and Behavioral Pediatrics, 31*(3), 209-216.

Bancroft, L., Silverman, J.G., and Ritchie, D. (2011). *The Batterer as Parent: Addressing the Impact of Domestic Violence on Family Dynamics*. Thousand Oaks, CA: Sage.

Barkley, R.A. (1997). *Defiant Children: A Clinician's Manual for Parent Training* (2nd ed.). New York: Guilford Press.

Barlow, J., Johnston, I., Kendrick, D., Polnay, L., and Stewart-Brown, S. (2006). Individual and group-based parenting programmes for the treatment of physical child abuse and neglect. *Cochrane Database of Systematic Reviews, 3*, CD005463.

Barlow, J., Bennett, C., Midgley, N., Larkin, S.K., and Wei, Y. (2015). Parent-infant psychotherapy for improving parental and infant mental health. *Cochrane Database of Systematic Reviews, 1*, CD010534.

Barnard, M., and McKeganey, N. (2004). The impact of parental problem drug use on children: What is the problem and what can be done to help? *Addiction, 99*(5), 552-559.

Barnet, B., Liu, J., DeVoe, M., Duggan, A.K., Gold, M.A., and Pecukonis, E. (2009). Motivational intervention to reduce rapid subsequent births to adolescent mothers: A community-based randomized trial. *Annals of Family Medicine, 7*(5), 436-445.

Barnet, B., Rapp, T., DeVoe, M., and Mullins, C.D. (2010). Cost-effectiveness of a motivational intervention to reduce rapid repeated childbearing in high-risk adolescent mothers: A rebirth of economic and policy considerations. *Archives of Pediatrics & Adolescent Medicine, 164*(4), 370-376.

Barnett, M.A., Mills-Koonce, W.R., Gustafsson, H., Cox, M., and Family Life Project Key Investigators. (2012). Mother-grandmother conflict, negative parenting, and young children's social development in multigenerational families. *Family Relations, 61*(5), 864-877.

Barrow, S.M., Alexander, M.J., McKinney, J., Lawinski, T., and Pratt, C. (2014). Context and opportunity: Multiple perspectives on parenting by women with a severe mental illness. *Psychiatric Rehabilitation Journal, 37*(3), 176-182.

Barth, R.P., and Liggett-Creel, K. (2014). Common components of parenting programs for children birth to eight years of age involved with child welfare services. *Children and Youth Services Review, 40*, 6-12.

Barth, R.P., Landsverk, J., Chamberlain, P., Reid, J.B., Rolls, J.A., Hurlburt, M.S., Farmer, E.M.Z., James, S., McCabe, K.M., and Kohl, P.L. (2005). Parent-training programs in child welfare services: Planning for a more evidence-based approach to serving biological parents. *Research on Social Work Practice, 15*(5), 353-371.

Batts, K., Pemberton, M., Bose, J., Weimer, B., Henderson, L., Penne, M., Gfroerer, J., Trunzo, D., and Strashny, A. (2014). *Comparing and Evaluating Substance Use Treatment Utilization Estimates from the National Survey on Drug Use and Health and Other Data Sources*. Washington, DC: Center for Behavioral Health Statistics and Quality.

Bavolek, S.J., Comstock, C.M., and McLaughlin, J. (1983). *The Nurturing Program: A Validated Approach for Reducing Dysfunctional Family Interactions*. Available: http://www.nurturingparenting.com/images/cmsfiles/the_nurturing_program_nimh_study.pdf [March 2016].

Bavolek, S.J., Henderson, H.L., and Schultz, B.B. (1988). *Reducing Chronic Neglect in Utah*. Salt Lake City: University of Utah, College of Health.

Bayer, J.K., Sanson, A.V., and Hemphill, S.A. (2006). Parent influences on early childhood internalizing difficulties. *Journal of Applied Developmental Psychology, 27*(6), 542-559.

Beardslee, W.R., Gladstone, T.R., Wright, E.J., and Cooper, A.B. (2003). A family-based approach to the prevention of depressive symptoms in children at risk: Evidence of parental and child change. *Pediatrics, 112*(2), e119-e131.

Beardslee, W.R., Ayoub, C., Avery, M.W., Watts, C.L., and O'Carroll, K.L. (2010). Family Connections: An approach for strengthening early care systems in facing depression and adversity. *The American Journal of Orthopsychiatry, 80*(4), 482-495.

Beardslee, W.R., Gladstone, T.R., and O'Connor, E.E. (2011). Transmission and prevention of mood disorders among children of affectively ill parents: A review. *Journal of the American Academy of Child and Adolescent Psychiatry, 50*(11), 1098-1109.

Bearss, K., Johnson, C., Handen, B., Smith, T., and Scahill, L. (2013). A pilot study of parent training in young children with autism spectrum disorders and disruptive behavior. *Journal of Autism and Developmental Disorders, 43*(4), 829-840.

Beasley, L.O., Silovsky, J.F., Owora, A., Burris, L., Hecht, D., DeMoraes-Huffine, P., Cruz, I., and Tolma, E. (2014). Mixed-methods feasibility study on the cultural adaptation of a child abuse prevention model. *Child Abuse and Neglect, 38*(9), 1496-1507.

Bee, P., Bower, P., Byford, S., Churchill, R., Calam, R., Stallard, P., Pryjmachuk, S., Berzins, K., Cary, M., Wan, M., and Abel, K. (2014). The clinical effectiveness, cost-effectiveness and acceptability of community-based interventions aimed at improving or maintaining quality of life in children of parents with serious mental illness: A systematic review. *Health Technology Assessment, 18*(8), 1-250.

Beeber, L.S., Schwartz, T.A., Holditch-Davis, D., Canuso, R., Lewis, V., and Hall, H.W. (2013). Parenting enhancement, interpersonal psychotherapy to reduce depression in low-income mothers of infants and toddlers: A randomized trial. *Nursing Research, 62*(2), 82-90.

Beeber, L.S., Schwartz, T.A., Martinez, M.I., Holditch-Davis, D., Bledsoe, S.E., Canuso, R., and Lewis, V.S. (2014). Depressive symptoms and compromised parenting in low-income mothers of infants and toddlers: Distal and proximal risks. *Research in Nursing & Health, 37*(4), 276-291.

Beeghly, M., and Tronick, E.Z. (1994). Effects of prenatal exposure to cocaine in early infancy: Toxic effects on the process of mutual regulation. *Infant Mental Health Journal, 15*(2), 158-175.

Benn, R., Akiva, T., Arel, S., and Roeser, R.W. (2012). Mindfulness training effects for parents and educators of children with special needs. *Developmental Psychology, 48*(5), 1476-1487.

Benson, M.L., Fox, G.L., DeMaris, A., and Van Wyk, J. (2003). Neighborhood disadvantage, individual economic distress and violence against women in intimate relationships. *Journal of Quantitative Criminology, 19*(3), 207-235.

Berger, L.M., Slack, K.S., Waldfogel, J., and Bruch, S.K. (2010). Caseworker-perceived caregiver substance abuse and child protective services outcomes. *Child Maltreatment, 15*(3), 199-210.

Berkovits, M.D., O'Brien, K.A., Carter, C.G., and Eyberg, S.M. (2010). Early identification and intervention for behavior problems in primary care: A comparison of two abbreviated versions of parent-child interaction therapy. *Behavior Therapy, 41*(3), 375-387.

Berlin, L.J., Shanahan, M., and Appleyard Carmody, K. (2014). Promoting supportive parenting in new mothers with substance-use problems: A pilot randomized trial of residential treatment plus an attachment-based parenting program. *Infant Mental Health Journal, 35*(1), 81-85.

Bernard, K., Dozier, M., Bick, J., Lewis-Morrarty, E., Lindhiem, O., and Carlson, E. (2012). Enhancing attachment organization among maltreated children: Results of a randomized clinical trial. *Child Development, 83*(2), 623-636.

Black, M.C., Basile, K.C., Breiding, M.J., Smith, S.G., Walters, M.L., Merrick, M.T., and Stevens, M. (2011). *National Intimate Partner and Sexual Violence Survey: 2010 Summary Report.* Atlanta, GA: Centers for Disease Control and Prevention.

Blegen, N.E., Hummelvoll, J.K., and Severinsson, E. (2010). Mothers with mental health problems: A systematic review. *Nursing & Health Sciences, 12*(4), 519-528.

Boden, J.M., Fergusson, D.M., and John Horwood, L. (2008). Early motherhood and subsequent life outcomes. *Journal of Child Psychology and Psychiatry, 49*(2), 151-160.

Boggs, S.R., Eyberg, S.M., Edwards, D.L., Rayfield, A., Jacobs, J., Bagner, D., and Hood, K.K. (2005). Outcomes of parent-child interaction therapy: A comparison of treatment completers and study dropouts one to three years later. *Child & Family Behavior Therapy, 26*(4), 1-22.

Borba, C.P.C., DePadilla, L., McCarty, F.A., von Esenwein, S.A., Druss, B.G., and Sterk, C.E. (2012). A qualitative study examining the perceived barriers and facilitators to medical healthcare services among women with a serious mental illness. *Women's Health Issues, 22*(2), e217-e224.

Bouris, A., Guilamo-Ramos, V., Cherry, K., Dittus, P., Michael, S., and Gloppen, K. (2012). Preventing rapid repeat births among Latina adolescents: The role of parents. *American Journal of Public Health, 102*(10), 1842-1847.

Boyle, C.A., Boulet, S., Schieve, L.A., Cohen, R.A., Blumberg, S.J., Yeargin-Allsopp, M., Visser, S., and Kogan, M.D. (2011). Trends in the prevalence of developmental disabilities in U.S. children, 1997-2008. *Pediatrics, 127*(6), 1034-1042.

Bromberg, S.R., Backman, T.L., Krow, J., and Frankel, K.A. (2010). The Haven Mother's House Modified Therapeutic Community: Meeting the gap in infant mental health services for pregnant and parenting mothers with drug addiction. *Infant Mental Health Journal, 31*(3), 255-276.

Brook, J., Akin, B.A., Lloyd, M.H., and Yan, Y. (2015). Family drug court, targeted parent training and family reunification: Did this enhanced service strategy make a difference? *Juvenile and Family Court Journal, 66*(2), 35-52.

Brooks-Gunn, J., Klebanov, P.K., and Liaw, F.-R. (1995). The learning, physical, and emotional environment of the home in the context of poverty: The Infant Health and Development Program. *Children and Youth Services Review, 17*(1), 251-276.

Brotman, L.M., Klein, R.G., Kamboukos, D., Brown, E.J., Coard, S.I., and Sosinsky, L.S. (2003). Preventive intervention for urban, low-income preschoolers at familial risk for conduct problems: A randomized pilot study. *Journal of Clinical Child and Adolescent Psychology, 32*(2), 246-257.

Brown, E. (2007). Women in the middle: The intersection of domestic violence and the child welfare system. *Columbia University Journal of Student Social Work, 5*(1), 21-29.

Browne, J.V., and Talmi, A. (2005). Family-based intervention to enhance infant-parent relationships in the neonatal intensive care unit. *Journal of Pediatric Psychology, 30*(8), 667-677.

Bruns, E.J., Pullmann, M.D., Weathers, E.S., Wirschem, M.L., and Murphy, J.K. (2012). Effects of a multidisciplinary family treatment drug court on child and family outcomes: Results of a quasi-experimental study. *Child Maltreatment, 17*(3), 218-230.

Burns, B.J., Phillips, S.D., Wagner, H.R., Barth, R.P., Kolko, D.J., Campbell, Y., and Landsverk, J. (2004). Mental health need and access to mental health services by youths involved with child welfare: A national survey. *Journal of the American Academy of Child and Adolescent Psychiatry, 43*(8), 960-970.

Byatt, N., Biebel, K., Friedman, L., Debordes-Jackson, G., Ziedonis, D., and Pbert, L. (2013). Patient's views on depression care in obstetric settings: How do they compare to the views of perinatal health care professionals? *General Hospital Psychiatry, 35*(6), 598-604.

Camp, J.M., and Finkelstein, N. (1997). Parenting training for women in residential substance abuse treatment. Results of a demonstration project. *Journal of Substance Abuse Treatment, 14*(5), 411-422.

Carrell, S.E., and Hoekstra, M.L. (2010). Externalities in the classroom: How children exposed to domestic violence affect everyone's kids. *American Economic Journal: Applied Economics, 2*(1), 211-228.

Casanueva, C., Dozier, M., Tueller, S., Jones Harden, B., Dolan, M., and Smith, K. (2012). *Instability and Early Life Changes among Children in the Child Welfare System.* No. 18. Washington, DC: Office of Planning, Research and Evaluation; Administration for Children and Families; U.S. Department of Health and Human Services.

Casanueva, C., Tueller, S., Smith, K., Dolan, M., and Ringeisen, H. (2014). *NSCAW II Wave 3 Tables.* OPRE Report No. 2013-43. Washington, DC: Office of Planning, Research and Evaluation; Administration for Children and Families; U.S. Department of Health and Human Services.

Catalano, S., Smith, E., Snyder, H., and Rand, M. (2009). *Female Victims of Violence.* Washington, DC: U.S. Department of Justice, Bureau of Justice Statistics.

Centers for Disease Control and Prevention. (n.d.). *Facts about Intellectual Disability.* Available: http://www.cdc.gov/ncbddd/actearly/pdf/parents_pdfs/IntellectualDisability.pdf [October 2016].

California Evidence-Based Clearinghouse. (2016a). *Adolescent Parenting Program (APP).* Available: http://www.cebc4cw.org/program/adolescent-parenting-program-app [March 2016].

California Evidence-Based Clearinghouse. (2016b). *Adult-Focused Family Behavior Therapy (Adult-Focused FBT).* Available: http://www.cebc4cw.org/program/adult-focused-family-behavior-therapy [March 2016].

California Evidence-Based Clearinghouse. (2016c). *Attachment and Biobehavioral Catch-up (ABC).* Available: http://www.cebc4cw.org/program/attachment-and-biobehavioral-catch-up [March 2016].

California Evidence-Based Clearinghouse. (2016d). *Computer-Assisted Motivational Intervention (CAMI).* Available: http://www.cebc4cw.org/program/computer-assisted-motivational-intervention [March 2016].

California Evidence-Based Clearinghouse. (2016e). *Family Connections (FC).* Available: http://www.cebc4cw.org/program/family-connections [March 2016].

California Evidence-Based Clearinghouse. (2016f). *The Family Growth Center (FGC).* Available: http://www.cebc4cw.org/program/the-family-growth-center-fgc [March 2016].

California Evidence-Based Clearinghouse. (2016g). *The Incredible Years (IY).* Available: http://www.cebc4cw.org/program/the-incredible-years [March 2016].

California Evidence-Based Clearinghouse. (2016h). *KEEP (Keeping Foster and Kin Parents Supported and Trained).* Available: http://www.cebc4cw.org/program/keeping-foster-and-kin-parents-supported-and-trained [March 2016].

California Evidence-Based Clearinghouse. (2016i). *Multisystemic Therapy for Child Abuse and Neglect (MST-CAN).* Available: http://www.cebc4cw.org/program/multisystemic-therapy-for-child-abuse-and-neglect [March 2016].

California Evidence-Based Clearinghouse. (2016j). *Nurturing Parenting Program for Parents and Their School-age Children 5 to 12 Years.* Available: http://www.cebc4cw.org/program/nurturing-parenting-program-for-parents-and-their-school-age-children-5-to-12-years [March 2016].

California Evidence-Based Clearinghouse. (2016k). *Parent-Child Interaction Therapy (PCIT).* Available: http://www.cebc4cw.org/program/parent-child-interaction-therapy [March 2016].

California Evidence-Based Clearinghouse. (2016l). *SafeCare®*. Available: http://www.cebc4cw. org/program/safecare [March 2016].

California Evidence-Based Clearinghouse. (2016m). *Treatment Foster Care Oregon for Pre-schoolers (TFCO-P)*. Available: http://www.cebc4cw.org/program/treatment-foster-care-oregon-for-preschoolers [March 2016].

California Evidence-Based Clearinghouse. (2016n). *Triple P—Positive Parenting Program® System (System Triple P)*. Available: http://www.cebc4cw.org/program/triple-p-positive-parenting-program-system [March 2016].

Center for Behavioral Health Statistics and Quality. (2015). *Behavioral Health Trends in the United States: Results from the 2014 National Survey on Drug Use and Health*. HHS Publication No. SMA 15-4927, NSDUH Series H-50. Rockville, MD: Substance Abuse and Mental Health Services Administration.

The Center for Community Partnerships in Child Welfare. (2006). *Families with Repeat Involvement with Child Welfare Systems: The Current Knowledge Base and Needed Next Steps*. New York: The Center for Community Partnerships in Child Welfare of the Center for the Study of Social Policy.

Chaffin, M., Silovsky, J.F., Funderburk, B., Valle, L.A., Brestan, E.V., Balachova, T., Jackson, S., Lensgraf, J., and Bonner, B.L. (2004). Parent-child interaction therapy with physically abusive parents: Efficacy for reducing future abuse reports. *Journal of Consulting and Clinical Psychology, 72*(3), 500-510.

Chaffin, M., Funderburk, B., Bard, D., Valle, L.A., and Gurwitch, R. (2011). A combined motivation and parent-child interaction therapy package reduces child welfare recidivism in a randomized dismantling field trial. *Journal of Consulting and Clinical Psychology, 79*(1), 84-95.

Chaffin, M., Hecht, D., Bard, D., Silovsky, J.F., and Beasley, W.H. (2012). A statewide trial of the SafeCare home-based services model with parents in child protective services. *Pediatrics, 129*(3), 509-515.

Chamberlain, P., Price, J., Reid, J. B., and Landsverk, J. (2008). Cascading implementation of a foster and kinship parent intervention. *Child Welfare, 87*(5), 27-48.

Chamberlain, P. (2014). *Comprehensive Review of Interventions for Children Exposed to Domestic Violence*. San Francisco, CA: Futures Without Violence.

Chamberlain, P., and Fisher, P.A. (2003). An application of multidimensional treatment foster care for early intervention. In P. Chamberlain (Ed.), *Treating Chronic Juvenile Offenders: Advances Made through the Oregon Multidimensional Treatment Foster Care Model* (pp. 129-140). Washington, DC: American Psychological Association.

Chavis, A., Hudnut-Beumler, J., Webb, M.W., Neely, J.A., Bickman, L., Dietrich, M.S., and Scholer, S.J. (2013). A brief intervention affects parents' attitudes toward using less physical punishment. *Child Abuse and Neglect, 37*(12), 1192-1201.

Chen, X.K., Wen, S.W., Fleming, N., Yang, Q., and Walker, M.C. (2007). Teenage pregnancy and congenital anomalies: Which system is vulnerable? *Human Reproduction, 22*(6), 1730-1735.

Child Welfare Information Gateway. (2014). *Parental Substance Use and the Child Welfare System*. Available: https://www.childwelfare.gov/pubPDFs/parentalsubabuse.pdf [January 2016].

Chorpita, B.F., Daleiden, E.L., and Weisz, J.R. (2005). Identifying and selecting the common elements of evidence based interventions: A distillation and matching model. *Mental Health Services Research, 7*(1), 5-20.

Clark, H.W. (2001). Residential substance abuse treatment for pregnant and postpartum women and their children: Treatment and policy implications. *Child Welfare, 80*(2), 179-198.

Cohen, J.A., and Mannarino, A.P. (1996). A treatment outcome study for sexually abused preschool children: Initial findings. *Journal of the American Academy of Child and Adolescent Psychiatry, 35*(1), 42-50.

Collins, K.S., Strieder, F.H., DePanfilis, D., Tabor, M., Freeman, P.A., Linde, L., and Greenberg, P. (2011). Trauma adapted family connections: Reducing developmental and complex trauma symptomatology to prevent child abuse and neglect. *Child Welfare, 90*(6), 29-47.

Collins, K.S., Freeman, P.A.C., Strieder, F.H., Reinicker, P., and Baldwin, C. (2015). A pilot study examining the reduction of trauma symptomatology in families to prevent child abuse and neglect: Trauma adapted family connections. *Journal of Public Child Welfare, 9*(5), 506-527.

Comer, J.S., Puliafico, A.C., Aschenbrand, S.G., McKnight, K., Robin, J.A., Goldfine, M.E., and Albano, A.M. (2012). A pilot feasibility evaluation of the CALM Program for anxiety disorders in early childhood. *Journal of Anxiety Disorders, 26*(1), 40-49.

Conger, R., Cui, M., and Lorenz, F. (2011). Intergenerational continuities in economic pressure and couple conflict in romantic relationships. In F. Fincham and M. Cui (Eds.), *Romantic Relationships in Emerging Adulthood* (pp. 101-122). New York: Cambridge University Press.

Conners, N.A., Bradley, R.H., Whiteside-Mansell, L., and Crone, C.C. (2001). A comprehensive substance abuse treatment program for women and their children: An initial evaluation. *Journal of Substance Abuse Treatment, 21*(2), 67-75.

Conroy, K., Engelhart, T., Arandia, P., and Forbes, P. (2013). Relationship between rapid repeat pregnancy and depression in low-income, minority teen mothers. *Journal of Adolescent Health, 52*(2 Suppl. 1), S109.

Cook, J.A., and Mueser, K.T. (2014). Improving services for parents with psychiatric disabilities: Three new opportunities in the field of psychiatric rehabilitation. *Psychiatric Rehabilitation Journal, 37*(1), 1-3.

Coren, E., Thomae, M., and Hutchfield, J. (2011). Parenting training for intellectually disabled parents: A Cochrane Systematic Review. *Research on Social Work Practice, 21*(4), 432-441.

Cowan, P.A., Cowan, C.P., Pruett, M.K., Pruett, K., and Gillette, P. (2014). Evaluating a couples group to enhance father involvement in low-income families using a benchmark comparison. *Family Relations, 63*(3), 356-370.

Craig, E.A. (2004). Parenting programs for women with mental illness who have young children: A review. *Australian & New Zealand Journal of Psychiatry, 38*(11-12), 923-928.

Crain-Thoreson, C., and Dale, P.S. (1999). Enhancing linguistic performance: Parents and teachers as book reading partners for children with language delays. *Topics in Early Childhood Special Education, 19*(1), 28-39.

Crean, H.F., Hightower, A.D., and Allan, M.J. (2001). School-based child care for children of teen parents: Evaluation of an urban program designed to keep young mothers in school. *Evaluation and Program Planning, 24*(3), 267-275.

Cress, C.J., Moskal, L., and Hoffmann, A. (2008). Parent directiveness in free play with young children with physical impairments. *Communication Disorders Quarterly, 29*(2), 99-108.

Cummings, E.M., and Davies, P.T. (2011). *Marital Conflict and Children: An Emotional Security Perspective.* New York: Guilford Press.

Dahinten, V.S., Shapka, J.D., and Willms, J.D. (2007). Adolescent children of adolescent mothers: The impact of family functioning on trajectories of development. *Journal of Youth and Adolescence, 36*(2), 195-212.

Dale, P.S., Crain-Thoreson, C., Notari-Syverson, A., and Cole, K. (1996). Parent-child book reading as an intervention technique for young children with language delays. *Topics in Early Childhood Special Education, 16*(2), 213-235.

d'Arlach, L., Olson, B.D., Jason, L.A., and Ferrari, J.R. (2006). Children, women, and substance abuse: A look at recovery in a communal setting. *Journal of Prevention & Intervention in the Community, 31*(1-2), 121-131.

Davies, P., and Cummings, E. (2006). Interparental discord, family process, and developmental psychopathology. In D. Cicchetti and D.J. Cohen (Eds.), *Developmental Psychopathology* (vol. 3, pp. 86-128). New York: Wiley & Sons.

Dawson, G., Rogers, S., Munson, J., Smith, M., Winter, J., Greenson, J., Donaldson, A., and Varley, J. (2010). Randomized, controlled trial of an intervention for toddlers with autism: The Early Start Denver Model. *Pediatrics, 125*(1), e17-e23.

Dawson, G., Jones, E.J., Merkle, K., Venema, K., Lowy, R., Faja, S., Kamara, D., Murias, M., Greenson, J., Winter, J., Smith, M., Rogers, S.J., and Webb, S.J. (2012). Early behavioral intervention is associated with normalized brain activity in young children with autism. *Journal of the American Academy of Child and Adolescent Psychiatry, 51*(11), 1150-1159.

Dean, K., Mortensen, P.B., Stevens, H., Murray, R.M., Walsh, E., and Agerbo, E. (2012). Criminal conviction among offspring with parental history of mental disorder. *Psychological Medicine, 42*(3), 571-581.

Deblinger, E., Stauffer, L.B., and Steer, R.A. (2001). Comparative efficacies of supportive and cognitive behavioral group therapies for young children who have been sexually abused and their nonoffending mothers. *Child Maltreatment, 6*(4), 332-343.

Dekker, M.C., Ferdinand, R.F., van Lang, N.D., Bongers, I.L., van der Ende, J., and Verhulst, F.C. (2007). Developmental trajectories of depressive symptoms from early childhood to late adolescence: Gender differences and adult outcome. *Journal of Child Psychology and Psychiatry, 48*(7), 657-666.

Dennis, C.L. (2014). Psychosocial interventions for the treatment of perinatal depression. *Best Practice & Research. Clinical Obstetrics & Gynaecology, 28*(1), 97-111.

DePanfilis, D., Dubowitz, H., and Kunz, J. (2008). Assessing the cost-effectiveness of family connections. *Child Abuse and Neglect, 32*(3), 335-351.

Dolan, M., Smith, K., Casanueva, C., and Ringeisen, H. (2011). *NSCAW II Baseline Report: Caseworker Characteristics, Child Welfare Services, and Experiences of Children Placed in Out-of-Home Care.* OPRE Report No. 2011-27E. Washington, DC: Office of Planning, Research and Evaluation; Administration for Children and Families; U.S. Department of Health and Human Services.

Dolan, M., Smith, K., Casanueva, C., and Ringeisen, H. (2012). *NSCAW II Wave 2 Report: Child and Caregiver Need and Receipt of Child Welfare Services Post-Baseline.* Washington, DC: Office of Planning, Research and Evaluation; Administration for Children and Families; U.S. Department of Health and Human Services.

Dolman, C., Jones, I., and Howard, L.M. (2013). Pre-conception to parenting: A systematic review and meta-synthesis of the qualitative literature on motherhood for women with severe mental illness. *Archives of Women's Mental Health, 16*(3), 173-196.

Donohue, B., Azrin, N.H., Bradshaw, K., Van Hasselt, V.B., Cross, C.L., Urgelles, J., Romero, V., Hill, H.H., and Allen, D.N. (2014). A controlled evaluation of family behavior therapy in concurrent child neglect and drug abuse. *Journal of Consulting and Clinical Psychology, 82*(4), 706-720.

Drake, B., and Jonson-Reid, M. (1999a). Some thoughts on the increasing use of administrative data in child maltreatment research. *Child Maltreatment, 4*(4), 308-315.

Drake, B., and Jonson-Reid, M. (1999b). *Substantiated and Unsubstantiated Cases: Patterns and Predictors of Recurrence. Year 2 Progress and Preliminary Findings.* Paper presented at the Children's Bureau Child Abuse and Neglect Discretionary Grants Meeting, Washington, DC.

Dunlap, G., and Fox, L. (2009). Positive behavior support and early intervention. In W. Sailor, G. Dunlap, G. Sugai, and R. Horner (Eds.), *Handbook of Positive Behavior Support* (pp. 49-71). New York: Springer.

Dunst, C.J., and Espe-Sherwindt, M. (2016). Family-centered practices in early intervention. In B. Reichow, B. Boyd, E. Barton, and S. Odom (Eds.), *Handbook of Early Childhood Special Education*. New York: Springer.

Dunst, C.J., and Trivette, C.M. (2010). Family-centered helpgiving practices, parent-professional partnerships, and parent, family and child outcomes. In S.L. Christenson and A.L. Reschley (Eds.), *Handbook of School-Family Partnerships* (pp. 362-379). New York: Routledge.

Durand, V.M., Hieneman, M., Clarke, S., Wang, M., and Rinaldi, M.L. (2013). Positive family intervention for severe challenging behavior I: A multisite randomized clinical trial. *Journal of Positive Behavior Interventions, 15*(3), 133-143.

Eckenrode, J., Ganzel, B., Henderson, C.R., Jr., Smith, E., Olds, D.L., Powers, J., Cole, R., Kitzman, H., and Sidora, K. (2000). Preventing child abuse and neglect with a program of nurse home visitation: The limiting effects of domestic violence. *Journal of the American Medical Association, 284*(11), 1385-1391.

Edleson, J.L. (1999). Children's witnessing of adult domestic violence. *Journal of Interpersonal Violence, 14*(8), 839-870.

Elliott, J.C., Lubin, D.A., Walker, C.H., and Johns, J.M. (2001). Acute cocaine alters oxytocin levels in the medial preoptic area and amygdala in lactating rat dams: Implications for cocaine-induced changes in maternal behavior and maternal aggression. *Neuropeptides, 35*(2), 127-134.

Eyberg, S.M., and Boggs, S.R. (1998). Parent-child interaction therapy: A psychosocial intervention for the treatment of young conduct-disordered children. In C.E. Schaefer and J.M. Briesmeister (Eds.), *Handbook of Parent Training: Parents as Co-therapists for Children's Behavior Problems* (2nd ed., pp. 61-97). New York: Wiley.

Fabiano, G.A., Chacko, A., Pelham, W.E., Jr., Robb, J., Walker, K.S., Wymbs, F., Sastry, A.L., Flammer, L., Keenan, J.K., Visweswaraiah, H., Shulman, S., Herbst, L., and Pirvics, L. (2009). A comparison of behavioral parent training programs for fathers of children with attention-deficit/hyperactivity disorder. *Behavior Therapy, 40*(2), 190-204.

Fals-Stewart, W., Klostermann, K., Yates, B.T., O'Farrell, T.J., and Birchler, G.R. (2005). Brief relationship therapy for alcoholism: A randomized clinical trial examining clinical efficacy and cost-effectiveness. *Psychology of Addictive Behaviors, 19*(4), 363-371.

Fals-Stewart, W., Klostermann, K., and Clinton-Sherrod, M. (2009). Substance abuse and intimate partner violence. In K.D. O'Leary and E.M. Woodin (Eds.), *Psychological and Physical Aggression in Couples: Causes and Interventions* (pp. 251-269). Washington, DC: American Psychological Association.

Feder, L., and Wilson, D. (2005). A meta-analytic review of court-mandated batterer intervention programs: Can courts affect abusers' behavior? *Journal of Experimental Criminology, 1*, 239-262.

Feinberg, E., Augustyn, M., Fitzgerald, E., Sandler, J., Ferreira-Cesar Suarez, Z., Chen, N., Cabral, H., Beardslee, W., and Silverstein, M. (2014). Improving maternal mental health after a child's diagnosis of autism spectrum disorder: Results from a randomized clinical trial. *Journal of the American Medical Association Pediatrics, 168*(1), 40-46.

Feldman, M.A. (1994). Parenting education for parents with intellectual disabilities: A review of outcome studies. *Research in Developmental Disabilities, 15*(4), 299-332.

Feldman, M.A., and Werner, S.E. (2002). Collateral effects of behavioral parent training on families of children with developmental disabilities and behavior disorders. *Behavioral Interventions, 17*(2), 75-83.

Feldman, M.A., Case, L., and Sparks, B. (1992). Effectiveness of a child-care training program for parents at-risk for child neglect. *Canadian Journal of Behavioural Science, 24*(1), 14.

Finkelhor, D., Turner, H., Ormrod, R., Hamby, S., and Kracke, K. (2009). Children's exposure to violence: A comprehensive national survey. *Juvenile Justice Bulletin* (October). Available: https://www.ncjrs.gov/pdffiles1/ojjdp/227744.pdf [March 2016].

Finkelhor, S., Turner, H.., Shattuck, A., Hamby, S., and Kracke, K. (2015). Children's exposure to violence, crime, and abuse: An update. *Juvenile Justice Bulletin* (September). Available: http://www.ojjdp.gov/pubs/248547.pdf [March 2016].

Finkelstein, N. (1994). Treatment issues for alcohol- and drug-dependent pregnant and parenting women. *Health and Social Work, 19*(1), 7-15.

Finkelstein, N. (1996). Using the relational model as a context for treating pregnant and parenting chemically dependent women. *Journal of Chemical Dependency Treatment, 6*(1-2), 23-44.

Fisher, P.A., Ellis, B.H., and Chamberlain, P. (1999). Early intervention foster care: A model for preventing risk in young children who have been maltreated. *Children's Services, 2*(3), 159-182.

Fisher, P.A., Burraston, B., and Pears, K. (2005). The Early Intervention Foster Care Program: Permanent placement from a randomized trial. *Child Maltreatment, 10*(1), 61-71.

Fisher, P.A., Gunnar, M., Dozier, M., Bruce, J., and Pears, K. (2006). Effects of therapeutic interventions for foster children on behavioral problems, caregiver attachment, and stress regulatory neural systems. *Annals of the New York Academy of Sciences, 1094,* 215-225.

Fisher, P.A., Kim, H.K., and Pears, K.C. (2009). Effects of Multidimensional Treatment Foster Care for Preschoolers (MTFC-P) on reducing permanent failures among children with placement instability. *Child and Youth Services Review, 31,* 541-546.

Fisher, P.A., Stoolmiller, M., Mannering, A.M., Takahashi, A., and Chamberlain, P. (2011a). Foster placement disruptions associated with problem behavior: Mitigating a threshold effect. *Journal of Consulting and Clinical Psychology, 79*(4), 481-487.

Fisher, P.A., Lester, B.M., DeGarmo, D.S., LaGasse, L.L., Lin, H., Shankaran, S., Bada, H.S., Bauer, C.R., Hammond, J., Whitaker, T., and Higgins, R. (2011b). The combined effects of prenatal drug exposure and early adversity on neurobehavioral disinhibition in childhood and adolescence. *Development and Psychopathology, 23*(3), 777-788.

Fletcher, R.J., Maharaj, O.N., Fletcher Watson, C.H., May, C., Skeates, N., and Gruenert, S. (2013). Fathers with mental illness: Implications for clinicians and health services. *The Medical Journal of Australia, 199*(Suppl. 3), S34-S36.

Fonagy, P., Bateman, A.W., and Luyten, P. (2012). Introduction and overview. In A.W. Bateman and P. Fonagy (Eds.), *Handbook of Mentalizing in Mental Health Practice* (pp. 3-42). Washington, DC: American Psychiatric Association.

Forman, D.R., O'Hara, M.W., Stuart, S., Gorman, L.K., Larsen, K.E., and Coy, K.C. (2007). Effective treatment for postpartum depression is not sufficient to improve the developing mother-child relationship. *Development and Psychopathology, 19*(2), 585-602.

Friesen, B.J., Nicholson, J., Kaplan, K., and Solomon, P. (2009). Parents with a mental illness and implementation of the Adoption and Safe Families Act. In O. Golden and J. Macomber (Eds.), *Intentions and Results: A Look Back at the Adoption and Safe Families Act* (pp. 102-114). Washington, DC: Urban Institute, Center for the Study of Social Policy.

Fung, M.P., and Fox, R.A. (2014). The culturally-adapted early pathways program for young Latino children in poverty: A randomized controlled trial. *Journal of Latina/o Psychology, 2*(3), 131-145.

Futures Without Violence. (2010). *Realizing the Promise of Home Visitations: Addressing Domestic Violence and Child Maltreatment.* San Francisco, CA: Family Violence Prevention Fund.

Gearing, R.E., Alonzo, D., and Marinelli, C. (2012). Maternal schizophrenia: Psychosocial treatment for mothers and their children. *Clinical Schizophrenia & Related Psychoses,* 6(1), 27-33.

Geeraert, L., Van den Noortgate, W., Grietens, H., and Onghena, P. (2004). The effects of early prevention programs for families with young children at risk for physical child abuse and neglect: A meta-analysis. *Child Maltreatment, 9*(3), 277-291.

Geffner, R., Igelman, R.S., and Zellner, J. (2014). *The Effects of Intimate Partner Violence on Children.* New York: Routledge.

Gershater-Molko, R.M., Lutzker, J.R., and Wesch, D. (2002). Using recidivism data to evaluate Project SafeCare: Teaching bonding, safety, and health care skills to parents. *Child Maltreatment, 7*(3), 277-285.

Gershater-Molko, R.M., Lutzker, J.R., and Wesch, D. (2003). Project SafeCare: Improving health, safety, and parenting skills in families reported for, and at-risk for child maltreatment. *Journal of Family Violence, 18*(6), 377-386.

Girolametto, L., Weitzman, E., and Clements-Baartman, J. (1998). Vocabulary intervention for children with Down syndrome: Parent training using focused stimulation. *Infant-Toddler Intervention: The Transdisciplinary Journal, 8*(2), 109-125.

Glazemakers, I., and Deboutte, D. (2013). Modifying the "Positive Parenting Program" for parents with intellectual disabilities. *Journal of Intellectual Disability Research, 57*(7), 616-626.

Goodmark, L. (2012). *A Troubled Marriage: Domestic Violence and the Legal System.* New York and London: New York University Press.

Gottman, J., Gottman, J., and Shapiro, A. (2010). A new couples approach to interventions for the transition to parenthood. In M.S. Schulz, M.K. Pruett, P.K. Kerig, and R.D. Parke (Eds.), *Strengthening Couple Relationships for Optimal Child Development: Lessons from Research and Intervention* (pp. 165-179). Washington, DC: American Psychological Association.

Grant, T.M., and Ernst, C.C. (2014). *Report to the Division of Behavioral Health and Recovery for Washington State PCAP Sites as of June 30, 2014. Fetal Alcohol and Drug Unit, Alcohol and Drug Abuse Institute.* Seattle: University of Washington Health Sciences Administration.

Grant, T.M., Ernst, C.C., Streissguth, A., and Stark, K. (2005). Preventing alcohol and drug exposed births in Washington state: Intervention findings from three parent-child assistance program sites. *The American Journal of Drug and Alcohol Abuse, 31*(3), 471-490.

Gray, B., Robinson, C., and Seddon, D. (2008). Invisible children: Young carers of parents with mental health problems—The perspectives of professionals. *Child and Adolescent Mental Health, 13*(4), 169-172.

Green, J., Charman, T., McConachie, H., Aldred, C., Slonims, V., Howlin, P., Le Couteur, A., Leadbitter, K., Hudry, K., Byford, S., Barrett, B., Temple, K., Macdonald, W., and Pickles, A. (2010). Parent-mediated communication-focused treatment in children with autism (PACT): A randomised controlled trial. *Lancet, 375*(9732), 2152-2160.

Greeno, J.E., Uretsky, M.C., Lee, B.R., Moore, J.E., Barth, R.P., and Shaw, T.V. (2016). Replication of the KEEP foster and kinship parent training program in a population of youth with externalizing behavior problems. *Children and Youth Services Review, 61*(Issue C), 75-82.

Grella, C.E., Joshi, V., and Hser, Y.I. (2000). Program variation in treatment outcomes among women in residential drug treatment. *Evaluation Review, 24*(4), 364-383.

Gruber, K.J. (2012). A comparative assessment of early adult life status of graduates of the North Carolina Adolescent Parenting Program. *Journal of Child and Adolescent Psychiatric Nursing, 25*(2), 75-83.

Guastaferro, K.M. (2011). *Teaching Young Mothers to Identify Developmental Milestones.* Thesis, Georgia State University, Atlanta, GA.

Hamilton, B.E., Martin, J.A., Osterman, M.J., and Curtin, S.C. (2015). Births: Final data for 2014. *National Vital Statistics Reports, 64*(12).

Harris, S.E., Fox, R.A., and Love, J.R. (2015). Early pathways therapy for young children in poverty: A randomized controlled trial. *Counseling Outcome Research and Evaluation, 6*(1), 3-17.

Hastings, R.P. (2002). Parental stress and behaviour problems of children with developmental disability. *Journal of Intellectual and Developmental Disability, 27*(3), 149-160.

Healy, S., Lewin, J., Butler, S., Vaillancourt, K., and Seth-Smith, F. (2015). Affect recognition and the quality of mother-infant interaction: Understanding parenting difficulties in mothers with schizophrenia. *Archives of Women's Mental Health, 19*(1), 113-124.

Heidari, H., Hasanpour, M., and Fooladi, M. (2013). The experiences of parents with infants in neonatal intensive care unit. *Iranian Journal of Nursing and Midwifery Research, 18*(3), 208-213.

Henderson, C., Evans-Lacko, S., and Thornicroft, G. (2013). Mental illness stigma, help seeking, and public health programs. *American Journal of Public Health, 103*(5), 777-780.

Herrera, V.M., and McCloskey, L.A. (2001). Gender differences in the risk for delinquency among youth exposed to family violence. *Child Abuse and Neglect, 25*(8), 1037-1051.

Hinden, B.R., Biebel, K., Nicholson, J., Henry, A., and Katz-Leavy, J. (2006). A survey of programs for parents with mental illness and their families: Identifying common elements to build the evidence base. *Journal of Behavioral Health Services & Research, 33*(1), 21-38.

Hirshfeld-Becker, D.R., Masek, B., Henin, A., Blakely, L.R., Pollock-Wurman, R.A., McQuade, J., DePetrillo, L., Briesch, J., Ollendick, T.H., Rosenbaum, J.F., and Biederman, J. (2010). Cognitive behavioral therapy for 4- to 7-year-old children with anxiety disorders: A randomized clinical trial. *Journal of Consulting and Clinical Psychology, 78*(4), 498-510.

Hoath, F.E., and Sanders, M.R. (2002). A feasibility study of enhanced group Triple P—Positive Parenting Program for parents of children with attention-deficit/hyperactivity disorder. *Behaviour Change, 19*(4), 191-206.

Hodgkinson, S.C., Colantuoni, E., Roberts, D., Berg-Cross, L., and Belcher, H.M.E. (2010). Depressive symptoms and birth outcomes among pregnant teenagers. *Journal of Pediatric and Adolescent Gynecology, 23*(1), 16-22.

Hodgkinson, S.C., Beers, L., Southammakosane, C., and Lewin, A. (2014). Addressing the mental health needs of pregnant and parenting adolescents. *Pediatrics, 133*(1), 114-122.

Hodnett, R.H., Faulk, K., Dellinger, A., and Maher, E. (2009). *Evaluation of the Statewide Implementation of a Parent Education Program in Louisiana's Child Welfare Agency: The Nurturing Parenting Program for Infants, Toddlers, and Pre-School Children.* Final Evaluation Report. Available: http://nurturingparenting.com/images/cmsfiles/nurturingparentprogram_exsum_fin_lo.pdf [March 2016].

Hoffman, S.D., and Maynard, R.A. (2008). *Kids Having Kids: Economic Costs & Social Consequences of Teen Pregnancy.* Washington, DC: Urban Institute.

Holt, S., Buckley, H., and Whelan, S. (2008). The impact of exposure to domestic violence on children and young people: A review of the literature. *Child Abuse and Neglect, 32*(8), 797-810.

Horwitz, S.M., Landsverk, J., Hurlburt, M., and Aarons, G.A. (2009). *Strategies to Increase Readiness to Adopt Evidence-Based Parent Training Programs in Child Welfare Agencies: Preliminary Findings.* Paper presented at the Child and Adolescent Mental Health Services: Issues and Solutions Conference, September 23-24, Nashville, TN.

Hotz, V.J., McElroy, S.W., and Sanders, S.G. (2005). Teenage childbearing and its life cycle consequences: Exploiting a natural experiment. *The Journal of Human Resources, 40*(3), 683-715.

Hughes, R.C., and Wilson, P.H. (1988). Behavioral parent training: Contingency management versus communication skills training with or without the participation of the child. *Child & Family Behavior Therapy, 10*(4), 11-23.

Huxley, A., and Foulger, S. (2008). Parents who misuse substances: Implications for parenting practices and treatment seeking behaviour. *Drugs and Alcohol Today, 8*(3), 9-16.

Ingersoll, B., and Wainer, A. (2013). Initial efficacy of Project ImPACT: A parent-mediated social communication intervention for young children with ASD. *Journal of Autism and Developmental Disorders, 43*(12), 2943-2952.

Ingoldsby, E.M. (2010). Review of interventions to improve family engagement and retention in parent and child mental health programs. *Journal of Child and Family Studies, 19*(5), 629-645.

Institute of Medicine and National Research Council. (2009). *Depression in Parents, Parenting, and Children: Opportunities to Improve Identification, Treatment, and Prevention.* M.J. England and L.J. Sim (Eds.). Committee on Depression, Parenting Practices, and the Healthy Development of Children; Division of Behavioral and Social Sciences and Education. Washington, DC: The National Academies Press.

Institute of Medicine and National Research Council. (2014). *New Directions in Child Abuse and Neglect Research.* A. Petersen, J. Joseph, and M. Feit (Eds.). Committee on Child Maltreatment Research, Policy, and Practice for the Next Decade: Phase II; Board on Children, Youth, and Families. Washington, DC: The National Academies Press.

Ippen, C., Harris, W.W., Van Horn, P., and Lieberman, A.F. (2011). Traumatic and stressful events in early childhood: Can treatment help those at highest risk? *Child Abuse and Neglect, 35*(7), 504-513.

Iqbal, M.M., Sobhan, T., and Ryals, T. (2002). Effects of commonly used benzodiazepines on the fetus, the neonate, and the nursing infant. *Psychiatric Services, 53*(1), 39-49.

Jackson, V. (2004). Residential treatment for parents and their children: The village experience. *Science and Practice Perspectives, 2*(2), 44-53.

Johnson, K. (2009). *State-Based Home Visiting: Strengthening Programs through State Leadership.* New York: Columbia University, National Center for Children in Poverty.

Jose, A., and O'Leary, K.D. (2009). Prevalence of partner aggression in representative and clinic samples. In K.D. O'Leary and E.M. Woodin (Eds.), *Psychological and Physical Aggression in Couples: Causes and Interventions* (pp. 15-35). Washington, DC: American Psychological Association.

Jutte, D.P., Roos, N.P., Brownell, M.D., Briggs, G., MacWilliam, L., and Roos, L.L. (2010). The ripples of adolescent motherhood: Social, educational, and medical outcomes for children of teen and prior teen mothers. *Academic Pediatrics, 10*(5), 293-301.

Kahng, S.K., Oyserman, D., Bybee, D., and Mowbray, C. (2008). Mothers with serious mental illness: When symptoms decline does parenting improve? *Journal of Family Psychology, 22*(1), 162-166.

Kaminski, J.W., Valle, L.A., Filene, J.H., and Boyle, C.L. (2008). A meta-analytic review of components associated with parent training program effectiveness. *Journal of Abnormal Child Psychology, 36*(4), 567-589.

Kandel, I., and Merrick, J. (2003). The birth of a child with disability. Coping by parents and siblings. *The Scientific World Journal, 3*, 741-750.

Karaaslan, O., and Mahoney, G. (2013). Effectiveness of responsive teaching with children with Down syndrome. *Intellectual and Developmental Disabilities, 51*(6), 458-469.

Karaaslan, O., Diken, I.H., and Mahoney, G. (2013). A randomized control study of responsive teaching with young Turkish children and their mothers. *Topics in Early Childhood Special Education, 33*(1), 18-27.

Kasari, C., Gulsrud, A.C., Wong, C., Kwon, S., and Locke, J. (2010). Randomized controlled caregiver mediated joint engagement intervention for toddlers with autism. *Journal of Autism and Developmental Disorders, 40*(9), 1045-1056.

Kelley, M.L., and Fals-Stewart, W. (2002). Couples- versus individual-based therapy for alcohol and drug abuse: Effects on children's psychosocial functioning. *Journal of Consulting and Clinical Psychology, 70*(2), 417-427.

Keltner, B., Finn, D., and Shearer, D. (1995). Effects of family intervention on maternal-child interaction for mothers with developmental disabilities. *Family & Community Health: The Journal of Health Promotion & Maintenance, 17*(4), 35-49.

Kennedy, S.J., Rapee, R.M., and Edwards, S.L. (2009). A selective intervention program for inhibited preschool-aged children of parents with an anxiety disorder: Effects on current anxiety disorders and temperament. *Journal of the American Academy of Child & Adolescent Psychiatry, 48*(6), 602-609.

Kenny, M., Conroy, S., Pariante, C.M., Seneviratne, G., and Pawlby, S. (2013). Mother-infant interaction in mother and baby unit patients: Before and after treatment. *Journal of Psychiatric Research, 47*(9), 1192-1198.

Kerwin, M.E. (2005). Collaboration between child welfare and substance-abuse fields: Combined treatment programs for mothers. *Journal of Pediatric Psychology, 30*(7), 581-597.

Kessler, R.C., Berglund, P., Demler, O., Jin, R., Merikangas, K.R., and Walters, E.E. (2005). Lifetime prevalence and age-of-onset distributions of DSM-IV disorders in the National Comorbidity Survey Replication. *Archives of General Psychiatry, 62*(6), 593-602.

Kitzman, H., Olds, D.L., Sidora, K., Henderson, C.R., Jr., Hanks, C., Cole, R., Luckey, D.W., Bondy, J., Cole, K., and Glazner, J. (2000). Enduring effects of nurse home visitation on maternal life course: A 3-year follow-up of a randomized trial. *Journal of the American Medical Association, 283*(15), 1983-1989.

Kitzmann, K.M., Gaylord, N.K., Holt, A.R., and Kenny, E.D. (2003). Child witnesses to domestic violence: A meta-analytic review. *Journal of Consulting and Clinical Psychology, 71*(2), 339-352.

Knerr, W., Gardner, F., and Cluver, L. (2013). Improving positive parenting skills and reducing harsh and abusive parenting in low- and middle-income countries: A systematic review. *Prevention Science, 14*(4), 352-363.

Koenen, K.C., Moffitt, T.E., Caspi, A., Taylor, A., and Purcell, S. (2003). Domestic violence is associated with environmental suppression of IQ in young children. *Development and Psychopathology, 15*(2), 297-311.

Krumm, S., Becker, T., and Wiegand-Grefe, S. (2013). Mental health services for parents affected by mental illness. *Current Opinion in Psychiatry, 26*(4), 362-368.

Kumpfer, K., Greene, J., Bates, R., Cofrin, K., and Whiteside, H. (2007). *State of New Jersey DHS Division of Addiction Services Strengthening Families Program Substance Abuse Prevention Initiative: Year Three Evaluation Report.* Reporting period: July 1, 2004-June 30, 2007. Salt Lake City, UT: LutraGroup.

Labriola, M., Bradley, S., O'Sullivan, C.S., Rempel, M., and Moore, S. (2010). *A National Portrait of Domestic Violence Courts.* Report submitted to the National Institute of Justice. New York: Center for Court Innovation.

Lacey, M., Paolini, S., Hanlon, M.C., Melville, J., Galletly, C., and Campbell, L.E. (2015). Parents with serious mental illness: Differences in internalised and externalised mental illness stigma and gender stigma between mothers and fathers. *Psychiatry Research, 225*(3), 723-733.

LaTaillade, J.J., Epstein, N.B., and Werlinich, C.A. (2006). Conjoint treatment of intimate partner violence: A cognitive behavioral approach. *Journal of Cognitive Psychotherapy, 20*(4), 393-410.

Lavigne, J.V., Gibbons, R.D., Christoffel, K.K., Arend, R., Rosenbaum, D., Binns, H., Dawson, N., Sobel, H., and Isaacs, C. (1996). Prevalence rates and correlates of psychiatric disorders among preschool children. *Journal of the American Academy of Child & Adolescent Psychiatry, 35*(2), 204-214.

Lavigne, J.V., Lebailly, S.A., Gouze, K.R., Cicchetti, C., Pochyly, J., Arend, R., Jessup, B.W., and Binns, H.J. (2008). Treating oppositional defiant disorder in primary care: A comparison of three models. *Journal of Pediatric Psychology, 33*(5), 449-461.

Leathers, S.J., Spielfogel, J.E., McMeel, L.S., and Atkins, M.S. (2011). Use of a parent management training intervention with urban foster parents: A pilot study. *Children and Youth Services Review, 33*(7), 1270-1279.

Lehner-Dua, L.L. (2001). *The Effectiveness of Russell A. Barkley's Parent Training Program on Parents with School-Aged Children Who Have ADHD on Their Perceived Severity of ADHD, Stress, and Sense of Competence* Ph.D. Dissertation, Hofstra University, Hempstead, NY.

Leung, D.W., and Slep, A.M. (2006). Predicting inept discipline: The role of parental depressive symptoms, anger, and attributions. *Journal of Consulting and Clinical Psychology, 74*(3), 524-534.

Lieberman, A.F., Van Horn, P., and Ippen, C.G. (2005). Toward evidence-based treatment: Child-parent psychotherapy with preschoolers exposed to marital violence. *Journal of the American Academy of Child & Adolescent Psychiatry, 44*(12), 1241-1248.

Lieberman, A.F., Ghosh Ippen, C., and Van Horn, P. (2006). Child-parent psychotherapy: 6-month follow-up of a randomized controlled trial. *Journal of the American Academy of Child & Adolescent Psychiatry, 45*(8), 913-918.

Lieberman, A.F., Chu, A., Van Horn, P., and Harris, W.W. (2011). Trauma in early childhood: Empirical evidence and clinical implications. *Development and Psychopathology, 23*(2), 397-410.

Linares, L.O., Montalto, D., Li, M., and Oza, V.S. (2006). A promising parenting intervention in foster care. *Journal of Consulting & Clinical Psychology, 74*(1), 32-41.

Linares, L.O., Li, M., and Shrout, P.E. (2012). Child training for physical aggression?: Lessons from foster care. *Children and Youth Services Review, 34*(12), 2416-2422.

Linares, L.O., Jimenez, J., Nesci, C., Pearson, E., Beller, S., Edwards, N., and Levin-Rector, A. (2015). Reducing sibling conflict in maltreated children placed in foster homes. *Prevention Science, 16*(2), 211-221.

Llewellyn, G., McConnell, D., Honey, A., Mayes, R., and Russo, D. (2003). Promoting health and home safety for children of parents with intellectual disability: A randomized controlled trial. *Research in Developmental Disabilities, 24*(6), 405-431.

Lloyd, E.C., and Barth, R.P. (2011). Developmental outcomes after five years for foster children returned home, remaining in care, or adopted. *Children and Youth Services Review, 33*(8), 1383-1391.

Luby, J.L. (2013). Treatment of anxiety and depression in the preschool period. *Journal of the American Academy of Child & Adolescent Psychiatry, 52*(4), 346-358.

Luby, J.L., Lenze, S., and Tillman, R. (2012). A novel early intervention for preschool depression: Findings from a pilot randomized controlled trial. *Journal of Child Psychology and Psychiatry, 53*(3), 313-322.

Lundgren, L.M., Schilling, R.F., Fitzgerald, T., Davis, K., and Amodeo, M. (2003). Parental status of women injection drug users and entry to methadone maintenance. *Substance Use and Misuse, 38*(8), 1109-1131.

Lussier, B.J., Crimmins, D.B., and Alberti, D. (1994). Effect of three adult interaction styles on infant engagement. *Journal of Early Intervention, 18*(1), 12-24.

Lutzker, J.R., and Chaffin, M. (2012). SafeCare®: An evidence-based constantly dynamic model to prevent child maltreatment. In H. Dubowitz (Ed.), *World Perspectives on Child Abuse* (10th ed., pp. 93-96). Canberra, Australia: International Society for the Prevention of Child Abuse and Neglect.

Mahoney, G., Perales, F., Wiggers, B., and Herman, B. (2006). Responsive teaching: Early intervention for children with Down syndrome and other disabilities. *Down Syndrome, Research and Practice, 11*(1), 18-28.

Malone, D.G., and Gallagher, P.A. (2008). Transition to preschool programs for young children with disabilities. *Journal of Early Intervention, 30*(4), 341-356.

Malone, D.G., and Gallagher, P.A. (2009). Transition to preschool special education: A review of the literature. *Early Education and Development, 20*(4), 584-602.

Manlove, J., Mariner, C., and Papillo, A.R. (2000). Subsequent fertility among teen mothers: Longitudinal analyses of recent national data. *Journal of Marriage and Family, 62*(2), 430-448.

Marcynyszyn, L.A., Maher, E.J., and Corwin, T.W. (2011). Getting with the (evidence-based) program: An evaluation of the Incredible Years parenting training program in child welfare. *Children and Youth Services Review, 33*(5), 747-757.

Marlowe, D.B., and Carey, S.M. (2012). *Research Update on Family Drug Courts.* Alexandria, VA: National Association of Drug Court Professionals.

Martin, J.A., Hamilton, B.E., Michelle, J., Curtin, S.C., and Matthews, T. (2015). Division of Vital Statistics births: Final data for 2013. *National Vital Statistics Reports, 64*(1).

Mayes, L., and Truman, S. (2002). Substance abuse and parenting. In M. Bornstein (Ed.), *Handbook of Parenting* (vol. 4, pp. 329-359). Mahwah, NJ: Lawrence Erlbaum Associates.

McCoy, B.M., Rickert, M.E., Class, Q.A., Larsson, H., Lichtenstein, P., and D'Onofrio, B.M. (2014). Mediators of the association between parental severe mental illness and offspring neurodevelopmental problems. *Annals of Epidemiology, 24*(9), 629-634.

McCurdy, K., and Daro, D. (2001). Parent involvement in family support programs: An integrated theory. *Family Relations, 50*(2), 113-121.

McGaw, S., Scully, T., and Pritchard, C. (2010). Predicting the unpredictable? Identifying high-risk versus low-risk parents with intellectual disabilities. *Child Abuse and Neglect, 34*(9), 699-710.

McIntyre, L.L. (2008). Parent training for young children with developmental disabilities: Randomized controlled trial. *American Journal of Mental Retardation, 113*(5), 356-368.

McKee, L., Colletti, C., Rakow, A., Jones, D.J., and Forehand, R. (2008). Parenting and child externalizing behaviors: Are the associations specific or diffuse? *Aggression and Violent Behavior, 13*(3), 201-215.

Meade, C.S., and Ickovics, J.R. (2005). Systematic review of sexual risk among pregnant and mothering teens in the USA: Pregnancy as an opportunity for integrated prevention of STD and repeat pregnancy. *Social Science & Medicine, 60*(4), 661-678.

Meade, C.S., Kershaw, T.S., and Ickovics, J.R. (2008). The intergenerational cycle of teenage motherhood: An ecological approach. *Health Psychology, 27*(4), 419-429.

Meier, J.S. (2015). Johnson's differentiation theory: Is it really empirically supported? *Journal of Child Custody, 12*(1), 4-24.

Melnyk, B.M., Alpert-Gillis, L.J., Hensel, P.B., Cable-Beiling, R.C., and Rubenstein, J.S. (1997). Helping mothers cope with a critically ill child: A pilot test of the COPE intervention. *Research in Nursing & Health, 20*(1), 3-14.

Melnyk, B.M., Crean, H.F., Feinstein, N.F., Fairbanks, E., and Alpert-Gillis, L.J. (2007). Testing the theoretical framework of the COPE program for mothers of critically ill children: An integrative model of young children's post-hospital adjustment behaviors. *Journal of Pediatric Psychology, 32*(4), 463-474.

Melnyk, B.M., Crean, H.F., Feinstein, N.F., and Fairbanks, E. (2008). Maternal anxiety and depression after a premature infant's discharge from the neonatal intensive care unit: Explanatory effects of the Creating Opportunities for Parent Empowerment Program. *Nursing Research, 57*(6), 383-394.

Menting, A.T., Orobio de Castro, B., and Matthys, W. (2013). Effectiveness of the Incredible Years parent training to modify disruptive and prosocial child behavior: A meta-analytic review. *Clinical Psychology Review, 33*(8), 901-913.

Metsch, L.R., Wolfe, H.P., Fewell, R., McCoy, C.B., Elwood, W.N., Wohler-Torres, B., Petersen-Baston, P., and Haskins, H.V. (2001). Treating substance-using women and their children in public housing: Preliminary evaluation findings. *Child Welfare, 80*(2), 199-220.

Middlemiss, W., and McGuigan, W. (2005). Ethnicity and adolescent mothers' benefit from participation in home-visitation services. *Family Relations, 54*(2), 212-224.

Mikami, A.Y., Lerner, M.D., Griggs, M.S., McGrath, A., and Calhoun, C.D. (2010). Parental influence on children with attention-deficit/hyperactivity disorder: II. Results of a pilot intervention training parents as friendship coaches for children. *Journal of Abnormal Child Psychology, 38*(6), 737-749.

Miller, B.A., Wilsnack, S.C., and Cunradi, C.B. (2000). Family violence and victimization: Treatment issues for women with alcohol problems. *Alcoholism, Clinical and Experimental Research, 24*(8), 1287-1297.

Mitchell, O., Wilson, D.B., Eggers, A., and MacKenzie, D.L. (2012). Assessing the effectiveness of drug courts on recidivism: A meta-analytic review of traditional and nontraditional drug courts. *Journal of Criminal Justice, 40*(1), 60-71.

Moore, B.A. (2012). *Handbook of Counseling Military Couples.* New York: Taylor & Francis.

Moore, J., and Finkelstein, N. (2001). Parenting services for families affected by substance abuse. *Child Welfare, 80*(2), 221-238.

Morinis, J., Carson, C., and Quigley, M.A. (2013). Effect of teenage motherhood on cognitive outcomes in children: A population-based cohort study. *Archives of Disease in Childhood, 98*(12), 959-964.

Mosher, W.D., Jones, J., and Abma, J.C. (2012). *Intended and Unintended Births in the United States: 1982-2010.* No. 55. Washington, DC: U.S. Department of Health and Human Services, Centers for Disease Control and Prevention, National Center for Health Statistics.

Najavits, L.M., Weiss, R.D., and Shaw, S.R. (1997). The link between substance abuse and posttraumatic stress disorder in women. A research review. *The American Journal on Addictions, 6*(4), 273-283.

National Association of County and City Health Officials. (2009). *Meeting the Needs of Pregnant and Parenting Teens: Local Health Department Programs and Services.* Available: http://www.dhs.state.mn.us/main/groups/agencywide/documents/pub/dhs16_148996.pdf [June 2016].

National Institute on Child Health and Human Development. (2012). *What Are Intellectual and Developmental Disabilities?* Available: https://www.nichd.nih.gov/health/topics/idds/conditioninfo/Pages/default.aspx [October 2016].

National Institute of Justice. (2016). *Drug Courts.* Available: http://www.nij.gov/topics/courts/drug-courts/pages/welcome.aspx [June 2016].

National Registry of Evidence-based Programs and Practices. (2016a). *SAMHSA's National Registry of Evidence-based Programs and Practices: Intervention Summary—Incredible Years (IY).* Available: http://legacy.nreppadmin.net/ViewIntervention.aspx?id=311 [March 2016].

National Registry of Evidence-based Programs and Practices. (2016b). *SAMHSA's National Registry of Evidence-based Programs and Practices: Intervention Summary—Nurturing Parenting Programs.* Available: http://legacy.nreppadmin.net/ViewIntervention.aspx?id=171 [March 2016].

National Registry of Evidence-based Programs and Practices. (2016c). *SAMHSA's National Registry of Evidence-based Programs and Practices: Intervention Summary—Parent-Child Interaction Therapy (PCIT)*. Available: http://legacy.nreppadmin.net/ViewIntervention. aspx?id=23 [March 2016].

National Registry of Evidence-based Programs and Practices. (2016d). *SAMHSA's National Registry of Evidence-based Programs and Practices: Intervention Summary—Strengthening Families Program*. Available: http://legacy.nreppadmin.net/ViewIntervention.aspx?id=44 [March 2016].

National Registry of Evidence-based Programs and Practices. (2016e). *SAMHSA's National Registry of Evidence-based Programs and Practices: Intervention Summary—Triple P-Positive Parenting Program*. Available: http://legacy.nreppadmin.net/ViewIntervention. aspx?id=1 [October 2016].

National Research Council. (1993). *Understanding Child Abuse and Neglect*. Panel on Research on Child Abuse and Neglect, Commission on Behavioral and Social Sciences and Education. Washington, DC: National Academy Press.

Neece, C.L. (2014). Mindfulness-based stress reduction for parents of young children with developmental delays: Implications for parental mental health and child behavior problems. *Journal of Applied Research in Intellectual Disabilities, 27*(2), 174-186.

Neger, E.N., and Prinz, R.J. (2015). Interventions to address parenting and parental substance abuse: Conceptual and methodological considerations. *Clinical Psychology Review, 39*, 71-82.

Niccols, A., and Sword, W. (2005). "New choices" for substance-using mothers and their children: Preliminary evaluation. *Journal of Substance Use, 10*(4), 239-251.

Nicholson, J., and Clayfield, J.C. (2004). Responding to depression in parents. *Pediatric Nursing, 30*(2), 136-142.

Nicholson, J., and Henry, A.D. (2003). Achieving the goal of evidence-based psychiatric rehabilitation practices for mothers with mental illnesses. *Psychiatric Rehabilitation Journal, 27*(2), 122-130.

Nicholson, J., Sweeney, E.M., and Geller, J.L. (1998). Mothers with mental illness: I. The competing demands of parenting and living with mental illness. *Psychiatric Services, 49*(5), 635-642.

Nicholson, J., Biebel, K., Katz-Leavy, J., and Williams, V. (2002). *The Prevalence of Parenthood in Adults with Mental Illness: Implications for State and Federal Policymakers, Programs, and Providers*. Paper 153. Rockville, MD: Substance Abuse and Mental Health Services Administration.

Nicholson, J., Finkelstein, N., Williams, V., Thom, J., Noether, C., and DeVilbiss, M. (2006). A comparison of mothers with co-occurring disorders and histories of violence living with or separated from minor children. *Journal of Behavioral Health Services & Research, 33*(2), 225-243.

Nixon, R.D., Sweeney, L., Erickson, D.B., and Touyz, S.W. (2003). Parent-child interaction therapy: A comparison of standard and abbreviated treatments for oppositional defiant preschoolers. *Journal of Consulting and Clinical Psychology, 71*(2), 251-260.

Nylen, K.J., Moran, T.E., Franklin, C.L., and O'Hara, M.W. (2006). Maternal depression: A review of relevant treatment approaches for mothers and infants. *Infant Mental Health Journal, 27*(4), 327-343.

Office of Adolescent Health. (2015). *OAH Vision and Strategic Priorities*. Available: http://www.hhs.gov/ash/oah/about-us [January 2016].

Obeidat, H.M., Bond, E.A., and Callister, L.C. (2009). The parental experience of having an infant in the newborn intensive care unit. *The Journal of Perinatal Education, 18*(3), 23-29.

O'Connor, M.J., and Paley, B. (2006). The relationship of prenatal alcohol exposure and the postnatal environment to child depressive symptoms. *Journal of Pediatric Psychology, 31*(1), 50-64.

Odom, S.L., and Chandler, L. (1990). Transition to parenthood for parents of technology-assisted infants. *Topics in Early Childhood Special Education, 9*(4), 43-54.

Odom, S.L., Boyd, B.A., Hall, L.J., Hume, K.A., Volkmar, F.R., Paul, R., Rogers, S.J., and Pelphrey, K.A. (2014). Comprehensive treatment models for children and youth with autism spectrum disorders. In F.R. Volkmar, R. Paul, S.J. Rogers, and K.A. Pelphrey (Eds.), *Handbook of Autism and Pervasive Developmental Disorders* (4th ed., pp. 770-787). Hoboken, NJ: John Wiley & Sons.

O'Hara, M.W., and McCabe, J.E. (2013). Postpartum depression: Current status and future directions. *Annual Review of Clinical Psychology, 9*, 379-407.

Olds, D.L., Robinson, J., O'Brien, R., Luckey, D.W., Pettitt, L.M., Henderson, C.R., Jr., Ng, R.K., Sheff, K.L., Korfmacher, J., Hiatt, S., and Talmi, A. (2002). Home visiting by paraprofessionals and by nurses: A randomized, controlled trial. *Pediatrics, 110*(3), 486-496.

Olds, D.L., Robinson, J., Pettitt, L., Luckey, D.W., Holmberg, J., Ng, R.K., Isacks, K., Sheff, K., and Henderson, C.R., Jr. (2004). Effects of home visits by paraprofessionals and by nurses: Age 4 follow-up results of a randomized trial. *Pediatrics, 114*(6), 1560-1568.

Olds, D.L., Sadler, L., and Kitzman, H. (2007). Programs for parents of infants and toddlers: Recent evidence from randomized trials. *Journal of Child Psychology and Psychiatry, 48*(3/4), 355-391.

Oyserman, D., Mowbray, C.T., Meares, P.A., and Firminger, K.B. (2000). Parenting among mothers with a serious mental illness. *American Journal of Orthopsychiatry, 70*(3), 296-315.

Pajulo, M., and Kalland, M. (2013). Mentalizing-based intervention with mother-baby dyads. In M. Pajulo and L.M. Mayes (Eds.), *Parenting and Substance Abuse* (pp. 282-302). New York: Oxford University Press.

Pajulo, M., Suchman, N., Kalland, M., and Mayes, L. (2006). Enhancing the effectiveness of residential treatment for substance abusing pregnant and parenting women: Focus on maternal reflective functioning and mother-child relationship. *Infant Mental Health Journal, 27*(5), 448.

Pajulo, M., Pyykkonen, N., Kalland, M., Sinkkonen, J., Helenius, H., Punamaki, R.L., and Suchman, N. (2012). Substance-abusing mothers in residential treatment with their babies: Importance of pre- and postnatal maternal reflective functioning. *Infant Mental Health Journal, 33*(1), 70-81.

Paradis, H.A., Sandler, M., Manly, J.T., and Valentine, L. (2013). Building healthy children: Evidence-based home visitation integrated with pediatric medical homes. *Pediatrics, 132*(Suppl. 2), S174-S179.

Parent-Child Interaction Therapy International. (2015). *About PCIT.* Available: http://www.pcit.org/resources-for-pcit-therapists/about [October 2016].

Park, J.M., Solomon, P., and Mandell, D.S. (2006). Involvement in the child welfare system among mothers with serious mental illness. *Psychiatric Services, 57*(4), 493-497.

Patterson, G.R., Chamberlain, P., and Reid, J.B. (1982). A comparative evaluation of a parent-training program. *Behavior Therapy, 13*(5), 638-650.

Perper, K., Peterson, K., and Manlove, J. (2010). *Diploma Attainment among Teen Mothers.* Fact Sheet. Publication No. 2010-01. Washington, DC: Child Trends.

Perrin, E.C., Sheldrick, R.C., McMenamy, J.M., Henson, B.S., and Carter, A.S. (2014). Improving parenting skills for families of young children in pediatric settings: A randomized clinical trial. *Journal of the American Medical Association Pediatrics, 168*(1), 16-24.

Petch, J.F., Halford, W.K., Creedy, D.K., and Gamble, J. (2012). A randomized controlled trial of a couple relationship and coparenting program (couple care for parents) for high- and low-risk new parents. *Journal of Consulting and Clinical Psychology, 80*(4), 662-673.

Pincus, D.B., Santucci, L.C., Ehrenreich, J.T., and Eyberg, S.M. (2008). The implementation of modified Parent-Child Interaction Therapy for youth with separation anxiety disorder. *Cognitive and Behavioral Practice, 15*(2), 118-125.

Pinzon, J.L., Jones, V.F., Blythe, M.J., Adelman, W.P., Breuner, C.C., Levine, D.A., Marcell, A.V., Murray, P.J., O'Brien, R.F., High, P.C., Donoghue, E., Fussell, J.J., Gleason, M.M., Jaudes, P.K., Rubin, D.M., and Schulte, E.E. (2012). Care of adolescent parents and their children. *Pediatrics, 130*(6), e1743-e1756.

Pogarsky, G., Thornberry, T.P., and Lizotte, A.J. (2006). Developmental outcomes for children of young mothers. *Journal of Marriage and Family, 68*(2), 332-344.

Pooblan, A.S., Aucott, L.S., Ross, L., Smith, W.C.S., Helms, P.J., and Williams, J.H.G. (2007). Effects of treating postnatal depression on mother-infant interaction and child development. *British Journal of Psychiatry, 191*, 378-386.

Porowski, A.W., Burgdorf, K., and Herrell, J.M. (2004). Effectiveness and sustainability of residential substance abuse treatment programs for pregnant and parenting women. *Evaluation and Program Planning, 27*(2), 191-198.

Powers, J.D., Bowen, N.K., and Bowen, G.L. (2010). Evidence-based programs in school settings: Barriers and recent advances. *Journal of Evidence-Based Social Work, 7*(4), 313-331.

Preece, P.M., and Riley, E.P. (2011). *Alcohol, Drugs and Medication in Pregnancy: The Long-Term Outcome for the Child*. Clinics in Developmental Medicine No. 188. London, UK: MacKeith Press.

Price, J.M., Chamberlain, P., Landsverk, J., and Reid, J. (2009). KEEP foster-parent training intervention: Model description and effectiveness. *Child & Family Social Work, 14*(2), 233-242.

Prinz, R. (2014). *Scaling Family-Focused Preventive Interventions: The Triple P System*. Presentation at the Workshop on Strategies for Scaling Tested and Effective Family-Focused Preventive Interventions to Promote Children's Cognitive, Affective, and Behavioral Health, April 1-2, Washington, DC.

Pruett, M.K., and Barker, R.K. (2010). Effectively intervening with divorcing parents and their children: What works and how it works. In M.S. Schulz, M.K. Pruett, P.K. Kerig, and R.D. Parke (Eds.), *Strengthening Couple Relationships for Optimal Child Development: Lessons from Research and Intervention* (pp. 181-196). Washington, DC: American Psychological Association.

Putnam-Hornstein, E., Simon, J.D., Eastman, A.L., and Magruder, J. (2015). Risk of re-reporting among infants who remain at home following alleged maltreatment. *Child Maltreatment, 20*(2), 92-103.

Rapee, R.M., Kennedy, S., Ingram, M., Edwards, S., and Sweeney, L. (2005). Prevention and early intervention of anxiety disorders in inhibited preschool children. *Journal of Consulting and Clinical Psychology, 73*(3), 488-497.

Read, J.P., Brown, P.J., and Kahler, C.W. (2004). Substance use and posttraumatic stress disorders: Symptom interplay and effects on outcome. *Addictive Behaviors, 29*(8), 1665-1672.

Reinders, H.S. (2008). Persons with disabilities as parents: What is the problem? *Journal of Applied Research in Intellectual Disabilities, 21*(4), 308-314.

Repetti, R.L., Taylor, S.E., and Seeman, T.E. (2002). Risky families: Family social environments and the mental and physical health of offspring. *Psychological Bulletin, 128*(2), 330-366.

Richmond, J.B. (1970). Disadvantaged children: What have they compelled us to learn? *Yale Journal of Biology and Medicine, 43*(3), 127-144.

Riggs, D.S., Caulfield, M.B., and Street, A.E. (2000). Risk for domestic violence: Factors associated with perpetration and victimization. *Journal of Clinical Psychology, 56*(10), 1289-1316.

Roberts, M.Y., and Kaiser, A.P. (2011). The effectiveness of parent-implemented language interventions: A meta-analysis. *American Journal of Speech-Language Pathology, 20*(3), 180-199.

Rogers, S.J., Estes, A., Lord, C., Vismara, L., Winter, J., Fitzpatrick, A., Guo, M., and Dawson, G. (2012). Effects of a brief Early Start Denver Model (ESDM)-based parent intervention on toddlers at risk for autism spectrum disorders: A randomized controlled trial. *Journal of the American Academy of Child and Adolescent Psychiatry, 51*(10), 1052-1065.

Rose, H.D., and Cohen, K. (2010). The experiences of young carers: A meta-synthesis of qualitative findings. *Journal of Youth Studies, 13*(4), 473-487.

Rosen, D., Warner, L.A., and Tolman, R.M. (2006). Comparing psychiatric service use among low-income women and women in a general household population. *Social Work Research, 30*(4), 223-232.

Rutherford, H., Potenza, M., and Mayes, L. (2013). Neurobiology of addiction and attachment. In N. Suchman, M. Pajulo, and L. Mayes (Eds.), *Parenting and Substance Abuse: Developmental Approaches to Intervention* (pp. 3-23). New York: Oxford University Press.

Ryan, J.P., Choi, S., Hong, J.S., Hernandez, P., and Larrison, C.R. (2008). Recovery coaches and substance exposed births: An experiment in child welfare. *Child Abuse and Neglect, 32*(11), 1072-1079.

Sadler, L.S., Swartz, M.K., and Ryan-Krause, P. (2003). Supporting adolescent mothers and their children through a high school-based child care center and parent support program. *Journal of Pediatric Health Care, 17*(3), 109-117.

Sadler, L.S., Swartz, M.K., Ryan-Krause, P., Seitz, V., Meadows-Oliver, M., Grey, M., and Clemmens, D.A. (2007). Promising outcomes in teen mothers enrolled in a school-based parent support program and child care center. *Journal of School Health, 77*(3), 121-130.

Sahler, O.J.Z., Varni, J.W., Fairclough, D.L., Butler, R.W., Noll, R.B., Dolgin, M.J., Phipps, S., Copeland, D.R., Katz, E.R., and Mulhern, R.K. (2002). Problem-solving skills training for mothers of children with newly diagnosed cancer: A randomized trial. *Journal of Developmental & Behavioral Pediatrics, 23*(2), 77-86.

Sahler, O.J.Z., Fairclough, D.L., Phipps, S., Mulhern, R.K., Dolgin, M.J., Noll, R.B., Katz, E.R., Varni, J.W., Copeland, D.R., and Butler, R.W. (2005). Using problem-solving skills training to reduce negative affectivity in mothers of children with newly diagnosed cancer: Report of a multisite randomized trial. *Journal of Consulting and Clinical Psychology, 73*(2), 272-283.

Sahler, O.J., Dolgin, M.J., Phipps, S., Fairclough, D.L., Askins, M.A., Katz, E.R., Noll, R.B., and Butler, R.W. (2013). Specificity of problem-solving skills training in mothers of children newly diagnosed with cancer: Results of a multisite randomized clinical trial. *Journal of Clinical Oncology, 31*(10), 1329-1335.

Sameroff, A.J., and Chandler, M.J. (1975). Reproductive risk and the continuum of caretaking casualty. In F.D. Horowitz, M. Hetherington, S. Scarr-Salapatek, and G. Siegel (Eds.), *Review of Child Development Research* (vol. 4, pp. 187-244). Chicago, IL: University of Chicago Press.

Sanders, M.R., and Prinz, R.J. (2005). The Triple P system: A multi-level, evidence-based, population approach to the prevention and treatment of behavioral and emotional problems in children. *The Register Report, 31*, 42-46.

Sanders, M.R., Markie-Dadds, C., Tully, L.A., and Bor, W. (2000). The Triple P-Positive Parenting Program: A comparison of enhanced, standard, and self-directed behavioral family intervention for parents of children with early onset conduct problems. *Journal of Consulting and Clinical Psychology, 68*(4), 624.

Sanders, M., Calam, R., Durand, M., Liversidge, T., and Carmont, S.A. (2008). Does self-directed and web-based support for parents enhance the effects of viewing a reality television series based on the Triple P-Positive Parenting Programme? *Journal of Child Psychology and Psychiatry, 49*(9), 924-932.

Sanders, M. R., Pickering, J. A, Kirby, J. N., Turner, K. M., Morawska, A., Mazzucchelli, T., Ralph, A., and Sofronoff, K. (2012). A commentary on evidence-based parenting programs: Redressing misconceptions of the empirical support for Triple P. *BMC Medicine, 10*, 145.

Sanders, M.R., Kirby, J.N., Tellegen, C.L., and Day, J.J. (2014). The Triple P-Positive Parenting Program: A systematic review and meta-analysis of a multi-level system of parenting support. *Clinical Psychology Review, 34*(4), 337-357.

Sandler, I., Ingram, A., Wolchik, S., Tein, J.-Y., and Winslow, E. (2015). Long-term effects of parenting-focused preventive interventions to promote resilience of children and adolescents. *Child Development Perspectives, 9*(3), 164-171.

Sangalang, B.B., and Rounds, K. (2005). Differences in health behaviors and parenting knowledge between pregnant adolescents and parenting adolescents. *Social Work in Health Care, 42*(2), 1-22.

Sangalang, B.B., Barth, R.P., and Painter, J.S. (2006). First-birth outcomes and timing of second births: A statewide case management program for adolescent mothers. *Health and Social Work, 31*(1), 54-63.

Santacruz, I., Méndez, F.J., and Sánchez-Meca, J. (2006). Play therapy applied by parents for children with darkness phobia: Comparison of two programmes. *Child & Family Behavior Therapy, 28*(1), 19-35.

Schaeffer, C.M., Swenson, C.C., Tuerk, E.H., and Henggeler, S.W. (2013). Comprehensive treatment for co-occurring child maltreatment and parental substance abuse: Outcomes from a 24-month pilot study of the MST-Building Stronger Families Program. *Child Abuse and Neglect, 37*(8), 596-607.

Schertz, H.H., Odom, S.L., Baggett, K.M., and Sideris, J.H. (2013). Effects of joint attention mediated learning for toddlers with autism spectrum disorders: An initial randomized controlled study. *Early Childhood Research Quarterly, 28*(2), 249-258.

Scholer, S.J., Hudnut-Beumler, J., and Dietrich, M.S. (2010). A brief primary care intervention helps parents develop plans to discipline. *Pediatrics, 125*(2), e242-e249.

Schrank, B., Moran, K., Borghi, C., and Priebe, S. (2015). How to support patients with severe mental illness in their parenting role with children aged over 1 year? A systematic review of interventions. *Social Psychiatry and Psychiatric Epidemiology, 50*(12), 1765-1783.

Schroeder, M., and Pridham, K. (2006). Development of relationship competencies through guided participation for mothers of preterm infants. *Journal of Obstetric, Gynecologic, and Neonatal Nursing, 35*(3), 358-368.

Schuetze, P., Eiden, R.D., and Coles, C.D. (2007). Prenatal cocaine and other substance exposure: Effects on infant autonomic regulation at 7 months of age. *Developmental Psychobiology, 49*(3), 276-289.

Schuhmann, E.M., Foote, R.C., Eyberg, S.M., Boggs, S.R., and Algina, J. (1998). Efficacy of parent-child interaction therapy: Interim report of a randomized trial with short-term maintenance. *Journal of Clinical Child Psychology, 27*(1), 34-45.

Seeman, M.V. (2012). Antipsychotic-induced somnolence in mothers with schizophrenia. *The Psychiatric Quarterly, 83*(1), 83-89.

Segre, L.S., Siewert, R.C., Brock, R.L., and O'Hara, M.W. (2013). Emotional distress in mothers of preterm hospitalized infants: A feasibility trial of nurse-delivered treatment. *Journal of Perinatology, 33*(12), 924-928.

Shadish, W.R., and Baldwin, S.A. (2005). Effects of behavioral marital therapy: A meta-analysis of randomized controlled trials. *Journal of Consulting and Clinical Psychology, 73*(1), 6-14.

Shanok, A.F., and Miller, L. (2007). Stepping up to motherhood among inner-city teens. *Psychology of Women Quarterly, 31*(3), 252-261.

Sharps, P., Alhusen, J.L., Bullock, L., Bhandari, S., Ghazarian, S., Udo, I.E., and Campbell, J. (2013). Engaging and retaining abused women in perinatal home visitation programs. *Pediatrics, 132*(Suppl. 2), S134-S139.

Siegel, R.S., and Brandon, A.R. (2014). Adolescents, pregnancy, and mental health. *Journal of Pediatric and Adolescent Gynecology, 27*(3), 138-150.

Siegenthaler, E., Munder, T., and Egger, M. (2012). Effect of preventive interventions in mentally ill parents on the mental health of the offspring: Systematic review and meta-analysis. *Journal of the American Academy of Child & Adolescent Psychiatry, 51*(1), 8-17.

Siller, M., Morgan, L., Turner-Brown, L., Baggett, K.M., Baranek, G.T., Brian, J., Bryson, S.E., Carter, A.S., Crais, E.R., Estes, A., Kasari, C., Landa, R.J., Lord, C., Messinger, D.S., Mundy, P., Odom, S.L., Reznick, J.S., Roberts, W., Rogers, S.J., Schertz, H.H., Smith, I.M., Stone, W.L., Watson, L.R., Wetherby, A.M., Yoder, P.J., and Zwaigenbaum, L. (2013). Designing studies to evaluate parent-mediated interventions for toddlers with autism spectrum disorder. *Journal of Early Intervention, 35*(4), 355-377.

Silverstein, M., Feinberg, E., Cabral, H., Sauder, S., Egbert, L., Schainker, E., Kamholz, K., Hegel, M., and Beardslee, W. (2011). Problem-solving education to prevent depression among low-income mothers of preterm infants: A randomized controlled pilot trial. *Archives of Women's Mental Health, 14*(4), 317-324.

Singer, G.H., Ethridge, B.L., and Aldana, S.I. (2007). Primary and secondary effects of parenting and stress management interventions for parents of children with developmental disabilities: A meta-analysis. *Mental Retardation and Developmental Disabilities Research Reviews, 13*(4), 357-369.

Sinha, R. (2001). How does stress increase risk of drug abuse and relapse? *Psychopharmacology, 158*(4), 343-359.

Smith, M.V. (2014). *The New Haven Moms Partnership: Combatting Depression, Reducing Stress and Building Foundational Skills for Success.* Available: http://www.buildingbetterprograms.org/wp-content/uploads/2014/03/New-Haven-MOMS-Partnership-Slides.pdf [February 2016].

Sofronoff, K., Jahnel, D., and Sanders, M. (2011). Stepping Stones Triple P seminars for parents of a child with a disability: A randomized controlled trial. *Research in Developmental Disabilities, 32*(6), 2253-2262.

Solantaus, T., Paavonen, E.J., Toikka, S., and Punamäki, R.-L. (2010). Preventive interventions in families with parental depression: Children's psychosocial symptoms and prosocial behaviour. *European Child & Adolescent Psychiatry, 19*(12), 883-892.

Solomon, R., and Liefeld, C.P. (1998). Effectiveness of a family support center approach to adolescent mothers: Repeat pregnancy and school drop-out rates. *Family Relations, 47*(2), 139-144.

Stadnick, N.A., Stahmer, A., and Brookman-Frazee, L. (2015). Preliminary effectiveness of Project ImPACT: A parent-mediated intervention for children with autism spectrum disorder delivered in a community program. *Journal of Autism and Developmental Disorders, 45*(7), 2092-2104.

Stepp, S.D., Whalen, D.J., Pilkonis, P.A., Hipwell, A.E., and Levine, M.D. (2012). Children of mothers with borderline personality disorder: Identifying parenting behaviors as potential targets for intervention. *Personality Disorders: Theory, Research, and Treatment, 3*(1), 76-91.

Stevens-Simon, C., Kelly, L., and Kulick, R. (2001). A village would be nice but . . . : It takes a long-acting contraceptive to prevent repeat adolescent pregnancies. *American Journal of Preventive Medicine, 21*(1), 60-65.

Stith, S.M., and McCollum, E.E. (2009). Couples treatment for psychological and physical aggression. In K.D. O'Leary and E.M. Woodin (Eds.), *Psychological and Physical Aggression in Couples: Causes and Interventions* (pp. 233-250). Washington, DC: American Psychological Association.

Stith, S.M., McCollum, E.E., Amanor-Boadu, Y., and Smith, D. (2012). Systemic perspectives on intimate partner violence treatment. *Journal of Marital and Family Therapy, 38*(1), 220-240.

Stover, C.S., Meadows, A.L., and Kaufman, J. (2009). Interventions for intimate partner violence: Review and implications for evidence-based practice. *Professional Psychology: Research and Practice, 40*(3), 223-233.

Strathearn, L., and Mayes, L.C. (2010). Cocaine addiction in mothers: Potential effects on maternal care and infant development. *Annals of the New York Academy of Sciences, 1187*, 172-183.

Strathearn, L., Li, J., Fonagy, P., and Montague, P.R. (2008). What's in a smile? Maternal brain responses to infant facial cues. *Pediatrics, 122*(1), 40-51.

Strauss, K., Mancini, F., and Fava, L. (2013). Parent inclusion in early intensive behavior interventions for young children with ASD: A synthesis of meta-analyses from 2009 to 2011. *Research in Developmental Disabilities, 34*(9), 2967-2985.

Substance Abuse and Mental Health Services Administration. (2014a). *Grants to Expand Services to Children Affected by Methamphetamine in Families Participating in Family Drug Court.* Available: https://ncsacw.samhsa.gov/files/CAM_Brief_2014-Final.pdf [January 2016].

Substance Abuse and Mental Health Services Administration. (2014b). *Results from the 2013 National Survey on Drug Use and Health: Summary of National Findings.* NSDUH Series H-48, HHS Publication No. (SMA) 14-4863. Rockville, MD: Substance Abuse and Mental Health Services Administration.

Suchman, N., Mayes, L., Conti, J., Slade, A., and Rounsaville, B. (2004). Rethinking parenting interventions for drug-dependent mothers: From behavior management to fostering emotional bonds. *Journal of Substance Abuse Treatment, 27*(3), 179-185.

Suchman, N., DeCoste, C., Castiglioni, N., Legow, N., and Mayes, L. (2008). The Mothers and Toddlers Program: Preliminary findings from an attachment-based parenting intervention for substance-abusing mothers. *Psychoanalytic Psychology, 25*(3), 499-517.

Suchman, N.E., DeCoste, C., Castiglioni, N., McMahon, T.J., Rounsaville, B., and Mayes, L. (2010). The Mothers and Toddlers Program, an attachment-based parenting intervention for substance using women: Post-treatment results from a randomized clinical pilot. *Attachment & Human Development, 12*(5), 483-504.

Suchman, N., DeCoste, C., Ordway, M.R., and Bers, S. (2013). Mothering from the inside out: A mentalization-based individual therapy for mothers with substance use disorders. In N.E. Suchman, M. Pajula, and L.M. Mayes (Eds.), *Parenting and Substance Abuse: Developmental Approaches to Intervention* (pp. 407-433). New York: Oxford University Press.

Sullivan, C.M. (2012). *Domestic Violence Shelter Services: A Review of the Empirical Evidence*, Harrisburg, PA: National Resource Center on Domestic Violence. Available: http://www.dvevidenceproject.org/wp-content/themes/DVEProject/files/research/DVShelterResearchSummary10-2012.pdf [January 2016].

Swenson, C.C., and Schaeffer, C.M. (2011). Multisystemic therapy for child abuse and neglect. In A. Rubin and D. Springer (Eds.), *Programs and Interventions for Maltreated Children and Families at Risk* (pp. 31-42). Hoboken, NJ: Wiley.

Swenson, C.C., Schaeffer, C.M., Tuerk, E.H., Henggeler, S.W., Tuten, M., Panzarella, P., Laue, C., Remmele, L., Foley, T., Cannata, E., and Guillorn, A. (2009). Adapting multisystemic therapy for co-occurring child maltreatment and parental substance abuse: The building stronger families project. *Emotional and Behavioral Disorders in Youth, 1*, 3-8.

Swenson, C.C., Schaeffer, C.M., Henggeler, S.W., Faldowski, R., and Mayhew, A.M. (2010). Multisystemic therapy for child abuse and neglect: A randomized effectiveness trial. *Journal of Family Psychology, 24*(4), 497-507.

Szuster, R.R., Rich, L.L., Chung, A., and Bisconer, S.W. (1996). Treatment retention in women's residential chemical dependency treatment: The effect of admission with children. *Substance Use and Misuse, 31*(8), 1001-1013.

Tajima, E.A., Herrenkohl, T.I., Moylan, C.A., and Derr, A.S. (2011). Moderating the effects of childhood exposure to intimate partner violence: The roles of parenting characteristics and adolescent peer support. *Journal of Research on Adolescence, 21*(2), 376-394.

Tandon, S.D., Leis, J.A., Mendelson, T., Perry, D.F., and Kemp, K. (2014). Six-month outcomes from a randomized controlled trial to prevent perinatal depression in low-income home visiting clients. *Maternal and Child Health Journal, 18*(4), 873-881.

Tellegen, C.L., and Sanders, M.R. (2013). Stepping Stones Triple P-Positive Parenting Program for children with disability: A systematic review and meta-analysis. *Research in Developmental Disabilities, 34*(5), 1556-1571.

Timmer, S.G., Ware, L.M., Urquiza, A.J., and Zebell, N.M. (2010). The effectiveness of parent-child interaction therapy for victims of interparental violence. *Violence and Victims, 25*(4), 486-503.

Tonge, B., Brereton, A., Kiomall, M., Mackinnon, A., King, N., and Rinehart, N. (2006). Effects on parental mental health of an education and skills training program for parents of young children with autism: A randomized controlled trial. *Journal of the American Academy of Child and Adolescent Psychiatry, 45*(5), 561-569.

Tsivos, Z.-L., Calam, R., Sanders, M.R., and Wittkowski, A. (2015). Interventions for postnatal depression assessing the mother-infant relationship and child developmental outcomes: A systematic review. *International Journal of Women's Health, 7*, 429-447.

Turner, K.M., and Sanders, M.R. (2006). Help when it's needed first: A controlled evaluation of brief, preventive behavioral family intervention in a primary care setting. *Behavior Therapy, 37*(2), 131-142.

U.S. Department of Education. (2015a). *Building the Legacy: IDEA 2004: Sec. 636 Individualized Family Service Plan*. Available: http://idea.ed.gov/explore/view/p/%2Croot%2Cstatute%2CI%2CC%2C636%2C [October 2016].

U.S. Department of Education. (2015b). *Building the Legacy: IDEA 2014: Sec. 632 Definitions*. Available: http://idea.ed.gov/explore/view/p/%2Croot%2Cstatute%2CI%2CC%2C632%2C [October 2016].

U.S. Department of Health and Human Services. (1999). *Blending Perspectives and Building Common Ground. A Report to Congress on Substance Abuse and Child Protection*. Washington, DC: U.S. Government Printing Office.

U.S. Department of Health and Human Services. (2014a). *Targeted Grants to Increase the Well-Being of, and to Improve the Permanency Outcomes for, Children Affected by Methamphetamine or Other Substance Abuse: Third Annual Report to Congress.* Washington, DC: U.S. Department of Health and Human Services; Administration for Children and Families; Administration on Children, Youth and Families; Children's Bureau.

U.S. Department of Health and Human Services. (2014b). *The Maternal, Infant, and Early Childhood Home Visiting (MIECHV) Program: Snapshot Reports of Benchmark Measures Selected by Grantees.* ORE Report No. 2014-26. Available: http://mchb.hrsa.gov/programs/homevisiting/ta/resources/snapshotbenchmarkmeasures.pdf [October 2016].

U.S. Preventive Services Task Force. (2009). Screening for depression in adults: U.S. Preventive Services Task Force recommendation statement. *Annals of Internal Medicine, 151*(11), 784-792.

Van Horn, P., and Reyes, V. (2014). Child-parent psychotherapy with infants and very young children. In S. Timmer and A. Urquiza (Eds.), *Evidence-Based Approaches for the Treatment of Maltreated Children* (pp. 61-77). New York: Springer.

Voisin, D., and Hong, J. (2012). A conceptual formulation examining the relationship between witnessing domestic violence and bullying behaviors and victimization among youth. *Educational Psychology Review, 24*(4), 479-498.

Wade, C., Llewellyn, G., and Matthews, J. (2008). Review of parent training interventions for parents with intellectual disability. *Journal of Applied Research in Intellectual Disabilities, 21*(4), 351-366.

Wahl, K., and Metzner, C. (2012). Parental influences on the prevalence and development of child aggressiveness. *Journal of Child and Family Studies, 21*(2), 344-355.

Webster-Stratton, C. (1984). Randomized trial of two parent-training programs for families with conduct-disordered children. *Journal of Consulting and Clinical Psychology, 52*(4), 666-678.

Weissman, M.M., Pilowsky, D.J., Wickramaratne, P.J., Talati, A., Wisniewski, S.R., Fava, M., Hughes, C.W., Garber, J., Malloy, E., King, C.A., Cerda, G., Sood, A.B., Alpert, J.E., Trivedi, M.H., and Rush, A.J. (2006). Remissions in maternal depression and child psychopathology: A STAR*D-child report. *Journal of the American Medical Association, 295*(12), 1389-1398.

What Works Clearinghouse. (2014). *What Works Clearinghouse: Procedures and Standards Handbook Version 3.0.* Washington, DC: U.S. Department of Education, Institute of Education Sciences.

Wildeman, C., Emanuel, N., Leventhal, J.M., Putnam-Hornstein, E., Waldfogel, J., and Lee, H. (2014). The prevalence of confirmed maltreatment among U.S. children, 2004 to 2011. *Journal of the American Medical Association Pediatrics, 168*(8), 706-713.

Wilson, P., Rush, R., Hussey, S., Puckering, C., Sim, F., Allely, C.S., Doku, P., McConnachie, A., and Gillberg, C. (2012). How evidence-based is an "evidence-based parenting program"? A prisma systematic review and meta-analysis of Triple P. *BMC Medicine, 10*, 130.

Wittkowski, A., McGrath, L., and Peters, S. (2014). Exploring psychosis and bipolar disorder in women: A critical review of the qualitative literature. *BMC Psychiatry, 14*(1), 1-14.

Wobie, K., Eyler, F.D., Conlon, M., Clarke, L., and Behnke, M. (1997). Women and children in residential treatment: Outcomes for mothers and their infants. *Journal of Drug Issues, 27*(3), 585-606.

Wolfe, D.A., Crooks, C.V., Lee, V., McIntyre-Smith, A., and Jaffe, P.G. (2003). The effects of children's exposure to domestic violence: A meta-analysis and critique. *Clinical Child and Family Psychology Review, 6*(3), 171-187.

Woodman, A.C. (2014). Trajectories of stress among parents of children with disabilities: A dyadic analysis. *Family Relations, 63*(1), 39-54.

Worcel, S.D., Furrer, C.J., Green, B.L., Burrus, S.W.M., and Finigan, M.W. (2008). Effects of family treatment drug courts on substance abuse and child welfare outcomes. *Child Abuse Review, 17*(6), 427-443.

Wu, J., DiCicco-Bloom, B., Greenberg, S., and Sahulhameed, F. (2012). Breaking the cycle of adolescent pregnancy: Can mothers influence their daughters' contraceptive behavior? *Contraception, 86*(2), 186.

Wulczyn, F., Hislop, K.B., and Harden, B.J. (2002). The placement of infants in foster care. *Infant Mental Health Journal, 23*(5), 454-475.

Yakima Valley Farm Workers Clinic. (2013). *Yakima Valley Farm Workers Clinic Enhanced Yakima County Nurse-Family Partnership (EYCNFP) Program at Children's Village: Final Report.* Grant No. 90CA1756. Available: https://library.childwelfare.gov/cwig/ws/library/docs/ gateway/Blob/89704.pdf;jsessionid=77C9A30DCC63FDD5597CA41BE0329685?w=NATIVE%28%27TITLE+ph+is+%27%27Final+Report%3A+Yakima+Valley+Farm+Workers+Clinic%27%27%2C%27%27Enhanced+Yakima+County+Nurse-Family+Partnership+%28EYCNFP %29+Program+at+Children%27%27%27%27s+Village%27%27%27%29&upp=0&order=native %28%27year%2FDescend%27%29&rpp=25&r=1&m=1 [January 2016].

Zubrick, S., Ward, K., Silburn, S., Lawrence, D., Williams, A., Blair, E., Robertson, D., and Sanders, M. (2005). Prevention of child behavior problems through universal implementation of a group behavioral family intervention. *Prevention Science, 6*(4), 287-304.

6

Elements of Effective Parenting Programs and Strategies for Increasing Program Participation and Retention

Parenting programs in the United States are reaching millions of parents and their children annually, but as discussed in Chapters 4 and 5, only a limited number of evidence-based, high-quality trials of the effects of these programs have been carried out. It is costly to conduct such evaluations, and they often are difficult to implement. Very few programs have undergone multiple evaluations using such designs. Other parenting interventions have been assessed through smaller studies, observational research, and case-control studies. Those studies indicate that these interventions may be effective, achieving improvements in outcomes similar to those found for the manualized parent training programs that have been studied experimentally (Chorpita et al., 2013).

This chapter identifies major elements of those programs that have been found to be effective through randomized controlled trials and other approaches. The identification of these elements is based on the committee's review of multiple studies, literature reviews (Axford et al., 2012), information provided by a number of invited speakers at open sessions held for this study, and committee members' own expertise and experiences. It should be noted that even those programs involving manualized interventions—with their relatively strict ordering of treatment components, each with a prescribed length—can be broken down into those components, which can be used more flexibly with success (Nakamura et al., 2014). Thus, in assessing current and developing new programs for strengthening and supporting parenting, a state policy maker or community service provider could use these components as benchmarks in determining the likelihood that a program will be effective. The identified elements may be especially important in programs aimed at strengthening parenting in families that face multiple adversities. Engaging and retaining these parents in parenting programs is a challenge. They often live in areas without sufficient evidence-based services, and they often lack the transportation needed to access such services. For these families, providing programs that have not been shown to be effective through experimental or quasi-experimental research but include elements that are common to such programs may be necessary. Given that parent participation and retention alone, however, cannot guarantee positive parent and child outcomes, these programs must have a sound theoretical approach to helping parents acquire the positive parenting knowledge, attitudes, and practices discussed in Chapter 2.

Clearly, a parenting program cannot be successful unless parents participate and remain in the program. As described earlier in this report and by Breitenstein and colleagues (2014), studies of face-to-face parent training interventions indicate that 10 to 34 percent of parents of children in the preschool to grade school age range enroll to participate (Baker et al., 2010; Garvey et al., 2006; Heinrichs et al., 2005; Thornton and Calam, 2011). Among those who do enroll, average attendance ranges from 34 to 50 percent of sessions (Breitenstein et al., 2012; Coatsworth et al., 2006; Scott et al., 2010). It has been estimated that between 20 and 80 percent of families drop out of mental health prevention and intervention programs prematurely with many of them receiving less than one-half of the intervention (Armbruster and Kazdin, 1994; Ingoldsby, 2010; Masi et al., 2003). Lower participation and retention rates limit program reach and dilute program benefits for parents and families. Throughout the discussion in this chapter of elements of effective parenting programs, therefore, approaches that have shown success in increasing parents' participation and retention in such programs are noted. The following section of the chapter then describes some additional strategies for increasing participation and retention. The final section presents a summary.

ELEMENTS OF EFFECTIVE PROGRAMS

The elements of effective parenting programs include parents being treated as partners with providers, tailoring of interventions to the needs of both parents and children, service integration and interagency collaborative care, peer support, trauma-informed services, cultural relevance, and inclusion of fathers.

Parents as Partners

A critical element of all parenting programs is viewing parents as equal partners with the provider, experts in what both they and their children need. The importance of this approach is evident in programs ranging from patient-centered medical care to joint decision-making interventions for parents' engagement in children's education (see Chapter 4).

Research has found that treating parents as partners enhances the quality of interactions between parents and providers and increases parents' trust in providers (Jago et al., 2013). This idea was supported by parent commentaries offered as part of the information gathering for this study. Findings from longitudinal and semi-structured interview research suggest that the level of therapeutic engagement with parents, empathic interaction style, and parents' feelings of being valued are related to participation in and completion of program activities (Jago et al., 2013; Orrell-Valente et al., 1999). In a review of 26 qualitative studies (Mytton et al., 2014), having an intervention delivered by individuals trusted by or already known to parents was important in parents' decisions to participate. (See also the discussion of participation and retention later in this chapter.)

Tailoring of Interventions to Parent and Child Needs

Because the needs of individual parents and children vary greatly and often depend on family context, strong programs, including those using manualized approaches, generally try to tailor the services to fit individual needs. The importance of such tailored approaches is widely recognized. For example, organizations providing Part C services under the Individuals with Disabilities Education Act (IDEA) look to individual family needs and child characteristics in designing interventions. The importance of personalized approaches to parenting skills also is central in working with parents with mental illness. Depressed parents, for example, may benefit particularly from training in dealing with conflict and difficult child behaviors, whereas those with borderline personality disorder may gain the most from education in providing a consistent routine and nurturing (Beeber et al., 2014; Stepp et al., 2012). Certain mental health disorders, such as schizophrenia, can lead to difficulty responding to emotional cues from infants and children, so programs that promote coaching to increase these skills may be particularly useful for individuals with those disorders, especially given the importance of early infant attachment (see Chapter 2) (Craig, 2004; Gearing et al., 2012; Nicholson and Miller, 2008; Stepp et al., 2012). This tailoring of treatment requires highly qualified and trained staff.

In addition, tailoring programs requires understanding and responding to gender differences in both the needs and the receptivity of parents. For example, mothers and fathers are likely to respond differently to program support based not only on their gender and role differences but also such factors as their engagement with the child and family, the level of responsiveness of program staff, the nature of familial and community expectations and supports, and their residential status.

As discussed in Chapter 1, many children are raised by a same-sex couple or a sexual minority parent. Few studies have explored the parenting experience of sexual minority adults. Studies that have been done suggest that lesbian and gay parents adjusting to parenthood generally experience levels of stress comparable to those experienced by their heterosexual counterparts (Goldberg and Smith, 2014). Lesbian and gay parents, particularly when new to parenthood, have many of the same concerns as any other new parents and could benefit from the same support structures (e.g., those provided by parent support groups/classes, medical professionals, teachers, or community groups). It is important for these programs to recognize that some parents whom they are serving might be sexual minorities and to adjust programming and terminology to be inclusive of sexual minority parents and nontraditional families more generally. Some studies have indicated that certain subsets of sexual minority parents (e.g., female partners of biological lesbian mothers) might have increased stress upon becoming parents, and it is important for programs to offer support to these groups in particular (Tornello et al., 2011; Wojnar and Katzenmeyer, 2014). In addition to experiencing the routine stresses of parenting, sexual minority parents and their children may face social stigma and discrimination.

Parents report that several of the barriers to participation in parenting programs are practical, such as not having transportation to reach the site where the intervention is being provided, being unable to arrange for child care, and having work and scheduling conflicts (Morawska et al., 2011). Many evidence-based parenting interventions provide transportation assistance and child care (Snell-Johns et al., 2004), and there is evidence that matching program scheduling with parents' own schedules is associated with higher rates of participation (Gross et al., 2001). In a recent systematic review of 26 qualitative studies in which parents were asked about why they did or did not enroll in or complete a parenting program, the time and place of the program delivery and the lack of collocation of classes with child care emerged as major factors related to participation (Mytton et al., 2014). Transportation is a primary barrier across multiple types of programs, not just those focused on parenting, particularly for those with limited income and access to personal and reliable public transportation.

Parent Voices

[One parent described transportation and child care-related challenges to participation.]

"For us, we want our kids to go to school as soon as possible. Transportation is a problem. Head Start programs can start at noon or nine o'clock in the morning. Time is a challenge for parents. Some women don't know how to drive. For our culture, we don't want to put kids in daycare either."

—Mother from Omaha, Nebraska

Service Integration and Inter-agency Collaborative Care

Service integration continues to be particularly important in the provision of services for families facing multiple challenges, including histories of trauma, substance use, relationship instability, and lack of social supports (Hernandez-Avila et al., 2004; Howell and Chasnoff, 1999). Integrated care often includes using a centralized access point for treatment of the parents' condition(s), combined with services to improve their parenting skills, such as parent training or child-related interventions (Niccols et al., 2012). Integration of services gives parents easier access to resources that address multiple needs and improves collaboration and continuity of care (Krumm et al., 2013; Schrank et al., 2015), and may help to reduce the stigma that can be associated with targeted interventions (Cortis et al., 2009). Service integration can also ease scheduling and transportation challenges for families (Ingoldsby, 2010).

Families contending with an array of adversities often also need services to address such needs as job training, housing, and income support, as well as active support to help them access and utilize those services (Gearing et al., 2012; Hinden et al., 2005, 2006). Helping parents deal with these stressors may free up personal resources, enabling them to focus better on improving their parenting skills (Ingoldsby, 2010). Indeed, lower economic stress and interparental conflict have been found to be associated with increased enrollment and participation in parenting interventions (Wong et al., 2013). Likewise, mothers in a study that included "family coaches" who helped link parents to other services in addition to direct parenting support reported strong satisfaction with the program (Nicholson et al., 2009). Conversely, interventions that fail to address coping mechanisms for family issues and parental stressors can drive families out of programs (Prinz and Miller, 1994).

Peer Support

Engagement in services and positive outcomes can be increased by linking behavioral supports with peer support (Axford et al., 2012; Barrett et al., 2008). Beyond increased engagement, strengthening social support among parents can have multiple benefits, including reduced stigma, increased sense of connection, and reduced isolation. For example, research using various methodologies indicates that interventions have successfully addressed both the stigma of mental illness and the social isolation of many parents by providing peer support via groups, classes, or even the Internet (Cook and Mueser, 2014; Craig, 2004; Kaplan et al., 2014; Schrank et al., 2015; Wan et al., 2008).

Parenting programs using a multifamily or multiparent group format allow participants to share their parenting experiences with others who serve as a source of social support and peer learning (Coatsworth et al., 2006; Levac et al., 2008; McKay et al., 1995). The opportunity to exchange ideas and receive support from peers may be an important reason why parents join and attend group parenting classes (Jago et al., 2012, 2013; Mytton et al., 2014). In experimental research, parents with serious mental illness, for example, report that peer groups help them feel understood and safe, and this may motivate them to return to the groups (Dixon et al., 2001, 2011). Peer support helps parents learn how others successfully provide guidance and set limits for and engage in other positive interactions with their children. Including spouses or partners in mental health visits is another way of decreasing stigma and encouraging support, based on findings from randomized controlled trials (Dennis, 2014). Notably, peer support services may be reimbursable by Medicare, Medicaid, states, and private health plans (Daniels et al., 2013). While peer support can be valuable in engaging and sustaining parent participation, however, it is not a substitute for professional staff with training in working with parents facing specific adversities.

Finally, it is important to note that, despite the limitations of evidence-based approaches for fathers, fatherhood programs incorporating peer support have shown success (Fagan and Iglesias, 1999). Evidence-based approaches now being implemented in fatherhood programs are likely to yield important data on the efficacy of peer support among fathers.

Parent Voices

[One parent described how she benefitted from peer support.]

"Sometimes you don't realize stuff until you talk about it. You don't realize how angry you was [sic] or how much you are over stuff or this or that until you talk about it. And then talking to people that don't know you. And not going to give you crazy feedback [from your family and friends]. And that advice never helps. Because as much as your family think [sic] they know you, they have no idea."

—Mother from Washington, DC

Trauma-Informed Services

Considerable research over the past 10 years has demonstrated the significant impact of traumatic experiences on a variety of outcomes during childhood and into adulthood. The Adverse Childhood Experiences (ACEs) study, which surveyed more than 17,000 members of a health maintenance organization in California, found that a large percentage had experienced traumatic experiences and demonstrated the connection between such experiences in early childhood and later adverse health outcomes (Anda et al., 2009). Relevant to the present context, trauma can have a significant impact on parenting ability. According to Banyard and colleagues (2003, p. 334) "cumulative exposure to trauma is associated with less parenting satisfaction, greater levels of neglect, child welfare involvement, and using punishment." Cumulative exposure to trauma is predictive of parents' potential for child abuse, more punitive behavior, and psychological aggression in correlational research (Cohen et al., 2008).

Trauma has a particularly damaging effect on children's development. Children exposed to trauma often experience problems with regulation of affect and impulses, constricted emotions, and an inability to express or experience feelings (Armsworth and Holaday, 1993; van der Kolk, 2005). Children who have experienced significant trauma without adequate parental support tend to have a heightened sense of vulnerability and sensitivity to environmental threats; experience high levels of guilt and shame; and have high rates of anxiety and depressive symptoms, including hypervigilance, hopelessness, anhedonia, suicidal ideation, and suicide attempts (Armsworth and Holaday, 1993; van der Kolk, 2005).

Based on these findings, many parenting programs now adopt a trauma-informed approach. Trauma-informed services are not about a specific intervention or set of interventions. According to the Substance Abuse and

Mental Health Services Administration, a trauma-informed approach "realizes the widespread impact of trauma and understands potential paths for recovery; recognizes the signs and symptoms of trauma in clients, families, staff, and others involved with the system; responds by fully integrating knowledge about trauma into policies, procedures, and practices; and seeks to actively resist re-traumatization" (Substance Abuse and Mental Health Services Administration, 2015b).

Trauma may affect provider relationships with parents and therefore their children. In trauma-informed services, an understanding of trauma permeates services, and all staff have the ability to view clients in the context of their life histories. It is important that providers be able to recognize signs and symptoms of trauma, a history of trauma, and traumatic stress, and have training in how to provide trauma-informed care (Institute for Health and Recovery, 2016). Interventions for parents may include present-focused trauma-specific therapies, such as Seeking Safety, Risking Connection, and Sanctuary. All of these are considered present-focused therapies, because they focus on developing skills to cope with trauma in the present. These therapies teach such skills as self-soothing, grounding, and engaging in healthy relationships, as well as other skills necessary for coping with trauma (Substance Abuse and Mental Health Services Administration, 2015b).

It is important to note that trauma can occur within typical interactions between parents and children or may be brought about as a result of unusual circumstances. In both instances, parents must find safe places for their children and navigate the turmoil that can have potentially deleterious effects on their children and themselves. Considering the high prevalence of trauma among at-risk parents and the impact of traumatic events on parenting and child development, assessing for past traumatic experiences and providing trauma-informed care for all at-risk parents can improve outcomes and may be cost effective in the long run (Hornby Zeller Associates, 2011).

Cultural Relevance

Parenting programs have historically had low utilization, especially among culturally diverse parents (Cunningham et al., 2000; Eisner and Meidert, 2011; Katz et al., 2007; Sawrikar and Katz, 2008). If intervention components and providers are not sensitive to cultural variations among families with respect to their coping styles and expression of problems, parents may be less likely to participate (Brondino et al., 1997; Moodie and Ramos, 2014; Prinz and Miller, 1994). Baumann and colleagues (2015) examine the extent to which researchers and developers of several commonly used evidence-based parent training programs (Parent-Child Interaction

Therapy [PCIT], Incredible Years, Parent Management Training-Oregon [PMT-O], and Triple P) have used culturally adapted models. Of 610 articles on these programs, only 8 document a rigorous cultural adaptation process, and just 2 of these programs used rigorous methods to test the program implementation. Recent efforts to rigorously test cultural adaptations of PCIT (McCabe and Yeh, 2009), PMT-O (Parra Cardona et al., 2012), and ParentCorps (Dawson-McClure et al., 2015) indicate growing awareness of the importance of developing and testing innovative ways to engage, retain, and educate Latino families.

At the same time, parenting programs delivered without significant modification and not incorporating tested cultural adaptations are sometimes viewed as highly attractive by local communities. This was the case with the implementation of SafeCare® in American Indian communities in Oklahoma, where researchers found that their manualized, structured, evidence-based model was a reasonable fit with American Indian parents in child welfare. SafeCare had higher client ratings of cultural competency, working alliance, service quality, and service benefit than services as usual (Chaffin et al., 2012). The Huey and Polo (2008) review of evidence-based psychosocial interventions for children found no pressing need for such adaptations. The culturally adapted interventions that have been tested have shown little added benefit, and outcomes for minority children and families who receive unadapted services generally are good, although this is not to minimize the need for cultural sensitivity and clinical expertise in order to engage families in treatment (Huey et al., 2014).

Inclusion of Fathers

As noted previously, fathers are underrepresented in research on parenting-related interventions. Moreover, relatively few fatherhood studies have examined the relationships between specific fathering behaviors and desired child outcomes. Although further research is needed, available studies indicate that parenting interventions would benefit from the use of approaches giving greater priority to fathers' participation, such as starting with an expectation that they will participate and using content and activities that they will find pertinent, in addition to using strategies that may improve participation more generally (e.g., providing financial incentives [discussed below] and scheduling sessions at times that are convenient) (Administration for Children and Families, 2015; Zaveri et al., 2015).

The data are clear and poignant regarding the lack of evidence-based strategies in fatherhood programs. In a study by Bronte-Tinkew and colleagues (2008), only 4 of 18 programs reviewed had rigorous enough designs to be considered model and promising. Much of the research on fathers and programs that include them has examined low-income, non-

BOX 6-1
A Father's Story

A proud husband and father of three children shared his story with the committee during one of its open sessions. His experience of becoming a father altered the direction of his life, influencing him to find the right path so as to be a role model for his children. During his journey as a father, he became part of a community in the Fatherhood Is Sacred Program in Sacramento. There he realized the importance of community support in helping him achieve his goal of becoming a good father.

He grew up in a tough neighborhood in North Sacramento, California. During his childhood and adolescence, he was forced to stick up for himself and his brothers. He came from a home in which the outward expression of love was rare. He pinpointed this, along with the fact that he did not have a role model at home, as the reason why he began hanging around with the wrong crowd. "I would say it was the wrong crowd of people to support me." He experienced a troubled adolescence: "I have been beat up, just been beat down by every obstacle that I can imagine."

The birth of his first child, a daughter who is now 10 years old, helped him start viewing his life from a different perspective—the perspective of a father. He worked toward becoming a better parent, but he struggled, as it was easy to fall back into the habits he had developed in the first 32 years of his life. "You learn so much of this terrible way of living. . . . Yes, I did fall back."

After the birth of his two sons, he recognized the need for support in keeping his family together and being a role model to his children, but this need was something he tried to ignore. It was then that other fathers in his neighborhood led him to Fatherhood Is Sacred, where he was immediately welcomed into a safe environment. "As a grown man, I felt safe and invited and welcomed, like I was at home." Once he became engaged in the program, he began doing the work to strengthen his parenting skills—work he had not been doing for 32 years. He has been actively involved with Fatherhood Is Sacred for nearly 3 years.

He views Fatherhood Is Sacred as more than a program; for him, it is a family. He works to engage families in the program throughout Sacramento, where he grew up. "For years, I took from our community. I was a big contributor to that [and] it is all positive now." Doing this work has helped him strengthen his ties, not only to his community, but also to his three children. In contrast with the household in which he was raised, he expresses to his children that he loves them. He educates them, and he believes that education starts in the home. "It is true, the saying, a father is a son's first hero . . . and a daughter's first love, because that's where it starts. . . . I am very proud to be here and to be where I am at today, for our next generation and generations to come for my family, for my friends, for the people that look up to me, [and] for my community."

SOURCE: "Perspectives from Parents," Open session presentation to the Committee on Supporting the Parents of Young Children, June 29, 2015, Irvine, California.

residential fathers but has not monitored effectively how fathers negotiate the core problems they face (e.g., unemployment, alienation of children and families, low schooling) or examined the effects of fathers' program participation on children over a sustained period of early development. Recent attention to programs for fathers and the need for systematic and grounded research should ultimately yield greater understanding of how fathers are affected by their involvement in such programs (see Box 6-1), but still may not illuminate with evidence-based data complex issues related to father-child interactions.

ADDITIONAL STRATEGIES FOR INCREASING PROGRAM PARTICIPATION AND RETENTION

As noted above, evidence indicates that parenting programs often experience substantial difficulty in engaging and retaining parents, especially those facing multiple adversities. Some of the reasons for this difficulty are discussed in Chapter 5 and above. In recent years, two strategies—monetary incentives and motivational interviewing—have been used to address this problem. Although these are promising practices, more research is needed to determine how they might best be utilized. Also important to engaging and retaining parents in parenting programs is appropriate preparation of the workforce, discussed in this section as well.

Monetary Incentives

Some parenting programs offer families modest monetary incentives in an effort to improve enrollment and retention, but few randomized studies have assessed the effectiveness of such incentives in increasing participation. In one randomized study, Dumas and colleagues (2010) evaluated the effect of a small monetary incentive on low-income parents' engagement in sessions of the Parent and Child Enrichment (PACE) Program over an 8-week period. (PACE is a manualized intervention designed to address parents' challenges related to childrearing.) The monetary incentive encouraged some parents to enroll but not to attend sessions. Among parents who both enrolled in the study and attended sessions (N = 483), attendance over eight sessions was comparable between groups who did and did not receive the incentive. There also was no major difference between the two groups in the percentage of parents who dropped out of the program at any point after the first session. Similarly, in a European randomized study (Heinrichs, 2006), low-income families who were offered a small payment to attend a series of Triple P parent trainings did not attend at a significantly higher rate than families who were not offered payment. Payment did appear to result in a large increase in recruitment compared with the unpaid condition, leading the authors to conclude that payment may be an effective strategy for increasing recruitment and initial attendance for some populations (see also Guyll et al., 2003). Older research on financial incentives and attrition in parent education has yielded mixed findings, with some studies showing a positive effect (Mischley et al., 1985; Rinn et al., 1975) and others not (Lochman and Brown, 1980; Sadler et al., 1976; Snow et al., 2002).

Some evidence indicates that the use of an incentive that exceeds an individual's perception of the value of an intervention may result in distrust and be counterproductive (Snow et al., 2002). Consistent with cognitive dissonance theory (Festinger and Carlsmith, 1959), if a potential participant thinks the incentive is too large, the value of the intervention may be compromised by the person's discomfort stemming from the feeling that his or her beliefs/values and behavior are incongruent. Moreover, while some experimental research suggests that modest monetary incentives help attract families that otherwise would not participate (Dumas et al., 2010; Guyll et al., 2003; Heinrichs, 2006; Heinrichs and Jensen-Doss, 2010), these payments do little to mitigate practical (e.g., child care, transportation) and other obstacles to parents' attendance and retention over time.

Another approach to incentives is the use of conditional cash transfers (CCTs). This approach entails providing cash payments to families living in poverty based on the parents' or children's engagement in specific activities. CCT programs traditionally have focused on improving children's health and well-being and conditioned families' receipt of cash transfers on receipt of recommended preventive health services or nutrition education and/or children's school attendance. CCTs are increasingly being used to promote other behaviors as well (Fernald, 2013).

Building on some successes in developing countries (Engle et al., 2011; Fernald, 2013; Rasella et al., 2013), the first demonstration of CCTs in the United States was launched in New York City in 2007. Called Opportunity NYC-Family Rewards, it provided cash assistance to families in the city's highest-poverty communities with the goal of reducing intergenerational economic hardship. Payments were conditioned on families' efforts to improve their health, increase parents' employment and income, and support children's education. Children also were paid in response to their educational activities and performance.

An experimental analysis of this program involving 4,800 families who participated for 3 years found that the families were transferred more than $8,700 during the 3-year period and that poverty, hunger, and housing-related hardships were reduced, but these effects weakened as the cash transfers ended. Parents' self-reported full-time employment also increased, but not in jobs covered by unemployment insurance (Riccio et al., 2013). Results for children varied by their age. Neither school attendance nor overall achievement improved among elementary and middle school students whose families received the payments. But children in these families who entered high school as proficient readers attended school more frequently, earned more course credits, were less likely to repeat a grade, scored higher on standardized tests, and had higher graduation rates. Families' receipt of preventive dental care increased, but there was no improvement in receipt of other preventive medical care (which was already high) or in health outcomes (Riccio et al., 2013).

Building on the findings from the Family Rewards demonstration, in 2011 Family Rewards 2.0 was initiated in the Bronx, New York, and Memphis, Tennessee. This version offers fewer rewards in each domain (health, employment/income, and child education), offers rewards for education only to high school students, provides payment on a more frequent basis (once a month), and offers families guidance on how to earn rewards. Findings from a randomized evaluation of the first 2 years of implementation involving 2,400 families show that by year 2, almost all families had received rewards (totaling $2,160 on average in year 2). Perhaps as a result of the guidance they received, moreover, parents understood the rewards more completely and were more likely to earn rewards than families in the original program. A follow-up analysis of Family Rewards 2.0 as an improvement over the earlier version is pending (DeChausay et al., 2014).

Significant gaps in knowledge about CCTs remain. These include, for example, differences in effects among subpopulations, strategies for increasing efficiency, how the programs can be adapted to cultural contexts, and longer-term outcomes (Marshall and Hill, 2015).

Motivational Interviewing

Motivational interviewing is an evidence-based, client-centered style of counseling. Based on the assumption that an ambivalent attitude is an obstacle to behavior change, motivational interviewing helps clients explore and resolve ambivalence to improve their motivation to change their behavior (Miller and Rollnick, 1991; Resnicow and McMaster, 2012; Substance Abuse and Mental Health Services Administration, 2015a). Key features of motivational interviewing include nonjudgmental reflective listening on the part of the counselor, with the client doing much of the work him- or herself. A concrete action plan for behavior change with measurable goals is developed, and sources of support are identified. Motivational interviewing was initially developed and is still used to treat addiction and recently has been used for other types of behavior change (Resnicow and McMaster, 2012; Substance Abuse and Mental Health Services Administration, 2015a).

Motivational interviewing has been proposed as a potential strategy for enhancing parents' motivation to engage and remain in parenting programs (Watson, 2011). Studies not focused specifically on parents have shown that individuals who receive motivational interviewing, or therapy based on its principles (e.g., motivational enhancement therapy), have improved treatment adherence (Montgomery et al., 2012). But only a few randomized trials have tested the use of motivational interviewing to improve parents' motivation to attend and adhere to mental health and substance use treatment, and these trials have yielded mixed findings.

Although motivational interviewing is a core component of effective programs designed for parents and families, such as Homebuilders and Family Check-Up, very little research has evaluated the specific effects of motivational practices on parents' participation. In a study of 192 parents that used a double randomized design, a self-motivational orientation intervention combined with PCIT increased retention in child welfare parenting services (Chaffin et al., 2009). The benefits were concentrated among parents whose initial level of motivation to participate was low to moderate; negative effects on participation were found for participants whose initial motivation was relatively high (Chaffin et al., 2009).

Drawing on research on motivation enhancement and barriers to treatment participation, Nock and Kazdin (2005) developed a brief intervention designed to increase parents' attendance at Parenting Management Training (PMT) sessions. (PMT is a well-supported program designed to help parents prevent internalizing and externalizing conduct behaviors in their children.) In a randomized controlled study, compared with controls who received PMT alone, families receiving the intervention in combination with PMT had greater treatment motivation, attended more sessions (completing 6.4 versus 5.2 sessions), and had higher retention in the training (56% versus 35%) in training according to parent and therapist reports (Nock and Kazdin, 2005).

Parent Voices

[Parents may not be naturally motivated to participate in programs, but participate when sought out and urged.]

"Like this [interview] is nice but I don't think I would have signed up for it. Like if this was somewhere else, I wouldn't have really signed up for it. . . . I don't think I'm good in a group. . . . I have thought about going to a lot of little groups like this but you've got to get yourself together before you go and sit in something like this."

—Mother from Washington, DC

Workforce Preparation

A central contributor to parents' participation and retention in evidence-based programs and services is a workforce that is appropriately trained in how to refer families to programs, engage them in receiving services, and deliver evidence-based parenting interventions.

As reviewed in earlier chapters, parents' engagement in their children's learning, both in the school environment and at home, is associated with improvements in measures of young children's development and academic readiness (Cabrera et al., 2007; Hart and Risley, 1995; Institute of Medicine and National Research Council, 2015; Rodriguez and Tamis-LeMonda, 2011). A central component of effective parental engagement in children's learning is reinforcement of classroom material in the home, which can be facilitated by positive relationships between families and teachers and other providers (Porter et al., 2012; U.S. Department of Health and Human Services and U.S. Department of Education, 2016). Thus, practitioners serving young children and their parents need skills in communicating and partnering with diverse families (Institute of Medicine and National Research Council, 2015). Parents' engagement in their children's health care also is important. In pediatric care, family engagement focuses on parents understanding and using information about their children's health, engaging in shared decision making, and participating in quality assessment aimed at improving care (Schuster, 2015). And enabling parents to play an effective role in reducing children's behavioral health problems likewise can benefit from professionals' understanding of the common elements of engagement (Lindsey et al., 2014) as well as of treatment (Barth and Liggett-Creel, 2014). The recent Institute of Medicine and National Research Council (2015) report *Transforming the Workforce for Children Birth through Age 8: A Unifying Foundation* reflects these research findings, identifying "the ability to communicate and connect with families in a mutually respectful, reciprocal way, and to set goals with families and prepare them to engage in complementary behaviors and activities that enhance development and early learning" as knowledge and competencies important for all professionals who provide direct, regular care and education for young children to support their development and early learning.

The importance of professionals having skills in working with families is currently reflected in several laws and policies pertinent to programs supporting children's education and in core competencies for care and education professionals. The U.S. Department of Education's Dual Capacity Building Framework for Family-School Partnerships offers research-based guidance to states, districts, and schools on improving staff and family capacity to work together to improve student outcomes (U.S. Department of Health and Human Services and U.S. Department of Education, 2016).

IDEA emphasizes that services for young children with disabilities involve children's families and that services provided should improve families' ability to meet their children's developmental needs. For 20 years, the Adoption and Safe Families Act has required that child welfare agencies engage families and endeavor to maintain children in their own families whenever it is reasonably safe to do so and, similarly, work to reunify children with their parents, when safe, as a preference over long-term foster care or adoption. Also, statements of core competencies for educators and health care providers who work with young children often identify partnering with families to support children's development as a core area of focus (Institute of Medicine and National Research Council, 2015). And as recommended in a recent policy statement on family engagement in children's education from the U.S. Department of Health and Human Services and the U.S. Department of Education, preservice and continuing in-service professional development should include concrete strategies for building positive relationships with families (U.S. Department of Health and Human Services and U.S. Department of Education, 2016).

Despite the important role of families in children's learning and development and the fact that family engagement is acknowledged in several laws, policies, and core competencies as central to the success of programs, workforce preparation for early childhood teachers and providers often does not address working with families. When family engagement is implemented, it may fail to take into account differences among families, such as culture and variations in family forms (U.S. Department of Health and Human Services and U.S. Department of Education, 2016). The committee's scan of state, territory, and tribal credentialing for early childhood education professionals revealed that only 12 states require a course or workshop on families, and just 5 states require a course on addressing ethnic and cultural difference or the needs of culturally and ethnically diverse families.

Professional schools (e.g., nursing, education, social work, medicine) training health and human service providers rarely offer courses that prepare students to work with parents of young children. For example, virtually all of nearly 250 graduate schools of social work have courses on working with families for their clinical students and taking diversity and difference into account in social work practice. These courses focus on family therapy, which is typically used for families with older children who can participate in family communication. Many also have courses in "school social work," which emphasize working with families in relation to special education services (Council on Social Work Education, 2012). Few have courses on parenting or working with parents of young children. A similar situation exists in education. Prospective teachers are required to take courses focused on diversity, multiculturalism, and families, but the requirement varies across context. In health care, challenges also have been identified with respect to communicating with children and families in the pediatric setting, such as about psychosocial and practical issues in families (Levetown, 2008).

There are indications that effective intervention approaches often are not used to the extent that they could be. For example, a recent Institute of Medicine report notes that evidence-based interventions frequently are not available as part of routine care for individuals with substance use and mental health disorders (Institute of Medicine, 2015). The story is similar with regard to parent training interventions in child welfare and other service settings (Barth et al., 2005; Garland et al., 2010). It is important for practitioners who work with families to be aware of evidence-based programs and services that support families and how they can refer families to and implement those programs and services. However, graduate schools that train providers of children's services and behavioral health (e.g., schools of social work and nursing) have limited or no coursework on leading evidence-based parenting programs. With few exceptions, health and human service professionals also are not trained in the common components that make up most evidence-based practices (Barth et al., 2014). One result of this neglect of appropriate training is that few child welfare agencies refer parents to parenting programs delivered by professionals trained in evidence-based practices (Barth et al., 2005). Indeed, mental health providers typically offer a low-intensity dose of treatments with inconsistent application of evidence-based components when working with children and their parents (Garland et al., 2010). Absent an expanded workforce prepared to deliver the evidence-based practices described in this report, these programs cannot be brought to scale.

SUMMARY

The following key points emerged from the committee's examination of elements of effective parenting programs and strategies for increasing participation and retention.

- Although no single approach is applicable to and will yield the same positive results for all parents, elements that the committee found to be successful across a wide-range of programs and services for parents are
  — viewing parents as equal partners in determining the types of services that would most benefit them and their children;
  — tailoring interventions to meet the specific needs of families;
  — integrating services for families with multiple service needs;
  — creating opportunities for parents to receive support from peers to increase engagement, reduce stigma, and increase their sense of connection to other parents with similar circumstances;

- — addressing trauma, which affects a high percentage of individuals in some communities and can interfere with parenting and healthy child development;
  - — making programs culturally relevant to improve their effectiveness and participation across diverse families; and
  - — enhancing efforts to involve fathers, who are underrepresented in parenting research.
- Studies of the effectiveness of the use of modest monetary incentives to improve participation and retention in parenting programs have had mixed findings. Some indicate that monetary incentives may enhance initial interest in and recruitment into programs for some parents, but do not necessarily lead to improvements in attendance.
- Preliminary experimental data on the use of conditional cash transfers to incentivize low-income families' engagement in behaviors that can enhance their well-being show an association between receipt of cash transfers and improvements in some economic outcomes, such as reduced poverty, food insecurity, and housing hardships and increased employment. These positive outcomes were not sustained when the cash transfers ended.
- Although available studies show that motivational techniques used in combination with other supportive strategies may improve attendance and retention in programs and services for some individuals, there is a lack of data focusing specifically on these outcomes in parents and identifying those populations of parents for which these techniques are most effective.
- Having a workforce that is trained in how to engage diverse families in activities and decision making pertaining to their children and how to refer parents to and implement evidence-informed parenting programs and services is essential to uptake. However, the committee found that professionals who work with young children and their families often lack appropriate training in these areas.

REFERENCES

Administration for Children and Families. (2015). *Fatherhood: Ongoing Research and Program Evaluation Efforts*. Washington, DC: U.S. Department of Health and Human Services, Office of Planning, Research and Evaluation.

Anda, R.F., Felitti, V.J., Dong, M., Brown, D.W., Felitti, V.J., Giles, W.H., Perry, G.S., Valerie, E.J., and Dube, S.R. (2009). The relationship of adverse childhood experiences to a history of premature death of family members. *BMC Public Health, 9*(1), 1-10.

Armbruster, P., and Kazdin, A.E. (1994). Attrition in child psychotherapy. In T.H. Ollendick and R.J. Prinz (Eds.), *Advances in Clinical Child Psychology* (vol. 16, pp. 81-108). New York: Plenum.

Armsworth, M.W., and Holaday, M. (1993). The effects of psychological trauma on children and adolescents. *Journal of Counseling and Development, 71*(4), 49-56.

Axford, N., Lehtonen, M., Kaoukji, D., Tobin, K., and Berry, V. (2012). Engaging parents in parenting programs: Lessons from research and practice. *Children and Youth Services Review, 34*(10), 2061-2071.

Baker, C.N., Arnold, D.H., and Meagher, S. (2010). Enrollment and attendance in a parent training prevention program for conduct problems. *Prevention Science, 12*(2), 1-13.

Banyard, V.L., Williams, L.M., and Siegel, J.A. (2003). The impact of complex trauma and depression on parenting: An exploration of mediating risk and protective factors. *Child Maltreatment, 8*(4), 334-349.

Barrett, M.S., Chua, W.-J., Crits-Christoph, P., Gibbons, M.B., and Thompson, D. (2008). Early withdrawal from mental health treatment: Implications for psychotherapy practice. *Psychotherapy: Theory, Research, Practice, Training, 45*(2), 247-267.

Barth, R.P., and Liggett-Creel, K. (2014). Common components of parenting programs for children birth to eight years of age involved with child welfare services. *Children and Youth Services Review, 40*, 6-12.

Barth, R.P., Landsverk, J., Chamberlain, P., Reid, J.B., Rolls, J.A., Hurlburt, M.S., Farmer, E.M.Z., James, S., McCabe, K.M., and Kohl, P.L. (2005). Parent-training programs in child welfare services: Planning for a more evidence-based approach to serving biological parents. *Research on Social Work Practice, 15*(5), 353-371.

Barth, R.P., Kolivoski, L.M., Lindsey, M.A., Lee, B.R., and Collins, K.S. (2014). Translating the common elements approach: Social work's experiences in education, practice, and research. *Journal of Clinical Child & Adolescent Psychology, 43*(2), 301-311.

Baumann, A.A., Powell, B.J., Kohl, P.L., Proctor, E.K., Tabak, R.G., Penalba, V., Domenech-Rodriguez, M.M., Cabassa, L.J., and Powell, B.J. (2015). Cultural adaptation and implementation of evidence-based parent-training: A systematic review and critique of guiding evidence. *Children and Youth Services Review, 53*, 113-120.

Beeber, L.S., Schwartz, T.A., Martinez, M.I., Holditch-Davis, D., Bledsoe, S.E., Canuso, R., and Lewis, V.S. (2014). Depressive symptoms and compromised parenting in low-income mothers of infants and toddlers: Distal and proximal risks. *Research in Nursing and Health, 37*(4), 276-291.

Breitenstein, S.M., Gross, D., Fogg, L., Ridge, A., Garvey, C., Julion, W., and Tucker, S. (2012). The Chicago Parent Program: Comparing 1-year outcomes for African American and Latino parents of young children. *Research in Nursing & Health, 35*(5), 475-489.

Breitenstein, S.M., Gross, D., and Christophersen, R. (2014). Digital delivery methods of parenting training interventions: A systematic review. *Worldviews on Evidence-Based Nursing, 11*(3), 168-176.

Brondino, M.J., Henggeler, S.W., Rowland, M.D., Pickrel, S.G., Cunningham, P., and Schoenwald, S. (1997). Multisystemic therapy and the ethnic minority client: Culturally responsive and clinically effective. In D.K. Wilson, J.R. Rodrigue, and W.C. Taylor (Eds.), *Health-Promoting and Health-Compromising Behaviors among Minority Adolescents* (pp. 229-250). Washington, DC: American Psychological Association.

Bronte-Tinkew, J., Burkhauser, M., and Metz, A. (2008). *Promising Teen Fatherhood Programs: Initial Evidence Lessons from Evidence-Based Research.* Gaithersburg, MD: National Responsible Fatherhood Clearinghouse.

Cabrera, N.J., Shannon, J.D., and Tamis-LeMonda, C. (2007). Fathers' influence on their children's cognitive and emotional development: From toddlers to pre-K. *Applied Development Science, 11*(4), 208-213.

Chaffin, M., Valle, L.A., Funderburk, B., Gurwitch, R., Silovsky, J., Bard, D., McCoy, C., and Kees, M. (2009). A motivational intervention can improve retention in PCIT for low-motivation child welfare clients. *Child Maltreatment, 14*(4), 356-368.

Chaffin, M., Bard, D., Bigfoot, D.S., and Maher, E.J. (2012). Is a structured, manualized, evidence-based treatment protocol culturally competent and equivalently effective among American Indian parents in child welfare? *Child Maltreatment, 17*(3), 242-252.

Chorpita, B.F., Weisz, J.R., Daleiden, E.L., Schoenwald, S.K., Palinkas, L.A., Miranda, J., Higa-McMillan, C.K., Nakamura, B.J., Austin, A.A., Borntrager, C.F., Ward, A., Wells, K.C., and Gibbons, R.D. (2013). Long-term outcomes for the Child Steps randomized effectiveness trial: A comparison of modular and standard treatment designs with usual care. *Journal of Consulting and Clinical Psychology, 81*(6), 999-1009.

Coatsworth, J.D., Duncan, L.G., Pantin, H., and Szapocznik, J. (2006). Retaining ethnic minority parents in a preventive intervention: The quality of group process. *Journal of Primary Prevention, 27*(4), 367-389.

Cohen, L.R., Hien, D.A., and Batchelder, S. (2008). The impact of cumulative maternal trauma and diagnosis on parenting behavior. *Child Maltreatment, 13*(1), 27-38.

Cook, J.A., and Mueser, K.T. (2014). Improving services for parents with psychiatric disabilities: Three new opportunities in the field of psychiatric rehabilitation. *Psychiatric Rehabilitation Journal, 37*(1), 1-3.

Cortis, N., Katz, I., and Patulny, R. (2009). *Engaging Hard-to-Reach Families and Children: Stronger Families and Communities Strategy 2004-2009*. Occasional Paper No. 26. Canberra, Australia: Department of Families, Housing, Community Services and Indigenous Affairs.

Council on Social Work Education. (2012). *Purpose: Social Work Practice, Education, and Educational Policy and Accreditation Standards*. Available: http://www.cswe.org/File.aspx?id=13780 [February 2016].

Craig, E.A. (2004). Parenting programs for women with mental illness who have young children: A review. *Australian & New Zealand Journal of Psychiatry, 38*(11-12), 923-928.

Cunningham, C.E., Boyle, M., Offord, D., Racine, Y., Hundert, J., Secord, M., and McDonald, J. (2000). Tri-ministry study: Correlates of school-based parenting course utilization. *Journal of Consulting and Clinical Psychology, 68*(5), 928-933.

Daniels, A.S., Cate, R., Bergeson, S., Forquer, S., Niewenhous, G., and Epps, B. (2013). Best practices: Level-of-care criteria for peer support services: A best-practice guide. *Psychiatric Services, 64*(12), 1190-1192.

Dawson-McClure, S., Calzada, E., Huang, K.-Y., Kamboukos, D., Rhule, D., Kolawole, B., Petkova, E., and Brotman, L.M. (2015). A population-level approach to promoting healthy child development and school success in low-income, urban neighborhoods: Impact on parenting and child conduct problems. *Prevention Science, 16*(2), 279-290.

DeChausay, N., Miller, C., and Quiroz-Becerra, V. (2014). *Implementing a Conditional Cash Transfer Program in Two American Cities: Early Lessons from Family Rewards 2.0*. New York: MDRC.

Dennis, C.-L. (2014). The process of developing and implementing a telephone-based peer support program for postpartum depression: Evidence from two randomized controlled trials. *Trials, 15*(1), 1-8.

Dixon, L.B., McFarlane, W.R., Lefley, H., Lucksted, A., Cohen, M., Falloon, I., Mueser, K., Miklowitz, D., Solomon, P., and Sondheimer, D. (2001). Evidence-based practices for services to families of people with psychiatric disabilities. *Psychiatric Services, 52*(7), 903-910.

Dixon, L.B., Lucksted, A., Medoff, D.R., Burland, J., Stewart, B., Lehman, A.F., Fang, L.J., Sturm, V., Brown, C., and Murray-Swank, A. (2011). Outcomes of a randomized study of a peer-taught family-to-family education program for mental illness. *Psychiatric Services, 62*(6), 591-597.

Dumas, J.E., Begle, A.M., French, B., and Pearl, A. (2010). Effects of monetary incentives on engagement in the PACE Parenting Program. *Journal of Clinical Child & Adolescent Psychology, 39*(3), 302-313.

Eisner, M., and Meidert, U. (2011). Stages of parental engagement in a universal parent training program. *The Journal of Primary Prevention, 32*(2), 83-93.

Engle, P.L., Fernald, L.C.H., Alderman, H., Behrman, J., O'Gara, C., Yousafzai, A., De Mello, M.C., Hidrobo, M., Ulkuer, N., Ertem, I., and Iltus, S. (2011). Strategies for reducing inequalities and improving developmental outcomes for young children in low-income and middle-income countries. *Lancet, 378*(9799), 1339-1353.

Fagan, J., and Iglesias, A. (1999). Father involvement program effects on fathers, father figures, and their Head Start children: A quasi-experimental study. *Early Childhood Research Quarterly, 14*(2), 243-269.

Fernald, L.C.H. (2013). Promise, and risks, of conditional cash transfer programmes. *Lancet, 382*(9886), 7-9.

Festinger, L., and Carlsmith, J.M. (1959). *Cognitive Consequences of Forced Compliance.* Washington, DC: American Psychological Association.

Garland, A.F., Brookman-Frazee, L., Hurlburt, M.S., Accurso, E.C., Zoffness, R.J., Haine-Schlagel, R., and Ganger, W. (2010). Mental health care for children with disruptive behavior problems: A view inside therapists' offices. *Psychiatric Services, 61*(8), 788-795.

Garvey, C., Julion, W., Fogg, L., Kratovil, A., and Gross, D. (2006). Measuring participation in a prevention trial with parents of young children. *Research in Nursing & Health, 29*(3), 212-222.

Gearing, R.E., Alonzo, D., and Marinelli, C. (2012). Maternal schizophrenia: Psychosocial treatment for mothers and their children. *Clinical Schizophrenia & Related Psychoses, 6*(1), 27-33.

Goldberg, A.E., and Smith, J.Z. (2014). Predictors of parenting stress in lesbian, gay, and heterosexual adoptive parents during early parenthood. *Journal of Family Psychology, 28*(2), 125-137.

Gross, D., Julion, W., and Fogg, L. (2001). What motivates participation and dropout among low-income urban families of color in a prevention intervention? *Family Relations, 50*(3), 246-254.

Guyll, M., Spoth, R., and Redmond, C. (2003). The effects of incentives and research requirements on participation rates for a community-based preventive intervention research study. *Journal of Primary Prevention, 24*(1), 25-41.

Hart, B., and Risley, T.R. (1995). *Meaningful Differences in the Everyday Experiences of Young American Children.* Baltimore, MD: Paul H. Brookes.

Heinrichs, N. (2006). The effects of two different incentives on recruitment rates of families into a prevention program. *Journal of Primary Prevention, 27*(4), 345-365.

Heinrichs, N., and Jensen-Doss, A. (2010). The effects of incentives on families' long-term outcome in a parenting program. *Journal of Clinical Child & Adolescent Psychology, 39*(5), 705-712.

Heinrichs, N., Bertram, H., Kuschel, A., and Hahlweg, K. (2005). Parent recruitment and retention in a universal prevention program for child behavior and emotional problems: Barriers to research and program participation. *Prevention Science, 6*(4), 275-286.

Hernandez-Avila, C.A., Rounsaville, B.J., and Kranzler, H.R. (2004). Opioid-, cannabis- and alcohol-dependent women show more rapid progression to substance abuse treatment. *Drug and Alcohol Dependence, 74*(3), 265-272.

Hinden, B.R., Biebel, K., Nicholson, J., and Mehnert, L. (2005). The Invisible Children's Project: Key ingredients of an intervention for parents with mental illness. *The Journal of Behavioral Health Services & Research, 32*(4), 393-408.

Hinden, B.R., Biebel, K., Nicholson, J., Henry, A., and Katz-Leavy, J. (2006). A survey of programs for parents with mental illness and their families: Identifying common elements to build the evidence base. *The Journal of Behavioral Health Services & Research, 33*(1), 21-38.

Hornby Zeller Associates. (2011). *Nebraska Family Helpline, Family Navigator and Right Turn Post Adoption/Post Guardianship Services.* Fiscal Year 2011 Evaluation Report July 1, 2010-June 30, 2011. Available: http://dhhs.ne.gov/behavioral_health/Documents/HZA-FY11-Evaluation-Report.pdf [July 2016].

Howell, E.M., and Chasnoff, I.J. (1999). Perinatal substance abuse treatment. Findings from focus groups with clients and providers. *Journal of Substance Abuse Treatment, 17*(1-2), 139-148.

Huey, S.J., and Polo, A.J. (2008). Evidence-based psychosocial treatments for ethnic minority youth. *Journal of Clinical Child & Adolescent Psychology, 37*(1), 262-301.

Huey, S.J., Tilley, J.L., Jones, E.O., and Smith, C.A. (2014). The contribution of cultural competence to evidence-based care for ethnically diverse populations. *Annual Review of Clinical Psychology, 10*, 305-338.

Ingoldsby, E.M. (2010). Review of interventions to improve family engagement and retention in parent and child mental health programs. *Journal of Child and Family Studies, 19*(5), 629-645.

Institute for Health and Recovery. (2016). *Child Witness to Violence Project.* Trauma-Informed Tips for EI Staff. Available: http://www.childwitnesstoviolence.org/table-of-cotents.html [October 2016].

Institute of Medicine. (2015). *Psychosocial Interventions for Mental and Substance Use Disorders: A Framework for Establishing Evidence-Based Standards.* M.J. England, A. Stith Butler, and M.L. Gonzalez (Eds.). Committee on Developing Evidence-Based Standards for Psychosocial Interventions for Mental Disorders, Board on Health Sciences Policy. Washington, DC: The National Academies Press.

Institute of Medicine and National Research Council. (2015). *Transforming the Workforce for Children Birth through Age 8: A Unifying Foundation.* L. Allen and B.B. Kelly (Eds.). Committee on the Science of Children Birth to Age 8: Deepening and Broadening the Foundation for Success. Board on Children, Youth, and Families. Washington, DC: The National Academies Press.

Jago, R., Steeds, J.K., Bentley, G.F., Sebire, S.J., Lucas, P.J., Fox, K.R., Stewart-Brown, S., and Turner, K.M. (2012). Designing a physical activity parenting course: Parental views on recruitment, content and delivery. *BMC Public Health, 12*(1), 1-10.

Jago, R., Sebire, S.J., Bentley, G.F., Turner, K.M., Goodred, J.K., Fox, K.R., Stewart-Brown, S., and Lucas, P.J. (2013). Process evaluation of the Teamplay parenting intervention pilot: Implications for recruitment, retention and course refinement. *BMC Public Health, 13*(1), 1-12.

Kaplan, K., Solomon, P., Salzer, M.S., and Brusilovskiy, E. (2014). Assessing an Internet-based parenting intervention for mothers with a serious mental illness: A randomized controlled trial. *Psychiatric Rehabilitation Journal, 37*(3), 222-231.

Katz, I., La Placa, V., and Hunter, S. (2007). *Barriers to Inclusion and Successful Engagement of Parents in Mainstream Services.* York, UK: Joseph Rowntree Foundation.

Krumm, S., Becker, T., and Wiegand-Grefe, S. (2013). Mental health services for parents affected by mental illness. *Current Opinion in Psychiatry, 26*(4), 362-368.

Levac, A.M., McCay, E., Merka, P., and Reddon-D'Arcy, M.L. (2008). Exploring parent participation in a parent training program for children's aggression: Understanding and illuminating mechanisms of change. *Journal of Child and Adolescent Psychiatric Nursing, 21*(2), 78-88.

Levetown, M. (2008). Communicating with children and families: From everyday interactions to skill in conveying distressing information. *Pediatrics, 121*(5), e1441-e1460.

Lindsey, M.A., Brandt, N.E., Becker, K.D., Lee, B.R., Barth, R.P., Daleiden, E.L., and Chorpita, B.F. (2014). Identifying the common elements of treatment engagement interventions in children's mental health services. *Clinical Child and Family Psychology Review, 17*(3), 283-298.

Lochman, J.E., and Brown, M.V. (1980). Evaluation of dropout clients and of perceived usefulness of a parent education program. *Journal of Community Psychology, 8*(2), 132-139.

Marshall, C., and Hill, P.S. (2015). Ten best resources on conditional cash transfers. *Health Policy and Planning, 30*(6), 742-746.

Masi, M.V., Miller, R.B., and Olson, M.M. (2003). Differences in dropout rates among individual, couple, and family therapy clients. *Contemporary Family Therapy, 25*(1), 63-75.

McCabe, K., and Yeh, M. (2009). Parent-child interaction therapy for Mexican Americans: A randomized clinical trial. *Journal of Clinical Child and Adolescent Psychology, 38*(5), 753-759.

McKay, M.M., Jude Gonzalez, J., Stone, S., Ryland, D., and Kohner, K. (1995). Multiple family therapy groups: A responsive intervention model for inner city families. *Social Work with Groups, 18*(4), 41-56.

Miller, W.R., and Rollnick, S. (1991). *Motivational Interviewing: Preparing People to Change Addictive Behavior*. New York: Guilford Press.

Mischley, M., Stacy, E.W., Mischley, L., and Dush, D. (1985). A parent education project for low-income families. *Prevention in Human Services Prevention in Human Services, 3*(4), 45-57.

Montgomery, L., Petry, N.M., and Carroll, K.M. (2012). Moderating effects of race in clinical trial participation and outcomes among marijuana-dependent young adults. *Drug and Alcohol Dependence, 126*(3), 333-339.

Moodie, S., and Ramos, M. (2014). *Culture Counts: Engaging Black and Latino Parents of Young Children in Family Support Programs*. Bethesda, MD: Child Trends.

Morawska, A., Sanders, M., Goadby, E., Headley, C., Hodge, L., McAuliffe, C., Pope, S., and Anderson, E. (2011). Is the Triple P-Positive Parenting Program acceptable to parents from culturally diverse backgrounds? *Journal of Child and Family Studies, 20*, 614-622.

Mytton, J., Ingram, J., Manns, S., and Thomas, J. (2014). Facilitators and barriers to engagement in parenting programs: A qualitative systematic review. *Health Education & Behavior, 41*(2), 127-137.

Nakamura, B.J., Mueller, C.W., Higa-McMillan, C., Okamura, K.H., Chang, J.P., Slavin, L., and Shimabukuro, S. (2014). Engineering youth service system infrastructure: Hawaii's continued efforts at large-scale implementation through knowledge management strategies. *Journal of Clinical Child & Adolescent Psychology, 43*(2), 179-189.

Niccols, A., Milligan, K., Sword, W., Thabane, L., Henderson, J., and Smith, A. (2012). Integrated programs for mothers with substance abuse issues: A systematic review of studies reporting on parenting outcomes. *Harm Reduction Journal, 9*, 14.

Nicholson, J., and Miller, L.J. (2008). Parenting. In K. Mueser and D.V. Jeste (Eds.), *The Clinical Handbook of Schizophrenia* (pp. 471-480). New York: Guilford Press.

Nicholson, J., Albert, K., Gershenson, B., Williams, V., and Biebel, K. (2009). Family options for parents with mental illnesses: A developmental, mixed-methods pilot study. *Psychiatric Rehabilitation Journal, 33*(2), 106-114.

Nock, M.K., and Kazdin, A.E. (2005). Randomized controlled trial of a brief intervention for increasing participation in parent management training. *Journal of Consulting and Clinical Psychology, 73*(5), 872-879.

Orrell-Valente, J.K., Pinderhughes, E.E., Valente, E., Laird, R.D., Bierman, K.L., Coie, J.D., Dodge, K.A., Greenberg, M.T., Lochman, J.E., McMahon, R.J., and Pinderhughes, E.E. (1999). If it's offered, will they come? Influences on parents' participation in a community-based conduct problems prevention program. *American Journal of Community Psychology, 27*(6), 753-783.

Parra Cardona, J.R., Domenech-Rodriguez, M., Forgatch, M., Sullivan, C., Bybee, D., Holtrop, K., Escobar-Chew, A.R., Tams, L., Dates, B., and Bernal, G. (2012). Culturally adapting an evidence-based parenting intervention for Latino immigrants: The need to integrate fidelity and cultural relevance. *Family Process, 51*(1), 56-72.

Porter, T., Guzman, L., Kuhfeld, M., Caal, S., Rodrigues, K., Moodie, S., Chrisler, A., and Ramos, M. (2012). *Family-Provider Relationship Quality: Review of Existing Measures of Family-Provider Relationships.* OPRE Report No. 2012-47. Washington, DC: Office of Planning, Research and Evaluation.

Prinz, R.J., and Miller, G.E. (1994). Family-based treatment for childhood antisocial behavior: Experimental influences on dropout and engagement. *Journal of Consulting and Clinical Psychology, 62*(3), 645-650.

Rasella, D., Aquino, R., Santos, C.A.T., Barreto, M.L., and Paes-Sousa, R. (2013). Effect of a conditional cash transfer programme on childhood mortality: A nationwide analysis of Brazilian municipalities. *Lancet, 382*(9886), 57-64.

Resnicow, K., and McMaster, F. (2012). Motivational interviewing: Moving from why to how with autonomy support. *International Journal of Behavioral Nutrition and Physical Activity, 9*(19), 1-9.

Riccio, J., Dechausay, N., Miller, C., Nuñez, S., Verma, N., and Yang, E. (2013). *Conditional Cash Transfers in New York City: The Continuing Story of the Opportunity NYC-Family Rewards Demonstration.* New York: MDRC.

Rinn, R.C., Vernon, J.C., and Wise, M.J. (1975). Training parents of behaviorally-disordered children in groups: A three years' program evaluation. *Behavior Therapy, 6*(3), 378-387.

Rodriguez, E.T., and Tamis-LeMonda, C.S. (2011). Trajectories of the home learning environment across the first 5 years: Associations with children's vocabulary and literacy skills at prekindergarten. *Child Development, 82*(4), 1058-1075.

Sadler, O.W., Seyden, T., Howe, B., and Kaminsky, T. (1976). An evaluation of "groups for parents": A standardization format encompassing both behavior modification and humanistic methods. *Journal of Community Psychology, 4*, 176-183.

Sawrikar, P., and Katz, I.. (2008). *Enhancing Family and Relationship Service Accessibility and Delivery to Culturally and Linguistically Diverse Families in Australia.* AFRC Issues No. 3. Canberra, Australia: Australian Family Relationships Clearinghouse, Australian Institute of Family Studies. Available: http://www.aifs.gov.au/afrc/pubs/resource/resource3. html [April 2016].

Schrank, B., Moran, K., Borghi, C., and Priebe, S. (2015). How to support patients with severe mental illness in their parenting role with children aged over 1 year? A systematic review of interventions. *Social Psychiatry and Psychiatric Epidemiology, 50*(12), 1765-1783.

Schuster, M.A. (2015). Pediatric clinicians and parents: Working together for the benefit of the child. *Academic Pediatrics, 15*(5), 469-473.

Scott, S., O'Connor, T.G., Futh, A., Matias, C., Price, J., and Doolan, M. (2010). Impact of a parenting program in a high-risk, multi-ethnic community: The PALS trial. *Journal of Child Psychology and Psychiatry and Allied Disciplines, 51*(12), 1331–1341.

Snell-Johns, J., Mendez, J.L., and Smith, B.H. (2004). Evidence-based solutions for overcoming access barriers, decreasing attrition, and promoting change with underserved families. *Journal of Family Psychology, 18*(1), 19-35.

Snow, J.N., Frey, M.R., and Kern, R.M. (2002). Attrition, financial incentives, and parent education. *Family Journal: Counseling and Therapy for Couples and Families, 10*(4), 373-378.

Stepp, S.D., Whalen, D.J., Pilkonis, P.A., Hipwell, A.E., and Levine, M.D. (2012). Children of mothers with borderline personality disorder: Identifying parenting behaviors as potential targets for intervention. *Personality Disorders: Theory, Research, and Treatment, 3*(1), 76-91.

Substance Abuse and Mental Health Services Administration. (2015a). *Motivational Interviewing*. Available: http://www.integration.samhsa.gov/clinical-practice/motivational-interviewing [January 2016].

Substance Abuse and Mental Health Services Administration. (2015b). *Trauma*. Available: http://www.integration.samhsa.gov/clinical-practice/trauma [January 2016].

Thornton, S. and Calam, R. (2011). Predicting intention to attend and actual attendance at a universal parent-training programme: A comparison of social cognition models. *Clinical Child Psychology and Psychiatry, 16*(3), 365–383.

Tornello, S.L., Farr, R.H., and Patterson, C.J. (2011). Predictors of parenting stress among gay adoptive fathers in the United States. *Journal of Family Psychology, 25*(4), 591-600.

U.S. Department of Health and Human Services and U.S. Department of Education. (2016). *Policy Statement on Family Engagement: From the Early Years to the Early Grades.* Available: https://www2.ed.gov/about/inits/ed/earlylearning/files/policy-statement-on-family-engagement.pdf [June 2016].

van der Kolk, B.A. (2005). Developmental trauma disorder—A more specific diagnosis than posttraumatic stress disorder should be considered for children with complex trauma histories. *Psychiatric Annals, 35*(5), 401.

Wan, M.W., Moulton, S., and Abel, K.M. (2008). A review of mother-child relational interventions and their usefulness for mothers with schizophrenia. *Archives of Women's Mental Health, 11*(3), 171-179.

Watson, J. (2011). Resistance is futile? Exploring the potential of motivational interviewing. *Journal of Social Work Practice, 25*(4), 465-479.

Wojnar, D. M., and Katzenmeyer, A. (2014). Experiences of preconception, pregnancy, and new motherhood for lesbian non-biological mothers. *Journal of Obstetric, Gynecologic, and Neonatal Nursing, 43*(1), 50-60.

Wong, J.J., Roubinov, D.S., Gonzales, N.A., Dumka, L.E., and Millsap, R.E. (2013). Father enrollment and participation in a parenting intervention: Personal and contextual predictors. *Family Process, 52*(3), 440-454.

Zaveri, H., Baumgartner, S., Dion, R. and Clary, L. (2015). *Parents and Children Together: Design and Implementation of Responsible Fatherhood Programs.* OPRE Report Number 2015-76. Washington, DC: Office of Planning, Research and Evaluation; Administration for Children and Families; U.S. Department of Health and Human Services.

7

Toward a National Framework

The statement of task for this study (Box 1-2 in Chapter 1) indicated that the committee's work "will inform a national framework for strengthening the capacity of parents (and other caregivers) of young children birth to age 8." In the preceding chapters, the committee has reviewed the evidence relevant to informing the structure and elements of such a framework. In this chapter, the committee looks to that evidence, coupled with the cumulative experience and expertise of its members, to describe what this framework might look like. The focus is on policies, programs, and systems that address both the general population of parents and parents who may need additional support in developing parenting knowledge, attitudes, and practices associated with positive developmental outcomes in children. While the committee's statement of task focused on a national framework, the elements identified in this chapter are applicable to all levels of government and can be enhanced by the participation of philanthropies, community-based organizations, and the business community.

As described in Chapters 3, 4, and 5, governments at all levels fund many programs designed to strengthen parenting, as well as a number of income and other support programs and policies designed to enable parents to better meet the needs of their children. The amount of support for parenting programs from federal and state resources has grown over the past 15 years, especially with respect to home visiting programs. Currently, many parents of young children have the opportunity to participate in an array of federally supported services designed to strengthen and support parenting, beginning with prenatal care and including well-baby care and educational services. Some programs, such as the Special Supplemental Nutrition Program for

Women, Infants, and Children (WIC), Early Head Start, Head Start, and prekindergarten and early elementary services, are delivered by thousands of local providers who are subject to differing degrees of federal regulation, oversight, technical assistance, and assessment. There also are thousands of other parenting programs, funded by state and local governments, as well as foundations and other contributors that focus on a variety of parenting skills. Some of these programs use the evidence-based approaches described in Chapters 4 and 5, but many programs, large and small, have not been evaluated to determine whether they are effective and meet their goals.

These programs do not serve all of the families and children that are eligible to participate, because of both inadequate funding and the choices of parents (Pew Research Center, 2015). Furthermore, while these programs are available to parents who seek them out or accept offers of service from home visitors or other providers, they are not coordinated and collectively do not form a system of services for families. Some parents, especially those who are more organized and self-directed, receive adequate services to enhance their knowledge, attitudes, and practices within the existing loose network of programs. A substantial portion of parents, however, especially those facing substantial personal challenges, need a more coordinated, ongoing set of services if they are to engage consistently in the types of parenting represented by the knowledge, attitudes, and practices discussed in Chapter 2 (Shonkoff, 2014; Wald, 2014). Thus, the suggested framework includes both a set of individual programs available at key points and a set of services that are connected and systematic. For families with ongoing needs, services would also be continuous.

CRITERIA TO CONSIDER IN DEVELOPING A SYSTEM FOR PARENTING SUPPORT

The committee considered several criteria in identifying the elements of a strong system for strengthening and supporting parents. First, a system that revolves around evidence-based programs is likely to be most effective in helping parents achieve the knowledge, attitudes, and practices identified in Chapter 2. Ideally this evidence would be derived from randomized controlled trials. As discussed in Chapter 1, however, programs that are theoretically sound that have been evaluated in high-quality studies using other research methodologies (e.g., quasi-experimental and longitudinal studies) can be used to test logical propositions inherent to causal inference, rule out potential sources of bias, and assess the sensitivity of results to assumptions regarding study design and measurement, and can work well in specific contexts (see, Center on the Developing Child at Harvard University, 2016; National Center for Parent Family and Community Engagement, 2015). The framework is founded on the concept that a system that starts with a clear set of desired outcomes, includes both evidence-based and evidence-informed programs, and applies a continuous quality improvement model in the context of existing service delivery platforms offers the greatest potential to reach and support families while at the same time improving programs and developing the evidence base (Center on the Developing Child at Harvard University, 2016; Mackrain and Cano, 2014; National Research Council and Institute of Medicine, 2009). Operationalizing this concept would require incorporating evidence reviews into the policy-making and funding system, promoting innovation and improvement, and supporting implementation research.

Second, as described in a recent Institute of Medicine and National Research Council workshop summary and other sources, issues of scalability and implementation should be taken into account in developing a system of effective, evidence-informed programs (Institute of Medicine and National Research Council, 2014; National Research Council and Institute of Medicine, 2000, 2009; Paulsell, et al., 2014). As noted above, services aimed at supporting parents generally are delivered by thousands of local entities, primarily nonprofit organizations. Implementing an effective system of services requires having structures for quality control, assessment, and technical support. In designing and implementing such a system, it may be easiest to build on existing programs that are widely available, working to enhance their quality and interconnectedness. Delivering services through large-scale, widely available programs also facilitates program evaluation and experimentation. A number of widely used, federally supported, locally administered programs—including prenatal care, WIC, home visiting programs, and Early Head Start and Head Start—can form the core of a strong, coordinated system with multiple opportunities to engage parents. These programs have been subjected to national and local impact evaluations and use the resulting information to improve performance. Enhancing well-baby care, which virtually all parents use, also would be central to developing a system that reaches all parents (National Institute for Children's Health Quality, 2016). Expanded parent engagement in state and local preschool and kindergarten through grade 3 education is another vehicle for reaching all parents, with kindergarten entry being a particularly important transition point for reaching out to all parents, especially those who have never had contact with any part of the system except well-baby and child health services. Through the graduated scale-up of proven programs and implementation of new programs utilizing continuous quality improvement methods, states and localities could create a set of programs "at scale."

Third, an effective system would be structured in a manner that fosters parent engagement in the services (Boller et al., 2014). Parents are likely to be most willing to engage in parenting programs, especially those that are intensive or home-based, when they believe that they and their children need and will benefit from those programs (National Research Council and Institute of Medicine, 2000; Pew Research Center, 2015). A number of factors that have proven most important in engaging and retaining parents are discussed in Chapter 6. Such programs are parent-centered and engage parents and communities in program design and operation to align services with the goals, needs, and culture of the parents (Fitzgerald and Farrell, 2012; Kreuter and Wang, 2015; Sarche and Whitesell, 2012). Parenting programs also benefit from including activities that parents find motivating and that treat them as "experts" with respect to their children. Services that arise from the universal or broadly available programs cited above, all of which have considerable parent buy-in, may have some advantages in this regard. Enhancing other widespread service delivery modes, such as community health clinics and family resource centers that are scalable and known in communities, is also likely to expand parental engagement. Federal and state quality standards and technical support for the organizations that administer the various types of parenting programs can be utilized to incorporate the core principles and elements identified in Chapter 6.

Fourth, if parenting programs are not made available to both mothers and fathers, program funders and operators cannot assume that what works for and appeals to mothers will do the same for fathers. The committee believes that including fathers is critical to the success of programs aimed at strengthening and supporting parents. Even when some components of a national framework (for example, prenatal office visits) may lend themselves more readily to serving mothers, staff could make services more father-focused and relevant by asking about fathers' participation, inviting fathers to participate directly, and engaging fathers in helping to design the services offered (Summers et al., 2004).

Fifth, an effective system requires a strong, well-trained workforce. Establishing and disseminating effective parenting programs requires bolstering the preparation of a workforce capable of engaging the highly diverse groups of parents in the United States (Coffee-Bordon and Paulsell, 2010; Institute of Medicine and National Research Council, 2015). Given the wide array of settings in which professionals now engage parents—including the health, education, and human service programs previously discussed—additional training opportunities addressing the skills needed to support parents are necessary (Center for the Developing Child at Harvard, 2016). Meeting this need will require new expectations, courses, and supports for health professionals in pediatrics and primary care (e.g., nurses and doctors), human service and behavioral health professionals (e.g., social workers), and staff in early education programs.

Although some trademarked parenting programs require that the personnel in organizations offering the intervention have training in the use of the program-specific intervention components, this requirement creates uneven availability of the training because there are not enough trainers to meet the need for training on these specific elements. As a result, programs that recognize the need for training in research-based parenting approaches may wait for the training to become available, the cost involved is high, and turnover among program staff leaves incoming staff without a ready source of training. Ultimately, the needs of many families remain largely unmet (Forgatch et al., 2013; Schurer et al., 2010). Given that a variety of similar parenting programs that are not delivered by specially trained or supervised therapists all appear to be effective in reducing disruptive child behavior, a less specialized approach may allow for broader availability of effective services to parents (Michelson et al., 2013). An alternative approach to training that consolidates the best parent training elements into more readily available training programs could reduce the gap in availability of effective parenting programs (Barth and Liggett-Creel, 2014).

Community colleges, 4-year colleges, and graduate programs could play a major role in the professional development of individuals who work with parents by providing training in the core skills that are commonly used in parent training. Universities could train more parent educators and therapists, thereby expanding the workforce, by instructing them in how best to deliver the core elements of interventions with fidelity. A small number of family science, social work, nursing, and clinical psychology programs already are providing extensive didactic training and practicum experiences in working with families, although these are often focused on therapy with families of older children. The committee knows of relatively few university programs that adequately prepare professionals for providing parent education or therapy for younger children. At present, existing programs are unable to accept and train enough students to meet the need (Stolz et al., 2013). To expand the training offered in these programs, more support both for teaching and student stipends may be beneficial.

Many members of the early care and education workforce who provide home visiting or classroom-based services that include parenting components come to their work through schools of education (Whitebook and Austin, 2015). The committee does not know of model postsecondary training programs in schools of education that provide specific certification in a parent engagement or parenting specialty concentration that would provide the level of skills and knowledge needed by a professional working with parents to implement existing evidence-based and evidence-informed programs in the settings suggested by a national framework. Nor could the committee find evidence that a significant proportion of social workers or nurses have specific specializations in work with parents of young children. Ideally, the workforce also would be trained in continuous quality improvement techniques. It may be beneficial as well for supervisors to have access to advanced training in the skills needed to conduct reflective supervision and support staff as they work to engage families and implement the models and continuous improvement and innovation strategies of the framework.

Sixth, the system would need to be cost efficient. Three key factors in determining approaches that are most cost efficient in helping children achieve the outcomes identified in Chapter 2 are as follows:

1. Examining whether the costs of generating benefits with respect to the outcomes exceed the costs of the program itself.
2. Examining whether it is necessary or desirable for a given approach (e.g., guidance in connection with well-child care) to be available universally, or it is more cost efficient to target a particular service to specific populations or through screening.
3. Examining whether the desired outcomes might be achieved most effectively through interventions focused on the child rather than the parent.

With respect to the latter factor, for example, while the nature and quality of parenting are important in helping children achieve all the identified outcomes, there are some outcomes, especially academic achievement, for which programs focused on the child (such as early education programs) rather than on the parent may be a more effective investment, at least when the parenting is minimally adequate (Duncan et al., 2010).

Finally, the evidence is clear that improving and expanding parenting programs represents just one investment to support achievement of the desired outcomes for children. Also essential are access to high-quality health care, child care, and preschool for children; adequate resources for parents; policies such as paid parental leave; and safe and active communities (National Research Council and Institute of Medicine, 2000). Parenting programs, while often valuable, are not a substitute for access to economic resources; parents who lack basic economic resources or who work in jobs that leave no time for being with their children often cannot engage in the types of parenting to which they aspire and that their children need (Halpern, 1990; Mullainathan and Shafir, 2013). As a result of the impact of stressors often associated with poverty, parents can be expected to experience diminished capacity to participate effectively in a range of activities, including the implementation of parenting practices learned in parenting programs that they do attend. Thus, the benefits that can be achieved through investments in programs designed to strengthen parents' knowledge, attitudes, and practices may be reduced or eliminated unless parents are provided with the resources needed to apply what those programs impart.

Based on the above considerations and the evidence discussed in Chapters 4 and 5, a system for strengthening and supporting parenting would include a variety of programs, ranging from universal to highly targeted and specialized services. It would include programs providing universal and low-intensity services and supports designed to reach a large percentage of families; targeted programs addressing the needs of parents and children with specific needs or risks, such as parents with low income or education and those with children with developmental delays or significant behavioral challenges; and still more specialized services for families experiencing multiple adversities. As discussed in Chapters 4 and 5, many of these programs and services can be delivered on a relatively short-term basis. A great challenge is developing a *system* of services for families with multiple needs or risk factors, such as parental mental health issues, substance abuse, and intimate partner violence. These families often need intensive, therapeutic strategies, such as parent-child psychotherapy, one-on-one parent guidance, and home visiting programs that are connected to psychotherapeutic interventions. Moreover, many of these families need more continuous and coordinated support among different services, including access to income supports, education, and other comprehensive services, such as housing assistance or job training.

In the discussion below, the committee explores the potential elements of a national and state framework by looking first at the types of programs and approaches that have proven effective at the universal and targeted levels, drawing on the assessments in Chapters 3-5. The committee then examines the factors to be addressed in developing a comprehensive approach to meeting the needs of families facing substantial and chronic adversities.

CORE ELEMENTS OF A FRAMEWORK

Universal and Near-Universal Programs and Supports

This section focuses on a set of universal programs that might constitute the core of a national and state framework for parenting services. The section is organized primarily in terms of "stages" of parenting; it begins by considering general parental education, and then looks at the prenatal period, postnatal services, services for parents with infants and toddlers, and finally, services connected with preschool and kindergarten through grade 3 education. While the discussion focuses on specific approaches and programs that would be offered to support parents of children at different stages of development, it is critical for many families that there be linkages of services across stages and that support be provided for families in transition periods.

General Parenting Information

Most parents seek advice about parenting from family, friends, and a variety of other sources (Pew Research Center, 2015). A strong system for strengthening parenting would include efforts at improving access to high-quality, culturally appropriate information on core aspects of parenting for all parents. Both the federal and state governments, plus a number of nonprofit organizations, now provide multiple types of information to parents through a variety of channels. As described in Chapter 4, new technologies can potentially increase access to such information. Ongoing evaluation of the reach of the information and the effectiveness of various means of conveying this information to parents can be expected to improve parental uptake.

While most new parents are likely to benefit from basic information on children's development and the parenting behaviors that promote it, no universal programs for providing this information to parents have been convincingly tested for effectiveness. Some communities are testing the implementation of level 1 of the Triple P-Positive Parenting Program, which offers parenting information through several channels, but definitive evaluations of this approach have not yet been conducted (Prinz, 2014; Prinz et al., 2009; Sanders et al., 2014). In addition, some states offer all new parents information kits, such as First 5 California's Kit for New Parents.[1]

The success of public health campaigns related to smoking cessation, obesity prevention, and use of car safety devices for children (see Chapter 3) indicates that further efforts to improve public education on specific parenting knowledge, attitudes, and practices may be warranted. For example, public education efforts have improved mothers' knowledge and behaviors regarding response to a crying baby (Barr et al., 2009) and have reduced unnecessary trips to the emergency room for healthy but crying babies (Barr et al., 2015). At the same time, the parenting information needs to be carefully crafted. Some public education efforts have failed to achieve some of the main targeted outcomes, such as reducing traumatic brain injury in infants in the case of public education on "shaken baby" syndrome (Runyan, 2008).

Additional efforts at providing general parenting information might focus on key transition points, such as the transition to kindergarten. Parents often need advice on helping their children make this transition and understanding their role in their child's education in this new setting. A number of communities now offer such guidance through programs provided by schools, including parent-accompanied classroom visits and teacher home visits. The opportunity for school staff to get to know parents at kindergarten entry can allow for assessment of both family risks and strengths. School staff also can help parents during this transition by fostering community among them, providing a channel for peer-to-peer supports.

Some high schools include information on parenting as part of health

---

[1] See http://www.first5california.com/services-support.aspx?id=21 [August 2016].

education or other courses. There is a paucity of research evidence on the effectiveness, including the cost effectiveness, of these efforts.

As stressed throughout this report, it is important that public education campaigns, efforts by schools, and all other universal strategies target fathers as well as mothers.

Support in Preventing Unintended Pregnancies

More than one-half of pregnancies in the United States are unintended. As discussed in Chapter 4, the evidence is clear that children born as a result of a planned pregnancy do better than those whose birth is unintended (Institute of Medicine, 1995; Sawhill and Venator, 2015). Parents whose pregnancies were planned are more likely to adopt parenting practices associated with favorable child outcomes, and child and parent outcomes are generally better in these cases (Sawhill and Venator, 2015). Short birth intervals place extra strain on parents. Therefore, systems designed to support parenting would benefit from including family planning as a key component. Cost-effective interventions for reducing rapid repeat subsequent births are available to support such efforts (Barnet et al., 2009, 2010).

Parenting Education and Support during Pregnancy

Parenting education and support during pregnancy, for both mothers and fathers, are a cornerstone of any framework of parenting services. In fact, programs offered at this point may have the greatest pay-off in increasing the chances that children will achieve healthy developmental trajectories (Currie and Reichman, 2015). As described in Chapter 4, programs that provide parenting education during pregnancy can be highly effective in increasing parental knowledge and improving behaviors related to producing positive outcomes for children (Currie and Reichman, 2015). Given that the vast majority of women receive prenatal care from obstetricians, family physicians, or midwives (although recent estimates indicate that 6% of women receive late or no prenatal care [Kids Count Data Center, 2015]), the most obvious channel for providing parenting information and support may be obstetricians or other staff or volunteers at obstetric offices and clinics. Expectant parents spend a great deal of time in those offices waiting for appointments, and that time could be used to provide parenting information in much the same way as time in pediatric offices is being used to provide services and information about generally accepted approaches to effective parenting.

At present, the extent to which obstetricians provide such information and support is variable, and little evidence exists on the impact of the efforts of those who do so. This is an area that might benefit from more experimentation and evaluation. States could support experiments in which obstetricians would use such tools as First 5 California's Kit for New Parents to determine whether different modes of delivering information or different types of information lead to improved parental knowledge and practices. Another possibility is the use of group programs to provide information and support. Although one program, Centering Parenting (see Chapter 4), has been shown to improve parental knowledge and behaviors associated with positive child outcomes, the limited studies of other programs have found no effects on parent or child outcomes. Labor and delivery classes are another universal setting that could be used to give parents important information about what to expect from their child and where to obtain additional resources in the community as needed.

In addition to general prenatal medical care, low-income women are eligible for WIC, which, in fiscal year 2015 served more than 8 million women, infants, and children, impacting about 53 percent of all children born in the United States (U.S. Department of Agriculture, 2015, 2016). Many interventions developed for WIC have improved outcomes for mothers, including birth outcomes and dietary intake (see Chapter 4). Since it is widely used and has been shown to support parenting, WIC may be ideally suited to serve as a central component of a system for supporting parents, especially given that parents may be eligible for WIC services until their child is age 5.

A key issue with respect to building on widely available prenatal services, whether in doctors' offices or WIC, is the importance of regular screening to identify significant issues that might affect parenting—such as conflictual relationships, substance use, and mental health problems—and then connecting these parents with treatment and, when needed, such supports as housing, income programs, and social services. Referrals for help in addressing any such issues would depend on the types of resources available in the community—perhaps in the health setting itself or in a managed care consortium or community health clinics. One possible approach for addressing this issue is use of a screening tool. For example, a recent adaptation of Family Check-Up (see Chapter 4) was administered to families using WIC (Dishion et al., 2014) and studied in a randomized clinical trial. In addition to screening and referral to needed auxiliary services, the intervention universally included behavioral parenting training. Researchers followed the children in these families through age 7.5 and found less increase in problem behavior among children in the Family Check-Up group as described by both parents and teachers (Dishion et al., 2014). Even though this experiment focused on mothers with toddlers, the approach could be used during pregnancy as well.

While there is a strong case to be made for the use of screening and referrals by health care providers in general and in WIC, a critical consideration is whether those services can be expanded without compromising their basic mission. The current staff in both health care settings and WIC generally are not trained to identify and respond to a broad range of problems. For example, WIC staff currently are very knowledgeable about issues related to nutrition, but indicate that they need additional training to communicate more effectively with parents about other concerns (Guerrero et al., 2013). It may be necessary to bring in different types of professionals to deliver broader family support. This issue was successfully addressed in the Family Check-Up experiment described above, because the WIC staff were not asked to engage in work that competed with their primary role. Thus, expansion of the services provided in these settings would need to be carefully planned and monitored.

In developing prenatal support services, careful attention also would need to be paid to involving fathers. Fathers—especially those in cohabiting unions—who are engaged during pregnancy, such as by attending prenatal classes and appointments or listening to sonograms, are more likely than those who are not thus engaged to be set on a path of committed involvement with both child and partner (Alio et al., 2013; Cabrera et al., 2008; McClain and DeMaris, 2013; Sandstrom et al., 2015).

Parenting Education and Support for Parents of Children Ages 0-1

Access to parenting support is especially important during a child's first year of life, given the extent of children's brain and neurological development during this period. This is also a period in which parents are especially open to preventive parenting support (Feldman, 2004) and in which it is particularly important to identify maternal (and paternal) depression and perhaps other problems, such as interpersonal violence and substance use (Golden et al., 2011), given the difficulty of intervening later and the high percentage (around 5% in California) of children referred to child welfare services by age 1 (Putnam-Hornstein et al., 2015). Two key systems—well-baby care and home visiting programs—now provide services and support to new parents. In addition, many communities offer a variety of parenting education and support programs.

Well-baby care As noted previously, preventive care visits for children are a mainstay of families' interaction with the health care system. These visits include basic health care, vaccination, developmental assessment, and anticipatory guidance for parents. Virtually all parents utilize this care. The anticipatory guidance can be provided to each family in an individual session or through group discussions in connection with individual visits.

Clearly, parents need access to regular, high-quality well-baby care to meet their children's health needs. However, there is currently very limited evidence that these visits positively impact other aspects of parenting. Anticipatory guidance obviously adds to the costs of the medical care provided. It is important to develop more effective means of conveying information and carrying out screening in connection with well-child visits (National Institute for Children's Health Quality, 2016).

There is evidence that this can be done. As discussed in Chapter 4, two programs—Healthy Steps for Young Children (which is physician based but can include six home visits over 3 years) and the Parent-focused Redesign for Encounters, Newborns to Toddlers (PARENT)—both of which link physician visits with screenings and guidance, have shown effectiveness in improving parenting behaviors, although there is less evidence on child outcomes. Assessments of these programs have found that they produce substantial savings in terms of reductions in emergency room visits. These programs might be implemented on a much wider scale, again with an evaluation looking at a variety of outcomes. If the findings on effectiveness and cost savings held as the programs were expanded, a case might be made for making them universal.

Home visiting Home visiting programs designed to support parenting during a child's first year (see Chapter 4) are now found in almost all states. By 2009, 40 states had a combined total of 70 state-based home visiting programs (Johnson, 2009).

As described in Chapter 4, some of these programs are offered to all new parents, while others are available to specific groups of new parents, usually based on income or age. There is some variation in the approaches and services offered by different programs, but there are also common approaches. Most home visitors provide parenting education directly and also use screening instruments to determine whether the parents may need additional supports. Those additional services may be provided by home visitors or via referral to such programs as WIC and Early Head Start that work closely with parents and children. Especially high-risk families may be referred to more intensive services, which may include full-day child care in special developmental centers (beginning at birth) and/or some form of parent-child therapy (Shonkoff, 2014; Wald, 2013, 2014). Some states such as New Jersey conduct universal screening to determine family needs and identify families that need specific types of home visiting services, and then do their best to match the families to those programs (Maternal Infant and Early Childhood Home Visiting: Technical Assistance Coordinating Center, 2014).

Home visiting can be a critical element of a system for strengthening and supporting parents. As described in Chapters 3 and 4, evaluations of home visiting programs have found several models with positive impacts on aspects of parenting and child outcomes. At least one model (Nurse-Family Partnership) has demonstrated significant effects on long-term as well as short-term positive outcomes for children (e.g., Kitzman et al., 2010; Olds et al., 2004, 2010). As discussed in Chapter 4, however, a number of approaches have shown no or minimal effects on parenting. The number of outcomes for which null effects have been found often exceeds the number for which impacts have been found. Few home visiting programs are universal, and programs—whether universal or not—often miss the highest-risk parents. In terms of producing significant child outcomes that reduce the need for additional services, only a few programs have demonstrated cost-effectiveness. This could, in part, be because these home visiting programs are not embedded in a larger framework that allows for longer-term and more varied ongoing services that help address a wide array of parenting situations.

As discussed in Chapter 4, the U.S. Department of Health and Human Services (HHS) currently is sponsoring a national evaluation of various home visiting models (Michalopoulos et al., 2013), while at the same time working with states to improve the programs through a Collaborative Improvement and Innovation Network focused on a range of specific outcomes and processes (Arbour, 2015). The existing research supports attempting to expand the programs with the most evidence while continuing to improve and study them, as the Health Resources and Services Administration and Office of Planning, Research, and Evaluation are doing. In terms of priorities for expansion, universal programs such as Durham Connects and Child First in Connecticut may warrant consideration because they capture parents often missed by other programs, including middle-class parents. They also incorporate screening for special parental needs and connect these parents to needed services. In addition, as discussed in Chapter 4, two specific programs—Play and Learning Strategies-Infant and My Baby and Me—have been found to have positive impacts on several important parent behaviors, including increasing contingent responsiveness, verbal stimulation, and warmth among socially disadvantaged mothers. Longitudinal follow-ups found later improvements in children's receptive and/or expressive language skills and complexity of play, as well as more prosocial play with their mothers and fewer behavior problems. Such programs might be especially appropriate for more targeted efforts.

Efforts at expansion would require careful consideration. It is not clear how transportable these models are and what it would take to implement them in other places. The most successful programs often were launched in university-connected settings with access to highly skilled workers. Such programs have proven difficult to replicate. Using tools developed by implementation science would be important to support adaptation from one community to another as evidence-based programs were scaled up (Metz and Bartley, 2012; Supplee and Metz, 2015).

By carefully evaluating the results from established home visiting programs (Michalopoulos et al., 2013), incorporating the training and technical assistance needed to support continuous improvement of these models (Arbour, 2015), and expanding programs based on evaluations, states and communities could build more effective home visiting systems that would best utilize available resources. If a model were selected for implementation that was not evidence based for a specific community or was new, a rigorous evaluation once key milestones had been met would be important.

In terms of parenting knowledge, attitudes, and practices, these programs could focus on attachment, sensitivity to cues and responsiveness, household organization and routines, and language development through creation of a stimulating home literacy environment.

Other general parenting education and support programs As discussed in Chapters 2 and 4, beyond well-baby care and home visitation, a number of parenting programs developed in recent years provide education and support on specific aspects of parenting, particularly behaviors that are associated with furthering children's academic preparedness, such as use of language and regular reading to children. These programs are generally run by nonprofits and supported by a combination of government funds, foundation support, and fees. Many are designed to serve particular cultural groups, are offered in the native languages of many parents, and are designed to suit the service networks and needs of local communities. These programs fill an important niche in a system of parenting education and support, warranting continued support by government and foundations. As with other components of the framework, significant additional, carefully designed research would be needed before the evidence would warrant taking these efforts to scale. The field would be improved if the relevant federal and state agencies continued to provide these organizations with information on the factors that have proven effective in parenting programs (see, e.g., National Center for Parent Family and Community Engagement, 2015), as well as economic support.

Providing Support in Selecting Child Care

Many parents returning to work will seek infant care in the first year of their child's life, and by the time most children are ages 5-8, they have been in some form of nonparental care. Helping parents identify and obtain quality child care is a key support element in any framework. Low-income families qualify for child care subsidies under the Child Care Development Block Grant (discussed in Chapter 3), administered by the states, and one of the many things states do with those funds is support local child care resource and referral (CCR&R) agencies. Parents can call such agencies or go online to find lists of licensed child care providers in their area, including providers that participate in the state subsidy system, as a first step in locating care. In the past 15 years, states also have used their child care funds for early care and education quality rating and improvement systems (QRIS), which help consumers know whether a child care setting is meeting state standards in a range of areas; this information also is available on CCR&R agency Websites. Some states have tried to incentivize families using subsidies to select care that is of higher quality according to the QRIS ratings. Given that the subsidy system and CCR&R agencies provide near-universal access for parents seeking a specific parenting support—child care information—this platform would appear to be a potential lever for providing additional information about parenting knowledge, attitudes, and practices, as well as for checking on family well-being. The committee is not aware of examples of these two specific child care programs being used for these purposes, and doing so would require developing and testing new information or program models.

Parenting Programs in Connection with Early Childhood Education

In addition to home visiting, the most widespread parenting programs, especially for parents of children under 5, are found in in the context of an early childhood care or education setting (Brooks-Gunn et al., 2000; Chase-Lansdale and Brooks-Gunn, 2014). As discussed in Chapter 4, these programs can be categorized as (1) primarily classroom-based services for children with some parenting education services, (2) primarily classroom-based services for children with some parent self-sufficiency services, and (3) comprehensive two-generation programs (such as Educare) that include multipronged, intensive classroom-based services for children, parenting education, and parent self-sufficiency programming.

The most widespread and extensive programs are those delivered in Head Start and Early Head Start; both of these federal programs were created to serve low-income children in a manner that includes parent involvement. Most programs focus on helping parents use several of the parenting practices discussed in Chapter 2, including those related to safety, discipline, and reading to children. Many of these programs also offer services for parents designed to strengthen their parenting ability. These services may include both English language and literacy and parenting classes. As noted in Chapter 4, however, the nature of the parenting component is highly variable in these programs, especially in Head Start.

Given the large number of families served by these programs (even though Early Head Start is available to only a small proportion of eligible families), the extensive technical assistance and oversight associated with the programs, the broad community support they command, the potential benefits of involving parents in their children's schooling and helping parents carry out reading and other educational activities at home, and the enrollment of especially disadvantaged children in Early Head Start, these programs are an important component of any framework. The evidence on the effectiveness of these programs in changing parenting behavior, usually maternal behavior, is mixed, especially with respect to Head Start (Love et al., 2002, 2005; Puma et al., 2012). Nonetheless, as detailed in Chapter 4, several programs focused on parent training and parent engagement in school have proven effective for changing both parent behavior and child outcomes, and much of this effectiveness has been demonstrated with Head Start children, a population commonly targeted in these intervention designs. Careful integration of proven parenting programs with Head Start and other early care and education programs serving low-income families is needed.

In 2011, HHS released the research-based Head Start Parent, Family, and Community Engagement Framework, which is intended to improve services, with the ultimate goal of having a greater impact on school readiness (U.S. Department of Health and Human Services, 2011). If these programs are to play a central role in providing high-quality early care and education with parenting components, continued quality improvement efforts and high-quality research on program effectiveness, including investigation of how to improve the parenting interventions and parent engagement, will be needed. Of particular benefit might be more experimentation with such programs as the Research-Based Developmentally Informed Parent Program and Parent Corps, which have shown success in enhancing parental activities that improve children's learning skills and school performance (Bierman et al., 2015; Brotman et al., 2013). It would be equally beneficial to examine programs, such as Head Start-based Educare, that are attempting to address the quality gap found in Head Start programs and to provide targeted, engaging activities and approaches with parents. Some technology-based add-on interventions also appear promising but would require close scrutiny and further consideration as enhancements to the parenting components of Head Start and Early Head Start.

In addition to Head Start and Early Head Start, there are a number of other two-generation approaches to helping children and improving parenting. As noted in Chapter 4, extensive evidence indicates that the Child-Parent Centers Program in Chicago improved outcomes for children, both through direct work with the children and by enhancing parenting, as well as by furthering the well-being of the parents (Reynolds, 1997, 2000). Several new models, described in Chapter 4, that focus on building both the parents' human capital and the child's cognitive and emotional development are being evaluated in a number of sites. Given the critical importance of helping parents build their own human capital while providing high-quality care and early education to their children, support for such programs by government agencies, philanthropies, and the business community is warranted.

Parent Engagement in Elementary Schools

As discussed in earlier chapters, the transition to kindergarten and the early years of school are key times for children's cognitive and social development (National Research Council and Institute of Medicine, 2000). Support and information help parents respond to developmental changes in their children as well as the new demands and rules of the school system. Parents' interactions with their children and with teachers can facilitate successful transition and contribute to a child's academic success.

As discussed in Chapter 6, education and family support policy has increasingly emphasized the central role of parent and family engagement in young children's learning and development. The Elementary and Secondary Education Act (reauthorized in 2015 as the Every Student Succeeds Act) requires that schools and districts have a written policy for engaging families and that families be included in joint decision making on the development of these policies. Moreover, recent frameworks for parent engagement and family-school partnerships have been promulgated by federal agencies. In 2013, the U.S. Department of Education released the evidence-based Dual Capacity-Building Framework for Family-School Partnerships, which places a central focus on relational and collaborative approaches to effective partnering of schools with parents and families (U.S. Department of Education, 2013). This framework also details present capacity challenges to family-school partnerships, necessary conditions for successful programs and policies for promoting such family-school partnerships, and recommendations for intermediate capacity goals and critical outcomes for these programs and policies.

As outlined in a recent policy statement from HHS and the U.S. Department of Education (U.S. Department of Health and Human Services and U.S. Department of Education, 2016), several obstacles presently impede the implementation and sustained use of best practices in parent engagement. These obstacles include enduring perceptions that parent engagement is a supplement to rather than a core element of high-quality early education; a dearth of official requirements or guidance at the local, state, and federal levels to ensure and incentivize the implementation of these best practices; a lack of attention to cultural and linguistic moderators of effective practices; and an early education workforce that lacks professional preparation in implementing these practices. These issues would need to be addressed in developing this aspect of a system for enhancing the role of parents in promoting the educational success of their children.

Targeted Programs

In addition to the universal and near-universal programs just discussed, a comprehensive set of parenting programs would include a variety of programs offering education and support to selected populations of families with children ages 0-8. These would include programs serving parents of children at special educational risk; parents requesting help in parenting children with special needs or evidencing severe behavioral problems; parents with chronic conditions, such as mental health or substance use problems that can negatively affect parenting; and families experiencing crises, such as intimate partner violence or divorce. As discussed in Chapter 5, a number of programs serving specific populations of parents and children have been widely studied and proven highly effective and cost efficient, at least for parents who seek these services. In providing targeted services, communities can choose among a number of evidence-based programs depending on the needs of the community's families. In the absence of these programs, many parents would experience great difficulty in helping their children attain the outcomes identified in Chapter 2.

Parents with Children with Special Needs or Behavioral Problems

As discussed in Chapter 5, there is strong evidence for the value of parenting programs that help parents meet the special needs of their children, including programs for parents who seek advice on parenting children with disabilities and children with behavioral problems.

Most training and support for parents of children with special needs is provided in connection with the Individuals with the Disabilities Education Act (IDEA) (Public Law No. 94-142). As discussed in Chapter 5, a number of effective program approaches are designed to meet the special needs of children with various disabilities. The basic issue is that these services are not available to all families who need them. Expanding the availability of parent-oriented services through IDEA could greatly enhance the effectiveness of a national system for supporting parenting.

With respect to helping parents work with children with behavioral problems, several well-researched programs, including the Incredible Years, Parent-Child Interaction Therapy, Triple P, and child-parent psychotherapy, described in Chapter 5, clearly produce good outcomes when parents are voluntarily engaged in participation. Providing access to one or more of these programs for all children and parents who need them could be expected to increase the number of children achieving the outcomes for child development described in Chapter 2 and also help avoid the need for more costly services.

Critical to serving many of these children and their parents is more support for children's mental health services. A strong children's mental health department or unit within local health departments or programs (e.g., federally qualified health centers) could provide the direction, oversight, and technical assistance needed to ensure that these services are adequate. Consistent, high-quality mental health consultation offered to primary care providers and nutrition and education programs such as WIC and Early Head Start also could be tested and, if found effective at diminishing developmental disruptions caused by child conduct problems, expanded.

Parents Needing Support for Their Special Needs

As discussed in Chapter 5, a significant number of parents struggle with conditions or circumstances that may impair their ability to engage in the positive parenting practices discussed in Chapter 2. These adversities include mental illness, substance use, and intimate partner violence.

The components of a system for supporting parents experiencing one or more of these adversities and protecting the development of their children would include quality care focused on the parents or family conditions and the addition or expansion of services designed to help these parents provide adequate parenting. Adequate treatment could be available to help these parents overcome or cope with mental illness or substance abuse problems. Provision of a comprehensive set of services for mothers and fathers experiencing intimate partner violence would also be important.

As discussed in Chapter 5, providers of treatment services for mental illness and substance abuse often do not determine whether individuals seeking treatment are parents, thereby missing an opportunity to provide them with parenting support. Offering these parents such support is likely to be beneficial not only for their children but also for the success of treatment. Evidence-based approaches for providing this support are discussed in Chapter 5. In addition, parents experiencing these problems would benefit if home visitors and staff in universal and near-universal programs like Early Head Start, WIC, and other early childhood programs were trained in identifying such parents and connecting them with treatment and parenting training services.

Support for Parenting Following Divorce

About one-half of children will experience a parental divorce, and one-half of those children will experience a second divorce (Centers for Disease Control and Prevention, 2015). Divorcing parents are, on average, 30 years old at the time of divorce, often having one or more children younger than age 8 (Centers for Disease Control and Prevention, 2015). Whereas most divorces do not entail a high level of conflict between the parents, many do, both during the divorce proceedings and thereafter (Fabricus et al.,

2012). Such conflict can be extremely harmful to children (Amato and Keith, 1991).

As noted in Chapter 5, a number of courts have introduced programs designed to minimize conflict and to improve parenting following divorce. A small number of states currently mandate that all divorcing parents participate in court-affiliated parenting education programs, with the goals of preventing future parental conflict and helping to minimize negative effects of the divorce on children (Sandler et al., 2015). Even though research has found that several high-quality programs can, to a modest degree, reduce conflict and improve parenting after divorce (Pruett and Barker, 2010; Sandler et al., 2015), these programs have not been successfully taken to scale. Given the potential for highly negative consequences from divorce, at least in cases of high conflict, states might want to develop and assess programs focused on these divorces. In situations involving intimate partner violence, however, safety needs to be a priority since continued contact with an abusive parent can harm both the nonabusive parent and the children.

Families with Persistent Adversities

The above framework is comprised largely of a set of separate programs that generally are not integrated, and many are short term. For many parents, participation in a single evidence-based program may be sufficient to help them acquire and effectively use the particular knowledge and skills they need to help their children achieve the desired outcomes discussed in Chapter 2, especially if they have access to ongoing support through well-child care providers, family, and community.

Some parents, however, would benefit from more intensive, longer-term, and more integrated services designed to strengthen and support their parenting. These are typically parents experiencing persistent adversities that often prevent them from providing parenting that is more than minimally sufficient, and, at times, even minimally sufficient care.

A variety of indicators led the committee to estimate that from 10 to 20 percent of all children reside in families that need considerable ongoing support if parents are to provide consistently sufficient parenting. One strong indicator is the number of parents reported to child welfare services. As noted in Chapter 5, approximately 12 percent of children experience a substantiated instance of maltreatment by the time they are age 18; nearly 6 percent do so by age 5 (Wildeman et al., 2014). The percentages are considerably higher for some subgroups of children. Several studies have found that the majority of these families are reported to child welfare services more than once in a 5-year period (Lohman et al., 2004; Putnam-Hornstein et al., 2015). Other evidence indicates that an additional 5 to 10 percent of parents need this support but are not reported to child welfare services (Wald, 2013).

As described in Chapter 5, the threats to children posed by the behaviors of some parents may require intervention through child welfare services to ensure children's basic safety. But as discussed in Chapter 5, child welfare services represent a residual system that is instituted when the parents already are evidencing highly problematic behavior that falls within a state's definition of child maltreatment or that constitutes a substantial risk of child maltreatment. These services are typically short term and are, primarily, invoked to make a decision about whether there is a sufficient safety concern to warrant court intervention. As discussed in Chapter 5, even when there is a finding of child maltreatment, child welfare services are not well designed to work with families experiencing chronic adversities and are often not successful in helping them—hence the high level of re-reporting to child welfare services.

Child welfare services experience considerable difficulty in responding to the needs of these families and children, beyond protecting the children from immediate harm. Child welfare services are not organized, or authorized, to provide ongoing, integrated services beyond a limited period of time, usually no more than 6-12 months (see Chapter 5 and Wald, 2013). One national study of parents receiving in-home services following a child abuse investigation found that the parent skills training lasted only 5 months (Casanueva et al., 2012). These parenting programs are focused primarily on the narrow challenge of helping parents interact more effectively with their children. There are no evidence-based practices for these children and families that last more than 1 year on average; only one program—child-parent psychotherapy—comes close to providing services of this duration. Most cases in which child welfare services are involved are responded to episodically and briefly. Rarely are children separated from their families and placed with foster parents, in guardianship, or in adoption (Wulczyn et al., 2005).

Further, many parents experiencing persistent adversities do not maltreat their children but could benefit from ongoing access to intensive services that would help them to address problems related to mental illness, substance abuse, intimate partner violence, and persistent poverty and homelessness. In addition to the need for longer-lasting support, many of these families need more coordinated support to maximize the benefit they receive from a variety of service providers, given their personal issues and the challenges entailed in navigating the current fragmented system of services. In general, parenting programs are designed to help well-resourced families change just one or a few of their children's problematic behaviors (especially externalizing behavior), not to assist children who may have developed multiple problems of their own and are living in exceptionally troubled families.

A system of services—one that facilitates ongoing access to needed services and encourages their utilization—is needed to support parents facing multiple adversities. Such a system is needed both for families that do not require intervention by child welfare services and to supplement the limited services offered to parents under the supervision of child welfare services. Such a system could facilitate the receipt of multiple interventions by parents and young children that are informed by screening, linked by personal care coordination and information technology, and provided in a timely way to reduce the burden of exceptional adversities.

The committee recognizes that there currently exist no available examples of a system at scale that uses screening to identify high-risk families and then provides continuous engagement, monitoring, and services. There are, however, elements of existing approaches that can provide the beginnings for the creation of such a system. In addition, as discussed in Chapter 5, a system of services is in place to help parents with children who have special needs. IDEA and other legislation require the establishment of a broad system, albeit not fully funded, that provides for screening and connection to services for these families. This structure might serve as a model for the development of a system for parents with special needs. Another promising model discussed earlier is health care for families who have children with chronic health conditions that require intensive monitoring and assistance. How these "family well-being" services might be configured could depend on state differences, but maternal and child health, well-child care, and early and elementary education programs would all need to have a significant role.

Such a system could begin with screening for significant adversities during pregnancy and at birth within prenatal and obstetric care, WIC, well-child visits, and home visiting programs, much like existing screening for children with disabilities. The goal would be to identify parents needing more intensive services and help them access these services. Linkages would be made to the universal or targeted parenting programs and types of support discussed above. Providers also would need sufficient time to perform this screening and linkage to other services. As discussed in Chapters 4 and 5, several programs, including Healthy Steps, Durham Connects, and Family Check-Up, currently perform such screening, and studies have found their approaches to be effective in helping parents and children (e.g., Dishion et al., 2014; Koniak-Griffin et al., 2003; Piotrowski et al., 2009). In addition, continued efforts to improve parenting interventions in Early Head Start, Head Start, and early childhood special education—and to have an available plan for ongoing receipt of services for families that have too many interfering experiences to be able to benefit from these parent training programs—would be necessary.

While the exact set of services offered to these parents and children would need to be individually tailored, many parents would need ongoing access to treatment for mental illness, substance use, or other problems, while their children would need to be enrolled in quality child care and early education services that include strong parenting programs. Recently there have been investments in programs aimed at providing high-quality education, job training, and career-building services for low-income parents, along with instruction in parenting skills (Chao et al., 2014). Several efforts to evaluate some of these programs are now under way (Haskins et al., 2014). Some evidence suggests that when parents with a history of maltreatment and their preschoolers participate in both Head Start and Incredible Years, the parents make significant improvements in their parenting practices (Hurlburt et al., 2013). Given that strong evidence on their impacts is currently unavailable, it is impossible to determine whether this new generation of programs will change parenting knowledge, attitudes, and practices or improve child well-being. The importance of serving these populations warrants continued support for conducting and evaluating these experiments, but it is unclear whether and how they might be incorporated into a national framework for supporting parenting.

Another important element of such a system might be having a method for periodic check-in with parents. Recent advances in information technology might enable staff of a neutral source, such as a health department or school-based program, to monitor the progress of children in these families, and to determine whether the children are experiencing developmental problems and whether they and their parents are receiving the supportive services they need. The monitoring entity could then reach out to families who needed services but with which the service system had lost contact. Another approach might be to use a care coordinator who would remain in contact with parents on an ongoing basis, help parents monitor their children's progress, encourage those who would benefit from additional services to seek those services out and help them do so, and collaborate with parent support professionals and relevant institutions (e.g., schools and mental health services) to implement effective parenting interventions. In addition, a number of organizations are establishing peer-to-peer support networks that help perform these functions. Such networks can serve to reduce the isolation often found among families facing chronic adversities and may be very attractive to parents, enhancing their engagement and retention in network activities. As discussed in Chapter 6, an important feature of all these approaches is that they be co-designed with parent representatives and communities so as to achieve the greatest potential for appealing to parents and not being viewed as threatening. At the same time, these support networks would need to be very clear with parents about the professionals' responsibility for making reports to child welfare services, as needed, if the risk to their child's well-being reached the mandated reporting threshold.

Information technologies and tools also could be used to assist in communicating across professional settings to facilitate continuous and coordinated parenting support mechanisms. Such an information infrastructure might have features characteristic of Facebook (voluntary and allowing multiple parties to communicate with a network of individuals concerned about a single individual) and combined with a linked information system that would capture information across health, human service, financial assistance, and correctional agencies. It might be hoped that parents would see the advantage of not needing to repeat information that had previously been gathered and the benefit of having better coordination between themselves and people trying to help them. As these tools were developed, parent support professionals could be trained to use them in an ethical and effective manner.

While the system outlined above entails attempting to connect with high-risk parents as early as possible, the system would be designed to engage parents whenever there were indications that more intensive and coordinated services might be needed. Children and families with such needs could be identified by health care providers, child care and early education personnel, and even family members. While earlier is better, research is clear that even when at-risk children are entering elementary school, it is not too late for effective programs to provide significant benefit. For example, children recruited into the Fast Track intervention during kindergarten because of their high level of problem behaviors were able to benefit from this school- and family-focused program (Conduct Problems Prevention Research Group, 2011). Although the advantages of the services were not evident at every follow-up period, important benefits with respect to decreased drug use, crime, and risky sexual behavior and increased well-being outcomes were seen even at age 25 (Conduct Problems Prevention Research Group, 2015).

CONCLUDING THOUGHTS

Governments at all levels currently invest substantial resources with the goal of helping children attain the outcomes identified in Chapter 2. Yet large numbers of children still do not attain one or more of the outcomes. As discussed in this and many other reports (Center on the Developing Child at Harvard University, 2016; National Research Council and Institute of Medicine, 2000, 2009), enhancing the ability of parents is a key component of a national strategy for promoting the well-being of children and families. Implementation of the framework outlined in this chapter could reduce the burden on parents seeking out the services they need and help programs focus on delivering services rather than filling their slots. By building on and improving existing service platforms, this framework could serve as an engine for enhancing parenting knowledge, attitudes, and practices associated with healthy child development and ultimately improving child and family well-being by helping all families, as well as providing access to more intensive services to those families that need them most.

REFERENCES

Alio, A.P., Lewis, C.A., Scarborough, K., Harris, K., and Fiscella, K. (2013). A community perspective on the role of fathers during pregnancy: A qualitative study. *BMC Pregnancy and Childbirth, 13*(1), 1-11.

Amato, P.R., and Keith, B. (1991). Parental divorce and the well-being of children: A meta-analysis. *Psychological Bulletin, 110*(1), 26-46.

Arbour, M. (2015). *Lessons on Home Visiting Program Implementation from the Collaborative for Improvement and Innovation Network (HV CoIIN).* Paper presented at the Committee on Supporting the Parents of Young Children: Meeting #3 Open Session, June 29, Irvine, CA.

Barnet, B., Liu, J., DeVoe, M., Duggan, A.K., Gold, M.A., and Pecukonis, E. (2009). Motivational intervention to reduce rapid subsequent births to adolescent mothers: A community-based randomized trial. *Annals of Family Medicine, 7*(5), 436-445.

Barnet, B., Rapp, T., DeVoe, M., and Mullins, C. (2010). Cost-effectiveness of a motivational intervention to reduce rapid repeated childbearing in high-risk adolescent mothers: A rebirth of economic and policy considerations. *Archives of Pediatrics & Adolescent Medicine, 164*(4), 370-376.

Barr, R.G., Barr, M., Fujiwara, T., Conway, J., Catherine, N., and Brant, R. (2009). Do educational materials change knowledge and behaviour about crying and shaken baby syndrome? A randomized controlled trial. *Canadian Medical Association Journal, 180*(7), 727-733.

Barr, R.G., Rajabali, F., Aragon, M., Colbourne, M., and Brant, R. (2015). Education about crying in normal infants is associated with a reduction in pediatric emergency room visits for crying complaints. *Journal of Developmental & Behavioral Pediatrics, 36*(4), 252-257.

Barth, R. P., and Liggett-Creel, K. (2014). Common components of parenting programs for children birth to eight years of age involved with child welfare services. *Children and Youth Services Review,* 40, 6-12.

Bierman, K.L., Welsh, J.A., Heinrichs, B.S., Nix, R.L., and Mathis, E.T. (2015). Helping Head Start parents promote their children's kindergarten adjustment: The Research-Based Developmentally Informed Parent Program. *Child Development, 86*(6), 1877-1891.

Boller, K., Daro, D., Del Grosso, P., Cole, R., Paulsell, D., Hart, B., Coffee-Borden, B., Strong, D., Zaveri, H., and Hargreaves, M. (2014). *Making Replication Work: Building Infrastructure to Implement, Scale-Up, and Sustain Evidence-Based Early Childhood Home Visiting Programs with Fidelity.* Washington, DC: Children's Bureau, Administration for Children and Families, U.S. Department of Health and Human Services.

Brooks-Gunn, J., Berlin, L., and Fuligni, A.S. (2000). Early childhood intervention programs: What about the family? In J.P. Shonkoff and S. Meisels (Eds.), *Handbook of Early Childhood Intervention* (2nd ed., pp. 549-587). New York: Cambridge University Press.

Brotman, L.M., Dawson-McClure, S., Calzada, E.J., Huang, K.Y., Kamboukos, D., Palamar, J.J., and Petkova, E. (2013). Cluster (school) RCT of ParentCorps: Impact on kindergarten academic achievement. *Pediatrics, 131*(5), e1521-e1529.

Cabrera, N.J., Fagan, J., and Farrie, D. (2008). Explaining the long reach of fathers' pre-natal involvement on later paternal engagement. *Journal of Marriage and Family, 70*(5), 1094-1107.

Casanueva, C., Wilson, E., Smith, K., Dolan, M., Ringeisen, H., and Horne, B. (2012). *NSCAW II Wave 2 Report: Child Well-Being.* OPRE Report 2012-38. Washington, DC: Office of Planning, Research, and Evaluation; Administration for Children and Families; U.S. Department of Health and Human Services.

Center on the Developing Child at Harvard University. (2016). *From Best Practices to Break-through Impacts: A Science-Based Approach to Building a More Promising Future for Young Children and Families.* Available: http://46y5eh11fhgw3ve3ytpwxt9r.wpengine. netdna-cdn.com/wp-content/uploads/2016/05/From_Best_Practices_to_Breakthrough_ Impacts-2.pdf [May 2016].

Centers for Disease Control and Prevention. (2015). *National Marriage and Divorce Rate Trends.* Available: http://www.cdc.gov/nchs/nvss/marriage_divorce_tables.htm; see also http://www.mckinleyirvin.com/Family-Law-Blog/2012/October/32-Shocking-Divorce-Statistics.aspx [January 2016].

Chao, R., Bertonaschi, S., and Gazmararian, J. (2014). Healthy Beginnings: A system of care for children in Atlanta. *Health Affairs (Millwood), 33*(12), 2260-2264.

Chase-Lansdale, P.L., and Brooks-Gunn, J. (2014). Two-generation programs in the twenty-first century. *The Future of Children, 24*(1), 13-39.

Coffee-Borden, B., and Paulsell, D. (2010). *Recruiting and Training Home Visitors for Evidence-Based Home Visiting (EBHV): Experience of EBHV Grantees.* Princeton, NJ: Mathematica Policy Research.

Conduct Problems Prevention Research Group. (2011). The effects of the fast track preventive intervention on the development of conduct disorder across childhood. *Child Develop-ment, 82*(1), 331-345.

Conduct Problems Prevention Research Group. (2015). Impact of early intervention on psychopathology, crime, and well-being at age 25. *The American Journal of Psychiatry, 172*(1), 59-70.

Currie, J., and Reichman, N. (2015). Policies to promote child health: Introducing the issue. *The Future of Children, 25*(1).

Dishion, T.J., Brennan, L.M., Shaw, D.S., McEachern, A.D., Wilson, M.N., and Jo, B. (2014). Prevention of problem behavior through annual family check-ups in early childhood: Intervention effects from home to early elementary school. *Journal of Abnormal Child Psychology, 42*(3), 343-354.

Duncan, G.J., Ludwig, J., and Magnuson, K.A. (2010). Child development. In P. Levine and D. Zimmerman (Eds.), *Targeting Investments in Children: Fighting Poverty When Resources Are Limited* (pp. 27-58). Chicago, IL: University of Chicago Press.

Fabricius, W.V., Sokol, K.R., Diaz, P., and Braver, S.L. (2012). Parenting time, parent conflict, parent-child relationships, and children's physical health. In K.F. Kuehnle and L.M. Drozd (Eds.), *Parenting Plan Evaluations: Applied Research for the Family Court* (pp. 188-213). New York: Oxford University Press.

Feldman, M.A. (2004). *Early Intervention: The Essential Readings.* Victoria, Australia: Blackwell.

Fitzgerald, H.E., and Farrell, P. (2012). Fulfilling the promise: Creating a child development research agenda with native communities. *Child Development Perspectives, 6*(1), 75-78.

Forgatch, M.S., Patterson, G.R., and Gewirtz, A.H. (2013). Looking forward: The promise of widespread implementation of parent training programs. *Perspectives on Psychological Science, 8*(6), 682-694.

Golden, O., Hawkins, A., and Beardslee, W. (2011). *Home Visiting and Maternal Depression: Seizing the Opportunities to Help Mothers and Young Children.* Washington, DC: Urban Institute.

Guerrero, A.D., Inkelas, M., Whaley, S.E., and Kuo, A.A. (2013). A WIC-based curriculum to enhance parent communication with healthcare providers. *Journal of Community Health, 38*(5), 958-964.

Halpern, R. (1990). Poverty and early childhood parenting: Toward a framework for intervention. *American Journal of Orthopsychiatry, 60*(1), 6-18.

Haskins, R., Garfinkel, I., and McLanahan, S. (2014). Introduction: Two-generation mechanisms of child development. *The Future of Children, 24*(1), 3-12.

Hurlburt, M.S., Nguyen, K., Reid, J., Webster-Stratton, C., and Zhang, J. (2013). Efficacy of the Incredible Years group parent program with families in Head Start who self-reported a history of child maltreatment. *Child Abuse & Neglect, 37*(8), 531-543.

Institute of Medicine. (1995). *The Best Intentions: Unintended Pregnancy and the Well-Being of Children and Families.* Washington, DC: National Academy Press.

Institute of Medicine and National Research Council. (2014). *Strategies for Scaling Effective Family-Focused Preventive Interventions to Promote Children's Cognitive, Affective, and Behavioral Health: Workshop Summary.* M. Patlak (Rapporteur). Forum on Promoting Children's Cognitive, Affective, and Behavioral Health; Board on Children, Youth, and Families. Washington, DC: The National Academies Press.

Institute of Medicine and National Research Council. (2015). *Transforming the Workforce for Children Birth through Age 8: A Unifying Foundation.* L. Allen and B.B. Kelly (Eds.). Committee on the Science of Children Birth to Age 8: Deepening and Broadening the Foundation for Success; Board on Children, Youth, and Families. Washington, DC: The National Academies Press.

Johnson, K. (2009). *State-Based Home Visiting: Strengthening Programs through State Leadership.* New York: Columbia University, National Center for Children in Poverty.

Kids Count Data Center. (2015). *Births to Women Receiving Late or No Prenatal Care.* Available: http://datacenter.kidscount.org/data/Tables/11-births-to-women-receiving-late-or-no-prenatal-care?loc=1&loct=1#detailed/1/any/false/36,868,867,133,38/any/265,266 [January 2016].

Kitzman, H.J., Cole, R.E., Anson, E.A., Olds, D.L., Knudtson, M.D., Holmberg, J.R., Hanks, C.A., Arcoleo, K.J., Luckey, D.W., and Henderson, C.R. (2010). Enduring effects of prenatal and infancy home visiting by nurses on children: Follow-up of a randomized trial among children at age 12 years. *Archives of Pediatric & Adolescent Medicine, 164*(5), 412-418.

Koniak-Griffin, D., Verzemnieks, I.L., Anderson, N.L., Brecht, M.L., Lesser, J., Kim, S., and Turner-Pluta, C. (2003). Nurse visitation for adolescent mothers: Two-year infant health and maternal outcomes. *Nursing Research, 52*(2), 127-136.

Kreuter, M.W., and Wang, M.L. (2015). From evidence to impact: Recommendations for a dissemination support system. *New Directions for Child and Adolescent Development, 2015*(149), 11-23.

Lohman, B.J., Pittman, L.D., Coley, R.L., and Chase, L.P. (2004). Welfare history, sanctions, and developmental outcomes among low-income children and youth. *Social Service Review, 78*(1), 41-73.

Love, J.M., Kisker, E.E., Ross, C.M., Schochet, P.Z., Brooks-Gunn, J., Paulsell, D., Boller, K., Constantine, J., Vogel, C., and Fuligni, A.S. (2002). *Making A Difference in the Lives of Infants and Toddlers and Their Families: The Impacts of Early Head Start.* Washington, DC: U.S. Department of Health and Human Services, Administration for Children and Families.

Love, J.M., Kisker, E.E., Ross, C., Raikes, H., Constantine, J., Boller, K., Brooks-Gunn, J., Chazan-Cohen, R., Tarullo, L.B., Brady-Smith, C., Fuligni, A.S., Schochet, P.Z., Paulsell, D., and Vogel, C. (2005). The effectiveness of Early Head Start for 3-year-old children and their parents: Lessons for policy and programs. *Developmental Psychology, 41*(6), 885-901.

Mackrain, M., and Cano, C. (2014). Home visiting collaborative improvement and innovation network. *Maternal Infant and Early Childhood Home Visiting Technical Assistance Coordinating Center Electronic Newsletter, 19.*

Maternal Infant and Early Childhood Home Visiting: Technical Assistance Coordinating Center. (2014). *MIECHV Issue Brief on Centralized Intake Systems.* Washington, DC: Health Resources and Services Administration.

McClain, L.R., and DeMaris, A. (2013). A better deal for cohabiting fathers? Union status differences in father involvement. *Fathering: A Journal of Theory, Research, and Practice about Men as Fathers, 11*(2).

Metz, A., and Bartley, L. (2012). Active implementation frameworks for program success: How to use implementation science to improve outcomes for children. *ZERO TO THREE Journal, 32*(4), 11-18.

Michalopoulos, C., Duggan, A., Knox, V., Filene, J.H., Lee, H., Snell, E.E., Crowne, S., Lundquist, E., Corso, P.S., and Ingels, J.B. (2013). *Revised Design for the Mother and Infant Home Visiting Program Evaluation.* OPRE Report No. 2013-18. Washington, DC: Office of Planning Research and Evaluation.

Michelson, D., Davenport, C., Dretzke, J., Barlow, J., and Day C. (2013). Do evidence-based interventions work when tested in the "real world?" A systematic review and meta-analysis of parent management training for the treatment of child disruptive behavior. *Clinical Child and Family Psychology Review, 16*(1), 18-34

Mullainathan, S., and Shafir, E. (2013). Decision making and policy in the context of poverty. In E. Shafir (Ed.), *The Behavioral Foundations of Public Policy* (pp. 281-300). Princeton, NJ: Princeton University Press.

National Center for Parent Family and Community Engagement. (2015). *Compendium of Parenting Interventions.* Washington, DC: National Center on Parent, Family, and Community Engagement; Office of Head Start; U.S. Department of Health and Human Services.

National Institute for Children's Health Quality. (2016). *Promoting Young Children's (Ages 0-3) Socioemotional Development in Primary Care.* Boston, MA: National Institute for Children's Health Quality.

National Research Council and Institute of Medicine. (2000). *From Neurons to Neighborhoods: The Science of Early Child Development.* J.P. Shonkoff and D.A. Phillips (Eds.). Committee on Integrating the Science of Early Childhood Development; Board on Children, Youth, and Families. Washington, DC: The National Academies Press.

National Research Council and Institute of Medicine. (2009). *Preventing Mental, Emotional, and Behavioral Disorders Among Young People: Progress and Possibilities.* M.E. O'Connell, T. Boat, and K.E. Warner (Eds.). Committee on the Prevention of Mental Disorders and Substance Abuse Among Children, Youth and Young Adults: Research Advances and Promising Interventions; Board on Children, Youth and Families; Division of Behavioral and Social Sciences and Education. Washington, DC: The National Academies Press.

Olds, D.L., Kitzman, H., Cole, R., Robinson, J., Sidora, K., Luckey, D.W., Henderson, C.R., Hanks, C., Bondy, J., and Holmberg, J. (2004). Effects of nurse home visiting on maternal life course and child development: Age 6 follow-up results of a randomized trial. *Pediatrics, 114*(6), 1550-1559.

Olds, D.L., Kitzman, H.J., Cole, R.E., Hanks, C.A., Arcoleo, K.J., Anson, E.A., Luckey, D.W., Knudtson, M.D., Henderson, C.R., Bondy, J., and Stevenson, A.J. (2010). Enduring effects of prenatal and infancy home visiting by nurses on maternal life course and government spending: Follow-up of a randomized trial among children at age 12 years. *Archives of Pediatrics & Adolescent Medicine, 164*(5), 419-424.

Paulsell, D., Del Grosso, P., and Supplee, L. (2014). Supporting replication and scale-up of evidence-based home visiting programs: Assessing the implementation knowledge base. *American Journal of Public Health, 104*(9), 1624-1632.

Pew Research Center. (2015). *Parenting in America: Outlook, Worries, Aspirations Are Strongly Linked to Financial Situation.* Washington, DC: Pew Research Center.

Piotrowski, C.C., Talavera, G.A., and Mayer, J.A. (2009). Healthy Steps: A systematic review of a preventive practice-based model of pediatric care. *Journal of Developmental and Behavioral Pediatrics, 30*(1), 91-103.

Prinz, R. (2014). *Scaling Family-Focused Preventive Interventions: The Triple P System.* Presentation at the Workshop on Strategies for Scaling Tested and Effective Family-Focused Preventive Interventions to Promote Children's Cognitive, Affective, and Behavioral Health, Washington, DC.

Prinz, R.J., Sanders, M.R., Shapiro, C.J., Whitaker, D.J., and Lutzker, J.R. (2009). Population-based prevention of child maltreatment: The U.S. Triple P system population trial. *Prevention Science, 10*(1), 1-12.

Pruett, M.K., and Barker, R.K. (2010). Effectively intervening with divorcing parents and their children: What works and how it works. In M.S. Schulz, M.K. Pruett, P.K. Kerig, and R.D. Parke (Eds.), *Strengthening Couple Relationships for Optimal Child Development: Lessons from Research and Intervention* (pp. 181-196). Washington, DC: American Psychological Association.

Puma, M., Bell, S., Cook, R., Heid, C., Broene, P., Jenkins, F., Mashburn, A., and Downer, J. (2012). *Third Grade Follow-Up to the Head Start Impact Study: Final Report.* OPRE Report 2012-45. Washington, DC: Administration for Children and Families.

Putnam-Hornstein, E., Simon, J.D., Eastman, A.L., and Magruder, J. (2015). Risk of re-reporting among infants who remain at home following alleged maltreatment. *Child Maltreatment, 20*(2), 92-103.

Reynolds, A.J. (1997). *The Chicago Child-Parent Centers: A Longitudinal Study of Extended Early Childhood Intervention.* Madison: Institute for Research on Poverty, University of Wisconsin–Madison.

Reynolds, A.J. (2000). *Success in Early Intervention: The Chicago Child Parent Centers.* Lincoln: University of Nebraska Press.

Runyan, D.K. (2008). The challenges of assessing the incidence of inflicted traumatic brain injury: A world perspective. *American Journal of Preventive Medicine, 34*(Suppl. 4), S112-S115.

Sanders, M.R., Kirby, J.N., Tellegen, C.L., and Day, J.J. (2014). The Triple P-Positive Parenting Program: A systematic review and meta-analysis of a multi-level system of parenting support. *Clinical Psychology Review, 34*(4), 337-357.

Sandler, I., Ingram, A., Wolchik, S., Tein, J.-Y., and Winslow, E. (2015). Long-term effects of parenting-focused preventive interventions to promote resilience of children and adolescents. *Child Development Perspectives, 9*(3), 164-171.

Sandstrom, H., Gearing, M., Peters, H.E., Heller, C., Healy, O., and Pratt, E. (2015). *Approaches to Father Engagement and Fathers' Experiences in Home Visiting Programs.* OPRE Report 2015-103. Washington, DC: Urban Institute.

Sarche, M.C., and Whitesell, N.R. (2012). Child development research in North American native communities—looking back and moving forward: Introduction. *Child Development Perspectives, 6*(1), 42-48.

Sawhill, I., and Venator, J. (2015). *Improving Children's Life Chances through Better Family Planning*. Washington, DC: Brookings Institution.

Schurer, J., Kohl, P.L., and Bellamy, J.L. (2010). Organizational context and readiness for change: A study of community-based parenting programs in one Midwestern city. *Administration in Social Work, 34*, 178-195.

Shonkoff, J.P. (2014). A healthy start before and after birth: Applying the biology of adversity to build the capabilities of caregivers. In K. McCartney, H. Yoshikawa, and L.B. Forcier (Eds.), *Improving the Odds for America's Children: Future Directions in Policy and Practice* (pp. 28-43). Cambridge, MA: Harvard Education Press.

Stolz, H., Brandon, M.D., Wallace, H., and Roberson, P. (2013). Understanding and addressing the needs of parenting educators: A focus group analysis. *Families in Society: The Journal of Contemporary Social Services, 94*(3), 203-210.

Summers, J.A., Boller, K., and Raikes, H. (2004). Preferences and perceptions about getting support expressed by low-income fathers. *Fathering: A Journal of Theory, Research, and Practice about Men as Fathers, 2*(1).

Supplee, L., and Metz, A. (2015). Opportunities and challenges in evidence-based social policy. *Social Policy Report, 28*(4).

U.S. Department of Agriculture. (2015). *WIC Program: Monthly Data—National Level*. Available: http://www.fns.usda.gov/sites/default/files/pd/37WIC_Monthly.pdf [October 2016].

U.S. Department of Agriculture. (2016). *WIC Program Participation and Costs*. Available: http://www.fns.usda.gov/sites/default/files/pd/wisummary.pdf [May 2016].

U.S. Department of Education. (2013). *The Dual Capacity Building Framework for Family-School Partnerships*. Available: http://www2.ed.gov/documents/family-community/partnership-frameworks.pdf [January 2016].

U.S. Department of Health and Human Services. (2011). *The Head Start Parent, Family, and Community Engagement Framework Promoting Family Engagement and School Readiness, from Prenatal to Age 8*. Available: http://eclkc.ohs.acf.hhs.gov/hslc/standards/im/2011/pfce-framework.pdf [January 2016].

U.S. Department of Health and Human Services and U.S. Department of Education. (2016). *Policy Statement on Family Engagement: From the Early Years to the Early Grades*. Available: http://www2.ed.gov/about/inits/ed/earlylearning/files/policy-statement-on-family-engagement.pdf [May 2016].

Wald, M.S. (2013). Taking the wrong message: The legacy of the identification of the battered child syndrome. In D.R. Krugman and E.J. Korbin (Eds.), *C. Henry Kempe: A 50-Year Legacy to the Field of Child Abuse and Neglect* (pp. 89-101). Dordrecht, Netherlands: Springer.

Wald, M.S. (2014). Beyond child protection: Helping all families provide adequate parenting. In K. McCartney, H. Yoshikawa and L.B. Forcier (Eds.), *Improving the Odds for America's Children: Future Directions in Policy and Practice* (pp. 135-148). Cambridge, MA: Harvard Education Press.

Whitebook, M., and Austin, L.J.E. (2015). *Early Childhood Higher Education: Taking Stock across the States*. Berkeley, CA: Center for the Study of Childcare Employment.

Wildeman, C., Emanuel, N., Leventhal, J.M., Putnam-Hornstein, E., Waldfogel, J., and Lee, H. (2014). The prevalence of confirmed maltreatment among U.S. children, 2004 to 2011. *Journal of the American Medical Association Pediatrics, 168*(8), 706-713.

Wulczyn, F., Barth, R. P., Yuan, Y. Y., Jones Harden, B., and Landsverk, J. (2005). *Beyond Common Sense: Evidence for Child Welfare Policy Reform*. New York: Transaction De Gruyter.

8

Conclusions and Recommendations

This chapter presents the committee's conclusions and recommendations. As directed in the statement of task for this study (Box 1-2 in Chapter 1), the recommendations focus on promoting the wide-scale adoption of parenting knowledge, attitudes, and practices associated with healthy child development and effective intervention strategies, as well as identifying priorities for future research.

SCALING EFFECTIVE INTERVENTIONS

Using Existing Platforms to Promote Parent Support

As described in Chapters 4 and 5, a number of intervention strategies currently have strong evidence of effectiveness for supporting parents' well-being and their use of practices associated with positive child outcomes. The committee was unable to identify a single intervention that supports all of the knowledge, attitudes, and practices identified in Chapter 2 for all groups of parents. However, intervention research has identified a number of strategies with robust evidence for supporting particular parenting practices in specific settings or among specific population groups. Yet many families who could benefit from these interventions neither seek out nor are referred to them. To better support parents and children, then, improved referral mechanisms are needed. Millions of parents interact with health care (e.g., well-child and mental and behavioral health care), education (e.g., early care and education and formal prekindergarten to grade 3), and other community services each year. Along with improvements in workforce preparation (see Recommendations 3 and 4 below), better leveraging the services with which many parents already have ongoing connections as points of intervention and referral would help improve the reach of effective strategies.

> **Recommendation 1: The U.S. Department of Health and Human Services, the U.S. Department of Education, state and local agencies, and community-based organizations responsible for the implementation of services that reach large numbers of families (e.g., health care, early care and education, community programs) should form a working group to identify points in the delivery of these services at which evidence-based strategies for supporting parents can be implemented and referral of parents to needed resources can be enhanced. Based on its findings, the working group should issue guidance to service delivery organizations on increasing parents' access to evidence-based interventions.**

Strengthening Evidence on How to Scale Parenting Programs

Research on how to bring effective parenting programs to scale is limited. Although a number of programs are effective in supporting parents, their potential for helping large numbers of families often depends on factors specific to the families served and to the organizations and communities in which they will be implemented (Axford et al., 2012; Katz et al., 2007). Additional evidence is needed to inform the creation of a system for efficiently disseminating evidence-based programs and services to the field and for ensuring that a wide range of communities learn about them, are able to assess their fit with community needs, develop needed adaptations, and monitor fidelity and progress toward targeted outcomes.

> **Recommendation 2:[1] The U.S. Department of Health and Human Services, the Institute of Education Sciences, the Patient-Centered Outcomes Research Institute, and private philanthropies should fund research focused on developing guidance for policy makers and program administrators and managers on how to scale effective parenting programs as widely and rapidly as possible. This research should take into account organization-, program-, and system-level factors, as well as quality improvement. Supports for scaling efforts developed through this research might include cost tools, measurement toolkits, and implementation guidelines.**

---

[1] This recommendation, along with Recommendations 4, 6, and 10 were modified following the transmittal of the report to the study sponsors. In particular, the U.S. Department of Health and Human Services (HHS) was inserted to replace the names of specific agencies within HHS to allow HHS to decide the most appropriate agencies to carry out the recommendations.

Implementation of this recommendation should not delay or preclude implementation of Recommendation 1. Rather, findings from this research could be used in an ongoing way to inform the integration of evidence-based interventions into widely used service platforms.

Enhancing Workforce Competence in Delivering Evidence-Based Parenting Interventions

A professional workforce with knowledge about and competencies for implementing evidence-based interventions to support parents is essential to the successful scale-up of effective approaches. The committee found that evidence-based parenting interventions often are not available as part of either routine services for parents or services, such as treatments for mental illness and substance abuse, not designed specifically for parents but with the potential to benefit many parents (Barth et al., 2005; Garland et al., 2010; Institute of Medicine, 2015). One reason for this is that providers of these services often lack knowledge and competencies in evidence-based parenting interventions. Graduate training for providers of children's services and behavioral health care (e.g., in schools of social work and nursing) generally includes limited or no coursework on evidence-based parenting programs or their core elements. A viable way to increase the availability of evidence-based parenting interventions is to build on the commonality of specific and nonspecific elements across interventions (Institute of Medicine, 2015). Although further research in this area is needed, the common elements approach has been shown to outperform usual care in at least one randomized clinical trial addressing children with mental health problems (Chorpita et al., 2013).

Recommendation 3: The U.S. Department of Health and Human Services should continue to promote the use of evidence-based parenting interventions. In so doing, it should support research designed to further operationalize the common elements of effective parenting interventions and to compare the benefits of interventions based on the common elements of effective parenting programs with the specific evidence-based programs from which the elements originated. These efforts also should encompass (1) development of a common terminology for describing common elements and creation and testing of corresponding training materials; (2) development of an open-source curriculum, fidelity-checking strategies, and sustainability strategies for use in educating health and human service professionals in the delivery of evidence-based parenting interventions; and (3) creation of a variety of incentives and training programs to ensure knowledge of effective parenting interventions among professional groups working with young children and their families.

Enhancing Workforce Knowledge and Competence in Parent Engagement

Parents' engagement in young children's learning is associated with improvements in children's literacy, behavior, and socioemotional well-being (Dearing et al., 2006; Fan and Chen, 2001; Fantuzzo et al., 2004; Gadsden, 2014; Jeynes, 2012; Sheridan et al., 2010). Engagement is a process that can be facilitated by provider skills in communication and joint decision making with diverse families about their children's education (U.S. Department of Health and Human Services and U.S. Department of Education, 2016). The Institute of Medicine and National Research Council (2015) report *Transforming the Workforce for Children Birth through Age 8* identifies as important competencies for all professionals providing direct, regular care for young children the ability to connect with families in a way that is mutually respectful and reciprocal, set goals with families, and prepare them to engage in behaviors and activities that enhance children's development and early learning. However, the committee found that programs designed to prepare individuals to work with young children do not always include evidence-informed strategies for creating successful partnerships with families. Despite growing recognition that partnerships with families contribute to the success of early childhood programs and schools in preparing children for academic success, as well as an emphasis on family engagement in statutes and policies, programs designed to prepare teachers and providers often do not include professional development related to working with parents (U.S. Department of Health and Human Services and U.S. Department of Education, 2016). Moreover, courses on interacting with diverse families show substantial variation. The committee's review of state/territory/tribal credentials for early education professionals revealed that only 12 states require a course or workshop on families, and just 5 states require a course on addressing the needs of culturally and ethnically diverse families.

> **Recommendation 4: The U.S. Department of Health and Human Services and the U.S. Department of Education should convene a group of experts in teaching and research and representatives of relevant practice organizations and research associations to review and improve professional development for providers who work with families of young children across sectors (e.g., education, child welfare, health). Professional development should be evaluated as to whether its core elements include best practices in engagement of and joint decision making with parents, across diverse family structures with other parental caregivers, as well as evidence-informed programs that support parents. The expert group should identify appropriate courses to address issues of parents and develop appropriate course plans and frameworks for professional development where they are lacking. Courses and course-**

work on parent engagement for educators of young children should be aligned with the knowledge and competencies outlined in the 2015 Institute of Medicine and National Research Council report *Transforming the Workforce for Children Birth through Age 8.*

Developing and Disseminating Best Practices in Parent Engagement

Studies have documented the effectiveness of joint decision making (parents as partners) and other approaches to parent-teacher collaboration in education (Dearing et al., 2015; Gadsden, 2014; Henderson and Mapp, 2002; Sheridan et al., 2010, 2014). Accordingly, the Elementary and Secondary Education Act requires that school districts develop and implement parent engagement policies designed to bolster student outcomes. Yet despite the availability of evidence-based approaches for increasing parent engagement in children's learning and thereby improving child development outcomes, limited official guidance is available on how to do so (U.S. Department of Health and Human Services and U.S. Department of Education, 2016). In addition to obstacles related to workforce preparation, the implementation and sustained use of best practices in parent engagement are limited by a dearth of official guidance at the local, state, and federal levels, as well as a lack of attention to how families' culture and language may moderate the effectiveness of school districts' engagement plans (U.S. Department of Health and Human Services and U.S. Department of Education, 2016).

Recommendation 5: The U.S. Department of Health and Human Services and the U.S. Department of Education should convene experts in parent engagement to create a toolbox of evidence-informed engagement and joint decision-making models, programs, and practices for implementation in early education settings. The U.S. Department of Health and Human Services and U.S. Department of Education should disseminate this toolbox to support state and district adherence to requirements for parent engagement such as those described in the Elementary and Secondary Education Act, as well as to support the effective use of parenting interventions by health, behavioral health, and community programs with which parents and their children often have sustained and important connections. Toolbox development and dissemination efforts should include parents from diverse language and cultural backgrounds.

COMMUNICATING EVIDENCE-BASED
PARENTING INFORMATION

Parents with knowledge of child development compared with parents without such knowledge have higher-quality interactions with their young children and are more likely to engage in parenting practices associated with children's healthy development (Benasich and Brooks-Gunn, 1996; Hess et al., 2004; Huang et al., 2005). Moreover, parents with versus those without knowledge of parenting practices that lead to healthy outcomes in children, particularly practices that facilitate children's physical health and safety, have been found to be more likely to implement those practices (Bryanton et al., 2013; Chung-Park, 2012; Corrarino et al., 2001; Katz et al., 2011). Although simply knowing about parenting practices that promote child development or the benefits of a particular parenting practice does not necessarily translate into the use of such practices, awareness is foundational for behavior that supports children.

When designed and executed carefully in accordance with rigorous scientific evidence, public health campaigns are a potentially effective low-cost way to reach large and heterogeneous groups of parents. Exemplar public health campaigns have addressed tobacco control, seat belt use, sudden infant death syndrome, and illicit drug use (Hornik, 2012). Moreover, information and communication technologies now offer promising opportunities to tailor information to the needs of parents based on their background and social circumstances.

Several important ongoing efforts by the federal government and private organizations (e.g., Centers for Disease Control and Prevention, 2016; ZERO TO THREE, 2016) communicate information to parents on developmental milestones and parenting practices grounded in evidence. Yet communication inequalities exist in how such information is generated, manipulated, and distributed among social groups and also at the individual level in the ability to access and take advantage of the information (Viswanath, 2006). Parenting information that is delivered via the Internet, for example, is more difficult to access for some parents, including linguistic minorities, families in rural areas, and parents with less education (File and Ryan, 2014).

> **Recommendation 6: The U.S. Department of Health and Human Services and the U.S. Department of Education, working with state and local departments of health and education and private partners, including businesses and employers, should lead an effort to expand and improve the communication to parents of up-to-date information on children's developmental milestones and parenting practices associated with healthy child development. This effort should place particular emphasis on communication to subpopulations that are often under-**

served, such as immigrant families; linguistic, racial, and ethnic minorities; families in rural areas; parents of low socioeconomic status; and fathers. Given the potential of public health campaigns to promote positive parenting practices, this effort should draw on the latest state of the science of such campaigns. The effectiveness of communication efforts also should be evaluated to enhance their success and to inform future efforts.

ADDRESSING GAPS IN THE
RESEARCH-TO-PRACTICE/PRACTICE-TO-RESEARCH PIPELINE

The committee identified a number of interventions that show promise in supporting the parenting knowledge, attitudes, and practices described in Chapter 2 for specific groups of parents and children. Further research is needed to understand whether and how these interventions should be scaled up to serve all parents who would benefit from them.

To best guide policy and practice, it is important that such research focus on major gaps in current knowledge and that it use those methodologies most likely to produce evidence that can inform policy or practice. These gaps include interventions previously subjected to rigorous evaluation but not tested in diverse populations; interventions that may have been limited by their mother-only focus; and the lack of interventions focused on parents needing services for personal issues, such as mental illness.

More research also is needed on cases in which parenting interventions have been layered onto another intervention and (1) their unique benefit (separate from that of the primary intervention) has not been adequately assessed or (2) the parenting component was found to have no impact. Examples of parenting interventions that fall into one or both of these categories are enhanced anticipatory guidance, which can be provided as part of well-child care; parenting interventions delivered in conjunction with treatment for parents who have mental illness or substance abuse or are experiencing interpersonal violence; parenting interventions delivered using new information and communication technologies; and parenting components in Head Start, Early Head Start, and the Special Supplemental Nutrition Program for Women, Infants, and Children (WIC). Although evaluation of these layered parenting interventions has been limited, many of them have shown promising initial findings and been supported by sizable public and private investment; thus it is important for both research and practice to optimize opportunities to learn from these investments and build on this existing work. Each of the above examples offers multiple opportunities for researchers to learn from practitioners and for practitioners to work with researchers to identify possibilities for improving both research and interventions and engaging parents.

To generate research that would produce policy-relevant findings, the federal government could sponsor a relatively small number of studies involving large and diverse samples. Most likely to produce findings that would be cumulative and translatable into policy and practice would be a research agenda based on three to five parenting behaviors clearly related to child outcomes, entailing studies that would utilize the same small number of measures and instruments. This research also could focus on evaluating the cost of programs and avenues through which evidence-based programs could be funded.

The evidence-based process used by the Department of Health and Human Services to design, fund, and implement the Maternal, Infant, and Early Childhood Home Visitation (MIECHV) Program (Health Resources and Services Administration, 2016), described in Chapter 4, could serve as a model for future research and practice aimed at improving programs designed to support parents and parenting knowledge, attitudes, and practices associated with positive child outcomes. MIECHV began with a systematic review of the evidence, followed by a state competition for funding that required the use of a consistent set of performance measures, rigorous local evaluation, and participation in a national evaluation. The Health Resources and Services Administration also has implemented collaborative improvement and innovation networks to facilitate ongoing learning and improve models for supporting parenting knowledge, attitudes, and practices in the areas of home visiting and infant mortality prevention (Arbour, 2015) that could inform the refinement and implementation of other types of parenting supports.

> **Recommendation 7: The secretary of the U.S. Department of Health and Human Services and the secretary of the U.S. Department of Education should launch a national effort to address major gaps in the research-to-practice/practice-to-research pipeline related to parenting.** This effort should be based on an assessment aimed at identifying the gaps in knowledge that if filled would most advance parenting-related policy and practice. The effort should include (1) systematic review of the evidence for the selected areas; (2) further development and testing of the most promising interventions; (3) research on newly developed and existing interventions conducted through collaborative improvement and innovation networks; and (4) rigorous efficacy, effectiveness, and implementation studies of promising programs and policies. In funding decisions, priority should be given to examining interventions delivered in the context of services that reach large numbers of families, such as prenatal care, well-child care, Head Start and Early Head Start, and parent engagement in the early grades.

Three important areas of need for additional research are described in Recommendations 8, 9, and 10 below, all of which address populations of parents on which relatively little evidence-based research has been conducted and for which few evidence-based interventions have been developed.

STRENGTHENING THE EVIDENCE ON STRATEGIES FOR SUPPORTING PARENTS WITH SPECIAL NEEDS

Many parents in the United States cope with personal challenges, such as mental illness, substance abuse, and intimate partner violence, as well as the stigma that is often associated with these challenges, that can reduce their ability to use effective parenting practices and their access to and participation in evidence-based parenting interventions. As reviewed in Chapter 5, relatively little is known about how best to support parents and parenting practices grounded in evidence for families with such special needs. Research is needed to realize the potential of available interventions that show promise for parents with special needs, as well as to develop new interventions that reflect emerging knowledge of how to support these parents. The strengths of evidenced-based training in parenting skills offer a foundation for improving existing and developing new interventions that can serve greater numbers of families with special needs, including by providing a setting of trust in which parents can reveal their needs.

Recommendation 8: The U.S. Department of Health and Human Services and the U.S. Department of Education, in coordination with private philanthropies, should fund research aimed at evaluating existing interventions that have shown promise with and designing and evaluating new interventions for parents with special needs. The design of new interventions should be informed by elements of successful programs, which include treating parents as equal partners, tailoring interventions to meet families' needs, making programs culturally relevant, ensuring service integration and collaboration for families with multiple needs, providing opportunities for peer support, addressing trauma, and targeting both mothers and fathers. Funders should incentivize the use of state and local data to support this research.

STRENGTHENING THE EVIDENCE ON FATHERS

Children's development is shaped by the independent and combined effects of myriad influences, especially their mothers and fathers and the interactions between them. During the early years, parents are the most proximal—and most important—influence on children's development.

Substantial evidence shows that young children have optimal developmental outcomes when they experience nurturing relationships with both fathers and mothers (Cabrera et al., 2006; Lamb, 2004; Pruett, 2000; Ramchandani et al., 2013; Rosenberg and Wilcox, 2006). Research also demonstrates that children benefit when parents who are living in the same household are supportive of each other and are generally consistent in their expectations for the child and in their parenting behaviors. Further, there is evidence that when parents live apart, children generally benefit if they have supportive relationships with each parent, at least in those cases in which the parents do not have negative relationships with each other. In contrast, children are placed at risk when their parents experience conflict or when they have very different expectations for the child, regardless of whether the parents are living together or apart. Yet despite the importance of the father-child relationship, fathers continue to be underrepresented in research on parenting and parenting support (Fabiano, 2007; Panter-Brick et al., 2014; Smith et al., 2012). Moreover, very few interventions aimed at improving mother-child relationships also target father-child or mother-father-child relationships, whether the parents are living together or apart. When parents are living apart, fatherhood programs typically focus on building fathers' economic capacity to parent, such as through employment or counseling, rather than on fostering father-child relationships that can support children's development.

More research is needed on how to design parenting programs so they better engage fathers and enhance the parenting of both parents. Few studies have evaluated how the dyadic and reciprocal interactions between parents and between fathers and their children affect children's development. Research is needed to identify promising interventions for parents both in their individual relationships with their children and in their co-parenting role.

Research also is needed to understand how nonresident fathers can establish long-lasting warm and nurturing relationships with their children. Although steps have been taken to increase evidence-based and empirically rigorous evaluations of fathering programs serving noncustodial fathers (e.g., the federally funded Fatherhood Research and Practice Network) (Fatherhood Research and Practice Network, 2016), these studies are still in their early stages and may be minimally focused on changes in child outcomes.

Recommendation 9: The U.S. Department of Health and Human Services, in coordination with the U.S. Department of Education and other relevant federal agencies, private philanthropies and foundations, researchers, and research associations focused on children and families, should increase support for studies that can inform the development

and improvement of parenting interventions focused on building parents' capacity to parent both individually and together. Such studies should be designed to identify strategies that can improve fathers' knowledge and use of parenting practices associated with positive child outcomes, and should examine the unique and combined effects of individual and co-parenting practices, with special attention to building strong relationships between parents and within diverse parenting relationships. The research should focus not only on adult but also on child outcomes, and should be designed to shed light on the specific ways in which greater investments in co-parenting can lead to better outcomes for children. Existing efforts to provide parenting support for both mothers and fathers should be reinforced and expanded in such programs as the Maternal, Infant, and Early Childhood Home Visitation program, Head Start, and Early Head Start.

STRENGTHENING THE EVIDENCE FOR DIVERSE POPULATIONS

The U.S. population of young children and their parents is demographically, culturally, linguistically, and socially diverse. Although research suggests that some parenting knowledge, attitudes, and practices vary across groups (Brooks-Gunn and Markman, 2005; Brooks et al., 2013; Burchinal et al., 2010; Leyendecker et al., 2002; Rowe, 2008), little is known about whether and how these differences matter for children's development. Moreover, relatively little is known about how engagement with, acceptance of, retention in, and the efficacy of interventions for parents vary across culturally and linguistically diverse subgroups. Finally, despite increasing diversity in family structure, data are lacking on how parenting, engagement in interventions and services, and efficacy of services may vary for diverse family forms (e.g., same-sex parents), kinship providers (e.g., grandparents), stepparents, and other adults assuming parental roles (e.g., foster or adoptive parents). Filling these gaps would improve the ability of evidence-based programs and policies to support the needs of the range of families and children while addressing the needs of parents from historically marginalized and underrepresented populations.

Recommendation 10: The U.S. Department of Health and Human Services and the U.S. Department of Education should launch a multipronged effort to support basic research on parenting and applied research on parenting interventions across diverse populations and family forms. Basic research should include the identification of (1) key constructs and measures related to successful parenting among different populations; (2) important gaps in knowledge of how parenting practices and parent-child interactions affect child outcomes in culturally, ethnically, and socially diverse groups; and (3) constraints that produce disparities in access to and utilization of resources that support parenting across groups and contribute to negative outcomes for parents and children. Applied intervention research should include the formation of a collaborative improvement and innovation network to develop new and adapt existing interventions for diverse groups, and support for rigorous efficacy, effectiveness, and implementation studies of the most promising programs and policies conducted in a manner consistent with Recommendation 7 above.

REFERENCES

Arbour, M. (2015). *Lessons on Home Visiting Program Implementation from the Collaborative for Improvement and Innovation Network (HV CoIIN): Promoting Wide-Scale Adoption of Evidence-Based Strategies with Continuous Quality Improvement Methodologies.* Presentation to the Committee on Supporting the Parents of Young Children, June 29, 2015, Irvine, CA.

Axford, N., Lehtonen, M., Kaoukji, D., Tobin, K., and Berry, V. (2012). Engaging parents in parenting programs: Lessons from research and practice. *Children and Youth Services Review, 34*(10), 2061-2071.

Barth, R.P., Landsverk, J., Chamberlain, P., Reid, J.B., Rolls, J.A., Hurlburt, M.S., Farmer, E.M.Z., James, S., McCabe, K.M., and Kohl, P.L. (2005). Parent-training programs in child welfare services: Planning for a more evidence-based approach to serving biological parents. *Research on Social Work Practice, 15*(5), 353-371.

Benasich, A.A., and Brooks-Gunn, J. (1996). Maternal attitudes and knowledge of child-rearing: Associations with family and child outcomes. *Child Development, 67*(3), 1186-1205.

Brooks, J.L., Holditch-Davis, D, and Landerman L.R. (2013). Interactive behaviors of ethnic minority mothers and their premature infants. *Journal of Obstetric, Gynecologic, & Neonatal Nursing, 42*(3), 357-368.

Brooks-Gunn, J., and Markman, L. (2005). The contribution of parenting to ethnic and racial gaps in school readiness. *The Future of Children, 15*(1), 139-168.

Bryanton, J., Beck, C.T., and Montelpare, W. (2013). Postnatal parental education for optimizing infant general health and parent-infant relationships. *Cochrane Database of Systematic Reviews, 11*, CD004068.

Burchinal, M., Skinner, D., and Reznick, J.S. (2010). European American and African American mothers' beliefs about parenting and disciplining infants: A mixed-method analysis. *Parenting: Science and Practice, 10*(2), 79-96.

Cabrera, N., Shannon, J.D., West, J., and Brooks-Gunn, J. (2006). Parental interactions with Latino infants: Variation by country of origin and English proficiency. *Special Issue on Race, Ethnicity, and Culture in Child Development, 74*, 1190-1207.

Centers for Disease Control and Prevention. (2016). *Essentials for Parenting Toddlers and Preschoolers.* Available: http://www.cdc.gov/parents/essentials/index.html [February 2016].

Chorpita, B.F., Weisz, J.R., Daleiden, E.L., Schoenwald, S.K., Palinkas, L.A., Miranda, J., Higa-McMillan, C.K., Nakamura, B.J., Austin A.A., Borntrager, C.F., Ward, A., Wells, K.C., Gibbons, R.D., and Research Network on Youth Mental Health. (2013). Long-term outcomes for the Child STEPs Randomized Effectiveness Trial: A comparison of modular and standard treatment designs with usual care. *Journal of Consulting and Clinical Psychology, 81*(6), 999-1009.

Chung-Park, M.S. (2012). Knowledge, opinions, and practices of infant sleep position among parents. *Military Medicine, 177*(2), 235-239.

Corrarino, J.E., Walsh, P.J., and Nadel, E. (2001). Does teaching scald burn prevention to families of young children make a difference? A pilot study. *Journal of Pediatric Nursing, 16*(4), 256-262.

Dearing, E., Kreider, H., Simpkins, S., and Weiss, H.B. (2006). Family involvement in school and low-income children's literacy: Longitudinal associations between and within families. *Journal of Educational Psychology, 98*(4), 653-664.

Dearing, E., Sibley, E., and Nguyen, H.N. (2015). Achievement mediators of family engagement in children's education: A family-school-community systems model. In S.M. Sheridan and K.E. Moorman (Eds.), *Processes and Pathways of Family-School Partnerships across Development* (pp. 17-39). New York: Springer.

Fabiano, G.A. (2007). Father participation in behavioral parent training for ADHD: Review and recommendations for increasing inclusion and engagement. *Journal of Family Psychology, 21*(4), 683-693.

Fan, X., and Chen, M. (2001). Parental involvement and students' academic achievement: A meta-analysis. *Educational Psychology Review, 13*(1), 1-22.

Fantuzzo, J., McWayne, C., and Perry, M.A. (2004). Multiple dimensions of family involvement and their relations to behavioral and learning competencies for urban, low-income children. *School Psychology Review, 33*(4), 467-480.

Fatherhood Research and Practice Network. (2016). *Who We Are.* Available: http://www.frpn.org/about/who-we-are [February 2016].

File, T., and Ryan, C. (2014). *Computer and Internet Use in the United States: 2013.* Available: https://www.census.gov/history/pdf/2013comp-internet.pdf [February 2016].

Gadsden, V.L. (2014). *Evaluating Family and Neighborhood Context for PreK-3.* Commissioned Peer-Reviewed Paper. New York: Foundation for Child Development.

Garland, A.F., Brookman-Frazee, L., Hurlburt, M.S., Accurso, E.C., Zoffness, R.J., Haine-Schlagel, R., and Ganger, W. (2010). Mental health care for children with disruptive behavior problems: A view inside therapists' offices. *Psychiatric Services, 61*(8), 788-795.

Health Resources and Services Administration. 2016. *Maternal, Infant, and Early Childhood Home Visiting.* Available: http://mchb.hrsa.gov/programs/homevisiting [February 2016].

Henderson, A.T., and Mapp, K.L. (2002). *A New Wave of Evidence: The Impact of School, Family, and Community Connections on Student Achievement.* Available: https://www.sedl.org/connections/resources/evidence.pdf [February 2016].

Hess, C.R., Teti, D. M., and Hussey-Gardner, B. (2004). Self-efficacy and parenting of high-risk infants: The moderating role of parent knowledge of infant development. *Journal of Applied Developmental Psychology, 25*(4), 423-437.

Hornik, R.C. (Ed.). (2012). *Public Health Communication: Evidence for Behavior Change.* New York: Lawrence Erlbaum Associates.

Huang, K.-Y., O'Brien Caughy, M., Genevro, J.L., and Miller, T.L. (2005). Maternal knowledge of child development and quality of parenting among white, African-American and Hispanic mothers. *Journal of Applied Developmental Psychology, 26*(2), 149-170.

Institute of Medicine. (2015). *Psychosocial Interventions for Mental and Substance Use Disorders: A Framework for Establishing Evidence-Based Standards.* Washington, DC: The National Academies Press.

Institute of Medicine and National Research Council. (2015). *Transforming the Workforce for Children Birth through Age 8: A Unifying Foundation.* L. Allen and B.B. Kelly (Eds.). Committee on the Science of Children Birth to Age 8: Deepening and Broadening the Foundation for Success; Board on Children, Youth, and Families. Washington, DC: The National Academies Press.

Jeynes, W. (2012). A meta-analysis of the efficacy of different types of parental involvement programs for urban students. *Urban Education, 47*(4), 706-742.

Katz, D.L., Katz, C.S., Treu, J.A., Reynolds, J., Njike, V., Walker, J., Smith, E., and Michael, J. (2011). Teaching healthful food choices to elementary school students and their parents: The Nutrition Detectives™ program. *Journal of School Health, 81*(1), 21-28.

Katz, I., La Placa, V., and Hunter, S. (2007). *Barriers to Inclusion and Successful Engagement of Parents in Mainstream Services.* York, UK: Joseph Rowntree Foundation.

Lamb, M.E. (2004). *The Role of the Father in Child Development* (4th ed). Hoboken, NJ: John Wiley & Sons.

Leyendecker, B., Lamb, M. E., Harwood, R. L., and Scholmerich, A. (2002). Mothers' socialization goals and evaluations of desirable and undesirable everyday situations in two diverse cultural groups. *International Journal of Behavioral Development, 26*(3), 248-258.

Panter-Brick, C., Burgess, A., Eggerman, M., McAllister, F., Pruett, K., and Leckman, J.F. (2014). Practitioner review: Engaging fathers—Recommendations for a game change in parenting interventions based on a systematic review of the global evidence. *Journal of Child Psychology, Psychiatry, and Allied Disciplines, 55*(11), 1187-1212.

Pruett, K. (2000). *Fatherneed: Why Father Care Is as Essential as Mother Care for Your Child.* New York: Broadway Books.

Ramchandani, P.G., Domoney, J., Sethna, V., Psychogiou, L., Vlachos, H., and Murray, L. (2013). Do early father-infant interactions predict the onset of externalising behaviours in young children? Findings from a longitudinal cohort study. *Journal of Child Psychology and Psychiatry, and Allied Disciplines, 54*(1), 56-64.

Rosenberg, J., and Wilcox, W.B. (2006). *The Importance of Fathers in the Healthy Development of Children: Fathers and Their Impact on Children's Well-Being.* Washington, DC: U.S. Children's Bureau, Office on Child Abuse and Neglect.

Rowe, M. L. (2008). Child-directed speech: Relation to socioeconomic status, knowledge of child development and child vocabulary skill. *Journal of Child Language, 35*(1), 185-205.

Sheridan, S.M., Knoche, L.L., Edwards, C.P., Bovaird, J.A., and Kupzyk, K.A. (2010). Parent engagement and school readiness: Effects of the Getting Ready intervention on preschool children's social-emotional competencies. *Early Education and Development, 21*(1), 125-156.

Sheridan, S.M., Knoche, L.L., Edwards, C.P., Kupzyk, K.A., Clarke, B.L., and Kim, E.M. (2014). The efficacy of the Getting Ready intervention and the role of parental depression. *Early Education and Development, 25*(5), 746-769.

Smith, T.K., Duggan, A., Bair-Merritt, M.H., and Cox, G. (2012). Systematic review of fathers' involvement in programmes for the primary prevention of child maltreatment. *Child Abuse Review, 21*(4), 237-254.

U.S. Department of Health and Human Services and U.S. Department of Education. (2016). *Policy Statement on Family Engagement: From the Early Years to the Early Grades.* Available: http://www2.ed.gov/about/inits/ed/earlylearning/files/policy-statement-on-family-engagement.pdf [June 2016].

Viswanath, K. (2006). Public communications and its role in reducing and eliminating health disparities. In Institute of Medicine, *Examining the Health Disparities Research Plan of the National Institutes of Health: Unfinished Business* (pp. 215-253). Committee on the Review and Assessment of NIH's Strategic Research Plan and Budget to Reduce and Ultimately Eliminate Health Disparities. G.E. Thomson, F. Mitchell, and M.B. Williams (Eds.). Board of Health Sciences Policy. Washington, DC: The National Academies Press.

ZERO TO THREE (2016). *Parent Portal.* Available: http://www.zerotothree.org/parenting-resources [February 2016].

Appendix A

Public Session Agendas

PUBLIC INFORMATION-GATHERING SESSION AGENDA

MEETING 1

January 29, 2015

Room 120
National Academy of Sciences Building
2101 Constitution Ave, NW, Washington, DC

1:00 p.m. **Welcome and Opening Remarks**
Vivian L. Gadsden, Ed.D., William T. Carter Professor of
Child Development and Education, School of Education,
University of Pennsylvania; Committee Chair

1:05 p.m. **Remarks on Study Statement of Task from Sponsors**
(5 minutes each)
Linda Smith, Administration for Children and Families
Bernadette Sangalang, David and Lucile Packard Foundation
Steven Hicks, Department of Education (Office of
Elementary and Secondary Education)
Carlos Martinez, Department of Education (Office of
English Language Acquisition)
Jacqueline Jones, Foundation for Child Development

David Willis, Health Resources and Services Administration
Holly Kreider, Heising-Simons Foundation
Larke Huang, Substance Abuse and Mental Health Services
    Administration
By phone:
Megan Wyatt, Bezos Family Foundation
Sarah Weber, Bill & Melinda Gates Foundation
Jennifer Kaminski, Centers for Disease Control and Prevention

2:00 p.m.   **Committee Discussion with Sponsors**

2:40 p.m.   **Public Comment**

3:10 p.m.   **Concluding Remarks**
             Vivian L. Gadsden

3:15 p.m.   **Adjourn Open Session**

PUBLIC INFORMATION-GATHERING SESSION AGENDA

MEETING 2

April 9, 2015

Room 120
National Academy of Sciences Building
2101 Constitution Ave, NW, Washington, DC

9:00 a.m.   **Welcome and Introductory Remarks**
             Vivian L. Gadsden, Ed.D., William T. Carter Professor of
                 Child Development and Education, School of Education,
                 University of Pennsylvania; Committee Chair

9:05 a.m.   **General and Specific Positive Parenting: Effects on Child
             Development**
             Marc Bornstein, Ph.D., Senior Investigator, Section on Child
                 and Family Research, National Institute of Child Health
                 and Human Development (20 minutes)
             Discussion and Q & A
             Facilitated by: William R. Beardslee, M.D., Gardner/Monks
                 Professor of Child Psychiatry, Harvard Medical School;
                 Committee Member

9:45 a.m.   **Effect of Changes in U.S. Policy on Parents and Parenting**
Kathryn Edin, Ph.D., Bloomberg Distinguished Professor,
Department of Sociology, Zanvyl Krieger School;
Department of Population, Family, and Reproductive
Health, Bloomberg School of Public Health, Johns
Hopkins University (20 minutes)
Discussion and Q & A
Facilitated by: Iheoma Iruka, Ph.D., Director of Research
and Evaluation, Buffet Early Childhood Institute,
University of Nebraska; Committee Member

10:25 a.m.   **Break**

10:40 a.m.   **Panel: Addressing the Needs of Specific Populations**
Moderator: Selcuk R. Sirin, Ph.D., Associate Professor of
Applied Psychology, New York University; Committee
Member

**Supporting Parents of Young Children in Native American
Communities: Cultural Contexts, Evidence Gaps, and the
Way Forward**
Nancy Rumbaugh Whitesell, Ph.D., Associate Professor of
Community and Behavioral Health; Associate Director,
Tribal Early Childhood Research Center; Colorado
School of Public Health, University of Colorado
Anschutz Medical Campus (20 minutes)

**Fragility in Affluent Families and Implications for Parenting
Research and Practice**
Suniya Luthar, Ph.D., Foundation Professor of Psychology,
Arizona State University; Professor Emerita, Teachers
College, Columbia University (20 minutes)

**Strategies for Supporting Low-Income and Welfare-
Dependent Parents of Young Children**
Aurora Jackson, Ph.D., Professor of Social Welfare, Lustin
School of Public Affairs, University of California, Los
Angeles (20 minutes)

Discussion and Q & A

12:10 p.m.   Implementing Evidence-Based Parenting Programs at Scale
Kenneth Dodge, Ph.D., Founding Director, Center for
Child and Family Policy; William McDougall Professor
of Public Policy and Professor of Psychology and
Neuroscience, Duke University (20 minutes)
Discussion and Q & A
Facilitated by: Michael Wald, J.D., M.A., Jackson Eli
Reynolds Professor of Law, Emeritus, School of Law,
Stanford University; Committee Member

12:50 p.m.   Public Comment (as needed)
Facilitated by: Vivian L. Gadsden, Ed.D., William T. Carter
Professor of Child Development and Education, School
of Education, University of Pennsylvania; Committee
Chair

1:10 p.m.   Concluding Remarks
Vivian L. Gadsden

1:15 p.m.   Adjourn Open Session

PUBLIC INFORMATION-GATHERING SESSION AGENDA

MEETING 3

June 29, 2015

Huntington Room
Arnold & Mabel Beckman Center
100 Academy Drive, Irvine, CA

8:30 a.m.   Welcome and Introductory Remarks
Vivian L. Gadsden, William T. Carter Professor of Child
Development and Education, School of Education,
University of Pennsylvania; Committee Chair

8:35 a.m.   Panel 1: Perspectives from Practitioners

Panelists will discuss their perspectives on how parents
and families use supports and services across various
organizations to meet diverse needs; how policies and
programs relevant to families may affect parenting

practices, with a particular focus on hard-to-reach families; and the trajectory of policies and programs in the near future and possible implications for families.

Moderator: Kim Boller, Senior Fellow, Mathematica Policy Research; Committee Member

Tammy Mann, President and Chief Executive Officer, The Campagna Center (via WebEx)
Albert Pooley, Founder and President, Native American Fatherhood and Families Association
Alyce Mastrianni, Director of Health Policy and Programs, Children and Families Commission of Orange County
Charles Avila, Executive Director, Yes2Kids; Founder, MENFOLK

9:35 a.m.   **Behavioral Insights and Parenting Knowledge, Attitudes, and Practices**
Ariel Kalil, Professor and Director of the Center for Human Potential and Public Policy, Harris School of Public Policy Studies, University of Chicago (15 minutes)
Discussion with Committee
Moderator: Clare Anderson, Policy Fellow, Chapin Hall; Committee Member

10:10 a.m.   **Break**

10:20 a.m.   **Panel 2: Perspectives from Parents**

Panelists will discuss their perspectives on the challenges that parents of young children experience, the types of services for parents of young children that should receive more support, and how services can be improved for families and parents.

Moderator: Elena Fuentes-Afflick, Professor and Vice Chair of Pediatrics; University of California, San Francisco; Committee Member

Clarissa Doutherd, Executive Director, Parent Voices Oakland
Sergio Hinojosa, Jr., Parent with Native Dads Network (NDN)

Maria Rosales, National Trainer for Abriendo Puertas/
Opening Doors
Stacy Williamson, State President, Missouri State Teachers
Association (MSTA)

11:35 a.m. **Lessons on Home Visiting Program Implementation from a
Collaborative Improvement and Innovation Network**
Mary Catherine Arbour, Associate Physician for Research,
Division of Global Health Equity, Brigham and Women's
Hospital; Senior Research Associate, Center on the
Developing Child, Harvard Medical School (15 minutes)
Discussion with Committee
Moderator: William R. Beardslee, Gardner/Monks Professor
of Child Psychiatry, Harvard Medical School; Committee
Member

12:10 p.m. **Parenting in the Context of Culture: Insights from Health
Research**
Marjorie Kagawa-Singer, Professor, Department of
Community Health Sciences and Department of Asian
American Studies, University of California, Los Angeles
(15 minutes)
Discussion with Committee
Moderator: Vish Viswanath., Professor of Health
Communications, Harvard School of Public Health;
Director, Health Communication Core, Dana-Farber/
Harvard Cancer Center; Committee Member

12:45 p.m. **Public Comment Session**
Moderator: Vivian L. Gadsden, William T. Carter Professor
of Child Development and Education, School of
Education, University of Pennsylvania; Committee Chair

1:00 p.m. **Final Remarks and Adjourn**
Vivian L. Gadsden

Appendix B

Clearinghouses Used to Identify Interventions with Evidence of Effectiveness

THE SUBSTANCE ABUSE AND MENTAL HEALTH SERVICES ADMINISTRATION'S NATIONAL REGISTRY OF EVIDENCE-BASED PROGRAMS AND PRACTICES[1]

The National Registry of Evidence-based Programs and Practices (NREPP) provides publicly available electronic access to information on more than 350 substance abuse and mental health interventions. NREPP's registry and review system was established to provide information to the public about evidence-based programs and practices that are available for implementation. NREPP's registry, run by the Substance Abuse and Mental Health Services Administration (SAMHSA), includes only interventions that undergo NREPP's review process, which provides information on research quality and impacts on individual outcomes. However, it should be noted that some, but not all, of the evidence presented online has been reviewed. Therefore, NREPP's registry is not fully comprehensive, and specific interventions are not recommended or supported. Instead, the registry is intended to be a tool for use in designing an intervention to meet specific needs.

The information provided by NREPP includes a program profile that gives

- a description of the program, the population(s) served, and the program's major components and goals;

---

[1] This section was compiled from information on SAMHSA's Website (http://nrepp.samhsa.gov) and NREPP's database (http://nrepp.samhsa.gov/AllPrograms.aspx) [October 2016].

- key study findings and ratings for outcomes (both positive and negative);
- a compilation of evaluations of the effectiveness of the program;
- dissemination and implementation information; and
- references.

The information is updated over time.

Typically, interventions that are candidates for inclusion in the registry are submitted by developers or other interested parties or found through environmental scans, such as literature searches by staff, or through agency nominations. NREPP then screens the interventions to determine whether they are eligible for review. To be eligible, an intervention must meet three minimum requirements:

1. The intervention's research or evaluation must either measure mental health or substance abuse outcomes or behavioral health-related outcomes for those with or at risk of mental health issues or substance use problems.
2. Evidence of outcomes must have been found in a minimum of one experimental or quasi-experimental study.
3. Results of the study/studies must have been published in a professional publication such as a peer-reviewed journal or included in an eligible comprehensive evaluation report.

NREPP recently revised its review criteria and ratings. The new review process is intended to improve the quality of the reviews themselves as well as the information they yield. Programs that are eligible for review are rated as effective, promising, or ineffective. These new ratings are intended to make it easier for users to find evidence-based programs that can address their specific needs. From September 2015 through June 2019, NREPP will be re-reviewing all programs currently in the registry.

Previously, programs were given a rating for the quality of research for each outcome assessed, as well as for the program's overall readiness for dissemination, on a scale of 0 to 4, with 4 being the highest rating. Higher scores indicated stronger, more persuasive evidence. Outcomes were rated individually since programs could aim to achieve more than one outcome (e.g., decreased substance use and improvement of parent-child relationships), and the evidence for each outcome could differ. A brief description of the criteria used to rate programs is provided in Box B-1, as until the updated reviews have been completed, the results of the previous review process will be the only information available.

Now, new interventions that qualify for the registry undergo a review process that begins with information gathering and a literature search for

---

BOX B-1
Previous National Registry of Evidence-based Programs and Practices (NREPP) Criteria for Rating Programs

All programs were previously reviewed using the following six criteria:

1. Reliability of measures: Outcome measures should have acceptable reliability to be interpretable. "Acceptable" here means reliability at a level that is conventionally accepted by experts in the field.

2. Validity of measures: Outcome measures should have acceptable validity to be interpretable. "Acceptable" here means validity at a level that is conventionally accepted by experts in the field.

3. Intervention fidelity: The "experimental" intervention implemented in a study should have fidelity to the intervention proposed by the applicant. Instruments that have tested acceptable psychometric properties (e.g., inter-rater reliability, validity as shown by positive association with outcomes) provide the highest level of evidence.

4. Missing data and attrition: Study results can be biased by participant attrition and other forms of missing data. Statistical methods as supported by theory and research can be employed to control for missing data and attrition that would bias results, but studies with no attrition or missing data needing adjustment provide the strongest evidence that results are not biased.

5. Potential confounding variables: Often variables other than the intervention may account for the reported outcomes. The degree to which confounds are accounted for affects the strength of causal inference.

6. Appropriateness of analysis: Appropriate analysis is necessary to make an inference that an intervention caused reported outcomes.

SOURCE: SAMHSA's National Registry of Evidence-based Programs and Practices (2016). Available: http://nrepp.samhsa.gov/04a_review_process.aspx [August 2016].

---

relevant evaluation studies and eligible outcomes that meet minimum criteria. Eligible outcomes presently include mental health, substance abuse, and wellness. Next, an expert review performed by two certified reviewers measures the rigor of the study and the impact on outcomes. The outcomes are reviewed using an NREPP outcome rating instrument and are judged on the basis of four dimensions: rigor, effect size, program fidelity, and conceptual framework (see Box B-2).

After all eligible measures or effects have been rated, the scores for each outcome are calculated, an evidence class for each measure is determined, and an outcome rating is determined (see Figure B-1).

BOX B-2
Four Dimensions Used to Review Outcomes in the
National Registry of Evidence-based Programs and Practices
(NREPP)

1. Rigor: A calculation of the study methodology strength, which consists of design/assessment; intent-to-treat original group assignment; statistical precision; pretest equivalence, pretest adjustment; analysis method; other threats to internal validity; measurement reliability; measurement validity; and attrition.

2. Effect size: A measurement of possible program impact and the impact on participants.

3. Program fidelity: A review of if the program was provided as anticipated to the target population, including service utilization and delivery.

4. Conceptual framework: A review of how well program components are expressed, consisting of program goals and components and utilization of a theory of change.

SOURCE: Excerpted from SAMHSA's National Registry of Evidence-based Programs and Practices (2016). Available: http://www.nrepp.samhsa.gov/02c_faq.aspx#12 [August 2016].

First, the evidence class is determined based on the evidence score (a combination of the rigor and fidelity dimensions) and the effect class (based on the confidence interval of the effect size). The evidence classes are as follows:

- Class A: highest-quality evidence with confidence interval completely within the favorable range
- Class B: sufficient evidence with confidence interval completely within the favorable range
- Class C: sufficient or highest-quality evidence with confidence interval spanning both the favorable and trivial ranges
- Class D: sufficient or highest-quality evidence with confidence interval completely within the trivial range
- Class E: sufficient or highest-quality evidence with confidence interval spanning both the harmful and trivial ranges
- Class F: sufficient or highest-quality evidence with confidence interval completely within the harmful range
- Class G: limitations in the study design preclude reporting further on the outcome

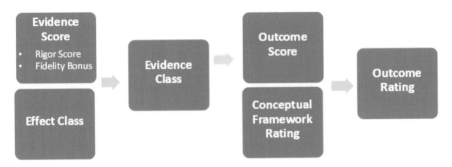

FIGURE B-1 Diagram of how the final outcome rating is determined for the National Registry of Evidence-based Programs and Practices.
SOURCE: SAMHSA's National Registry of Evidence-based Programs and Practices (2016). Available: http://nrepp.samhsa.gov/04a_review_process.aspx [August 2016].

Next, the outcome rating is determined on the basis of the outcome scores and the conceptual framework. The outcome scores are calculated from the evidence classes of each component measure, and the rating of the conceptual framework is a determination of whether a program has clear goals, activities, and a theory of change. The possible outcome ratings are

- Effective: strong evidence of a favorable effect
- Promising: sufficient evidence of a favorable effect
- Ineffective: sufficient evidence of a negligible effect OR sufficient evidence of a possibly harmful effect
- Inconclusive: study design limitations or a lack of effect size information precludes reporting further on the effect

BLUEPRINTS FOR HEALTHY YOUTH DEVELOPMENT[2]

Blueprints for Healthy Youth Development is a registry of evidence-based programs for positive youth development created by the Center for the Study and Prevention of Violence at the University of Colorado Boulder. The registry is intended to be a source of information for decision makers investing in programs with a goal of promoting positive youth development. Positive youth development includes academic performance and success, health and well-being, and positive relationships. Programs can be family-, school-, or community-based and can have a variety of different goals (e.g., violence prevention, reduced school delinquency, reduced sub-

---

[2]This section was compiled from information on the Blueprints Website. Available: http://www.blueprintsprograms.com/ [October 2016].

stance use, improved mental and physical health, improved self-regulation, higher educational achievement). The registry is intended to provide users with information on evidence-based programs with high standards. Thus far, more than 1,300 programs have been reviewed, with less than 5 percent having been found to meet the review criteria. For programs that have met the criteria, users can find a program description as well as information on outcomes, target population, risk and protective factors, training and tech-

---

BOX B-3
Basic Criteria for Inclusion in the Blueprints Registry

1. **Evaluation Quality:** The evaluation produces valid and reliable findings from a minimum of one high-quality randomized control trial (RCT) or two high-quality quasi-experimental (QED) evaluations. The evaluation also meets the following criteria:

- Assignment to the intervention is at a level appropriate to the intervention
- Valid and reliable measures that are appropriate for the intervention population of focus and desired outcomes are used
- Analysis is based on 'intent-to-treat'
- Appropriate statistical methods are used to analyze results

Additional requirements include the following:

- A clear statement of the demographic characteristics of the targeted intervention population
- Documentation of what participants actually received in the intervention condition/s and description of any significant departures from the intervention as designed and the nature of the control condition
- No evidence of significant differential attrition
- Outcome measures must be independent of the content of the intervention
- Outcome measures cannot be rated solely by the individual(s) delivering the intervention

2. **Intervention Impact:** Evidence from high-quality evaluations indicates significant positive change in intended outcomes that are attributed to the program with no evidence of harmful effects. There must be

- Evidence of a consistent and statistically significant positive impact on a Blueprints outcome in a preponderance of studies that meet the Evaluation Quality criteria above
- An absence of iatrogenic effects for intervention participants, including all subgroups and Blueprints outcomes

3. **Intervention Specificity:** The program identifies intended program outcomes, risks and protective factors linked to this change in outcome, target population

nical assistance, evaluation methodology, program costs, funding strategies, benefits and costs, and references.

Program reviews are conducted by staff and then an advisory board of seven youth development experts to determine whether a program meets the criteria of (1) evaluation quality, (2) intervention impact, (3) intervention specificity, and (4) dissemination readiness. (See Box B-3 for more detail.) Programs meeting these criteria have demonstrated at least some effective-

---

and how intervention components work to produce this change. Specifically the program

- Identifies the intended subjects or clients to receive the intervention
- Specifies the outcomes of the intervention which must be one of the Blueprints outcomes
- Identifies the risk and protective factors that the program seeks to change along with the program's theoretical rationale or logic model explaining how the intervention is expected to have a positive effect on these factors and how this change in risk or protection will affect the specified outcome(s).
- Documents the intended intervention structure, content and delivery process, and includes a description of the planned intervention, including what service, activity or treatment is provided, to whom, by whom, over what period, with what intensity and frequency, and in what setting.

4. **Dissemination Readiness:** The program is available for dissemination with the appropriate organizational capability, manuals, training, technical assistance, and support necessary for implementation with fidelity. This includes having

- explicit processes for insuring the program gets to the right persons.
- training materials, protocols and explicit implementation procedures which specify the program content and guide the implementation of the intervention. This includes materials specifying in detail what the intervention comprises; levels of formal training or qualifications for those delivering the intervention; and typically includes training and technical assistance
- specifications on the financial resources required to deliver the intervention including a description of costs associated with implementing the program (start-up costs; intervention implementation costs; intervention implementation support costs, costs associated with fidelity monitoring and evaluation).
- information on the human resources required to deliver the intervention (staff resources, qualifications and skill requirements for staff, and staff time required to cover delivery, training, supervision, preparation and travel)
- a program that is still available for sites wishing to implement it with up-to-date materials

SOURCE: Excerpted from Blueprints for Health Youth Development (2016). Available: http://www.blueprintsprograms.com/criteria [August 2016].

ness at changing targeted behavior and developmental outcomes. These programs are then added to the registry with a rating of Model or Promising.

Model Programs

Model programs meet higher standards than those met by Promising programs and offer greater confidence in the program's ability to modify behavior and developmental outcomes. These programs are suggested for use in large-scale implementation, such as at the national or state level. Model programs meet the four criteria above and two additional requirements:

1. Evaluation Quality: Evidence is required from two high-quality randomized controlled trials (RCTs) or one RCT and one quasi-experimental evaluation.
2. Intervention Impact: A minimum of one long-term follow-up (at least 12 months after the intervention has ended) on at least one outcome measure must indicate that results have been sustained following the intervention. Data on sustainability are required for both program and control groups. For interventions designed to extend over many years, evidence is required that effects have been sustained after several years of participation in the program even though participation is continuing and will be accepted as evidence of sustainability.

Programs rated as Model that also have been independently replicated in a high-quality manner are designated Model Plus.

Promising Programs

Promising programs meet the four criteria elaborated in Box B-3 and are recommended for local community and system adoption. Promising programs do not have to meet the additional evaluation quality and intervention impact requirements for Model programs listed above.

THE CALIFORNIA EVIDENCE-BASED CLEARINGHOUSE FOR CHILD WELFARE[3]

The California Evidence-Based Clearinghouse for Child Welfare (CEBC), funded by the California Department of Social Services' Office of Child Abuse Prevention, is a database of child welfare-related programs in-

---

[3] This section was compiled from information on CEBC's Website. Available: http://www. cebc4cw.org/ [October 2016].

tended to provide information and resources for child welfare professionals. The mission of the clearinghouse is to advance the effective implementation of evidence-based practices for children and families involved in the child welfare system. CEBC provides descriptions of and information on research evidence for specific programs, as well as implementation guidance. All programs are categorized by topic area. Assignment to topic areas is based on clear definitions and requirements that programs must meet. Requirements also are specified for which program outcomes the research evidence must demonstrate for programs to be rated within each topic area.

The CEBC review process starts with the selection of topic areas, which is performed annually by an advisory committee. A list of possible programs to be included in each topic area is then generated based on information from topic experts and literature searches conducted by staff. Each of these programs is then contacted with a list of screening questions. If the program passes the screening, it receives a questionnaire to complete, and a literature search is conducted for any relevant published peer-reviewed research literature. A program outline is then created, and study outcomes are summarized from the research literature. Outcomes of focus relate to child welfare and include safety, permanency, and child/family well-being. Program outlines that meet one of the five categories of the CEBC Scientific Rating Scale (see Figure B-2) are then sent to raters (usually the topic expert and two staff). The scale's purpose is to assess each program based on the available research evidence.

Scientific Rating Scale

The Scientific Rating Scale is a 1 to 5 rating of the strength of the research evidence supporting a program. A scientific rating of 1 represents a program with the strongest research evidence, while a 5 represents a con-

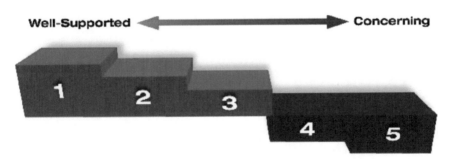

FIGURE B-2 Scientific Rating Scale for the California Evidence-Based Clearinghouse for Child Welfare.
SOURCE: California Evidence-Based Clearing House for Child Welfare (2016).

cerning practice that appears to pose substantial risk to children and families. A rating of 2 indicates the program is supported by research evidence, 3 indicates promising research evidence, and 4 indicates that the evidence fails to demonstrate effect. Specific criteria for each rating are presented in Box B-4. Some programs currently lack strong enough research evidence to be rated on the Scientific Rating Scale and are classified as NR (Not Able to Be Rated). A rating of NR does not mean a program is not effective.

Program ratings are evaluated on an ongoing basis as new research is published, and programs are rerated if necessary. Intermittent re-reviews are conducted to look for new published, peer-reviewed research on programs already rated. Program representatives also can submit new published, peer-reviewed studies to initiate the re-review process at any time.

Child Welfare System Relevance Levels

In addition to its assigned rating, each program included in the database is reviewed to determine how child outcomes are addressed in the program's research evidence. The topic expert and staff review the target population and goals of the program to determine a Child Welfare System Relevance Level of high, medium, or low. Programs rated high are designed or commonly used to meet the needs of children and families receiving child welfare services. Those rated medium are designed or commonly used to serve children and families similar to child welfare populations and likely include current and former child welfare participants. Finally, programs rated low serve children and families with little or no apparent similarity to child welfare participants.

BOX B-4
Specific Criteria for Each CEBC Classification System Category

1 = Well-Supported by Research Evidence
- A minimum of *two rigorous randomized controlled trials* (RCTs) in published, peer-reviewed literature have found the practice to be superior to an appropriate comparison practice, and at least one RCT has found a sustained effect at minimum *one year* after treatment ended.
- Reliable and valid outcome measures are administered consistently and accurately across all subjects.
- If multiple outcome studies have been published, the total weight of the evidence must *support* the value of the practice.

continued

BOX B-4 Continued

- No data suggest a risk of harm that (a) was probably caused by the treatment and (b) the harm was severe or frequent.
- There is no legal or empirical basis suggesting that, compared to its likely benefits, the practice constitutes a risk of harm to those receiving it.
- The practice has a book, manual, and/or other available writings that specify components of the service and describe how to administer it.

2 = Supported by Research Evidence
- A minimum of *one rigorous randomized controlled trials* (RCTs) in published, peer-reviewed literature have found the practice to be superior to an appropriate comparison practice, and at least one RCT has found a sustained effect at minimum *6 months* after treatment ended.
- Reliable and valid outcome measures are administered consistently and accurately across all subjects.
- If multiple outcome studies have been published, the total weight of the evidence must *support* the value of the practice.
- No data suggest a risk of harm that (a) was probably caused by the treatment and (b) the harm was severe or frequent.
- There is no legal or empirical basis suggesting that, compared to its likely benefits, the practice constitutes a risk of harm to those receiving it.
- The practice has a book, manual, and/or other available writings that specify components of the service and describe how to administer it.

3 = Promising Research Evidence
- A minimum of *one study* in published, peer-reviewed literature utilizing some form of control have found the practice to have a benefit over the control, or found it comparable to a practice rated 1, 2, or 3, or superior to an appropriate comparison practice.
- Reliable and valid outcome measures are administered consistently and accurately across all subjects.
- If multiple outcome studies have been published, the total weight of the evidence must *support* the value of the practice.
- No data suggest a risk of harm that (a) was probably caused by the treatment and (b) the harm was severe or frequent.
- There is no legal or empirical basis suggesting that, compared to its likely benefits, the practice constitutes a risk of harm to those receiving it.
- The practice has a book, manual, and/or other available writings that specify components of the service and describe how to administer it.

4 = Evidence Fails to Demonstrate Effect
- A minimum of *two randomized controlled trials* (RCTs) in published, peer-reviewed literature have found the practice has not resulted in improved outcomes, when compared to usual care.

continued

BOX B-4 Continued

- If multiple outcome studies have been conducted, the total weight of evidence (based on published peer-reviewed studies, not a systematic review or meta-analysis) *does not support* the benefit of the practice.
- Reliable and valid outcome measures are administered consistently and accurately across all subjects.
- If multiple outcome studies have been published, the total weight of the evidence must support the value of the practice.
- No data suggest a risk of harm that (a) was probably caused by the treatment and (b) the harm was severe or frequent.
- There is no legal or empirical basis suggesting that, compared to its likely benefits, the practice constitutes a risk of harm to those receiving it.
- The practice has a book, manual, and/or other available writings that specify components of the service and describe how to administer it.

5 = Concerning Practice
- If multiple outcome studies have been conducted, the total weight of evidence suggests the intervention has a *negative effect* upon clients served; and/or there are data suggesting a risk of harm that (a) was probably caused by the treatment and (b) the harm was severe or frequent.
- There is a legal or empirical basis suggesting that, compared to its likely benefits, the practice constitutes a risk of harm to those receiving it.
- The practice has a book, manual, and/or other available writings that specify the components of the practice protocol and describe how to administer it.

NR = Not Able to Be Rated
- The practice does not have any published, peer-reviewed study utilizing some form of control that has established the practice's benefit over the placebo or found it to be comparable to or better than an appropriate comparison practice.
- The practice is generally accepted in clinical practice as appropriate for use with children receiving services from child welfare or related systems and their parents/caregivers.
- Practice does not meet criteria for any other level on the CEBC Scientific Rating Scale.
- There are no case data suggesting a risk of harm that (a) was probably caused by the treatment and (b) the harm was severe or frequent.
- There is no legal or empirical basis suggesting that, compared to its likely benefits, the practice constitutes a risk of harm to those receiving it.
- The practice has a book, manual, and/or other available writings that specify the components of the practice protocol and describe how to administer it.

SOURCE: Excerpted from The California Evidence-Based Clearinghouse for Child Welfare (2016). Available: http://www.cebc4cw.org/ratings/scientific-rating-scale/ [August 2016].

Appendix C

Table of Parenting Interventions

The committee used the National Registry of Evidence-based Programs and Practices (NREPP), the Blueprints for Youth Development registry, and the California Evidence-Based Clearinghouse for Child Welfare (CEBC) to identify parenting programs with strong evidence of effectiveness for supporting parenting knowledge, attitudes, or practices[1] for parents of children ages 0-8. The following table draws on those sources to present information on the parenting support interventions that are discussed in this report. Some of the programs the committee determined to be important to include in the table, such as Adult-Focused Family Behavior Therapy and Child and Family Traumatic Stress Intervention, are not included in the report text. See Appendix B for a description of the criteria used by the clearinghouses for reviewing programs.

---

[1] This appendix was compiled from information on the National Registry of Evidence-based Programs and Practices (NREPP) (http://nrepp.samhsa.gov/AllPrograms.aspx), Blueprints for Youth Development registry (http://www.blueprintsprograms.com/programs), and the California Evidence-Based Clearinghouse for Child Welfare (CEBC) (http://www.cebc4cw.org/home/). Some of the information provided in the table is used verbatim from the above Websites.

TABLE C-1 Evidence-Based Interventions That Support Parenting

Program Name	Target Population	Intervention Description
1-2-3 Magic: Effective Discipline for Children 2-12	Parents, grandparents, teachers, babysitters, and other caretakers working with children approximately ages 2-12 with behavior problems involving compliance and oppositional issues	Group-format discipline program that divides parenting responsibilities into three straightforward tasks: controlling negative behavior, encouraging good behavior, and strengthening the child-parent relationship. The program seeks to encourage gentle, but firm, discipline without arguing, yelling, or spanking. By effectively addressing behavior problems, the program also attempts to improve the adult-child relationship. One or two sessions per week for 4-8 weeks, each 1.5 hours

Targeted Knowledge, Attitudes, and Practices	Qualifications of Staff	Cost	Rating
The program defines two basic kinds of problems that children present to adults—Stop Behavior and Start Behavior. When adults are frustrated with their children, the children are either (1) doing something the adults want them to Stop or (2) not doing something the adults want them to Start. Start behavior tactics (behavioral management techniques) include using positive verbal feedback, a kitchen timer method, a docking system, natural consequences, and charting.	Mental health professionals or teachers	None noted	CEBC: 3 CEBC: Medium Child Welfare

Three simple steps:
(1) Control Obnoxious Behavior—
Parents learn a simple technique for getting their children to Stop doing what they do not want them to do (whining, arguing, tantrums, sibling rivalry, etc.).
(2) Encourage Good Behavior—Parents learn several effective methods for getting their children to start doing what they do want them to do (cleaning their room, going to bed, homework, etc.).
(3) Strengthen Relationships—Parents learn powerful techniques that reinforce their bond with their children.

1-2-3 Magic utilizes a counting technique that is clearly understood by children so they know the consequences of their actions. The secret is not just in the counting, however. The real secret or "magic" comes from parents learning when to keep quiet.

The "Little Adult Assumption" explores the notion that children are not little adults and do not have the same reasoning capacity as an adult.

Parents also learn about managing the Six Kinds of Testing and Manipulation: badgering, intimidation, threats, martyrdom, butter-up, and physical.

Program Name	Target Population	Intervention Description
Adolescent Parenting Program (APP)	First-time pregnant and parenting youth ages 12-19 who must be enrolled in school or a GED completion program, and their children ages 0-5	Support to first-time pregnant and parenting teens through intensive home visiting and peer group education Monthly home visits, along with 24 hours of group education

Targeted Knowledge, Attitudes, and Practices	Qualifications of Staff	Cost	Rating
The program supports adolescent parents to prevent a repeat pregnancy, complete their high school education, acquire job skills, and improve their parenting skills, helping them become self-sufficient and better able to support themselves and their families. It also establishes a strong, stable foundation upon which their children will be raised. The program is designed to increase the self-sufficiency outcomes for participants by increasing the time to a subsequent pregnancy; increasing rates of graduation from high school with a diploma or completion of GED; increasing successful transition to adulthood, including enrollment in postsecondary education, vocational training, or employment at a livable wage; and living in safe and stable housing after graduation from the program. The program also aims to improve developmental outcomes for the children of participants by increasing healthy births; increasing the incidence of appropriate discipline, of nurturing behavior, and of children who are well cared for; and increasing age-appropriate physical, emotional, cognitive, and social development, including readiness for school success.	Staff must have a history of working with at-risk youth and must be trained in either the Partners for a Healthy Baby or Parents as Teachers home visiting curriculum. Staff must also complete at least 18 hours of professional development training annually, aimed at improving program outcomes.	Not provided	CEBC: 3 CEBC: Medium Child Welfare

Program Name	Target Population	Intervention Description
Adult-Focused Family Behavior Therapy (Adult-Focused FBT)*	Adults with drug abuse and dependence, as well as other coexisting problems, such as depression, family dysfunction, trauma, child maltreatment, noncompliance, employment, HIV/ sexually transmitted infection risk behavior, and poor communication skills	More than a dozen treatments, including management of emergencies, treatment planning, home safety tours, behavioral goals and rewards, contingency management skills training, communication skills training, child management skills training, job-getting skills training, financial management, self-control, environmental control, home safety and aesthetics tours, and teletherapy to improve session attendance Starts with 1- to 2-hour initial outpatient or home-based sessions once or twice in the first week, then declines in frequency depending on multiple factors that are determined among the client, the client's family, and the treatment provider (e.g., population, setting, intensity of treatment plan, effort) Typically lasts 6 months to 1 year. The length varies depending on multiple factors (e.g., population, setting, intensity of treatment plan, effort) that are determined by the client, client's family, and treatment provider

Targeted Knowledge, Attitudes, and Practices	Qualifications of Staff	Cost	Rating
Goals are to decrease alcohol and drug use, depression, conduct problems, family dysfunction, and days absent from work/school. Treatment components: program orientation; behavioral goals and rewards through establishing family support systems; treatment planning; communication skills training; child management skills training, where parents learn to discipline their children by catching them being good, engaging in positive practice learning exercises, and when necessary, providing firm directives and undesired consequences; training in job-getting skills, financial management; self-control intervention; assurance of basic necessities, home safety and aesthetics tour, environmental control. Addresses the following: alcohol and drug misuse, depression, school/work attendance problems, parenting stress, poor child management and communication skills, family dysfunction, HIV prevention, child abuse and neglect, home hazards, management of emergencies, and conduct problems in children.	Supervisors must be state-licensed mental health professionals with an interest in supervising the intervention. They should ideally have experience in conducting evidence-based therapies, particularly cognitive-behavioral therapies, and should have professional therapeutic experience serving the population that is being targeted for treatment. Therapists should be state-licensed mental health professionals. They should ideally have experience serving the population that is being targeted for treatment, and must have an interest in conducting therapy utilizing the intervention.	None noted	CEBC: 2 CEBC: High Child Welfare

Program Name	Target Population	Intervention Description
Attachment and Biobehavioral Catch-up (ABC)*	Caregivers of infants ages 6 months to 2 years who have experienced early adversity	Targets several key issues that have been identified as problematic among children who have experienced early maltreatment and/or disruptions in care. The first intervention component helps caregivers reinterpret children's behavioral signals so that they provide nurturance even when it is not elicited. Second, many children who have experienced early adversity are dysregulated behaviorally and biologically. The second intervention component helps caregivers provide a responsive, predictable environment that enhances young children's behavioral and regulatory capabilities. The third intervention component helps caregivers decrease behaviors that could be overwhelming or frightening to a young child. 10 weekly 1-hour sessions

Targeted Knowledge, Attitudes, and Practices	Qualifications of Staff	Cost	Rating
Goals: increase caregiver nurturance, sensitivity, and delight; decrease caregiver frightening behaviors; increase child attachment security and decrease disorganized attachment; increase child behavioral and biological regulation. Targets several key issues: Child behaves in ways that push caregiver away—caregiver is helped to override tendencies to respond "in kind" and to provide nurturance regardless. Child is dysregulated at behavioral and biological levels—caregiver is helped to provide an environment that helps the child develop regulatory capabilities. This includes the parent following the child's lead and showing delight in the child. Caregiver is helped to decrease behaviors that may be frightening or overwhelming to the child. Provides services to parents/caregivers and addresses the following: Has child that pushes caregivers away or has difficulty being soothed; has child with behavioral and biological dysregulation; has difficulty in providing parental nurturance, following the lead, or delighting; has tendency to be frightening or overwhelming; has own history of care that may interfere with parenting. The child is involved in the home visits to show the parents new skills, and the parents are expected to observe and note the child's behavior and practice new skills between sessions.	There is no educational requirement for parent coaches. Potential parent coaches participate in a screening prior to training. If they pass the short screening, coaches attend a 2- to 3-day training and are subject to a year of supervision.	None noted	CEBC: 1 CEBC: High Child Welfare

Program Name	Target Population	Intervention Description
Behavioral Couples Therapy for Alcoholism and Drug Abuse*	Substance-abusing patient together with the spouse or live-in partner seeking help for alcoholism or drug abuse	Components include a recovery or sobriety contract between the partners and therapist 15-20 hour-long sessions over 5-6 months
Caring Dads: Helping Fathers Value Their Children	Fathers (including biological, step, and common-law) who have physically abused, emotionally abused, or neglected their children, have exposed their children to domestic violence, or are deemed to be at high risk for these behaviors	Combines elements of parenting, fathering, and child protection practice to address the needs of maltreating fathers 17 2-hour weekly sessions

Targeted Knowledge, Attitudes, and Practices	Qualifications of Staff	Cost	Rating
Activities and assignments are designed to increase positive feelings, shared activities, and constructive communication; relapse prevention planning.	Providers must be therapists in outpatient facilities.	*Behavioral Couples Therapy for Alcoholism and Drug Abuse* guidebook, $38 each Average per-couple cost estimated in 1997 to be about $1,400; included clinician training, staff salaries, overhead, workbooks, etc.	NREPP: 3.54
Combination of motivation enhancement, parent education (including skills training and behavioral practice), and cognitive-behavioral therapy. Aims are to improve men's recognition and prioritization of children's needs; improve men's understanding of developmental stages; improve men's respect and support for children's relationships with their mothers; improve men's listening and using praise; improve men's empathy for children's experiences of maltreatment, and identify and counter the distortions underlying men's past, and potentially ongoing, abuse of their children and/or children's mothers.	No specific formal qualifications needed, although as a group, the cofacilitation team needs training and experience in working with men (particularly men who are resistant to intervention), a firm understanding of the dynamics of abuse against women, knowledge of child development, and experience in cognitive-behavioral therapy.	None provided	CEBC: NR CEBC: High Child Welfare

Program Name	Target Population	Intervention Description
Chicago Parent Program (CPP)	Parents of children ages 2-5 originally for low-income African American and Latino parents in urban communities	Parenting-skills training program designed to improve parenting self-efficacy and promote positive parenting behavior and child discipline strategies. Uses video vignettes to depict parent-child interactions at home and in various community settings Eleven 2-hour group sessions, followed by a booster session 4-8 weeks later

Targeted Knowledge, Attitudes, and Practices	Qualifications of Staff	Cost	Rating
The vignettes present challenging situations parents typically face with their children and stimulate discussion and problem solving related to child behavior and parenting skills. Sessions focus on building positive relationships with children (e.g., having child-centered time, maintaining family routines and traditions, using praise and encouragement), child behavior management skills (e.g., following through with consequences, using effective forms of discipline), stress management, and problem-solving skills.	Sessions are facilitated by two trained group leaders who must have a minimum of a high school degree or equivalent and must successfully complete a 2-day CPP group leader training.	Group leader set costs $699 each; 2-day, onsite group leader training in the Chicago metropolitan area costs $2,500 for up to 20 participants, plus travel expenses; in other cities, $3,000 for up to 20 participants, plus travel expenses	NREPP: 3.43

Program Name	Target Population	Intervention Description
Child and Family Traumatic Stress Intervention (CFTSI)*	Families with children ages 7-18 who have either recently experienced a potentially traumatic event or recently disclosed the trauma of physical or sexual abuse	Aims to reduce early posttraumatic stress symptoms, to decrease the likelihood of traumatized children developing long-term posttraumatic psychiatric disorders, and to assess children's need for longer-term treatment. The intervention focuses on increasing communication between the caregiver and child about the child's traumatic stress reactions and on providing skills to the family to help cope with traumatic stress reactions

Four to eight weekly sessions lasting 45-60 minutes each |

Targeted Knowledge, Attitudes, and Practices	Qualifications of Staff	Cost	Rating
In session 1, the clinician provides education about trauma and children's typical reactions to traumatic exposure and explains the protective role of communication and family support. In session 2, the clinician first meets with the child alone to provide education about trauma and children's typical reactions to traumatic exposure and to use standardized assessment instruments to obtain the child's assessment of his or her traumatic stress reactions. Next, the clinician meets with the caregiver and the child together. In this session, the clinician uses the child's and caregiver's responses to the standardized assessment instruments as a basis for discussion. The discussion focuses on ways of improving communication, including encouraging greater awareness of when traumatic stress reactions are occurring; helping the child to better communicate with and inform his or her caregiver about feelings, symptoms, and behaviors; and helping the caregiver to be more aware, receptive, and supportive of the child. The clinician works with the child and caregiver collaboratively to identify specific traumatic stress reactions as the areas of focus, which are based on symptom clusters identified by the child and caregiver as being the most problematic (e.g., anxiety, sleep disturbance, depressive withdrawal, intrusive thoughts, oppositionality, tantrums, aggressive behaviors). The clinician then introduces skills, techniques, and behavioral interventions for the child and caregiver to practice to help the child cope with and master traumatic stress reactions. Sessions 3 and 4 are held with the child and caregiver together, and the clinician focuses on continuing to improve communication between the child and caregiver and on practicing the skills introduced in session 2. Sessions 5-8 are provided on an as-needed basis and may be used for additional meetings with the child and caregiver together or with the caregiver or child alone.	Providers must be trained clinicians (master's, Ph.D., or M.D. level).	CFTSI implementation guide for providers: free electronic copy or $15 for hard copy; 2-day training costs $3,000 per day for up to 30 participants, plus travel expenses; 6 months of biweekly consultation calls: $200 per hour for up to 15 participants per call	CEBC: 3 CEBC: High Child Welfare NREPP: 3.0

Program Name	Target Population	Intervention Description
Child-Parent Psychotherapy (CPP)	Children ages 0-5 who have experienced at least one traumatic event and are experiencing behavior, attachment, and/ or mental health problems	Aims to support and strengthen the relationship between a child and his or her parent (or caregiver) as a vehicle for restoring the child's sense of safety, attachment, and appropriate affect and improving the child's cognitive, behavioral, and social functioning Weekly 1- to 1.5-hour sessions for approximately a year

Targeted Knowledge, Attitudes, and Practices	Qualifications of Staff	Cost	Rating
(1) Focus on safety: focus on safety issues in the environment as needed; promote safe behavior; legitimize feelings while highlighting the need for safe/appropriate behavior; foster appropriate limit setting; help establish appropriate parent-child roles. (2) Affect regulation: provide developmental guidance regarding how children regulate affect and emotional reactions; support and label affective experiences; foster parent's ability to respond in helpful, soothing ways when child is upset; foster child's ability to use parent as a secure base; develop/foster strategies for regulating affect. (3) Reciprocity in relationships: highlight parent's and child's love and understanding for each other; support expression of positive and negative feelings for important people; foster ability to understand the other's perspective; talk about ways that parent and child are different and autonomous; develop interventions to change maladaptive patterns of interactions. (4) Focus on the traumatic event: help parent acknowledge what child has witnessed and remembered; help parent and child understand each other's reality with regard to the trauma; provide developmental guidance acknowledging response to trauma; make linkages between past experiences and current thoughts, feelings, and behaviors; help parent understand link between her own experiences and current feelings and parenting practices; highlight the difference between past and present circumstances; support parent and child in creating a joint narrative; reinforce behaviors that help parent and child master the trauma and gain a new perspective. (5) Continuity of daily living: foster prosocial, adaptive behavior; foster efforts to engage in appropriate activities; foster development of a daily predictable routine. (6) Reflective supervision.	The therapist must be a master's- or doctoral-level psychologist, a master's-level social worker or counselor, or a supervised trainee.	*Psychotherapy with Infants and Young Children: Repairing the Effects of Stress and Trauma on Early Attachment* (manual) costs $35.79 for hardcover, $28 for paperback, or $21.95 for Kindle version; *Don't Hit My Mommy!: A Manual for Child-Parent Psychotherapy with Young Witnesses of Family Violence* costs $24.95 each. One training option is required: free 1-year full-time internship at specialized National Child Traumatic Stress Network (NCTSN) sites, or free (except travel) 1.5-year training through the NCTSN Learning Collaborative Model, or 1.5-year training for a learning community or an individual agency at a cost of $1,500-$3,000 per day of training for up to 30 participants, plus travel expenses	CEBC: 2 CEBC: High Child Welfare

[continued]

Program Name	Target Population	Intervention Description
Child-Parent Psychotherapy (CPP) continued		
Clinician-Based Cognitive Psychoeducational Intervention for Families (Family Talk)	Families with parents with significant mood disorders	Based on public health models. Core elements of the intervention are (1) an assessment of all family members, (2) teaching information about affective disorders and risks and resilience in children, (3) linking information to the family's life experience, (4) decreasing feelings of guilt and blame in children, and (5) helping children to develop relationships within and outside the family to facilitate their independent functioning in school and in activities outside the home.

6-11 modules that include separate meetings with parents and children, family meetings, and telephone contacts or refresher meetings at 6- to 9-month intervals |

Targeted Knowledge, Attitudes, and Practices	Qualifications of Staff	Cost	Rating
Provides services to children/adolescents and addresses exposure to trauma, internalizing and externalizing symptoms, and/or symptoms of posttraumatic stress disorder (PTSD).			
Provides services to parents/caregivers to address negative attributions about the child, problems in the parent-child relationship, and maladaptive parenting strategies. In addition, when appropriate, the program targets parental symptoms of PTSD (avoidance, intrusion, and hyperarousal), depression, and anxiety.			
Designed to provide information about mood disorders to parents, equip parents with skills they need to communicate this information to their children, and open dialogue in families about the effects of parental depression.	Sessions are conducted by trained psychologists, social workers, and nurses.	Implementation manual: free; online training: free; 2-day initial training: $500 per day; ongoing biweekly supervision and consultation: $100 per hour Delivery of the intervention requires 7-10 hours of clinician time per family, including parent, child, and family sessions	NREPP: 3.5

Program Name	Target Population	Intervention Description
Cognitive-Behavioral Intervention for Trauma in Schools (CBITS)*	Primarily children in grades 3 through 8 who screened positive for exposure to a traumatic event and symptoms of PTSD related to that event	School-based group and individual intervention designed to reduce symptoms of PTSD, depression, and behavioral problems; improve peer and parent support; and enhance coping skills among students exposed to traumatic life events, such as community and school violence, physical abuse, domestic violence, accidents, and natural disasters 10 45-minute group sessions and 1-3 30-minute individual sessions for students, 2 parent psychoeducational sessions, and a teacher educational session

Targeted Knowledge, Attitudes, and Practices	Qualifications of Staff	Cost	Rating
Relies on cognitive and behavioral theories of adjustment to traumatic events and uses cognitive-behavioral techniques such as psychoeducation, relaxation, social problem solving, cognitive restructuring, imaginal exposure, exposure to trauma reminders, and development of a trauma narrative. Uses a mixture of didactic presentation, examples, and games to solidify concepts. Components of the program include relaxation training, combating negative thoughts, reducing avoidance, developing a trauma narrative, and building social problem-solving skills.

This program involves the family or other support systems in the individual's treatment. The program includes extensive outreach to parents and two parent sessions to keep them informed about what is happening in the groups, as well as to teach them some of the same skills the child is learning. | Delivered in the school setting by mental health professionals (with a master's or doctoral degree in a clinical field) working in close collaboration with school personnel. | Manual costs $40

One professional can screen students and select those with elevated symptoms, serving up to 30 CBITS groups per academic year (6-8 students per group, for about 210 students). Assuming an approximate staffing cost of $90,000 per year for a full-time social worker, the estimated cost per participant is $430.

Cost for implementation in 10 schools in year 1: $5,000 for training, $500 for manuals, $900,000 for 10 mental health professional salaries; so at a ratio of 30 groups serving 6-8 children per mental health professional, the above costs would support CBITS for 2,100 children and youth at a per youth cost of $431 for year 1. | Blueprints: Promising

CEBC: 3
CEBC: Medium Child Welfare

NREPP: 3.17 |

Program Name	Target Population	Intervention Description
Computer-Assisted Motivational Intervention (CAMI)	Pregnant and/ or parenting adolescents ages 18 and younger	Aims to increase motivation among adolescent mothers to use condoms and contraception consistently, with the long-term goal of reducing rapid repeat births 60-minute sessions conducted in two parts
Early Head Start (EHS)	Low-income families	Federally funded early childhood development program providing comprehensive child development services in a center-based setting, supplemented with home visits Weekly home visits and bimonthly group socialization experiences
Families and Schools Together (FAST)*	Families with children transitioning into elementary school	Multifamily group intervention designed to build relationships between and within families, schools, and communities (particularly in low-income areas) to increase all children's well-being 8 weeks of multifamily group meetings, each about 2.5 hours long; and 2 years of monthly parent-led group meetings

Targeted Knowledge, Attitudes, and Practices	Qualifications of Staff	Cost	Rating
During the first part of each session, participants use the computer-based CAMI program to answer questions about current sexual relationships and contraceptive use intentions and behaviors. Based on the responses generated, CAMI counselors conduct a stage-matched motivational interviewing session to enhance participants' motivation to use condoms and contraception consistently in order to reduce the risk for a repeat pregnancy.	It is recommended that agencies seek individuals who possess empathetic qualities, excellent communication skills, experience working with adolescents, and familiarity with the community. There is no set minimum educational requirement.	Not specified	CEBC: 3 CEBC: Medium Child Welfare
Also serves children through locally designed family child care options, in which certified child care providers care for children in their homes. Services include early education both in and out of the home, parenting education, comprehensive health and mental health services for mothers and children, nutrition education, and family support services.	Teacher and other EHS staff	Not specified	CEBC: 3 CEBC: Medium Child Welfare
Objectives: (1) enhance parent-child bonding and family functioning while reducing family conflict and isolation and child neglect; (2) enhance school success through more parent involvement and family engagement at school, improved school climate, and reduced school mobility; (3) prevent substance use by both adults and children by building protective factors and referring appropriately for treatment; and (4) reduce the stress that children and parents experience in daily life situations in their communities by empowering parents, building social capital, and increasing social inclusion.	Sessions are led by a trained team that includes at least one member of the school staff in addition to parents and professionals from local social service agencies in the community. FAST teams must be culturally representative of the families served.	Licensing fee is $550 per site; training package costs $4,295 per site (serving approximately 1 to 10 families), plus travel expenses; ongoing technical assistance costs $200 per site; evaluation package costs $1,100 per site	NREPP: 3.7

Program Name	Target Population	Intervention Description
Family Check-Up (FCU) for Children	Families with children ages 2-17	Strengths-based, family-centered intervention that motivates parents to use parenting practices in support of child competence, mental health, and reduced risk for substance use; can be integrated into a variety of service settings, including schools, primary care, and community mental health Phase 1 involves 3 1-hour sessions. Phase 2 can be limited to 1 to 3 Everyday Parenting sessions; as a treatment approach, Phase 2 can range from 3 to 15 Everyday Parenting sessions.
Family Check-Up (FCU) for Toddlers	Families with children ages 17 months-2	Strengths-based, family-centered intervention that motivates parents to use parenting practices in support of child competence, mental health, and reduced risk for substance use; can be integrated into a variety of service settings, including schools, primary care, and community mental health Phase 1 involves 3 1-hour sessions. Phase 2 can be limited to 1 to 3 Everyday Parenting sessions; as a treatment approach, Phase 2 can range from 3 to 15 Everyday Parenting sessions.

Targeted Knowledge, Attitudes, and Practices	Qualifications of Staff	Cost	Rating
Two phases: (1) initial interview, assessment, and feedback; and (2) Everyday Parenting as a follow-up service that builds parents' skills in positive behavior support, healthy limit setting, and relationship building.	Providers with a master's degree in education, social work, counseling, or related areas generally implement the program; however, bachelor's- and paraprofessional/nonbachelor's-level providers, with the appropriate consultation and supervisory support, may also implement the program.	Manual costs $21; training manual costs $104.25 per provider; 2-day FCU training costs $4,194 + trainer travel costs for 1 trainer and up to approximately 8-10 trainees; 2-day Everyday Parenting training costs $4,194 + trainer travel costs for 1 trainer and up to approximately 8-10 trainees; additional costs incurred if the site wants providers to become certified.	NREPP: 3.1
Two phases: (1) initial interview, assessment, and feedback; and (2) Everyday Parenting as a follow-up service that builds parents' skills in positive behavior support, healthy limit setting, and relationship building.	Providers must have a master's degree in education, social work, counseling, or related areas.	Example cost: For one community agency serving 400 families, the first-year expense would be $476 per family. The costs would decrease significantly in subsequent years as the initial readiness, training, and certification costs are start-up costs that would not be incurred beyond year 1.	Blueprints: Promising

Program Name	Target Population	Intervention Description
Family Connections (FC)	Families at risk for child maltreatment	Multifaceted, community-based service program that works with families in their homes and in the context of their neighborhoods to help them meet the basic needs of their children and prevent child maltreatment
		A minimum of 1 hour of face-to-face contact between the social worker and clients weekly for 3-4 months, with an optional 90-day extension if needed
Family Foundations*	Adult couples expecting their first child	Aims to help establish positive parenting skills and adjustment to the physical, social, and emotional challenges of parenthood. Program topics include coping with postpartum depression and stress, creating a caring environment, and developing the child's social and emotional competence.
		Delivered to groups of couples through four prenatal and four postnatal classes of 2 hours each. Prenatal classes are started during the fifth or sixth month of pregnancy, and postnatal classes end when children are 6 months old.

Targeted Knowledge, Attitudes, and Practices	Qualifications of Staff	Cost	Rating
Nine practice principles guide FC interventions: ecological developmental framework, community outreach, individualized family assessment and tailored interventions, helping alliance, empowerment principles, strengths-based practice, cultural competence, outcome-driven service plans with SMART goals, and a focus on the competence of the practitioner. Individualized family intervention is geared to increase protective factors; decrease risk factors; and target child safety, well-being, and permanency outcomes. Addresses the following: Poor household conditions, financial stress, inadequate social support, parenting stress and poor parenting attitudes, unsafe caregiver/child interactions, poor family functioning, poor adult functioning (e.g., mental health problems/substance abuse) that impacts parenting, poor family resources.	Master's-level or bachelor's-level workers are supervised by a staff member with a master's degree or higher.	None provided	CEBC: 3 CEBC: High Child Welfare
Foster and enhance the coparenting relationship through conflict resolution strategies, information and communication exercises to help parents develop realistic and positive expectations about parenthood, and videos presenting couples discussing the family and personal stresses they have experienced as well as the successful strategies they have employed. Key aspects of parenting addressed include fostering child emotional security, attending to infant cues, and promoting infant sleep.	Delivered in a community setting by childbirth educators who have received 3 days of training from Family Foundations staff. It is recommended, but not required, that classes be codelivered by a male and a female. The female leader is a childbirth educator, and male leaders are from various backgrounds, but experienced in working with families and leading groups.	Facilitator manual (includes PowerPoint slides, facilitator DVDs, and participant feedback forms) costs $325 each; pre- and postnatal parent handbooks (include DVDs) cost $300 for materials for 10 couples	NREPP: 3.65

Program Name	Target Population	Intervention Description
Family Spirit	American Indian teenage mothers, who generally experience high rates of substance use, school dropout, and residential instability, receive services from pregnancy through 36 months postpartum	Culturally tailored home visiting intervention with lessons designed to correspond to the changing developmental needs of the mother and child during this period, addressing such topics as prenatal care, infant care, child development, family planning, and healthy living 63 structured lessons delivered one on one by health educators in participants' homes, starting at about 28 weeks of gestation and continuing to 36 months postpartum. Each home visit lasts about an hour and includes a warm-up conversation, lesson content, a question-and-answer period, and review of summary handouts. The 63 lessons can be delivered in 52 home visits, which occur weekly through 3 months postpartum and gradually become less frequent thereafter.

Targeted Knowledge, Attitudes, and Practices	Qualifications of Staff	Cost	Rating
Designed to increase parenting competence (e.g., parenting knowledge and self-efficacy), reduce maternal psychosocial and behavioral risks that could interfere with effective parenting (e.g., drug and alcohol use, depression, externalizing problems), and promote healthy infant and toddler emotional and social adjustment (i.e., avoid internalizing and externalizing behaviors). The program also aims to prepare toddlers for early school success, promote parents' coping and life skills, and link families to appropriate community services.	Health educators are trained American Indian paraprofessionals	1-week, on- or off-site training in curriculum content and implementation costs $3,000 per person for up to 30 participants, plus travel expenses; tailored training development and implementation affiliation fee (includes access to all training resources; 3-year membership to the Web-based FS Connect; and consultation and technical assistance before training to establish needs and after training to support program implementation, sustainability, and data collection) is $9,600 per program, plus travel expenses.	NREPP: 3.22

Program Name	Target Population	Intervention Description
Head Start REDI		Enrichment intervention that can be integrated into the existing framework of Head Start programs that are already using the High/Scope or Creative Curriculum. The intervention is delivered by classroom teachers and integrated into their ongoing classroom programs.

Targeted Knowledge, Attitudes, and Practices	Qualifications of Staff	Cost	Rating
Includes curriculum-based lessons, center-based extension activities, and training and weekly classroom coaching in "teaching strategies" to use throughout the day. It is focused primarily on social-emotional skill enrichment using the Preschool PATHS curriculum and language/emergent literacy skill enrichment. Parents also receive take-home materials describing the importance of positive support, emotion coaching, and interactive reading, with parenting tips and learning activities to use at home.	Prerequisites: Attendance at a Preschool PATHS Workshop/ REDI Workshop; high-quality performance for at least 2 years as a Preschool PATHS/REDI teacher or PATHS/REDI coach; master's degree (or comparable credentials); classroom experience with students in a learner role (teaching, administration, and school counseling preferred); training experience with educators	Example cost: With three classrooms of 17 students each, the REDI program would serve 51 students in the first year. The year 1 cost per student would be $599.55.	Blueprints: Promising

Program Name	Target Population	Intervention Description
Healthy Families America (Home Visiting for Child Well-Being) (HFA)	Overburdened families who are at risk for child abuse and neglect and other adverse childhood experiences. Families are determined eligible for services once they have been screened and/or assessed for the presence of factors that could contribute to increased risk for child maltreatment or other poor childhood outcomes (e.g., social isolation, substance abuse, mental illness, parental history of abuse in childhood). Home visiting services must be initiated either prenatally or within 3 months after the birth of the baby.	Home visiting program model offering services voluntarily, intensively, and over the long term (3 to 5 years after the birth of the baby) Families are to be offered weekly home visits for a minimum of 6 months after the birth of the baby. Home visits typically last 50-60 minutes. Once the defined criteria for family functioning have been met, visit frequency is reduced to biweekly, monthly, and quarterly, and services are tapered off over time. Typically, families receive two to four visits per month during pregnancy. During times of crisis, families may be seen two or more times per week. Services are offered prenatally or at birth until the child is at least age 3 and can be offered until he/she is age 5.

Targeted Knowledge, Attitudes, and Practices	Qualifications of Staff	Cost	Rating
Goals: Build and sustain community partnerships to systematically engage overburdened families in home visiting services prenatally or at birth. Cultivate and strengthen nurturing parent-child relationships. Promote healthy childhood growth and development. Enhance family functioning by reducing risk and building protective factors. Parent Survey (formerly Kempe Family Stress Checklist) is administered to identify the family strengths as well as family history and/or issues related to higher risk of child maltreatment and/or poor childhood outcomes. Services focus on supporting the parent as well as parent-child interaction and child development. All families are linked to a medical provider to ensure optimal health and development (e.g., timely immunizations, well-child care). Depending on the family's needs, the program may also be linked to additional services, such as financial, food, and housing assistance programs; school readiness programs; child care; job training programs; family support centers; substance abuse treatment programs; and domestic violence shelters. Provides services to expectant or new parents screened and/or assessed as at moderate to high risk for child maltreatment and/or poor early childhood outcomes (e.g., mental health issues, domestic violence, substance abuse, poverty, housing, lack of education, lack of social support).	Direct service staff should have qualifications including, but not limited to, experience in working with or providing services to children and families, an ability to establish trusting relationships, acceptance of individual differences, experience and willingness to work with the culturally diverse populations that are present among the program's target population; and knowledge of infant and child development. Training is provided in person either in state or regionally: 4 days for direct service staff.	None noted	CEBC: 1 CEBC: Medium Child Welfare

[continued]

Program Name	Target Population	Intervention Description
Healthy Families America (Home Visiting for Child Well-Being) (HFA)		

(continued)

Targeted Knowledge, Attitudes, and Practices	Qualifications of Staff	Cost	Rating
Involves the family or other support systems in the individual's treatment. Given that children develop within the context of a relationship, relationship-based early intervention focuses on strengthening the parent (or caregiver)-child relationship. HFA takes advantage of teachable moments to encourage the healthy parent-child relationship. Three key aspects of building a relationship must be present to grow a mentally and emotionally healthy child: parents or caregivers must touch the child, have eye contact, and give quality time to the child. Children must experience, regulate, and express emotions to form close and secure interpersonal relationships and to explore their environment and learn. The end result is formation of a strong attachment to the parent or caregiver. It is critical that early caregivers know how to promote healthy social and emotional well-being through nurturing and consistent relationships.			

Program Name	Target Population	Intervention Description
Highscope Preschool*	Preschool students from disadvantaged families and at high risk of school problems	Educational approach aims to promote active learning by providing many opportunities for children to initiate their own activities and take responsibility for completing them. Classroom program meets for half-days (2.5 hours per day), 5 days a week for 7 months of the year, with 90-minute weekly home visits by preschool teachers.

Targeted Knowledge, Attitudes, and Practices	Qualifications of Staff	Cost	Rating
Program aims to enhance children's cognitive, social-emotional, and physical development, imparting skills that will help them succeed in school and be more productive and responsible throughout their lives.	Delivered by preschool teachers. The staff-to-child ratio is one adult for every five or six children.	Three steps, each with training options. Initial onsite training averages $1,930 per participant for groups of more than 30. Each of the implementation steps requires the purchase of materials for each classroom. The curriculum costs approximately $800 per classroom. Estimated cost for consumable is $500-$1,000 per classroom per year. Each student is evaluated using the HighScope Child Observation Record at an annual cost of $10.95-19.95 per student. Program example: Cost for a preschool program with 10 teachers in five classrooms of 20 children would be $295.50 per student in year 1.	Blueprints: Promising NREPP: 3.55

Program Name	Target Population	Intervention Description
Home Instruction for Parents of Preschool Youngsters (HIPPY)	Parents with young children ages 3-5 and with limited formal education and resources	Home-based and parent-involved school readiness program that helps parents prepare their children for success in school and beyond. The parent is provided with carefully developed curriculum, books, and materials designed to strengthen the child's cognitive and early literacy skills, as well as social, emotional, and physical development. Home visitors engage their assigned parents on a weekly basis. Service delivery is primarily through home visits. A home visit consists of a 1-hour, one-on-one interaction between the home visitor and the assigned parents. Parents then engage their children in educational activities for 5 days per week for 30 weeks. At least six times per year, one or more cohorts of parents meet in a group setting with the coordinator and their assigned home visitor(s). Group meetings feature enrichment activities for parents and their children and last approximately 2 hours. A minimum of 30 weeks of interaction with the home visitor; curriculum available for up to 3 years of home visiting services

Targeted Knowledge, Attitudes, and Practices	Qualifications of Staff	Cost	Rating
In the developmentally appropriate curriculum, role play is the method of instruction. Staff consisting of coordinators and home visitors engage parents through home visits and group meetings. Parent-child educational interactions are encouraged through the use of the HIPPY curriculum. The scripted curriculum serves as a lesson plan for parents and is designed to support parents with limited formal education. The curriculum is based on exposure to skills, rather than mastery. Provides services to children/adolescents that address limited exposure to reading readiness skills. Provides services to parents/caregivers that address low literacy level and limited English proficiency.	The home visitors live in the community they serve and work with the same group of parents for 3 years. They receive weekly comprehensive training to equip them to serve their assigned families effectively. The training also encourages them to seek further education. Many home visitors earn degrees in early childhood education. Educational requirements are established by the implementing agency and are usually a high school diploma or GED. Home visitors must be able to read in and speak the language of the families they serve. The coordinator, who trains the home visitors and oversees the local program, is required to have a minimum of a bachelor's degree.	None noted	CEBC: 2 CEBC: Medium Child Welfare

Program Name	Target Population	Intervention Description
Homebuilders	Families with one or more children (up to age 18) who are at imminent risk of out-of-home placement or who have been placed out of the home and need intensive services to reunify with their family. Family is usually experiencing such problems as child abuse and neglect, other family violence, juvenile delinquency, mental illness, and/or substance abuse.	Home-based intensive family preservation services program designed to improve family functioning and children's behavior and to prevent out-of-home placement of children into foster or group care, psychiatric hospitals, or correctional facilities. 4 to 6 weeks; extensions are offered, and two booster sessions are offered in the 6 months after services end.

Targeted Knowledge, Attitudes, and Practices	Qualifications of Staff	Cost	Rating
Drawing on social learning and crisis intervention theories, the program is structured to reduce barriers to family support services and maximize opportunities for family members to learn new personal and social skills. Services provided by therapists include social support (e.g., transportation, budgeting, household maintenance and home repair services), counseling, modeling of parenting skills, extensive interagency treatment planning, and family advocacy within the community context.	Families are typically referred by protective services, foster care and adoption agencies, community mental health professionals, probate courts, or domestic violence shelters. Within 24 hours of referral, families begin receiving services from master's-level therapists who meet with them in their homes and neighborhoods during sessions that are scheduled on a flexible basis. Each therapist serves two or three families at a time, typically spending 40 or more hours in face-to-face contact with family members. In addition, therapists are on call for families 24 hours per day, 7 days per week.	Site development and implementation readiness consultation for all training costs $1,250 (up to 15 participants) or $2,500 (up to 30 participants), plus travel expenses. Core Curriculum training costs $120 per participant for materials. Goal-Setting and Paperwork training costs $20 per participant. Motivational Interviewing training costs $40 per participant. Relapse Prevention training costs $20 per participant. Utilizing Behavioral Principles and Strategies with Families costs $20 per participant. Teaching Skills to Families costs $15 per participant. Improving Decision Making through Critical Thinking costs $25 per participant. Fundamentals of Supervising Homebuilders: Intensive Family Preservation costs $275 per participant.	NREPP: 3.05

[continued]

Program Name	Target Population	Intervention Description
Homebuilders (continued)		

Targeted Knowledge, Attitudes, and Practices	Qualifications of Staff	Cost	Rating
		Program Consultation and Quality Assurance Skills for Homebuilders Supervisors costs $75 per participant. Online Data Manager training costs $15 per participant. Phone consultations (held weekly in the first 2 years of implementation, monthly in year 3, and quarterly thereafter) cost $100 per hour. 3- to 4-day onsite visits (twice per year) cost $1,250 per day, plus travel expenses. Access to the Online Data Manager: $4,900 activation fee (year 1 only); $350 monthly fee; $980 annual upgrade fee.	

Program Name	Target Population	Intervention Description
Incredible Years (IY)	Young children and their parents and teachers Programs for parents target key developmental stages: IY Babies Program (0-9 months); IY Toddlers Program (ages 1-3); IY Preschool Program (ages 3-5); IY School Age Program (ages 6-12) There are two Social and Emotional Skills Programs for Children (Dinosaur School Program): IY Classroom Child Program (ages 3-8); IY Treatment Small Group Child Program (ages 4-8) One Classroom Management Program for Teachers (early childhood and elementary school, ages 3-8)	Child, parent, and teacher developmentally based programs designed to promote emotional and social competence and to prevent, reduce, and treat behavioral and emotional problems in young children. The Dinosaur School Program consists of more than 60 classroom lesson plans (approximately 45 minutes each) for three age levels, beginning in preschool through second grade (ages 3-8). Lesson plans are delivered by the teacher at least twice weekly over consecutive years. The small-group treatment program consists of 18-22 weekly sessions (2 hours each) offered in conjunction with the training programs for parents of preschoolers or school-age children. Lengths of the parent and child programs vary from 12 to 20 weekly group sessions (2-3 hours each). Teacher sessions can be completed in 5-6 full-day workshops or 18 to 21 2-hour sessions. The Basic Parent Training Program is 14 weeks for prevention populations, and 18-20 weeks for treatment. The Child Training Program is 18-22 weeks. For the treatment version, the Advance Parent Program is recommended as a supplemental program. Basic plus Advance takes 26-30 weeks. The Child Prevention Program is 20-30 weeks and may be spaced over 2 years. The Teachers Program is 5-6 full-day workshops spaced over 6-8 months.

Targeted Knowledge, Attitudes, and Practices	Qualifications of Staff	Cost	Rating
The child program aims to strengthen children's social and emotional competencies, such as understanding and communicating feelings, using effective problem-solving strategies, managing anger, practicing friendship and conversational skills, and behaving appropriately in the classroom. The parent programs focus on strengthening parent-child interactions and relationships; reducing harsh discipline; and fostering parents' ability to promote children's social, emotional, and language development. In the programs for parents of preschoolers and school-age children, participants also learn how to promote school readiness skills; in addition, these parents are encouraged to partner with teachers and become involved in their children's school experiences to promote children's academic and social skills and emotional self-regulation and to reduce conduct problems. Each program includes protocols for use as a prevention program or as a treatment program for children with conduct problems and attention deficit hyperactivity disorder (ADHD). The teacher program focuses on strengthening teachers' classroom management strategies; promoting children's prosocial behavior, emotional self-regulation, and school readiness; and reducing children's classroom aggression and noncooperation with peers and teachers. The training also helps teachers collaborate with parents to support parents' school involvement and promote consistency between home and school.	Trained facilitators with a master's degree (or equivalent) use videotaped vignettes to structure the content and stimulate group discussions, problem solving, and practices related to participants' goals.	Program materials cost $1,150-$1,895, depending on the series selected. Ongoing costs include $476 for each parent in parent groups, $775 for each child in child treatment groups, $15 for each child receiving the Dinosaur curriculum in school, and $30 for each teacher receiving the teacher training. These costs vary by location.	CEBC: 1 CEBC: Medium Child Welfare NREPP: 3.5

Program Name	Target Population	Intervention Description
Incredible Years (IY)-Child Treatment	Families of children ages 4-8 with conduct problems, ADHD, and internalizing problems	Small-group treatment program designed to enhance social competence, positive peer interactions, conflict management strategies, emotional literacy, and anger management. 18-22 weekly 2-hour sessions

Targeted Knowledge, Attitudes, and Practices	Qualifications of Staff	Cost	Rating
Emphasizes training children in such skills as emotional literacy, empathy or perspective taking, friendship skills, anger management, interpersonal problem solving, school rules, and how to be successful at school. The child program is organized to dovetail with the IY parent training programs.	Trained facilitators use videotaped scenes to encourage group discussion, problem solving, and sharing of ideas.	Initial workshop training costs typically include a 3-day training for approximately $1,100-$2,000. A set of program DVDs and materials costs $1,150 for the Small-Group Treatment version of the Dinosaur Child Program. With 18 children participating, the initial cost of the program is approximately $2,150.60/child for the Small-Group Treatment version; however, after one-time up-front costs have been paid, subsequent groups in future years cost less: $1,117.95.	Blueprints: Promising

Program Name	Target Population	Intervention Description
Incredible Years (IY)-Parent	Families and teachers of children ages 2-8 with behavioral and emotional problems	Three BASIC parent training programs target key developmental stages: Baby and Toddler Program, Preschool Program, and School Age Program. Program length varies, but generally lasts between 3-5 months: Baby and Toddler Program (0-2.5 years; 9-13 sessions), Preschool Program (3-5 years; 18-20 sessions), and School Age Program (6-12 years; 12-16+ sessions).

Targeted Knowledge, Attitudes, and Practices	Qualifications of Staff	Cost	Rating
Programs emphasize developmentally appropriate parenting skills known to promote children's social competence, emotional regulation, and academic skills and to reduce behavior problems. The BASIC parent program is the core of the parenting programs and must be implemented, as Blueprints recognition is based on evaluations of this program. This BASIC parent training component emphasizes such parenting skills as child-directed play with children; academic, persistence, social, and emotional coaching methods; use of effective praise and incentives; establishment of predictable routines and rules and effective limit setting; handling misbehavior with proactive discipline; and teaching children to problem solve.	Trained facilitators use video scenes to encourage group discussion, self-reflection, modeling and practice rehearsals, problem solving, sharing of ideas, and support networks.	Initial training and technical assistance costs typically include a 3-day training for group leaders for approximately $1,100-$2,000. A set of program DVDs costs $1,595 for Preschool BASIC ($1,895 for dual-language English/ Spanish). With 108 parents participating, the initial cost of the program is approximately $643/parent; however, after one-time up-front costs have been paid, subsequent groups in future years cost less.	Blueprints: Promising

Program Name	Target Population	Intervention Description
Kids' Club & Moms' Empowerment*	Children ages 6-12 and their mothers exposed to intimate partner violence in the last year	Preventive intervention program that targets children's knowledge about family violence, their attitudes and beliefs about families and family violence, their emotional adjustment, and their social behavior in the small group. Later sessions address responsibility for violence, managing emotions, family relationship paradigms, and conflict and its resolution. 10 weeks of 1-hour sessions where groups of mothers and children meet concurrently

Targeted Knowledge, Attitudes, and Practices	Qualifications of Staff	Cost	Rating
Provides support to mothers by empowering them to discuss the impact of the violence on their child's development, building parenting competence, providing a safe place to discuss parenting fears and worries, and building connections for the mother in the context of a supportive group. Goals of Kids' Club are reducing children's internalizing and externalizing behavioral adjustment problems, reducing children's harmful attitudes and beliefs about the acceptability of violence, enhancing children's ability to cope with violence by learning safety skills and additional conflict resolution skills, and enhancing children's ability to identify and regulate emotions related to violence. The goals of Moms' Empowerment are reducing the level of mothers' traumatic stress and violence exposure, enhancing mothers' safety and ability to parent under stress, and providing support and resources in a group setting.	Therapists have a master's in social work (MSW), are licensed clinical social workers, or have a master's or Ph.D. in psychology. Therapists also can be in training to receive a professional degree, in which case they are subject to regular supervision by a licensed professional.	None noted	CEBC: 3 CEBC: Medium Child Welfare

Program Name	Target Population	Intervention Description
Nurse-Family Partnership (NFP)	First-time, low-income mothers (no previous live births)	Prenatal and infancy home visiting by nurses beginning during pregnancy and continuing through the child's second birthday. Designed to link families with needed health and human services, promote good decision making about personal development, assist families in making healthy choices during pregnancy and providing proper care to their children, and help women build supportive relationships with families and friends. Weekly home visits for the first month after enrollment and then every other week until the baby is born. Visits are weekly for the first 6 weeks after the baby is born and then every other week until the baby is 20 months old. The last four visits are monthly until the child is 2 years old. Visits typically last 60-75 minutes.

Targeted Knowledge, Attitudes, and Practices	Qualifications of Staff	Cost	Rating
Goals are to improve pregnancy outcomes by promoting health-related behaviors; to improve child health, development, and safety by promoting competent caregiving; and to enhance parent life-course development by promoting pregnancy planning, educational achievement, and employment. The program also has two secondary goals: to enhance families' material support by providing links with needed health and social services, and to promote supportive relationships among family and friends.

Objectives include improving women's diets; helping women monitor their weight gain and eliminate the use of cigarettes, alcohol, and drugs; teaching parents to identify the signs of pregnancy complication; encouraging regular rest, appropriate exercise, and good personal hygiene related to obstetric health; and preparing parents for labor, delivery, and early care of the newborn. | Nurse home visitors must be registered nurses with a bachelor's degree in nursing, as a minimum qualification.

Nurse supervisors must be registered nurses with a bachelor's degree in nursing as a minimum qualification, with a master's degree in nursing preferred.

Implemented by teams of eight nurse home visitors with one supervisor. | The cost to prepare one team to begin offering the program is approximately $77,000.

Estimated annual salary and benefit costs for a team of eight nurses and one supervisor serving 200 families total $711,000 but costs vary based on local salary levels.

Travel is a significant expense, estimated at $21,000 for a nursing team annually. Ongoing training is estimated at $1,526 annually for a nursing team, and replacement training as a result of turnover is $7,750 per supervisor and $6,000 per nurse. Annual quality improvement and technical assistance services total $8,816 per nursing team.

With 8 nurses and a caseload of 25 families per nurse, 200 families would be served at a cost of $5,074 per family for 1 year of services.

[continued] | CEBC: 1 CEBC: Medium Child Welfare

NREPP: 3.38

Blueprints: Model |

Program Name	Target Population	Intervention Description
Nurse-Family Partnership (NFP) (continued)		
Nurturing Parenting Program (NPP)	Families who have been identified by child welfare agencies for past child abuse and neglect or who are at high risk for child abuse and neglect; includes families of children ages 0-12	Instruction-based program for the prevention and treatment of child abuse and neglect is based on psychoeducational and cognitive-behavioral approaches to learning and focuses on "reparenting," or helping parents learn new patterns of parenting to replace their existing, learned abusive patterns. Participating families attend sessions either at home or in a group format with other families. Group sessions combine concurrent separate experiences for parents and children with shared "family nurturing time." In home-based sessions, parents and children meet separately and jointly during a 90-minute lesson once per week for 15 weeks.

Targeted Knowledge, Attitudes, and Practices	Qualifications of Staff	Cost	Rating
		NFP costs approximately $4,500 per family per year, with a range of $2,914 to $6,463 per family per year.	
By completing questionnaires and participating in discussion, role play, and audiovisual exercises, participants learn how to nurture themselves and in turn build their nurturing family and parenting skills as dads, moms, sons, and daughters. Participants develop awareness, knowledge, and skills in five areas: age-appropriate expectations; empathy, bonding, and attachment; nonviolent nurturing discipline; self-awareness and self-worth; and empowerment, autonomy, and healthy independence. Multiple NPPs have been developed for various age groups and family circumstances.	Two group facilitators are recommended for every seven adults participating in the program. Two additional group facilitators are recommended for every 10 children participating. NPP can be implemented by professionals or paraprofessionals in such fields as social work, education, recreation, and psychology who have undergone NPP facilitator training and have related experience.	Materials set (includes all materials needed for implementation and quality assurance) costs $300-$2,000, depending on the program selected; 3-day, on- or off-site facilitator training costs $250-$325 per participant. The cost of running a high-quality NPP varies based on the program format and number of sessions provided. The initial set of materials can be used to implement the program for approximately 15 families. The majority of program materials are reusable.	NREPP: 3.05

Program Name	Target Population	Intervention Description
Parent Management Training-Oregon Model (PMT-O)*	Recently separated single mothers of children ages 2-18 with disruptive behaviors, such as conduct disorder, oppositional defiant disorder, and antisocial behaviors	Group- or individual-based parent training program that teaches effective family management strategies and parenting skills, including skill encouragement, setting limits/positive discipline, monitoring, problem solving, and positive involvement, aimed at reducing antisocial and behavior problems in children. Delivered in group and individual family formats, in diverse settings (e.g., clinics, homes, schools, community centers, homeless shelters), over varied lengths of time depending on families' needs. Can be tailored for specific clinical problems, such as antisocial behavior, conduct problems, substance abuse, and child neglect and abuse. 1.5- to 2-hour weekly parent group sessions and 60-minute weekly individual/family sessions; 14 group sessions and 20-25 individual/family sessions, depending on severity; individual family treatment is not typically provided together with group treatment. The time frame can be 5-6 months or longer, depending on circumstances.

Targeted Knowledge, Attitudes, and Practices	Qualifications of Staff	Cost	Rating
Teach and coach parents in the use of effective parenting strategies: skill encouragement, setting limits or effective discipline, monitoring, problem solving, and positive involvement. In addition to the core parenting practices, PMT-O incorporates the supporting parenting components of identifying and regulating emotions, enhancing communication, giving clear directions, and tracking behavior. PMT-O also includes strategies designed to help parents decrease coercive exchanges with their children and use contingent positive reinforcements (e.g., praise, incentives) to promote prosocial behavior. Promoting school success is woven into the program throughout relevant components. Goals include improving parenting practices; reducing family coercion; reducing and preventing in youth internalizing and externalizing behaviors, substance use and abuse, delinquency and police arrests, out-of-home placements, and deviant peer associations; and improving in youth academic performance, social competency, and peer relations.	Providers must have a bachelor's degree with 5 years of appropriate clinical experience or master's degree in a relevant field. During the first phase, therapists are trained and certified over a period of 18-24 months.	Estimated cost is $1,000 per participant, based on 10-15 participants per group, with 2 group facilitators and 14 sessions. Estimated total training and technical assistance cost for Phase 1 for 16 clinicians is $515,000 in year 1 and $310,000 in year 2. Beyond Phase 3 costs an estimated $12,000 yearly. Estimated cost over 3 years to become a qualified independent Fidelity of Implementation Rating System (FIMP) team is $11,780 (Phase 4). $2,500-$4,000 will be needed for testing before independent operation starts. An organization with 16 clinicians could expect to incur estimated costs of $1,170,000 in year 1.	Blueprints: Model CEBC: 1 CEBC: Medium Child Welfare NREPP: 3.56

Program Name	Target Population	Intervention Description
Parent-Child Interaction Therapy (PCIT)	Parents of children ages 2-7 with behavior and parent-child relationship problems	Didactic and coaching sessions focus on decreasing externalizing child behaviors (e.g., defiance, aggression), increasing child social skills and cooperation, and improving the parent-child attachment. Parents learn to use traditional play-therapy skills as social reinforcers of positive child behavior and traditional behavior management skills to decrease negative child behavior. Parents learn and practice these skills with their child in a playroom while coached by a therapist. The coaching provides parents with immediate feedback on their use of the new parenting skills, which enables them to apply the skills correctly and master them rapidly. Typically one or two 1-hour sessions per week with the therapist. The average number of sessions is 14, but varies from 10 to 20. Treatment continues until the parent masters the interaction skills to meet preset criteria and the child's behavior has improved to within normal limits.

Targeted Knowledge, Attitudes, and Practices	Qualifications of Staff	Cost	Rating
Parents are taught specific skills to establish or strengthen a nurturing and secure relationship with their child while encouraging prosocial behavior and discouraging negative behavior. This treatment has two phases, each focusing on a different parent-child interaction: child-directed interaction (CDI) and parent-directed interaction (PDI). In each phase, parents attend one didactic session to learn interaction skills and then attend a series of coaching sessions with the child in which they apply these skills. During the CDI phase, parents learn nondirective play skills similar to those used in play therapy and engage their child in a play situation with the goal of strengthening the parent-child relationship. During the PDI phase, parents learn to direct the child's behavior with clear, age-appropriate instructions and consistent consequences, with the aim of increasing child compliance.	Generally administered in an outpatient clinic by a licensed mental health professional with experience working with children and families.	Treatment materials cost $1,000 per set; 1-week, offsite training plus 100 hours of additional training/ consultation over 12 months costs $3,000-$4,000 per person; certification costs $200 per organization. The model often requires modification of space at an estimated cost of $1,000-$1,500. An Eyberg Child Behavior Inventory is administered weekly to each parent at a cost of $40 for 25 forms. Each therapist receives weekly consultation from the purveyor for the first year at a cost of $1,000 per therapist for the year. A study of high-risk families involved in the child welfare system estimated the cost for each parent-child pair completing the program at $2,208-$3,638. *[continued]*	NREPP: 3.375 CEBC: 1 CEBC: Medium Child Welfare Blueprints: Promising
Teaches parents traditional play-therapy skills to improve parent-child interactions and problem-solving skills that can be used to manage new problem behaviors. Parents are taught and practice communication skills and behavior management with their children in a playroom while coached by therapists. Most parenting programs for abusive parents treat parents separately from their children and use an instructive approach, but PCIT treats parents with their children. Skills are behaviorally defined, directly coached, and practiced in parent-child sessions. Parents are shown directly how to implement specific behavioral skills with their children. Therapists observe parent-child interactions through a one-way mirror and coach. Live coaching and monitoring of skill acquisition are cornerstones of PCIT. *[continued]*			

Program Name	Target Population	Intervention Description
Parent-Child Interaction Therapy (PCIT)		

(continued)

Targeted Knowledge, Attitudes, and Practices	Qualifications of Staff	Cost	Rating
Child goals include building close relationships with parents using positive attention strategies; helping children feel safe and calm by fostering warmth and security between parents and children; increasing children's organizational and play skills; decreasing children's frustration and anger; educating parents about ways to teach their child without frustration for parent and child; enhancing children's self-esteem; improving children's social skills, such as sharing and cooperation; and teaching parents how to communicate with young children who have limited attention spans.		If each therapist had a caseload of 20 families for an average of 15 weeks per family, 280 families could be served in the first year at a cost of $1,210 per family.	
Parent goals include teaching parents specific discipline techniques that help children listen to instructions and follow directions, decreasing problematic child behaviors by teaching parents to be consistent and predictable, and helping parents develop confidence in managing their children's behaviors at home and in public.			
Provides services to children/adolescents that address noncompliance, aggression, rule breaking, disruptive behavior, dysfunctional attachment with parents, and internalizing symptoms.			
Provides services to parents/caregivers that address ineffective parenting styles (e.g., permissive, authoritarian, and overly harsh parenting).			

Program Name	Target Population	Intervention Description
ParentCorps	Parents and their young children ages 3-6 living in low-income communities	Family-centered preventive intervention designed to foster healthy development and school success of young children Weekly series of 14 2-hour group sessions that occur concurrently for parents and children

Targeted Knowledge, Attitudes, and Practices	Qualifications of Staff	Cost	Rating
Parent groups present a specific set of parenting strategies: establishing structure and routines for children, providing opportunities for positive parent-child interactions during nondirective play, using positive reinforcement to encourage compliance and social and behavioral competence, selectively ignoring mild misbehaviors, and using effective forms of discipline for misbehavior (e.g., time-outs, loss of privileges). Parenting strategies are introduced through group discussions, role plays, an animated video series, and a photography-based book of ParentCorps family stories and homework. In a manner that is sensitive to and respectful of parents' readiness for change, facilitators help parents anticipate barriers and generate solutions so that families can implement the strategies successfully. Child groups focus on promoting social, emotional, and self-regulatory skills through interactive lessons, experiential activities, and play. In support of individualized goals that parents set for children, teachers promote skills and shape behaviors using strategies that complement the parenting strategies being introduced to parents.	Delivered in parent and child groups facilitated by trained professionals. Groups include approximately 15 participants and are held in early childhood education or child care settings. Parent groups are facilitated by trained mental health professionals. Child groups are led by trained classroom teachers.	ParentCorps training and start-up materials (include leader's manuals and resource guides for use with the child and parent groups; props, puppet, and music CD for use with the child group; and DVD for use with the parent group) cost $2,000 (for up to 4 child group leaders and 1 parent group leader). Family group materials (include parent workbooks, parent toolkit, and wordless picture book) cost $30 per family. ParentCorps 101 Web-based training costs $50 per user. 5-day training at New York University costs $5,000 per site (for up to 4 participants). 2-day, onsite consultation costs $5,000 plus travel expenses. Group leader coaching (14 hours during the first cycle of implementation) costs $2,000. Quality assurance measures are included in the cost of implementation materials.	NREPP: 3.36

Program Name	Target Population	Intervention Description
Parenting Wisely	Parents of children ages 3-18 at risk for or with behavior problems, substance abuse problems, or delinquency	A set of self-instructional interactive, computer-based training programs based on social learning, cognitive-behavioral, and family systems theories, the program aims to increase parental communication and disciplinary skills. All nine sessions can be completed in 2-3 hours.

Targeted Knowledge, Attitudes, and Practices	Qualifications of Staff	Cost	Rating
Parents use this self-instructional program on an agency's personal computer or laptop, either onsite or at home, using the CD-ROM or online format. The program utilizes a DVD for group administration or an interactive online program for individual administration, with 10 video scenarios depicting common challenges with adolescents. Parents choose from among three solutions to these challenges and are able to view the scenarios enacted while receiving feedback about each choice. Parents are quizzed periodically throughout the program and receive feedback. The program operates as a supportive tutor, pointing out typical errors parents make and highlighting new skills that will help them resolve problems.	None required	Program kit (includes service provider's guide and program integrity guide) costs $659 each. Additional parent workbooks cost $6.75-$9.00 each, depending on the quantity purchased.	CEBC: 3 CEBC: Medium Child Welfare NREPP: 2.73

Program Name	Target Population	Intervention Description
Parents as Teachers (PAT)	Parents of children ages 0-5	Early childhood family support and parent education home visiting program includes optional group connection formats with family activities, presentations, community events, parent cafes, and ongoing groups. Annual health, hearing, vision, and developmental screenings, beginning within 90 days of enrollment, are a third component of the model. Home visits of approximately 60 minutes delivered weekly, every 2 weeks, or monthly, depending on family needs; optional monthly or more frequent group connections

Targeted Knowledge, Attitudes, and Practices	Qualifications of Staff	Cost	Rating
Parent educators work with parents to strengthen protective factors and ensure that young children are healthy, safe, and ready to learn. The goals of the model are to increase parent knowledge of early childhood development, improve parenting practices, provide early detection of developmental delays and health issues, prevent child abuse and neglect, and increase children's school readiness and school success. Parent-child interaction focuses on promoting positive parenting behaviors and child development through parent-child activities. Development-centered parenting focuses on the link between child development and parenting and on key developmental topics (i.e., attachment, discipline, health, nutrition, safety, sleep, transitions/routines, healthy births). Family well-being includes a focus on family strengths, capabilities, skills, and building of protective factors.	Parent educators ideally hold a bachelor's degree in an area, such as early childhood education, human services, or a related field; however, a high school diploma and 2 years of supervised work experience with young children and/or parents is acceptable. Different curriculum materials are used for those working with families of children up to age 3 and those working with families of children from age 3 to kindergarten.	5-day, offsite parent educator foundational and model implementation training (includes all program materials and 1-year access to online materials for serving families prenatally to age 3) costs about $800 per parent educator, but varies by location. 2-day, offsite parent educator training for the 3 Years to Kindergarten Entry curriculum (includes printed curriculum) costs about $225-$450. Annual recertification and online access fee is $75 per parent educator. After initial start-up expenses have been paid, the cost to provide PAT services to families is estimated to be approximately $2,500 per family for twice-monthly visits. PAT provides resources to help new affiliates build a realistic and comprehensive budget.	NREPP: 3.175

Program Name	Target Population	Intervention Description
Period of PURPLE Crying	All mothers and fathers of new infants and society in general with respect to understanding early increased infant crying and shaken baby syndrome	Shaken baby syndrome prevention program educates parents and caretakers on normal infant crying, the most common trigger for shaking an infant. The program was designed to be used primarily in universal, primary prevention settings, but is applicable to secondary prevention as well. Three 3- to 10-minute "doses": (1) in the maternity ward, provided separately from other materials; (2) either pre- or postbirth as a second "dose" (e.g., in prenatal classes and in the first pediatric office visit); (3) via media and social networking campaigns. With these three doses, the duration of the program is at least a week and can be much longer since the infant crying period lasts up to 4-5 months, and a key element of the program is that each parent receives a copy of the DVD and booklet to take home.
Play and Learning Strategies-Infant Program (PALS I)	Children ages 5-15 months and their families	Preventive intervention program to strengthen the bond between parent and baby and to stimulate early language, cognitive, and social development The program consists of 90-minute individual sessions in the family's home and lasts about 11 weeks.

Targeted Knowledge, Attitudes, and Practices	Qualifications of Staff	Cost	Rating
Goals include supporting caregivers in their understanding of early increased infant crying and reducing the incidence of shaken baby syndrome/abusive head trauma.	There are no educational requirements, but providers must take the training online or in person and be in a position where they have the authority to provide the program to new parents. Providers should protect the fidelity of the program by complying with the protocol required.	Not specified	CEBC: 3 CEBC: Medium Child Welfare
The aim is to facilitate parents' mastery of specific skills for interacting with their young children, including paying attention to and correctly interpreting babies' signals, responding contingently to signals, and using rich language. Goals include increasing parents' contingent responsiveness behaviors, rich language input, emotional/affective support, and ability to maintain their child's focus of attention, and improving children's language, cognitive, and social outcomes.	It is recommended that a trained PALS I home visitor have at least an associate's degree in early childhood (or a related field) or work experience commensurate with that education. PALS I home visitors are supervised by a person with at least a bachelor's degree in early childhood education or a related field with 3-5 years' experience in parent education.	Not specified	CEBC: 3 CEBC: Medium Child Welfare

Program Name	Target Population	Intervention Description
Play and Learning Strategies-Toddler/ Preschool Program (PALS II)	Children ages 18 months to 4 years and their families	Preventive intervention program designed to strengthen the bond between parent and child and to stimulate early language, cognitive, and social development through positive language input, use of language and activities to encourage children's problem-solving skills, and positive discipline strategies. The program consists of 90-minute individual sessions in the family's home and lasts about 14 weeks.
SafeCare®	Parents at risk for or with a history of child neglect and/or abuse	In-home parenting program that targets risk factors for child neglect and physical abuse. Parents are taught (1) how to interact in a positive manner with their children, plan activities, and respond appropriately to challenging child behaviors; (2) how to recognize hazards in the home to improve the home environment; and (3) how to recognize and respond to children's symptoms of illness and injury, in addition to keeping good health records. 18-20 weekly sessions of approximately 1-1.5 hours each

Targeted Knowledge, Attitudes, and Practices	Qualifications of Staff	Cost	Rating
Facilitate parents' mastery of specific skills for interacting with their young children, such as understanding children's signals, responding contingently, guiding children's behavior, and using rich language. Goals include increasing parents' contingent responsiveness behaviors, rich language input, emotional/affective support, and ability to maintain the child's focus of attention, and improving the child's language, cognitive, and social outcomes.	It is recommended that a trained PALS II home visitor have at least an associate's degree or higher in early childhood (or a related field) or work experience commensurate with that education. PALS II home visitors are supervised by a person with at least a bachelor's degree in early childhood education or a related field with 3-5 years' experience in parent education.	Not specified	CEBC: 3 CEBC: Medium Child Welfare
Goals are to reduce future incidents of child maltreatment, increase positive parent-child interaction, improve how parents care for their children's health, and enhance home safety and parent supervision.	A college education is preferred, but the most important qualification is that staff be trained to performance criteria.	Not specified	SafeCare® CEBC: 2 CEBC: High Child Welfare SafeCare® [Home Visiting for Child Well-Being] CEBC: 3 CEBC: High Child Welfare

Program Name	Target Population	Intervention Description
Strengthening Families Program (SFP)	Children ages 3-16	Family skills training program designed to increase resilience and reduce risk factors for behavioral, emotional, academic, and social problems 14 weekly 2-hour sessions

Targeted Knowledge, Attitudes, and Practices	Qualifications of Staff	Cost	Rating
Comprises three life-skills courses. The Parenting Skills sessions are designed to help parents learn to increase desired behaviors in children by using attention and rewards, clear communication, effective discipline, substance use education, problem solving, and limit setting. The Children's Life Skills sessions are designed to help children learn effective communication, understand their feelings, improve social and problem-solving skills, resist peer pressure, understand the consequences of substance use, and comply with parental rules. In the Family Life Skills sessions, families engage in structured family activities, practice therapeutic child play, conduct family meetings, learn communication skills, practice effective discipline, reinforce positive behaviors in each other, and plan family activities together. Participation in ongoing family support groups and booster sessions is encouraged to increase generalization and use of skills learned.	Not specified	CD containing materials for one age group (3-5, 6-11, 7-17, or 12-16) costs $450 each (or is included in training fee). Small agencies may find it economical to attend a training hosted by a nearby agency. Lutra Group, Inc., the entity that coordinates SFP training and technical assistance, can help in locating other trainings. Training in the United States is available in English and Spanish. Implementation requires a minimum of five trained staff: two group leaders for the parents, two group leaders for the children, and a site coordinator.	NREPP: 3.1

Program Name	Target Population	Intervention Description
Systematic Training for Effective Parenting (STEP)*	Parents dealing with frequently encountered challenges with their children (ages 0-12) that often result from autocratic parenting styles. Designed for use with parents facing typical parenting challenges; however, all the studies reviewed for this summary targeted families with an abusive parent, families at risk for parenting problems and child maltreatment, or families with a child receiving mental health treatment.	Skills training that promotes a more participatory family structure by fostering responsibility, independence, and competence in children; improving communication between parents and children; and helping children learn from the natural and logical consequences of their own choices. Presented in a group format, with optimal group sizes ranging from 6 to 14 parents. Typically taught in 8 or 9 weekly 1.5-hour study groups

Targeted Knowledge, Attitudes, and Practices	Qualifications of Staff	Cost	Rating
Four current versions of STEP: Early Childhood STEP for parents of children up to age 6; STEP for parents of children ages 6-12; STEP/Teen for parents of teens; and Spanish STEP, a complete translation of the STEP program for parents of children ages 6-12. Using the STEP multimedia kit, lessons are taught to parents on how to understand child behavior and misbehavior, practice positive listening, give encouragement (rather than praise), explore alternative parenting behaviors and express ideas and feelings, develop their child's responsibilities, apply natural and logical consequences, convene family meetings, and develop their child's confidence.	Facilitated by a counselor, social worker, or individual who has participated in a STEP workshop.	STEP kit costs $345 each. Parent's handbook costs $16.99 per participant (quantity discounts are available).	NREPP: 2.86

Program Name	Target Population	Intervention Description
Trauma-Focused Cognitive-Behavioral Therapy (TF-CBT)*	Children with a known trauma history who are experiencing significant PTSD symptoms, whether or not they meet full diagnostic criteria. In addition, children with depression, anxiety, and/or shame related to their traumatic exposure. Children experiencing childhood traumatic grief can also benefit from the treatment.	Psychosocial treatment model designed to address traumatic experiences. Initially provides parallel individual sessions with children and their parents (or guardians), with conjoint parent-child sessions increasingly incorporated over the course of treatment. Sessions are conducted once a week. Each session is 30-45 minutes for the child, 30-45 minutes for the parent. The conjoint child-parent sessions toward the end of treatment last approximately 30-45 minutes. Treatment lasts 12-18 sessions.

Targeted Knowledge, Attitudes, and Practices	Qualifications of Staff	Cost	Rating
Goals include improving child PTSD, depressive, and anxiety symptoms; improving child externalizing behavior problems (including sexual behavior problems if related to trauma); improving parenting skills and parental support of the child and reducing parental distress; enhancing parent-child communication, attachment, and ability to maintain safety; improving child's adaptive functioning; and reducing shame and embarrassment related to the traumatic experiences.

Components include psychoeducation and parenting skills, relaxation techniques, affective expression and regulation, cognitive coping, trauma narrative and processing, in vivo exposure, conjoint parent-child sessions, and enhancing personal safety and future growth.

Provides services to children/adolescents that address feelings of shame, distorted beliefs about self and others, acting-out behavior problems, and PTSD and related symptoms.

Provides services to parents/caregivers that address inappropriate parenting practices and parental trauma-related emotional distress. | Master's degree and training in the treatment model; experience working with children and families | 10-hour online introductory training is free. 2- to 3-day onsite full clinical training (introductory and advanced training) varies depending on site needs. Consultation call twice a month for at least 6 months costs $200-$260 per hour. | CEBC: 1 CEBC: High Child Welfare

NREPP: 3.72 |

Program Name	Target Population	Intervention Description
Treatment Foster Care Oregon for Preschoolers (TFCO-P)	Preschool foster children ages 3-6 who exhibit a high level of disruptive and antisocial behavior and cannot be maintained in regular foster care or may be considered for residential treatment	Foster care treatment model effective at promoting secure attachment in foster care and facilitating successful permanent placements. TFCO-P is delivered through a treatment team approach in which foster parents receive training and ongoing consultation and support. For foster parent(s), the program typically entails a minimum of seven contacts per week that include five 10-minute contacts, one 2-hour group session, and additional contacts based on the amount of support or consultation required. For the child in treatment, the program includes two contacts per week that comprise a 2-hour therapeutic playgroup and a 2-hour skills training session. For the biological family or other long-term placement resource, the program includes one contact per week in the form of a 1-hour skill-building session. Designed with an overall treatment duration of 6-9 months.

Targeted Knowledge, Attitudes, and Practices	Qualifications of Staff	Cost	Rating
Children receive individual skills training and participate in a therapeutic playgroup, and birth parents (or other permanent placement caregivers) receive family therapy. TFCO-P emphasizes the use of concrete encouragement for prosocial behavior; consistent, nonabusive limit setting to address disruptive behavior; and close supervision of the child. In addition, the TFCO-P intervention employs a developmental framework in which the challenges of foster preschoolers are viewed from the perspective of delayed maturation. Goals include eliminating or reducing child problem behaviors; increasing developmentally appropriate normative and prosocial behavior in children; transitioning children to a birth family, adoptive family, or lower-level aftercare resource; improving children's peer associations; improving parent-child interaction and communication; and improving children's coping and social skills.	Program supervisors must have a master's-level education and relevant experience in behavior management approaches. Foster parent consultants/ recruiters/ trainers must have knowledge of foster parents and a clear understanding of the model. Prior experience as a foster/adoptive parent is strongly desirable. Family therapists must have a master's-level education. Knowledge of parent management training or related behaviorally based parenting techniques is highly desirable. Playgroup leaders and skills trainers must have a bachelor's-level education.	None noted	CEBC: 2 CEBC: High Child Welfare

Program Name	Target Population	Intervention Description
Triple P-Positive Parenting Program® System (Triple P)	Families with children ages 0-12, with extensions to families with teenagers ages 13-16	Triple P is a multitiered system of five levels of education and support for parents and caregivers of children and adolescents. Although Triple P can be used in parts (e.g., using only one level of the five or a group version versus the standard version), this entry on the CEBC reviews Triple P as a whole (i.e., using all five levels) in its standard version and includes only evidence from research that evaluated the whole system. As a prevention program, Triple P helps parents learn strategies that promote social competence and self-regulation in children. Parents become better equipped to handle the stress of everyday childrearing, and children become better able to respond positively to their individual developmental challenges. As an early intervention, Triple P can assist families in greater distress by working with parents of children who are experiencing moderate to severe behavior problems. Throughout the program, parents are encouraged to develop a parenting plan that makes use of a variety of Triple P strategies and tools. Triple P practitioners are trained, therefore, to work with parents' strengths and to provide a supportive, nonjudgmental environment in which parents can continually improve their parenting skills. Level 1, Universal/Stay Positive, uses variable outreach strategies (Websites, parent newspaper, brochures, posters, and radio/TV spots) that are designed to reach the entire population at planned intervals. Level 2, Selected Seminars/Selected Seminars Teen, includes three 2-hour seminars that may be offered as standalone events or together in a series, and brief primary care, which consists of one to two brief consultations lasting up to 30 minutes. Level 3, Primary Care/Primary Care Teen/Primary Care Stepping Stones, consists of one to four brief consultations lasting approximately 30 minutes each and four 2-hour discussion groups that may be offered as standalone events or together in a series. [continued]

Targeted Knowledge, Attitudes, and Practices	Qualifications of Staff	Cost	Rating
The overall goal of Triple P is to prevent development or worsening of severe behavioral, emotional, and developmental problems in children and adolescents by enhancing the knowledge, skills, and confidence of parents. Practitioners are trained to create a supportive learning environment in which parents receive and discuss practical information about parenting skills that they can incorporate into everyday interactions with their children. Specific expected outcomes include increasing parents' competence in promoting healthy development and managing common behavior problems and developmental issues; reducing parents' use of coercive and punitive methods of disciplining children; increasing parents' use of positive parenting strategies in managing their children's behavior; increasing parents' confidence in raising their children; decreasing child behavior problems (for families experiencing difficult child behavior); improving parenting partners' communication about parenting issues; and reducing parenting stress associated with raising children.

Level 1 is a comprehensive media campaign and distribution strategy for delivering positive parenting information to all families within a given community.

Level 2 interventions are delivered to parents through low-intensity seminars or single-session meetings.

Level 3 interventions are brief in duration (one to four sessions) and focus on identifying and resolving commonly encountered behavior problems in childhood. Level 3 interventions may be offered in a variety of settings that parents naturally visit.

[continued] | Formal training on each of the five program levels is available to organizations implementing this program.

Provider training courses are usually offered to practitioners with a post-high school degree in health, education, child care, or social services. In exceptional circumstances, this requirement is relaxed when the prospective practitioners are actively involved in "hands-on" roles dealing with the targeted parents, children, and teenagers. These particular practitioners have developed, through their workplace experience, some knowledge of child/adolescent development and/or have experience working with families.

[continued] | Parent workbooks cost $20-$32 per participant. Positive parenting booklets cost $6.50 per participant. Parenting tip sheets cost $8-$11 for a set of 10.

2- to 3-day on-site training and half-day follow-up training (includes session fidelity checklists and pre-and post-test assessment measures) costs $21,415-$26,195 per site for up to 20 practitioners, depending on their level of training.

Costs are based on preparing a site to serve 100,000 families: Level 2, $160,300; Level 3, $537,900 (includes $66,800 for preaccreditation cost); Level 4, $301,000 (includes $33,400 for preaccreditation cost); Level 4 (Standard), $210,700 (includes $23,380 for preaccreditation cost); Level 4 (Standard Stepping Stones), $32,155 (includes $3,340 for preaccreditation cost);

[continued] | CEBC: 2 CEBC: Medium Child Welfare

NREPP: 2.93

Blueprints: Promising |

Program Name	Target Population	Intervention Description
Triple P-Positive Parenting Program® System (Triple P) (continued)		Level 4 can consist of a variety of options: (1) Group/Group Teen/Group Stepping Stones, which includes five 2-hour group sessions and three 20-minute individual telephone consultations for each family, offered over 8 consecutive weeks; (2) Triple P Online, which comprises eight self-paced online modules; (3) a self-directed workbook, which is self-paced; or (4) Standard/Standard Teen/Standard Stepping Stones, which comprises ten 1-hour sessions that occur weekly.

Level 5 can consist of a variety of options: (1) Enhanced, which consists of three to ten 60- to 90-minute sessions; (2) Pathways, which includes four sessions lasting 60-90 minutes each when offered individually or 2 hours each when offered in group format; (3) Family Transitions, which consists of ten 2-hour group sessions plus two individual telephone consultations for each family lasting 30 minutes; or (4) Group Lifestyle, which consists of ten 90-minute group sessions plus four individual telephone consultations for each family lasting 30 minutes.

Level 1 may be planned for intermittent distribution of materials throughout the course of Levels 2-5. Level 1 is typically planned as a 3-year intervention; Levels 2-3 may include one to four encounters that take place over 1-6 weeks; Levels 4-5 typically take place over 4-5 months. If accommodations are needed (e.g., low-literacy clients), the duration may be longer. |

Targeted Knowledge, Attitudes, and Practices	Qualifications of Staff	Cost	Rating
Level 4 interventions are delivered in eight to ten sessions and offer parents a more comprehensive set of strategies for improving family functioning and parent-child relationships in any situation. The interventions have sufficient impact to address moderate to severe behavior problems in children. Level 5 interventions offer further support for parents with specific risk factors (e.g., families at high risk for child maltreatment, families going through a divorce or separation, or families with overweight or obese children) or for parents with continuing needs following a Level 4 intervention. Directly provides services to parents/caregivers that address management of child behavior problems; management of stress, mild to moderate depression symptoms, anxiety, and anger; parenting partner conflict; and negative attributional thinking.	Trainers are master's- or doctorate-level professionals (mainly clinical or educational psychologists) who are practitioners (Triple P providers) trained to implement Triple P programs with the parents with whom they work. Professionals invited to become Triple P trainers undergo an intensive 2-week training program.	Level 5, $81,740. Total for training and preaccreditation workshops is $1,323,795. Implementation resources cost $723,598 (including freight and handling). To summarize the above costs, which represent the year-1 investment in a Triple P program serving 100,000 families: training courses, $1,323,795; implementation costs, $723,598; Stay Positive communications campaign, $320,000; total year-1 cost, $2,367,393. The total dollar value of $2,367,393 represents a cost of $23.67 per family in a community serving 100,000 families.	

Program Name	Target Population	Intervention Description
Triple P-Positive Parenting Program® Level 4 (Level 4 Triple P)	For parents and caregivers of children and adolescents with moderate to severe behavioral and/or emotional difficulties or for parents that are motivated to gain a more in-depth understanding of positive parenting. Level 4 Triple P is applicable to parents of children and adolescents ages 0-12.	Level 4 Triple P helps parents learn strategies that promote social competence and self-regulation in children as well as decrease problem behavior. Parents are encouraged to develop a parenting plan that makes use of a variety of Level 4 Triple P strategies and tools. Parents are then asked to practice their parenting plan with their children. During the course of the program, parents are encouraged to keep track of their children's behavior, as well as their own behavior, and to reflect on what is working with their parenting plan and what is not working so well. They then work with their practitioner to fine tune their plan. Level 4 Triple P practitioners are trained to work with parents' strengths and to provide a supportive, nonjudgmental environment in which parents can continually improve their parenting skills. Level 4 Triple P is offered in several different formats (e.g., individual, group, self-directed, online). The CEBC evaluated the standard version of Level 4 Triple P as described above and no other variations (including early teen versions or those for children with developmental delays). The program has a variety of delivery options: (1) three group versions that include five 2-hour group sessions and three 20-minute individual telephone consultations for each family offered over 8 consecutive weeks; (2) an online version that comprises eight self-paced online modules; (3) a self-directed workbook, which is self-paced; or (4) three individual or standard versions consisting of ten 1-hour weekly sessions. Program interventions typically take place over 2-3 months. If accommodations are needed (e.g., low-literacy clients), the duration may be longer.

*Program that is not mentioned in the report text.

Targeted Knowledge, Attitudes, and Practices	Qualifications of Staff	Cost	Rating
The aim is to prevent worsening of severe behavioral, emotional, and developmental problems in children and adolescents by enhancing the knowledge, skills, and confidence of parents. Practitioners are trained to create a supportive learning environment in which parents receive and discuss practical information about parenting skills they can incorporate into everyday interactions with their children. Specific expected outcomes include increasing parents' competence in promoting healthy development and managing common behavior problems and developmental issues; reducing parents' use of coercive and punitive methods of disciplining children; increasing parents' use of positive parenting strategies in managing their children's behavior; increasing parents' confidence in raising their children; decreasing child behavior problems (for families experiencing difficult child behavior); improving parenting partners' communication about parenting issues; and reducing parenting stress associated with raising children. Provides services to parents/caregivers that address parents with children with moderate to severe behavior problems, significant difficulty managing these behaviors, and lack of positive parenting skills. Typically includes management of stress, mild to moderate depression symptoms, anxiety, and anger; parenting partner conflict; and negative attributional thinking.	Level 4 Triple P provider training courses are usually offered to practitioners with a post-high school degree in health, education, child care, or social services. In exceptional circumstances, this requirement is relaxed when the prospective practitioners are actively involved in "hands-on" roles dealing with the targeted parents, children, and teenagers. These particular practitioners have developed, through their workplace experience, some knowledge of child/adolescent development and/or have experience working with families.	None noted	CEBC: 1 CEBC: Medium Child Welfare

Appendix D

Biographical Sketches of Committee Members

Vivian L. Gadsden, Ed.D. *(Chair)* is William T. Carter professor of child development and professor of education at the University of Pennsylvania. She is also on the faculties of Africana Studies and of Gender, Sexuality, and Women's Studies; serves as director of the National Center on Fathers and Families; and served as associate director of the National Center on Adult Literacy. Her research and scholarly interests focus on children and families across the life course, particularly those at the greatest risk for academic and social vulnerability by virtue of race, gender, ethnicity, poverty, and immigrant status. In addition to serving on the Board of the Foundation for Child Development, she has served or serves on various foundation and congressionally mandated review committees. She has held leadership roles in the American Educational Research Association, of which she is a fellow, and the Society for Research in Child Development. She received her Ed.D. in educational psychology and policy from the University of Michigan.

Clare Anderson, M.S.W., is a policy fellow at Chapin Hall, University of Chicago. Her work focuses on using research, policy, and fiscal levers to improve outcomes for vulnerable children and families. She works with state child welfare systems to implement evidence-based screening, assessment, and interventions and better integrate the goals of children's safety, permanency, and well-being. Prior to joining Chapin Hall, she was deputy commissioner at the U.S. Department of Health and Human Services' Administration on Children, Youth, and Families (ACYF), responsible for federal programs addressing child abuse and neglect, runaway and homeless

499

youth, domestic and intimate partner violence, and teen pregnancy prevention. Prior to joining ACYF, she spent a decade at the Center for the Study of Social Policy, helping states and local jurisdictions change policies and practices to improve outcomes for vulnerable children and families. She holds an M.S.W. from the University of Alabama.

Oscar A. Barbarin, III, Ph.D., is Wilson H. Elkins professor and chair of the African American Studies Department (with a joint faculty appointment in the Department of Psychology) at the University of Maryland, College Park. He is former Lila L. and Douglas J. Hertz endowed chair, Department of Psychology, Tulane University. He has served on the faculties of the Universities of Maryland, Michigan, and North Carolina. His research has focused on the social and familial determinants of ethnic and gender achievement gaps beginning in early childhood. He has developed a universal mental health screening system for children from prekindergarten to age 8. He was principal investigator for a national study focused on the socioemotional and academic development of boys of color. His work on children of African descent includes a 20-year longitudinal study of the effects of poverty and violence on child development in South Africa. He served as editor of the *American Journal of Orthopsychiatry*, 2009-2014, and on the Governing Council of the Society for Research in Child Development, 2007-2013. He earned a Ph.D. in clinical psychology at Rutgers University in 1975.

Richard P. Barth, M.S.W., Ph.D., is dean, School of Social Work, at the University of Maryland. He previously served as Frank A. Daniels distinguished professor, School of Social Work, University of North Carolina, Chapel Hill, and as Hutto Patterson professor, School of Social Welfare, University of California, Berkeley. He was the 1986 winner of the Frank Breul Prize for Excellence in Child Welfare Scholarship from the University of Chicago; a Fulbright Scholar in 1990 and 2006; the 1998 recipient of the Presidential Award for Excellence in Research from the National Association of Social Workers; the 2005 winner of the Flynn Prize for Research; and the 2007 winner of the Peter Forsythe Award for Child Welfare Leadership from the American Public Human Services Association. He is a fellow of the American Psychological Association, and was a founding board member and president of the American Academy of Social Work and Social Welfare. He served on the Board of the Society for Social Work Research, 2002-2006, and has also served on the boards of numerous child-serving agencies. His A.B., M.S.W., and Ph.D. degrees are from Brown University and the University of California, Berkeley.

William R. Beardslee, M.D., directs the Baer Prevention Initiatives at Boston Children's Hospital and is senior research scientist at the Judge Baker Children's Center; chairman emeritus, Department of Psychiatry, Boston Children's Hospital; and Distinguished Gardner-Monks professor of child psychiatry at Harvard Medical School. His long-standing research interest has centered on the development of children at risk because of parental adversities such as mental illness or poverty. He and his colleagues adapted the principles of his work on public health interventions for families facing depression in a teacher training and empowerment program for use in Head Start and Early Head Start called Family Connections. He directed the Boston site of a multisite study on the prevention of depression in adolescents that demonstrated prevention of episodes of major depression in high-risk youth fully 60 months after intervention delivery. He has received numerous awards, including the Blanche F. Ittleson Award of the American Psychiatric Association for outstanding published research contributing to the mental health of children, the Catcher in the Rye Award for Advocacy of the American Academy of Child and Adolescent Psychiatry, the Human Rights Award from the Department of Mental Health of the Commonwealth of Massachusetts and the Judge Baker Children's Center World of Children Award. He received an honorary doctor of science degree from Emory University.

Kimberly Boller, Ph.D., is a senior fellow at Mathematica Policy Research. She studies the effects of early childhood care and education, parenting programs, and policy on children and parents. Her expertise includes measurement of program fidelity, implementation, and quality; child outcomes from infancy through early elementary school; and parent well-being and self-sufficiency. Her current research in the United States focuses on Early Head Start, the cost of quality early childhood services, and informal child care. As director of testing and learning for the Early Learning Lab, she supports research-informed innovation and improvement of programs for children and families. She has conducted research on early childhood and parenting programs and systems in more than 10 countries. A recent project in Tanzania included an evaluability assessment of a preprimary teacher training intervention designed to improve grade 2 outcomes. She recently guest co-edited a special issue of *Early Childhood Research Quarterly* on early childhood care and education quality rating and improvement systems. She received her Ph.D. in developmental and cognitive psychology from Rutgers University.

Natasha J. Cabrera, Ph.D., is a professor in the Department of Human Development and Quantitative Methodology, College of Education, University of Maryland, College Park. Previously, she had several years of experience as an executive branch fellow and expert in child development with the National Institute of Child Health and Human Development (NICHD). Her research focuses on father involvement and children's social development, ethnic and cultural variations in fathering and mothering behaviors, family processes in a social and cultural context, and the mechanisms that link early experiences to children's school readiness. In her previous position with NICHD, she developed a major initiative called Developing a Daddy Survey, which coordinated measures of father involvement across major studies in the field and provided a set of measures for others to use. She is associate editor of *Child Development* and *Early Childhood Research Quarterly* and recipient of the National Council on Family Relations award for best research article regarding men in families. She is a 2015-2016 visiting scholar at the Russell Sage Foundation. She holds a Ph.D. from the University of Denver, Colorado, in educational and developmental psychology.

Eric Dearing, Ph.D., is a professor in the Department of Counseling, Developmental, and Educational Psychology at Boston College's Lynch School of Education. He is also a senior researcher at the Norwegian Center for Child Behavioral Development, University of Oslo. His work is focused on the consequences of children's lives outside of school for their performance in school. He has a special interest in the power of families, early education and care, and neighborhood supports to bolster achievement and well-being for children growing up poor. He is currently principal investigator for a study investigating the importance of parents' engagement in their children's early math learning for children's long-term achievement. He holds a Ph.D. in psychology from the University of New Hampshire.

Greg J. Duncan, Ph.D., is distinguished professor of education at the University of California, Irvine. Previously, he was a professor at the University of Michigan and director of the Panel Study of Income Dynamics. His recent work has focused on understanding the relative importance of early academic skills, cognitive and emotional self-regulation, and health in promoting children's eventual success in school and the labor market. He has also investigated how families, peers, neighborhoods, and public policy affect the life chances of children and adolescents. He has served as president of the Population Association of America and of the Society for Research in Child Development. He received the 2013 Klaus J. Jacobs Research Prize of the Jacobs Foundation, given for scientific work of high social relevance to the personality development of children and young people. He is a member of the National Academy of Sciences and holds a Ph.D. in economics from the University of Michigan.

Norma Finkelstein, Ph.D., M.S.W., is founder and executive director of the Institute for Health and Recovery, a Massachusetts statewide services, policy, program development, training, and research organization. Previously, she was founder and executive director of the Women's Alcoholism

Program/CASPAR, Inc., a comprehensive prevention, education, and treatment program for chemically dependent women and their families. Her work has focused on substance use prevention and treatment, with specific emphasis on women, children, and families; pregnancy; co-occurring disorders, including integrated care for women with substance use disorders, mental illness, and histories of violence; trauma-informed services; services for youth and young adults; tobacco education and cessation; and family-centered care. She has received numerous awards, including, most recently, the National Center on Substance Abuse and Child Welfare's National Collaborative Leadership Award, the National Organization on Fetal Alcohol Syndrome's Erin Frey Advocacy Award, and the Women's Service Network's and National Association of State Alcohol and Drug Abuse Directors' Women's Services Champion Award. She received her M.S.W. from the University of Michigan and her Ph.D. from Brandeis University.

Elena Fuentes-Afflick, M.D., M.P.H., is chief of pediatrics at San Francisco General and professor and vice chair of pediatrics and vice dean for academic affairs at the University of California, San Francisco (UCSF). Her research has focused on the broad themes of acculturation and immigrant health, with specific emphasis on perinatal and neonatal health disparities. She has served as chair of the UCSF Academic Senate and served on national committees of the Society for Pediatric Research, the National Institutes of Health, and the Robert Wood Johnson Foundation. She served as president of the Society for Pediatric Research, 2008-2009, and has served or is serving as a member of numerous advisory councils and committees. In 2010, she was elected to the National Academy of Medicine. She obtained her undergraduate education and medical degree at the University of Michigan. She completed her residency training at UCSF, where she served as chief resident, followed by a research fellowship at the Phillip R. Lee Institute for Health Policy Studies. She also completed an M.P.H. at the University of California, Berkeley.

Iheoma U. Iruka, Ph.D., is director of research and evaluation, Buffett Early Childhood Institute, University of Nebraska. Her research focuses on determining how early experiences impact poor and ethnic minority young children's health, learning, and development and the role of the family and education environments and systems in this process. She is engaged in projects and initiatives focused on how evidence-informed policies, systems, and practices in early education can support the optimal development and experiences of low-income and ethnic minority children, such as through quality rating and improvement systems, home visiting programs, and high-quality preschool programming. In addition to being a former scientist and associate director at the Frank Porter Graham Child

Development Institute, University of North Carolina, Chapel Hill, she serves on several national committees and boards. She holds a Ph.D. in applied developmental psychology from the University of Miami, Florida.

Samuel L. Odom, Ph.D., is director of the Frank Porter Graham Child Development Institute, University of North Carolina, Chapel Hill, and principal investigator, National Professional Development Center on Autism Spectrum Disorders and Center on Secondary Education for Students with Autism Spectrum Disorders (ASD). His current research is addressing treatment efficacy for children and youth with ASD, early intervention for toddlers with disabilities and their families, and professional development for teachers of children and youth with ASD. In 2013, he received the Arnold Lucius Gesell Prize for career achievement in research on social inclusion and child development from the Theordor Hellbrugge Foundation, Munich, Germany. He holds a Ph.D. in special education from the University of Washington.

Barbara Rogoff, Ph.D., is distinguished professor of psychology, University of California, Santa Cruz. She received the 2013 Award for Distinguished Lifetime Contributions to Cultural and Contextual Factors in Child Development from the Society for Research in Child Development. She is a fellow of the Association for Psychological Science, the American Anthropological Association, the American Psychological Association, and the American Educational Research Association. Her research focuses on cultural aspects of learning, with special emphasis on collaboration and observation and indigenous-heritage, Mexican, Guatemalan, and other communities of the Americas. She has held the University of California Presidential Chair and has been a fellow of the Center for Advanced Study in the Behavioral Sciences, a Kellogg fellow, a Spencer fellow, and an Osher fellow of the Exploratorium. She holds a Ph.D. in developmental psychology from Harvard University.

Mark A. Schuster, M.D., Ph.D., is William Berenberg professor of pediatrics, Harvard Medical School, and chief of general pediatrics and vice chair for health policy, Department of Medicine, Boston Children's Hospital. He conducts research on child, adolescent, and family issues and has studied the role of parents in influencing and addressing their children's health. He has conducted research on health disparities, family leave for parents with chronically ill children, adolescent sexual health, obesity prevention, children with HIV-infected parents, parental reports of family experience of health care, and other aspects of quality of health care. He is an elected member of the National Academy of Medicine and a recipient of the Society for Pediatric Research's Richardson Award for lifetime achievement in perinatal and pediatric health care research, and was president of the Academic Pediatric Association (2014-2015). He received his B.A. from Yale University, his M.D. and M.P.P. from Harvard University, and his Ph.D. in public policy analysis from the Pardee RAND Graduate School.

Selcuk R. Sirin, Ph.D., is associate professor of applied psychology, New York University (NYU). His research focuses primarily on the lives of immigrant and minority children and their families and ways to increase professionals' ability to better serve them. He conducted a major meta-analytical review of research on socioeconomic status and co-produced the Racial and Ethical Sensitivity Test and accompanying training program for school professionals. He also served as research coordinator for the Partnership for Teacher Excellence project at NYU in collaboration with New York City School of Education. His most recent research focused on immigrant youth in general and Muslim American children and adolescents in particular. He is the recipient of a Teaching Excellence Award from Boston College; a Young Scholar Award from the Foundation for Child Development for his project on immigrant children; and a Review of Research Award from the American Educational Research Association, given in recognition of an outstanding article published in education. He holds a Ph.D. in applied developmental and educational psychology (minor in methodology) from Boston College.

Kasisomayajula "Vish" Viswanath, Ph.D., is professor of health communication, Department of Social and Behavioral Sciences, Harvard School of Public Health and McGraw-Patterson Center for Population Sciences, Dana-Farber Cancer Institute. He is also faculty director of the Health Communication Core of the Dana-Farber/Harvard Cancer Center (DF/HCC) and leader of the DF/HCC's Cancer Risk and Disparities Program. He is founding director of DF/HCC's Enhancing Communications for Health Outcomes Laboratory. His work focuses on the use of translational communication science to influence public health policy and practice. His primary research emphasis is on documenting the relationship among communication inequalities, poverty and health disparities, and knowledge translation to address health disparities. He is a member of the U.S. Department of Health and Human Services' National Vaccine Advisory Committee and chairs its Working Group on Vaccine Acceptance, and is a member of the Board of Scientific Counselors, Office of Public Health Preparedness, Centers for Disease Control and Prevention. He holds a Ph.D. in mass communications from the University of Minnesota, Minneapolis.

Michael S. Wald, J.D., M.A., is Jackson Eli Reynolds professor of law, emeritus, at Stanford University. His teaching and research focus on public policy concerning children and families. In addition to his teaching and research, he has extensive experience in designing and implementing public policy related to parents and children, including holding a number of government positions at the federal, state, and local levels related to social services for children and families, and he has helped author legislation related to child welfare at the federal and state levels. He has served as director of the San Francisco Human Services Agency, deputy general counsel of the U.S. Department of Health and Human Services (1993-1995), and member of the U.S. Advisory Board on Child Abuse and Neglect. He is currently a member of the San Francisco Our Children Our Families Council, which develops child and family policy for San Francisco, and has been a member of the World Economic Forum's Global Agenda Council on the Welfare of Children; the Board of Directors, Chapin Hall Children's Center, University of Chicago; and the Carnegie Foundation's Commission on Children 0-3. He received his B.A. from Cornell University, his M.A. in political science from Yale University Graduate School of Arts and Sciences, and his LL.B from Yale Law School.